Finding the Knowledge of God

The Role of Imitation in Proverbs 1–9

Jesse W. Harris

Edition Notice: First Printing

Hardcover: 979-8-9909268-0-6
Paperback: 979-8-9909268-1-3
eBook: 979-8-9909268-2-0

Library of Congress Number: 2024912946

Gever Hakam
545 NW 68th Ave
Ocala, FL 34482

Original version published in ProQuest Dissertations & Theses Global.

―――――――――――――――――――――――――

Publisher's Cataloging-in-Publication Data

Names: Harris, Jesse W., 1985- .
Title: Finding the knowledge of God : the role of imitation in Proverbs
    1-9 / Jesse W. Harris.
Description: Ocala, FL: Gever Hakam, 2024. | Includes bibliographic
    references. | Summary: Analyzes the topic of imitation of God in
    Proverbs 1-9, including a historical survey of the topic through
    several related traditions, a literary structure for Proverbs 1-9,
    and a detailed commentary on the role of imitating God in
    Proverbs 1-9.
Identifiers: LCCN 2024912946 | ISBN 9798990926806 (hardcover) |
    ISBN 9798990926813 (pbk.) | ISBN 9798990926820 (ebook)
Subjects: LCSH: Bible. Proverbs, I-IX – Commentaries. | Bible.
    Proverbs, I-IX – Criticism, interpretation, etc. | Bible. Proverbs, I-
    IX – Language, style. | God – Knowableness. | Imitation –
    Religious aspects. | BISAC: RELIGION / Biblical Commentary /
    Old Testament / Poetry & Wisdom Literature. | RELIGION /
    Biblical Studies / Old Testament / Poetry & Wisdom Literature. |
    RELIGION / Theology.
Classification: LCC BS1465.52.H37 2024 | DDC 223.706 H--dc23
LC record available at https://lccn.loc.gov/2024912946

In dedication to my father, an exemplary and biblical model of humility, generosity, and faithfulness.

Proverbs 20:7

CONTENTS

PART ONE

PART TWO

ACKNOWLEDGMENTS

A project of this magnitude is not possible in a vacuum. Many gracious and collegial partners have played a role in its final fruition. First of all, my father Bruce Harris has been a constant source of support in so many ways, from encouragement to prayer to finances to spiritual guidance. His consistent devotion to the heart of God has been a constant reminder to stay focused on the eternal. Second, my PhD advisor, Dr. Phil Long, was an incredibly gracious and insightful guide throughout the original development of this study. His patience and careful attention to detail allowed this project to grow and flourish without hindrance. Dr. Long's collegiality and commitment to scripture are a formidable and biblical example to follow. Third, Dr. Paul Wegner and Dr. Rick Melick have been wonderful mentors who took an interest in me, shared many conversations, and genuinely sought to see me succeed. Through their friendship, love for the Lord, and commitment to academic excellence, I am fortunate to have them as models, those worthy of emulation for all who seek to teach God's word. Finally, there have been countless friends and classmates along the way who provided helpful dialogue regarding the various languages, topics, and passages that appear in this work. In fact, my introduction to Proverbs came through exegetical classes under the guidance of Dr. Chip Hardy and later with Dr. Tremper Longman, alongside a number of exceptional students in both classes who fostered an environment of focused academic rigor and genuine biblical fellowship. As it is said, "The one who walks with the wise will become wise" (Prov 13:20). This adage is indeed true and this study is a testament to the immeasurable value of being surrounded by such a great cloud of witnesses.

ABBREVIATIONS

General

ANE	Ancient Near East	Ms(s)	Manuscripts
BCE	Before the Common Era	MT	Masoretic Text
BHS	Biblia Hebraica Stuttgartensia	NT	New Testament
		OT	Old Testament
c.	Century	pl.	Plural
ca.	Circa	Q	Qumran / Dead Sea Scrolls
CE	Common Era		
GNT	Greek New Testament	sg.	Singular
Grk.	Greek	SP	Samaritan Pentateuch
HB	Hebrew Bible	Syr.	Syriac/Peshitta
Heb.	Hebrew	Tg.	Targum(s)
LXX	Septuagint	Vulg.	Vulgate

Bibliographic

AB	Anchor Bible
ABIG	Arbeiten zur Bibel und ihrer Geschichte
ABR	*Australian Biblical Review*
AcBib	Academia Biblica
AJSR	*Association for Jewish Studies*
AJSL	*American Journal of Semitic Languages and Literatures*
ANF	*The Ante-Nicene Fathers*
ATD	Das Alte Testament Deutsch
AUSS	*Andrews University Seminary Studies*
AYBC	Anchor Yale Bible Commentary
AYBD	*Anchor Yale Bible Dictionary*
BASOR	*Bulletin of the American Schools of Oriental Research*
BBR	*Bulletin for Biblical Research*

BCOTWP	Baker Commentary of the Old Testament: Wisdom & Psalms
BETL	Bibliotheca Ephemeridum Theologicarum Lovaniensium
Bib	*Biblica*
BIS	Biblical Interpretation Series
BKAT	Biblischer Kommentar, Altes Testament
BN	*Biblische Notizen*
BNTC	Black's New Testament Commentaries
BO	*Bibliotheca Orientalis*
BSac	*Bibliotheca Sacra*
BTB	*Biblical Theology Bulletin*
BZAW	Beihefte zur Zeitschrift fur die alttestamentliche Wissenshaft
CBQ	*Catholic Biblical Quarterly*
CBQMS	*Catholic Biblical Quarterly Monograph Series*
CurBR	*Currents in Biblical Research*
DOTPe	*Dictionary of the Old Testament: Pentateuch*
DOTPr	*Dictionary of the Old Testament: Prophets*
DOTWPW	*Dictionary of the Old Testament: Wisdom, Poetry, & Writings*
ETL	*Ephemerides Theologicae Lovanienses*
EvT	*Evangelische Theologie*
ExpTim	*Expository Times*
FAT	Forschungen zum Alten Testament
FOTL	Forms of the Old Testament Literature
FRLANT	Forschungen zur Religion und Literatur des Alten und Neuen Testament
HBT	*Horizons in Biblical Theology*
HCOT	Historical Commentary on the Old Testament
HdO	Handbuch der Orientalistik
HeyJ	*Heythrop Journal*
HS	*Hebrew Studies*
HTR	*Harvard Theological Review*
HvTSt	*HTS Theological Studies*
HUCA	*Hebrew Union College Annual*
IBC	Interpretation: A Bible Commentary for Teaching & Preaching
ICC	International Critical Commentary
IDS	*In die Skriflig*
Int	*Interpretation*
ITC	International Theological Commentary
IVP	Intervarsity Press
JANER	*Journal of Ancient Near Eastern Religions*

JAOS	*Journal of the American Oriental Society*
JBL	*Journal of Biblical Literature*
JBR	*Journal of Bible and Religion*
JESOT	*Journal for the Evangelical Study of the Old Testament*
JJS	*Journal of Jewish Studies*
JNSL	*Journal of Northwest Semitic Languages*
JPSTC	The Jewish Publishing Society Torah Commentary
JPT	*Journal of Psychology and Theology*
JQR	*Jewish Quarterly Review*
JSJSup	Supplements to the Journal for the Study of Judaism
JSOT	*Journal for the Study of Old Testament*
JSOTSup	Journal for the Study of Old Testament Supplement Series
JTS	*Journal of Theological Studies*
KTU	Die keilalphabetischen Texte aus Ugarit
LHBOTS	The Library of Hebrew Bible/Old Testament Studies
LNTS	The Library of New Testament Studies
LTJ	*Lutheran Theological Journal*
MT	*Modern Theology*
MVAG	Mitteilungen der Vorderasiatisch-agyptischen Gesellschaft
NAC	New American Commentary
NCBC	The New Century Bible Commentary
NICNT	New International Commentary on the New Testament
NICOT	New International Commentary on the Old Testament
NIDNTTE	*New International Dictionary of New Testament Theology and Exegesis*
NIDOTTE	*New International Dictionary of the Old Testament Theology & Exegesis*
NIGTC	New International Greek Testament Commentary
NIVAC	New International Version Application Commentary
NovTSup	Supplements to Novum Testamentum
NPNF	*The Nicene and Post-Nicene Fathers*
NSBT	New Studies in Biblical Theology
NTL	New Testament Library
NTS	*New Testament Studies*
OBT	Overtures to Biblical Theology
OTE	*Old Testament Essays*
OTL	Old Testament Library
OTM	*Old Testament Message*
PNTC	Pillar New Testament Commentaries
Proof	*Prooftexts: A Journal of Jewish Literary History*
RB	*Revue biblique*
RBPH	*Revue belge de philologie et d'histoire*
RevExp	*Review and Expositor*

RevQ	*Revue de Qumran*
RP	Religious Perspectives
SBJT	*The Southern Baptist Journal of Theology*
SBL	Society of Biblical Literature
SBLDS	Society of Biblical Literature Dissertation Series
SBS	Stuttgarter Bibelstudien
SBT	Studies in Biblical Theology
Semeia	*Semeia*
SHBC	Smyth & Helwys Bible Commentary
SJT	*Scottish Journal of Theology*
StBibLit	Studies in Biblical Literature
TB	*Theologische Bucherei*
TDOT	*Theological Dictionary of the Old Testament*
Text	*Textus*
Theology	*Theology*
TOTC	Tyndale Old Testament Commentaries
TS	*Theological Studies*
TWOT	*Theological Wordbook of the Old Testament*
TynBul	*Tyndale Bulletin*
TZ	*Theologische Zeitschrift*
VT	*Vetus Testamentum*
VTSup	Supplements to Vetus Testamentum
WBC	Word Biblical Commentary
WMANT	Wissenschaftliche Monographien zum Alten und Neuen Testament
WUNT	Wissenschaftliche Untersuchungen zum Neuen Testament
WW	*Word and World*
ZAW	*Zeitschrift fur die alttestamentliche Wissenschaft*
ZBK	Zurcher Bibelkommentare
ZNW	*Zeitschrift fur die neutestamentliche Wissenschaft und die Kunde der alteren Kirche*

Old Testament / Hebrew Bible

Gen	Genesis	Prov	Proverbs
Exod	Exodus	Eccl	Ecclesiastes
Lev	Leviticus	Song	Song of Songs
Num	Numbers	Isa	Isaiah
Deut	Deuteronomy	Jer	Jeremiah
Josh	Joshua	Lam	Lamentations
Judg	Judges	Ezek	Ezekiel
Ruth	Ruth	Dan	Daniel
1-2 Sam	1-2 Samuel	Hos	Hosea
1-2 Kgdms	1-2 Kingdoms (LXX)	Joel	Joel
		Am	Amos
1-2 Kgs	1-2 Kings	Obad	Obadiah
3-4 Kgdms	3-4 Kingdoms (LXX)	Jon	Jonah
		Mic	Micah
1-2 Chr	1-2 Chronicles	Nah	Nahum
Ezra	Ezra	Hab	Habakkuk
Neh	Nehemiah	Zeph	Zephaniah
Esth	Esther	Hag	Haggai
Ps/Pss	Psalms	Zech	Zechariah
Job	Job	Mal	Malachi

New Testament / Greek

Matt	Matthew	1-2 Thess	1-2 Thessalonians
Mark	Mark	1-2 Tim	1-2 Timothy
Luke	Luke	Titus	Titus
John	John	Phlm	Philemon
Acts	Acts	Heb	Hebrews
Rom	Romans	Jas	James
1-2 Cor	1-2 Corinthians	1-2 Pet	1-2 Peter
Gal	Galatians	1-2-3 John	1-2-3 John
Eph	Ephesians	Jude	Jude
Phil	Philippians	Rev	Revelation
Col	Colossians		

Apocrypha and Other Ancient Sources

1–2 Macc	1–2 Maccabees
Ahiqar	Ahiqar
Sir	Sirach/Ecclesiasticus
TgJ	Targum Jonathan
Tg. Neof	Targum Neofiti
Tg. Onq.	Targum Onqelos
TgProv	Targum Proverbs
Wis	Wisdom of Solomon
Alleg. Interp.	*Allegorical Interpretation*
Creation	*On the Creation of the World*
Decalogue	*On the Decalogue*
Embassy	*On the Embassy to Gaius*
Flight	*On Flight and Finding*
Virtues	*On the Virtues*
Spec. Laws	*On the Special Laws*

PREFACE

B efore engaging in this book, I want to provide you with a framework and some practical guidance for its use. This project began as an academic endeavor with a scholarly audience in mind. It has been adapted in order to make it more accessible for the typical pastor and Bible student engaged in ministry. The overall tone, however, remains descriptive with an aim toward demonstrating the presence of *imitatio Dei* (imitation of God) and its relationship to knowing God in Proverbs 1–9. Over the course of this book, I believe the case is sufficiently made to warrant this interpretive framework. While this certainly has scholarly value, it also upholds practical value for the study and use of Proverbs. All too often, zealous Bible students devour portions of scripture and set out to preach or lead Bible studies with their church, ministry, or college group. Yet, when they get to Proverbs, there is often a sense of perplexity and confusion. Unlike the Torah or Prophets, there is not a clear sense of "Thus says the Lord." Rather, it is typically approached as though the formative wisdom book were merely for attaining earthly success or for the practicality of a good life. While success and a good life are an aspect of Proverbs, its aim and goal are far more sublime and divine. The authorial intent is to lead the eager, or at least willing, wisdom student down a winding and complex path in order to develop their skill in discernment. Recitation of mere information is not enough, nor impressive in the largely oral ancient world. Knowing how to properly utilize information was far more important. In this way, Prov 1–9 provides a great curriculum for training a student in the way of wisdom, a program designed to provoke contemplation and rumination. Furthermore, it is essential to understand that such an endeavor must begin with God and end in God. Any other orientation toward wisdom is foolishness and perhaps even wickedness according to Proverbs.

So, how might you make the most of this book? The first use is simply to read it with the desire of knowing and understanding a key biblical theology theme central to the Bible, particularly as it is expressed in Proverbs. This approach is noble and will take the reader through a wide array of passages that express the theme of imitating and knowing God. With this orientation, the book will provide a great context for understanding the importance of this theme throughout the Bible. The second use would be as a tool or resource. For the pastor preaching through Proverbs, the first fifteen to twenty sermons would easily follow the basic lesson outline of this book.

While not every verse or word is fully discussed, it would serve as a great place to derive the internal structures and connections, many helpful insights and interpretations, additional resources to consult, and the running theme of God's presence and engagement in the wisdom endeavor. Likewise, the book could serve as a tool for someone preparing Bible studies or who is working on their own writing project, either on Prov 1–9 or the topic of *imitatio Dei* more broadly. In any of these, the reader must take the time to understand the discussion and implications that arise from the many interpretive points made, even taking the time to look through the copious additional insights found in the footnotes. Although I do not give a quick list of practical applications for the preacher or teacher, the theological and biblical principles illuminated throughout this book are primed and ready for a myriad of practical uses.

Overall, though, my hope for the reader is that you would come away glorifying God and deeply challenged in your own faith journey. In the process of writing this book, there were countless times I was struck by the disconnect between my fingers as they typed and the reality of my own heart and life. The heartbeat of this book is the emulation of God and his ways, in purity and with passion. Yet, all too often as I reflect on my own weaknesses, I am struck by the wonder of God's grace and patience in treating me as a son, providing guidance and restoration in love. With this in mind, there is an important distinction briefly mentioned in this book that clarifies the difference between discipline for the son versus the wicked. For the wicked, he ought to fear discipline in the sense of judgement and punishment. There is a finality to it and a sense of justice for the offended. Yet, the son can joyfully receive discipline as one grateful to a father who provides wise instruction. In this way, the father's discipline is not a whip for the purpose of pain and justice. It is discipline as a teacher in the hope that the student will grow and learn, ultimately being shaped into the very image of his father and teacher. From the English, and generally true for the words in Hebrew and Greek, "discipline" is derived from "disciple." Disciple means "student." Student implies there is a teacher. And what is the goal of a student? He is to become more and more like the teacher until he himself is a teacher for someone else. Thus, discipline is intimately related to the discipleship process, particularly in the sense of instruction and emulation. This distinction is important and often missed by both the casual Bible student and professional scholar.

So, as we work through the various sections of this book, I hope you will persist with a heart set on learning from God as a good and gracious father. I hope that you will reflect on the implications for your own life and the importance of walking in the ways of the Lord. Finally, I hope that this book will serve you in your ministry as a preacher or teacher as you yourself grow in emulation and knowledge of our supremely wise and righteous teacher, the creator of heaven and earth. May he guide you with grace in your journey along this divine path.

Jesse W. Harris
California
July 2024

PART ONE

INTRODUCTION

I n a profound ancient inquiry, the author of Job asked, "Where is wisdom found? Where is the place of understanding? Man does not know its value. It is not found among the land of the living" (Job 28:12–13). The elusiveness of wisdom in human lives and societies has been an ever-present problem throughout history. Not only is life complicated on the individual level but with the vast array of competing views and desires its complexity can be compounded beyond human capacity. How are humans to navigate the world, society, and all the complexity? What is wisdom? How might one acquire such a thing, if at all possible? While no individual guide can remove or address all the challenges of human life, as the central and formative work of biblical wisdom, Proverbs does attempt to provide a framework, or perhaps a roadmap, for engaging these common concerns. The whole book is valuable in this regard. Yet, within the first nine chapters, the proverbial father provides an especially coherent pedagogical program in order to guide and shape the proverbial son in his development to be one of the wise. As a wise father, he leads the son through a collection of images and metaphors for warning, encouragement, instruction, and growth. In some areas, the instruction is simple and concrete, accessible to even the uninitiated. In other areas, though, it is a deep well of profound pursuit, teeming with complex literary connections and allusions, even riddles, interwoven with inexhaustible theological and philosophical threads. Through these, the introductory wisdom program in Prov 1–9 serves the son as a guide that only deepens and broadens as he matures and develops into the kind of person who is capable of receiving the instruction, one with a proper heart and ability to discern. The core of this fatherly instruction is more than just pragmatism and rules for mundane success. There is an understanding that if human capacity and earthly knowledge are the end, then the human experience is inherently limited and feeble. Instead, the vision from the proverbial father extends beyond the tangible into the divine. God himself is the point of reference for wisdom and thus for all mundane existence. So, as a good teacher, the father desires the son to look beyond himself in order to walk the path that reflects God and his ways. This, as Prov 1–9 teaches, is the way of wisdom.

The objective of this study, then, is to show that Prov 1–9 utilizes the formative process of imitation in its pedagogy. For the novitiate, this process begins with mundane human exemplars. While these models are indeed vital, they are not the goal. The wise who have walked the righteous path are worthy examples but they too are limited. Rather, the wisdom program of Prov 1–9 intends for the son to grow along the wisdom trajectory, that is, to travel the path that leads from human exemplars through the intermediate figure of Wisdom ultimately reaching to God. It is the biblical God who serves as the primary father and teacher of wise instruction and as the prime exemplar of those ideal traits that he proffers. While God is the ultimate example, the wise teacher of Proverbs understands the inherent developmental process that the son must travel through. To address this process, he provides a number of positive and negative figures for the student to observe, both directly and indirectly, as he develops along this wise, divine path. At its core, then, this study analyzes the presence of imitative elements within the pedagogical program of Prov 1–9 and illuminates how they ultimately point to *imitatio Dei* (imitation of God).

Over the last century, the role of imitation has received little focus in studies of the HB. In fact, there have even been some scholars who deny the role of *imitatio Dei* in the HB. These skeptical scholars have questioned a variety of aspects in imitating God, giving reasons such as God's wholly transcendent nature, humanity's inability to fully know or replicate his nature and ways, God's harsh or even barbaric actions, and the lack of explicit biblical address of the topic, just to name a few.[1] Despite the presence of criticism, a few scholars have used and developed the idea of *imitatio Dei* in the HB, particularly from the Torah.[2] So, the goal of this study is to expand on the work of these positive evaluations and to illuminate *imitatio Dei* in the book of Proverbs, a book that has largely been overlooked in the scholarly world of

---

[1] For examples, see Cyril S. Rodd, "Shall Not the Judge of All the Earth Do What Is Right? (Gen 18:25)," *ExpTim* 83.5 (1972): 137–39; Barnabas Lindars, "Imitation of God and Imitation of Christ: Duty and Discernment," *Theology* 76.638 (1973): 394–402; Mary E. Mills, *Images of God in the Old Testament* (Collegeville, MN: Liturgical, 1998); David Penchansky, *What Rough Beast?: Images of God in the Hebrew Bible* (Louisville: John Knox, 1999); Cyril S. Rodd, *Glimpses of a Strange Land: Studies in Old Testament Ethics*, OTS (Edinburgh: T&T Clark, 2001); John H. Walton and J. Harvey Walton, *The Lost World of the Torah: Law as Covenant and Wisdom in Ancient Context* (Downers Grove: IVP, 2019).

[2] E.g., Christopher J. H. Wright, *Old Testament Ethics for the People of God* (Downers Grove: IVP, 2004); Ryan O'Dowd, *The Wisdom of Torah: Epistemology in Deuteronomy and the Wisdom Literature*, FRLANT 225 (Göttingen: Vandenhoeck & Ruprecht, 2009).

biblical theology. [3] This endeavor will provide a suitable framework for knowing God through imitating him, particularly through sensitivity to linguistic, socio-historical, philosophical, and theological elements within Proverbs and its HB context. The relational nature of wisdom and growth in the knowledge of God will be illuminated as core aspects of *imitatio Dei* in the wisdom program. Daniel Estes argues that the "knowledge of God," implying both reverence and relationship, is the central educational goal of Prov 1–9.[4] In other words, the proverbial father understands that the way of wisdom is intrinsically and inextricably intertwined with God himself. One cannot be wise apart from God, which necessitates a proper knowledge or relationship with him. Likewise, as one grows in true proverbial wisdom, one will also grow in likeness to God, walking the path marked by his ways. This spiral of growth and knowledge is a path traversed by all the wise and righteous figures throughout biblical history, perhaps most expressively imaged in King David. Ryan O'Dowd rightly emphasizes this embodied form of knowledge in his study of HB epistemology, "The sort of knowledge that Israel is to acquire is more than purely intellectual … [and] may be said to be relational."[5] Our study, then, will draw from and build upon the work of those who have paved the way in exploring the inherent role of *imitatio Dei* and divine knowledge within the HB in order to develop the concept as it is embedded within Prov 1–9.

To properly understand and observe the role of imitation in Prov 1–9, Part One will first walk through a historical survey of *imitatio Dei* and the complex structure of Prov 1–9. The historical survey is an essential, though limited, overview of the presence and role of *imitatio Dei* in ANE, Greco-Roman, Judaic, and Christian traditions, including modern positive and negative evaluations over the past century. Although the concept has been expressed in a number of contexts and in a variety of ways, its presence has remained consistent. As a framework, these traditions serve to highlight the likelihood of *imitatio Dei* in both the HB and Prov 1–9. Thus, while critical evaluations are not without some merit, it would be a mistake to reject the pedagogical and theological notion of divine imitation. Following the historical survey, we will consider the highly intentional and poetic structure of Prov 1–9. Despite a trove of scholarly attention to this popular section of scripture, we will see that a simple yet central literary feature has been overlooked, one that sheds light on the whole wisdom program. Although a few scholars have come close, this study proposes a fifteen-lesson chiastic structure that highlights Prov 4:20–27 as the center passage. This center passage contains a

---

[3] Cf. Tremper Longman III, *The Fear of the Lord Is Wisdom: A Theological Introduction to Wisdom in Israel* (Grand Rapids: Baker Academic, 2017), xv, 24–25.

[4] Daniel J. Estes, *Hear, My Son: Teaching and Learning in Proverbs 1–9*, NSBT 4 (Grand Rapids: Eerdmans, 1997), 84–86.

[5] He says elsewhere, "Knowledge, therefore, is intrinsically participatory, or a product of discovering God and his world by living in it. To know is to live in ethical conformity with God's ordered reality, not to escape from it into objective analysis. It is only in late wisdom literature that we find the slightest of allusions to Greek knowledge in an abstract sense" (O'Dowd, *The Wisdom of Torah*, 48).

common motif that served the proverbial father's purpose in pointing the son to examples worthy of following so that he would carefully consider his own ways. While subtle, the structure illuminates a number of parallel features that also help interpret many otherwise seemingly simplistic or misunderstood instructions.

After these introductory matters in Part One, we will then engage in a focused and exegetical analysis of Prov 1–9. In Part Two, we will systematically analyze the nine chapters according to the fifteen sections of the proposed chiasm, those outlined in the structural analysis. Within these chiastic sections, the literary and theological tapestry of Prov 1–9 will be analyzed with several threads in focus. The proverbial father does not desire for the son to grow merely in information. Rather, he understands that the true path of wisdom is growth in discernment, character, and the knowledge of God. Thus, although many useful principles are accessible on the cursory level, there is a deep and complex web of intertextual allusions and theological instruction that require growth in discernment. To this end, the pedagogical process in Prov 1–9 desires for the son to grow in his ability to discern, or to read between the lines in modern idiom. This endeavor is clearly stated from the outset of Proverbs (Prov 1:1–7). It is only the wise student with the right starting point and end goal who can rightly read and understand the subsequent proverbial instructions. So, to teach the son all the essential principles for life on the right path with God, the proverbial father utilizes a variety of metaphors. One of the metaphors central to *imitatio Dei* is the fatherhood of God. Although this image is only explicitly given in one place (Prov 3:11–12), the underlying notion of the divine Father permeates the entirety of the wisdom program. Indeed, the divine Father is the ultimate source of the instruction and ways that the proverbial father presents to the son. Even the figure of Wisdom is utilized in her many forms to point the son to God as the paragon of wisdom. Likewise, the instruction in these sections relies heavily on the intrinsic biblical metaphor of a "path," or more specifically the two ways. With expansive versatility, this pathway image presents both admirable and abominable figures who have chosen and walked their relative paths. The two paths are further represented by the enigmatic figures of Wisdom and Folly, who embody the characteristics and results of their paths. Although Folly is not given a clear referent, Wisdom is masterfully interwoven as a representative figure bridging the proverbial father and the divine Father. With a variety of roles, perhaps most importantly she serves as an exalted teacher above the father and as a close companion or representative of God. In both, she is a vital aspect of the *imitatio Dei* process and the wisdom trajectory. Furthermore, the proverbial father instructs the son on a number of desirable traits. These traits are not arbitrary or merely humanistic. They are indirect attributions of the biblical God and his ways. In other words, the son is to grow in the character, actions, and desires that were ultimately found in God by those who reflect him and walk in his ways. While many of these qualities are presented by way of allusion or intertextual illumination, they are paradigmatic for the wisdom program of Prov 1–9.

Methodological Considerations

Before moving into the study, a few relevant methodological considerations are in order. To start, there are the textual and intertextual aspects at the heart of this primarily exegetical study. By saying exegetical, I only mean that there is a sensitivity to the text, its original context, and its embedded intent for interpretational purposes.[6] However, despite a sensitivity to the context of the text, the historical context and potential compositional history will be left largely to other more exhaustive studies. The historical survey at the start will serve as the foundation for the context since this study is focused primarily on the topic of *imitatio Dei* rather than of Proverbs generally. That said, this study works from the presupposition that Proverbs is not a Hellenistic product but rooted in the monarchic period of Israel (ca. 950–600 BCE).[7] Although much of the content may originate with Solomon, editorial factors and lexical usage place its composition, compilation, or final form sometime during or after Hezekiah (ca. 700 BCE; cf. Prov 25:1). For our purposes in this study, it is not necessary to ascribe an exact date or final editor. Rather, there is a strong presence of both intertextuality and a shared conceptual framework with the other biblical authors from this pre-exilic period, especially with the Psalms and eighth-century prophets. There have been various attempts to show Proverb's intertextual relationship with other biblical works.[8] Although many of the connections suggest direct reliance, many of the ideas and images are widespread enough in the HB to suggest a shared conceptual framework. Thus, while some sensitivity to diachronic textual development is followed, there is a more theological, thematic, and synchronic approach to the primary topic and the relevant passages that appear to illuminate its proper interpretation.

As a second consideration, metaphorical language plays an essential role in this study, formally developed in modern scholarship with metaphor theory.[9] As Dru Johnson notes about this type of language in the OT, "Metaphors and analogs are not decorative … but function cognitively in a way that supposedly 'literal' discourse cannot."[10] These tools propose the

---

[6] Cf. Andreas J. Köstenberger and Richard Duane Patterson, *Invitation to Biblical Interpretation: Exploring the Hermeneutical Triad of History, Literature, and Theology*, 2nd ed. (Grand Rapids: Kregel Academic, 2021); Grant R. Osborne, *The Hermeneutical Spiral: A Comprehensive Introduction to Biblical Interpretation*, 2nd ed. (Downers Grove: IVP, 2006).

[7] Cf. Bruce K. Waltke, *The Book of Proverbs: Chapters 1–15*, NICOT (Grand Rapids: Eerdmans, 2004), 32–36.

[8] E.g., Moshe Weinfeld, *Deuteronomy and the Deuteronomic School* (Winona Lake: Eisenbrauns, 1972); Scott L. Harris, *Proverbs 1–9: A Study of Inner-Biblical Interpretation*, SBLDS 150 (Atlanta: Scholars, 1996); Bernd U. Schipper, *Proverbs 1–15: A Commentary on the Book of Proverbs 1:1–15:33*, Hermeneia (Minneapolis: Fortress, 2019).

[9] For the initial theory and its modern expansions, see George Lakoff and Mark Johnson, *Metaphors We Live By* (Chicago: University of Chicago Press, 1980); Zoltán Kövecses, *Metaphor: A Practical Introduction*, 2nd ed. (New York: Oxford University Press, 2010).

[10] Dru Johnson, *Biblical Philosophy: A Hebraic Approach to the Old and New Testaments* (Cambridge: Cambridge University Press, 2021), 107. Erin Heim states regarding the function of biblical metaphor, "[They] are capable of shaping how a person conceives of

conceptualization of particular linguistic patterns with the mental frameworks they follow.[11] With careful attention to texts and contexts, they can serve to highlight the importance of the particular terms, syntagmatic relationships, semantic domains, and conceptual connections.[12] Thus, this study will utilize a web of important terms and phrases that overlap in many places conceptually and textually, e.g., fatherhood and paths.[13] While each metaphor has independent and unique meanings, the terms often appear in overlapping relationships within a broader conceptual framework. These connections will show the value and usage within Prov 1–9 from the biblical corpus regarding *imitatio Dei* and the knowledge of God.

Regarding imitation, modern scholarship has developed a vast trove of literature derived from "mimetic theory," which fundamentally highlights the inherent role of imitation within humanity.[14] Humans instinctively imitate other's actions and even their desires. Despite some shared underlying principles, however, modern theories that follow René Girad have largely focused on modern sociological concerns in human-to-human imitation and typically go beyond the interests of this study. In more relevant ways, modern pedagogical studies have arrived at similar conclusions for their basic models of human development, which demonstrate the necessity of imitation.[15] Thus,

---

reality; a truly creative metaphor communicates truths which have no literal paraphrase" (Erin M. Heim, *Adoption in Galatians and Romans: Contemporary Metaphor Theories and the Pauline Huiothesia Metaphors*, BIS 153 (Leiden: Brill, 2017), 70).

[11] Dru Johnson develops six qualities of ancient Hebraic philosophy: style (pixelated, networked) and conviction (mysterionist, creationist, ritualist, transdemographic). These qualities approach and develop the thought-world of the Biblical authors in distinct ways from the formal Greek qualities later (linear, autonomous, domesticationist, abstractionist, classist, mentalist). He later expands on seven basic categories of methods employed by the biblical authors, "The essential toolbox for many biblical authors to advocate philosophical methodology: 1. narratives as an argument; discursive and presentational 2. definition by genus and differentia 3. analogical reasoning and metaphor 4. ritualized learning environments 5. taxonomical paradigm creation 6. pre-Aristotelian logic not restricted to a binary notion of truth 7. presumption of discernible cause and effect relationships" (Johnson, *Biblical Philosophy*, 83, 100).

[12] Some elements of cognitive-linguistic principles, as found in Ruark's study, will be adapted for the metaphors particular to this study (Joel D. Ruark, "Toward an Old Testament Theology of Light: From Physical Concept to Metaphysical Analogy" (PhD diss., Stellenbosch University, 2019), 33).

[13] Cf. Raymond C. Van Leeuwen, "Liminality and Worldview in Proverbs 1–9," *Semeia* 50 (1990): 111–44; Eryl W. Davies, "Walking in God's Ways: The Concept of Imitatio Dei in the Old Testament," in *In Search of True Wisdom* (Sheffield: Sheffield Academic, 1999), 100. Davies notes the rabbinic history of interpretation for the metaphorical phrase "walking after the Lord" as indicative of imitation.

[14] For a few relevant endeavors within this field, see Scott R. Garrels, ed., *Mimesis and Science: Empirical Research on Imitation and the Mimetic Theory of Culture and Religion*, Studies in Violence, Mimesis, and Culture (East Lansing, MI: Michigan State University Press, 2011); Wolfgang Palaver, *René Girard's Mimetic Theory*, Studies in Violence, Mimesis, and Culture (East Lansing: Michigan State University Press, 2013); Erich Auerbach, *Mimesis: The Representation of Reality in Western Literature*, trans. Willard R. Trask, 50th ed. (Princeton: Princeton University Press, 2013); Michael Hardin, *Mimetic Theory and Biblical Interpretation: Reclaiming the Good News of the Gospel*, Cascade Companions (Eugene: Wipf & Stock, 2017).

[15] E.g., Michael Tomasello, Ann C. Kruger, and Hilary H. Ratner, "Cultural Learning," *Behavioral & Brain Sciences* 16.3 (1993): 495–511; Michael Tomasello, "Emulation Learning and

this pedagogical tool provides an undergirding for the centrality of imitation in Prov 1–9, discussed more formally by later philosophers and theologians but readily present among their ANE and biblical predecessors.[16]

Philosophical Considerations for the "Knowledge of God"

Finally, in order to address the enigmatic phrase "knowledge of God" used in Prov 2:5 (cf., Hos 4:1, 6:6), a few brief philosophical considerations are needed, particularly with sensitivity to the contextual nature of the idea in the OT.[17] Since the modern exegete is not endowed with a right to "chronological snobbery," it is helpful to have had many eras of philosophical and theological inquiry from which to work.[18] Countless bright minds and searching souls have sought to open a window into what is really meant when one speaks of knowing God. Is such a thing possible? And if so, how or what might this be? Inevitably, "knowledge" as a technical pursuit is terribly complex and elusive, despite being one of the most foundational aspects of the human experience.[19] So, while describing the precise nature of knowledge and epistemology is

Cultural Learning," *Behavioral & Brain Sciences* 21 (2002): 703–4; Gergely Csibra and György Gergely, "Sylvia's Recipe: The Role of Imitation and Pedagogy in the Transmission of Cultural Knowledge," in *Roots of Human Sociality: Culture, Cognition, and Human Interaction* (Oxford: Berg, 2006), 229–55; Adrian E. Hinkle, *Pedagogical Theory of Wisdom Literature: An Application of Educational Theory to Biblical Texts* (Eugene: Wipf & Stock, 2017).

[16] Gregory E. Sterling, "Imitatio Dei (Eph 5:1–2): The Soteriological Basis for Ethics," in *Sōtēria: Salvation in Early Christianity and Antiquity: Festschrift in Honour of Cilliers Breytenbach on the Occasion of His 65th Birthday*, ed. Cilliers Breytenbach et al., NovTSup 175 (Leiden: Brill, 2019), 351–56.

[17] Biblical wisdom literature has often been read and categorized as secular in nature and origin. However, scholars have turned to the wisdom literature once again to find theological connections to the rest of the biblical corpus. Alongside this endeavor, there has been interest in understanding the HB according to philosophical inquiry and analysis. When done responsibly and with keen attention to texts and contexts, such an analysis can bring to light naturally embedded concepts without superimposing modern ones. For a few examples of this endeavor, see Craig G. Bartholomew and Ryan O'Dowd, *Old Testament Wisdom Literature: A Theological Introduction* (Downers Grove: IVP Academic, 2011); Mary Healy and Robin A. Parry, eds., *The Bible and Epistemology: Biblical Soundings on the Knowledge of God* (Milton Keynes: Paternoster, 2007); Jaco Gericke, *The Hebrew Bible and Philosophy of Religion*, SBL 70 (Atlanta: SBL, 2012); Yoram. Hazony, *The Philosophy of Hebrew Scripture: An Introduction* (New York: Cambridge University Press, 2012); Zoltán S. Schwáb, *Toward an Interpretation of the Book of Proverbs: Selfishness and Secularity Reconsidered*, JTISup 7 (Winona Lake: Eisenbrauns, 2013); Arthur J. Keefer, *The Book of Proverbs and Virtue Ethics: Integrating the Biblical and Philosophical Traditions* (Cambridge: Cambridge University Press, 2021); Johnson, *Biblical Philosophy*.

[18] C. S. Lewis, *Surprised by Joy: The Shape of My Early Life* (San Francisco: HarperOne, 2017), 254. He describes this as, "The uncritical acceptance of the intellectual climate common to our own age and the assumption that whatever has gone out of date is on that account discredited."

[19] It is perhaps similar to Augustine's musings on the issue of time, saying, "What then is time? If no one asks me, I know: if I wish to explain it to one that asks, I know not" (Augustine of Hippo, *The Confessions of St. Augustine* 11.14.17 (*NPNF* 1.1:168).

beyond the scope of this study, consideration of a few relevant aspects will help us approach a proper framework with some inherent implications for the rest of the study regarding *imitatio Dei*.

Modern philosophers and theologians generally identify four types of knowledge – "knowledge by acquaintance," "knowledge of persons," "know-how," and "knowledge by description."[20] The first is a kind of direct access to information through sensory experience. As an extension of the first, knowledge of persons is a form of knowledge special to personally knowing other sentient beings that encompasses a quality beyond mere information. The third is simply a skill or procedural knowledge. The fourth is "propositional knowledge," which is acquired logically and deductively through a "justified true belief."[21] Within this framework, several competing epistemologies address how one engages with God. One approach is called "foundationalism," which attempts to build a house of knowledge on "basic beliefs" and logical "inferences." This has a long history in the Christian tradition, proposing that certain "basic beliefs" are a priori and evidence is unnecessary.[22] Utilizing another classic approach, Alvin Plantinga appeals to the *sensus divinitatis*, which he defines as "a disposition or set of dispositions to form theistic beliefs in various circumstances, in response to the sorts of conditions or stimuli that trigger the working of this sense of divinity."[23] This Latin phrase suggests that the sense of God is experienced either through spiritual interaction or perhaps through a universal faculty, similar to eyesight, through which humans are able to know or sense God.[24] Another interesting approach is proposed by Esther Meeks. With the ultimate goal of illuminating the knowledge of God, she disparages the atomistic and false dichotomy often placed between faith and reason.[25] Her argument is that all human knowledge is limited in its certainty yet can still be trusted and legitimate. She views all knowledge as inherently relational, entering into a relationship that involves trust and engagement. In other words, knowledge

---

[20] James P. Moreland, *Philosophical Foundations for a Christian Worldview* (Downers Grove: IVP Academic, 2017), 62; John M. Frame, *The Doctrine of the Knowledge of God* (Phillipsburg, NJ: P&R, 1987), 45–46. John Frame adds "knowledge of persons" to the more common three types.

[21] Moreland, *Philosophical Foundations*, 63.

[22] Craig G. Bartholomew and Michael W. Goheen, *Christian Philosophy: A Systematic and Narrative Introduction* (Grand Rapids: Baker Academic, 2013), 215–16, 20. Here, it is important to note that Foundationalism and Classical Foundationalism are countered by the equally prominent approach of Evidentialism, which proposes that all beliefs must be justified by verifiable evidence. However, it does not seem this approach addresses the knowledge of God. As Bartholomew and Goheen explain, Wolterstorff also proposes a mediating theory integrating belief with reason referred to as "reason within the bounds of religion." This too seems an extraneous approach for this study, though.

[23] Alvin Plantinga, *Warranted Christian Belief* (New York: Oxford University Press, 2000), 173; Zoltán S Schwáb, "The Value of a Curious Translation: Revisiting Proverbs 2:5," *JBL* 133.4 (2014): 741; Moreland, *Philosophical Foundations*, 148–49. Origen was perhaps the first to use this phrase but the idea was later popularized in the writings of Calvin.

[24] Moreland questions the exegetical and conceptual value of the universal faculty (Moreland, *Philosophical Foundations*, 153–54).

[25] Esther L. Meek, *Longing to Know* (Grand Rapids: Brazos, 2003), 41.

is a perpetual process based on humility and desire.[26] Within this model, the particulars are necessary components to seeing the broader picture and are incoherent in isolation without integration.[27] So, within this philosophical view, all types of knowledge would be necessary for genuine knowledge, equally valid in pursuing the "knowledge of God." This would mean, then, that knowing God involves knowing and deducing information about God, participating in the skills of God, and knowing God by personal acquaintance.

The biblical corpus, of course, speaks of the "knowledge of God" in present and real terms rather than in the abstract, theoretical, or purely transcendent.[28] The experiences of those in the Bible suggest that God was not far off but immanent throughout the world (e.g., Deut 4:7; Jer 23:23; Ps 139:7–9). In this way, the OT demonstrates a well-constituted sense of knowing God, though not in full for finite creaturely humans.[29] Thus, there is a great deal of commonality between modern categories of knowledge and the scriptures.[30]

So, what is the nature of this knowledge then? Meek puts it well in saying, "Our knowing [God] is as a lover, a husband to his people, whom to know involves interpersonal, unfolding, covenantal relationship. ... The covenant mutuality of God and his people is paradigmatic for all human knowing ... interpersonal, pledge-based, calling for respect and humility and patience."[31] The OT is replete with imagery relating the knowledge of God to marriage, though inherently communal in nature.[32] As will be discussed later, the conceptual framework for Proverbs and Hosea elicits this type of imagery. The inherent problem, however, is that although the knowledge of God is possible there are necessary conditions, all of which God has provided from his side of the relationship.[33] So, as both the father and the figure of Wisdom indicate in Proverbs, the goal of the instruction and warnings is that the son will fulfill his side of the necessary conditions for proper knowledge and relationship. While the father can tell the son about God and the path to knowing him, it is the responsibility of the son to pursue and achieve the personal experience and knowledge of God for himself (cf. Job 42:5),[34] primarily found in becoming like him.

---

[26] Meek, *Longing to Know*, 64.

[27] Meek, *Longing to Know*, 50.

[28] E. Schutz, "Knowledge, Experience, Ignorance," in *NIDNTTE*, ed. Colin Brown (Grand Rapids: Zondervan, 1976), 395–96.

[29] Daniel T. Niles, *We Know in Part* (Philadelphia: Westminster, 1964), 30.

[30] Frame, *The Doctrine of the Knowledge of God*, 46.

[31] Meek, *Longing to Know*, 179.

[32] Gustave Weigel and Arthur G. Madden, *Religion and The Knowledge of God* (Englewood Cliffs, NJ: Prentice-Hall, 1961), 52–53; Frame, *The Doctrine of the Knowledge of God*, 41.

[33] Brevard S. Childs, *Old Testament Theology in a Canonical Context* (Philadelphia: Fortress, 1994), 41.

[34] As Job states, "I heard of you by ear but now my eye has seen you." This is likely an important epistemological point implying that Job's knowledge about God developed from informational to an experiential and personal knowledge of God.

One of the central themes in the HB is conformity to the will and nature of God. As Childs insightfully writes, "Israel did not first know God, and then later discover what God wants. Knowledge of his person and will are identical, and both are grounded in his self-revelation."[35] In particular, this correspondence between knowing God and his will is evidenced in the ideal characteristics of justice, righteousness, uprightness, goodness, turning from evil, devotion, faithfulness, mercy, and loving-kindness. Obedience or commitment to a covenant relationship is, therefore, central and should be seen as an "experiential, reverential response to God's greatness." [36] Naturally, those who know and fear God "turn away from evil" (Prov 3:7, 16:6; cf. Job 28:28; Ps 34:15). The reality of this relationship, then, is that it is all-consuming for the person.[37] While knowing information or a skill can be compartmentalized, personal knowledge of the infinite God is a much deeper reality. Concerning this theological point, John Murray says, "Knowledge is not simply an affair of intelligence; it is an affair of the heart, in the biblical sense of the heart as the center and source of the whole inner life in its full complex of thought, desire, and moral decision."[38] Therefore, to know God is to love God with one's whole heart, which requires both obeying God and conforming to his own character and will.[39] As Frame proposes, "Knowledge of God produces obedience" and "obedience to God leads to knowledge."[40]

As patristic and medieval theologians believed, "All knowledge ultimately finds its final goal in God, beginning now in faith and culminating in the beatific vision of God."[41] Despite the danger of anachronism, the biblical witness seems to espouse and demonstrate a multifaceted view of knowledge, which parallels modern scholarship. Thus, according to our study, knowing God involves privileged information, personal interaction and commitment, and the skills to properly live in consideration of the other two forms of knowledge. Second, central to the message of the proverbial father, wisdom and knowledge are essentially theocentric with God as the beginning and end of both. The kind of wisdom proffered in Prov 1–9 is meant to orient the entirety of one's life toward reflecting the divine qualities, particularly justice, righteousness, faithfulness, and goodness. These elements are not optional or ancillary but vitally interwoven with what it means to be wise and to know God, necessarily dependent on imitating God and walking in his ways.

---

[35] Childs, *Old Testament Theology in a Canonical Context*, 51.

[36] Steven B. Sherman, *Revitalizing Theological Epistemology: Holistic Evangelical Approaches to the Knowledge of God* (Eugene: Wipf & Stock, 2008), 160.

[37] Childs, *Old Testament Theology in a Canonical Context*, 29.

[38] John Murray, *The Problem of God: Yesterday and Today* (New Haven: Yale University Press, 1965), 21.

[39] Samuel L. Terrien, *The Elusive Presence: Toward a New Biblical Theology*, RP 26 (San Francisco: Harper & Row, 1978), 42.

[40] Frame, *The Doctrine of the Knowledge of God*, 43.

[41] Bartholomew and Goheen, *Christian Philosophy*, 89.

So, with these foundational ideas established, our next section will analyze the presence and use of divine imitation throughout history. This study will provide a substantive historical context for *imitatio Dei* over many millennia and establish its value for understanding the biblical text, particularly Prov 1–9.

A HISTORICAL SURVEY
OF *IMITATIO DEI*

Since the time of the ANE myths, humanity has had an intimate self-identification with the divine. The human-divine relationship has followed a number of expressions over the millennia, persisting as a central foundation for human behavior and aspiration. Even to the present, many scholars often place the roots of morality and ethics in the nature of God, particularly based on the scope of the OT and NT. This position, however, has not been without its criticisms and caveats. In modern times, critical scholars have sought to undermine the concept of *imitatio Dei* on a number of fronts. These indictments include claims such as God's wholly other nature, a lack of explicit command to do so in the OT, human limitations, and God's own questionable actions or character, just to name a few. As this historical survey will illuminate, people throughout the millennia have understood human nature in parallel to the divine. Despite some exceptions raised in all of the traditions, *imitatio Dei* serves as a valid and useful conceptual framework for biblical thinking, seemingly an innate concept to thinkers across time. This framework and the related discussion will serve to better understand and ground the underlying centrality of this topic within Proverbs and its OT context. The survey will highlight several salient and important examples along with developments within several traditions: ANE, Greek, NT, Rabbinic, Church, and modern scholarship. Each tradition has unique qualities and particular interests that make them distinct; yet all seem to explicitly or intuitively rely on the viability of *imitatio Dei*. Although this historical survey is arranged by tradition, it also follows a broad, temporal progression as well. The analysis begins with the ANE and Greek traditions. The survey concludes with discussions in modern scholarship. Due to focus, this survey will not be exhaustive or comprehensive but only illustrative and representative.

Mesopotamia and the ANE

In the 1980s, William Hallo proposed the contextual model of ANE comparison.[1] This approach intended to illuminate the cultural, religious, and literary world in which the Hebrew people lived yet without overly drawing causative implications. As Mark Smith has claimed, scholarship since the 1970s has reduced its view of direct correspondence or causation between Canaanite and Israelite cultures, part of a larger debate regarding biblical polemics.[2] Despite the ongoing discussion, this study will highlight the presence of imitation within the ANE. While it can be debated whether the Canaanites formed their practices from the divine or if they formed the divine myths according to their practices, there is good reason to believe they saw an overlapping, imitative relationship between the two realms.[3]

According to Smith, there has also been a debate regarding the relationship between myth and ritual within Ugaritic studies and the ANE.[4] Until relatively recent, the prevailing notion was that a direct correlation existed between the rituals and the myths, the former flowing from the latter. While some nuance has been introduced regarding the directionality and relationship of these, there still remains general agreement that the ANE had a close conceptual connection between the heavenly and mundane.[5] The overlap and connections were achieved in various ways such as cultic practice, idols, divination, and ritual procedures. As Smith argues, there was at times

---

[1] William W. Hallo, "Biblical History in Its Near Eastern Setting: The Contextual Approach," in *Israel's Past in Present Research: Essays on Ancient Israelite Historiography*, ed. V. Philips. Long, Sources for Biblical and Theological Study 7 (Winona Lake: Eisenbrauns, 1999), 77–97; C. D. Evans, W. W. Hallo, and J. B. White, *Scripture in Context: Essays on the Comparative Method* (Pittsburgh: Pickwick, 1980), 1–26.

[2] Mark S. Smith, *The Rituals and Myths of the Feast of the Goodly Gods of KTU/CAT 1.23: Royal Constructions of Opposition, Intersection, Integration, and Domination*, Society of Biblical Literature Resources for Biblical Study 51 (Atlanta: SBL, 2006), 153, 155; Gregorio del Olmo Lete, *Canaanite Religion: According to the Liturgical Texts of Ugarit* (Winona Lake: Eisenbrauns, 2004), 315; William W. Hallo and K. Lawson Younger, *The Context of Scripture* (New York: Brill, 1997), 422.

Ann K. Guinan notes in *COS* regarding biblical correspondence to divination, "While the biblical record preserves clear evidence of familiarity with Mesopotamian practices, there is no biblical corollary to the divinatory texts produced in Mesopotamia. There are a few direct references to Mesopotamian practices (Ezek 21:21; Isa 47:12–13; Dan 5:11). Echoes of, or perhaps, direct references to Mesopotamian texts, find their way into other conceptually very different genres. In contrast with Mesopotamia, there was no scholarly tradition associated with divination nor any systematic observation of omens" (422).

[3] For more discussion on imitative elements in Ugaritic myth and ritual, see, Olmo Lete, *Canaanite Religion*, 161.

[4] Smith, *Rituals and Myths*, 128, 135. Smith notes, "It was commonly assumed in many circles of classical and NE studies that myth was part of ritual, that it was the spoken part of the acted rite ... by the 1960s, this view came in for strong criticism ... NE specialists have strongly criticized the 'myth and ritual' approach (see Xella) and it has largely passed from the field."

[5] Clifford Geertz, "Religion as a Cultural System," in *Anthropological Approaches to the Study of Religion*, ed. M. Banton, ASA Monographs 3 (London: Tavistock, 1966), 28; Smith, *Rituals and Myths*, 160–61.

a sense that the participants of the rituals – particularly royalty and priests – were transcending the mysterious boundaries of the divine and participating in godly affairs.[6] There has also been some discussion of the imitative function of the various ritualistic and cultic practices that sought not only to breach the realm of the gods but to assert control over them, though a case for appeasement or pleading may also be appropriate.[7] The rituals worked to form and engender conceptual realities that would lead human participants "to act analogously to deities and be similar to them."[8] While not explicit about philosophical inquiry as found in later Greek culture, the convergence of myth and ritual served as a foundation for their understanding of reality.[9] Sarah Iles Johnston notes, "What we would call philosophy was integrated with science, magic, and divination or that philosophy was dependent on the religious system ... theological and philosophical essay was unknown in Syro-Canaanite culture; instead, thinkers used narratives to explore the great questions."[10]

As evidenced in the texts, much of the ANE practices and theology included some imitative correspondence between the human and the divine.[11] One example is the mythic story of Baal's death which elicits mourning from El and Anat. Such ritualized laments are the same as those performed by the Canaanite peoples.[12] As the text says of El,

---

[6] Smith, *Rituals and Myths*, 140. As Smith notes, "The human participants may have imagined that their world connects to this mythic world, but not simply as ritual imitation. Instead, the text offers a representation of an imagined divine reality in which the situation on the ground, as conceived by the royal elite, is reflected."

[7] Nicolas Wyatt, *Religious Texts from Ugarit*, BibSem 53 (London: Sheffield Academic, 2003), 128.

[8] Smith, *Rituals and Myths*, 141–42. Smith draws from prior scholarship to say, "As metaphorical meaning is imparted to symbol by our minds in the first place, there is then an engagement of the mind's products with the mind's sensibilities. ... when this engagement occurs within well defined, and orchestrated, ritual sequences that are socially supported, an inordinate impetus for behavioral transformation is engineered."

[9] Smith, *Rituals and Myths*, 159–60. Smith makes a couple of intriguing statements regarding the basis of reality for the ANE, "The ancients did not write systematic treatises about ontology. In Kunin's words (2004:105), 'mythology ... is creator of ontology.' Instead, the ancient texts expressed relations and causation, in reality, through a narration of divine familial ties. ... In sum, reality is experienced on the cosmic and terrestrial planes as a series of oppositions. ... It may be said that the beginning and end-points signal a vision of reality that is ultimately monistic ... This mythological structure arguably corresponds analogically to later neo-Platonic theories of divine emanation. An important difference between this text and later philosophical accounts of reality is that 1.23 expresses its theory of cosmic reality embedded within its rituals and myths."

[10] Sarah Iles Johnston, *Religions of the Ancient World: A Guide*, Harvard University Press Reference Library (Cambridge: Harvard University Press, 2004), 536–37.

[11] G. K. Beale, *We Become What We Worship: A Biblical Theology of Idolatry* (Downers Grove: IVP Academic, 2008), 101, 120.

[12] KTU 1.19:4; Wyatt, *Religious Texts from Ugarit*, 308–9. The human story of Danilu and Aqhatu accounts, "Wailing women had come into his palace mourning women into his dwelling. Those who lacerate the flesh wept for Aqhat the hero; they sobbed for the child of Danel the man of healing. ... Then he offered a sacrifice to the gods, he offered up their incense among the heavenly ones."

The Wise One, the perceptive god, went down from his throne ... He poured the ashes of affliction on his head, the dust of groveling on his skull. For clothing he put on a loin-cloth. His skin with a stone he scored, his side-locks with a razor; he gashed cheeks and chin. He ploughed his collar-bones, he turned over like a garden his chest, like a valley he ploughed his breast. He lifted up his voice and cried: 'Baal is dead!'[13]

Wyatt notes regarding this myth, the mythic procession of El is itself an imitation or recapitulation of death or Baal's descent to the underworld which was "modelled on real burial rites."[14] As a ritual, the biblical text explicitly forbids many of these mourning practices, which imitated the peoples and the gods of Canaan.[15] In Lev 21:5, the text addresses the priests saying, "They shall not make bald patches on their heads, nor shave off the edges of their beards, nor make any cuts on their body."[16] While not expressly connected to mourning rituals, Lev 19:28 does create the link, "You shall not make any cuts on your body for the dead or tattoo yourselves." Likewise, from Jer 16:6, the text mentions such practices as though commonly understood, "They shall not be buried, and no one shall lament for them or cut himself or make himself bald for them." A similar prohibition in Deut 14:1 seems to fit within its broader context, a warning against pagan assimilation, "When Yhwh your God will cut off the nations which you are going to inherit them from before you, ... guard yourself lest you be ensnared to follow after them ... lest you inquire about their gods, saying, 'How do these nations serve their gods, that I also may do the same?'" (Deut 12:29–30).

Although many stories and practices could be analyzed, which imply or describe divine imitation, the general sentiment within the ANE is one of participation and convergence, expressed in reflective or imitative

---

[13] KTU 1.5:6; cf. 1.6:1; Wyatt, *Religious Texts from Ugarit*, 126–31. Wyatt notes, "This is probably a fairly accurate description of actual mourning behaviour, in effect an expression on the one hand of solidarity with the deceased, and on the other of the hope that by going through the ritual motions of death, the catastrophe itself can be averted, with regard both to the dead and the mourner."

[14] Wyatt, *Religious Texts from Ugarit*, 126; Olmo Lete, *Canaanite Religion*, 161. Wyatt says of this myth, "El's descent is a ritual counterpart to Baal's. This element is not present in the parallel description of Anat's response. ... Note also that El recapitulates in his mourning behaviour the descent of Baal into the underworld." However, Olmo Lete contends against this view, saying, "[This] cannot be used as a reflection of practices in ordinary life."

[15] Saul Olyan points out there is some debate as to the correspondence between the biblical prohibitions and the Canaanite practices. He takes the position that these practices are prohibited merely because of their symbolic implications of death and unholiness rather than their association with pagan practices. See, Saul M. Olyan, "The Biblical Prohibition of the Mourning Rites of Shaving and Laceration: Several Proposals," in *A Wise and Discerning Mind: Essays in Honor of Burke O. Long*, ed. Saul M. Olyan and Robert C. Culley, 2nd ed., Brown Judaic Studies 325 (Providence: Brown Judaic Studies, 2020), 181; B. B. Schmidt, *Israel's Beneficent Dead* (Winona Lake: Eisenbrauns, 1996), 166–78; E. S. Gerstenberger, *Das dritte Buch Mose: Leviticus* (Gottingen: Vandenhoeck & Ruprecht, 1993), 252–85.

[16] Unless otherwise noted, quotations of the HB and GNT are the author's translation based on the BHS, LXX, Syr., Vulg, or GNT.

patterning. [17] Perhaps the most extensive category is the correspondence between royal hierarchy and affairs with the divine. [18] As Johnston notes regarding the complexity of gods, "The divine [reflected] the increased centralization of Mesopotamian national and imperial states."[19] Among the overlapping realms, royal banquets were a regular component of the divine and human intersection, often considered "communal meals." These meals were held in temples or palaces with the king as the central intermediary.[20] In one text, the completion of Baal's Palace prompts a royal celebration feast which is described in great detail.[21] Wyatt comments regarding the details and attendants, "These are evidently classes of minor deities, the apotheosis of the cultural and economic realities of Ugarit. … I take it that these minor deities are the attendants and mythic personnel of Baal's palace, corresponding to the human personnel in the Ugarit temple. Every item of furniture and cult is deified, or in more modern parlance, has its prototype in heaven."[22] Likewise, del Olmo Lete provides additional commentary, stating, "This is a mythologeme that undoubtedly reflects the multiplicity of sanctuaries and the varied uses to which they were put as the cultic texts attest. … The myth outlines the building of the 'heavenly' temple, model of the 'earthly' temple and its execution by commission and with divine intervention."[23] In fact, the overlap of realms in divine meals was more than just an excuse for festivities but served to engender and dramatize "cosmic coherence."[24] Such mediation was thought to be central to the role of the royalty and priests for the sake of the broader society.[25]

In one Hittite ritualistic guide to a divine meal, the text describes actions of both participants and gods, "The master of the estate libates [the goat] with wine before the table for Šantaš. Then … they bring the raw liver and the heart and the master of the estate holds them out for the gods. Further, he takes a bite (and) they imitate (him). … They place the liver and

---

[17] Smith, *Rituals and Myths*, 46, 51, 127, 132, 139, 146; Julian Obermann, *Ugaritic Mythology: A Study of Its Leading Motifs* (New Haven: Yale University Press, 1948), 4, 20.

[18] Smith, *Rituals and Myths*, 140. He states here, "The human participants may have imagined that their world connects to this mythic world, but not simply as ritual imitation. Instead, the text offers a representation of an imagined divine reality in which the situation on the ground, as conceived by the royal elite, is reflected." It is apparent Smith prefers the term 'reflect' over 'imitate,' likely due to its particular use as 'mimesis' in the 'myth and ritual school' (135).

[19] Johnston, *Religions of the Ancient World*, 536.

[20] Johnston, *Religions of the Ancient World*, 539.

[21] KTU 1.4:6. Regarding this story as a whole, Obermann says that it "formed the central theme of the mythological folklore." He goes on to say, "An alliance-enmity motif appears to dominate the building saga and indeed Ugaritic mythology as a whole." While avoiding a definitive parallel between the human and divine, he does raise the likelihood (Obermann, *Ugaritic Mythology: A Study of Its Leading Motifs*, 1, 4, 20.)

[22] Wyatt, *Religious Texts from Ugarit*, 107.

[23] Olmo Lete, *Canaanite Religion*, 28.

[24] Smith, *Rituals and Myths*, 163.

[25] Discussing another Ugaritic text, Wyatt says, "A mythic paradigm is established … implicit identification of his offspring with kings becomes the means whereby royal duties are represented as actualizing the theological programme" (Nicolas Wyatt, *Religious Texts from Ugarit*, 325; cf. Smith, *Rituals and Myths*, 128).

heart and he sets them back on the table and says as follows: 'Eat, O Sun God of Heaven above and below. Let the gods of the father of the house eat!'"[26] The implication of the ritual is to instantiate a meal with parallel parts between the human and the divine. In fact, there was a sense that participation in the affairs of the gods helped to secure good fortune. As one Egyptian ritual intimated, the reciprocal nature of the actions was central, "Act for the god, that he may act similarly for thee."[27]

Within the human royalty paradigm, sacred marriage served as another area of participation within divine affairs.[28] Sacred marriage (*hieros gamos*)[29] has been defined as, "Sexual relations between humans as ritual imitation of the sexual relations on the divine plane designed to promote fertility, or at least symbolic representation."[30] While there is a wide range of opinions on the specifics of the topic and these have led to much disagreement about possible rituals associated,[31] there are some examples that point to the broader worldview within the ANE. Some of the more explicit examples come from the Ur III period involving Inanna and Dumuzi.[32] These stories involved

---

[26] "The Ritual of Zarpiya," COS 1.64:7–12.

[27] James B. Pritchard, ed., *The Ancient near Eastern Texts Relating to the Old Testament, with Supplements*, 3rd ed. (Princeton: Princeton University Press, 1969), 417.

[28] Olmo Lete states regarding a royal enthronement text, "Ritual comes to us in the form of a sacred marriage of the king with the goddess Pidrayu, the 'underworld' daughter of Ba'lu, patron goddess of the dynasty … Myth can be considered the transcendent expression of all sacred marriage. … It is the first liturgy … As supreme officiant of the Ugaritic cult, the liturgy of his own 'installment' … the king 'becomes related by marriage' to the gods" (*Canaanite Religion*, 207).

[29] See Aphrodite A. Avagianou, "Hieros Gamos in Ancient Greek Religion: The Human Aspect of a Sacralized Ritual," in *Sacred Marriages: The Divine-Human Sexual Metaphor from Sumer to Early Christianity*, ed. Martti Nissinen and Risto Uro (Winona Lake: Eisenbrauns, 2008), 145–71; Ruben Zimmermann, *Geschlechtermetaphorik und Gottesverhaltnis: Traditionsgeschichte und Theologie eines Bildfelds im Urchristentum und antiker Umwelt*, WUNT 2 (Tubingen: Mohr Siebeck, 2001), 62–76; Jacob Klein, "Sacred Marriage," in *AYBD*, ed. David Noel Freedman (New York: Doubleday, 1992), 5:866.

[30] Smith, *Rituals and Myths*, 127; Moshe Weinfeld, "Feminine Features in the Imagery of God in Israel: The Sacred Marriage and the Sacred Tree," *VT* 46 (1996): 523, 525.

[31] Sir James George Frazer, *The Golden Bough* (London: Macmillan, 1890); Johannes C. de Moor, *New Year with Canaanites and Israelites* (Kampen: Kok, 1972); J. Ivan Trujillo, "The Ugaritic Ritual for a Sacrificial Meal Honoring the Good Gods" (PhD diss., Johns Hopkins University, 1973); F. R. Kraus, "Das altbabylonische Konigtum," in *Le Palaise et la Royaute*, ed. P. Garelli, Archaeology et Civilisation (Paris: Geuthner, 1974); Eduard Lipinski, "Fertility Cult in Ancient Ugarit," in *Archaeology and Fertility Cult in the Ancient Mediterranean: Papers Presented at the First International Conference on Archaeology of the Ancient Mediterranean, the University of Malta, 2–5 Semptember 1985*, ed. Anthony Bonanno (Amsterdam: Gruner, 1986); R. F. G. Sweet, "A New Look at the 'sacred Marriage' in Ancient Mesopotamia," in *Corolla Torontonensis: Studies in Honor of Ronald Morton Smith*, ed. E. Robbins and S. Sandahl (Toronto: TSAR, 1994); Wyatt, *Religious Texts from Ugarit*; John Maier, "Sacred Marriage(s) in Mesopotamian Literature," *Proceedings EGL & MWBS* 24 (2004): 17–34; Nicole Brisch, "The Priestess and the King: The Divine Kingship of Šū-Sîn of Ur," *JAOS* 126.2 (2006): 161–76; Pierre de Miroschedji, "At the Origin of Canaanite Cult and Religion: The Early Bronze Age Fertility Ritual in Palestine," *Eretz-Israel* 7 (2011): 74–103.

[32] David R. Kinsley, *The Goddesses' Mirror: Visions of the Divine from East and West* (Albany: State University of New York Press, 1989), 114; Mary K. Wakeman, "Sacred Marriage," *JSOT* 22 (1982): 24.

a convergence between the divine and mundane. The story "Iddin-Dagan" (ca. 1900 BCE) in poetic form describes Inanna and Dumuzi involved in a romantic and sexual relationship on the divine plane. This then turns to a relationship between King Iddin-Dagan and his queen who is embodied by the goddess.[33] In this story, there is a parallel in the divine occurring between gods which is then being symbolically and even literally evoked into the human realm. In another related hymn, "The Joy of Sumer" (ca. 2000 BCE) which explicitly parallels Dumuzi and Inanna, upon sexual union between the king and the queen she embraces him and calls him Dumuzi "her love."[34] It is uncertain whether these accounts were indicative of literal rituals or simply represented a conceptualization of the world and royalty. Likewise, though the practice was maintained for millennia across many cultures, the exact purpose of the imitative convergence in sacred marriage is debated. It may have been a regular practice to promote fertility,[35] a symbolic practice to coronate a king by intermarrying with the gods,[36] a practice in hopes of a royal offspring secured by its relation to the gods,[37] or perhaps merely to provide festival banquets that reflected the divine realm.[38]

In a later narrative from Ugarit, the story "Gracious Gods: A Sacred Marriage Liturgy" (ca. 1550–1200 BCE) clearly narrates divine relationships, which in Wyatt's view may parallel a "royal marriage."[39] Mark Smith, however, titles it as the "Feast of the Goodly Gods" and contends that the story should simply be seen as a banquet rather than as a sacred marriage ritual.[40] Despite involving divine sexual aspects, Smith argues that a clear ritualistic reenactment of sexual partners on the human level is not present. Instead, according to Smith, the purpose of the narrative is to shape the community's conception of reality,

> The power and nature of the human royalty are effectual to the extent that they ritually share or participate in the power and nature of the divine beneficial powers that are evoked in the narrative. … We might suppose that the ritual and mythic behaviors directed the royal participants' attention and action toward the deities named or alluded to in the rituals. As suggested above, we can easily surmise what this

---

[33] *Iddin-Dagan A,* 187–202; Philip Jones, "Embracing Inana: Legitimation and Mediation in the Ancient Mesopotamian Sacred Marriage Hymn Iddin-Dagan A," *JAOS* 123.2 (2003): 293, 294, 296.

[34] Diana Wolkstein and Samuel Noah Kramer, *Inanna: Queen of Heaven and Earth* (New York: Harper & Row, 1983), 107–14; Kinsley, *Goddesses' Mirror*, 121.

[35] Kinsley, *Goddesses' Mirror*, 121; Douglas R. Frayne, "Notes on the Sacred Marriage Rite," *BO* 42 (1985): 12–22; Klein, "Sacred Marriage," 5:868.

[36] Jones, "Embracing Inana," 291; Olmo Lete, *Canaanite Religion*, 207.

[37] Brisch, "The Priestess and the King," 169; William W. Hallo, "The Birth of Kings," in *Love and Death in the Ancient Near East. Essays in Honor of Marvin H. Pope.*, ed. J. H. Marks and R. M. Good (Guilford: Four Quarters, 1987), 45–52.

[38] Smith, *Rituals and Myths*, 141; Marten Stol, *Women in the Ancient Near East* (Boston: De Gruyter, 2016), 435.

[39] Wyatt, *Religious Texts from Ugarit*, 324–25.

[40] Smith, *Rituals and Myths*, 140, 141.

ritual process impressed on its human participants: in particular, that they should act analogously to the deities and be similar to them. ... The rituals and the myths together generate and express a symbolic worldview that allows the human royal patrons to participate in and intersect with the divine world, thus securing their place in the cosmos.[41]

Although not denying the sexual aspects or the divine parallels, his vision of the story points to a goal beyond such acts as merely ritual. In this, he does not deny sacred marriage so much as he nuances the relationship between ritual and myth along with re-evaluating the function of this particular narrative within its historical context.[42]

In Egypt, the worldview was similar to the one espoused in Mesopotamia, despite some nuanced differences between ritualistic practices. [43] The convergence between the divine and mundane, however, was more explicitly connected to royalty and priests.[44] While it is uncertain if specific sacred marriage rituals were conducted, there was a cultic setting and mythology that saw great importance in the parallel and convergence between the human and the divine realms.[45] Amidst many figures from the Egyptian corpus, the goddess Isis serves as a prime example of imitative ideals from the divine realm. She was considered a devoted wife, embodying love and passion for Osiris. Because of this, she became the "model of affection that is supportive of society and the family" and was revered as the "model spouse."[46] Likewise, she was considered a patron deity for motherhood and parenting because of her care for Horus and his model of reciprocal "filial piety."[47] These highly desired qualities in society earned her a great deal of esteem, particularly among women and family units. Although many of the divine convergences were restricted to royalty and priests, unlike in Mesopotamia, her devotees developed art and worship that praised her as central to civilization and all of human society.[48] Important to note regarding Isis is the broadly and intuitively accepted notion that gods possessed qualities or

---

[41] Mark S. Smith, "Sacred Marriage in the Ugaritic Texts? The Case of KTU/CAT 1.23," in *Sacred Marriages: The Divine-Human Sexual Metaphor from Sumer to Early Christianity*, ed. Martti Nissinen and Risto Uro (Winona Lake: Eisenbrauns, 2008), 112–13.

[42] Smith, *Rituals and Myths*, 135, 139, 140, 141.

[43] For discussion on a different but related ritualistic practice found in both Mesopotamia and Egypt, see, Michael B. Dick, *Born in Heaven, Made on Earth: The Making of the Cult Image in the Ancient Near East* (Winona Lake: Eisenbrauns, 1999), 57, 68–71, 140; C.B.F. Walker and Michael B. Dick, *The Induction of the Cult Image in Ancient Mesopotamia: The Mesopotamian Mīs Pî Ritual*, vol. 1 of *State Archives of Assyria Literary Texts, 1457–9189* (Helsinki: University of Helsinki Press, 2001), 7, 12–13.

[44] Kinsley, *Goddesses' Mirror*, 167.

[45] Mia Rikala, "Sacred Marriage in the New Kingdom of Ancient Egypt: Circumstantial Evidence for a Ritual Interpretation," in *Sacred Marriages: The Divine-Human Sexual Metaphor from Sumer to Early Christianity*, ed. Martti Nissinen and Risto Uro (Winona Lake: Eisenbrauns, 2008), 115–44.

[46] Kinsley, *Goddesses' Mirror*, 173, 175.

[47] Kinsley, *Goddesses' Mirror*, 173.

[48] Kinsley, *Goddesses' Mirror*, 175–77.

engaged in activities that humans desired or sought to emulate. Isis was an example that persisted over a great span of time, at times associated with Hathor and Aphrodite but within a paradigm of fidelity.[49]

The picture painted by these examples within the ANE moves the modern scholar to appreciate a widespread framework. This framework early in human history took for granted the idea that the affairs of the gods paralleled those on the human level, or perhaps vice versa. The gods engaged in seemingly mundane acts such as building homes and palaces, engaging in various rituals, sending emissaries and communications, engaging in war, and were involved in complex sexual and familial webs that often paralleled royal patterns for purposes of treaty or hegemony.[50] While these actions were mythically envisioned in narratives and possibly embodied in ritual, they more affirmatively ensigned the ancient concept of the relationship between the divine and mundane realms.

Greco-Roman

Perhaps one of the most enduring aspects of ancient Greek culture has been its philosophical influence. Greek thinkers at that time were unique in many respects but most in their systematic and metaphysical analyses. These professional thinkers and rhetoricians sought to unravel the universe and display its orderly nature by means of logic. However, this does not imply that other people groups never had philosophical-type thoughts. Rather, the mode and interests of other people groups did not pursue the same questions or produce the same level of analytical scrutiny. Sarah Iles Johnston writes,

> It is often said ... that Mesopotamia did not produce a philosophy. This is true insofar as philosophy is defined according to the ancient Greek model ... However, if we define philosophy more generally as reflection on the human condition and as the investigation of the structure of the cosmos and the laws governing its workings, then it may be claimed that the entire corpus of Mesopotamian literary, religious, and scientific texts constitutes a philosophy.[51]

[49] Kinsley, *Goddesses' Mirror*, 173.

[50] Obermann, *Ugaritic Mythology: A Study of Its Leading Motifs*, 1, 4; Wyatt, *Religious Texts from Ugarit*, 325; John C.L. Gibson and Godfrey Rolles Driver, eds., *Canaanite Myths and Legends*, 2nd ed. (New York: T&T Clark, 2004), 41–42, 99, 406; Olmo Lete, *Canaanite Religion*, 269, 308, 331; Smith, *Rituals and Myths*, 139, 140, 162, 163; Harold W. Attridge, "Pollution, Sin, Atonement, Salvation," in *Ancient Religions*, ed. Sarah Iles Johnston (Cambridge: Harvard University Press, 2007), 73; Johannes C. de Moor, ed., *An Anthology of Religious Texts from Ugarit*, vol. 16 of *Nisaba* (New York: Brill, 1987), 19; Hallo and Younger, *The Context of Scripture*, 163.

[51] Johnston, *Religions of the Ancient World*, 536.

Johnston goes on to describe how the Greek system of philosophy itself was not a monolith, having both religious and non-religious avenues of investigation. The initial contention was between Pythagoras and Xenophanes (6th c. BCE). The Pythagoreans held to a permeable view between the divine and mundane realms, which allowed for the efficacy of religious practice. Such a view was much more akin to those of the ANE. However, Xenophanes was skeptical of cultic practices and knowledge of the divine, holding to a less permeable view of the relationship between the two realms.[52] To him, the realms were quite distinct and the higher order could only be accessed via the mind. Parmenides then took Xenophanes a step further, rejecting any communicability between the two realms.[53]

At this point in the philosophical movement, Plato (5th c. BCE) developed notions of the ideal form which he believed were necessarily transcendent, as Johnston notes, "The fundamental split between the world of the sense, which lacks certainty, truth, and permanence, and the transcendental world of forms, which are eternal and true, locates the divine beyond our world."[54] This view of metaphysical realities led to the view of a poorly conditioned human realm, characterized by dejection and severe limitation. As Buber writes regarding the Greek concept of the human condition, "The soul is a fallen godlike being ... when souls will purify in the course of their transmigrations and back to their likeness to God, they free themselves from the compulsion to re-enter the corporeal life and enter anew the world of the gods. God is, then, the model of the soul that purifies itself in order to return home."[55]

Within this Greek milieu of philosophical inquiry, metaphysical analysis, and epistemological doubt, the topic of imitation and *imitatio Dei* arose quite naturally. Perhaps first in the Greek tradition, the Pythagoreans were credited with the phrase, "Follow after god."[56] This particular phrase was used to promote the ultimate purpose of man: to become like the gods.[57] Writing many centuries later, Josephus contended, though difficult to prove, that Pythagoras actually developed much of his philosophy and idea of following after the gods from Jewish theology and scripture, "This [Pythagoras] did and said in imitation of the doctrines of the Jews and Thracians, which he transferred into his own philosophy. For it is very truly affirmed of this Pythagoras, that he took a great many of the laws of the Jews into his own philosophy."[58] It seems, Plato later picked up on this Pythagorean

[52] Xenophanes is credited with a scathing repudiation of man's recreation of the gods in his image: "The Ethiopian gods have Ethiopian lips, bronze cheeks, and woolly hair; the Grecian gods are like the Greeks, as keen-eyed, cold, and fair" (Israel Abrahams, *Studies in Pharisaism and the Gospels* (1917; repr., New York: Ktav, 1967), 140).

[53] Johnston, *Religions of the Ancient World*, 543.

[54] Johnston, *Religions of the Ancient World*, 543.

[55] Martin Buber, *Israel and the World: Essays in a Time of Crisis* (New York: Schocken Books, 1948), 66.

[56] Buber, *Israel and the World*, 66.

[57] Abrahams, *Studies in Pharisaism*, 155.

[58] Josephus, *Ag. Ap.* 1.163; Flavius Josephus, *The Works of Josephus: Complete and Unabridged*, trans. William Whiston (Peabody: Hendrickson, 1987), 783. Josephus writes: "

idea and developed it into his own philosophy, as well. In an allegory of a charioteer, Plato describes in *Phaedrus* the successful journey of the soul as "that which best follows after God and is most like him."[59] In fact, he goes on to discuss the nature of particular followers of different gods. For followers of Ares, they desire and emulate love. For Zeus, they desire and pursue a "philosophical and lordly nature" and of Hera a "kingly nature." The followers of Apollo seek "youth."[60] This thinking fits well with his statements from Socrates in *Theaetetus* emphasizing the phrase "likeness to God" (ὁμοίωσις θεῷ), which in his view meant pursuit of the divine virtues.[61] The mundane world is irredeemably and necessarily replete with evil. Thus, the goal of man is to escape, which is possible only through imitating the gods in divine qualities. Similarly, he writes regarding a human imitative relationship with a wise person, "Him I follow after and 'walk in his footsteps as if he were a god.'"[62] The implication, of course, is man ought to aspire to emulate those of

---

[59] Plato, *Phaedrus* 247–48; Plato, *Euthyphro; Apology; Crito; Phaedo; Phaedrus*, trans. Harold North Fowler (1914; repr., Cambridge: Harvard University Press, 2005), 477. Additionally, he says, "But the region above the heaven ... is visible only to the mind, the pilot of the soul."

[60] Plato, *Phaedrus*, 252–53. Plato in *Phaedrus*, "Now he who is a follower of Zeus, when seized by Love can bear a heavier burden of the winged god; but those who are servants of Ares and followed in his train, when they have been seized by Love and think they have been wronged in any way by the beloved, become murderous and are ready to sacrifice themselves and the beloved. [d] And so it is with the follower of each of the other gods; he lives, so far as he is able, honoring and imitating that god, so long as he is uncorrupted, and is living his first life on earth, and in that way, he behaves and conducts himself toward his beloved and toward all others. Now each one chooses his love from the ranks of the beautiful according to his character, and he fashions him and adorns him [e] like a statue, as though he were his god, to honor and worship him. The followers of Zeus desire that the soul of him whom they love be like Zeus; so, they seek for one of philosophical and lordly nature, and when they find him and love him, they do all they can to give him such a character. If they have not previously had experience, they learn then from all who can teach them anything; [253] they seek after information themselves, and when they search eagerly within themselves to find the nature of their god, they are successful, because they have been compelled to keep their eyes fixed upon the god, and as they reach and grasp him by memory they are inspired and receive from him character and habits, so far as it is possible for a man to have part in God. Now they consider the beloved the cause of all this, so they love him more than before, and if they draw the waters of their inspiration from Zeus, like the bacchantes, they pour it out upon the beloved and make him, so far as possible, like their god. [b] And those who followed after Hera seek a kingly nature, and when they have found such an one, they act in a corresponding manner toward him in all respects; and likewise the followers of Apollo, and of each of the gods, go out and seek for their beloved a youth whose nature accords with that of the god, and when they have gained his affection, by imitating the god themselves and by persuasion and education they lead the beloved to the conduct and nature of the god, so far as each of them can do so; they exhibit no jealousy or meanness toward the loved one, but endeavor by every means in their power to lead him to the likeness [c] of the god whom they honor."

[61] Plato writes of Socrates, "We ought to try to escape from earth to the dwelling of the gods as quickly as we can; and to escape is to become like God, so far as this is possible; and to become like God is to become righteous and holy and wise" (Plato, *Theaetetus*, 176b–d; Gregory E. Sterling, "Imitatio Dei (Eph 5:1–2): The Soteriological Basis for Ethics," in *Sōtēria: Salvation in Early Christianity and Antiquity: Festschrift in Honour of Cilliers Breytenbach on the Occasion of His 65th Birthday*, ed. Cilliers Breytenbach et al., NovTSup 175 (Leiden: Brill, 2019), 352).

[62] Plato, *Euthyphro; Apology; Crito; Phaedo; Phaedrus*, 535.

greater capacity or being, whether they be gods or men. Despite this great aspiration, Plato was cognizant that creaturely beings had limitations. Thus, they were to imitate the gods as far as it was possible, reasonable, and virtuous.

The discussion of imitating the gods did not end with Pythagoras and Plato, however.[63] Rather, the thinking and terminology strengthened. Moving into Middle Platonism, philosophers began discussing *imitatio Dei* as the human *telos* rather than just a means for escape. One author stated in discourse with Plato's writings, "Having achieved this likeness one attains finally to that *telos* of the best life which is set before humans by the gods, both for the present and for the time to come."[64] Following Plato, these philosophers emphasized that this imitation was primarily in the sense of divine virtues. The likeness envisioned was achieved through "nature, habits, and practice that is according to law and … reason, instruction, and philosophical tradition."[65] Epicurus opined on the ideal life that imitation of the gods led to the total annihilation of suffering, which transcends human existence and assimilates to the divine.[66] Another important shift occurred with these philosophers toward a strong sense of division between the transcendent and mundane. In this era, the idea developed further that the transcendence of the divine was impenetrable and thus required an intermediary. This fostered a long tradition of identifying or qualifying this intermediary. Early on, the being was called the "heavenly god" (ἐπουράνιος) or the "Craftsman," in distinction from the transcendent god. Later, the intermediary was referred to as the "Logos" or "Wisdom."[67] The primary role was both to bridge the communicative and epistemological barrier between the ideal and mundane but also to serve as the imitative bridge to the divine as well. By following this imitative ideal, humans could approximate a likeness to the divine ideal, one beyond normal human capacity.

The Greek picture of imitation of the gods is more explicit than the mythic and ritualistic narratives found in the ANE. However, the principal concepts regarding the imitative value of the gods permeated both. While the philosophers sought virtue and metaphysics, their earlier ANE counterparts sought prosperity, stability, and blessing. While this has only been a small

---

[63] It should be noted at this point that Aristotle discussed "imitation" (μίμησις), as well. However, he was primarily interested in the idea as it pertained to literature and the arts. W. H. Frye notes regarding this use of *mimesis*, "Life 'presents' to the artist the phenomena of sense, which the artist 're-presents' in his own medium, giving coherence, designing a pattern." Plato discussed imitation in the arts but found particular relevance in imitation of the gods as well. See Aristotle, "Poetics," in *Aristotle in 23 Volumes*, trans. W. H. Frye (Cambridge: Harvard University Press, 1932), 1447a; Michael Davis, *The Poetry of Philosophy: On Aristotle's Poetics* (South Bend: St. Augustine's, 1999), 3.

[64] Sterling, "Imitatio Dei (Eph 5:1–2)," 353.

[65] See Alcinous, *Didaskalikos*, 28.1–4; 181.19–182.14; J. Whittaker and Pierre Louis, *Alcinous: Enseignementdes Doctrines de Platon*, Collection Des Universités De France (Paris: Belles Lettres, 1990); Sterling, "Imitatio Dei (Eph 5:1–2)," 353.

[66] Johnston, *Religions of the Ancient World*, 544.

[67] Johnston, *Religions of the Ancient World*, 539–44; Sterling, "Imitatio Dei (Eph 5:1–2)," 354.

window into the broad field of Greek philosophy, culture, and religion, it does serve to provide an additional perspective into the widespread, imitative framework within the ancient world. Although particularities may have differed, the Greeks understood that their world was parallel with the transcendent and that the purpose of humanity was assimilation with the divine realm.

Jewish

Philo of Alexandria

As such a pivotal thinker, it is perhaps difficult to know the extent of influence Philo had on both Rabbinic and Church theology and philosophy. However, it is generally agreed that he himself was deeply influenced by both Greek philosophy and Jewish literature. [68] On the topic of imitation, his Greek influence is directly evident when he quotes Plato's *Theaetetus*. Here, Philo discusses the two paths or patterns, condemning the godless who are not becoming like God but imitating one another in foolishness. [69] Such a perspective orients many of his views and serves as the basis for many of his applications. For example, he praises and commends virtuous actions, such as generosity and mercy, by appealing to the imitation of God.[70] As he states in reference to a common aphorism, "Men never act in a manner more resembling the gods than when they are bestowing benefits; and what can be a greater good than for mortal men to imitate the everlasting God?" [71] Likewise, he points to imitating God's own action in Gen 1 to support the Sabbath commandment in Exod 20.[72] In fact, he says quite explicitly, "The commandment, in effect says: Always imitate God; let that one period of seven days in which God created the world, be to you a complete example of the way in which you are to obey the law, and an all-sufficient model for your actions."[73] In a few places, he appeals to imitation of pagan gods, particularly for the absurdity of idolatry.[74] On one hand, he condemned the inhumane and

---

[68] Abrahams, *Studies in Pharisaism*; Buber, *Israel and the World*; Johnston, *Religions of the Ancient World*; Howard Kreisel, "Imitatio Dei in Maimonides' Guide of the Perplexed," *AJS Review* 19.2 (1994): 169–211; Arthur Marmorstein, *The Doctrine of Merits in Old Rabbinical Literature; and The Old Rabbinic Doctrine of God: I. The Names and Attributes of God and II. Essays in Anthropomorphism* (1920; repr., New York: Ktav, 1968); Hindy Najman, "Imitatio Dei and the Formation of the Subject in Ancient Judaism," *JBL* 140.2 (2021): 309–23; Sterling, "Imitatio Dei (Eph 5:1–2)."

[69] Philo, *Flight*, 63; Philo of Alexandria, *The Works of Philo: Complete and Unabridged*, trans. Charles Duke Yonge (Peabody: Hendrickson, 1995).

[70] Philo, *Virtues*, 66, 168–69; *Spec. Laws 4*, 72–74, 188–89; Philo of Alexandria, *The Works of Philo*.

[71] Philo, *Spec. Laws 4*, 73; Philo of Alexandria, *The Works of Philo*.

[72] Philo, *Decalogue*, 98–100; Philo of Alexandria, *The Works of Philo*.

[73] Philo, *Decalogue*, 100; Philo of Alexandria, *The Works of Philo*.

[74] Philo, *Decalogue*, 75; Philo of Alexandria, *The Works of Philo*.

idolatrous practices of the Greeks and Romans.[75] Conversely, Philo invoked pagan divine imitation for the sake of seeking mercy, "Have you imitated the twin sons of Jupiter in their brotherly affection, that I may begin with that point? Did you not rather, O hard-hearted and most pitiless of men inhumanly slaughter your brother."[76] Central to his theology and philosophy regarding human ethics was its inherent parallel with the divine realm.

Rooted in the Platonic tradition, he also held to a strong view for a mediating bridge between the realms.[77] This mediator was "Wisdom" or "Logos" and the "mind" was the location of convergence with the divine.[78] Furthermore, in regards to the "image of God," he believed man was made in likeness to the "image" of God, which he referred to as the "Archetype."[79] Because of this view, he rejected any sense of physical or embodied resemblance between God and man. Rather, Philo was interested in the path toward perfection. Like the Greek philosophers before, Philo sought this assimilation to God by means of imitating the Logos through virtue.[80] Such a path was not to become God, nor Moses, but simply to grow in the likeness of God.[81] Accordingly, though, there was a limit to how similar one might attain. As Plato also believed, Philo taught that man should imitate as far as it is possible. So, while deeply impacted by a late Greek philosophical framework, he understood that humanity acted in accordance with the nature and actions of the divine.

Rabbinic

The rabbinic tradition broke from Philo with an important distinction, ultimate priority was given to scripture and subsequent rabbinic interpretations. Philo was of course deeply influenced by Greek philosophy and sought to harmonize the two traditions.[82] However, rabbinic tradition until Maimonides largely sought internally developed ideas and interpretations, rather than those rooted in non-Jewish philosophy. Because

---

[75] Philo, *Decalogue*, 65–82; Philo of Alexandria, *The Works of Philo*; Arthur Marmorstein, *Studies in Jewish Theology; the Arthur Marmorstein Memorial Volume*, ed. J. Rabbinowitz and M. S. Lew (New York: Oxford University Press, 1950), 117. Marmorstein discusses rabbinic theology stating, "Philo uses the doctrine of the *Imitatio Dei* to reduce to an absurdity the worship of idols."

[76] Philo, *Embassy*, 87; Philo of Alexandria, *The Works of Philo*.

[77] Sterling, "Imitatio Dei (Eph 5:1–2)," 356–57.

[78] Abrahams, *Studies in Pharisaism*, 143, 150; Philo of Alexandria, *The Works of Philo*, 675. Philo says of the mind, "This is the mind which has drunk strong draughts of the beneficent power of God, and has feasted on his sacred words and doctrines. This is the mind in which the prophet says that God walks as in his palace; for the mind of the wise man is in truth the palace and the house of God" (675).

[79] Philo, *Creation*, 25, 139; *Alleg. Interp. 2*, 4–5; Abrahams, *Studies in Pharisaism*, 141; Sterling, "Imitatio Dei (Eph 5:1–2)," 356.

[80] Sterling, "Imitatio Dei (Eph 5:1–2)," 356–57.

[81] Najman, "Imitatio Dei," 320–22.

[82] Abrahams, *Studies in Pharisaism*, 156–57.

of this focus, the rabbis spent centuries pouring over the HB in order to provide important and relevant interpretations for the life of the Jewish community. Part of this discussion was the imitation of God. In fact, it has been claimed that such was the center or basis of rabbinic ethics.[83] This central idea was rooted in the rabbinic theology that God did not prescribe things he himself did not do.[84] In other words, God's character was consistent with his word.

The rabbinic discussion around imitation of God primarily involved a few key ideas: walking in the ways of God (e.g., Deut 13:5[4]),[85] the name and attributes of God (e.g., Exod 34:6–7), and the image of God (e.g., Gen 1:26). The first is preeminent in the book of Deuteronomy and characterized much of rabbinic thinking regarding the legal code and ethics. In the Talmud, Rabbi Hama and Rabbi Hanina (ca. 4th c. CE) provided commentary on Deut 13:5, "After the Lord your God you shall walk." Regarding this passage, they said, "Is it actually possible to follow the Divine Presence? ... the meaning is that one should follow the attributes of the Holy One."[86] In some practical examples, they note how God clothed the naked (Gen 3:21), visited the sick (Gen 18:1), consoled mourners (Gen 25:11), and buried the dead (Deut 34:6). Abrahams adds a couple passages to their list to further illuminate the idea. In Gen 17:1, which is similar to the account of Noah (Gen 6:9), God says, "I am God almighty; walk before me and be perfect (תמים)." According to Abrahams, this is equivalent to the Platonic and Pythagorean idea of "imitation" (μίμησις) and the trajectory of divine perfection.[87] Likewise, he connects this to Matthew's account of Jesus, "Be perfect as your father in heaven is perfect" (5:48).

From a critical perspective, Cyril Rodd contends against the connection between "walk in the ways of Yhwh" and imitation of God, claiming it is merely a command statement.[88] According to rabbinic tradition, however, walking in the ways of God was not understood to be merely a command.[89]

[83] Peter Nasuti, "Identity, Identification, and Imitation: The Narrative Hermeneutics of Biblical Law," *Journal of Law and Religion* 4.1 (1986): 20; Buber, *Israel and the World*, 71; Marmorstein, *Doctrine of Merits*, 7; Abrahams, *Studies in Pharisaism*, 138.

[84] Cohen quotes from a rabbinic source, "With the Holy One, blessed be He ... when He makes a decree, He performs it first" (Abraham Cohen, *Everyman's Talmud* (1932; repr., Hawthorne: BN, 2007), 291–92).

[85] Marmorstein notes that in the Tannaim the rabbis closely associated this phrase with the Hebrew verb דמה often used as "to be like." Rabbi ibn Ezra provided commentary on this verse saying, "You shall do your utmost to imitate God's deeds and pursue His paths." See Marmorstein, *Studies in Jewish Theology*, 115; Abraham ben Meïr Ibn Ezra, *Ibn Ezra's Commentary on the Pentateuch*, trans. H. Norman Strickman and Arthur M. Silver (New York: Menorah, 1988), Deut 13:5.

[86] Adin Even-Israel Steinsaltz, *Sota*, ed. Tzvi Hersh Weinreb, Shalom Zvi Berger, and Joshua Schreier, Koren Talmud Bavli 20 (Jerusalem: Koren, 2012), §Sota 14a.

[87] Abrahams, *Studies in Pharisaism*, 155–56.

[88] Cyril S. Rodd, *Glimpses of a Strange Land: Studies in Old Testament Ethics*, OTS (Edinburgh: T&T Clark, 2001), 70. His contention is specifically related to Eryl Davies use of the rabbinic phrase in his article on *imitatio Dei*.

[89] Buber says in a discussion about Rashi and Rabbi Shaul's interpretation of Exod 15:2, "To imitate God means then to cleave to his ways, to walk in his ways. By these are meant

Rather, it was reflective of God's own character. Cohen opines on the rabbinic theology of "walk after the Lord" saying, "Not only in His commandments did God provide the human being with guidance to the true way of life, but in Himself He set the example which is to be followed. The Imitation of God is, in Rabbinic literature, set forward as the ideal after which man should strive. God is the Pattern after which human life must be delineated."[90] In many other instances, the command to Abraham (Gen 17:1) and the commendation of Noah (Gen 6:9) are connected to Deut 11:22, which further includes the ideas "to love" (אהב) and "to cling" (דבק) to the Lord. Deuteronomy 11:22 was often connected with Exod 34:6–7, the moral attributes of God's name.[91] In his revelation to Moses, God declared his name, which included "merciful, gracious, slow to anger, and abounding in steadfast love and faithfulness" (רחוּם וְחַנּוּן אֶרֶךְ אַפַּיִם וְרַב־חֶסֶד וֶאֱמֶת). So, in rabbinic thinking, one fulfills the command in Deut 11:22 and 13:4, along with other places which use "walk in the ways of Yhwh," by taking on his name and its attributes (e.g., Deut 28:9; Joel 3:5). Similarly, the list of attributes was related to Mic 6:8 which says, "Do justice and love steadfast love and walk humbly with your God" (עֲשׂוֹת מִשְׁפָּט וְאַהֲבַת חֶסֶד וְהַצְנֵעַ לֶכֶת עִם־אֱלֹהֶיךָ).[92] To walk "with God" (e.g., Gen 5:24, 6:9), "after God" (e.g., Deut 13:5), or "in his ways" (e.g., Deut 5:33, 10:12) were essentially overlapping in function, always implying a call to do as God does, particularly according to his moral attributes. In fact, it has been said that the rabbinic tradition of Halakah is based on this phrase.[93] In one Haggadic passage, the rabbinic teaching on Song 1:15 expounds on a simple phrase saying, "My beloved, he who walks in God's ways is called beloved and the friend of God. As God is gracious and merciful, long-suffering and full of love, so be thou also like God, give charity and practice beneficence."[94] Rabbi Saul also used similar

---

not the ways which God has commanded man as man to walk in, they are really God's own ways" (*Israel and the World*, 75).

[90] Cohen, *Everyman's Talmud*, 292–93.

[91] As the *Sifre Devarim 49* says, "'To Walk in all His ways' (11:22): These are the ways of 'the Lord, God, merciful and gracious' (Exod 34:6). Scripture says, 'And it shall come to pass, that whosoever shall call by the name of the Lord shall be delivered' (Joel 3:5) – how is it possible for man to be called by the name of the Lord? Rather, as God is called 'merciful,' so should you be merciful, as the Holy One, blessed be He, is called 'gracious,' so too should you be gracious, as it is said, 'The Lord is gracious and full of compassion' (Ps 145:8), and grants free gifts. As God is called righteous, 'For the Lord is righteous, He loveth righteousness' (Ps 11:7), so you too should be righteous. As God is called merciful, as it is said, 'For I am merciful, saith the Lord' (Jer 3:12), so too should you be merciful." Hammer adds the note, "Rabbinic tradition calls upon man to imitate God by living in accordance with his qualities of mercy and justice, not those of punishment" (Reuven Hammer, *Sifre: A Tannaitic Commentary on the Book of Deuteronomy*, Yale Judaica Series 24 (New Haven: Yale University Press, 1986), 105–6, 418).

[92] Abrahams notes that several writers such as Cordovero find a total of thirteen attributes of God to be imitated, which is further completed with Mic 7:18–20. See, Abrahams, *Studies in Pharisaism*, 145; Menachem Kellner, "Ethics of Judaism," in *The Encyclopaedia of Judaism*, 2nd ed., ed. Jacob Neusner, Alan J. Avery-Peck, and William S. Green (Boston: Brill, 2005), 745.

[93] Erich Fromm, *You Shall Be as Gods: A Radical Interpretation of the Old Testament and Its Tradition* (New York: Holt, Rinehart, and Winston, 1966), 179.

[94] Marmorstein, *Studies in Jewish Theology*, 114.

language to discuss his unique interpretation of Exod 15:2 saying, "As he is merciful and gracious, so be thou merciful and gracious."[95]

The image of God was also a prominent fixture in rabbinic thought, particularly as it relates to imitating God. The appeals to Gen 1:26–27 are extensive but primarily include several views such as a physical likeness, a likeness in function, or likeness in character. Rabbi Chaim of Tchernovitz claimed, "The fundamental reason for the creation of man is that he is to make himself as much like his Creator as he can."[96] He then quoted Rabbi Hizkiah (3rd c. CE) saying, "They make themselves like their Creator by unifying all their limbs to resemble his unity, and driving all share of evil out of themselves that they may be perfect with the Lord their God ... That is why God said, 'Let us make man in our image and after our likeness'—out of his love for man he created him in his own image, so that man should be able to make himself like his Creator."[97] Regarding man's likeness to God, Rabbi Donnolo (10th c. CE) understood this to be primarily a functional likeness, just as God governs and creates so does man.[98] In a somewhat different perspective, possibly due to a reverence for the transcendence of God, much of the medieval rabbinic literature took the "image" (צלם) to be a metaphor for intellect, similar to Philo in the first century.[99] In a debate over the greatest teaching in Torah, Rabbis Aqiba and Azzai both agreed that the image of God was central. Rabbi Aqiba believed this was primarily realized in ethical conduct as found in Lev 19:18, "You shall love your neighbor as yourself."[100] However, Rabbi Azzai placed a higher value on the basis of human relationships because, as he taught, all of humanity shares a common ancestor who was formed according to the likeness of God.[101]

Now, despite a great deal of rabbinic support for the imitation of God, there were some that rejected the idea or provided caveats. In a satirical statement, Rabbi Levi says, "'Only he who can accomplish My works is like Me' ... God has created heaven and earth. Do the same, and then canst thou also be called God, then wilt thou be like Him."[102] Similarly, Rabbi Simon ben Lakish (3rd c. CE) provided a caution on Lev 19:2, questioning the possibility of a human being as holy as God is. With a more guarded caveat, Abrahams proposes that rabbinic literature does not support man's imitation of the

---

[95] Buber, *Israel and the World*, 75.

[96] Buber, *Israel and the World*, 74.

[97] Buber, *Israel and the World*, 74.

[98] Abrahams, *Studies in Pharisaism*, 144.

[99] Mayer I. Gruber, "Image of God," in *The Encyclopaedia of Judaism*, 2nd ed., ed. Jacob Neusner, Alan J. Avery-Peck, and William S. Green (Boston: Brill, 2005), 871–72.

[100] Kellner, "Ethics of Judaism," 742.

[101] Cohen, *Everyman's Talmud*, 293.

[102] Marmorstein, *Studies in Jewish Theology*, 117; Abrahams, *Studies in Pharisaism*, 148–49. Abrahams discusses the issue of equality in respect to absorption, endorsed by some scholars like Thomas and Albertus, saying, "Unless the copy becomes as the model, the Imitation is imperfect. If Imitation is likeness, the likeness must eventually be of equals The Lord will answer: 'Am I not like you?' Or in another passage (Pesiqta Rabbathi 46b): 'In this world Israel cleaves to the Holy One; hereafter they will be and be like Him.' The goal is reached, not in absorption but in equality, the copy and the original are of one order, though the idea of reverence remains."

"sterner of the Old Testament attributes of God." [103] In his reading of the rabbis, divine qualities such as anger, which even Moses failed to properly imitate, are not meant to be models to imitate. Likewise, Cohen notes that although God was the prime example to be followed, according to rabbinic theology some things such as jealousy were not to be imitated. This caveat was based on Exod 20:5, "I am a jealous God," to which rabbis opined was unique to God who could not be mastered by jealousy. [104] In later Jewish theology, rabbis such as Azkari proposed that imitation was only for his moral attributes and not God directly, due to a theological view of God's transcendence. [105]

One last important voice in the rabbinic tradition was Moses ben Maimon (12th c. CE), also known as Maimonides. He was within the rabbinic tradition but far more akin to Philo in his thinking. [106] Much like Philo, Maimonides sought to bridge the gap between Greek philosophy and biblical interpretation. [107] With this in mind, it is helpful to approach his views on *imitatio Dei* as unique within the rabbinic tradition. He held to a transcendent and simple view of God which led to his view of "pure intellect" as the goal of imitation. [108] Thus, the attributes of God to be imitated were only known indirectly. [109] Furthermore, in parallel with Greek thinking, he held that the goal of humanity was assimilation to divine character, expressed in ethical actions. [110] In other words, one grows in intellectual perfection through ethical purity. [111] So, according to Maimonides, both knowledge of God and imitation of God were to be understood through the lens of practical ethics rather than speculation of his essence. [112]

As the Jewish and Rabbinic tradition attest, the idea of imitating God was central. It served as the basis for much of the theological and ethical reasoning. Likewise, it served as the foundation for the nature and purpose of humanity, which guided all of human society. The framework for divine imitation was not derived from Greek philosophy or ANE myth but through the interpretation of their sacred scriptures. Yet, in many respects, it reflected familiar sentiments found throughout the ancient and medieval world.

---

[103] Abrahams, *Studies in Pharisaism*, 152.

[104] Cohen, *Everyman's Talmud*, 293.

[105] Abrahams, *Studies in Pharisaism*, 169.

[106] Abrahams, *Studies in Pharisaism*, 157.

[107] Gruber, "Image of God," 872.

[108] Kreisel, "Imitatio Dei in Maimonides' Guide of the Perplexed," 174.

[109] Najman, "Imitatio Dei," 314.

[110] Kreisel, "Imitatio Dei in Maimonides' Guide of the Perplexed," 190.

[111] Kellner, "Ethics of Judaism," 744.

[112] Fromm, *You Shall Be as Gods*, 67.

Christianity

The New Testament

Although written in Greek, the New Testament is deeply reliant on the HB and its Jewish context, shaped by the first century. Having explored in brief both the Greek and Jewish traditions surrounding *imitatio Dei*, it is important to understand this idea as it appeared in the NT and subsequently in the Church. There are perhaps many places to begin this overview. However, the best place is in the single appearance in the Old or New Testaments of the phrase "imitators of God" (μιμηταὶ τοῦ θεοῦ) (Eph 5:1). Scholars have speculated whether Paul was drawing directly from Greek philosophy or not.[113] Regardless of Paul's influence, he immediately explained what he intended by the phrase. First, Paul qualifies his command to "be imitators of God" within the analogy of a paternal relationship, children to their father, a paradigm foundational for rabbinic theology as well (Prov 10:1).[114] Just as children imitate or resemble their fathers (e.g., Gen 5:1), so the Ephesians were to resemble their heavenly father.[115] This is particularly salient in light of Paul's prior claim that the new humanity was created κατὰ θεὸν or "Godlike" (Eph 4:24).[116] However, avoiding Greek transcendent philosophical categories, Paul uses the phrase as the fundamental basis for his audience to live a certain

---

[113] Ernest Best provides a brief excursus on identifying the source and context of Paul's phrase, "It is unnecessary to trace the origin of the concept in the Greek world where it was widespread, being used in philosophy (the material world an imitation of the ideal, man a microcosm of the macrocosm), in art (artistic creation imitates reality), in the Mysteries (the experience of the initiate imitates that of the god). In brief, some kind of model is set up for imitation and this appears in varying forms. Important for v. 1 are those places where one person is regarded as imitating, or exhorted to imitate, another: (1) sons to imitate fathers (Isocrates, *To Demonicus* 4:11); (2) subjects, rulers (Xenophon, *Cyropedeia*, VIII 1:21, 24); (3) pupils, teachers (Dio Chrys, *Discourses* 55:4, 5; Seneca, Ep 6:5–6); (4) the good are also to be imitated (Isocrates, *To Nicocles* 22:38; 38:61). Parallels exist to most of these in Judaism: (1) 1 Macc 2:51; Philo, *Sacrif Abel* 64; (3) Philo, *Mosis* 1:158; (4) *T Benj* 3:1; 4:1; 4 Macc 9:23; Philo, *Spec. Laws* 4, 83; *Ps-Phoc* 77 speaks more abstractly of not imitating evil. Philo provides, if not the bridge from the Hellenistic world to Judaism, an example of how Judaism could adopt the theme. In him, we find both the philosophical and cosmological aspects and the personal (in addition to the above references see also *Congressu* 59; cf. *Jos Ant* 3:123; *T Asher* 4:3; *Ep Arist* 188, 210, 281)."

However, Best goes on to propose that the idea of imitating God was a late, Hellenistic philosophy not original to the OT. His argument claims as evidence the disapproval of Adam and Eve's desire to be like God (Gen 3:1–7), the admonition against making anything in the likeness of God (Exod 20:4–6; Deut 5:8–10), and the causal rather than comparative aspect of Lev 19:2. For a more in-depth look at the relationship between Ephesians, Philo, and Plato, see Robert A. Wild, "'Be Imitators of God': Discipleship in the Letter to the Ephesians," in *Discipleship in the New Testament*, ed. Fernando F. Segovia (Philadelphia: Fortress, 1985), 127–38; Ernest Best, *A Critical and Exegetical Commentary on Ephesians* (Edinburgh: T&T Clark, 1998), 466.

[114] Marmorstein, *Doctrine of Merits*, 202.

[115] Best provides a caveat to the command, "Naturally a widening to imitation can only be partial for it is impossible to imitate God in everything" (Best, *A Critical and Exegetical Commentary on Ephesians*, 465).

[116] Wild, "Be Imitators of God," 135.

way, following in God's ways. Second, much like later rabbinic focus,[117] Paul follows his command for them to "imitate" with the command to "walk in love" (περιπατεῖτε ἐν ἀγάπῃ) (Eph 5:2).[118] He then qualifies what he means by "walk." The Ephesians were to "walk in love" in imitative cohesion with Christ, who did the same for them, "just as Christ also loved you" (καθὼς καὶ ὁ Χριστὸς ἠγάπησεν ἡμᾶς). Paul's command could perhaps be rephrased to say 'walk in the ways of Christ' meaning both Christ's command to "love one another" and according to his own example "just as I have loved you" found in John 13:34. This type of imitative reflection is found most clearly in Deut 10:17–19.[119] In fact, Paul uses this imitative, reciprocal paradigm in the previous verse, "Be kind to one another, compassionate, being gracious to each just as God in Christ was gracious to you" (Eph 4:32).[120] Thus, in Ephesians, Paul teaches the importance of forgiving and loving one another by the appeal to imitate both God and Christ, the prime exemplars of such divine characteristics.

Elsewhere, Paul also explicitly commands or commends his first century audience to imitate him (1 Cor 4:16, 11:1; Phil 3:17; 1 Thess 1:6; 2 Thess 3:7, 9). In two of these instances, Paul implicates their imitation of him as a link to imitating Christ, "Be imitators of me just as I am of Christ" (1 Cor 11:1) and "You became imitators of us and of the Lord" (1 Thess 1:6).[121] Likewise, Paul praises these believers for becoming models themselves that others could imitate in their Paul-like and Christ-like obedience amidst difficulty (1 Thess 1:7).[122] Gene Green says, "Unlike many modern students, the ancients deeply appreciated the value of imitating model lives as a means of moral education, whether those models were parents, heroes, or teachers."[123] In other words, Paul's imitative pattern was not novel in the least but fit quite neatly within a very broad and long history of such modeling.

---

[117] Marmorstein comments on the center of rabbinic theology saying, "God's love to His creatures, whether good or bad, Gentiles or Jews, is as we see, one of the most emphatic and characteristic doctrines of Rabbinic theology. ... Rabbinic teachings extend God's love and grace, goodness and mercy, to sinners. God is the Father of all beings, of the whole world. 'A wise son makes a glad father' (Prov 10:1). The father is God, who is the Father of the whole world!" (Marmorstein, *Doctrine of Merits*, 201).

[118] The idea of "walking" (περιπατέω) as a metaphor relating to ethical and godly pattern of life is popular in Pauline scripture, occurring 30x (Rom 6:4, 8:4, 13:13, 14:15; 1 Cor 3:3, 7:17; 2 Cor 4:2, 5:7, 10:2, 3, 12:18; Gal 5:16; Eph 2:2, 10, 4:1, 17, 5:2, 8, 15; Phil 3:17, 18; Col 1:10, 2:6, 3:7, 4:5; 1 Thess 2:12, 4:1, 12; 2 Thess 3:6, 11).

[119] Walter J. Houston, "The Character of YHWH and the Ethics of the Old Testament: Is Imitatio Dei Appropriate?" *JTS* 58.1 (2007): 11; Rodd, *Glimpses of a Strange Land*, 67. Despite deep skepticism of *imitatio Dei*, even Rodd says this of Deut 10:17–19, "The two texts where the 'model' is 'particularly visible' are Deuteronomy 10:17–19 and Leviticus 19:2."

[120] γίνεσθε εἰς ἀλλήλους χρηστοί, εὔσπλαγχνοι, χαριζόμενοι ἑαυτοῖς, καθὼς καὶ ὁ θεὸς ἐν Χριστῷ ἐχαρίσατο ὑμῖν (Eph 4:32). A parallel idea is found in Col 3:13, "just as the Lord has forgiven you, so also ought you."

[121] μιμηταί μου γίνεσθε καθὼς κἀγὼ Χριστοῦ (1 Cor 11:1); ὑμεῖς μιμηταὶ ἡμῶν ἐγενήθητε καὶ τοῦ κυρίου (1 Thess 1:6).

[122] Andrew D. Clarke, "'Be Imitators of Me': Paul's Model of Leadership," *TB* 49.2 (1998): 333–35; Ernest Best, *A Commentary on the First and Second Epistles to the Thessalonians*, BNTC (London: Continuum, 1986), 76–79.

[123] Gene L. Green, *The Letters to the Thessalonians*, PNTC (Grand Rapids: Eerdmans, 2002), 97. Green goes on to say, "Xenophon, for example, described the role of the teacher, saying,

Finally, Paul's idea of imitation is reflective of the view proposed by the Gospel writers as well. Paul's imitative, paternal pattern in Eph 5:1 was primarily built on the idea that Christ imitated his father. Buber comments on the imitative pattern in 1 Cor 11:1, "The imitation is made easier and possible by intermediary links. We need only transfer ourselves from mediacy to immediacy, from the imitation of Jesus to his imitation of our Father, and we are standing on Jewish soil."[124] Jesus makes it clear that his work was not arbitrary or original but in perfect accord with the nature and works of his father (John 5:19–26).[125] Jesus says, "For whatever [the Father] may do, this also the Son does the same ... For just as the father raises the dead and gives life, so also the Son gives life to those he desires" (John 5:19, 21).[126] Jesus also commended his audience to follow him in imitating the Father, that they might also be "sons of the Father" (υἱοὶ τοῦ πατρὸς) (Matt 5:45; cf. John 1:12). The imitative path Jesus teaches here is the principle, "love your enemies" (ἀγαπᾶτε τοὺς ἐχθροὺς ὑμῶν) (5:44).[127] Likewise, he concludes this teaching by saying, "You yourselves shall be perfect as your heavenly Father is perfect" (Matt 5:48).[128] His teaching could either be an adaptation of Gen 17:1 or Lev 19:2 (cf. Lev 11:44–45, 20:26; Deut 18:13). In Gen 17:1, God commends Abraham to "be blameless." However, Lev 19:2 which is reproduced by 1 Pet 1:16, says, "Be holy for I am holy."[129] The implication in both Matt 5 and 1 Pet 1 is an ethical teaching for proper conduct and character, one in which "God represents the moral standard."[130] The one potentially significant difference in Jesus's command is the Greek term "as" (ὡς) rather than "for" (ὅτι). In this

'Now the professors of other subjects try to make their pupils copy their teachers.' In Jewish literature the imitation of model lives was a commonplace in moral instruction, whether one imitated the conduct of a person (*Wis.* 4:2; *T. Ben.* 3:1; 4:1), a person's sufferings (4 Macc. 13:9), or the character of God himself (*T. Asher* 4:3; *Ep. Arist.* 188, 210, 280–81)."

[124] Buber, *Israel and the World*, 71.

[125] Borchert says, "The first *gar* ... reminds the reader that the Father is the model for the Son's activity (5:19). The point is that the Son copied the Father. Paul employed a similar idea in the theme of imitation to suggest that Christians were to copy him and his model of authentic life (cf. Phil 3:17; 1 Cor 4:16) as he copied or imitated Christ (1 Cor 11:1)."

Contra this view, Leon Morris quotes Westcott saying, "'not in imitation, but in virtue of His sameness of nature' (Westcott). The verse contains the thought of subordination." However, Morris does not seem to be dismissing Jesus's copying of the Father but simply saying it is not merely mimicry but revelation of his deity, willful subordination. As he says in a note, "It is not a question of copying: the Son does the same deeds as the Father does." See Gerald L. Borchert, *John 1–11*, NAC 25A (Nashville: B&H, 1996), 237; Leon Morris, *The Gospel According to John*, Rev. ed., NICNT (Grand Rapids: Eerdmans, 1995), 277.

[126] ἃ γὰρ ἂν ἐκεῖνος ποιῇ, ταῦτα καὶ ὁ υἱὸς ὁμοίως ποιεῖ and ὥσπερ γὰρ ὁ πατὴρ ἐγείρει τοὺς νεκροὺς καὶ ζῳοποιεῖ, οὕτως καὶ ὁ υἱὸς οὓς θέλει ζῳοποιεῖ (John 5:19, 21).

[127] Morris comments regarding this relationship, "Love and membership in God's family go together. ... There is a sense in which those members are ... all characterized by dependence on and likeness to the Father ... God loves like that, and his sons come to love in some measure like that, too" (Leon Morris, *The Gospel According to Matthew*, PNTC (Grand Rapids: Eerdmans, 1992), 131).

[128] Ἔσεσθε οὖν ὑμεῖς τέλειοι ὡς ὁ πατὴρ ὑμῶν ὁ οὐράνιος τέλειός ἐστιν (Matt 5:48).

[129] For further discussion of Lev 19:2 (11:44–45, 20:26), see Excursus: Leviticus and the Holiness of God.

[130] Craig S. Keener, *The Gospel of Matthew: A Socio-Rhetorical Commentary* (Grand Rapids: Eerdmans, 2009), 2005.

Sermon on the Mount, Jesus regularly seeks to unveil the true essence of an OT teaching.[131] This slight variation strengthens the comparative sense and moves away from the perception of mere obedience by fiat. Instead, Jesus proposes the true essence of this statement is genuine sonship in following him as he imitates the Father.[132]

Despite the brevity of this overview, it is sufficient to see the general perspective of the NT regarding imitation and *imitatio Dei*. As seen, the NT teaches imitation of character, desire, and conduct. It teaches that Christian believers are to imitate examples such as Paul and Jesus with the heavenly Father as the ultimate ideal or foundation. Likewise, NT Christians were to be examples themselves for others to see and imitate in their Christ-like and God-like conduct. The NT writers also taught that identity and conformity were intertwined aspects which could not be fully parsed from the other. In other words, walking in the ways of Christ was equivalent to imitating him and central to the formation of his followers.

The Church

Building on the teachings of the NT, the Church era followed closely regarding imitation. In a logical fashion, Patristic and medieval writers often focused on *imitatio Christi*, partly because according to Christian theology he was the revelation of God to humanity (e.g., John 1:18; Heb 1:3). Despite a focus on Christ, the imitation of God or the Father was still a prominent theme and often interconnected.

In an early Christian-era letter (2nd c. CE), one writer commended the Jewish people as imitators of God. The *Apology of Aristides* says, "Let us come now, O King, to the history of the Jews … they imitate God by the philanthropy which prevails among them; for they have compassion on the poor, and they release the captives, and bury the dead, and do such things as these, which are acceptable before God and well-pleasing also to men."[133] Likewise, the letter also condemns the immoral practices of humans who imitate their pagan gods. He says, "[They] become adulterous men and

---

[131] Morris states regarding Jesus's Sermon on the Mount, "Jesus' understanding of keeping the law meant a great deal more than making sure that the letter of the law was not infringed. For him, it was important that the deeper implications of what God had commanded be understood and put into practice. He brings this out with reference to specific commands that the Pharisees had no difficulty in keeping in the literal sense. He shows that in each case a principle is involved" (Morris, *The Gospel According to Matthew*, 112).

[132] France comments, "[5:48] appropriately rounds off the final example in vv. 43–47, picking up from v. 45 the theme of the children's imitation of their heavenly Father … The disciple's lifestyle is to be different from other people's because it draws its inspiration not from the norms of society but from the character of God. … Jesus is demanding a different approach, not via laws read as simply rules of conduct but rather by looking behind those laws to the mind and character of God himself" (R. T. France, *The Gospel of Matthew*, NICNT (Grand Rapids: Eerdmans, 2007), 228–29).

[133] Aristides, *The Apology of Aristides the Philosopher* 14 (*ANF* 9:276).

lascivious women ... workers of other terrible iniquities, through the imitation of their god. ... For if he who is said to be the chief and king of their gods do these things how much more should his worshippers imitate him? And great is the folly which the Greeks have brought forward in their narrative concerning him."[134] Although the letter does not give indications as to his source for this perspective, it does mean that at least some in the early church had a clear concept of imitating the divine realm. Yet, the letter does not directly mention imitation of God or Christ regarding Christians, though it might be assumed through syllogistic comparisons between Christians and the Greeks.

The Christian tradition continued the basic tenets of imitation and expanded it to include a great deal of explicit applications. Objects of imitation could be either positive or negative examples. Positive exemplars included God, Christ, apostles, angels, biblical persons, philosophers, Christian teachers, and other noteworthy examples. As for negative ones, Satan and demons along with pagans, evildoers, and false teachers were used as foils in the teaching of many authors. For example, Athanasius condemned moral evils saying, "They imitated their gods with like misdoings, thinking the imitation of superior beings ... was a credit to themselves."[135] The evils that he goes on to mention involve such things as murder and fornication, which are in imitation of gods such as Zeus, Aphrodite, Rhea, and Ares. Likewise, Justin Martyr condemned the followers of Epicurus as "imitating Jupiter and the other gods in sodomy and shameless intercourse."[136]

Since there are a great many positive examples of imitation, only an overview of notable examples particularly related to imitation of God and Christ can be discussed. These appeals to imitation comprise a variety of modes such as literal facets of Jesus's life to moral virtues. In the more literal mode, one author commended virginity claiming, "Virgins rejoice at all times in becoming like God and his Christ ... Dost thou wish to be a Christian? Imitate Christ in everything."[137] Also, the death and baptism of Christ were seen by Christian authors as either commendable or necessary for full conformity and imitation for his followers. [138] Such teachings included suffering more generally, as Leo the Great intimated, "Christ's passion provided a saving mystery and an example for us to follow," and commended willful martyrdom as an imitation of Christ. [139] Cyril of Jerusalem even defended nakedness in baptism as "imitating Christ, who was stripped naked on the Cross."[140]

---

[134] Aristides, *The Apology of Aristides the Philosopher* 9 (*ANF* 9:270).
[135] Athanasius of Alexandria, *Against the Heathen* 1.24 (*NPNF* 2.4:17–18).
[136] Justin Martyr, *The Second Apology of Justin* 12 (*ANF* 1:192).
[137] Pseudo-Clement of Rome, *Two Epistles Concerning Virginity* 8 (*ANF* 8:57).
[138] Basil of Caesarea, *The Book of Saint Basil on the Spirit* 35 (*NPNF* 2.8:21).
[139] Leo the Great, *Sermon* 63.4 (*NPNF* 2.12:176, 197).
[140] Cyril of Jerusalem, *The Catechetical Lectures* 20.2 (*NPNF* 2.7:147).

In more practical qualities, authors in this tradition also taught they were to be generous and help the poor.[141] As Chrysostom taught, "For nothing can so make a man an imitator of Christ as caring for his neighbors."[142] Chrysostom seems to echo an earlier teaching, "He who takes upon himself the burden of his neighbor ... he is an imitator of God."[143] They were also to pray for the salvation of all and those who were their enemies, imitating both the will of God and the actions and teachings of Jesus.[144]

Beyond just the literal or practical imitations, the Christian tradition also commended imitation of God and Christ for their moral or virtuous qualities. Athanasius understood imitation as a trajectory, though it could not result in equality, "For we too, albeit we cannot become like God in essence, yet by progress in virtue imitate God."[145] In a similar sentiment, Augustine commended Plato's perspective on the topic, "Plato determined the final good to be to live according to virtue, and affirmed that he only can attain to virtue who knows and imitates God."[146] Though not related to Greek philosophy, Augustine appealed to the source of wisdom to teach imitation, "It is not therefore to be wondered at, if, on account of the example which the Image, which is equal to the Father, gives to us, in order that we may be refashioned after the image of God; Scripture, when it speaks of wisdom, speaks of the Son, whom we follow by living wisely."[147] Polycarp taught of patience, "Let us then be imitators of His patience ... For He has set us this example in Himself."[148] Augustine taught of righteousness, "All His saints, also, imitate Christ in the pursuit of righteousness ... [He offers] Himself as an example of righteousness to those who imitate Him."[149] He also taught of forgiveness, "Lest ye should think it too high a thing to imitate Christ, hear the Apostle saying, 'Forgiving one another, even as God in Christ hath forgiven you'"[150] Ambrose taught about mercy, "Mercy, also, is a good thing, for it makes men perfect, in that it imitates the perfect Father."[151] John Cassian taught of love, "For in what can a weak and fragile human nature be like Him, except in always showing a calm love in its heart towards the good and evil, the just and the unjust, in imitation of God, and by doing good for the love of goodness

---

[141] John Chrysostom, *Homily 19* (*NPNF* 1.13:142–43); Ambrose of Milan, *Three Books on the Duties of the Clergy* 1.38 (*NPNF* 2.10:7).

[142] John Chrysostom, *Homily 25* (*NPNF* 1.12:53).

[143] *The Epistle of Mathetes to Diognetus* 10 (*ANF* 1:29).

[144] Ignatius of Antioch, *The Second Epistle of Ignatius to the Ephesians* (*ANF* 1:101); Pseudo-Clement of Rome, *Book* 5.5 (*ANF* 8:154); Augustine of Hippo, *Tractates on the Gospel According to St. John* 4.6 (*NPNF* 1.7:27); John Chrysostom, *Homily 7* (*NPNF* 1.13:430).

[145] Athanasius of Alexandria, *To the Bishops of Africa* 7 (*NPNF* 2.4:492).

[146] Augustine of Hippo, *City of God* 8.8.1 (*NPNF* 1.2:150).

[147] Augustine of Hippo, *On the Trinity* 7.3.5 (*NPNF* 1.3:108).

[148] Polycarp of Smryna, *The Epistle of Polycarp to the Philippians* 8 (*ANF* 1:35).

[149] Augustine of Hippo, *A Treatise on the Merits and Forgiveness of Sins, and on the Baptism of Infants* 1.10 (*NPNF* 1.5:18–19).

[150] Augustine of Hippo, *Sermons on Selected Lessons of the New Testament* 64.3 (*NPNF* 1.6:453).

[151] Ambrose of Milan, *On the Duties of the Clergy* 1.11.38 (*NPNF* 2.10:7). Cf. John Chrysostom, *Homilies on the epistle of St. Paul the Apostle to the Ephesians* 17 (*NPNF* 1.13:129).

itself."[152] Leo the Great and Pseudo-Clement taught of goodness as a return to the image of God, "We shall find that man was made in God's image, to the end that he might imitate his Creator, and that our race attains its highest natural dignity, by the form of the Divine goodness being reflected in us, as in a mirror."[153] Chrysostom taught of meekness, "Christ Himself saith, 'Learn of Me, for I am meek and lowly in heart.' (Matt 11:29). And this He taught, not by words alone, but by actions also."[154] In all of these examples, the authors seemed to use imitation as a generally accepted concept without need of defense, despite some logical caveats.

Centuries later, however, Thomas Aquinas interacted with the idea but with a more defensive approach. In his treatise on "Whether any creature can be like God?," he lays out a logical explanation why man can imitate God's likeness without infringing on his essence, saying, "Likeness of creatures to God is not affirmed on account of agreement in form according to the formality of the same genus or species, but solely according to analogy, inasmuch as God is essential being, whereas other things are beings by participation."[155] In another place, he contends that a desire for likeness to God is not the problem but pride, "Pride is the desire for inordinate exaltation: and hence it is that, as he asserts, pride imitates God inordinately: for it hath equality of fellowship under Him, and wishes to usurp His."[156] In many places he echoes the sentiments of those earlier writers relating imitation to wisdom and divine goodness. [157] Quoting and building on Augustine, Aquinas commends the necessity of imitation for virtue, "The soul needs to follow something in order to give birth to virtue: this something is God: if we follow Him we shall live aright. Consequently, the exemplar of human virtue must needs pre-exist in God."[158] He also applied the notion of imitation to other areas. Regarding sins of the fathers being visited upon the children, he says, "[They] are more prone to sin through being brought up amid their parents' crimes, both by becoming accustomed to them, and by imitating their parents' example."[159] Regarding government he says, "Human government is derived from the Divine government, and should imitate it." [160] As seen in this brief assessment, Aquinas went beyond assuming the natural or scriptural validity of imitating God from earlier Christian writers by providing philosophical treatises.

In all, the Church held to a strong and clear sense of imitating God and Christ, which they believed was a principle derived from scripture. This view, though including Christ as a mediator, parallels many of the views and sources found in rabbinic circles. At the heart, it was a generally accepted

---

[152] John Cassian, *The Conferences* 2.11.9 (*NPNF* 2.11:419). Cf. Augustine of Hippo, *Our Lord's Sermon on the Mount according to Matthew* 1.19 (*NPNF* 1.6:27).

[153] Leo the Great, *Sermons* 12.1 (*NPNF* 2.12:121). Cf. Pseudo-Clement of Rome, *Recognitions of Clement* 5.13 (*ANF* 8:146).

[154] John Chrysostom, *Homilies on the Gospel of John* 69.3 (*NPNF* 1.14:256).

[155] Thomas Aquinas, *Summa Theologica* 1.4.3.

[156] Thomas Aquinas, *Summa Theologica* 2-2.162.1, 2-2.163.2.

[157] Thomas Aquinas, *Summa Theologica* 1.9.1, 1.65.2, 1-2.19.9.

[158] Thomas Aquinas, *Summa Theologica* 1-2.61.5, 2-2.152.5, 2-2.31.3.

[159] Thomas Aquinas, *Summa Theologica* 1-2.87.8.

[160] Thomas Aquinas, *Summa Theologica* 2-2.10.11.

reality, even intuitively true, that humans imitate and reflect the divine realm and those human exemplars further along on the divine pathway. Such patterns of imitation were not unique to Christianity but intrinsic to humanity.

Modern Evaluations

Over the past century, a great deal of literature has appeared either directly or indirectly discussing *imitatio Dei*, from many areas of interest. Subsequently, the conversation regarding imitation of God has developed in a number of directions. Initially, scholars simply followed along with the prevalent ideas and themes found in Rabbinic, Christian, and Greco-Roman traditions. In essence, imitation of God was intuitive and central to ethics and theology. Humans did not derive elements of morality or proper behavior out of a vacuum or by mere fiat, though natural order and divine command were important. Humanity was primarily learning to be like God, or according to the divine model, on a trajectory of progression. However, beginning in the mid-20th c., scholars began questioning the validity of this notion and unraveling it from prior biblical and theological studies. Criticisms primarily began by questioning *imitatio Dei* within moral philosophy generally and more specifically as the core of biblical and OT ethics. This gave way to more critical analyses that questioned even the possibility and ethicalness of imitating God. Despite some negative perspectives, the role of imitating God has remained a core tenant for many scholars up to the present, even providing a foundation for character formation studies.[161]

Early 1900s

A few notable scholars, all Jewish in heritage and orientation, helped popularize the idea of imitating God in the early-to-mid 1900s. Israel Abrahams published, in 1917, a constructive analysis on rabbinic and Christian traditions, one section specifically addressing "Imitation of God." He addressed the topic because of "the greatness of the idea itself; second, its ubiquity."[162] Regarding ubiquity, he had in mind "all religions" but goes on to

---

[161] For a few examples, see Arthur J. Keefer, *The Book of Proverbs and Virtue Ethics: Integrating the Biblical and Philosophical Traditions* (Cambridge: Cambridge University Press, 2021); Najman, "Imitatio Dei"; Ryan O'Dowd, *The Wisdom of Torah: Epistemology in Deuteronomy and the Wisdom Literature*, FRLANT 225 (Göttingen: Vandenhoeck & Ruprecht, 2009); Christopher J. H. Wright, *Old Testament Ethics for the People of God* (Downers Grove: IVP, 2004); Anne W. Stewart, *Poetic Ethics in Proverbs: Wisdom Literature and the Shaping of the Moral Self* (New York: Cambridge University Press, 2016).

[162] Abrahams, *Studies in Pharisaism*, 138.

say that imitation "forms the crown of Judaism and of Christianity." [163] Although he begins his historical analysis for *imitatio Dei* in the rabbinic tradition with the Greeks, this was not to imply that the notion actually began with the Greeks. Rather, as he shows, the rabbis developed their teachings from studying the ancient writings in the OT. Likewise, around the same time, Arthur Marmorstein was writing and teaching within Jewish circles. Through expounding rabbinic teachings, he also based the center of biblical ethics on the imitation of God. In his view of the Haggadists, "[They] made it their endeavour to bring the divine nearer to man and man nearer to the divine … and to cultivate in man a resemblance to God." [164] He went on to interact with and affirm the long rabbinic tradition of *imitatio Dei*. However, Marmorstein believed a distinction between Judaism's view and the Greek or Christian view is the direct imitation of God rather than through a mediator, such as the Logos or Christ. [165]

As an influential scholar, Martin Buber also interacted with imitation of God around the same time, initially publishing a short essay that was republished and translated several times. [166] In this essay, Buber provides a historical survey of *imitatio Dei* and its centrality in rabbinic interpretation which he understood to be central in Christianity as well. [167] While following closely with the rabbinic view, he states, "To imitate God means then to cleave to his ways, to walk in his ways. By these are meant not the ways which God has commanded man as man to walk in, they are really God's own ways." [168] Finally, building on this trend, Erich Fromm, a notable Jewish philosopher, published his views on OT theology. In the book, he spoke in length about the centrality of imitating God, the title of the book implying as much. [169] In his understanding, imitation was not an end in itself. Rather, "Imitation of God by acting like God acts means becoming more and more like God; it means at the same time knowing God. … knowing God and being like God means to imitate his actions." [170] Here, he ties together a deeper essence of imitation, namely growing in the knowledge of God. This was not a novel idea, however. He was building on the writings of the rabbis and others who believed imitation was as much about relational knowledge as it was ethical behavior. [171]

---

[163] Abrahams, *Studies in Pharisaism*, 138.

[164] Marmorstein, *Studies in Jewish Theology*, 106. This volume was published posthumously but is a collection of his writings from the first half of the century.

[165] Marmorstein, *Studies in Jewish Theology*, 119–20.

[166] Martin Buber, "Nachahmung Gottes," *Der Morgen* Jahrgang I.6 (1926): 638–47; Martin Buber, *Kampf um Israel: Reden und Schriften* (Berlin: Schocken Verlag, 1933).

[167] Buber, *Israel and the World*, 68–71.

[168] Buber, *Israel and the World*, 75.

[169] Fromm, *You Shall Be as Gods*.

[170] Fromm, *You Shall Be as Gods*, 67.

[171] Fromm, *You Shall Be as Gods*, 67; Buber, *Israel and the World*, 67; Marmorstein, *The Doctrine of Merits in Old Rabbinical Literature*, 202; Abrahams, *Studies in Pharisaism*, 157.

Critical Evaluations

Despite the popularity and general acceptance of *imitatio Dei*, a debate began with Barnabas Lindars when he questioned the viability of the idea. In particular, he was addressing two works that presumed *imitatio Dei* in the role of *imitatio Christi*.[172] Lindars argued that the characteristics of God from Exod 34:6 were not to be imitated but were simply conditions for covenantal harmony between groups.[173] Similarly, he believed this was true for holiness (Lev 19:2).[174] Furthermore, he argued that many commands, like to be just and rule properly, were simply in the sense of delegation as emissaries.[175] However, despite this negative perspective, he does concede that much of the Deuteronomic literature includes instruction to imitate God.[176] Yet, even here, he holds such a view in abeyance, noting that it was more for emotive rhetoric and didactic aim than for teaching imitation of God as a principle.

Following in the critical perspective of Lindars, other scholars added to the skepticism of *imitatio Dei* in the OT and biblical ethics. One of the more notable critics has been Cyril Rodd. In an early article on Gen 18:25 not directly focused on the imitation of God, he questioned the legitimacy of God as the model and source of good and ethical behavior.[177] A primary contention was the rejection that "morality is what God commands." [178] Through a questionable interpretation of Gen 18,[179] Rodd proposed Abraham was right to question God and attempt to steer God toward being just. Almost three decades later, Rodd published more extensively and specifically on the topic of *imitatio Dei*.[180] In his book *Glimpses of a Strange Land*, he analyzed OT ethics more broadly with a focused section on many of the proposed *imitatio*

---

[172] E. J. Tinsley, *Imitation of God in Christ: An Essay on the Biblical Basis of Christian Spirituality* (Philadelphia: Westminster, 1960); Don Cupitt, "God and Morality: Duty and Discernment, 6," *Theology* 76.637 (1973): 356–64. Cupitt is more concerned in this article with moral philosophy generally than OT ethics. He proposes "imitation" and "response" as the primary paradigmatic themes (357). Lindars focuses on the imitation aspect of the article, though Cupitt does not provide extensive coverage on the topic. Cupitt also acknowledges difficulties with the idea of *imitatio Dei* but only provides one example, *apatheia* (358).

[173] Barnabas Lindars, "Imitation of God and Imitation of Christ: Duty and Discernment," *Theology* 76.638 (1973): 396.

[174] Lindars, "Imitation of God and Imitation of Christ," 400. See Excursus: Leviticus and the Holiness of God.

[175] Lindars, "Imitation of God and Imitation of Christ," 399.

[176] Lindars, "Imitation of God and Imitation of Christ," 400.

[177] Cyril S. Rodd, "Shall Not the Judge of All the Earth Do What Is Right? (Gen 18:25)," *ExpTim* 83.5 (1972): 137–39; Houston, "The Character of YHWH and the Ethics of the Old Testament," 25. Houston is moderately skeptical of *imitatio Dei* as the primary driver of OT ethics. But he critiques Rodd as excessively skeptical, "The character and actions of YHWH may function more widely as models for human conduct than Rodd's excessively skeptical analysis may suggest, but I concur entirely with Barton that *imitatio Dei* is not a key to unlock all doors in the ethics of the Old Testament."

[178] Rodd, "Shall Not the Judge of All the Earth Do What Is Right? (Gen 18:25)," 139.

[179] Houston, "The Character of YHWH and the Ethics of the Old Testament," 4; Nathan MacDonald, "Listening to Abraham—Listening to Yhwh: Divine Justice and Mercy in Genesis 18:16–33," *CBQ* 66 (2004): 25–43.

[180] Rodd, *Glimpses of a Strange Land.*

Dei passages and his critiques of those who had espoused the view. As might be expected from his earlier article, he rejects Barton's view that God is a moral being bound to the same laws he dictates. He believes instead that God is wholly other and the OT explicitly describes God as different and distinct from humans.[181] Rodd goes on to critique the Deuteronomic passages often lauded as explicit proof of imitation. Similar to Lindars, though with a much more definitive rejection, he claimed these are simply "motive clauses" unrelated to the character or nature of God.[182] Additionally, he critiqued Davies' article regarding both "holiness" and the phrase "walk in the ways of the Lord."[183] Much like Lindars, he rejects Lev 19:2 as comparative, instead favoring the grammatical sense for causal (כִּי).[184] In his view, divine holiness and human holiness do not overlap, the human version being commanded within mundane social settings. Likewise, for the phrase discussed by Davies, which was favored within the rabbinic tradition, he claims it is only meant in the sense of obedience by fiat.[185] As he argues, God does not walk or have ways that could be followed imitatively, only obediently. At one point, he does concede that some passages and the parallel between Pss 111 and 112 are perhaps meant to signify relationship and mirroring. However, he maintains that mirroring only means "parallel" and does not imply "imitation," which he defines as "to attempt to recreate in the life of Israel ... the virtues and actions of God."[186] In another critique of Davies' view, Rodd laments a seemingly negative statement by him, "When God's behaviour appeared vindictive, tyrannical and capricious the command to imitate him would inevitably be seen as morally perverse."[187] Yet, Davies' explains in the footnote that it was common among the rabbis to accept there are things humanity cannot or perhaps should not imitate due to natural limitations or sinful tendencies.[188] In summation of his section on *imitatio Dei* in the OT, he states, "[It] rests ultimately on the belief in a God who has been brought down to the human level, and this God is never found in the Old Testament."[189] So it would appear, in an attempt to elevate the place God, perhaps anachronistically, he eliminates humanity's relation to him.

John H. Walton and J. Harvey Walton make a case for the basis of *torah*, or Israelite law, in ANE wisdom. In the process, they reject the notion

---

[181] Rodd, *Glimpses of a Strange Land*, 67, 68.

[182] Rodd, *Glimpses of a Strange Land*, 65.

[183] Eryl W. Davies, "Walking in God's Ways: The Concept of Imitatio Dei in the Old Testament," in *In Search of True Wisdom* (Sheffield: Sheffield Academic, 1999), 99–114.

[184] Rodd, *Glimpses of a Strange Land*, 69. See Excursus: Leviticus and the Holiness of God.

[185] Rodd, *Glimpses of a Strange Land*, 70.

[186] Rodd, *Glimpses of a Strange Land*, 72–75.

[187] Rodd, *Glimpses of a Strange Land*, 75; Davies, "Walking in God's Ways," 113; Esias E. Meyer, "The Dark Side of the Imitatio Dei. Why Imitating the God of the Holiness Code Is Not Always a Good Thing," *OTE* 22.2 (2009): 376, 377, 379. Meyer agrees with Rodd's criticism of Davies, including many negative images of God such as slave owner and landlord. Yet, his views on God and slavery seem to be anachronistic and misguided.

[188] Davies, "Walking in God's Ways," 113.

[189] Rodd, *Glimpses of a Strange Land*, 76.

of *imitatio Dei* in the OT and biblical ethics more generally.[190] What is interesting, however, is that John Walton had previously espoused the traditional view.[191] Apparently, at some point in the intervening years he evolved on the topic.[192] In *The Lost World of the Torah*, Walton and Walton primarily reject *imitatio Dei* because of their view on holiness. Focusing on Lev 19:2, they propose it is merely a conferred status for Israel and is not at all moral, equivalent to the term "divine."[193] While holiness may imply status, the literary context contrasts this myopic view suggesting that it is hortatory and comparative as well (cf. Lev 11:44–45, 20:7, 26; Matt 5:48; 1 Peter 1:16).[194] Furthermore, they reject *imitatio Dei* because, as he believes, it would require humanity to have a full list of expectations and a full revelation of his character in order to know what and how to imitate him.[195] At the heart of his issue, however, is a broad rejection of "objective morality," which includes both *imitatio Dei* and divine command theory.[196] Instead, they favor descriptive rather than prescriptive exegesis. This leads to a form of cultural relativism referred to as "wise living," often relying on the image of navigating a "cultural river."[197] The Waltons' views are typical of those who critique or reject *imitatio Dei* and reflect earlier scholars such as Lindars and Rodd.

Positive Evaluations

While there have been some notable scholars against *imitatio Dei*, there are many more who hold to the viability and presence of the topic in OT and biblical ethics. A few years after Lindars, John Barton added to the

---

[190] John H. Walton and J. Harvey Walton, *The Lost World of the Torah: Law as Covenant and Wisdom in Ancient Context* (Downers Grove: IVP, 2019), 54, 203.

[191] John H. Walton, *Ancient Near Eastern Thought and the Old Testament: Introducing the Conceptual World of the Hebrew Bible*, 1st ed. (Grand Rapids: Baker Academic, 2006), 110, 311.

[192] In 2006, Walton wrote, "In Israel, people are called upon to imitate the holiness of God, and, while that holiness includes a cultic dimension, it stretches across the entire range of covenant stipulations and has a moral element to it." However, in 2018, Walton changed it to say, "In Israel, people are identified as Yahweh's holy people and as such have become part of his constellation. They are called upon to reflect the status that he has given them both in the way they order their society and in their maintenance of sacred space." Likewise, in 2006, he wrote, "Live a life of obedience to the covenant informed by the demands of holiness, in imitation of your holy God." In 2018, he changed it to say, "Live a life of covenant observance informed by the demands of having been co-identified with a holy God" (Walton, *Ancient Near Eastern Thought* (2006), 110, 311; John H. Walton, *Ancient Near Eastern Thought and the Old Testament: Introducing the Conceptual World of the Hebrew Bible*, 2nd ed. (Grand Rapids: Baker Academic, 2018), 71, 292).

[193] Walton and Walton, *Lost World of the Torah*, 54–55, 203–4.

[194] For further discussion on this (11:44–45, 20:26), see Excursus: Leviticus and the Holiness of God.

[195] Walton and Walton, *Lost World of the Torah*, 203.

[196] Walton and Walton, *Lost World of the Torah*, 206.

[197] Walton and Walton, *Lost World of the Torah*, 11, 44.

conversation, primarily addressing models of OT ethics in scholarship.[198] After surveying Hempel's and Eichrodt's works, he concluded that primarily they found ethics to be rooted in obedience and natural law.[199] However, he went on to add the possibility of *imitatio Dei* to this set of viable models for ethics drawing on the influence of Buber. It was a few years later, writing again on biblical ethics, that he adopted a more robust view. Here, he proposed that the center of ethics is rooted in "imitating the pattern of God's own actions … though he is transcendent … he is nonetheless knowable."[200] He goes on to say, "Ethics is not so much a system of obligations as a way of communion with God."[201] Almost a decade later, he wrote again on OT ethics, revisiting the models and exploring more the imitation of God. Despite uncertainty of the topic's prevalence in the OT, he draws on Hempel to say that God himself is a moral being and a basis for human moral behavior.[202] Rather than simply deontological, he believed that OT ethics was teleological, which included the wisdom literature.[203] While reiterating much from his previous writings on the topic, he states that an intent in this article is to further his nascent idea in that 1978 article.[204] Here, he argues mainly that God is bound to moral norms, "Yahweh asks of human agents nothing that is not also self-imposed."[205] Despite making a case for the legitimacy of imitation, he only sees this as one of the models present in the OT. Accordingly, he states, "Obedience to the declared will of God is probably the strongest model for ethical obligation in most of the books of the Hebrew Scriptures."[206] In a later essay, while still affirming the presence and necessity of *imitatio Dei*, Barton considers several of Rodd's criticisms.[207] Rodd thinks the idea is perhaps more a result of anthropomorphism, God condescending or the writers

---

[198] John Barton, "Understanding Old Testament Ethics," *JSOT* 3.9 (1978): 44–64.

[199] Barton, "Understanding Old Testament Ethics," 59–60; Walther Eichrodt, *Theology of the Old Testament*, trans. J. A. Baker, OTL (Philadelphia: Westminster, 1967), II:373. Despite the emphasis, it is important to note that Eichrodt did hold to a more traditional, intuitive notion that morality was sourced in God's nature. Eichrodt says, "The ultimate motive of moral action into the desire to be modelled on the pattern of the divine."

[200] John Barton, "Approaches to Ethics in the Old Testament," in *Beginning Old Testament Study*, ed. John Rogerson (Philadelphia: Westminster, 1982), 130.

[201] Barton, "Approaches to Ethics in the Old Testament," 130.

[202] John Barton, "The Basis of Ethics in the Hebrew Bible," *Semeia* 66 (1994): 17–18; Bruce C. Birch, "Moral Agency, Community, and the Character of God in the Hebrew Bible," *Semeia* 66 (1994): 30. Birch commends Barton's position and takes it further, "Attention to the moral significance of the character of God can significantly enrich our understanding of key moments in the biblical story."

[203] Barton, "The Basis of Ethics in the Hebrew Bible," 19.

[204] He states, "In my 1978 article I mentioned a third possible model for theological ethics in ancient Israel: the imitation of God. … Subsequently, I have begun to think that it is more common, and more important, than I then allowed. It is particularly visible in [Deut 10:17–19; Lev 19:2]" (Barton, "The Basis of Ethics in the Hebrew Bible," 17).

[205] Barton, "The Basis of Ethics in the Hebrew Bible," 18.

[206] Barton, "The Basis of Ethics in the Hebrew Bible," 13.

[207] Barton states, "The sense of affinity between God and humanity upon which it depends is seen as a central assertion … Thus, a good deal is at stake theologically if one attacks the idea of *imitatio Dei*" (John Barton, "Imitation of God in the Old Testament," in *The God of Israel*, ed. R. P. Gordon (Cambridge: Cambridge University Press, 2007), 38, 40–46).

conceptualizing him humanly, than a call for man to imitate God. Barton, however, agrees there is a danger of making God in the image of man but maintains that the biblical writers did believe in a real affinity between God and man. [208] Regarding the foundations of biblical ethics in God's own character and nature, he says,

> Even though some of the things God does in the Old Testament show that the parallelism between divine and human action can never be complete, the biblical writers do insist that God is indeed bound by moral laws just as human beings are, and this is a central plank in Otto's own position, namely that there is a shared moral agenda between human beings and God in Israel, which is an unusual if not a unique feature in the ancient Near East. ... YHWH is a good God, in some sense that is cognate with what people in Israel thought of as good in human beings, and it therefore made sense to try to imitate him. This might thus be one of the implications or meanings of being made 'in the image of God'; God and humankind share a common ethical perception, so that God is not only the commander but also the paradigm of all moral conduct. This implies an affinity between the divine and the human, and it makes the human *capax Dei*.[209]

Likewise, he addresses Rodd's use of Davies' quote in representing God in a very negative and capricious manner, which humans ought not imitate.[210] Barton responds to Rodd by agreeing that scholars and biblical writers alike were able to distinguish the limitations of *imitatio Dei*. Finally, he takes a more cautious position in this later essay on the prevalence of *imitatio Dei* in the OT than he did in his previous, more optimistic writings.[211]

Continuing the sentiments of Barton and others, Harry Nasuti published on imitation and its relational implications within a covenant. While discussing many common passages highlighted by the rabbinic and Christian traditions, he notes that there are limitations to human imitation

---

[208] In response to Rodd's view, he says, "This is true because God did indeed make us in his own image, and we are therefore not deluded when we suppose that he is in some very remote sense like ourselves. But, of course, from a God's-eye view this really means that we are like him: in the order of knowing, we reason from humans to God. But this is only legitimate because, in the order of being, we derive all our good qualities from him in the first place" (Barton, "Imitation of God in the Old Testament," 40).

[209] Barton, "Imitation of God in the Old Testament," 37, 38; Eckart Otto, *Theologische Ethik des Alten Testaments*, Theologische Wissenschaft (Stuttgart: W. Kohlhammer, 1994), 85–85, 89, 185. Barton refers to Eckart Otto for much of his thinking in this later essay, which largely aligns with his earlier writings on the topic.

[210] Barton, "Imitation of God in the Old Testament," 42; Davies, "Walking in God's Ways," 113; Rodd, *Glimpses of a Strange Land*, 75. Davies wrote, "'There was obviously no problem with the concept of *imitatio Dei* while it was confined to such exemplary characteristics as God's mercy, justice and compassion, but when God's behaviour appeared vindictive, tyrannical and capricious the command to imitate him would inevitably be seen as morally perverse."

[211] Barton, "Imitation of God in the Old Testament," 39.

of God, which should not imply supernatural powers.[212] Rather, he believes, quoting H. H. Rowley, "Yahweh asks of men that they shall reflect his own character, so far as it can be reflected within the limitations of human life."[213] It was not the expectation to "imitate any individual action" but rather to "imitate a key divine attribute."[214] In his study, he discusses and relies upon the rabbinic tradition, appealing to earlier interpretations of OT passages for his study. Despite some reticence from scholars, together these passages paint the picture that "Who we are is determined by narrative and the community formed by that narrative. ... [which] entails need for Israel not only to remember, but also to imitate such actions."[215]

Another important contribution was through Eryl Davies. Though brief, his essay tackles the idea of *imitatio Dei* and its relevance for OT studies. As Davies argues, the idea of *imitatio Dei* builds on the biblical phrase, addressed by the rabbis, "walk in the ways of the Lord." The phrase is found especially in Deuteronomy and, in his view, is a helpful conceptual metaphor for imitating God, though Lev 19 is the clearest example of *imitatio Dei*.[216] In a desire to provide a basis for biblical and OT ethics, Davies believes this theme is not only present but central. Accordingly, God's activity serves as a "blueprint."[217] Along with imitable actions, Davies proposes it is also necessary to imitate his character, particularly God's virtuous qualities.[218] Despite the strong insistence on *imitatio Dei*, he unfortunately argues that it is not related to *imago Dei*, which he proposes was a late concept.[219]

Perhaps the most formidable and extensive address of imitation of God is found in Christopher Wright's work on biblical ethics. In *Old Testament Ethics for the People of God*, Wright formulates an ethical foundation rooted in God himself, rather than in natural law or as a result of mere fiat.[220] In this, he builds a case for imitating God, particularly with respect to the Torah, though he prefers the language of "reflect" due to scholarly misconceptions about "imitation."[221] On this point he notes, "It would be misleading to think in terms of mere mimickry – attempting to do whatever the LORD did or does,

---

[212] Nasuti, "Identity, Identification, and Imitation," 18.

[213] H. H. Rowley, *The Unity of the Bible* (Westport, CT: Greenwood, 1978), 25.

[214] Nasuti, "Identity, Identification, and Imitation," 17.

[215] Nasuti, "Identity, Identification, and Imitation," 21; Stanley Hauerwas, *The Peaceable Kingdom: A Primer in Christian Ethics* (Notre Dame: University of Notre Dame Press, 1983), 76–77; Tinsley, *Imitation of God in Christ*, 25, 31, 35, 55. Nasuti relies on and quotes Stanley Hauerwas, who was heavily influenced by E. J. Tinsley.

[216] Davies, "Walking in God's Ways," 101.

[217] Davies, "Walking in God's Ways," 103.

[218] Davies, "Walking in God's Ways," 101, 103.

[219] Davies, "Walking in God's Ways," 110.

[220] Wright says, "The relationship between God's command and God's previous actions on behalf of Israel is even more clearly shown in Deuteronomy, where the whole historical prologue, chapters 1–4, precedes the Decalogue in chapter 5. It has even been argued that the mainly legal section of the book, chapters 12–26, is deliberately reflective of the mainly theological section, chapters 1–11. Israel's response to the LORD is meant to be, in broad social terms, a mirroring of the LORD's own actions towards Israel" (Wright, *Old Testament Ethics for the People of God*, 28).

[221] Wright, *Old Testament Ethics for the People of God*, 38.

for clearly there are whole areas of the activity of God that are not available or appropriate for human replication."[222] The bulk of his focus and emphasis, however, is on ethics as primarily an outflow of knowing God. For him, knowing and being like God are necessarily intertwined, rather than mutually exclusive.[223] The most central passages for his divine imitation paradigm are Gen 1, Lev 19, and Deut 10, though many more are addressed.[224] Likewise, the clearest example of imitation of God as it relates to knowledge is in Jer 22:15–16.[225] While he touches on the notion of overlap between imitation and knowledge, he does not go into depth on how or why this is nor does he address the ANE or biblical context in depth. He does briefly mention that knowledge through imitation is likely an intentional feature in Proverbs but does not spend much time unpacking this insight.[226] Commenting on the central phrase of biblical wisdom that "the fear of the Yahweh is the beginning of wisdom" (Ps 111:10; Prov 1:7, 9:10), he adds his interpretive implication stating, "The imitation of the LORD is the application of wisdom."[227] Though Wright does not provide a detailed analysis of Proverbs as he did for the Torah, he does give his view of how they are aligned,

> The Wisdom literature has a deep social concern, like the law and the prophets, but the bulk of its sayings are directed at the individual. These proverbs are collected to inform, forewarn, correct and guide the individual Israelite in that path of life which is both pleasing to God and in his or her own best interests. Although the prevailing interest of Proverbs appears to be anthropocentric (concerned about the affairs of human life), there is an interesting and indirect God-centredness underlying it. So many of the human character traits, behaviour patterns and moral values commended in the Wisdom texts do in fact reflect the known character of God, as described elsewhere in the Old Testament. In this respect the personal ethics of Proverbs bear out the point made in [the Torah] about Old Testament ethics embodying a strong element of imitation of the ways of God himself.[228]

Additionally, he provides a number of general *imitatio Dei* categories which he thinks Proverbs teaches: God created man in his image, God is the divine parent, God is righteous as a king and judge, God is love, God is compassionate and generous, God is a worker, God speaks, and God is sovereign.[229] After formulating a detailed analysis of the Torah and an overview of the rest of the

---

[222] Wright, *Old Testament Ethics for the People of God*, 37.

[223] Wright states in response to the critical view of Cyril Rodd, "Obedience to the law and the imitation of God are not mutually exclusive categories: the one is an expression of the other" (Wright, *Old Testament Ethics for the People of God*, 40).

[224] Wright, *Old Testament Ethics for the People of God*, 38, 40, 121, 168.

[225] Wright, *Old Testament Ethics for the People of God*, 274.

[226] Wright, *Old Testament Ethics for the People of God*, 368–71.

[227] Wright, *Old Testament Ethics for the People of God*, 41.

[228] Wright, *Old Testament Ethics for the People of God*, 369.

[229] Wright, *Old Testament Ethics for the People of God*, 369–71. Unfortunately, almost all of his citations come from Prov 10–31, which highlights the necessity of this study.

OT, Wright provides a lengthy critical analysis of many fellow scholars and their views on biblical ethics, including some quite critical against *imitatio Dei*.[230]

G. K. Beale published a full biblical theological work on idolatry. As his thesis states, "What people revere, they resemble, either for ruin or restoration."[231] The primary basis for this claim is that humans are image bearers, created to reflect and worship. Thus, "It is not possible to be neutral on this issue: we either reflect the Creator or something in creation."[232] An interesting aspect of Beale's study is that he focuses more on the negative aspect of imitation. In other words, since he is interested in idolatry, he assesses many passages that imply improper imitation, whether in the Garden of Eden (Gen 3) or the craftsman who foolishly put their skills to vain use (Isa 42, 44).[233] Similarly, building on the sexual immorality implicit in the metaphors of idolatry, Beale discussed Hosea and the Israelites' improper imitation of Canaanite practices based on Baal and Asherah rather than in the ways of Israel's God.[234] In essence, the OT presents both a positive and negative picture of *imitatio Dei*. Thus, humanity will necessarily imitate either the creation or the Creator.

In a published version of his dissertation, Ryan O'Dowd analyzed the epistemology of Torah. In addition to Torah, his work includes some consideration of the three books commonly deemed wisdom literature. The focus of his study is on the primary view of knowledge (epistemology), which he believes is through recitation or "actualization" of Israel's history. This actualization was captured in the Torah and required to be enacted through reading and festivals in order to perpetuate the knowledge of God. In several places, specifically speaking to the Torah, he includes the idea of imitation, even claiming that it is a form of knowing God, "Imitation of God by acting the way God acts means becoming more and more like God; it means at the same time knowing God. ... Knowing, in fact, is a matter of divine-imitation where creating, or imagining, is at one and the same time obeying God and knowing God."[235] This particular point was not the sole focus of his study but does serve

---

[230] E.g., Mary E. Mills, *Images of God in the Old Testament* (Collegeville, MN: Liturgical, 1998); David Penchansky, *What Rough Beast? Images of God in the Hebrew Bible* (Louisville: John Knox, 1999); Rodd, *Glimpses of a Strange Land*. Mills is not directly opposed to *imitatio Dei* but provides a complex picture of the God presented in scripture. The implication is that such an image would be difficult to imitate. Penchansky, however, is much more critical of humans imitating God, describing his nature as insecure, irrational, vindictive, dangerous, malevolent, and abusive (3). He discusses through several OT stories that the character of God is quite frightful, hardly a reasonable picture for people to imitate. Despite presenting some indeed curious passages, his hermeneutic is myopic preferring the question, "If all you knew about God you knew from this passage?" (1). With this methodology, whatever conclusions he may arrive at are at best limited or perhaps more realistically misguided since they do not consider the wider literary, historical, and theological context for viewing the God of the OT.

[231] Beale, *We Become What We Worship*, 16.

[232] Beale, *We Become What We Worship*, 16.

[233] Beale, *We Become What We Worship*, 21, 41, 44, 46, 129–34.

[234] Beale, *We Become What We Worship*, 101, 120.

[235] O'Dowd, *The Wisdom of Torah*, 15, 24; Fromm, *You Shall Be as Gods*, 167. O'Dowd draws this idea primarily from similar quotes in Erich Fromm's work.

as a helpful foundation for this study. Furthermore, despite noticing the role of imitation in divine knowledge in Torah, O'Dowd does not bring over any of the imitative or divine epistemology ideas while surveying the epistemology of Proverbs. This seems to be a strange and unfortunate oversight in assessing the central wisdom book, which is rooted in Torah language and ideals. Between the writing and publishing of his dissertation, he contributed to an edited volume on epistemology in the Bible, as well. The primary focus of the book was the knowledge of God mediated through experience and "actualization in the present through a corporate memory." [236] Despite including imitation within his earlier published dissertation, there is no direct mention of imitation here, perhaps due to a focus on Wisdom Literature as he had in his dissertation. Regardless of why, the focus of his contribution is on obedience and memory. [237] This historicized knowledge is passed on from generation to generation. The relational reality of the knowledge of God is acknowledged while a mundane, empiricist type of epistemology is dismissed. [238] Yet, particularly regarding Proverbs, there is little grounding in what the knowledge of God is or its purpose. In sum, while O'Dowd provides insightful analysis and conclusions in the Torah, his contribution to Proverbs seems to be an oversight of the cohesion between the two corpora.

Several scholars have used *imitatio Dei* and its elements with studies on Proverbs and character formation more generally. For most, the issue is different than the debate within OT ethics over the preceding three decades. The insight of imitation becomes more expansive and is taken almost as intuitive and as though present prima facie. Likewise, the term "emulate" becomes more common than "imitate," perhaps in hopes of avoiding some scholarly baggage. With an indirect address in his dissertation, Dali Luo has the goal of understanding the role of kingship in Prov 16. While the focus is on the ideal king, the study seeks to understand the king as an intermediary between the people and God. [239] As such, the king serves as a model for the people to emulate, himself imitating God. [240] To build a case for this in Prov 16, the dissertation briefly addresses the notion in Prov 1–9. Here, he mentions the role of imitation as part of the goal in wisdom, a formative process with likeness as the telos. [241] The author even briefly connects this emulation to the knowledge of God, as seen with other scholars. [242] Luo's study focuses primarily on Prov 16 and only indirectly addresses chapters 1–9 as grounds for understanding the paradigmatic role of Israel's king in the

---

[236] Mary Healy and Robin A. Parry, "Introduction," in *The Bible and Epistemology: Biblical Soundings on the Knowledge of God* (Milton Keynes: Paternoster, 2007), xiv.

[237] Ryan O'Dowd, "A Chord of Three Strands," in *The Bible and Epistemology: Biblical Soundings on the Knowledge of God* (Milton Keynes: Paternoster, 2007), 68, 83.

[238] O'Dowd, "A Chord of Three Strands," 66, 73.

[239] Dali Luo, "Proverbs 16:1–15: An Invitation to Adopt the Royal Way of Life" (PhD diss., Trinity International University, 2010), 36, 44–45.

[240] Luo, "Proverbs 16:1–15," 194; Wright, *Old Testament Ethics for the People of God*, 121. Wright also spends time unpacking the role of the kingship in its intermediatory role for Israel to know and imitate God.

[241] Luo, "Proverbs 16:1–15," 34–36.

[242] Luo, "Proverbs 16:1–15," 46–47.

wisdom tradition. Within his discussion of imitation, he does provide caveats as seen elsewhere, such as limitations for humanity, levels of imitation, and that it is "impossible to imitate God in everything."[243]

In her book on poetic ethics, as she calls it, Anne Stewart investigates Proverbs through the lens of character formation, which she believes Proverbs teaches "can and must be cultivated."[244] For her, it is a "process that does not end" and involves "the whole person … emotions, motivations, desires, and imagination."[245] Furthermore, she argues in this book from the perspective that "knowledge of God cannot be divorced from human knowledge of the self … to alter one's perspective of God and the world is to shape and reshape character, the goal of sapiential rhetoric."[246] A primary way she addresses character formation is through desires, which is "assumed to be an innate part of the human" in Proverbs.[247] The student or son in Proverbs is intended to emulate the idealized desires and character of the righteous, the father, Wisdom, and God.[248] With these models, examples, and guides, the student grows in wisdom, able to discern proper desires from dangerous ones.[249]

Arthur Keefer has published two works on Proverbs. One addressed the function of Prov 1–9 for the rest of the book while the other addressed "virtue ethics" in Proverbs. For his book on virtue, he sets out to analyze Proverbs through the lens of moral philosophy, particularly compared to Aristotelian virtue.[250] In part, he aims to place the OT moral tradition within the broader history of ethics, which often begins with the Greek tradition rather than Israel.[251] Within this analysis, he holds that "God himself … exemplified what was right and good."[252] This foundation assumes the God of Israel as the prime model or source of goodness and proper behavior. As he discusses, the book of Proverbs provides a number of character types which serve as models to emulate, both positively and negatively.[253] Although holiness is not explicitly commanded, with the reference to Yhwh as "the Holy

---

[243] Luo, "Proverbs 16:1–15," 223; Best, *A Critical and Exegetical Commentary on Ephesians*, 240.

[244] Stewart, *Poetic Ethics in Proverbs*, 15, 42, 53. Regarding the relationship between ethics and poetry, she says, "Poetry has the ability to convey something about the process of learning as much as the content of instruction … the poetry of Proverbs is not simply a literary form but is a central means by which the sages teach one how to think, to discern, and to seek wisdom" (42). Furthermore, she claims, "Figurative language is not simply a clever way to say what could be said otherwise. Rather, it communicates ways of conceptualizing the world" (53).

[245] Stewart, *Poetic Ethics in Proverbs*, 3.

[246] Stewart, *Poetic Ethics in Proverbs*, 12; William P. Brown, *Wisdom's Wonder: Character, Creation, and Crisis in the Bible's Wisdom Literature* (Grand Rapids: Eerdmans, 2014), 21.

[247] Stewart, *Poetic Ethics in Proverbs*, 129, 136.

[248] Stewart, *Poetic Ethics in Proverbs*, 121, 142, 166; Sun Myung Lyu, *Righteousness in the Book of Proverbs*, FAT 55 (Tübingen: Mohr Siebeck, 2012), 62.

[249] Stewart, *Poetic Ethics in Proverbs*, 66.

[250] Keefer, *The Book of Proverbs and Virtue Ethics*, 5–6, 10–11.

[251] See Yoram. Hazony, *The Philosophy of Hebrew Scripture: An Introduction* (New York: Cambridge University Press, 2012), 4, 9–10, 17–18, 279.

[252] Keefer, *The Book of Proverbs and Virtue Ethics*, 2.

[253] Keefer, *The Book of Proverbs and Virtue Ethics*, 46, 153.

One" (Prov 9:10, 30:3) it is implicit. The student's aim, then, is similar to Lev 19.[254] Furthermore, though Keefer believes the ethical nature of Proverbs is largely on the human level, he does acknowledge that Prov 3:5–12 indicates *imitatio Dei* is in view also. Building on Aquinas, he says that "humans who know God also act similarly to God" and are thought to be participating in the divine life.[255] While Wisdom and Yhwh are not necessarily "character types" they do serve as models to be emulated in both behavior and attitude.[256] In his book on Prov 1–9, a publishing of his dissertation, he aims to show that many of the points found in 10–31 are only understandable through the hermeneutic lens of the first nine chapters, the introduction. In particular, character types found within the richer literary section help provide the reader necessary tools for the more terse proverbs, particularly as they stress the two-paths metaphor central to Proverbs.[257] The introduction of Proverbs "encourages emulation of one while portraying the other as unattractive: be like the wise; the fool is not appealing."[258] However, despite a focus on the human or "character type" aspect of emulation, Keefer discusses the importance of relationship and knowledge of God in the pedagogical purposes of Prov 1–9.[259] Furthermore, he argues that Wisdom serves as a "mediator between God and humans, bridging the gap." [260] More than just an informational conduit, Wisdom actually provides "fellowship with God."[261] This is because, Yhwh and Wisdom are seen as overlapping in speech, action, and desires. [262] The Lord, as Keefer states, "saturates the educational process."[263] It is not just his actions but his feelings or attitudes that must be imitated, which includes his disdain for wickedness.[264] While only indirectly discussing *imitatio Dei*, Keefer utilizes many of its tenets to understand the role of character formation and pedagogy in Proverbs.

Finally, an article by Hindy Najman has appeared on the topic of *imitatio Dei*. The focus of the essay is the "self" and formation in ancient Judaism, particularly through Hellenized views of the Second Temple period. [265] Her primary paradigm is the image of God language found in Genesis.[266] God serves as the ultimate exemplar for humans to become their

---

[254] Keefer, *The Book of Proverbs and Virtue Ethics*, 157.

[255] Keefer, *The Book of Proverbs and Virtue Ethics*, 178; Zoltán S. Schwáb, *Toward an Interpretation of the Book of Proverbs: Selfishness and Secularity Reconsidered*, JTISup 7 (Winona Lake: Eisenbrauns, 2013), 146; Eberhard Schockenhoff, "The Theological Virtue of Charity (IIa IIae, Qq. 23–46)," in *The Ethics of Aquinas*, ed. Stephen J. Pope (Washington, DC: Georgetown University Press, 2002), 247.

[256] Keefer, *The Book of Proverbs and Virtue Ethics*, 206.

[257] Keefer, *The Book of Proverbs and Virtue Ethics*, 61–64.

[258] Arthur J. Keefer, *Proverbs 1–9 as an Introduction to the Book of Proverbs* (London: T&T Clark, 2020), 79.

[259] Keefer, *Proverbs 1–9 as an Introduction to the Book of Proverbs*, 100–102.

[260] Keefer, *Proverbs 1–9 as an Introduction to the Book of Proverbs*, 44.

[261] Keefer, *Proverbs 1–9 as an Introduction to the Book of Proverbs*, 106.

[262] Keefer, *Proverbs 1–9 as an Introduction to the Book of Proverbs*, 156–61.

[263] Keefer, *Proverbs 1–9 as an Introduction to the Book of Proverbs*, 111.

[264] Keefer, *Proverbs 1–9 as an Introduction to the Book of Proverbs*, 174, 176, 178–79.

[265] Najman, "Imitatio Dei," 309, 322.

[266] Najman, "Imitatio Dei," 313.

most complete self. This imitative aspiration is "always incomplete" but exists on a pathway that utilizes lesser human examples for "expansion, refinement, and extension."[267] Likewise, she provides a caveat to *imitatio Dei*, humans emulate God as far as it is possible and reasonable.[268] In this way, the human is "constructed as a copy and never as a form."[269] The process of becoming perfect involves both internalization of the law and an "earthly context ... which revolves around the community."[270] Although she bases her article on Hellenistic Judaism, her basic premise aligns with the sentiments of the rabbinic tradition and the OT.

Conclusion

As observed in this brief survey, the topic of *imitatio Dei* has persisted in a relatively consistent form throughout a number of cultural and religious contexts, through thousands of years, and amidst countless individual perspectives. Many of the reasons and underlying assumptions, such as the fatherhood of God or the basis of morality, have been found in all the traditions. Likewise, caveats and limitations have been raised in all the traditions, indicating thoughtful engagement with the subject rather than mere shallow or primitive assertions. The picture observed in this historical survey points to a shared conceptual framework among many people over many years. While this does not directly imply that the OT did indeed teach *imitatio Dei,* or Proverbs for that matter, it does place the goal of this study within its proper context and supports its plausibility. If the OT and Proverbs did not conceptualize imitation and *imitatio Dei* at the heart of their pedagogical program, they would be anomalous and disconnected from the myriad of teachers and thinkers throughout the generations. Instead, just as the ANE, Greco-Roman, Jewish, and Christian traditions viewed humanity as children of God who ought to imitate and walk in the ways of their divine father, so Proverbs and the OT used these metaphors as foundational tools for their own instruction.

As we will see in the following section, Proverbs not only espouses these general sentiments but is quite developed and complex in its literary artistry and intertextuality, particularly as the father points the son to follow in the ways of Yhwh. The son's imitation of God is not automatic or easy. Yet, it is the path that all the wise and righteous must walk, those figured by the straight-way motif at the center of Prov 1–9.

---

[267] Najman, "Imitatio Dei," 313, 314.

[268] Najman, "Imitatio Dei," 316.

[269] Najman, "Imitatio Dei," 323.

[270] Najman, "Imitatio Dei," 320.

THE STRUCTURE
OF PROVERBS 1– 9

T o understand the logic of Proverbs on a microscale, which will be the pursuit of Part Two, it will be important to understand the macro-structure, as well. Proverbs has been analyzed for generations and over time has accumulated a broad range of postulations on its macrostructure. Typically, scholars have opted to categorize sections or subsections based on proposed compositional history or according to literary cohesion within presumed units.[1] Although a great deal of discussion has occurred regarding the whole of Proverbs, for the sake of attention and value, our analysis here will focus on Prov 1–9. Despite near consensus,[2] our study will propose a new approach to these nine chapters. This approach utilizes a common feature in Hebrew and ANE literature known as chiasm, or palistrophe more generally.[3] If correct, the final structure of Prov 1–9 fits nicely into a fifteen-unit chiasm, hinging on the middle unit in 4:20–27.[4] In this center unit, the proverbial teacher emphasizes the straight-way motif. In fact, as it will be discussed further, the final verse of this unit presents a

---

[1] The term "compositional history" is used here to mean the scholarly pursuit of source, form, and redactional criticisms, which seek to understand the diachronic and progressive process of accumulation and composition for the text both as a whole and according to authorship, compilation, and editorial elements in its subunits. The term "literary cohesion" is used here to mean the internal, synchronic, literary, and thematic elements that purportedly cohere to create a logical unit of thought. These particular categories are followed generally but in unique ways by individual scholars.

[2] See Arndt Meinhold, *Die Sprüche*, ZBK (Zürich: Theologischer Verlag, 1991); Michael V. Fox, *Proverbs 1–9: A New Translation with Introduction and Commentary*, AYBC 18A (New York: Doubleday, 2000); Bruce K. Waltke, *The Book of Proverbs: Chapters 1–15*, NICOT (Grand Rapids: Eerdmans, 2004); James Alfred Loader, *Proverbs 1–9*, HCOT (Leuven: Peeters, 2014); Bernd U. Schipper, *Proverbs 1–15: A Commentary on the Book of Proverbs 1:1–15:33*, Hermeneia (Minneapolis: Fortress, 2019).

[3] See P. Overland, "Chiasm," in *Dictionary of the Old Testament: Wisdom, Poetry, Writings* (Downers Grove: IVP Academic, 2008), 54–57; John W. Welch, ed., *Chiasmus in Antiquity: Structures, Analyses, Exegesis* (Hildesheim: Gerstenberg, 1981).

[4] Weeks follows the same divisions proposed in this study up through Lesson 8 (4:20–27). After this, however, he follows the typical divisions proposed by most other scholars. In this perspective, he adopts the common ten-section structure of Prov 1–9 and does not observe the fifteen-lesson chiasm. See Stuart Weeks, *Instruction and Imagery in Proverbs 1–9* (New York: Oxford University Press, 2007), 51.

parallel phrase common and unique to Deuteronomy and Deuteronomistic history (Prov 4:27; cf. Deut 5:32–33, 17:20, 28:14; Josh 1:7, 23:6; 2 Kgs 22:2; [2 Chron 34:2]). In all occurrences, the focus is on covenant fidelity to God. However, before exploring this particular passage, our analysis will first highlight structural approaches that have been taken over the years for Prov 1–9. Only a brief overview of notable scholars and approaches will be addressed. The majority of our structural study will focus on the fifteen units of the chiastic structure with a brief analysis for each of the corresponding units.

Patterns of Division for Proverbs 1–9

To begin, there are a number of observable divisions indicated throughout the book, according to the MT. Unfortunately, there is no reasoning provided to further illuminate the purpose or logic behind these divisions. In the Leningrad Codex, the divisions are marked either by an open line or one or two *pᵉṭûḥā'* are included below the last line or above the first line, if occurring at the end of a page. This symbol is considered the open or soft dividing marker.[5] The MT divisions in Prov 1–9, according to the Leningrad Codex, are as follows:

> **1**:1–7, 8–19, 20–33,
> **2**:1–22,
> **3**:1–10, 11–18, 19–35,
> **4**:1–19, 20–**5**:6, 7–23,
> **6**:1–5, 6–11, 12–15, 16–19, 20–26, 27–35,
> **7**:1–23, 24–27,
> **8**:1–21, 22–31, 32–**9**:9, 10–18

This totals up to twenty–two sections within the first nine chapters. While only speculative, it is possible the number of sections is meant to coordinate with the number of Hebrew letters, typical of acrostic poetic patterning.[6] According to the BHS editors, the divisions are only slightly amended, perhaps to accommodate alternate mss or preferred readings. In this schema, there are twenty–four divisions within Proverbs 1–9:[7]

---

[5] William R. Scott, *A Simplified Guide to BHS: Critical Apparatus, Masora, Accents, Unusual Letters & Other Markings*, 4th ed. (North Richland Hills, TX: Bibal, 2007), 1.

[6] The correspondence could be coincidental or intentional. For instance, Prov 2 has twenty-two lines, which could be happenstance or have poetic implications. Schipper argues that Prov 2 is the "table of contents" or "hermeneutical key" to Prov 1–9 and is "reminiscent" of such a poetic pattern, used explicitly in Prov 31:10–31 (Schipper, *Proverbs 1–15*, 54, 60, 103).

[7] Scott notes, regarding the *pᵉṭûḥā'* in the BHS, "Increasing inconsistency developed concerning this difference in format, and it was largely ignored by the time of Codex

1:1–7, 8–19, 20–33,
2:1–22,
3:1–4, 5–10, 11–18, 19–35,
4:1–19, 20–**5**:6, 7–23,
6:1–5, 6–11, 12–15, 16–19, 20–26, 27–35,
7:1–23, 24–27,
8:1–21, 22–31, 32–36,
9:1–9, 10–18

While the 19th century was embroiled by an array of scholarly and newly formulated disciplines, Franz Delitzsch produced a commentary on Proverbs. He was not alone in his pursuits but was a substantial figure during the era. Despite the popular criticism underway in Germany, he sided with a scholar from a previous generation, G. H. A. Ewald, noting that the whole of Prov 1–9 was likely composed by a single author.[8] This in his estimation was to provide an introduction to the Solomonic collections in the latter part of the book. Regarding chapters 1–9, Delitzsch worked from his broader literary interests which focused on the poetic structuring of lines or "stichs." Furthermore, this led him to assess portions within Prov 1–9 as both literary and thematic units, or "independent Mashals." [9] These units were not mechanically or strictly adherent to a "symmetrically chiseled form" but nevertheless did have coherent thought and "systematic internal unity."[10] In order to identify these units, he categorized them as "hortatory discourses." According to Delitzsch, there are fifteen "Mashal strains" that comprise the structure of Prov 1–9.[11] However, despite arguing for internal unity within each Mashal, he did not propose a particular macrostructure for the whole of Prov 1–9.

Beginning in the mid-20th century, the ideas of form criticism were well underway in biblical scholarship, incorporating the interests of sapiential literature as well. Several scholars sought to compare biblical wisdom literature to those of the ANE, Egyptian wisdom in particular.[12] In doing so, they believed there were ten sections able to be isolated and paralleled externally. The general sentiment of this scholarly movement was rooted in a complex compositional history. Such methodology led many to presume that the whole of Prov 1–9 was an "unsystematically compiled school text without

---

Leningradensis ... These marks are added by the editors of BHS" (Scott, *A Simplified Guide to BHS*, 1).

[8] Despite this affirmation, he subtly espoused some amount of openness to the issue of authorship regarding potential poetic insertions for individual units (Franz Delitzsch, *The Book of Proverbs*, trans. M. G. Easton (Grand Rapids: Eerdmans, 1950), 3, 12, 15).

[9] Delitzsch, *The Book of Proverbs*, 12.

[10] Delitzsch, *The Book of Proverbs*, 14.

[11] Delitzsch, *The Book of Proverbs*, xii, 12.

[12] R. N. Whybray, *Wisdom in Proverbs: The Concept of Wisdom in Proverbs 1–9* (Naperville: SCM, 1965); William McKane, *Proverbs: A New Approach*, OTL (London: SCM, 1970); Bernhard Lang, *Wisdom and the Book of Proverbs: A Hebrew Goddess Redefined* (New York: Pilgrim, 1986).

a coherent structure, thematic unity, or progression of content."[13] This pattern of identifying ten units became a staple among Proverbs scholarship. Terms such as "lecture" or "lesson" were applied to the units, along with the old term "discourse." [14] Along with the ten lectures, several additional units were identified and have been generally agreed upon despite varying terminologies and categorizations. Meinhold identified four wisdom poems and three interludes added to the instructional sections.[15] Fox identified seven major interludes, six minor insertions, and seven LXX additions beyond the typical ten lectures.[16] Waltke likewise identified ten lectures with three interludes and two framing sections.[17] Loader followed the ten units but referred to them as "lessons," also identifying five poems and a preface.[18]

Finally, Schipper broke from the established pattern of ten lectures by identifying eight instructional units, an introduction, two wisdom poems, a table of contents, three interludes, and two antithetical sapiential poems.[19] According to him, these units are primarily due to compositional and redactional history. This process was an incremental authorial or editorial accumulation rather than the splicing of disparate materials. In the structuring system argued by Schipper, broad thematic similarities are considered intentional and a result of progressive development. The "table of contents" in Prov 2 was a second level of authorship which helped define many key aspects of the content found in the following eight instructions. Likewise, there was intentional mirroring of language between many of the sections, either signaling forward or backward to other content. In his language, the theology and concepts between them, however, do not always cohere perfectly but were an intentional component of what he calls "discursive" pedagogy.[20] So, while not particularly unique in his identification of units, his attempt to amend the standard scholarly program is an interesting departure, particularly regarding the potential for intra-textuality within Proverbs and inter-textuality with Deuteronomy.[21]

In the following chart, the unit divisions are compared between the Leningrad Codex, the "my son" units, Delitzsch, Whybray, Meinhold, Loader, and Schipper. The "my son" units will serve as the basis for the new structural

---

[13] Schipper, *Proverbs 1–15*, 45; Bernhard Lang, *Die weisheitliche Lehrrede: eine Untersuchung von Sprüche 1–7*, SBS 54 (Stuttgart: KBW-Verlag, 1972), 28. Schipper translates Lang's original comment, "unsystematisch kompiliertes Stück Schulliteratur ohne planvollen Aufbau, ohne gedankliche Einheit und ohne inhaltlichen Fortschritt."

[14] Meinhold, *Die Sprüche*; Fox, *Proverbs 1–9*; Waltke, *Proverbs (1–15)*; Loader, *Proverbs 1–9*.

[15] Meinhold, *Die Sprüche*, 43–46.

[16] Fox, *Proverbs 1–9*, 322–30.

[17] Waltke, *Proverbs (1–15)*, 10–13.

[18] Loader, *Proverbs 1–9*, 7–8.

[19] Schipper, *Proverbs 1–15*, 60.

[20] Schipper, *Proverbs 1–15*, 51.

[21] Schipper states, "Within Proverbs 1–9, this redefinition of wisdom is combined with another phenomenon: the critical engagement with a Deuteronomistic concept of wisdom. ... The detailed commentary on Proverbs 3, 6, and 7 shows that introductory verses of these three instructions (3:1–5; 6:20–24; and 7:1–5) were composed against the backdrop of Deut 6:6–9 // 11:18–20" (Schipper, *Proverbs 1–15*, 37).

approach discussed later in this section. It is interesting and important to notice both the similarities and differences between these scholarly views.

L Codex	"My son"	Delitzsch	Whybray[22]	Meinhold[23]	Loader	Schipper
1:1–7	*Preface* 1:1–7	*Preface* 1:1–7	*Preface* 1:1–5	*Preface* 1:1–7	*Preface* 1:1–7	*Preface* 1:1–7
1:8–19	**Lesson 1** 1:8–33	**Discourse 1** 1:8–19	**Discourse 1** 1:8–19	**Lecture 1** 1:8–19	**Lesson 1** 1:8–19	*Interlude* 1:8–19
1:20–33		**Discourse 2** 1:20–33	*Poem* 1:20–33	*Poem* 1:20–33	*Poem* 1:20–33	*Poem* 1:20–33
2:1–22	**Lesson 2** 2:1–22	**Discourse 3** 2:1–22	**Discourse 2** 2:1,9,16–19	**Lecture 2** 2:1–22	**Lesson 2** 2:1–22	*TOC* 2:1–22
3:1–10	**Lesson 3** 3:1–10	**Discourse 4** 3:1–18	**Discourse 3** 3:1–10	**Lecture 3** 3:1–12	**Lesson 3** 3:1–12	**Lecture 1** 3:1–12
3:11–18	**Lesson 4** 3:11–20		*Poem* 3:13–20	**Lecture 4** 3:13–20	**Lesson 4** 3:13–26	*Interlude* 3:13–20
3:19–35	**Lesson 5** 3:21–35	**Discourse 5** 3:19–26	**Discourse 4** 3:21–35	*Interlude* 3:21–35		**Lecture 2** 3:21–35
		Discourse 6 3:27–35			*Poem* 3:27–35	
4:1–19	**Lesson 6** 4:1–9	**Discourse 7** 4:1–5:6	**Discourse 5** 4:1–9	**Lecture 5** 4:1–9	**Lesson 5** 4:1–9	**Lecture 3** 4:1–9
	Lesson 7 4:10–19		**Discourse 6** 4:10–19	**Lecture 6** 4:10–19	**Lesson 6** 4:10–19	**Lecture 4** 4:10–19
4:20–5:6	**Lesson 8** 4:20–27		**Discourse 7** 4:20–27	**Lecture 7** 4:20–27	**Lesson 7** 4:20–27	**Lecture 5** 4:20–27
	Lesson 9 5:1–6		**Discourse 8** 5:1–23	**Lecture 8** 5:1–23	**Lesson 8** 5:1–23	**Lecture 6** 5:1–23
5:7–23	**Lesson 10** 5:7–23	**Discourse 8** 5:7–23				
6:1–5	**Lesson 11** 6:1–19	**Discourse 9** 6:1–5	*Interlude* 6:1–19	*Interlude* 6:1–19	*Poem* 6:1–19	*Interlude* 6:1–19
6:6–11		**Discourse 10** 6:6–11				
6:12–15		**Discourse 11** 6:12–19				
6:16–19						

[22] Whybray, *Wisdom in Proverbs*, 33–52; R. N. Whybray, *The Composition of the Book of Proverbs*, JSOT 168 (Sheffield: JSOT, 1994), 11–30. Whybray evaluates the original "kernel" and subsequent additions according to those parts which he considers to be mundane, Elohistic, and Yahwistic each a result of stages in development. The progression is from a-theological to primarily theological. Longman follows closely the divisions of Whybray and Meinhold. However, he deviates in his naming of the seventeen divisions, calling them "Extended Discourses," which includes the "prologue" (1:1–7) (Tremper Longman III, *Proverbs*, BCOTWP (Grand Rapids: Baker Academic, 2006), 37–38).

[23] Meinhold, *Die Sprüche*, 43–46; Michael V. Fox, "Ideas of Wisdom in Proverbs 1–9," *JBL* 116.4 (1997): 614; Fox, *Proverbs 1–9*, 44–45; Waltke, *Proverbs (1–15)*, 10; Knut Martin Heim, *Poetic Imagination in Proverbs: Variant Repetitions and the Nature of Poetry*, BBRSup 4 (Eisenbrauns, 2013), 40–41. Fox and Waltke follow the same structuring scheme without notable difference. Heim provides a detailed comparison chart for Fox and Waltke.

	Lesson 12	Discourse 12	Discourse 9	Lecture 9	Lesson 9	Lecture 7
6:20–26	6:20–35	6:20–35	6:20–35	6:20–35	6:20–35	6:20–35
6:27–35						
7:1–23	Lesson 13 7:1–23	Discourse 13 7:1–27	Discourse 10 7:1–27	Lecture 10 7:1–27	Lesson 10 7:1–27	Lecture 8 7:1–27
7:24–27	Lesson 14 7:24–8:31					
8:1–21		Discourse 14 8:1–36	*Poem* 8:1–36	*Poem* 8:1–36	*Poem* 8:1–36	*Poem* 8:1–36
8:22–31						
8:32–9:9	Lesson 15 8:32–9:18	Discourse 15 9:1–18	*Prologue* 9:1–6, 13–18	*Poem* 9:1–6	*Poem* 9:1–18	*Interlude* 9:1–6
9:10–18			*Interlude* 9:7–12	*Interlude* 9:7–12		*Interlude* 9:7–12
				Poem 9:13–18		*Interlude* 9:13–18
22 units	**16 units**	**16 units**	**17 units**	**18 units**	**16 units**	**18 units**

As observed in this structural comparison, there are a few notable departures. In particular, the major departures occur primarily at four literary demarcations (Prov 3:11, 5:7, 7:24, 8:32). It is understandable why all these scholars opt to begin their units only slightly off from these verses (Prov 3:13, 5:1, 8:1, 9:1). The thematic content at Prov 3:13, 8:1, and 9:1 seem quite pronounced, and in all likelihood do represent new thematic units. Yet, with the chiastic pattern proposed in this study, it becomes more apparent that their divisions are misplaced. The difficulty with defining units in Prov 1–9 thematically is the great deal of conceptual and metaphorical, even lexical, overlap between sequential units and between more distant sections within chapters 1–9.[24] Despite great confluence of language, however, the proposed divisions and chiastic parallels in this study provide clarity to the purpose of some seemingly odd phrases and units. According to most scholars, one important departure with "my son" occurs at Prov 3:11.[25] The unit is normally

---

[24] For extensive analyses of repetitions and intratextuality, see Daniel C. Snell, *Twice-Told Proverbs and the Composition of the Book of Proverbs* (Winona Lake: Eisenbrauns, 1993); Heim, *Poetic Imagination in Proverbs*, 51–207. Heim proposes three reasons for repetition: 1) to link subunits to other units within Prov 1–9; 2) to "create coherence" within units and subunits; and 3) to create connections between Prov 1–9 and the rest of the book (43).

[25] See Whybray, *Composition of the Book of Proverbs*, 18–19; Dermot Cox, *Proverbs with an Introduction to Sapiential Books*, OTM 17 (Wilmington: Michael Glazier, 1982), 115–24. Whybray proposed that Prov 3:11–12 were a later addition, slightly divergent from the focus of 3:1–10. In his view, though, it is the fourth admonition. Cox breaks the section at Prov 3:10 but makes 3:11–18 and 19–20 separate sections.

divided at Prov 3:13. However, it more coherently begins with Prov 3:11, as observed for Lesson 4 (3:11–20).[26]

Hebrew	v.	Translation	Structure
מוּסַר יְהוָה בְּנִי אַל־תִּמְאָס וְאַל־תָּקֹץ בְּתוֹכַחְתּוֹ	11	Discipline of Yhwh, my son, do not refuse and do not despise his rebukes.	A Inclusio with Yhwh 3:11–12 // 19–20
כִּי אֶת אֲשֶׁר יֶאֱהַב יְהוָה יוֹכִיחַ וּכְאָב אֶת־בֵּן יִרְצֶה	12	For Yhwh reproves the one whom he loves and as a father, he delights in the son.	(Overlays father with Fatherhood of God)
אַשְׁרֵי אָדָם מָצָא חָכְמָה וְאָדָם יָפִיק תְּבוּנָה	13	Blessed is a man that finds wisdom and a man that obtains understanding.	B Blessed to get wisdom
כִּי טוֹב סַחְרָהּ מִסְּחַר־כָּסֶף וּמֵחָרוּץ תְּבוּאָתָהּ	14	For her gain is better than gain of silver and her produce than gold.	C Extols value of wisdom
יְקָרָה הִיא מִפְּנִיִּים וְכָל־חֲפָצֶיךָ לֹא יִשְׁווּ־בָהּ	15	She is more precious than pearls and all your desires do not compare with her.	
אֹרֶךְ יָמִים בִּימִינָהּ בִּשְׂמֹאולָהּ עֹשֶׁר וְכָבוֹד	16	Long life is in her right hand in her left hand are wealth and honor.	C' Reason wisdom is valuable
דְּרָכֶיהָ דַרְכֵי־נֹעַם וְכָל־נְתִיבוֹתֶיהָ שָׁלוֹם	17	Her ways are ways of pleasantness and all her paths are peace.	
עֵץ־חַיִּים הִיא לַמַּחֲזִיקִים בָּהּ וְתֹמְכֶיהָ מְאֻשָּׁר	18	She is a tree of life for those grasping her and those holding her are Blessed.	B' Blessed to get wisdom
יְהוָה בְּחָכְמָה יָסַד־אָרֶץ כּוֹנֵן שָׁמַיִם בִּתְבוּנָה	19	Yhwh by wisdom founded the earth; he established the heavens by understanding.	A' Inclusio with Yhwh 3:11–12 // 19–20
בְּדַעְתּוֹ תְּהוֹמוֹת נִבְקָעוּ וּשְׁחָקִים יִרְעֲפוּ־טָל	20	In his knowledge the deeps broke open and clouds dripped dew.	(Overlays Yhwh with "Blessed" poem 3:13)

As you can see, this lesson is more properly structured with three parts, Prov 3:11–12, 13–18, and 19–20. The middle section is a standalone poem of the

---

26 Weeks and Kidner both divide the sections as Prov 3:1–10 and 11–20. See Derek Kidner, *Proverbs: An Introduction and Commentary*, TOTC (IVP, 1964), 60–62; Weeks, *Instruction and Imagery in Proverbs 1–9*, 51.

"blessed" (אַשְׁרֵי).[27] This word serves as an inclusio, appearing as the first and last word of the 6–verse poem. Interestingly, the poem contains mostly 7–word lines, comprised of two stiches. The first three verses (Prov 3:13–15) extol wisdom as precious with the other three verses (3:16–18) declaring the reason why. Furthermore, within this poem, Prov 3:13 and 18 serve as book ends with the same basic import, get and hold onto wisdom! Altogether, the unit creates a 10–verse lesson (Prov 3:11–20), which of course has its symbolic numerical implication of completion found throughout the biblical corpus.

Likewise, there is a secondary bookend or inclusio with Prov 3:11–12 and 19–20.[28] The divine name "Yhwh" (יהוה) appears in both. The first part (Prov 3:11–12) overlays the teaching of the proverbial "father" with the fatherhood of God, an important implication behind the proverbial father's teachings. This point will be further explored later in the study. The last part of the lesson (Prov 3:19–20) overlays the source of the "blessed" with Yhwh in his creative acts of "wisdom" and "understanding" before anything existed. This point will also be further explored later in the study.[29] The "blessed-Wisdom" poem marked by an inclusio is couched within the Yhwh inclusio book ends, pointing to an important and central tenet. Wisdom is found in Yhwh and he is the source that one seeks for wisdom and to be "blessed." Verses 11–12 would be a somewhat abrupt end to Prov 3:1–10 if it were meant to be read this way. However, if intended to be read with Prov 3:13–20, it serves as a smooth and poetic bridge between the sections. Likewise, if the primary lesson for the son is to gracefully receive Yhwh's discipline (Prov 3:11–12), the poem (3:13–18) and final inclusio (3:19–20) provide the grounds for why.

In the proposed macro-chiasm, another point of departure from prior scholarly divisions occurs at Prov 5:7, 7:24, and 8:32.[30] For all three, scholars have followed apparent thematic content rather than acknowledging the literary breaks.[31] This is perhaps because such breaks make more sense if one is aware that these literary markers signal the macro-chiasm.

---

[27] Whybray, *Composition of the Book of Proverbs*, 36.

[28] Schipper mistakenly states, "Whereas 3:1–12 spoke of Yhwh, now the focus is on personified wisdom." Although wisdom is certainly important in the poem, his statement overlooks the use of Yhwh in Prov 3:19. Including Prov 3:11–12 in this unit eliminates the inconsistency of his analysis and a missed key concept (Schipper, *Proverbs 1–15*, 138).

[29] See Lessons 6 and 14.

[30] The LXX (Vulg.) has an altered form, which reads as "listen son" rather than the plural. The plural in Heb. does not fit the sg. context of the following verses for Prov 5:7 or 7:24. It has been proposed that Prov 5:7 and 7:24 were inserted (Schipper, *Proverbs 1–15*, 195; Rolf Schäfer, *Die Poesie der Weisen: Dichotomie als Grundstruktur der Lehr und Weisheitsgedichte in Proverbien 1–9*, WMANT 77 (Neukirchen-Vluyn: Neukirchener Verlag, 1999), 136).

[31] Whybray views a correspondence between Prov 1:20–33 and 8:1–36. While there are similarities and the content is analogous, as will be seen in the discussion regarding chiastic alignments, his assessment is misplaced (Whybray, *Composition of the Book of Proverbs*, 38–40).

5:7	7:24	8:32
וְעַתָּה בָנִים שִׁמְעוּ־לִי וְאַל־תָּסוּרוּ מֵאִמְרֵי־פִי	וְעַתָּה בָנִים שִׁמְעוּ־לִי וְהַקְשִׁיבוּ לְאִמְרֵי־פִי	וְעַתָּה בָנִים שִׁמְעוּ־לִי וְאַשְׁרֵי דְּרָכַי יִשְׁמֹרוּ
And now, sons, listen to me and do not turn from the words of my mouth.	And now, sons, listen to me and consider the words of my mouth.	And now, sons, listen to me and the blessed guard my ways.

It is possible, as well, that all three of these, including Prov 3:11–12, serve as a bridge between units rather than as hard breaks, which seems to apply in all four situations. Each includes elements from the units both before and after. Regardless, there is certainly an observable pattern between these units.[32] As will be observed in the following discussion regarding the macro-chiasm, the lessons beginning at these divisions function well for the overall vision of the editor for Prov 1–9. In particular, Prov 5:7 seems to be an odd insertion and difficult to explain apart from the chiasm proposed here. Why would an editor make such an arbitrary insertion? The answer likely lies in the intentional demarcation of literary units for an important and functional macro-chiasm.

The Chiasm of Proverbs 1–9

Despite general scholarly agreement on coherent units and structural analysis, there is little agreement or even discussion on a macro-structure for Prov 1–9. The common feature of Hebrew literature known as chiasm has been identified and studied for generations found in various genres, both on small and large scales.[33] However, this common literary feature has had minimal analysis when it comes to Proverbs, developed on a macro-scale by only Skehan, Waltke, and Dorsey.[34] Waltke's proposed macro-chiasm for Prov

---

[32] See analysis by Heim, *Poetic Imagination in Proverbs*, 141–48.

[33] See N. W. Lund, "The Presence of Chiasmus in the Old Testament," *AJSL* 46.2 (1930): 104–26; Overland, "Chiasm," 54; Bernard M. Levinson, "The Significance of Chiasm as a Structuring Device in the Hebrew Bible," *WW* 40.3 (2020): 271–80; Loader, *Proverbs 1–9*, 76–77. Levinson provides discussion of both micro and macro level chiasms. In each, there is reliance on both lexical and thematic elements, as well as similarities and contrasts. Of chiasms, he states, "Once this pattern is recognized within a chapter or literary unit, an ostensibly haphazard or difficult-to-follow textual sequence gains a sense of order, as a logical structure emerges from the text. ... In the skilled hands of the editors of ancient Israelite literature, the device was also an agent of the theological imagination, of literary and religious creativity, and of cultural change" (273, 280).

[34] For examples in Proverbs, Trible and Overland have proposed two micro-chiasms within Prov 1 (1:10–19, 20–33), see Phyllis Trible, "Wisdom Builds a Poem: The Architecture of Proverbs 1:20–33," *JBL* 94.4 (1975): 3; Paul B. Overland, "Literary Structure in Proverbs 1–9" (PhD diss., Brandeis University, 1988), 168, 209, 378–797. For the first chiasm, Overland places the center and emphasis on Prov 1:15–18 with the title "Warning" and the second center

1–9 was thematically based, finding only eight large parallel sections in his formulation.[35]

A (1:8–19) "Rival invitations of the father and the gang"
 B (1:20–33) "Wisdom's rebuke of the gullible"
  C (2:1–22) "Janus: The father's command to heed teaching"
   D (3:1–4:27) "The father's commands to heed teaching"
   D' (5:1–6:35 "The father's warnings against the unchaste wife"
  C' (7:1–27) "Janus: The father's warnings against Wisdom's rival"
 B' (8:1–36) "Wisdom's invitation to the gullible"
A' (9:1–18) "Rival invitations of Wisdom and the foolish woman"

His chiasm is essentially a broad summary of content, though. While his thematic overview is apropos, the chiastic parallels are general and oversimplify a great deal of material. So, despite a valid and useful attempt, this structuring does not seem to fully capture the macrostructure of Prov 1–9. Dorsey also proposed a macro-chiasm but was more complete finding fourteen units.[36]

A (1:8–19) "invitation of folly"
 B (1:20–33) "invitation of wisdom"
  C (2:1–9) "invitation to call out for wisdom"
   D (2:10–22) "the loose woman"
    E (3:1–20) "good consequences of wise living"
     F (3:21–35) "practical advice about right social behavior"
      G (4:1–27) "embrace wisdom"
      G' (5:1–23) "don't embrace the adulteress"
     F' (6:1–19) "practical advice about wrong social behavior"
    E' (6:20–35) "bad consequences of adultery"
   D' (7:1–27) "the loose woman"
  C' (8:1–36) "invitation of wisdom who calls out"
 B' (9:1–12) "invitation of wisdom"
A' (9:13–18) "invitation of Lady Folly to her house"

His structure and organization for Prov 1–9 is primarily based on the "woman" metaphor, which contrasts Wisdom and Folly. Within these chapters, he also proposes several other units of variously formulated poetic structures,

---

at 1:27 with the focus on "Description of disaster." Trible deals only with the second chiasm in this chapter placing the center in 1:26–27 and providing the title "Announcement of derisive judgment."

[35] Waltke, *Proverbs (1–15)*, 12.

[36] The schema articulated by Dorsey was fortuitously discovered after the pattern indicated in this study was independently developed. As will be seen, the similarities lend credibility to the schema generally while the differences illuminate this study's important and intrinsic contributions more broadly. See David A. Dorsey, *The Literary Structure of the Old Testament: A Commentary on Genesis–Malachi* (Grand Rapids: Baker Academic, 2004), 187–91.

primarily based on the "woman" metaphor as well.[37] Like Waltke, he observes the general correspondence of positive versus negative between the two halves. As seen in his schema, Dorsey partially utilizes the "my son" literary markers but mostly relies on general thematic aspects, similar to Waltke and others.[38] In doing so, the centralizing purposes of Prov 1–9 are overlooked. While his analysis is a good attempt, he misses the multitude of chiastic correspondences, which will be explored in this study.

Prior to both Waltke and Dorsey, Skehan developed a structural approach to the whole of Proverbs, which included chapters 1–9.[39] In his assessment, there were fifteen units within these introductory chapters. These "columns" in his view were akin to or derived from Solomon's Temple and its proposed arrangement. This referent helped direct his structure based on versification and numerical divisions. In doing so, he forced verses into specific units to create the proper alignments.

1. 1:2–7 (6 verses)
2. 1:8–19 (11 verses)
3. 1:20–33 (15 verses)
4. 6:1–19 (20 verses)
5. 2:1–22 (22 verses)
6. 3:1–12, 25–34 (22 verses)
7. 4:1–9, 3:13–24, 35 (22 verses)
8. 4:10–27, 5:21–23 (22 verses)
9. 5:1–19, 6:22, 5:20 (22 verses)
10. 6:20–21, 6:23–7:6 (22 verses)
11. 7:7–27 (22 verses)
12. 8:1–21 (20 verses)
13. 8:22–36 (15 verses)
14. 9:1–11 (11 verses)
15. 9:12–18 (7 verses)

While Skehan's contribution is certainly intriguing, his reasoning for division and versification for the "columns" is highly questionable. This is perhaps why the macro-structure has not been more broadly analyzed.[40] With little explanation, he appears to pick verses and move them around based loosely on topics, literary markers, and perhaps most importantly verse numbers to

---

[37] Dorsey, *Literary Structure of the Old Testament*, 189–90. Dorsey sees a variety of overlapping chiasms in 1:8–2:22, 3:1–6:35, and 7:1–9:18.

[38] Dorsey, *Literary Structure of the Old Testament*, 188.

[39] The pattern provided by Skehan was fortuitously discovered after the schema indicated in this study was independently developed. While the similarities give credibility to the pattern generally, the differences illuminate many important and intrinsic contributions of this study. See P. Skehan, *Studies in Israelite Poetry and Wisdom*, CBQMS 1 (Washington, DC: Catholic Biblical Association of America, 1971), 9–14, 15–26, 27–45.

[40] Skehan also developed numerical values for the whole of Proverbs, building upon the work of prior observers. In Gematria, his values may allude to several biblical names, including Solomon. These observations are more likely than his view on versification in Prov 1–9, though both are uncertain (Skehan, *Studies in Israelite Poetry and Wisdom*, 25).

properly fit his structure.[41] As this study will demonstrate, Skehan was on to something with the fifteen-unit structure but was not able to properly see the natural structuring present. While his versification schema does create a very neat and orderly pattern, there can be little confidence in his divisions.

It is perhaps surprising that the macro-chiasm of Prov 1–9 has not been more expansively explored despite all of the analysis that has occurred throughout the years.[42] Though speculative, this could be due to the high focus on source, form, redaction, and compositional history which tended to overlook the whole or final form of these introductory chapters. In our current analysis, the macro-chiasm will be presented and each corresponding section briefly discussed to highlight the features that point towards the chiastic alignment. Although some interpretive implications will be discussed, much of the thematic and theological aspects will be dealt with in later chapters, particularly as they serve the broader intent of this project.

As previously mentioned, there are fifteen lessons presented in Prov 1–9, with a middle hinge at Prov 4:20–27. The primary indicator at the beginning of each lesson is either "my son" or the plural "sons."[43]

שְׁמַע בְּנִי מוּסַר אָבִיךָ וְאַל־תִּטֹּשׁ תּוֹרַת אִמֶּךָ	1:8[44] (L1)	Listen, my son, to your father's *musar* and do not turn from the *torah* of your mother.
בְּנִי אִם־יְפַתּוּךָ חַטָּאִים אַל־תֹּבֵא	[1:10]	*My son, if sinners fool you, do not go.*
בְּנִי אַל־תֵּלֵךְ בְּדֶרֶךְ אִתָּם מְנַע רַגְלְךָ מִנְּתִיבָתָם	[1:15]	*My son, do not walk in the way with them; restrain your foot from their path.*

---

[41] Skehan, *Studies in Israelite Poetry and Wisdom*, 30–35.

[42] While Heim does not see or mention a macro-chiasm, his chart for parallel variants in Prov 1–9 has an incidental chiastic appearance (Heim, *Poetic Imagination in Proverbs*, 45).

[43] The Hebrew phrase "my son" (בְּנִי) appears at the beginning of eleven lessons (Prov 1:8, 2:1, 3:1, 11, 21, 4:10, 20, 5:1, 6:1, 20, 7:1). The Hebrew phrase "and now sons" (וְעַתָּה בָנִים) appears at the beginning of three lessons (Prov 5:7, 7:24, 8:32). Additionally, the term "sons" (בָּנִים) appears at the beginning of one lesson (Prov 4:1) In addition, the phrase "my son" occurs within a lesson rather than as the beginning of a new instructive section four times (Prov 1:10, 15, 5:20, 6:3). It is interesting the first lesson contains three instances of "my son," two not at the start of a new lesson. The occurrences at Prov 1:15 and 5:20 are not found in the LXX, which could indicate they were a later addition to the MT. The occurrences at Prov 1:10 and 6:3 serve as a rhetorical aspect of the introduction to their lessons. Murphy only tentatively accepts the phrase "my son" as a reliable literary marker due to its apparent misuse in Prov 1:8–15. Yet, this phrase does appear at the start for most of Whybray's "discourses." However, he further noted that these literary markers were accompanied by an imperative or hortatory import. See Roland E. Murphy, *Proverbs*, WBC 22 (Dallas: Thomas Nelson, 1998), 9; Whybray, *Composition of the Book of Proverbs*, 11, 13, 15.

[44] This chart shows the beginning of the fifteen lessons (L1–15), plus four additional, rhetorical occurrences (Prov 1:10, 15, 5:20, 6:3).

בְּנִי אִם־תִּקַּח אֲמָרָי וּמִצְוֹתַי תִּצְפֹּן אִתָּךְ	2:1 (L2)	My son, if you receive my words and my *mitsvah* you treasure up with you,
בְּנִי תּוֹרָתִי אַל־תִּשְׁכָּח וּמִצְוֹתַי יִצֹּר לִבֶּךָ	3:1 (L3)	My son, do not forget my *torah* and my *mitsvah* guard in your heart.
מוּסַר יְהוָה בְּנִי אַל־תִּמְאָס וְאַל־תָּקֹץ בְּתוֹכַחְתּוֹ	3:11 (L4)	Yhwh's *musar*, my son, do not refuse and do not despise his rebukes.
בְּנִי אַל־יָלֻזוּ מֵעֵינֶיךָ נְצֹר תֻּשִׁיָּה וּמְזִמָּה	3:21 (L5)	My son, do not stray from your eyes; guard prudence and discretion.
שִׁמְעוּ בָנִים מוּסַר אָב וְהַקְשִׁיבוּ לָדַעַת בִּינָה	4:1 (L6)	Listen, my sons, to a father's *musar* and attend to know insight.
שְׁמַע בְּנִי וְקַח אֲמָרָי וְיִרְבּוּ לְךָ שְׁנוֹת חַיִּים	4:10 (L7)	Listen, my son, and receive my words and they will multiply for you years of life.
בְּנִי לִדְבָרַי הַקְשִׁיבָה לַאֲמָרַי הַט־אָזְנֶךָ	4:20 (L8)	My son, attend to my words, turn your ear to my sayings.
בְּנִי לְחָכְמָתִי הַקְשִׁיבָה לִתְבוּנָתִי הַט־אָזְנֶךָ	5:1 (L9)	My son, attend to my wisdom, turn your ear to my understanding.
וְעַתָּה בָנִים שִׁמְעוּ־לִי וְאַל־תָּסוּרוּ מֵאִמְרֵי־פִי	5:7 (L10)	And now, sons, listen to me and do not turn from the sayings of my mouth.
וְלָמָּה תִשְׁגֶּה בְנִי בְזָרָה וּתְחַבֵּק חֵק נָכְרִיָּה	[5:20]	*And why should you be intoxicated, my son, with a foreigner and you should embrace a stranger's lap.*
בְּנִי אִם־עָרַבְתָּ לְרֵעֶךָ תָּקַעְתָּ לַזָּר כַּפֶּיךָ	6:1 (L11)	My son, if you pledged to your neighbor, you have gripped your palm to a foreigner

עֲשֵׂה זֹאת אֵפוֹא| בְּנִי וְהִנָּצֵל כִּי בָאתָ בְכַף־רֵעֶךָ לֵךְ הִתְרַפֵּס וּרְהַב רֵעֶיךָ	[6:3]	*Do this too, my son, and be saved for you have gone into the palm of your neighbor; go, make a disturbance and press your neighbor.*
נְצֹר בְּנִי מִצְוַת אָבִיךָ וְאַל־תִּטֹּשׁ תּוֹרַת אִמֶּךָ	6:20 (L12)	Guard, my son, your father's *mitsvah* and do not abandon your mother's *torah*
בְּנִי שְׁמֹר אֲמָרָי וּמִצְוֹתַי תִּצְפֹּן אִתָּךְ	7:1 (L13)	My son, guard my words and treasure up my *mitsvah* with you.
וְעַתָּה בָנִים שִׁמְעוּ־לִי וְהַקְשִׁיבוּ לְאִמְרֵי־פִי	7:24 (L14)	And now, sons, listen to me and attend to the words of my mouth.
וְעַתָּה בָנִים שִׁמְעוּ־לִי וְאַשְׁרֵי דְּרָכַי יִשְׁמֹרוּ	8:32 (L15)	And now, sons, listen to me and blessed are those who guard my ways.

Throughout the scholarly history of Proverbs, these terms have been identified as key markers for many of the sections. However, it does not appear that they have been followed closely in any of the analyses.[45] Additionally, chapters 1–9 include what has often been deemed the preface to the book as a whole (Prov 1:1–7).[46] Many of the terms and phrases in the "preface" unit are key to the intentions of the following chapters, such as, "the fear of Yhwh is the beginning" (Prov 1:7 // 9:10). Since the preface is not part of the lesson schema, it is omitted from the chiasm and the following discussion.

In typical chiastic form, the macro-chiasm of Prov 1–9, as proposed in this study, has corresponding units, which serve to highlight the central unit (Prov 4:20–27). Although providing summary statements for large chiastic units is always a matter of personal nuance, the core intent or message of

---

[45] It is easy to understand that the occurrences in Prov 5:20 and 6:3 are not meant to be literary divisions. In Prov 5:20, "my son" is a passing emphatic reference, without admonition. For Prov 6:3, the phrase is an extension of 6:1–2, which altogether serves as the opening of Lesson 11. It seems, however, that Prov 1:10 and 15 serve a similar function as 6:1–3. All other literary divisions for the lessons include the admonition to follow the instruction from the father, Wisdom, or Yhwh (Prov 3:11, 8:32). Schipper and Fox build on prior scholarship to propose Prov 1:10 and 15 are simply emphatic uses rather than literary markers for independent lessons. Verse 15 is a "consequential" extension of 1:10, both of which fall within the instructional purview of Lesson 1. Likewise, since these verses do not invoke the words or teachings of the father as stated in Prov 1:8, it is preferable to see 1:8–19 as a single unit within Lesson 1 (1:8–33). It is possible the triplet occurrence signals poetically the complexity of contending voices vying for the son's attention, which sets the scope of Prov 1–9. See Schipper, *Proverbs 1–15*, 73–74; Fox, *Proverbs 1–9*, 79–80; Johnny E. Miles, *Wise King · Royal Fool: Semiotics, Satire and Proverbs 1–9* (New York: T&T Clark, 2004), 48.

[46] See Schipper, *Proverbs 1–15*, 61.

these units do seem to correspond, either in kind or contrast. As evidenced in Waltke's large general chiasm, he also observes a broad movement of correspondence. Generally, Lessons 3–7 are more positive in nature while 9–13 are more negative in nature. In other words, a lesson given in the first half will typically correspond but with a negative parallel in the second half. Furthermore, Prov 1–9 is a trove of poetic, literary, and parallelistic repetition. [47] Despite the multiplicity of possible connections, this study highlights those that in the aggregate signal the subtle literary structuring feature. In some cases, the parallel is exclusive. Yet, in others, it is but one of several possible parallels, many of which are intentional as well. The author of Prov 1–9 crafted both chiastic ties and sequential transitions between the lessons. In doing so, the array of literary and lexical connections is often muted or lost, necessitating careful analysis of their corresponding qualities. For the following analyses, only brief attention is given to a few salient chiastic features. Some, however, will be further addressed or developed in subsequent chapters, particularly as they point to the underlying imitative pedagogy.

> **Lesson 1**: Seek Wisdom, find life (1:8–33)
>> **Lesson 2**: Seek Yhwh as Wisdom (2:1–22)
>>> **Lesson 3**: Keeping commandments is life (3:1–10)
>>> **Lesson 4**: Wisdom is a tree of life (3:11–20)
>>>> **Lesson 5**: Yhwh is with the righteous (3:21–35)
>>>> **Lesson 6**: The wise embraces Wisdom (4:1–9)
>>>>> **Lesson 7**: The way of Wisdom is life (4:10–19)
>>>>> **Lesson 8**: *Walk the straight-way (4:20–27)*
>>>> **Lesson 9**: The way of Folly is death (5:1–6)
>>>> **Lesson 10**: The fool embraces disaster (5:7–23)
>>> **Lesson 11**: Yhwh is against the wicked (6:1–19)
>>> **Lesson 12**: Torah is the path of life (6:20–35)
>> **Lesson 13**: Keeping commandments is life (7:1–23)
> **Lesson 14**: Seek Wisdom as Yhwh (7:24–8:31)
Lesson 15: Seek Wisdom, find life (8:32–9:18)

In this structural format, the chiastic shape is evident and highlights the middle point of the macro-structure. Alternatively, the corresponding structural components can be placed in parallel or side-by-side. In this structure, the form is typically referred to more generally as a palistrophe. While the first structure is true to the sequence of Prov 1–9, this latter structure facilitates a clear view of the parallel columns or Lessons.

---

[47] E.g., Snell, *Twice-Told Proverbs and the Composition of the Book of Proverbs;* Heim, *Poetic Imagination in Proverbs.*

Lesson 1 Seek Wisdom, find life (1:8–33)	**Lesson 15** Seek Wisdom, find life (8:32–9:18)
Lesson 2 Seek Yhwh as Wisdom (2:1–22)	**Lesson 14** Seek Wisdom as Yhwh (7:24–8:31)
Lesson 3 Keeping commandments is life (3:1–10)	**Lesson 13** Keeping commandments is life (7:1–23)
Lesson 4 Wisdom is a tree of life (3:11–20)	**Lesson 12** Torah is the path of life (6:20–35)
Lesson 5 Yhwh is with the righteous (3:21–35)	**Lesson 11** Yhwh is against the wicked (6:1–19)
Lesson 6 The wise embraces Wisdom (4:1–9)	**Lesson 10** The fool embraces disaster (5:7–23)
Lesson 7 The way of Wisdom is life (4:10–19)	**Lesson 9** The way of Folly is death (5:1–6)
Lesson 8 Walk the straight-way (4:20–27)	

Chiastic Analysis of Lessons 1 & 15

The first (Prov 1:8–33) and last (8:32–9:18) units in the chiasm share several paralleling features. Perhaps the most important phrase in Proverbs is provided in the preface to the book (Prov 1:7), "fear of Yhwh" (יראת יהוה).[48] While many have noted the corresponding reference between Prov 1:7 and 9:10,[49] which use similar language, it is most curious that the key phrase only occurs five times in Prov 1–9 ([1:7], 1:29, 2:5, 8:13, 9:10). This might seem arbitrary on the surface. Yet, it is likely not a coincidence these occurrences are only

---

[48] Whybray not only notes the paucity of the phrase but its primary appearance in what might be deemed wisdom literature and psalms, only appearing outside the genre a few times (Isa 11:2, 3, 33:6; 2 Chron 19:9). He goes on to call the preface to Proverbs the "syllabus of the wisdom school" in its pedagogical curriculum. See Whybray, *Wisdom in Proverbs*, 95–98; Whybray, *Composition of the Book of Proverbs*, 61.

[49] Von Rad discusses the phrase and its potential import, noting, "It contains in a nutshell the whole Israelite theory of knowledge" (Gerhard von Rad, *Wisdom in Israel* (Nashville: Abingdon, 1972), 65–68).

within the first two and last two chiastic sections. This paradigmatic phrase helps to signal the poetic structure through chiastic correspondence. Another central feature of these two sections is the motif of "wisdom" calling out (Prov 1:20–21, 9:1–3). The plural form used here "wisdoms" (חָכְמוֹת) is only attested a few times in the HB (Ps 49:4; Prov 1:20, 9:1, 24:7), further strengthening the intentional alignment between these lessons.[50] In the first lesson, Wisdom does the calling herself in the "streets," "markets," and "gates." However, in the last lesson, she sends out her "maids" to call from the "heights." The message is for the "naïve" (פתי, פתים) in both (Prov 1:22, 9:4). However, the first lesson does not mention "woman folly" (אשת כסילות), which parallels "wisdom" in calling from the heights at the end (Prov 9:3 // 9:14). The only other place "wisdom" calls out is at the beginning of Lesson 14, which seems to intensify the emphasis on listening to Wisdom's call in Lesson 15.

Between these two lessons, there are several other connections that help to signal their correspondence. A rebuke of "scoffers" (לֵץ) is paralleled between these sections, only occurring one other time outside of these two lessons (Prov 1:22 [2x], 3:34, 9:7, 8). The placement of Prov 9:7–12 seems to be an aphoristic unit, not explicitly coming from Wisdom as it does in Prov 1:22.[51] This could imply the editor intentionally placed this unit here to parallel the first lesson. Likewise, there is a contrasting correspondence between these lessons regarding "seeking" and "finding." The idea of seeking and finding occurs several times in Prov 1–9 (שחר 1:28, 7:15, 8:17; בקש 2:4; חפש 2:4; מצא 1:13, 1:28, 2:5, 3:4, 3:13, 4:22, 6:31, 33, 7:15, 8:9, 8:12, 8:17, 35, 36). However, Wisdom claims in Lesson 1 that the wicked "will seek me but not find me" (Prov 1:28). In the last lesson, "Wisdom" (or the father or Yhwh) states that those who "find me will find life" but those who fail "love death" (Prov 8:35–36).[52] In other words, those who fail to find Wisdom are those who have

---

[50] As Waltke discusses, it is unclear why this form is used (Prov 1:20, 9:1). Building on the work of Albright, he proposes it is either derived from a Phoenician singular form, an abstract noun, or an intensive plural form (Waltke, *Proverbs (1–15)*, 197; Bruce K. Waltke and M. O'Connor, *An Introduction to Biblical Hebrew Syntax* (Winona Lake: Eisenbrauns, 1990), 120–21; Schipper, *Proverbs 1–15*, 91; Murphy, *Proverbs*, 96–97).

[51] The LXX has an addition after Prov 9:10 and 12. The latter addition is rather long. As noted by scholars, the placement of Prov 9:7–12 is curious but bridges 9:1–6 and 9:13–18. The lexical and conceptual connection between Prov 9:10 and 1:7 implies intentional editorial alignment (Schipper, *Proverbs 1–15*, 59–60, 321; Murphy, *Proverbs*, 57–58). The LXX additions read: "for a mind knowing law is good" (9:10a); "one who is fixed on a lie, this one shepherds wind, and is one pursuing a flying bird, for he abandons the ways of his vineyard, and the paths of his own field he leaves, and he passes through a dry desert and a land appointed in thirst, and he brings together fruitless hands" (9:12a–c). For further discussion, see Lesson 15.

[52] For Prov 8:32–36, most read it as the end of 8:1–36. In this reading, the first singular grammar fits with "Wisdom" (חכמה) from earlier verses. "Wisdom" may indeed be the subject of Prov 8:32–36. Yet, Prov 9:1 introduces "Wisdom" (חכמות) in the third plural (cf. 1:20). Also, as previously mentioned, Prov 5:7 and 7:24 parallel 8:32 but certainly refer to the proverbial "father." So, it could be possible to read Prov 8:32–36 as the "father" or even Yhwh, since the import of these verses is quite theologically rich. The overlay of "Wisdom" here with the "father" in Prov 5:7 and 7:24 is likely an intentional signal of the indistinguishable nature of Wisdom's and the father's teachings. These possibilities and their implications will be explored more in later sections.

rejected her calls (Prov 1:25, 30).[53] Amidst the various occurrences of seek-find in Prov 1–9, only three occur with Wisdom in the first person (Prov 1:28, 8:17, 35–36).

Finally, there is a connection between lessons one and fifteen with the idea of "fools" and "knowledge." Lesson 1 states, "Fools hate knowledge" (Prov 1:22, 29). Then in the last lesson, it says that "Woman Folly … does not know anything" (Prov 9:13). Following this, it reiterates that the one seduced by "Folly" goes to her house because "he does not know" it leads to Sheol (Prov 9:18). The negative view of knowledge occurs in Prov 1:22, 29, 4:19, 5:6, 7:23, 9:13, 18. Although the first and last lessons are not the only occurrences, they help to strengthen the poetic signal alongside the other corresponding elements. Another motif that may point toward the parallel is the term "Sheol" (שְׁאוֹל). It only occurs four times in Prov 1–9 (1:12, 5:5, 7:27, 9:18).[54] On its own, it may not be enough to propose a chiastic correspondence. But, in light of the other elements, it provides additional support for alignment.

The summary phrase for these chiastic lessons is "Seek Wisdom, find life." While any number of summary words may have been chosen, there is a strong emphasis on the dire situation in both lessons.[55] Lesson 1 negatively warns that "[the wicked] lay an ambush on their own soul" and "unjust gain takes away the soul of its possessor" (Prov 1:18, 19). Similarly, Wisdom warns that "the naïve are killed in their turning away" but "those who listen dwell securely" (Prov 1:32, 33). In a parallel manner, lesson fifteen explicitly states that the one who "finds me, finds life" but the one who "misses me, harms his soul" (Prov 8:35, 36). After this, Wisdom beckons to the "naïve, turn here … turn away from your naïve ways and live" (Prov 9:4, 6). So, there is both a lexical and conceptual parallel occurring between these lessons, emphasizing the importance of finding Wisdom. Although Wisdom desires to be heard and sought, contending voices seek to lead the son astray.

Chiastic Analysis of Lessons 2 & 14

The second level of the chiasm, Lesson 2 (Prov 2:1–22) and Lesson 14 (7:24–8:31), displays several correspondences as well. As discussed in lessons one and fifteen, the paradigmatic phrase "fear of Yhwh" occurs only five times in Prov 1–9. Excluding the preface to the book (Prov 1:1–7), the only lessons

---

[53] Daniel J. Estes, *Hear, My Son: Teaching and Learning in Proverbs 1–9*, NSBT 4 (Grand Rapids: Eerdmans, 1997), 45–46.

[54] See Lessons 1, 2, 9, 14, and 15 for more focused attention on this thematic emphasis.

[55] Regarding the value of life in Proverbs, Estes comments, "Proverbs 1–9, in keeping with the emphasis of the entire biblical wisdom corpus, places a high value upon life. Life, however, is not mere physical existence, but it is viewed as a substantial, meaningful existence within Yahweh's ordered boundaries. In recommending genuine life, the wisdom teacher contrasts it with the counterfeits that only purport to give life. The wise person values genuine life in its substantial qualities, but the foolish person is attracted to and destroyed by superficial pleasures that only appear to make life meaningful" (Estes, *Hear, My Son*, 52–53).

containing the phrase are 1–2 and 14–15. This could be a mere coincidence but with the level of importance placed on the phrase in 1:7, this would seem unlikely.

(1:7)	1:29	2:5	8:12b, 13a	9:10
The <u>fear of Yhwh</u> is the beginning of <u>knowledge</u>	They hated <u>knowledge</u> and did not choose the <u>fear of Yhwh</u>	You will understand the <u>fear of Yhwh</u> and find the <u>knowledge of God</u>	I find <u>knowledge</u> and discretion. The <u>fear of Yhwh</u> is hatred of evil	The <u>fear of Yhwh</u> is the beginning of wisdom, and the <u>knowledge</u> of the Holy One is insight

Apparent from this comparison, all five emphasize "fear of Yhwh" and "knowledge."[56] However, in lessons two and fourteen, there is a correlation between finding knowledge of God and the fear of Yhwh. Together, they paint a cohesive picture that is not simply mechanistic but intuitive and overlapping.[57]

Another parallel of these lessons involves the "foreign woman" and the path of her "house" (Prov 2:16–19 // 7:24–27). In the second lesson, the female antagonist is called a "foreign woman" (אִשָּׁה זָרָה). In the fourteenth, she is anaphorically referenced with the third feminine singular pronoun, which goes back to Prov 7:5 for the phrase (אִשָּׁה זָרָה).[58] Furthermore, compare the wording between Prov 2:18 and 7:27.[59]

---

[56] See Murphy and Longman for discussion on the phrase Murphy, *Proverbs*, 254–58; Tremper Longman III, *The Fear of the Lord Is Wisdom: A Theological Introduction to Wisdom in Israel* (Grand Rapids: Baker Academic, 2017), xv, 12–14, 15.

[57] Waltke, *Proverbs (1–15)*, 181; Dave L. Bland, *Proverbs and the Formation of Character* (Eugene: Cascade Books, 2015), 3–5. Waltke discusses the overlapping and parallel relation between "fear of Yhwh," "wisdom," and "knowledge." Bland echoes this by stating, "'Knowledge' and 'wisdom' in Proverbs are parallel concepts, and the terms are often used synonymously."

[58] Interestingly, there is a clear parallel between Prov 2:16 "to deliver you from a foreign woman, from the smooth words of a stranger" (לְהַצִּילְךָ מֵאִשָּׁה זָרָה מִנָּכְרִיָּה אֲמָרֶיהָ הֶחֱלִיקָה) and 7:5 "to guard you from a foreign woman, from the smooth words of a stranger" (לִשְׁמָרְךָ מֵאִשָּׁה זָרָה מִנָּכְרִיָּה אֲמָרֶיהָ הֶחֱלִיקָה). The overlap between the content is clear, also coordinating with Prov 7:27. The dual parallel between Prov 7:5 and 7:27 with 2:16–19 is perhaps due to the bridging function of 7:24–27 for Lessons 13 and 14 (cf. 3:11–12). Chiastic alignment is likely occurring in tandem with sequential cohesion as well. These need not be thought of as contradictory but aesthetically and rhetorically complementary. For further discussion, see Schipper, *Proverbs 1–15*, 104–5.

[59] A similar phrase occurs in Prov 5:5, "Her feet descend to death, her steps hold to Sheol" (רַגְלֶיהָ יֹרְדוֹת מָוֶת שְׁאוֹל צְעָדֶיהָ יִתְמֹכוּ).

2:18	7:27
שָׁחָה אֶל־מָוֶת בֵּיתָהּ וְאֶל־רְפָאִים מַעְגְּלֹתֶיהָ	דַּרְכֵי שְׁאוֹל בֵּיתָהּ יֹרְדוֹת אֶל־חַדְרֵי־מָוֶת
Her house sinks to death and her paths to the Rephaim	Her house is the paths of Sheol, those descending to the chambers of death

Although not exactly the same, they are surprisingly similar in the Heb., forming a parallel between the units.[60] They essentially say the same thing with slightly altered lexemes and word order, as often found in parallel poetic lines.

These lessons also parallel the idea that wisdom is like treasure. This idea only occurs in four places (Prov 2:4, 3:14–15, 8:10–11, 18–19). Although the idea is not exclusive between these two lessons, it is rare and alongside the other corresponding elements helps signal the poetic parallel. Beyond the notion of wisdom as treasure, there are several corresponding phrases between the lessons. In Prov 2:8, 9, and 20, the son is exhorted, "For those guarding (נצר) just (משפט) paths (ארח) ... you will understand righteousness (צדק), justice (משפט), and uprightness (ישר), every good (טוב) path (עגל) ... You will walk (הלך) in the way (דרך) of the good (טוב) and guard the paths (ארח) of the righteous (צדק)." In Prov 8:20, wisdom claims, "I walk (הלך) in the righteous (צדק) path (ארח), in the midst of the just (משפט) road (נתיבה)." While there is a mix of terms between these verses, there is an especially strong connection between "walking" and "the path of the righteous."

2:20	8:20
תֵּלֵךְ בְּדֶרֶךְ טוֹבִים וְאָרְחוֹת צַדִּיקִים תִּשְׁמֹר	בְּאֹרַח־צְדָקָה אֲהַלֵּךְ בְּתוֹךְ נְתִיבוֹת מִשְׁפָּט
You will walk in the way of the good and guard the paths of the righteous	I walk in the righteous path, in the midst of the just road

In addition to these, there are two parallel phrases between Prov 2:12 and 8:13. In Prov 2:12, the text uses the phrases "evil way" (דרך רע) and "perverse speech" (דבר תהפכות). In Prov 8:13, the text uses the phrases "evil way" (דרך רע) and "perverse mouth" (פי תהפכות). The term for "perverse" only occurs in Prov 2:12, 14, 6:14, and 8:13. The exact phrase "evil way" only occurs between in Prov 2:12 and 8:13, with only one other similar use in 4:14 (דרך רעים). Finally, there is similar verbiage between Prov 2:3 and 8:1.

---

60 Schipper, *Proverbs 1–15*, 118.

2:3	8:1
אִם לַבִּינָה תִקְרָא לַתְּבוּנָה תִּתֵּן קוֹלֶךָ	הֲלֹא־חָכְמָה תִקְרָא וּתְבוּנָה תִּתֵּן קוֹלָהּ
If you cry out for insight, you give your voice for understanding	Does wisdom not cry out and understanding give her voice?

The lexical and structural correspondence is quite obvious in the Hebrew.[61] In particular, the second half of the verses are almost exactly the same. In the first half, there is a grammatical word-play since the imperfect (*yiqtol*) patterns for a second masculine singular and third feminine singular are the same in Hebrew. The only real aberration is the use of "wisdom" (חָכְמָה) instead of "insight" (בִּינָה) in Prov 8:1. It is not clear why this happens. Perhaps the switch to "wisdom" is meant to further emphasize the theme of Lesson 14, which exalts "wisdom" and puts her proximity to Yhwh on display for the proverbial son. Though perhaps coincidental, these elements help point the reader to the poetic structure in coordination with the other parallel features of this chiastic level.

As for the title of this section, "Seek Yhwh as Wisdom // Seek Wisdom as Yhwh," there is a strong emphasis on the parallel and complementary nature of Wisdom and Yhwh.[62] For Lesson 2, Yhwh seems to be the mediator of Wisdom. Yet, for Lesson 14, Wisdom seems to be the mediator for Yhwh. The son is to pursue Wisdom with the "fear of Yhwh" and "knowledge of God" as the result (Prov 2:5). This is because God is the source and dispenser of wisdom, knowledge, and understanding (Prov 2:6). Yet, in the parallel lesson, Wisdom speaks in the first person and presents herself as an exemplar, near and dear to Yhwh (Prov 8:12–31). In this lesson, it is Wisdom who is the dispenser of gifts for those who "love me," "seek me," and "find me" (Prov 8:17–21). While many words or ideas may be chosen for these lessons, there is a thematic correspondence in an inverse or complementary manner.

---

[61] See Heim, *Poetic Imagination in Proverbs*, 90–93. Heim comments on the complementary contexts of the two sections. The reason the son ought to call out for "understanding" (//wisdom) is because "Wisdom" will hear and respond accordingly (93).

[62] Longman, *The Fear of the Lord Is Wisdom*, 19–20.

Chiastic Analysis of Lessons 3 & 13

The third level of the chiastic structure contains a strong parallel element. Lesson 3 (Prov 3:1–10)[63] and Lesson 13 (7:1–23)[64] both contain an almost identical and unique phrase in the Heb.

3:3	7:3
קָשְׁרֵם עַל־גַּרְגְּרוֹתֶיךָ כָּתְבֵם עַל־לוּחַ לִבֶּךָ	קָשְׁרֵם עַל־אֶצְבְּעֹתֶיךָ כָּתְבֵם עַל־לוּחַ לִבֶּךָ
Bind them around your neck (גרגרות), write them on the tablet of your heart	Bind them around your fingers (אצבע), write them on the tablet of your heart

The term for "neck" is uncommon, only appearing in Proverbs (1:9, 3:3, 22, 6:21). It is not clear why there is a lexical difference between the units, unless for parallelistic patterning.[65] Likewise, the idea that the son is commanded to "tie" (קשר) is likely alluding to Deut 6:8 and 11:18: "You (sg.) shall tie (קשר) them on your hand (יד) for a sign" and "You (pl.) shall tie (קשר) them on your hand (יד) for a sign."[66] Perhaps not coincidental, the primary term for what is

---

[63] The LXX has a different construction of Prov 3:3, "Mercy and faith shall not forsake you, but you are to bind them on your neck, and you will find grace." The Vulg., Syr., and Tg. follow the MT construction. There is no scholarly consensus but those who favor the LXX dismiss this tri-stich as a later addition. Overland rejects the LXX as original arguing that tri-stiches are a common feature elsewhere in Proverbs. In particular, he builds the case that the parallel between Proverbs and Deuteronomy emphasizes the centrality of the "heart" and the action of "writing." See, Paul Overland, "Did the Sage Draw from the Shema?: A Study of Proverbs 3:1–12," *CBQ* 62.3 (2000): 428; Waltke, *Proverbs (1–15)*, 236; Murphy, *Proverbs*, 20; Whybray, *Composition of the Book of Proverbs*, 18.

[64] There is one other place outside these two lessons where a similar phrase occurs, "Tie (קשר) them on your heart (לב) continually, bind them on your neck (גרגרות)" (Prov 6:21). Two of the terms from Prov 3:3 are present. The correspondence is perhaps a poetic echo while providing a cohesive transition to the thematic scene of the "stranger" (נכריה) for Lessons 12 and 13.

[65] Fox, *Proverbs 1–9*, 146–47; Schipper, *Proverbs 1–15*, 128–29; Angelika Berlejung, "Zeichen der Verbundenheit und Medien der Erinnerung: Zur Religionsgeschichte und Theologie von Dtn 6,6–9 und verwandten Texten," in *Ex oriente Lux: Studien zur Theologie des Alten Testaments*, ABIG 39 (Leipzig: Evangelische Verlagsanstalt, 2012), 131–65; J. M. LeMon and B. A. Strawn, "Parallelism," in *DOTWPW* (Downers Grove: IVP Academic, 2008), 502–3, 510–11. Fox attributes the use of a "necklace" here to a real mnemonic device students would wear. While perhaps the physical backdrop of the metaphor is legitimate, it does not explain why "neck" is used here but "fingers" and "hand" are used in Prov 7:3 and Deut 6:8, 11:18. Alternatively, as known in parallelism, corresponding lines can provide poetic complementarity rather than mere repetition.

[66] For further discussion, see Overland, "Did the Sage Draw from the Shema?" 427–33; McKane, *Proverbs*, 291–92; Otto Plöger, *Spruche Salomos (Proverbia)*, BKAT 17 (Neukirchen-Vluyn: Neukirchener Verlag, 1984), 32–35. Overland builds on previous scholarship to construct a strong case for the correspondence between the language and concepts of Prov 3:1–12 and Deut 6:4–9.

to be "tied" in Deut 6:8 and 11:18 is the "commandment" (מצוה) from Yhwh,[67] which is also a primary term for what the son is to "tie" to his "neck" and "fingers" in Prov 3:1 and 7:1. Additionally, both passages in Deuteronomy include within the "commandment" an instructive hortatory phrase: "love Yhwh your God and serve him with all your heart and with all your soul." The phrase "tablet of your heart" is exclusive to Prov 3:3 and 7:3, with only one other similar phrase in the HB, "tablet of their heart" (Jer 17:1).[68] The language of writing on a "tablet" is, of course, the foundational place Yhwh himself inscribed his instructions for Israel (Exod 24:12, 31:18, 32:15–19, 34:1, 4, 28–29; Deut 4:13, 5:22, 9:9–17, 10:1–5).

Between lessons three and fourteen, there is also a subtle contrast. Lesson three exhorts the son to "trust" (בטח) in Yhwh and to "know" (ידע) him, a word often laden with intimate relational implications (Prov 3:5, 6). The son is promised healing and refreshment in following the teaching of the father (Prov 3:8). More than that, he is promised fulfillment (מלא), satisfaction (שבע), and excessive blessing (Prov 3:9). However, in lesson thirteen, the son is warned about the deception of the "strange" woman. She promises delights and love in the absence of her husband (Prov 7:16–19). Yet, in going to her he is actually going to "slaughter" (טבח) and does not "know" (ידע) that she will take his "soul" (נפש) like a foolish animal (Prov 7:22, 23). While it is not necessary to have exact parallels to create poetic chiasm, the essence of the passages and a few of their lexemes do present correspondence and contrast.

Finally, the title of the two lessons, "Keeping commandments is life," captures the purpose and introductory emphasis of the father's teaching in both, particularly due to their roots in Deuteronomy. Lesson 3 focuses in Prov 3:1–2 on "guarding" (נצר) his "commandments" (מצוה) and "teaching" (תורה).[69] This, as it is claimed, will result in "length of days" (ארך ימים) and "years of life" (שנות חיים). Lesson 13 exhorts in Prov 7:1–2 that the son treasures his "commandments" (מצוה) and "guards" (שמר) his "commandments" (מצוה) and "teaching" (תורה). By these, the son is promised he will "live" (חיה).[70] As

---

[67] See Fox, *Proverbs 1–9*, 79. Fox notes on 1:8, "With regard to Torah and commandments, G. Baumann (1996:295) observes that outside Proverbs, *torah* and *mitsvah* with the possessive suffix are (with one exception each) always divine. Thus, the suffixed forms in Proverbs 'transgress or blur the border between human and divine commandments.'"

[68] Couroyer makes an argument that this did not imply an internal reality "in" the heart but literally "on" (על) the heart. This argument stems from the Hebrew preposition used, which he proposes implied an actual schoolboy placard hung around the neck resting over the heart (Bernard Couroyer, "La Tablette Du Coeur," *RB* 90.3 (1983): 416–34). While a plausible image, the import of an internalization on the heart is not foreign to biblical thinking. In Deut 10:16 and 30:6, the command and expectation were for Israel to circumcise their hearts (cf. Jer 4:4). Then in Jer 31:33, Yhwh gives a prophecy, "I will place my law within them and I will write on (על) their heart." It would not make sense in Jer 31 to suppose that Yhwh would write his law on a schoolboy placard and hang it around Israel's neck.

[69] The combination of *torah* (תורה) and "command" (מצוה) occurs in four places (Prov 3:1, 6:20, 23, 7:2). All three contexts have similar imagery, though 6:20 seemingly echoes 1:8.

[70] See Heim, *Poetic Imagination in Proverbs*, 137–41; Schipper, *Proverbs 1–15*, 260. In Prov 4:4c and 7:2a, the same phrase occurs, "Guard my commandments and live." The occurrence in Prov 7:2 may be a conceptual echo substantiating the following lesson in the generational wisdom passed on from the grandfather in 4:3–4.

mentioned, lesson thirteen conversely provides a negative example or warning if the son were to depart from his teaching, namely losing his "soul" (Prov 7:23). Therefore, the two lessons primarily teach the son the mortal importance of the father's moral instruction.

Chiastic Analysis of Lessons 4 & 12

For Lesson 4 (Prov 3:11–20) and Lesson 12 (6:20–35), the introductory exhortations of both emphasize the parental structure. Lesson 4 mentions that his "discipline" (מוסר) is from Yhwh, who is teaching him like a "father" (אב) to a son. Therefore, he should not reject these divine "rebukes" (תוכחת). Then in lesson twelve (Prov 6:20), the instruction begins with a similar phrase that began in lesson one. He mentions the "commands" (מצוה) and "teaching" (תורה) are from the "father" (אב) and "mother" (אם), as also found in Prov 10:1. Then in Prov 6:23, the father gives perhaps the primary emphasis of the lesson. It repeats "command" and "teaching" but also mentions in this verse the phrase "rebukes of discipline" (תוכחת מוסר). Between the two passages, the same idea is overlaid poetically, implicating the divine role of father and mother in teaching (מוסר, מצוה, and תורה).

Also, as a general theme, the two lessons provide a contrast. The son is to "hold fast" (תמך/חזק) to Wisdom like a wife (Prov 3:18) but lesson twelve (6:25, 32) describes the dangers of "adultery" (נאף), rooted in "desire" (חמד). Likewise, Wisdom is exalted as worth an immense value, more than anything (Prov 3:14–15). Yet, in Prov 6:24–26, the adulterous woman – called the "evil woman" (אשה רע), "prostitute" (זונה), and a "stranger" (נכריה) – is only worth a "round of bread" (ככר לחם). In other words, she is worthless. The value of Wisdom is not unique to Lesson 4 (Prov 2:4, 3:14–15, 8:18–19). But it does serve in this instance as a persuasive parallel in order to contrast foolish choices in Lesson 12.

Regarding the title of these lessons, "Wisdom is a tree of life // Torah is the path of life," the two lessons seem to build on these poetic images. As mentioned, Prov 6:23 appears to be a central instruction for lesson twelve. The text says, "For a lamp of commandment and a teaching of light and a path of life (דרך חיים) are the rebukes of discipline." In Prov 3:18, Wisdom is called a "tree of life" (עץ חיים).[71] Interestingly, looking at Gen 3:24 there is a similar but conflated phrase, "he placed cherubim ... to guard the path of the tree of life (דרך עץ החיים)." The "tree of life" is itself a rare phrase (Gen 2:9, 3:22, 24; Prov 3:18, 11:30, 13:12, 15:4; cf. Rev 2:7, 22:2, 14, 19), as is the path of life (Gen

---

[71] Waltke, *Proverbs (1–15)*, 259–60. Waltke notes, "The concept of a tree of life ('ēṣ-ḥayyîm; see 11:30) to represent eternal life is part of the ancient Near Eastern culture in which Israel participated. ... The Genesis narrative represents 'ādām seeking a wisdom independent from God by reaching for the tree of knowledge of good and evil (i.e., to formulate his own laws of right and wrong, a right that belongs exclusively to God). ... Proverbs functions symbolically (and provisionally) as the 'tree of life' that was lost in Gen. 2:22–24."

3:24; Prov 6:23, Jer 21:8; cf. [ארח חיים] Ps 16:11, Prov 2:19, 5:6, 15:24). In these lessons, there appears to be a poetic signal to the *torah* path of life – restoration of the Edenic world – found in the Torah.[72] Through the lens of the proverbial father, this path requires wisdom, discipline, understanding, commandments, rebukes, and teaching, which will result in life.

Chiastic Analysis of Lessons 5 & 11

Lessons 5 (Prov 3:21–35) and 11 (6:1–19) may not appear parallel initially.[73] However, upon closer inspection, several features point toward their intentional alignment. First, both emphasize consideration for the "neighbor" (רע). The word only occurs in five verses in Prov 1–9 (3:28, 29, 6:1, 3, 29). Only 6:29 is outside of lessons five and eleven, which focuses on adultery rather than neighbor care. Interestingly, Lesson 5 approaches the issue of "neighbor" from a positive view. In other words, the son should treat them well. The primary issue, here, is when the son has the upper hand, presumably in possession of the neighbor's pledge (cf. Exod 22:26–27). Lesson 5 describes this indirectly, "Do not tell your neighbor, 'Go and return, tomorrow I will give,' when it is with you" (Prov 3:28). Lesson 11 approaches the issue of the "neighbor" from a negative view when they have the upper hand.[74] Here, the son is exhorted to free himself from the trap of his "neighbor" to whom he is "pledged" (ערב). While one might hope the neighbor would treat the son righteously, it is not guaranteed. Thus, it is a concern and a dangerous liability. Lessons 5 and 11 are the only ones in Prov 1–9 that provide direct instruction regarding neighbor care. Perhaps not surprisingly, they do so in a contrasting or complementary fashion.

---

[72] J. Scott Duvall and J. Daniel Hays, *God's Relational Presence: The Cohesive Center of Biblical Theology.* (Grand Rapids: Baker Academic, 2019), 105–6. Duvall and Hays comment, "The mention of the 'tree of life' seems to be a clear reference back to the tree of life in Genesis 2–3. Ironically, while it was the unauthorized and disobedient desire for knowledge that resulted in the banishment of Adam and Eve from the garden, the tree of life, and the presence of God in Genesis 2–3, in Proverbs God offers a way back to the garden, to his presence, and to the tree of life, through Woman Wisdom."

[73] Fox is quite baffled by the use and placement of Prov 6:1–19, saying, "I do not see any literary explanation for the location of Interlude C. ... The placement of Interlude C seems to have been adventitious, with the interpolator giving little thought to its location, except insofar as he inserted the interlude on the boundary between two units" (Fox, *Proverbs 1–9*, 226). While Lesson 11 may seem arbitrary in its placement for Fox's schema, it provides balance to the macro-chiasm for Prov 1–9.

[74] Fox makes the case that the phrase implies "giving surety for a loan" to the neighbor (Fox, *Proverbs 1–9*, 212). Schipper proposes the opposite reading, preferring "vouch for" in the sense of taking responsibility for the neighbor's liabilities (Schipper, *Proverbs 1–15*, 221). With the parallel of Prov 3:28–29 in view, 6:1–2 would likely read with Fox. In Prov 3:28–29, this passage seems to intentionally elide what the son must not withhold, perhaps broadening the implications to any form of "good" (טוב) in 3:27. The two lessons together provide a complementary teaching.

Found in these lessons is also the important topic of the "abomination of Yhwh" (תועבה יהוה).[75] In Prov 3:32, the phrase references a "devious person (לוז). In Prov 6:16, the phrase is split up into parallel lines, "Six things Yhwh hates; seven are an abomination of his soul." The only other place "abomination" occurs in Prov 1–9 is 8:7, but without reference to Yhwh. So, clearly lessons five and eleven are presenting parallel correspondence. Likewise, both occurrences of "abomination" begin similar passages. For Prov 3:33–35, there are three negative "curses" (מארה) given to the wicked (רשע), scornful (לץ), and foolish (כסיל). Intermixed are three positive blessings given to the righteous (צדיק), humble (עני), and wise (חכם).[76] For Prov 6:16–19, there are six or seven abominations of Yhwh. These are prideful eyes, a lying tongue, hands that shed innocent blood, a heart devising evil, feet that run to evil, a false witness, and one who creates strife between brothers. While these need not be comprehensive, a lying tongue and false witness are perhaps overlapping, making six abominations out of seven poetic phrases (cf., Exod 20:16, 23:1–3; Deut 19:16–20; Prov 19:5, 9). Although Lesson 5 provides a set of three blessings and three curses, Lesson 11 only provides six abominations. Finally, the words "devise evil" (חרש רע) only occur in lessons five and eleven (Prov 3:29, 6:14, 18), two of which are within these sets of abominations to Yhwh.

Another parallel between these lessons is the subject of "sleep" (שנה). This particular term only occurs five times in Prov 1–9 (3:24, 4:16, 6:4, 9, 10). While Prov 4:16 mentions sleep, it is only a passing description of the wicked. However, lessons five and eleven provide instructions to the son that highlight "sleep." Interestingly, though perhaps not surprising at this point, the lessons approach "sleep" from contrasting perspectives. In Prov 3:24, the father promises peace and good sleep if the son will hold to Wisdom. Conversely, in Prov 6:4 and 9–10, the father warns of the anxiety associated with giving a pledge and the danger of being lazy. Both instances are negative in Lesson 11. In fact, Prov 6:9–10 is an ironic reversal from 3:24. For Prov 6:9–10, what the lazy might presume is peaceful sleep is actually foolishness and will result in poverty.[77] Together, the passages provide a holistic and balanced view of rest, either through Wisdom or through Folly.

---

[75] Schipper notes the Deuteronomistic roots of the phrase, seen in Deut 7:25; 12:31; 17:1; 18:12; 22:5; 23:19; 25:16; 27:16. He goes on to say, "In the book of Proverbs, this expression describes things that are unacceptable to God: false weights (11:1), people with a false heart (11:20), lying lips (12:22), and so on (see also 15:8, 9, 26; 16:5; 17:15; 20:10, 23). As in 15:8, 9, the expression 'abomination to Yhwh' in 3:32 refers to a type of person" (Schipper, *Proverbs 1–15*, 161).

[76] Longman comments on the potential echo of these verses from Deuteronomy, "Curse and blessing bring the language of the covenant to play here. However, it may be doubted that we should make a major connection, considering that covenant is rarely an explicit concept in the book, though there may be an implicit association. ... Even so, if we reflect on similar language in places like Deut. 28 and remember the language of reward and punishment throughout Proverbs, we are likely right to think of blessing as including things like long life, health, material wealth, happiness, and curse as the opposite" (Longman, *Proverbs*, 144).

[77] Several features of Prov 6:1–11 are reminiscent of 24:28–34. These passages discuss both the "neighbor" and the "sluggard." In Prov 24:30–34, there is a strong parallel to 6:6–11, with 24:33–34 as an exact parallel to 6:10–11. In 24:30–34, the sage is observing and

Finally, the titles for these lessons are "Yhwh is with the righteous" and "Yhwh is against the wicked." Really the message is essentially the same between the two lessons. But lesson five is from a more positive perspective and lesson eleven is from a more negative one. In Prov 3:26, it says, "Yhwh will be with your way/naivety."[78] Similarly, as mentioned, in Prov 3:33–35, it says, "Yhwh ... will bless the dwelling of the righteous ... give favor to the humble." Lesson 11, of course, only provides the things and people Yhwh hates. Together, the final sections of these two lessons provide a primary emphasis for the instruction.

Chiastic Analysis of Lessons 6 & 10

Although Proverbs is full of familiar ideas and repeating motifs, there are salient instances in the lessons that highlight structural artistry. For Lessons 6 (Prov 4:1–9) and 10 (5:7–23), several points overlap between them. To begin, lesson six exhorts the sons (pl.) to "hear a father's discipline (מוסר)." While the term appears often in Prov 1–9 (13x), Lesson 10 makes it a central feature, particularly in the negative sense. In 5:12, the father warns of those on the foolish way who say, "How I hated discipline (מוסר)." Likewise, the lesson ends (Prov 5:23) with a prediction of the wicked, "He dies when there is no discipline (מוסר)." Lesson 6 begins with a positive view towards discipline but Lesson 10 ends with a stark negative warning for the lack of discipline.[79]

Another important and parallel idea between the two lessons involves adherence to generational instruction.[80] Lesson 6 says to "hear a father's

---

understanding the correlation between self-deception, laziness, and poverty. For Prov 6:6–11, the father conveys similar wisdom in a hortatory manner. Kidner notes, "[The sluggard] does not commit himself to a refusal but deceives himself by the smallness of his surrenders. So, by inches and minutes, his opportunity slips away." As Longman discusses, Proverbs is clear in its "intolerance of lazy people," mentioning the subject often (Prov 6:6–11; 10:4, 5, 26; 12:11, 24, 27; 13:4; 14:23; 15:19; 18:9; 19:15, 24; 20:4, 13; 21:25; 22:13, 29; 24:30–34; 26:13–16; 27:23–27; 28:19; 31:27). See Schipper, *Proverbs 1–15*, 227–28; Longman, *Proverbs*, 561–62; Kidner, *Proverbs*, 42.

[78] Schipper determines this to be a *beth essentiae*, which implies the sense of "as," following Delitzsch and Wildboer. In this verse, he reads, "Yhwh will be your confidence." However, in analyzing occurrences of the verb "to be" (היה) with the preposition בְּ, it does not seem this occurs elsewhere in the HB. It is perhaps to be read as a circumstantial *beth* or accompaniment, "in" or "with." HALOT identifies this use of the preposition as "expresses the sharing of an act: a) (together) with" (HALOT, 105). Alternatively, if the term "confidence" (כסל) were actually the term "foolishness" (כסיל) then the *beth* would perhaps be adversative, "against." The LXX has the phrase "for the Lord is on/with your path" (ὁ γὰρ κύριος ἔσται ἐπὶ πασῶν ὁδῶν σου), possibly translating "in your ways" (בְמְסִלֹתֶיךָ), according to the BHS. Regardless, it would seem Prov 3:26a is conveying to the son Yhwh will assist his walking the path safely, which parallels 3:23. See Schipper, *Proverbs 1–15*, 157; Waltke and O'Connor, *Introduction to Biblical Hebrew Syntax*, 197–98; Ronald J. Williams and John C. Beckman, *Williams' Hebrew Syntax*, 3rd ed. (Toronto: University of Toronto Press, 2007), 96–101.

[79] Schipper also sees continuity with Prov 4 regarding the topic of "discipline" (Schipper, *Proverbs 1–15*, 207).

[80] Schipper discusses the dual setting of this passage. On one hand, it mentions father and mother. Yet, it directs the instruction to "sons," which Schipper proposes could refer to a

discipline" (Prov 4:1). Then he goes on to explain that his father "taught" (ירה) him, also mentioning his mother (Prov 4:3, 4). In contrast, Lesson 10 (Prov 5:13) describes that a foolish son does not "hear" (שמע) his "teachers" (מרה) nor his "instructors" (מלמד).[81] Lesson 10 is the only place where the idea of "teachers" is used and Lesson 6 is the only where transgenerational instruction occurs, the father learning from his father. Despite the proverbial father and mother occurring elsewhere (Prov 1:8, 6:20), there is not another explicit reference to generational instruction.

Furthermore, there is a similar phrase repeated in both lessons. The only difference in Prov 5:7 is the synonymous word "turn" (סור) instead of "turn" (נטה).[82]

4:5	5:7
וְאַל־תֵּט מֵאִמְרֵי־פִי	וְאַל־תָּסוּרוּ מֵאִמְרֵי־פִי
Do not turn (נטה) from the words of my mouth	Do not turn (סור) from the words of my mouth

This is the only occurrence of the phrases, including "words of my mouth."[83] Additionally, both lessons use the idea of "heart" (לב).[84] While the term is not unique, these two lessons use the term in similar but contrasting instances. Lesson 6 exhorts the son, "May your heart hold fast to my words" (Prov 4:4). Lesson 10 describes a foolish son who says, "My heart rejects rebuke" (Prov 5:12). In many ways, this contrast fits within the two lessons' imagery of a wife versus adulteress.[85] Lesson 6 urges the son to "obtain" (קנה) Wisdom (Prov 4:5). He then (Prov 4:6, 8) instructs him not to "forsake her" (תעזבה) but to "love her" (אהבה) and "embrace her" (תחבקנה). In other words, he is to treat Wisdom like a beloved wife.[86] This becomes more evident when compared with Lesson

---

scribal school such as in Egypt or Sir 6:32–37, 51:23. However, despite the possibility of these settings, Schipper rightly prefers to view this passage through the lens of Deut 6:6–9 (Schipper, *Proverbs 1–15*, 167).

[81] The LXX translates these terms in the singular since the consonantal forms (מלמדי, מרי) could be read as either singular or plural. Fox argues that the singular would imply the "father" but the plural would perhaps imply the generational teachers rather than in the sense of teachers at formal "universities," as Toy proposed (Fox, *Proverbs 1–9*, 197–98).

[82] These terms play a key role and artistic interplay in Lesson 8, as well.

[83] As discussed previously, Prov 5:7 parallels the literary division at 7:24. This phrase occurs in similar forms at Prov 4:5, 5:7, [6:2], and 8:8.

[84] The term "heart" (לב) occurs nineteen times in Prov 1–9 (2:2, 10, 3:1, 3, 5, 4:4, 23, 5:12, 6:14, 18, 21, 32, 7:3, 7, 10, 25, 8:5, 9:4, 16).

[85] The topic of "adultery" is likely described or implied in seven passages in Prov 1–9 (2:16–19, 4:5–9, 5:3–6, 15–19, 6:24–35, 7:4–23, 24–27).

[86] Murphy notes that the four-fold use of the term "obtain" (קנה) is also used by Boaz in reference to acquiring Ruth as his redeemed wife. Likewise, he connects the term for "crown" (עטרה) to Song 3:11, which is perhaps related to Solomon's wedding. Altogether, Murphy calls Prov 4:4–9 a "love engagement" pairing the metaphor of marriage and covenantal fidelity, "fidelity to wisdom means fidelity to God" (Murphy, *Proverbs*, 26, 29).

10, particularly in Prov 5:15–20.[87] This section in lesson ten focuses on the "foreigner" (זרה) and "stranger" (נכריה) whom he should avoid (Prov 5:20). He is to rejoice in the "wife of his youth" (Prov 5:18) and to be intoxicated in "her love" (אהבתה) (Prov 5:19). Likewise, he must not be "intoxicated" with the "foreign" woman nor should he "embrace" her (תחבק) (Prov 5:20). The uses of "embrace" in Lessons 6 and 10 are the only occurrences in Proverbs (4:8, 5:20). Lesson six uses the term positively for Wisdom but lesson ten uses it negatively for the "foreigner." The imagery of the two women fits within the broader warnings and exhortations of the two paths.[88]

Finally, the lessons emphasize the benefits or disgrace inherent in the two paths. In Prov 4:6–9, not only will wisdom "guard" (שמר) and "protect" (נצר) the son, she will "exalt" (רום) and "honor" (כבד) with a "garland" (לויה) and "crown" (עטרה) the one who treats her as a beloved wife. For those who approach the door of the stranger's house (Prov 5:8–11), they will lose "honor" (הוד), "years" (שנה), "strength" (כח), "labors" (עצב), will "groan" (נהם), and their body will "cease" (כלה). So, the titles of the lessons, "The wise embrace Wisdom" and "The fool embraces disaster," bring out the parallel emphases within the lessons. The son in Lesson 6 is emphatically commanded to "obtain" (קנה) Wisdom and "embrace" her like a beloved wife. In Lesson 10, he is warned of adulterous desires that lead to "embracing" the stranger instead of his wife.

Chiastic Analysis of Lessons 7 & 9

For Lesson 7 (Prov 4:10–19) and Lesson 9 (5:1–6), there is a warning of the two paths theme.[89] In Prov 4:11, the father mentions the "path of wisdom" (דרך חכמה) and the "path of uprightness" (מעגלי־ישר).[90] Then in Prov 4:14, he

---

[87] Schipper summarizes Prov 5:1–23 (Lessons 9 and 10) saying, "The imagery of Proverbs 5 has an erotic/sexual level of meaning. By drawing on the imagery of the Song of Songs and ancient Near Eastern love poetry, a contrast is created between the strange woman and one's own wife. The image of love and intoxication describes the danger associated with the female figure. ... There are also allusions to sapiential knowledge using metaphors such as water and wells. Whoever gives in to a 'strange woman' squanders one's sapiential knowledge (v. 16) and sets out on a path that ultimately leads to death. By the end of the instruction, it is clear that 5:1–23 has to do with two paths—the path of life and the path of death. ... The concluding reference to Yhwh in vv. 21–23, however, connects seamlessly to what precedes, making explicit the instruction's previously implicit religious dimension. Whoever gives in to a foreign woman does more than give in to sexual desire and erotic fantasy; what is at stake is also faith in Yhwh and belonging to the community" (Schipper, *Proverbs 1–15*, 215–16).

[88] Estes discusses the subtle and poetic elements of the father's instruction, "[This is a] tale of two ethical systems ... which are pictured by the Strange Woman and Woman Wisdom" (Daniel J. Estes, "What Makes the Strange Woman of Proverbs 1–9 Strange? Ethical and Unethical in the Old Testament: God and Humans in Dialogue," in *Ethical and Unethical in the Old Testament: God and Humans in Dialogue* (New York: T&T Clark, 2010), 165).

[89] As Fox notes, "In Prov 1–9, there are two archetypal ways, the way of life and the way of death. They are both timeless realities" (Fox, *Proverbs 1–9*, 180).

[90] Schipper points out the echoes to Deuteronomy in this lesson, "The connections to Deuteronomy are found especially in 4:10–13, where the path of wisdom is described in terms

warns of the "path of the wicked" (ארח רשעים) and the "path of the evil" (דרך רעים). For Lesson 9, the father mentions two paths as well. He warns, in Prov 5:5–6, that the feet of the "foreigner" (זרה) descend to "death" and "Sheol" and that she does not consider the "path of life" (ארח חיים).[91] Conversely, the father says of Wisdom (with uprightness and discipline) that "she is your life" (Prov 4:13).[92] Lesson 9 only provides the negative perspective of the two paths and life. Lesson 7 provides both possibilities but emphasizes the way to attain life. A primary metaphor of lesson seven is the contrast between light and dark. In fact, it seems both lessons seven and nine use contrasting metaphors to emphasize the point of their lesson. In Prov 4:18–19, the father describes that the "path of the righteous" (ארח צדיקים) is like the "light of dawn" (אור נגה) and "shines bright" (אור).[93] But, the "path of the wicked" (דרך רשעים) is compared to "deep darkness" (אפלה). Lesson 9 uses the imagery of sweet and bitter. In Prov 5:3–4, the "foreigner" is deceptive with lips as "honey" (נפת) and words as "oil" (שמן). Yet, it is a ruse since in the end, they are "bitter" (מרה) and "sharp" (חדה). While the lessons are different in their metaphors, they both utilize a unique and important contrast.[94]

There are two more interesting parallels between these lessons. Both lessons use the term "step" (צעד) which only occurs in these lessons of Proverbs 1–9. They are used in opposing perspectives, though. Lesson 7 assures the son that his "steps" will not be hindered and that he will not "stumble" (כשל), an important theme in this lesson (Prov 4:12). However, Lesson 9 assures the son that the "steps" of the foreigner descend to Sheol and death without hindrance or consideration (Prov 5:5). Thus, they affirm the certainty of the "steps" in both situations. Following the "foreigner" will surely lead to Sheol while following the "way of wisdom" will surely prevent stumbling and lead to life. Additionally, there is a congruent parallel between Prov 4:19 and 5:6.[95] Lesson 7 mentions that the wicked "do not know" (לא ידעו) why they "stumble" (כשל). Likewise, Lesson 9 affirms that the foreigner "does not know" (לא תדע) that her

---

similar to portrayals of Israel's relationship to Yhwh in Deuteronomy. By combining 'teaching' (ירה) with the metaphor of the path, Prov 4:11 bears a similarity to Deuteronomy 8, where Israel is instructed not to forsake the path of Yahweh (Deut 8:7–20). The statement in 4:13 that wisdom 'is your life' (כי־היא חייך) resembles Deut 30:20 (Yhwh 'is your life,' כי הוא חייך), instructing the audience to love (אהב) Yhwh, to listen (שמע) to his voice, and to hold fast (דבק) to him" (Schipper, *Proverbs 1–15*, 177).

[91] Lesson 12 (Prov 6:23) also mentions the "path of life" (דרך חיים) in regards to the metaphor of "light" (אור). In this case, it is in reference to the father's *mitsvah* and *torah* (6:20).

[92] Murphy notes the parallel emphasis on life through the *torah* path, "The emphasis on a long life (cf. v 13, and also 3:2); this is an emphasis of Deuteronomistic theology as well; cf. Deut 30:16, 19" (Murphy, *Proverbs*, 27–28).

[93] Fox argues Prov 4:18–19 are not ancillary, as McKane has postulated, but a typical and necessary conclusion to the lesson. Whybray has argued the verses should be inverted. However, Schäfer and Schipper maintain the MT should be preferred as it is. See Fox, *Proverbs 1–9*, 182; McKane, *Proverbs*, 309; Whybray, *Composition of the Book of Proverbs*, 22; Schäfer, *Die Poesie der Weisen*, 115; Schipper, *Proverbs 1–15*, 175.

[94] Discussing parallelism more generally, Heim argues that it is "structured by variation and difference just as much as it is structured by 'equality'" (Heim, *Poetic Imagination in Proverbs*, 29–35, 67).

[95] Schipper, *Proverbs 1–15*, 203.

path is "unstable" (נוע). In this case, they both negatively describe the reason for stumbling, which is a lack of knowledge. Regarding the titles "The path of Wisdom is life" and "The path of Folly is death," both lessons emphasize the importance of the two paths, which are antithetical.[96] One leads to stumbling, bitterness, and death. The other leads to life and light.

Chiastic Analysis of Lesson 8

The eighth lesson (Prov 4:20–27) serves as the emphatic middle of the chiastic structure. This means there are seven lessons before and seven lessons after, making fifteen total. The number "seven" appears three times in Prov 1–9 and three times in Prov 10–31. The first occurs with the "seven abominations" to Yhwh (Prov 6:16). The second occurs as the punishment for stealing, "sevenfold he will give" (Prov 6:31).[97] The last occurrence in chapters 1–9 is perhaps more significant and symbolic. In Prov 9:1, the text poetically declares, "Wisdom built her house; she has hewn her seven pillars" (cf. Num 23:1, 14, 29).[98] While some scholarly discussion has been raised to this reference,[99] it may in fact be an oblique hint to the chiastic structure of Prov 1–9.[100]

In the latter portion of Proverbs, 24:16 mentions, "The righteous fall seven times and rise." In Prov 26:16, it says, "The lazy is wiser in his eyes than seven who return discernment." Finally, in Prov 26:25, in reference to those

---

[96] As Waltke opines, "The road metaphor does not depict life from the cradle to the grave, but the road to eternal life versus the road to eternal death" (Waltke, *Proverbs (1–15)*, 289).

[97] The term "sevenfold" (שִׁבְעָתַיִם) is rare, first occurring with Cain and Lamech and their punishment (Gen 4:15, 24). Regarding the punishment for stealing, in Exodus the law is "five oxen for one and four sheep for one" (Exod 21:37 [22:1, 3, 6]). In Leviticus, the law requires full return for what is stolen plus an additional "fifth" to the victim of the theft (Lev 5:15–16). There is not a clear legal precedence for the "sevenfold" of Prov 6:31. However, it may be a more poetic injunction or simply echo the symbolic implications for "seven" elsewhere in the HB (Joran Friberg, "Numbers and Counting," in *AYBD*, ed. David Noel Freedman (New York: Doubleday, 1992), 4:1145).

[98] For discussion of the symbolic use of "seven," see George B. Gray, *A Critical and Exegetical Commentary on Numbers*, ICC (New York: C. Scribner's Sons, 1903), 342; Jacob Milgrom, *Numbers*, JPSTC (Philadelphia: JPS, 1990), 194; Roy Gane, *Leviticus, Numbers*, NIVAC (Grand Rapids: Zondervan, 2004), 700.

[99] For further discussions and potential referents, see Whybray, *Wisdom in Proverbs*, 90–92; Fox, *Proverbs 1–9*, 297–98; Schipper, *Proverbs 1–15*, 326–27; Longman, *Proverbs*, 216.

[100] Stuart Weeks notes that the "seven pillars" in Prov 9:1 could allude to the seven sections of Proverbs as a whole. Although he does not connect this with Prov 1–9, the idea provides some grounding for the possibility. Though speculative, the phrase in Prov 9:1 perhaps serves as a dual allusion to both the chiastic structure of Prov 1–9 and the whole book. Similarly, Skehan argues for a fifteen-column structure for Prov 1–9, similar to the findings of this study, which implies the seven-column imagery. For discussion of the many theories for Wisdom's "seven columns," see Weeks, *Instruction and Imagery in Proverbs 1–9*, 40; Skehan, *Studies in Israelite Poetry and Wisdom*, 27–35; Murphy, *Proverbs*, 58–59; Fox, *Proverbs 1–9*, 297–98; Schipper, *Proverbs 1–15*, 326–27.

who hide hate, "You ought not trust him, for there are seven abominations in his heart." As seen in these occurrences throughout Proverbs, there is a generally symbolic use of the number seven. The phrase "seven abominations" occurs twice but not in any strict sense. The reference to paying "sevenfold" for theft, the righteous falling "seven times," and a lazy man wiser than "seven" are certainly not absolute but symbolic in nature. In fact, numbers are not very common in Proverbs. The numbers "three" and "four" only occur in poetic numerical addition passages (Prov 30:15, 18, 21, 24, 29). The number "two" is used several times mostly to refer to a set of items in an aphorism (Prov 17:15, 20:10, 12, 24:22, 27:3, 29:13, 30:7, 15). The number "six" only occurs once (Prov 6:16). The number "one" only occurs once (Prov 1:14). With this in mind, it is clear that numbers do not play a prominent role in Proverbs but as occasional poetic and symbolic elements.

Regarding Lesson 8, this passage plays a pivotal or central role in the structure of Prov 1–9. The most significant aspect of Prov 4:20–27 is its parallel to Deuteronomy and the subsequent motif catalyzed by Deut 5:32–33. There are several observable links between the passages. Of particular importance is the context of Deut 5:32–33,[101] the re-giving of the Sinai code (Exod 20:1–21; Deut 5:6–27). This means the expectations of Deut 5:32–33 are in reference to the basic tenets of the *torah* and God's covenant commands. If Prov 4:20–27 is pointing the "son" to Deut 5, then the emphasis is on the essential place of God's covenant and subsequent instruction from the Torah. In other words, the path of the wise is the path of Torah. The Shema in Deut 6 immediately follows this passage. The Shema, of course, exhorts Israel to pass on the Torah way to their children, a central transgenerational and imitative pedagogical pattern.

Prov 4:20–27	Deut 5:32–33

20b <u>Turn</u> (נטה) your ear to my words
21b <u>Guard them</u> in the midst of your heart
22a For <u>they are life</u> (חיים)
  to those finding them.
24a <u>Turn</u> (סור) from you wrongness of mouth
26 <u>Consider the path of your feet</u>
  and <u>all your ways</u> will be established.
27 <u>Do not turn</u> (נטה) <u>right or left</u>.
  <u>Turn</u> (סור) <u>your feet</u> from evil.
	32 <u>You shall guard to do</u> just as Yhwh your God commanded you. <u>You shall not turn</u> (סור) <u>right or left</u>.
	33 <u>In all the way</u> which Yhwh your God commanded you, <u>you shall walk</u>; in order that, <u>you may live</u> (חיה) and it be well for you and you will have lengthened days in the land which you possess.

---

[101] Interestingly, Murphy sees a connection with Prov 4:20–27 and Deut 5:29 which reads, "May this heart be for them to fear me and to guard all my commands all days in order that it be well for them and their sons forever" (Murphy, *Proverbs*, 28). It is curious he does not make the connection with Deut 5:32. Regardless, there are certainly many connections between Deut 5 and Prov 4:20–27.

20 בְּנִי לִדְבָרַי הַקְשִׁיבָה לַאֲמָרַי הַט־אָזְנֶךָ׃	32 וּשְׁמַרְתֶּם לַעֲשׂוֹת כַּאֲשֶׁר צִוָּה יְהוָה
21 אַל־יַלִּיזוּ מֵעֵינֶיךָ שָׁמְרֵם בְּתוֹךְ לְבָבֶךָ׃	אֱלֹהֵיכֶם אֶתְכֶם לֹא תָסֻרוּ יָמִין וּשְׂמֹאל׃
22 כִּי־חַיִּים הֵם לְמֹצְאֵיהֶם וּלְכָל־בְּשָׂרוֹ מַרְפֵּא׃	33 בְּכָל־הַדֶּרֶךְ אֲשֶׁר צִוָּה יְהוָה אֱלֹהֵיכֶם
23 מִכָּל־מִשְׁמָר נְצֹר לִבֶּךָ כִּי־מִמֶּנּוּ תּוֹצְאוֹת חַיִּים׃	אֶתְכֶם תֵּלֵכוּ לְמַעַן תִּחְיוּן וְטוֹב לָכֶם
24 הָסֵר מִמְּךָ עִקְּשׁוּת פֶּה וּלְזוּת שְׂפָתַיִם הַרְחֵק מִמֶּךָּ׃	וְהַאֲרַכְתֶּם יָמִים בָּאָרֶץ אֲשֶׁר תִּירָשׁוּן׃
25 עֵינֶיךָ לְנֹכַח יַבִּיטוּ וְעַפְעַפֶּיךָ יַיְשִׁרוּ נֶגְדֶּךָ׃	
26 פַּלֵּס מַעְגַּל רַגְלֶךָ וְכָל־דְּרָכֶיךָ יִכֹּנוּ׃	
27 אַל־תֵּט־יָמִין וּשְׂמֹאול הָסֵר רַגְלְךָ מֵרָע׃	

The idea of proper adherence to the path of God's instruction in the Torah is strengthened by the parallel phrases between Prov 4:27 and Deut 5:32. The phrase "right and left" occurs twenty-six times together in some variation.[102] However, seven of those form a clear motif, which all harken back to Deut 5:32. In these occurrences, the sense is metaphorical and covenantal. The phrase either exhorts all of Israel (Deut 5:32, 28:14, Josh 23:6) or the leader of Israel (Deut 17:20; Josh 1:7; 2 Kgs 22:2 [2 Chron 34:2]). Likewise, all occurrences use the term "turn" (סור) except Prov 4:27, which uses "turn" (נטה) in that particular phrase. In Prov 4:20–27, both lexemes appear twice (4:20, 24, 27). For poetic flare, perhaps, Prov 4:27 uses both terms but uses "turn" (נטה) with the phrase "do not turn right or left," placing "turn" (סור) in the parallel line, "turn your feet from evil." Since the lesson begins with the exhortation "turn (נטה) your ear to my words," the author may have intentionally linked this covenantal motif, "do not turn (נטה) to the right or left," with his own instruction as a whole.

Deut 5:32–33	You shall guard to do just as Yhwh your God commanded you. You shall not turn (סור) right or left. In all the way which Yhwh your God commanded you, you shall walk; in order that, you may live and it be well for you.
Deut 17:19–20	And it [a copy of this torah] will be with him and he read it all the days of his life; in order that, he will learn to fear Yhwh his God, to guard all the words of this Torah and to do these statutes, to not exalt his heart more than his brothers and to not turn (סור) from the commandment, right or left; in order that he extend days over his kingdom, he and his sons, in the midst of Israel.

---

102 Although the words for "right" and "left" occur much more, only about twenty-six times do they occur together as a phrase (Gen 24:49; Exod 14:22, 29; Num 20:17, 22:26; Deut 2:27, 5:32, 17:11, 17:20, 28:14; Josh 1:7, 23:6; 1 Sam 6:12; 2 Sam 2:19, 21, 16:6; 1 Kgs 22:19; 2 Kgs 22:2; Isa 54:3; Jon 4:11; Zech 4:11, 12:6; Prov 3:16; Eccl 10:2; Dan 12:7; 2 Chron 34:2). Most of these passages use the terms in their more practical sense for direction or hands.

Deut 28:13b-14	"… if you listen to the commands of Yhwh your God which I command you today, to guard and to do. And you shall not turn (סור) from all the words which I command you today, right or left, to walk after other gods, to serve them.
Josh 1:7	Only, be strengthened and be very strong, to guard to do as all the Torah which Moses my servant commanded you. Do not turn (סור) from it, right or left, in order that you may prosper in all which you walk.
Josh 23:6–8	You all will be very strong to guard and to do all writing in the scroll of the Torah of Moses, to not turn (סור) from it, right or left, to not enter with these nations these remaining with you and in the name of their gods you shall not cause remembrance and you shall not make an oath and you shall not serve them and you shall not bow to them. Rather, you shall cling to Yhwh your God just as you have done until this day.
2 Kings 22:2	And [Josiah] did upright in the eyes of Yhwh and he walked in all the way of David his father and he did not turn (סור) right or left.
2 Chron 34:2	And [Josiah] did upright in the eyes of Yhwh and he walked in all the ways of David his father and he did not turn (סור) right or left.

The broader yet important motif of "walking" from Deut 5 will be discussed more in Lesson 8, particularly in regard to sons reflecting their fathers. In a key passage, Moses exhorts Israel in Deut 10:12–13, "What does Yhwh your God ask from you except to fear Yhwh your God, to walk in all his ways, to love him, and to serve Yhwh your God with all your heart and with all of your soul, to guard the commands of Yhwh and his statutes." In brief, the metaphor of walking the proper path is also central to Proverbs and especially chapters 1–9.[103] With the context of passages such as Deut 5 and 10, the metaphor of "path" illuminates the metaphorical and covenantal relationship Israel was to maintain with Yhwh, particularly central to instruction in wisdom. In relation to the Deuteronomic motif for covenantal obedience and relationship, "do not

---

[103] Fox provides a lengthy discussion on the concept of metaphor in Prov 1–9, as described by Lakoff and Johnson. He states, "BEHAVIOR IS A PATH is the ground metaphor of Prov 1–9, or, as N. Habel (1972) designates it, the 'nuclear symbol' that unifies its teachings. A ground metaphor is an image that organizes other perceptions and images and conveys a way of perceiving the world. … Another way of thinking of our movement through life is by the metaphor of TWO PATHS. While in one sense we can go on a limitless number of 'paths,' from another perspective there are really only two paths, or types of path, of fatal importance. The path that wisdom teaches, the one the righteous take, is the WAY OF LIFE. … Proverbs splits the world along a moral fault line that runs between two classes, the wicked/foolish and the righteous/wise" (Fox, *Proverbs 1–9*, 129–31; George Lakoff and Mark Johnson, *Metaphors We Live By* (Chicago: University of Chicago Press, 1980); Norman C. Habel, "Symbolism of Wisdom in Proverbs 1–9," *Int* 26.2 (1972): 131–57).

turn right or left," the metaphor gives clarity to the conceptual, cultural, and theological context behind Prov 1–9, particularly Prov 4:20–27. Therefore, in accordance with typical chiastic purposes, Lesson 8 provides the poetic, rhetorical center of the father's instruction for the proverbial son.

Conclusion

A central feature of biblical wisdom is not merely attention to informational transmission but the persuasive power of imagery and conceptualization. While the proverbial father could have provided the same material in a less poetically structured and chiastic form, the additional layer of complexity and artistry propels the son to continual reflection and growth in his pursuit of understanding. The very terms that orient the whole book, "proverb" (משל) and "riddle" (חידה), are themselves signals to the underlying nature of the instruction (Prov 1:6).[104] In other words, the implication is that one is not wise by merely possessing information but in proper discernment.[105] Furthermore, at the heart of this proper discernment are the necessary relational and expressive aspects. These aspects are couched in covenantal fidelity to the ways of the wise who have preceded and to Yhwh who both gives and expresses the fullest forms of ideal qualities. While Lesson 8 is not the only essential principle of instruction, it does serve as a centralizing image and motif for what it means to "follow after" or reflect one's "father." Yet, a wise, mundane fatherly example is itself only a lesser version of the greater model found in God and his ways. So, as the chiasm of this study proposes, the pedagogical implications for the book of Proverbs are not simply for practical knowledge and skill but to instill a deeply theological, Torah way of life. This special way of life and its inextricable relation to *imitatio Dei* will be thoroughly explicated in the ensuing analysis of Lessons 1–15.

---

[104] As Sandoval rightly observes, "They function to highlight the figurative and literary qualities of the book's discourse. They alert the reader to the interpretive efforts one will need to undertake as one continues reading the book" (Timothy J. Sandoval, "Revisiting the Prologue of Proverbs," *JBL* 126.3 (2007): 469).

[105] Anne W. Stewart, *Poetic Ethics in Proverbs: Wisdom Literature and the Shaping of the Moral Self* (New York: Cambridge University Press, 2016), 15, 42, 53.

PART TWO

INTRODUCTION

Now that we have understand the history of *imitatio Dei* and the structure of Prov 1–9, we will turn our attention to analyzing the proverbial father's fifteen lessons in sequence. Fundamental to this thematic and exegetical examination are questions such as, "What is the essence of wisdom and the father's teaching?" and "What role does imitation play in developing wisdom?" While many have attempted to define "wisdom," Graeme Goldsworthy's concise yet broadly encompassing explanation is an appropriate starting point for this study, "[Wisdom] is a way of thinking and a way of doing. ... On one hand, it is to know man and the world, and on the other, it is both the way to know God and the reward for knowing him."[1] According to Goldsworthy, wisdom is both internal (mental) and external (physical). It is moreover inherently relational and interconnected with God. By growing in wisdom, a person grows in the knowledge of God. As one grows in the knowledge of God, one likewise grows in wisdom. This dynamic movement implies a subtle process whereby a person moves along a trajectory of likeness. First, the likeness is to parents and sages, and then to Wisdom, who is closely identified with Yhwh God. As it will be illuminated through the analysis of the following fifteen lessons, the aim or 'Lehrprogramm'[2] of Prov 1–9 is not simply that the wisdom student will dwell in the land,[3] achieve

---

[1] Graeme Goldsworthy, *The Goldsworthy Trilogy: Gospel & Kingdom, Wisdom & Revelation* (Milton Keynes: Paternoster, 2013), 342.

[2] Arndt Meinhold, *Die Sprüche*, ZBK (Zürich: Theologischer Verlag, 1991), 43–47.

[3] Schipper argues that the land is the central goal and motivation for the proverbial instruction (Bernd U. Schipper, *Proverbs 1–15: A Commentary on the Book of Proverbs 1:1–15:33*, Hermeneia (Minneapolis: Fortress, 2019), 120–21).

mundane success,[4] attain immortality,[5] or develop wise character.[6] Yhwh, as the God of Israel and of all creation,[7] is the ultimate goal and example. He is likewise the means for developing in wisdom and to receive the various blessings associated, though only incidental as one walks on the divine path. Such an aim is achieved through imitating God's ways, that is, by following in the patterns presented by *torah,* Wisdom, and the numerous wise exemplars on the path of wisdom.

As our study will show, the wisdom program in Lessons 1–15 utilizes a number of rhetorical tools to teach and instill within the son a desire and ability both to imitate and to know God. As outlined in the Introduction chapter, the proverbial father weaves together a variety of images, metaphors, allusions, and motifs in order to achieve this aim. As a key metaphor, the proverbial father instructs the son to emulate Yhwh as the ultimate Father (parent and teacher). The father also presents the figure of Wisdom as a worthy model and source of instruction. She serves as a multifaceted and rhetorical thread throughout the wisdom program. Among her various roles, she is a divine tool to be used, a path to walk, a wise figure to emulate, and a representative of Yhwh himself. Likewise, the father uses a number of positive and negative examples to lead the son along the wisdom trajectory, which ultimately derives from and concludes in God. As it will be seen in many of the lessons, the proverbial father even alludes to a number of intertextual concepts and historical figures in order to further emphasize the role of imitation and the nature of God (e.g., Abraham, Moses, David). Altogether, these threads are an integral aspect of the father's wisdom training in the knowledge of God and *imitatio Dei.*

---

[4] Wilson builds a case for connections between Proverbs, Qoheleth, and Deuteronomy. In conclusion, he affirms mere success cannot be the point of Proverbs, "The canonical editor insists that the 'words of the wise[men]' cannot be rightly understood apart from the 'commandments of God/YHWH.' While this single exhortation by itself might be overlooked, it seems to bring out the implicit connections made between Proverbs 1–9 and Deuteronomy, which cannot so easily be dismissed. Where are these 'commandments' hammered out but in the Torah and Prophets? On the basis of this 'canonical' statement, Proverbs-Qoheleth can no longer be read simply as practical advice on how to succeed in life, wisdom that could easily pass across national and religious boundaries. They are now inextricably bound up with the Torah and Israel's God, YHWH – his commandments – and cannot be read apart from them" (Gerald H. Wilson, "'The Words of the Wise': The Intent and Significance of Qoheleth 12:9–14," *JBL* 103 (1984): 192.

[5] Waltke both argues for the presence of immortality and for the mundane purpose of wisdom in Proverbs, "The schools where wisdom was taught in Egypt were called 'Schools of Life.' Since Proverbs shows a heavy dependence on Egyptian instructions, it would be surprising if 'life' meant less with the living God than the Egyptian hope of life with a 'no-god' (Deut. 32:21). … Nevertheless, it must be admitted that Proverbs and the Egyptian instructions focus on health, prosperity, and social honor in this life" (Bruce K. Waltke, *The Book of Proverbs: Chapters 1–15,* NICOT (Grand Rapids: Eerdmans, 2004), 106–7).

[6] Arthur J. Keefer, *Proverbs 1–9 as an Introduction to the Book of Proverbs* (London: T&T Clark, 2020), 127.

[7] Commenting on the reference to "my son," Murphy notes, "This book is for all Israel, and the observations deal with universal human experience" (Roland E. Murphy, *Proverbs,* WBC 22 (Dallas: Thomas Nelson, 1998), 12).

LESSON 1

Analysis of Proverbs 1:8–33
"Seek wisdom, find life"

As a wisdom program designed to instruct youth or the naïve, the proverbial father first establishes the foolishness of those who stray from wise instruction and Wisdom's call. Though a modern person might prefer a happier start and finish, the father instead begins and ends the program with dire warnings (Prov 1:10–33, 9:13–18). While broadly negative in tone, the initial warning in Lesson 1 sets an essential foundation for the following lessons. Here, the path of sinners, a group representative of their foolish ways, is first encountered. The wise son must not become like them but must walk as a son reflecting his wise father. Next, the mysterious figure of Wisdom is introduced in this lesson, who instructs the son as a prophet. She is also associated with Yhwh through her unique, overlapping language and behavior, which is important for the rest of the wisdom program. As an anthropomorphic embodiment of God, then, the son must listen to and emulate her as he would Yhwh. This is a vital step in the son's growth along the wisdom trajectory. Over the course of the program, there is a movement from the father and the righteous to Wisdom and Yhwh as the primary examples for the son to follow, that is, from the mundane to the divine. This movement begins first with the fatherly call of Lesson 1 (Prov 1:8–9). Thus, this first lesson serves the father's purpose in establishing the core elements of imitation along with several supporting images and metaphors. While the wisdom program provides a full picture of those to imitate and those to avoid, this first lesson primarily gives negative examples. In their reflection of Yhwh, however, both Wisdom and the parents are proffered as positive examples in contrast to the fools. Lesson 2, though, will provide a more balanced and positive tone against the negative one here.

Structure of Lesson 1

Traditionally, two prominent sections have been identified in Prov 1 following the preface (Prov 1:1–7). These sections are thematically apportioned in Prov 1:8–19 and 1:20–33. The first unit is typically understood as an instruction while the second unit is often deemed a separate Wisdom Poem. While the thematic sentiment is generally true, it is unfortunate the two have not often been understood together as the father's first lesson to the son.[1] In fact, it is important to note that there is logical coherence to the words spoken: first the call of the father and mother, then by the sinners, then by Wisdom. It is likely a subtle, conceptual metaphor for the progression of influences on a person. Parents are the first influence in a person's life, as children.[2] This is followed by the naïve influence of peers and even heroes. If a person is diligent and wise, they will go on to greater influences such as the sages and Wisdom itself. As will be further explored, this inevitably leads along a trajectory to Yhwh who is the paragon of wisdom and the ultimate model for imitation.

The structure of Lesson 1 can be broken into six sections. The first is a positive exhortation to the son which serves as both an introduction and a promise of blessing (Prov 1:8–9).[3] In the second, the dramatized call of sinners is presented, providing the core teaching of the lesson (Prov 1:10–14). This is then followed by the father's warning of the sinners' fate (Prov 1:15–19).[4] Wisdom enters the scene to provide a call as well (Prov 1:20–25). Yet, like the

---

[1] The use of father-son imagery is attested in ANE wisdom literature such as in Mesopotamia and Egypt. While a familial setting is the metaphorical picture, the terms need not be understood in an overly strict manner, whether for a family or schoolhouse. Loader notes, "Father often designates the authoritative position of men such as priests, prophets, and counsellors over 'sons' other than their own (cf. Judg 17:10, 18:19; 2 Kgs 2:3ff., 4:1, 38, 5:22, 6:1, 21, 9:1, 13:14). Ahiqar is not only the father of his 'conventional' son Nadin, but also explicitly called 'father of all Assyria.'" However, Lang goes too far in claiming an absolute dichotomy between the family and school setting, "The mention of the parents must not lead to the mistaken conclusion that the instructional poem relates to family education. Instruction takes place not in the family but in the school." Likewise, Whybray goes too far in making an absolute claim the "domestic situation" is the only intended setting and audience, due to his view that there is not a "compelling reason to doubt that they are intended to represent the teaching of a real father given to his son." See James Alfred Loader, *Proverbs 1–9*, HCOT (Leuven: Peeters, 2014), 69–70; Bernhard Lang, "Schule und Unterricht im alten Israel," in *La Sagesse de l'Ancien Testament*, ed. Maurice Gilbert, 2nd ed., BETL 51 (Leuven: Leuven University Press, 1990), 194; R. N. Whybray, *The Intellectual Tradition in the Old Testament*, BZAW 135 (New York: De Gruyter, 1974), 42; R. N. Whybray, *The Composition of the Book of Proverbs*, JSOT 168 (Sheffield: JSOT, 1994), 56.

[2] Cupitt commenting on the picture of father-to-son as God-to-man, says, "The formation of our personalities vis-a-vis our parents is a complex and beautiful interweaving of patterns of imitation and response" (Don Cupitt, "God and Morality: Duty and Discernment, 6," *Theology* 76.637 (1973): 357; Dave L. Bland, *Proverbs and the Formation of Character* (Eugene: Cascade Books, 2015), 57).

[3] Rolf Schäfer, *Die Poesie der Weisen: Dichotomie als Grundstruktur der Lehr und Weisheitsgedichte in Proverbien 1–9*, WMANT 77 (Neukirchen-Vluyn: Neukirchener Verlag, 1999), 25.

[4] See Paul B. Overland, "Literary Structure in Proverbs 1–9" (Brandeis University, PhD diss., 1988), 167–87.

father's message, Wisdom uses the fate of fools as a rhetorical device in the lesson (Prov 1:26–32), not only to persuade those who would listen but to establish the role of Wisdom. Finally, the lesson concludes with a brief promise of blessing from Wisdom (Prov 1:33). Though almost entirely negative, the lesson ends with a positive and theologically rich statement.

I.   Introduction: the father's call (1:8–9)
II.   Warning: the sinners' call (1:10–14)
III.   Warning: the fate of sinners (1:15–19)
IV.   Warning: Wisdom's call (1:20–25)
V.   Warning: the fate of fools (1:26–32)
VI.   Conclusion: Wisdom's blessing (1:33)

Paul Overland proposed a chiastic structure to Prov 1:8–19.[5] According to his analysis, he rightly identifies a number of corresponding words and ideas that structure the two contrasting calls in the first half of this lesson. In his view, the emphasis is Prov 1:15–18.[6] While his analysis illuminates a number of legitimate correspondences, according to his chiastic layout there is not a clear center. Instead, the palistrophe centers on the dual contentions or persuasions (Prov 1:14, 15). In Prov 1:14, the sinners call for the son to join them. At Prov 1:15, the father warns the son not to join them. This is a restatement of the father's warning in Prov 1:10. As for the emphasis of Lesson 1, however, the call from the sinners serves as the primary foil against which the father and Wisdom contend (Prov 1:15–19, 20–33). Such a connection is often lost due to a scholarly disconnect between the two sections of Lesson 1. Thematically, Schipper emphasizes that Prov 1:10 and 15 introduce the "two paths" motif developed throughout Prov 1–9.[7] Several scholars have also proposed similar chiasms for Prov 1:20–33.[8] For all, there is an emphatic focus around Prov 1:27, which declares judgment or disaster. If the Wisdom Poem is meant to complement the father's teaching of Prov 1:8–19, then Lesson 1 provides not only the father's warning to the son but Wisdom's as well. The negative tone of Wisdom matches the father's tone in Prov 1:15–19.[9] However, Wisdom provides a positive bent (Prov 1:23, 33) similar to the initial call by the father

---

[5] Overland, "Literary Structure in Proverbs 1–9," 168, 378.

[6] Schipper calls these verses the apodosis of the protasis (Prov 1:10–14) due to the uses of אם "if" (Schipper, *Proverbs 1–15*, 74.

[7] Schipper, *Proverbs 1–15*, 74–75.

[8] Bálint Károly Zabán, *The Pillar Function of the Speeches of Wisdom: Proverbs 1:20–33, 8:1–36 and 9:1–6 in the Structural Framework of Proverbs 1–9*, BZAW 429 (Berlin: Walter de Gruyter, 2012), 63; Overland, "Literary Structure in Proverbs 1–9," 191, 379; Phyllis Trible, "Wisdom Builds a Poem: The Architecture of Proverbs 1:20–33," *JBL* 94.4 (1975): 511. All three place the center on 1:26–27, emphasizing judgement.

[9] Murphy notes that there is a prophetic tone familiar to the prophets such as Jer 7 and 20. In his view, Wisdom takes the teaching a step further than the father in Prov 1:15–19, providing a condemnatory pronouncement (Murphy, *Proverbs*, 8).

(1:8–9). This creates literary symmetry and cohesion within Lesson 1, Wisdom and the father echoing one another (Prov 1:8–33).[10]

The Father's Call: Following Father & Mother (1:8–9)

The opening stanza helps set the tone and trajectory for the whole of Proverbs by mentioning "father" (אב) and "mother" (אם) in the context of *musar* and *torah* (Prov 1:8). In Prov 10:1, a similar father-mother paradigm begins the latter portion of Proverbs, serving as an appeal for an emotional-relational motivation, perhaps invoking Deut 5:16. Likewise, father and mother surface in Prov 4:3 and 6:20. The combination of these familial terms occurs twelve times in the whole of Proverbs.[11] While this has led some scholars to focus on the familial setting of education in ancient Israel, Schipper contends the implication is to signal Proverbs' correspondence with Deuteronomy.[12] In Deut 6:6–9 and 11:18–21, the Torah makes clear that every covenantal member of Israel must pass on the teachings of Yhwh from generation to generation, necessarily beginning in childhood.[13] It is perhaps not a coincidence that in Prov 1:8 the first word of the fifteen-lesson program is the

---

[10] Moss argues that the fatherly or parental message throughout these chapters is further highlighted by Wisdom's poems. In essence, they present a unified message, blurring the lines between Wisdom and the father (Alan Moss, "Wisdom as Parental Teaching in Proverbs 1–9," *HeyJ* 38.4 (1997): 432; Anne W. Stewart, *Poetic Ethics in Proverbs: Wisdom Literature and the Shaping of the Moral Self* (New York: Cambridge University Press, 2016), 59).

[11] Prov 1:8, 4:3, 6:20, 10:1, 15:20, 19:26, 20:20, 23:22, 25, 28:24, 30:11, 17.

[12] Walton and Walton, among others, have argued that the proper conceptual setting for *torah* is wisdom, "The Torah was intended to give the king wisdom for doing his job. The Torah (like the legal lists in the ANE) embodies wisdom; it does not establish legislation" (38). For discussion on the relationship between wisdom-*torah* and Deut-Prov, see C. F. Keil and Franz Delitzsch, *Commentary on the Old Testament*, rev. ed. (Peabody: Hendrickson, 1996), VI: 25, 110; Moshe Weinfeld, *Deuteronomy and the Deuteronomic School* (Winona Lake: Eisenbrauns, 1972), 244–319; Roland E. Murphy, *The Tree of Life: An Exploration of Biblical Wisdom Literature*, 2nd ed. (Grand Rapids: Eerdmans, 1996), 104–6; Paul Overland, "Did the Sage Draw from the Shema?: A Study of Proverbs 3:1–12," *CBQ* 62.3 (2000): 424–40; Ryan O'Dowd, *The Wisdom of Torah: Epistemology in Deuteronomy and the Wisdom Literature*, FRLANT 225 (Göttingen: Vandenhoeck & Ruprecht, 2009), 111; Tremper Longman III, *The Fear of the Lord Is Wisdom: A Theological Introduction to Wisdom in Israel* (Grand Rapids: Baker Academic, 2017), 163–75; John H. Walton and J. Harvey Walton, *The Lost World of the Torah: Law as Covenant and Wisdom in Ancient Context* (Downers Grove: IVP, 2019), 37–45; Schipper, *Proverbs 1–15*, 1–4, 75; Bernd U. Schipper, "'Teach Them Diligently to Your Son!' The Book of Proverbs and Deuteronomy," in *Reading Proverbs Intertextually*, ed. Katharine J. Dell and Will Kynes (London: T&T Clark, 2019), 21–34.

[13] O'Dowd says, "This relational knowledge cascades across past, present and future generations as parents 'teach' children through continuous cycles of life in the land. Loving Yahweh means 'knowing' and embracing the relationship initiated by God in his loving redemptive work (cf. 7:6–9) by keeping the torah. Obeying the torah means loving Yahweh and thereby actualizing those experiences perpetually in Israel" (Ryan P. O'Dowd, "Memory on the Boundary: Epistemology in Deuteronomy," in *The Bible and Epistemology: Biblical Sounding on the Knowledge of God*, ed. Mary Healy and Robin A. Parry (Colorado Springs: Paternoster, 2007), 10).

Heb. imperative *Shema* (שְׁמַע), known most famously from the beginning of Deut 6:4 (cf. Deut 4:1, 5:1).[14]

With this in mind, the proverbial teaching develops the Deuteronomic view of *torah* through the means of *musar* as the essential foundation for Israelite wisdom.[15] In other words, the proverbial father is not conveying mere personal experience but principles derived and congruent with God's covenantal instruction for all of Israel.[16] The term *musar* (discipline or instruction) only occurs once in Deuteronomy (11:2), "*musar* of Yhwh your God" (מוּסַר יְהוָה אֱלֹהֵיכֶם).[17] In Proverbs, the term occurs many times, functioning as a central tenet on the path of wisdom.[18] Of importance, as will be discussed further in Lesson 4, the phrase "*musar* of Yhwh" occurs in Prov 3:12, which overlays the proverbial father with the fatherhood of God.[19] The intent of Prov 1:7–8 is further highlighted by a similar phrase later in Proverbs, perhaps serving as the editorial catalyst for Prov 1:2–7, "Fear of Yhwh is *musar* and wisdom, and before honor is humility" (15:33).[20]

---

[14] Cf. Keil and Delitzsch, *Commentary on the Old Testament*, VI: 25; Loader, *Proverbs 1–9*, 68.

[15] Stewart remarks, "Behind the concept of mûsār is a sophisticated moral psychology that presumes the complexity of the human person. Accordingly, mûsār is a task not only of verbal or physical correction, but of training the student's intellect, emotion, and perception such that his faculties are equipped for navigating the world. Thus, the effect of mûsār is not described simply as intellectual assent to certain principles, but rather it is a process of acquiring right perception, the proper perspective to see and experience the world" (Stewart, *Poetic Ethics in Proverbs*, 78).

[16] Crenshaw has been a proponent of the empirical, experiential model for wisdom literature, along with others who have followed. As he states, "Wisdom is 'the ability to cope,' 'the art of steering;' it is 'practical knowledge of the laws of life and of the world, based on experience;' wisdom constitutes 'parents' legacy to their children;' it is 'the quest for self-understanding and for mastery of the world.'" Frydrych proposes that sapiential knowledge involves two components, "Collection of data followed by its assessment ... based on observation ... [and] reoccurring experience." While a level of experiential pragmatism exists within biblical wisdom, it is limited and can only be understood properly through the broader lens of life within God's supervening covenant relationship with Israel and his special revelation. As Goldsworthy rightly notes, even Solomon who was the exemplar of wisdom received it as a gift (1 Kgs 3:12). Divorcing wisdom from God is precisely the opposite purpose of Proverbs. See James L. Crenshaw, *Old Testament Wisdom: An Introduction*, Rev. and enl. (Louisville: Westminster John Knox, 1998), 9; Tomáš Frydrych, *Living under the Sun: Examination of Proverbs and Qoheleth*, VTSup 90 (Boston: Brill, 2002), 53–54; Goldsworthy, *The Goldsworthy Trilogy*, 339, 342, 399, 461.

[17] This holds true in the LXX with the equivalent term παιδεία "guidance, training, discipline" (BDAG).

[18] Frydrych rightly comments, "Wisdom in Proverbs is not so much about intellectual knowledge or abilities, but rather, it is a commitment to a way of life" (Frydrych, *Living under the Sun*, 26–27).

[19] Loader discusses the literary presence of two fathers in Prov 1–9. There is the father who addresses "my son" and the third-person father with "your father" (Loader, *Proverbs 1–9*, 68–69). While reference to "your father" may only be a poetic, rhetorical comment, the underlying fatherhood of God does permeate the proverbial lessons and may account for the dual-fatherhood expressed.

[20] Bruce K. Waltke, *The Book of Proverbs: Chapters 16–31*, NICOT (Grand Rapids: Eerdmans, 2004), 8.

Building on the generational imagery from Deuteronomy, it is important to consider the implications for parental pedagogy.[21] Modern scholarship has established that imitating the actions, words, and attitudes of parents – as well as any authority figure – is essential to the formation of a person.[22] While certain capacities are inherent, the development of many, such as language or social norms, are largely acquired through observing and attempting to emulate father and mother. Of course, such theoretical scholarship is rather intuitive and has been understood throughout human history.[23] Yet, it must be seen here as the foundational method for Israelite instruction in God's way. Both passages in Deut 6 and 11 declare that Yhwh, or Moses the mediator, taught the people of Israel. These recipients were adults at the time but were to teach the way of Yhwh to subsequent generations.[24] Important to note about these exhortations is the holistic nature of the command. In both, the emphasis is on loving and obeying Yhwh with their whole being and life (Deut 6:5, 11:13). Likewise, they were to teach God's ways holistically. Parents were to pass on the *torah* way while in their house, in their walking, in their resting, and in their rising (Deut 6:7, 11:19). In other words, Deuteronomy prescribes instruction to take place at all times, in all areas, and in all their ways.[25] Such a pedagogy can only be accomplished

---

[21] Ansberry discusses the importance of the familial framework, whether the actual setting or conceptual, "Israelite fathers not only passed their vocations on to their sons, but they were also responsible for their social, moral, and religious training (Gen 18:19; Exod 12:24; Deut 4:9–11; 6:20–25). The domestic sense of the father-son designation is also apparent in the sapiential lectures. The inclusion of the mother within the instructions is a significant feature of the discourse (Prov 1:8; 6:20). Though the maternal voice is not given expression in the lectures (cf. 31:1–9), the appellation seems to indicate a domestic setting, for it assumes a relational dimension that transcends the teacher-pupil relationship." See Christopher B. Ansberry, "Be Wise, My Son, and Make My Heart Glad: An Exploration of the Courtly Nature of the Book of Proverbs" (Wheaton College, PhD diss., 2009), 61–62; Bruce K Waltke, "The Book of Proverbs and Ancient Wisdom Literature," *BSac* 136.543 (1979): 232.

[22] Gunter Gebauer and Christoph Wulf, *Mimesis: Culture, Art, Society* (Berkeley: University of California Press, 1995), 326–27; Scott R. Garrels, ed., *Mimesis and Science: Empirical Research on Imitation and the Mimetic Theory of Culture and Religion*, Studies in Violence, Mimesis, and Culture (East Lansing, MI: Michigan State University Press, 2011); Wolfgang Palaver, *René Girard's Mimetic Theory*, Studies in Violence, Mimesis, and Culture (East Lansing: Michigan State University Press, 2013), 43.

[23] Aristotle comments on the instinctual nature of imitation for children, "Imitation is natural to man from childhood, one of his advantages over the lower animals being this, that he is the most imitative creature in the world, and learns at first by imitation." See Aristotle, *Poetics*, 1448b; Palaver, *René Girard's Mimetic Theory*, 41.

[24] Fox creates an unnecessary dichotomy between Proverbs and Deuteronomy regarding the term *torah* (Prov 1:8), saying "These are basically secular words and carry with them no allusion to divine law. With regard to Torah and commandments, G. Baumann (1996:295) observes that outside Proverbs, *torah* and *mitsvah* with the possessive suffix are (with one exception each) always divine. Thus the suffixed forms in Proverbs 'transgress or blur the border between human and divine commandments.' But theological conclusions cannot be deduced from this incidental grammatic phenomenon. The distribution of the forms has nothing to do with theology" (Michael V. Fox, *Proverbs 1–9: A New Translation with Introduction and Commentary*, AYBC 18A (New York: Doubleday, 2000), 79; Gerlinde Baumann, *Die Weisheitsgestalt in Proverbien 1–9*, FAT 16 (Tübingen: Mohr Siebeck, 1996), 295).

[25] As Craigie comments, "The commandments were to permeate every sphere of the life of man" (Peter C. Craigie, *The Book of Deuteronomy*, NICOT (Eerdmans, 1976), 170).

through intentional instruction from the older generation to the younger through imitation of their entire life. As Beale observes, "Children only begin what we continue to do as adults. We imitate. We reflect, sometimes consciously, sometimes unconsciously."[26] In this sense, then, *musar* and *torah* are not relegated to special educational settings or topics. The father-mother paradigm signifies that proverbial wisdom is inherently a full-life, imitative process. In reality, though, the Deuteronomic charge for generational instruction in the way of Yhwh began with Abraham, "I have known him in order that he might command his sons and his sons after him that they will guard the way of Yhwh doing righteousness and justice" (Gen 18:19). Bland opines on the topic, saying, "The book of Proverbs offers a valuable perspective on the efforts of a community to educate those with open hearts and minds in the formation and transformation of character."[27] In his view, Proverbs draws its holistic view of instruction from the Torah. He takes it a step further, though, implying that the context and setting for the father-mother paradigm was not just the nuclear family but the village or town.[28]

Furthermore, the imagery of father-mother and head-neck in Prov 1:8–9 is likely meant to be in a metaphorical, parallel relationship.[29] In Prov 10:1, the parallel between father and mother, a "stereotyped phrase," [30] strengthens the notion of their singular function, "A wise son gladdens a father, but a fool is his mother's grief." It would be wrong to create a division between father and mother since the opposite is intended here. Being wise makes both parents rejoice while foolishness grieves both parents. Likewise, while one might mistakenly assume *torah* and *musar* are independent or mutually exclusive, Prov 1:9 creates a lexical and poetic bond. In Prov 1:9, the author uses the term "they" (הֵם), a third masculine plural pronoun, as an anaphoric pronominal composite for *musar* and *torah* from 1:8. For the poetic function, the author parallels the "father's *musar*" with a "garland of grace for your head" and the "mother's *torah*" with a "necklace for your neck." The metaphor insinuates that honor, royalty, and blessing are associated with following *musar* and *torah*. [31] The metaphorical relationship between head and neck is valuable as well. As a head and neck are related, the metaphor reflects the complementary relationship between a father and mother and

---

[26] G. K. Beale, *We Become What We Worship: A Biblical Theology of Idolatry* (Downers Grove: IVP Academic, 2008), 15.

[27] Bland, *Proverbs and the Formation of Character*, 19.

[28] Murphy takes father-mother to be a metaphor for teachers (Murphy, *The Tree of Life*, 16).

[29] See Fox, *Proverbs 1–9*, 82.

[30] Waltke, *Proverbs (1–15)*, I: 451.

[31] Miles comments on this metaphor, "The parents are only the medium of the instruction. The poet's emphasis upon Torah observance suggests that by complying with the מוסר of the father (Yahweh) and the תורה of the mother (Wisdom), Solomon dons the proper insignia of royalty. Torah becomes the royal crown and symbol of wealth that shall surround the monarch and protect him" (Johnny E. Miles, *Wise King - Royal Fool: Semiotics, Satire and Proverbs 1–9* (New York: T&T Clark, 2004), 48).

likewise between *musar* and *torah*.[32] Furthermore, the proverbial instruction for the son begins with a positive motivation to follow in the ways of his parents, which is the *torah* way. Positive reinforcement is a powerful pedagogical tool.[33] Although most of Lesson 1 is quite negative, the proverbial father begins and ends the lesson with a positive inclusio (Prov 1:8, 33), providing a conceptual overlay between Wisdom and the father.

Warning: Following after Sinners (1:10–19)

At the heart of his lesson, the father provides two negative exhortations to the son, "Do not go … Do not walk in the way with them" (Prov 1:10, 15).[34] As Overland notes, Prov 1:5 had already "named two exemplary individuals whom the youth would do well to emulate. These were the 'wise man' (חכם) and 'man of understanding' (נבון)." [35] In the first section (Prov 1:10–14), two conditionals are indicated by "if" (אִם). The first is generic, implying Prov 1:10 and 15 ought to be understood together, "if sinners persuade you" (1:10).[36] The second conditional is specific and provides a compounding plan or scheme from Prov 1:11–14, "if they say …" (1:11).[37] The call of the sinners is a clear request for the son to do as they do, or imitate them. Repeatedly, the perspective is first plural (i.e., we, us, our). In everything, they will function cohesively,

---

[32] Kövecses says, "Metaphor, far from being a superfluous though pleasing linguistic ornament, is an inevitable process of human thought and reasoning" (Zoltán Kövecses, *Metaphor: A Practical Introduction*, 2nd ed. (New York: Oxford University Press, 2010), xi).

[33] See Philip A. Captain, "Effect of Positive Reinforcement on Comprehension, Attitudes, and Rate of Bible Reading in Adolescents," *JPT* 3.1 (1975): 49–55.

[34] The term "go" (בוא) could be read as "willing" (אבה). If it were אבה, this would be the only example in the HB with this form. Rendsburg argues that the unusual form of the word here (תבא) is derived from the first letters of the words in Prov 1:15 (תֵּלֵךְ בְּדֶרֶךְ אִתָּם). This speculative suggestion is tenuous at best. Regardless, though, both terms would imply the same intent and fit with the logic of the father's exhortation. Loader regards the sense of "willing" as preferential to the overall ethical intent of Proverbs. In his view, this avoids the potential simplification of wisdom to eudemonism. See Loader, *Proverbs 1–9*, 76; Gary A. Rendsburg, "Literary and Linguistic Matters in the Book of Proverbs," in *Perspectives on Israelite Wisdom: Proceedings of the Oxford Old Testament Seminar*, ed. John Jarick, LHBOTS 618 (London: T&T Clark, 2016), 123–24.

[35] Overland, "Literary Structure in Proverbs 1–9," 184.

[36] Ploger notes the initial danger of persuasion comes from this group of sinners which also takes on the form of a foreign woman later (Otto Plöger, *Spruche Salomos (Proverbia)*, BKAT 17 (Neukirchen-Vluyn: Neukirchener Verlag, 1984), 13).

[37] Longman notes, "This language is a subtle way by which the parents associate the gang with the 'dark side.' They are those who model themselves after their master Death" (Tremper Longman III, *Proverbs*, BCOTWP (Grand Rapids: Baker Academic, 2006), 107). Furthermore, Loader discusses the well-known trope in ANE and the HB for Sheol, "In Ugaritic mythological texts the motif of being swallowed alive occurs as an image of death. The god Mot swallows his victims by opening his mouth wide (CTA 5. II. 1–6; cf. Isa 5:14; Hab 2:5) and the victims are likened to lambs (CTA 4. VIII. 17–20; cf. Prov 7:23). … The criminals are thereby criticized for usurping the divine prerogative to decide over life and death" (Loader, *Proverbs 1–9*, 78–79).

"Throw your lot in our midst" (Prov 1:14). While the son has not yet partaken or participated in the hypothetical scenario, the possibility of his following in the ways of sinners and becoming like them is a serious threat. In Deut 18:9, Moses provides a similar warning for those entering the land, "You shall not learn to do (imitate) the abominations of those nations." [38] Likewise, he provides a similar warning in Lev 20:23, "You shall not walk in the customs of the nations that I am driving out." While it cannot be known if the "sinner" group in the father's example were Israelites or foreigners, their aberration from the Torah would place them outside the covenant community, as though they were foreigners. Thus, the father exhorts the son that he must not "walk in the way with them" or in "their paths" (Prov 1:15). This metaphor is used as literary imagery to indicate many of the kings' behavior and choices, for good or evil.[39] They either walked in the way of their fathers through their faithfulness to God and restoration of Israel to Yhwh or by practicing the wickedness and idolatry of their ancestors. As this one example demonstrates, "[Nadab] did evil in the eyes of Yhwh and he walked in the way of his father and in his sin which he caused Israel to sin" (1 Kgs 15:26; cf. 14:8, 15:34, 16:2, 19, 22:53; 2 Kgs 8:18, 27, 13:2, 16:3, 21:22, 23:3). For the son to walk in the way of sinners is to emulate and know them, which necessarily means he is not like God and does not know him (cf. Hos 4:1–2, 6, 5:4, 6:6–9).

Regarding the scheme of the sinners, the statement "let us lie in ambush for blood ... we shall fill our houses with plunder" (Prov 1:11, 13) directly violates the Torah, "If a man hates his neighbor and lies in wait for him and rises against him and strikes his life and he dies ... the elders shall ... hand him over ... and he will die ... you shall purge the innocent (נקי) blood from Israel and it will be well for you" (Deut 19:10–11, 13; cf. Exod 23:7; Deut 27:25). In Prov 1:11, it is perhaps even worse than Deut 19 since they will "ambush the innocent (נקי) without reason (חנם)." This is not to mention the clear violation of covenantal commandments five and ten, "You shall not murder ... You shall not covet" (Exod 20:13, 17; Deut 5:17, 21).[40] While the call of the sinners makes no mention of a path, the father's response (Prov 1:15–19) makes clear that their call is a call to a way of life.[41] By becoming like them in their disregard for God's way, the son will join them in their ways of destruction. The sinners mention "innocent" victims in this call. While "innocent" is a generic term, Jeremiah helps provide the fuller syntagm, "If you do not oppress the sojourner, fatherless, and widow and do not spill

---

[38] The context of the passage in Deut appears to be religious evil rather than social. However, Prov 3:31–35 and 6:15–19 connect "abomination" (תועבות) with social and civil evil, those shedding "innocent" (נקי) blood. As Fox notes, the sense of "abomination" is not exclusive to cultic violations. But, in the HB, it is almost exclusively used this way, Proverbs being the exception. Regardless, the sense is always repulsion or separation. Although Deut 18 focuses on improper communication or attempted manipulation, for both Deut and Prov, the centralizing issue is walking in ways aberrant or repulsive to Yhwh's way. See Daniel I. Block, *Deuteronomy*, NIVAC (Grand Rapids: Zondervan, 2012), 434–35; Fox, *Proverbs 1–9*, 166–67.

[39] See the discussion in Lesson 8.

[40] Moss, "Wisdom as Parental Teaching in Proverbs 1–9," 429.

[41] Longman, *Proverbs*, 105.

innocent blood ... I will let you dwell" (Jer 7:6–7).[42] Also, he says, "Do justice and righteousness ... do no harm the sojourner, fatherless, and widow and do not shed innocent (נקי) blood" (Jer 22:3; cf. Isa 58:7).[43] For the proverbial father, the call to attack innocent lives implied not only a violation of the Deut 19 covenant stipulation but a violation of a much broader motif in the Torah and beyond.[44] In Exod 22:21–23, Moses provides Yhwh's covenant code to Israel, "You shall not harm any widow and fatherless ... my wrath will burn and I will kill you with the sword and your wives will become widows and your sons fatherless." Apparently, God has a special concern for the vulnerable and innocent.[45] So much so, he himself is the paradigm of such care and concern, "[Yhwh] makes justice for the fatherless and widow and he loves the sojourner giving to him food and a cloak" (Deut 10:18; cf. Ps 10:14, 18, 146:9).[46] In fact, Yhwh is called the "father of the fatherless and judge of the widow" by the psalmist (Ps 68:6).[47] Isaiah's prophecy to Judah starts off with this motif, as well, "Learn to do good, seek justice, correct oppression, judge the fatherless, plead for the widow" (Isa 1:17; cf. 1:23). In an interesting reversal, Isaiah claims Yhwh has ceased to care for the innocent, "[Yhwh] has no compassion for the fatherless and widow for all are godless and evil" (Isa 9:16). In other

---

[42] For further discussion on the relationship between Prov 1 and Jer 7, see Zabán, *The Pillar Function of the Speeches of Wisdom*, 100–105; Scott L. Harris, *Proverbs 1–9: A Study of Inner-Biblical Interpretation*, SBLDS 150 (Atlanta: Scholars, 1996), 87–88.

[43] The TDOT entry for "fatherless, orphan" acknowledges the widespread nature of the idiom and idea in the ANE, "Orphans were considered especially helpless and needy. To care for such people was the duty of the king and the monarchs. In the Peasant's Lament, the speaker addresses the chief administrator Rensi as follows: 'For you are the father of the orphan (*nmḥw*), the husband of the widow, the brother of the outcast.' It is characteristic that helpless orphans and widows are mentioned in the same breath" (Helmer Ringgren, "יתום," *TDOT* 6:478).

[44] This motif extends across a broad range of biblical literature, though largely found in the Torah and the prophetic tradition: Exod 22:21, 23; Deut 10:18, 14:29, 16:11, 14, 24:17, 19, 20, 21, 26:12, 13, 27:19; Isa 1:17, 23, 9:16, 10:2; Jer 5:28, 7:6, 22:3, 49:11; Ezek 22:7; Hos 14:4; Zech 7:10; Mal 3:5; Ps 10:14, 18, 68:6, 82:3, 94:6, 109:9, 12, 146:9; Job 6:27, 22:9, 24:3, 9, 29:12, 31:17, 21; Prov 23:10; Lam 5:3.

[45] As Carroll notes, "Fundamental to the ethical call to the nation to defend and provide for the orphan is the very character of Yahweh himself, who, though he is the incomparable and omnipotent God, had demonstrated unmerited grace in his election and redemption of Israel (Deut 10:14–22). Attitudes and actions toward the orphan, then, were to be rooted in an appreciation of the divine mercy manifested toward Israel throughout its history" (R. M. D. Carroll, "Orphan," in *DOTP* (Downers Grove: IVP, 2003), 620).

[46] As Wright properly understands, "The commands of God are not autonomous or arbitrary rules; they are frequently related to the character or values or desires of God. So to obey God's commands is to reflect God in human life. Obedience to the law and the imitation of God are not mutually exclusive categories: the one is an expression of the other. One of the clearest model passages for this is Deuteronomy 10:12–19. It begins with a rhetorical flourish, rather like Micah 6:8, summarizing the whole law in a single chord of five notes: fear, walk, love, serve and obey (note that love, the most relational and personal of them all is at the centre of the five). ... And what are the ways of the LORD in which Israel is to walk? ... At last the passage gets down to detail. [Deut 10:17–19]. The concluding line of the verse clearly expresses an ethic of imitation" (Christopher J. H. Wright, *Old Testament Ethics for the People of God* (Downers Grove: IVP, 2004), 40–41).

[47] Frank-Lothar Hossfeld and Erich Zenger, *Psalms 2: A Commentary on Psalms 51–100*, Hermeneia (Minneapolis: Fortress, 2005), 164. Hossfeld and Zenger draw connections here between the Deuteronomic and Wisdom traditions.

words, Isaiah says it may seem like God has abandoned his nature and his way but the reality is that Judah is so corrupt even the innocent are not innocent.[48] Near the end of the prophetic tradition, Malachi confirms God's impending judgment for those violating this cause, one dear to Yhwh, "I will draw near to you to judge ... against sorcerers, adulterers, liars, oppressors of widows and fatherless and those turning against the sojourner and who do not fear me" (Mal 3:5). Altogether, the consistent picture throughout the HB is that Yhwh protects and cares for the innocent and vulnerable. To take advantage of or harm such persons is not only a violation of the Torah but of God's own way. It is to reject him and his word, therefore, abandoning the very purpose for which man was created, to reflect and imitate his character as the righteous, compassionate ruler (Gen 1:26–28).[49] Thus, the sinners' scheme contrasts the divine way, implying the son ought to imitate the wise ways of Yhwh instead.

Within the father's warning against this sinners' path, an interesting parallel occurs between Prov 1:16 and Isa 59:7a, "Their feet run to evil, and they hasten to shed innocent (נקי) blood."[50] Strengthening the connection between these passages is the occurrence of "path" (נְתִיבָה), a fairly uncommon term (Prov 1:15; Isa 59:8b). The instructional import of Prov 1:15–19 seems to find a broader context in this passage of Isaiah,[51] which has connections to Wisdom's call as well. Isaiah 59 begins with a divine declaration, "Your iniquities have made divisions between you and your God" (Isa 59:2a).[52] In Isa 59:8, Isaiah's prophetic rebuke states, "The way of peace they do not know and there is no justice in their paths; they make crooked their paths (נְתִיבָה), the one walking in it he does not know peace."[53] This contrasts with Wisdom in Prov 3:17, "All her paths (נְתִיבָה) are peace." Isaiah builds a web of connections between sinful actions and their path of life as tantamount to relational disconnect from God.[54] However, this is not accidental or incidental. In Prov

---

[48] See Mark Gray, *Rhetoric and Social Justice in Isaiah*, LHBOTS (New York: T&T Clark, 2006), 131–54; Christopher R. Seitz, *Isaiah 1–39: Interpretation: A Bible Commentary for Teaching and Preaching*, Interpretation (Louisville: Presbyterian, 2011), 90; John F. A. Sawyer, *Isaiah* (Philadelphia: Westminster, 1986), I:104–05.

[49] Wright, *Old Testament Ethics for the People of God*, 369.

[50] For discussions on the originality of this verse, see BHQ; Whybray, *Composition of the Book of Proverbs*, 14; Fox, *Proverbs 1–9*, 88, 369; Loader, *Proverbs 1–9*, 81–82; Harris, *Proverbs 1–9*, 42–45.

[51] Loader, *Proverbs 1–9*, 81.

[52] Oswalt connects this passage lexically to Gen 1:6, saying, "Just as the firmament separated the waters above from the waters below, preventing any commingling, so iniquity and sins prevent any intercourse between God and his people" (John N. Oswalt, *The Book of Isaiah*, NICOT (Grand Rapids: Eerdmans, 1986), 513).

[53] Oswalt discusses the high concentration of 'path' language and purpose here, "Throughout the book of Isaiah words for 'way' and 'highway' have been prominent. Here all the words are collected in one place. This collection is for the purpose of showing how utterly futile all human ways are apart from the Lord's intervention. His highways are peace and redemption (Isa 11:16; 19:23; 35:8; 40:3; 49:11; 62:10), but the human highways are destruction and confusion (7:3; 33:8; 36:2; 59:7)" (Oswalt, *The Book of Isaiah*, 516).

[54] As Goldingay rightly observes, "The notion of the way recurs in the Old Testament. Its assumption is that humanity is on a journey ... that individuals and communities walk whose point lies as much in the traveling as in the arriving, because it is a journey that follows a moral

59:13, Isaiah provides a poetic confession from those running after evil, much like the sinners' call from the proverbial father in Prov 1:11–14. They say, "[We] transgress and deny Yhwh and turn from after our God" (Isa 59:13; cf. Zeph 1:6).[55] Here, a clear link is formed between social evil and religious fidelity and affections.[56] The confession negatively echoes Deut 13:4, "You shall walk after Yhwh your God and fear him and guard his commandment and listen to his voice and serve him and cling to him." Later, Josiah is said to have committed to this way in his reforms, "The king stood by the pillar and made the covenant before Yhwh to walk after Yhwh and to guard his commandment ... with all his heart and soul" (2 Kgs 23:3). Taking these passages together, the father warns, "Do not walk in the way with them," which becomes quite dire due to the implications regarding God and his way.[57] The path of sinners is not just in error but in opposition to the way espoused by the father, ultimately rooted in Yhwh himself and his ways (cf. Judg 2:11–22, 3:27–28). Thus, if the son chooses to imitate the way of sinners, he is simultaneously refusing to reflect Yhwh.

Furthermore, in order to drive home the incredulity of the sinners' scheme and path, the father mocks them as more foolish than birds, "In vain (חנם) a net is set in the sight of any bird but these men lie in wait for their own blood" (Prov 1:17–18).[58] This is the first use of a lesser-to-greater metaphor found in Proverbs (e.g., 6:5–15).[59] As it will be discussed elsewhere, this type of metaphor utilizes a simple or undesirable comparison for the son. Underlying the metaphor, the author assumes a wisdom hierarchy present in

---

route laid out by God. 'The figure of the way is a central symbol of biblical ethics'" (John Goldingay, *A Critical and Exegetical Commentary on Isaiah 56 - 66*, ICC (London: Bloomsbury, T&T Clark, 2014), 195–97).

[55] Motyer remarks on this passage, "There cannot be a true relationship with the Lord that is not at the same time a genuine relationship with people. Equally, to offend against other people is to sin against God" (J. A. Motyer, *The Prophecy of Isaiah: An Introduction & Commentary* (Downers Grove: IVP, 1993), 488).

[56] Goldingay, *A Critical and Exegetical Commentary on Isaiah 56 - 66*, 215–16.

[57] As Wegner notes regarding Isaiah's warning, similar to the warning from the proverbial father, "Those who walk in the ways of wickedness will never know peace ... The people have become so hardened by sin that they can no longer remember what it is like to act in ways that are pleasing to God (i.e., the way of peace)" (Paul D. Wegner, *Isaiah: An Introduction and Commentary*, TOTC (Downers Grove: IVP Academic, 2021), 430).

[58] Birds, though cunning in ways, are not imagined as more intelligent than humans generally (Job 39:13–18; Hos 7:11). Loader prefers to see the intent of the bird metaphor as simply "innocent," here implying naïve, relating to the biblical metaphor of doves (Loader, *Proverbs 1–9*, 83). Although innocent or naïve is perhaps implied with birds generally, the fact that it is vain to set a trap visible to a bird implies that even a bird is more observant and wiser than the fools who set traps for themselves and cannot see it.

[59] This form of metaphor is perhaps subtly related to the "better-than" sayings elsewhere in Proverbs (e.g., 12:17, 21:19). In these examples, there is an implicit belief that one circumstance is preferable to the other. However, in the lesser-to-greater examples in Prov 1–9, the animals are not incidental and possess a quality that is contrasted with humans, positively or negatively, for rhetorical emphasis. Forti notes an ANE metaphor with ants, "Ahiqar humbles himself before the king by describing his position 'as one of the loathsome ants in the kingdom.'" This example demonstrates a simple metaphor rather than a "better-than" or lesser-to-greater metaphor. For a discussion on animal imagery and metaphor, see Tova Forti, *Animal Imagery in the Book of Proverbs*, VTSup 118 (Leiden: Brill, 2008), 17.

Proverbs, fixed from highest to lowest: Yhwh/Wisdom, the father/wise, creatures, and then fools/wicked at the bottom. By implication, this type of metaphor is meant to evoke a desire in the "naïve" or "simple," portrayed in a neutral position,[60] to not be like the lesser but instead the greater. The instructive implication for the son in this particular example is the disgrace inherent to the sinners' way. They are not only covenant violators but descending on the foolish pathway away from God, becoming lower than even the animal/creature order. This reality is in spite of their own delusions of grandeur, which the father emphatically corrects. Thus, the father is teaching the son that walking in the way with sinners is to imitate them and their foolish behaviors. The son is charged not to imitate such fools, which will result in descending rather than ascending in the wisdom hierarchy. Instead, he is to be a son after his father (Gen 5:3),[61] who is presented as supremely wise and on the path of the wise. Though not explicit, neither the father nor God acts the way these sinners or fools do.

Finally, the way of sinners is not only in contradiction to the ways of the father and God but ultimately it leads to death (Prov 1:19).[62] Death of course is not at all the way of the father, Wisdom, or Yhwh. In a similar warning from God to his people, he declares that he desires all would experience life and contends that he himself is the ultimate source of life (Deut 30:15–20).[63] At this point, it is important to ask the question, what is meant by the self-harm from the sinners' path? Is it simply an impersonal, reciprocal principle of cause-and-effect, one reaps what they sow, or divine judgment? Habakkuk 2:6–20 expresses five woes that characterize similar types of evil espoused by the sinners' circle in Prov 1. On the one hand, it seems as though the calamity that will befall them is simply a natural result of afflicting those who eventually turn the whip on their oppressor, "Since you plundered many nations all the remaining people will plunder you" (Hab 2:8). Yet, a few verses later, the prophet clarifies the calamity is judgment in the hands of Yhwh, "The cup in Yhwh's right hand will surround you and dishonor will be over

---

[60] Waltke identifies the neutrality of the naïve, though not without its dangers, "Until the gullible—not a correlative term with fool—make a decisive decision for wisdom, they suffer the fate of fools (1:22–33). Though the gullible, unlike fools, do not despise wisdom, they have not made a commitment as those who fear the LORD, the spiritual foundation of the wise" (Waltke, *Proverbs (1–15)*, 93).

[61] As taught in Genesis, Hamilton says there is a "transmission of the divine image and likeness from generation to generation ... stressing his point about the operations of divine grace" (Victor P. Hamilton, *The Book of Genesis*, NICOT (Grand Rapids: Eerdmans, 1990), 255–56). Wright connects the "image" in Gen 1–5 with humanity reflecting or imitating the righteous, wise character and dominion of God. Both are inherent to the purpose of humanity as well (Wright, *Old Testament Ethics for the People of God*, 121).

[62] While commenting on the two-path metaphor, which he calls the "ground metaphor," Loader notes that the cause-effect relationship between the two-paths and their results is the "nexus of deed and consequence" or "Tun-Ergehen-Zusammenhang." Likewise, he notes that the conclusion of this section also metaphorically signals "the end of their road," keeping with the pathway metaphor inherent (Loader, *Proverbs 1–9*, 67, 84–85).

[63] Weinfeld comments, "'Life' in the book of Deuteronomy, as in both Israelite and non-Israelite wisdom literature, constitutes the framework of reward" (Weinfeld, *Deuteronomy and the Deuteronomic School*, 307).

your honor" (Hab 2:16; cf. Jer 25:15–29).[64] Here in the father's lesson, it seems as though there is a natural progression and conclusion.[65] Elsewhere, though, there is an emphasis on the righteous and wicked receiving their due reward from God (e.g., Prov 3:33–35, 5:21–22, 6:16–19, 8:34–36; cf. 16:4, 19:17).[66] It must be concluded, then, that judgment is the natural end of the sinner's way, which is not an escape from Yhwh but a foolish trap leading one directly into Yhwh's judgment (cf. Judg 9:56–57). In other words, the two paths both lead to Yhwh, one for blessing and proper relationship but the other for judgment and death. As for the educational program, the goal is conformity to the father's way as he follows in the way of Yhwh, unlike the sinners here.[67] He hopes to lead the son along an incrementally expanding pathway,[68] one which begins in simple, concrete terms but blossoms into knowledge beyond the mundane understanding of the "naive."

---

[64] O. Palmer Robertson, *The Books of Nahum, Habakkuk, and Zephaniah*, NICOT (Grand Rapids: Eerdmans, 1990), 186–88, 202–3.

[65] Waltke notes, "All agree that Proverbs presents a 'world order' involving 'deed and destiny,' that is to say, 'What you do now will determine what will happen then.' A more precise formulation is a character > conduct > consequence connection—that is, what you are determines what you will become. At issue here is the relationship of the LORD to this nexus. K. Koch and others remove God altogether from involvement in the world, or at best reduce him to a first cause within a deistic view of reality (a so-called synthetische Lebensauffassung). ... Many sayings represent the character-consequence nexus without appealing to the LORD's involvement, but Proverbs aims to protect itself against interpreting the deed-destiny connection as being fatalistic in several ways. ... Goldingay pointed out that the sequence of observations on righteousness and wickedness (10:2) is followed by an observation about the LORD's involvement in people's lives (10:3) and he found the same sequence as in 10:2–5 again in 10:23–27, 12:1–14, 14:1–4, and 15:2–7. ... The discussion on structure also noted that Collection I functions as a hermeneutical key to the rest of the book. The key to the book and to wisdom as presented in its own preamble is 'the fear of the LORD,' ... Suffice it here to note that 'piety toward God,' a religious lifestyle, not a rational understanding of an impersonal order, shapes the character and destiny of the truly wise. In the book's prologue, the father's first lecture places the blame for final and certain death on the sinner (1:19), and to this Woman Wisdom adds that this came about because they refused to fear the LORD (1:29). Protection against sinners, according to the father's second lecture, depends on accepting the teachings involved in the fear of the LORD (2:1–5). The third lecture represents the LORD and the faithful as each having covenant obligations (3:1–10), concluding with the truth that the LORD himself takes over the father's role in disciplining his children. The fourth sermon concludes by showing the connection between the LORD's retribution and human social behavior (3:27–35). The first full lecture against the unfaithful wife certifies the adulterer's death as due to the LORD's omnivision (5:21–23)" (Waltke, *Proverbs (1–15)*, 73).

[66] Waltke, *Proverbs (1–15)*, 69–72.

[67] Loader, *Proverbs 1–9*, 63.

[68] Cf. Hindy Najman, "Imitatio Dei and the Formation of the Subject in Ancient Judaism," *JBL* 140.2 (2021): 317. Najman notes the role of *torah* and *musar* in the trajectory of self-definition, following the example of sages or fathers in an imitative pattern, though she attributes this to a Hellenistic development as seen in Dan 9.

Following after Wisdom as Yhwh (1:20–33)

In the latter half of Lesson 1 (Prov 1:20–33), the father's call and warning leads to Wisdom's call and warning. As it will be seen, several claims by Wisdom are things true of God elsewhere in scripture, interweaving language and ideas both in Proverbs and the HB.[69] If taken alone, these claims might seem merely incidental but taken together they paint a substantive picture of what or who Wisdom is. In Prov 1–9, Wisdom serves as both a metaphor and an anthropomorphism.[70] On the one hand, Wisdom is pictured as a teacher, wife, mother, sister, prophet, and sage.[71] On the other, Wisdom is the metaphorical embodiment of Yhwh.[72] This is perhaps analogous, though metaphorically, to the angel of Yhwh (e.g., Judg 2:1–5).[73] The son is to desire, obey, and follow Wisdom, since Wisdom speaks, does, and gives as Yhwh

---

[69] As Murphy elucidates, "An astonishing feature of Wisdom's speeches in chaps. 1–9 is that she speaks like the Lord, no less. The references to the prophetic language given above are an indication of this. What was referred to God is now referred to her. It is she who feels rebuffed, and who threatens those who refuse to listen. She has divine authority, and she hands out reward and punishment. She does not mention the Lord; she does not urge conversion to God, but to herself." (Murphy, *Proverbs*, 12).

[70] The distinction made here is that personification typically implies an upward movement in characterization from inanimate to animate or attributing human characteristics to nonhuman objects and creatures. Anthropomorphism often implies a descent in characterization from divine to mundane or attributing human and creaturely characteristics to the ineffable God. Against typical characterization, Prov 1–9 presents Wisdom as a human figuration of God rather than mere poetic animation of an abstract concept. Koptak provides a typical and incomplete identification of Wisdom in Proverbs as "characterized personification," incidentally diminishing the functional import of this unique and mysterious figure. See Paul E. Koptak, "Personification," in *Dictionary of the Old Testament: Wisdom, Poetry, & Writings*, ed. Tremper Longman III (Downers Grove: IVP Academic, 2008), 516–19; Elaine T. James, *An Invitation to Biblical Poetry* (New York: Oxford University Press, 2022), 106–37; David Stern, "Imitatio Hominis: Anthropomorphism and the Character(s) of God in Rabbinic Literature," *Proof* 12.2 (1992): 151–74; John Bowker, "Anthropomorphism," in *The Oxford Dictionary of World Religions* (Oxford: Oxford University Press, 1997), 74; Shalom Bar-Asher, "Anthropomorphism," in *The Oxford Dictionary of the Jewish Religion*, eds. R. J. Zwi Werblowsky and Geoffrey Wigoder (Oxford: Oxford University Press, 1997), 51–52; Merrill C. Tenney and Moisés Silva, eds., *The Zondervan Encyclopedia of the Bible*, rev. ed. (Grand Rapids: Zondervan, 2009), 1:202–04.

[71] Fox outlines a number of reasons for seeing Wisdom as a prophetic figure. Though, he does not think this image fully captures the role of Wisdom, despite it providing a "few pigments for Wisdom's portrait." In his view, the similarity between Wisdom and prophets is their overlap as teachers (Fox, *Proverbs 1–9*, 333–34).

[72] Longman notes that "Woman Wisdom is a poetic personification of Yahweh's wisdom; indeed, as indicated by her house's location on the high point of the city, Wisdom ultimately represents Yahweh himself" (Longman, *The Fear of the Lord Is Wisdom*, 111).

[73] See Stephen L White, "Angel of the LORD: Messenger or Euphemism?," *TynBul* 50.2 (1999): 299–305; Andrew S Malone, "Distinguishing the Angel of the Lord," *BBR* 21.3 (2011): 297–314; René López, "Identifying the 'angel of the Lord' in the Book of Judges: A Model for Reconsidering the Referent in Other Old Testament Loci," *BBR* 20.1 (2010): 1–18; Carl Judson Davis, *The Name and Way of the Lord: Old Testament Themes, New Testament Christology*, LNTS 129 (London: Bloomsbury, 1996), 30–38; Tenney and Silva, *The Zondervan Encyclopedia of the Bible*, I:186–87; Stephen F. Noll, "מַלְאָךְ," in *NIDOTTE*, ed. Willem VanGemeren (Grand Rapids: Zondervan, 1997), II:941–43.

does.[74] As Longman notes, "[Woman Wisdom] ultimately stands for Yahweh. As we listen to her, we listen to God himself."[75] To this we may add, if the son imitates Wisdom, he necessarily imitates Yhwh as well.

Warning: Wisdom's call (1:20–25)

To begin this latter instruction, Wisdom provides either an imperative (conditional) "turn to my rebuke"[76] or a continuation of Prov 1:22 "[how long] will you turn from my rebuke" (1:23).[77] In both, the emphasis is on "my rebuke" (לְתוֹכַחְתִּי), spoken by Wisdom three times here (Prov 1:22, 25, 30) but occurs three more times in Prov 1–9 (3:11, 5:12, 6:23). In Prov 3:11, the "rebuke" is from Yhwh and connected to *musar,* a dominant picture for Proverbs (cf. 10:17, 12:1, 13:18, 15:5, 10, 32). Externally, the verb form appears in a very important passage, with strong connections to Prov 3:11 as well, "I will be his father and he will be my son; in his guilt, I will rebuke (וְהֹכַחְתִּיו) him with a rod of men" (2 Sam 7:14). In Prov 5:12, the source of "rebuke" is ambiguous, perhaps intentionally, "I hated *musar,* my heart despised rebuke" (וְתוֹכַחַת). Here, it is followed by Prov 5:13, which speaks of teachers but not directly. Lastly, in Prov 6:23, "rebuke of *musar*" appears in a tri-parallel line with commandments and *torah* which are coupled with "lamp," "light," and "path of life" (cf. Ps 119:105). In Prov 1–9, the dominant use of "rebuke" is from Wisdom. This front-loading of the term in Lesson 1 may imply that the others are instantiations of Wisdom's rebuke. Together these uses describe the great importance of "rebuke" and its integral coupling with *musar,* particularly as a tool by Wisdom and Yhwh. The goal in all instances is to bring the proverbial son in line with the proper *torah* way.[78]

A phrase attributed to "Wisdom" in Prov 1:24 is attributed to God elsewhere in the HB, "I called and you refused (מאס)."[79] In several prophetic passages,[80] a similar phrase comes from God to Israel, "I called and you did not answer; I spoke and you did not listen" (Isa 65:12, 66:4; cf. Jer 23:18). The metaphor carries over from Prov 1:20, where Wisdom calls out, paralleled in 8:1 and 9:3. While Prov 1:24 might be taken only as a metaphor, 1:28 provides a strong connection to Yhwh.[81] Due to rejection, Wisdom will reject those who would not listen, saying, "They will call for me but I will not answer" (Prov

---

[74] Cf. Schipper, *Proverbs 1–15,* 317–18; Plöger, *Spruche Salomos (Proverbia),* 19.

[75] Longman, *Proverbs,* 79.

[76] Waltke, *Proverbs (1–15),* 198, 203–4; Fox, *Proverbs 1–9,* 98–99; C. H. Toy, *A Critical and Exegetical Commentary on the Book of Proverbs,* ICC (New York: C. Scribner's Sons, 1899), 24.

[77] Murphy, *Proverbs,* 7–8; Schipper, *Proverbs 1–15,* 93.

[78] Wilson, "The Words of the Wise," 192.

[79] Schipper connects the volitional rejection of Yhwh's call to Pharaoh and the plagues in Exod 4–16 (Schipper, *Proverbs 1–15,* 94).

[80] For a variety of prophetic parallels, see Loader, *Proverbs 1–9,* 90–91.

[81] Schipper, *Proverbs 1–15,* 96.

1:28).[82] As seen here, Wisdom is not just a personification of an abstract concept. The will of Wisdom implies a strong anthropomorphic response reflective of Yhwh.[83] In Mic 3:4, a similar phrase is expressed by Yhwh against the rulers of Israel. Likewise, God's refusal to answer Israel was prophesied by Samuel when the people "rejected" (מאס) God as their king (1 Sam 8:7, 18). The call-rejection motif between God and humans is a powerful and prominent refrain throughout the HB.[84] Yet, the language of calling on God is typical of a prayer for rescue or salvation. Isaiah prophesies, "Then you will call and Yhwh will answer ... Yhwh will lead (נחה) you continually" (Isa 58:9, 11). His prophecy is a gracious reversal of the wicked rejection from earlier generations. Likewise, it demonstrates the intimacy and personal guidance from Yhwh, a reality rooted in Israel's earliest days as a people under the covenant (cf. Exod 13:21, 15:13, 33:14; Deut 32:12).[85] In many places, God's response is given, though conditioned towards the righteous, to those who trust in him and walk in his way. But, here in Prov 1:28, Wisdom will not grant an answer to the fool.[86] Rather they will suffer the consequences of their prior rejection (Prov 1:24–27). This is the exact opposite of Ps 50:15, where Yhwh says, "Call upon me in the day of trouble; I will deliver you" (cf. Ps 11:17, 17:6, 18:6, 20:9, 40:1).

Warning: the fate of fools (1:26–32)

Perhaps most striking in this section is Wisdom's response to calamity by "laughing" (שׂחק) and "mocking" (לעג) the "trouble" (איד) experienced by those who refused to listen (Prov 1:26). The idea of laughing/mocking is also used of God in several places.[87] Perhaps most prominently, Ps 2:4 uses both laughing" (שׂחק) and "mocking" (לעג) of God, "The one sitting in heaven laughs, Adonai mocks him."[88] Similarly, in Ps 59:9, it says, "You, Yhwh, will laugh at them; you will mock all the nations." For Ps 2:4, it is in response to kings and nobles conspiring against Yhwh and his anointed (Ps 2:2). Later in the psalter, the psalmist says, "Adonai laughs at [the wicked] for he sees his day" (Ps 37:13). This particular psalm has a number of connections to Proverbs and the

---

[82] Cf. Hos 9:17, "My God will reject (מאס) them because they did not listen to him."

[83] As Whybray states, "To choose Wisdom is synonymous with choosing obedience to Yahweh." Similarly, Waltke says, "Submission to Wisdom is equated with submission to God." Plöger, however, prefers to see Wisdom as a prophet with a special word from Yhwh, creating a level of separation. See Whybray, *Composition of the Book of Proverbs*, 39; Plöger, *Spruche Salomos (Proverbia)*, 20; Waltke, *Proverbs (1–15)*, 210.

[84] Schipper connects several phrases from Wisdom to the prophetic tradition for Israel's rejection of the "divine will," also noting the overlaying relationship between Yhwh and Wisdom. See Schipper, *Proverbs 1–15*, 94–96; Plöger, *Spruche Salomos (Proverbia)*, 19.

[85] See Lesson 12 and Excursus: Exodus and God's Leading in His Way.

[86] Waltke, *Proverbs (1–15)*, I:209.

[87] Paul E. Koptak, *Proverbs: From Biblical Text to Contemporary Life*, NIVAC (Grand Rapids: Zondervan, 2003), 86.

[88] Cf. Longman, *Proverbs*, 113.

father's teaching.[89] In Ps 37:3 and 5, it commands, "Trust in Yhwh" (// Prov 3:5). Likewise, in 37:23, it says, "Yhwh establishes the steps (צעד) of man" (// Prov 3:6, 16:9). In 37:27, there is a command to "turn (סור) from evil ... so you will dwell forever" (// Prov 4:27, 1:33). There is also a promise for security in the "land" for those who are righteous (Ps 37:3, 9, 11, 22, 29, 34 // Prov 1:33, 2:21, 22). A central quality of this righteous person is that the "*torah* of his God is in his heart" (Ps 37:31 // Prov 3:1–3, 7:2–3). Finally, there is a significant emphasis on keeping the way of Yhwh (Ps 37:5, 23, 34). Yet, in contrast to these examples, Prov 17:5 states, "The one mocking (לעג) the poor disgraces his maker; the one rejoicing for calamity (איד) will not be set free." On its face, this presumably condemns Wisdom in 1:26. However, the latter proverb seems to imply a sense of pride and pleasure in the downfall of the innocent.[90] The earlier proverb relates Wisdom to Yhwh, highlighting the foolishness of only calling on Wisdom/Yhwh once trouble has come. As Ps 37 elicits, there is a holistic pathway for the righteous to which God will respond. Such a path involves the whole of life, one who "delights in the way of Yhwh" (Ps 37:23), not just as a last resort. The lesson for the son in Prov 1, then, is to follow in the way of the father, Wisdom, and Yhwh.

Another important phrase used by "wisdom" condemns those who refuse to listen, "They will seek (שׁחר) me but not find (מצא) me" (1:28). The idea of seeking or finding occurs with a variety of lexemes several times elsewhere in Prov 1–9 (cf. 2:4–5, 3:13, 4:22, 7:15, 8:9, 17, 35–36). This particular phrasing 'seek and find' connects to an important conceptual and linguistic web used between God and his people, rooted in the Torah, implicit for relational knowledge (e.g., Ps 24:6, 63:1, 119:1–2, 10; Hos 5:6; 1 Chron 28:9; 2 Chron 15:2). The first and central instance of this motif is in Deut 4:29, "From there, you will seek (בקשׁ) Yhwh your God and you will find (מצא) him when you seek (דרשׁ) with all your heart and all your soul."[91] The context is a prophetic prediction of apostasy, exile, and restoration (Deut 4:25–28; cf. 28:36–37, 64–68, 30:1–10). Conversely, there is an exhortation in all of these passages regarding idolatry, as Deut 12:30 warns, "Guard yourself lest you be ensnared after them ... lest you seek (דרשׁ) their gods saying, 'How do these nations serve their gods?'" It is vital to note that Prov 1:28 does not imply that Israel is to seek something or someone other than Yhwh, which would be an affront to his exclusivity.[92] The addressees in Prov 1 are simply wrong in their timing and motivation. While idolatry is not explicit in Proverbs, it is likely implicit with

---

[89] William P. Brown, "'Come, O Children . . . I Will Teach You the Fear of the Lord' (Psalm 34:12): Comparing Psalms and Proverbs," in *Seeking out the Wisdom of the Ancients: Essays Offered to Honor Michael V. Fox on the Occasion of His Sixty-Fifth Birthday* (Winona Lake: Eisenbrauns, 2005), 86–90.

[90] Waltke identifies the one mocked as "pitiful" and a "victim" (Waltke, *Proverbs (16–31)*, 42).

[91] Cf. Schipper, *Proverbs 1–15*, 305.

[92] Lang incorrectly identifies Wisdom and fundamentally misses the import here, "In monotheistic Judaism it would have been either blasphemous or meaningless to call on Wisdom in the same sense as one would call on God in prayer. Yet in polytheistic circles of preexilic Israel, Wisdom must have been regarded as a goddess" (Bernhard Lang, *Wisdom and the Book of Proverbs: A Hebrew Goddess Redefined* (New York: Pilgrim, 1986), 39, 126–31).

the many notions of adultery and turning from the path, typical imagery in Deuteronomic and prophetic literature for idolatry.[93] As Longman notes regarding Folly (Prov 9:13–18),

> She is best understood as a metaphor for all the false gods and goddesses that provided such a tremendous illicit attraction to Israelites. In a word, she represents the idols, perhaps no one specific idol, but any false god that lured the hearts of the Israelites. Among the ones that we know pulled the hearts of the Israelites are Marduk, Asherah, Anat, Ishtar, and perhaps most notoriously Baal. Thus, in the same way that personification gives wisdom a theological dimension, so also folly is more than simply a mistaken way to act or speak. They represent diametrically opposed relationships with the divine and alternative worldviews.[94]

If Longman is correct that "Folly" is a metaphorical representation of the gods and ways of the nations, it would naturally follow that Wisdom is the inverse parallel, representing God and his ways.

Furthermore, Jeremiah expresses the Deuteronomic idea in a personal manner, very similar to Prov 1:28, "You will call on me … and I will hear you. You will seek (בקש) me and find (מצא) me when you seek (דרש) with all your heart. I will be found (מצא) by you declares Yhwh" (Jer 29:12–14). This is a positive version of Wisdom's pronouncement, explicitly identifying Yhwh as the one who will be sought and found. In a similar tone as Wisdom, the prophet in Hos 5:6 states, "They will go to seek (בקש) Yhwh and they will not find (מצא); he has withdrawn from them." This is because, as Hosea rebukes, "they do not know Yhwh" since their "deeds will not permit them" and a "spirit of prostitution is within them" (Hos 5:4). Interestingly, several verses later, Hosea says of Yhwh, "I will go, I will return to my place when they … seek (בקש) my face, in their distress they seek (שחר) me" (Hos 5:15).[95] This seems to be a reversal of both Hos 5:6 and Prov 1:28. While Hosea envisions a merciful restoration, Proverbs sees only the righteous judgment of those who have rejected Wisdom/Yhwh. For Wisdom, there are apparently two, diametrically opposed paths.[96] There are those who listen and those who do not (Prov 1:23–

---

[93] Perdue remarks about metaphors, "For the sages, metaphors are ambiguous, since they are capable of having a surplus of meaning that rejects concrete, simple, and unilateral understanding. This variety of significations means that metaphors by nature reject any one-dimensional interpretation" (Leo G. Perdue, *Wisdom Literature: A Theological History* (Louisville: Westminster John Knox, 2007), 11).

[94] Longman, *Proverbs*, 59.

[95] Cf. Fox, *Proverbs 1–9*, 102.

[96] This is not to imply a fixity of character as Barton seems to imply. As Stewart elaborates, Proverbs teaches that "formation is a process that does not end" (John Barton, *Understanding Old Testament Ethics: Approaches and Explorations* (Louisville: Westminster John Knox, 2003), 67; Stewart, *Poetic Ethics in Proverbs*, 2–3). The fixed perspective here in Prov 1:28 simply emphasizes the end of the foolish path. Those who commit their way to folly cannot claim grace after judgement has been issued. In many ways, the trouble or blessing

24, 33). However, if Wisdom's pronouncement is meant to be rhetorically persuasive, then there is a sense of hope.[97] Likewise, Hosea's judgment and restoration are targeted at the nation as a whole while Wisdom and the father seem to have the individual in focus. The difference of perspective provides both hope for the naïve to seek and find the way of Wisdom but also a warning for failing to do so. This message is strengthened later in Lesson 15, "Blessed is the one who listens to me ... for the one finding (מצא) me, finds life ... but the one missing me, harms his soul" (Prov 8:34–36). In other words, some will seek (Prov 2:4, 8:17) and find (2:5, 3:13, 8:9, 35) but many will not and be lost.

In the following verse, Wisdom explains that those who refused to listen will not find her because, "They hated knowledge and did not choose the fear of Yhwh" (1:29; cf. Judg 10:14). Regarding the volitional aspect, Ansberry and Stewart criticized the so-called "Socratic principle" which presumes "no one does wrong willingly and that, accordingly, lack of knowledge is the fundamental cause of vice." In other words, "Unethical behavior is not simply the product of ignorance."[98] The phrase "fear of Yhwh" only occurs five times in Prov 1–9 (1:7, 1:29, 2:5, 8:13, 9:10).[99] In each, the phrase is associated with "knowledge" (דעת). Twice this knowledge is of God (אלהים) or the Holy one (קדשים), implying an intimate, relational knowledge.[100] By implication, Prov 1:7 and 1:29 could be read as though "knowledge" were an elided form for "knowledge of God/Holy one."

1:7	*Fear of Yhwh* is the beginning of *knowledge* [of God], fools despise wisdom and *musar*.
1:29	They hate *knowledge* [of God] and do not choose *fear of Yhwh*.
2:5	You will understand *fear of Yhwh* and *knowledge of God* you will find
8:12b-13a	I find *knowledge* and discretion. *Fear of Yhwh* is hating evil, pride, arrogance, the way of evil, and a perverse mouth I hate[101]

experienced is the natural results of either walking in the way of God with God or rejecting him and his way.

[97] See Lesson 15.

[98] Christopher B. Ansberry, "What Does Jerusalem Have to Do with Athens? The Moral Vision of the Book of Proverbs and Aristotle's Nicomachean Ethics," *HS* 51 (2010): 162; Stewart, *Poetic Ethics in Proverbs*, 7.

[99] Loader believes this is "the oldest description in the Bible and even in the whole semitic world of religion as such." Likewise, he notes that Prov 1:7 indicates, "The principal authority (ראשית) is God himself. The enterprise of wisdom is, therefore, religious" (Loader, *Proverbs 1–9*, 63).

[100] See Fox, *Proverbs 1–9*, 111–13.

[101] In Prov 8:12, Wisdom declares, "I am Wisdom, I dwell with prudence and knowledge; I find discretion." While the "fear of Yhwh" is not directly paralleled with "knowledge," it is closely associated with the person and nature of Wisdom who embodies these vital traits.

9:10	The beginning of wisdom is *fear of Yhwh* and *knowledge of the Holy One* is insight

In the one instance this does not work directly (Prov 8:13), the passage parallels "fear of Yhwh" with "hatred of evil." While it may be an inverse of Prov 1:29, Ps 97:10 provides an instructive parallel, "The one who loves Yhwh hates evil."[102] Thus, it can be presumed that a polar opposite is intended to underly "hatred of evil" in Prov 8. As mentioned previously, a key covenantal phrase was to "love Yhwh" with all one's heart (Deut 6:5, 7:9, 10:12, 11:1, 13, 22, 13:4, 19:9, 30:6, 16, 20). Along with this, Deuteronomy mentions that Yhwh initiated this cycle by loving his people, indicating the imitative and reciprocal nature of this covenantal love (Deut 7:9, 10:15, 23:6). In other words, just as Yhwh loved them, so they were to love him. Furthermore, the prophet Isaiah, in a fascinating use of the phrase, claims of the coming messianic figure, "The Spirit of Yhwh will come upon him, the Spirit of Wisdom and Insight, the Spirit of Counsel and Power, the Spirit of Knowledge and Fear of Yhwh" (Isa 11:2). The verse appears to create a string of appositional clauses further explaining the "Spirit of Yhwh."[103] With the presence of the Spirit, there are a number of identifiable results, representative of God's own nature and actions. This implication is further strengthened by Isaiah's claim that this messianic figure will judge properly and righteously (Isa 11:3–5; cf. Gen 18:25; Judg 11:27).[104] At the heart of Prov 1–9's conceptual framework, "fear of Yhwh" is the subtle complementary parallel to "knowledge of God" and "love of Yhwh." The father and Wisdom are instructing the son in a deeply theological pathway, one inextricably intertwined with Yhwh and reflecting his ways.

Additionally, in the broader book of Proverbs, the phrase "fear of Yhwh" is often associated with life or its loss (Prov 1:29, 9:10, 10:27, 14:27, 19:23, 22:4, 23:17). The fear of Yhwh, though limited in usage within the HB,[105] finds a curious occurrence in Ps 34:11–14, "Come, sons, listen to me; I

---

[102] Tate sees a connection in this passage between the Deuteronomic and Wisdom traditions. In this case, the emphasis is on the kingship of Yhwh and those in proper worship through covenant fidelity (Marvin E. Tate, *Psalms 51–100*, WBC 20 (Waco: Word Books, 2000), 519–21).

[103] Childs comments, "The coming ruler is equipped with the spirit of knowledge and the fear of Yahweh. The knowledge of God (*da'at*) is the essence of the right relationship of a creature to its creator (Hos. 2:22[20]; 4:1). It is based on love and devotion that is able to recognize the works of God in the world, constant with his own glory and the welfare of humanity. The fear of the Lord expresses both the beginning and end of life, and issues in reverence and worship" (Brevard S. Childs, *Isaiah: A Commentary*, OTL (Louisville: Westminster John Knox, 2001), 102–3).

[104] For a few example passages that explicitly mention God as judge: "God is a righteous judge" (Ps 7:11), "He establishes his throne for justice, and he judges the world in righteousness, he judges the peoples in uprightness" (Ps 9:8–9), "the fear of Yhwh is pure, standing forever, the justice of Yhwh is true and together righteous" (Ps 19:9), "the heavens declare his righteousness for God is indeed a judge" (Ps 50:6), "you judge the peoples with uprightness and lead the peoples of the earth" (Ps 67:5).

[105] The nominal phrase "fear of Yhwh" (יראת יהוה) occurs twenty-two times (Isa 11:1, 3, 33:6; Ps 19:10, 34:12, 111:10; Prov 1:7, 29, 2:5, 8:13, 9:10, 10:27, 14:26, 27, 15:16, 33, 16:6, 19:23,

will teach you the fear of Yhwh. Who is the man delighting in life, loving days ... turn (סור) from evil and do good."[106] The first line in Ps 34:11 parallels Prov 5:7, 7:24, and 8:32. The rest highlights the relationship between fear of Yhwh and life. It is clear the biblical implications for fear of Yhwh are more than just mundane piety.[107] It evokes a perpetual covenantal relationship with Yhwh that results in life.[108] In Prov 1:29, then, the proverbial father and Wisdom teach the son that rejecting Wisdom and her words is equivalent to "hating knowledge" and rejecting "fear of Yhwh."[109] Such a lesson emphasizes the ambiguity between Wisdom and Yhwh, that is, who is the primary figure and example.[110] It seems that following or rejecting one is akin to following or rejecting the other, true also in the ambiguous overlap between the father and Wisdom.

Near the end of Wisdom's warning, a metaphor is presented, "They will eat from the fruit of their ways" (Prov 1:31). The metaphor is a recognizable agricultural picture linked to the pathway metaphor. While at times eating the fruit of something is literal, there is almost always an implication or a metaphor intended. Here, it is probable that the metaphor was intended to evoke the Garden scene when Adam and Eve ate fruit which determined the "way" they were choosing (Gen 3:6). As discussed in Lesson 4, the two trees were paradigmatic of the wise and foolish or righteous and wicked (cf. Prov 3:18).[111] Their way was to abandon God's way. In fact, their primary sin was a desire to be like God in an improper manner, to supplant him.[112] Rather than humility, obedience, and faithfulness, they refused to listen to God's single command. They could have chosen to eat from the tree of life, a path symbolizing harmony and relationship with God. Instead, they "hated knowledge and did not choose the fear of Yhwh." Later, in Jer 6:19, the

---

22:4, 23:17; 2 Chron 19:9). The verbal phrase "to fear Yhwh" (ירא יהוה) occurs forty-eight times (Exod 9:30, 14:31; Deut 6:2, 13, 24, 8:6, 10:12, 20, 13:5, 14:23, 17:19, 28:58, 31:12, 13; Josh 4:24, 24:14; 1 Sam 12:14, 18, 24; 2 Sam 6:9; 1 Kgs 18:3, 12; 2 Kgs 4:1, 17:25, 28, 32, 33, 34, 36, 39, 41; Isa 59:19; Jer 5:22, 24, 26:19; Hos 10:3; Jon 1:16; Hag 1:12; Mal 3:5; Ps 33:8, 34:10, 96:4, 102:16, 112:1; Job 1:9; Prov 3:7, 24:21; 1 Chron 16:25). Additionally, the nominal or verbal phrase with "God" substituted occurs thirty-three times (Gen 20:11, 22:12, 42:18; Exod 1:17, 21, 18:21; Lev 19:14, 32, 25:17, 36, 43; Deut 4:10, 25:18; 2 Sam 23:3; Ps 55:19, 66:16, 67:7, 89:7; Job 1:1, 8, 2:3, 4:6, 15:4; Eccl 3:14, 5:7, 7:18, 8:12, 13, 12:13; Neh 5:9, 15, 7:22; 2 Chron 26:5).

[106] Tanner et al. rightly understand the close connection this psalm has with Prov 1–9. They define "fear of Yhwh" as, "The proper attitude of one with whom God has established a right relationship. ... Those who gathered for worship did so not only to experience the divine presence and blessings, but to be schooled by elders and fellow community members." Furthermore, they see a strong connection with the character of God conveyed in the psalm. See Nancy L. DeClaissé-Walford, Rolf A. Jacobson, and Beth LaNeel Tanner, *The Book of Psalms*, NICOT (Grand Rapids: Eerdmans, 2014), 326–27; Brown, "Come, O Children," 85–102.

[107] See Longman, *The Fear of the Lord Is Wisdom*, 12–20.

[108] DeClaissé-Walford, Jacobson, and Tanner, *Book of Psalms*, 327.

[109] Trible, "Wisdom Builds a Poem," 515; William McKane, *Proverbs: A New Approach*, OTL (London: SCM, 1970), 275.

[110] See Moss, "Wisdom as Parental Teaching in Proverbs 1–9," 433.

[111] See Tova Forti, "The Polarity of Wisdom and Fear of God in the Eden Narrative and in the Book of Proverbs," *BN* 149 (2011): 45–57.

[112] O'Dowd, *The Wisdom of Torah*, 15; Forti, "The Polarity of Wisdom and Fear of God in the Eden Narrative and in the Book of Proverbs," 55.

prophet speaks of coming judgment for Israel due to their rejection of God's way, "Ask for the ancient path... where is the good way and walk in it ... but they said 'We will not walk. ... I am bringing disaster to this people, the fruit of their devices for ... they rejected (מאס) my *torah*." In fact, many of the indictments by Jeremiah in this section are reminiscent of Prov 1–9, condemning the entirety of the nation, "They do not know the way of Yhwh, the justice of their God" (Jer 5:4). The phrasing and conceptual connections reflect the prophets' similar vision and intention. Although Jeremiah speaks of Yhwh's rejection directly, Lesson 1 in Proverbs utilizes the metaphorical embodiment of Wisdom to convey the danger of abandoning the way of Yhwh.

Conclusion: Wisdom's blessing (1:33)

Finally, the father ends the lesson with Wisdom's abrupt but positive conclusion. If the son will adhere to "my words," implicitly also the father's, he will "dwell securely" (Prov 1:33). This claim, from a theological perspective, is only true and valuable if it is rooted in one who can assure its validity.[113] Otherwise, it is a meaningless claim. While the father can convey a promise of God, he cannot guarantee such a claim. Wisdom is presented as the source of this particular promise to the son which means it must signify a greater source of blessing, namely Yhwh himself. The idea of "dwelling secure" originates in the Torah as a blessing and promise from God to those who would walk in his way. Moses provides Israel with the words of Yhwh, "You shall do my statutes and my justice you shall guard and you shall do them and you will dwell *securely* on the land" (Lev 25:18; cf. 26:5; Deut 12:10, 33:12, 28; Prov 2:21).[114] With the installment of Solomon, the author of Kings describes the fulfillment of God's promises for Israel in the land.[115] In 1 Kgs 4:20–5:5, it mentions that Judah and Israel were "as many as the sand of the sea ... Solomon ruled over all the kingdoms from the River, the land of the Philistines, and until Egypt. ... He had peace on all sides around. And Judah

---

[113] Lang misses the depth of this point by placing the entirety of the teaching within pedagogical tradition, "The wisdom communicated by teachers does not originate in them nor is it a product of their brilliance. It is the tradition, and nothing else, that is being passed from teacher to student. ... The assertion [Prov 1:33] does not imply that the teacher is an all-powerful individual, but sees him as one who communicates tradition" (Lang, *Wisdom and the Book of Proverbs*, 36–37). Such a stunted claim creates an infinite regression to which one must ask from whence does the tradition originate?

[114] The promise of blessing, particularly security, was a direct result of Israel's covenantal fidelity with Yhwh. As Hartley and Milgrom observe, the combination of blessings between Lev 25 and 26 describe financial, military, and social *shalom*. Such *shalom* is only promised to those who "walk" (26:3) in the way of Yhwh. See John E. Hartley, *Leviticus*, WBC 4 (Dallas: Word Books, 1992), 462; Jacob Milgrom, ed., *Leviticus 23–27: A New Translation with Introduction and Commentary*, AB 3B (New York: Doubleday, 2001), 179–80, 293–94.

[115] Marvin A. Sweeney, *I & II Kings: A Commentary*, OTL (Louisville: Westminster John Knox, 2007), 9798; Walter Brueggemann, *1 & 2 Kings*, SHBC (Macon: Smyth & Helwys, 2000), 63.

and Israel dwelt *securely*" (cf. Gen 15:18, 22:17; Exod 23:31; Lev 26:6; Deut 12:10, 33:28; Josh 1:4).[116] Dwelling securely was a blessing directly related to covenant fidelity and God's promises, which necessitated listening to the word of Yhwh and rejecting the ways and gods of the nations. As the positive inclusio to this lesson, listening to Wisdom (Prov 1:33) is equated with listening to the father's *musar* and not abandoning the mother's *torah*,[117] which emphasizes the metaphorical and conceptual pathway or trajectory for the son to walk. In other words, following after one is following both.

Conclusion

In Lesson 1, both the proverbial father and Wisdom present a call and a warning. Their overlap in this regard points to their shared role as wise teachers, who are both worthy examples. Their unified call, then, is for the son to conform to the ancient and divine way, one that warns the son against following sinners in their aberrations. Such aberrations are in reality a relational break and rejection of the father and of Wisdom. As it has been argued, if Yhwh is envisioned and more than just wise advice is being given,[118] then rejecting the father and Wisdom is ultimately equivalent to rejecting the path of Yhwh, or ceasing to follow after him and imitate his ways. As Longman notes, the rejection of Wisdom likely implied following after and becoming like the nations and their gods, who were not gods at all (cf. Ps 115:8, 135:18; Isa 37:19; Jer 16:20; Hos 8:4).[119] Abandoning God's way is akin to destruction, death, and foolishness. It is essential, then, to love knowledge and choose the fear of Yhwh in order to attain wisdom, life, and security. All of these blessings are inherent to following the proper path of God. So, as the father teaches in this lesson, the son ought to emulate the proverbial father and Wisdom, which necessitates not imitating the way of sinners. In doing so, he will grow and move along the wisdom trajectory toward Yhwh. While Yhwh is only indirectly alluded to in this first lesson, Lessons 2–5 bring him into sharp focus.

---

[116] Christensen claims Deut 33:26–29 is a central, thematic passage for Deut, emphasizing the security of Israel due to the kingship, salvation, and incomparability of their God Yhwh. See Paul House, *1, 2 Kings*, NAC (Nashville: B&H, 1995), 118–20; Duane L. Christensen, *Deuteronomy 21:10 - 34:12*, WBC 6B (Nashville: Nelson, 2002), 833–35, 858–61.

[117] Moss, "Wisdom as Parental Teaching in Proverbs 1–9," 426.

[118] Moss, "Wisdom as Parental Teaching in Proverbs 1–9," 430.

[119] Cf. Longman, *Proverbs*, 59.

LESSON 2

Analysis of Proverbs 2:1–22
"Seek Yhwh as Wisdom"

After a rather dire and demoralizing warning in Lesson 1, the second lesson serves the wisdom program by giving the first lengthy, positive instruction and by describing the inherent benefits of seeking wisdom. By walking in the path of Yhwh, the wise son will not only find safety (Prov 2:21; cf. 1:33) but will grow in his knowledge of God (2:5). As the chiastic parallel to Lesson 14, this lesson teaches that the son must seek Yhwh through Wisdom. This divine path, however, is neither linear nor lonely. On it, there are many positive examples – "righteous," "good," "upright," and "blameless" – those who have also sought the wisdom of God and are, consequently, characterized by his ways. These travelers are drawn into the wisdom spiral of both knowing and imitating Yhwh. Likewise, by walking in ways that reflect Yhwh and positive examples, the son will be delivered from the dangers on the bad path, which is represented by seven models of foolishness and the seductive *zarah*.

Structure of Lesson 2

Scholars have long noted the unique 22–verse structure of Prov 2, illuminating the potential acrostic poetic intent. [1] Although an acrostic structure is possible, there is not a clear indicator.[2] In his argument for the acrostic, Schipper calls this chapter the "table of contents" of the "didactic program."[3] Structurally this second lesson contains three main movements

---

[1] See Murphy, *Proverbs*, 14; P. Skehan, *Studies in Israelite Poetry and Wisdom*, CBQMS 1 (Washington, DC: Catholic Biblical Association of America, 1971), 9–16; L. S. Hermann, *Die Sprüche Salomos*, 2nd ed. (Munich: Beck, 1899), 313.

[2] Longman doubts the acrostic while Waltke says it simply implies "completeness." See Longman, *Proverbs*, 117; Waltke, *Proverbs (1–15)*, 216.

[3] Schipper, *Proverbs 1–15*, 47–49, 52–53, 102–3. In his view, the chapter can be broken into six structural strophes. The first three begin with א (Prov 2:[1], 5, 9) and the last three with

with subordinated sections. It begins with the typical "my son" phrase (Prov 2:1). While most other lessons use an imperative or hortatory call, this lesson departs from that pattern with a conditional "if" (אם).[4] While literarily and thematically distinct from Lesson 1, it does echo the secondary occurrence of "my son" in its conditional tone, "My son, if sinners persuade you" (Prov 1:10). The subtle echo may signal the supervening role of Prov 1:8–10 for this lesson and perhaps the other lessons of Prov 1–9. Conditionals appear three times (Prov 2:1, 3, 4) in the first call section (2:1–4). These conditionals are complemented by the resultative adverbs "then" (אז) in two apodoses (Prov 2:5, 9), which both begin with the same phrase "then you will understand" (אז תבין). These adverbs are further complemented with the causal, motive particles "for" (כי) in two verses (Prov 2:6, 10),[5] which also begin with parallel, complementary phrases: "for Yhwh will give Wisdom" (כי־יהוה יתן חכמה) and "for Wisdom will enter" (כי־תבוא חכמה). The second apodosis (Prov 2:9–19) also contains two symmetrical sub-sections (2:12–15, 16–19), which both begin with the phrase "to deliver you" (לְהַצִּילְךָ). Then, in Prov 2:20, the causal preposition "in order that" (למען) is used to complement both the conditionals and resultative adverbs with the logical sense, "if … then … then … in order that." These final consequential verses (Prov 2:20–22) provide the summation of the two paths described by the father in the preceding verses.

Scholars have rightly observed six structural divisions for the lesson as Prov 2:1–4, 5–8, 9–11, 12–15, 16–19, 20–22, identifying the number of verses per unit as 4, 4, 3, 4, 4, 3.[6] This structure creates a noticeable symmetry.[7] However, while Prov 2:20–22 is the concluding three-verse unit structurally, the content within it functions as a summary of the apodoses (2:5–19), both for the good path and the bad path. Thus, though structurally separated, the verses of Prov 2:20–22 are subsumed under their respective thematic units in this analysis. In terms of thematic content, there is the good path (Prov 2:5–11, 20–21) and the bad path (2:12–19, 22). Both thematic units contain nine verses, which creates symmetry for the centralizing two-paths imagery.

ל (2:12, 16, 20). However, the first strophe only works if בְּנִי is an addition originally beginning with אם. Regardless, the chapter is certainly highly structured and balanced.

[4] Perdue notes the similarity this construction has with "Israelite and Jewish legal codes," by which he means Torah. See Leo G. Perdue, *Proverbs*, IBC (Louisville: John Knox, 2000), 88; Whybray, *Composition of the Book of Proverbs*, 15; McKane, *Proverbs*, 280.

[5] Whybray, *Composition of the Book of Proverbs*, 16.

[6] See Schipper, *Proverbs 1–15*, 102–3; Murphy, *Proverbs*, 14; Stuart Weeks, *Instruction and Imagery in Proverbs 1–9* (New York: Oxford University Press, 2007), 61.

[7] Waltke believes the extreme level of structure and balance of this chapter matches "the ordered, divine world the encomium represents" (Waltke, *Proverbs (1–15)*, 217).

I. The Father's Call to Seek Wisdom (2:1–4)
II. The Wise Find the Knowledge of God (2:5–8)
   a. The Result of Seeking (2:5)
   b. The Source of Wisdom (2:6–8)
III. The Two Paths (2:9–22)
   a. Walking on the Good Path (2:9–11, 20–21)
   b. Deliverance from the Bad Path (2:12–19, 22)

The initial section gives the conditional call from the father (Prov 2:1–4). Of utmost importance, the teacher provides the primary result and blessing for adhering to his call in the second section (Prov 2:5–8), namely that the son "find the knowledge of God" (2:5). God is not only the gift of seeking wisdom but the source of all wisdom and blessing (Prov 2:6–8; cf. Job 28:12, 20, 23, 28).[8] In the third thematic section (Prov 2:9–22), the lesson highlights the two-paths metaphor, more fully developed from Lesson 1.[9] Between Prov 2:7–20, there are a variety of pathway terms that appear sixteen times. The third section complements the second by giving further explanation and expansion for the protective benefits on the good path (Prov 2:9–11). Additionally, the bad path is characterized as something that God and Wisdom will deliver the wise son from if he responds rightly. On the bad path, there are two structural units (Prov 2:12–15, 16–19), which emphasize the harmful, deceptive, and deadly ways of those on this path. The two bad path units focus on the bad group – likely reflecting the sinners of Lesson 1 – and the "foreign woman." Together the bad group and the "foreigner" represent complementary aspects of the bad path. Finally, the lesson concludes with the consequences of the two paths (Prov 2:20–21, 22). The son will either reflect the life and blessing of the wise or the death and destruction of the wicked. Of course, the hope and

---

[8] Perdue believes Prov 2:6–8 is the primary purpose of this instruction, appealing to the divine versus mundane origins of wisdom (Perdue, *Proverbs*, 89). If mere wisdom were the purpose rather than proper relation to Yhwh, then this presumption would work. Yet, building on Lesson 1 and the broader network of the seek/find metaphor it is preferable to understand finding the knowledge of God as primary. Wisdom is a consequential and requisite aspect of knowing and reflecting Yhwh.

[9] Keefer comments, "As Proverbs 1–2 clarifies, 'ways' functions as a metaphor that represents the collective behaviours of persons. ... One is associated with the Lord and wisdom, trodden by good characters and leading to life, the other associates with folly and its character types, ending in death. ... The way constitutes the metaphorical substructure of Proverbs 1–9. And what are its main characteristics? According to Proverbs, all individual ways, which stand for behaviours embodied in characters, fall onto either the way of wisdom or folly and result in either life or death. For in addition to consolidating the two groups of characters in Proverbs, the ways are, in turn, even defined by them – 'the path of the righteous' and 'way of the wicked'" (Keefer, *Proverbs 1–9 as an Introduction to the Book of Proverbs*, 62–63).

expectation from the father is that the son will follow him in knowing and walking with Yhwh on the good path.

The Father's Call to Seek Wisdom (2:1–4)

The second lesson (Prov 2:1–22) for the son continues several ideas from the first, which help structure this lesson. Right away, the teacher implores the son in Prov 2:1–4 to pursue his wise and righteous way, couched in the language of "words," "command," and "wisdom." He uses metaphorical terms such as "ear" and "heart." It is likely the "ear" implies external obedience, a double entendre for hearing and obeying. The heart represents the conceptual seat of human will and desire.[10] The son's adoption and reflection of the teacher's instruction were to be total, both externally and internally. This idea coheres with the lament of Isa 29:13, "This people draws near with its mouth and honors me with its lips but its heart is far from me. Their fear of me is a commandment taught by men."[11] The teacher did not want to incidentally condemn the student to fallacious, hypocritical practices separated from a proper relationship and inner orientation to God (cf. Deut 10:16, 30:6).[12]

As discussed in Lesson 1, the topic of "seeking" is quite central to the whole program of Prov 1–9. Parallels arise in Prov 1:28, 2:4, 3:14–15, 8:10–11, 19, 32–36 (Lessons 1, 2, 4, 14, 15). Wisdom commends the son to seek her in Lessons 1 and 14.[13] Lesson 4 commends the son to seek Wisdom but in an impersonal poem. Lesson 15 does not clarify who the speaker is in Prov 8:32–36, but likely overlays Wisdom with the father and God, the ultimate teacher. For Lesson 2, the teacher provides a conditional statement that serves as a

---

[10] In a discussion about ANE and Egyptian philosophy, Dru Johnson briefly mentions the role of human organs as the "seat of logic and volition," found also throughout the HB and Israelite thought. See Dru Johnson, *Biblical Philosophy: A Hebraic Approach to the Old and New Testaments* (Cambridge: Cambridge University Press, 2021), 65; Aubrey R. Johnson, *The Vitality of the Individual in the Thought of Ancient Israel*, 2nd ed. (Cardiff: University of Wales Press, 1964), 75–81; Fox, *Proverbs 1–9*, 109; Waltke, *Proverbs (1–15)*, 90–92.

[11] Whybray notes the correspondence between Isa 29 and Prov 1–9. However, he believes this sparked an attempt "to reconcile the wisdom tradition with the will of God." While right to note the overlap, he unnecessarily drives a wedge between the prophetic and wisdom genres, largely due to his presupposition that Israelite wisdom was derived from secular ANE wisdom that later became theological. See R. N. Whybray, *The Book of Proverbs* (New York: Cambridge University Press, 1972), 7–10.

[12] Oswalt says of Isa 29:13, "The charge is one of hypocritical religion. Because the prophets have not been faithful to declare God's word, 'this people' has lapsed into the manipulative style of religion typical of paganism. This concern that Israel's religion be one involving the very seat of the personality, the heart, is typical of the Bible. Thus the 'fear of the Lord' is a way of life which involves an accurate understanding of who God is and a corresponding ordering of one's affairs. To speak of reducing this to a set of 'do's' and 'don'ts' is to move one's faith from the center to the periphery of life." In this way, then, the proverbial father teaches the same message as Isaiah. See Oswalt, *The Book of Isaiah*, 532.

[13] McKane notes the personified sense of "call" and "seek" for "insight" and "understanding" which parallels Wisdom in 1:20–33 (McKane, *Proverbs*, 282).

rhetorical call to action.[14] The conditional call is twofold. In Prov 2:1–2, the son is to "receive my words … treasure my *mitsvah* … make your ear consider wisdom … turn your heart to understanding." For Prov 2:3–4, the conditional call is for the son to "call out for insight … cry out for understanding … seek her like silver and search for her as treasure." Although these appear as a simple, undifferentiated chain, Prov 2:5 illuminates the structure or purpose of the preceding verses. The verbs "understand" and "find" control the two lines of Prov 2:5. These terms are the logical result of the conditional calls in Prov 2:1–4. The line Prov 2:5a parallels 2:1–2 with the refrain to receive the father's words. By doing so, the son will attain understanding (2:5a). The second line (2:5b) parallels Prov 2:3–4 with the call to seek. By seeking, the son will find, namely the knowledge of God.

The Wise Find the Knowledge of God (2:5–8)

The Result of Seeking (2:5)

The father structurally ties the conditionals in Prov 2:1–4 to their results in 2:5. If the son listens to the father's words, he will understand the "fear of Yhwh" (Prov 2:5a).[15] If he seeks wisdom, he will find the "knowledge of God" (Prov 2:5b). At the theological center, the phrase "knowledge of God" (דַעַת אֱלֹהִים) in Prov 2:5b is an essential instruction for the son's growth in true wisdom, though it only appears twice elsewhere in the HB (Hos 4:1, 6:6).[16] The phrase does, however, parallel a couple elsewhere in Proverbs, which help illuminate Prov 2:5.

To better understand Prov 2:5, several parallels will illuminate the verse and its phrases. Likewise, there is an inherent syntactical logic and an interesting textual history, which serve to identify the father's intent as well. In brief, the verse serves as the theological center for the whole lesson, giving the primary benefit of traversing the wise path. By walking on the wise path, the son will ultimately join himself to Yhwh, since he is its primary source and the paragon of the wise.

---

[14] Fox rightly observes that the teacher's tone or approach is not as militant as some have presumed ancient education to be. Rather, it is persuasive and perceptive. Regarding the conditionals, Waltke notes the intent is hortatory or imperatival. See Michael V. Fox, "The Pedagogy of Proverbs 2," *JBL* 113.2 (1994): 233; Lorenz Dürr, *Das Erziehungswesen im Alten Testament und im antiken Orient*, MVAG (Leipzig: J. C. Hinrichs, 1932), 114–15; Waltke, *Proverbs (1–15)*, 219.

[15] Newsom mentions, "Allegiance precedes understanding, not the other way around." While proper ordering is present in this lesson, the sense of "allegiance" may be too impersonal for this context since the next line invokes knowing God. See Carol A. Newsom, "Woman and the Discourse of Patriarchal Wisdom: A Study of Proverbs 1–9," in *Gender and Difference in Ancient Israel*, ed. Peggy L. Day (Minneapolis: Fortress, 1989), 147.

[16] For a more detailed analysis, see Excursus: Hosea and the Knowledge of God. Cf. Murphy, *Proverbs*, 15.

Regarding this central verse, there is a network of phrases in Proverbs that help illuminate the phrase "knowledge of God" (2:5b).

Prov 2:5	אָז תָּבִין יִרְאַת יְהוָה וְדַעַת אֱלֹהִים תִּמְצָא	then you will understand the fear of Yhwh and you will find the *knowledge of God*
Prov 9:10	תְּחִלַּת חָכְמָה יִרְאַת יְהוָה וְדַעַת קְדֹשִׁים בִּינָה	the beginning of wisdom is the fear of Yhwh and the *knowledge of the Holy One* is insight
Prov 30:3	וְלֹא־לָמַדְתִּי חָכְמָה וְדַעַת קְדֹשִׁים אֵדָע	and I have not learned wisdom nor do I know the *knowledge of the Holy One*

In Prov 9:10, the phrase "knowledge of the Holy" is instructively paralleled with "fear of Yhwh," as well.[17] As Keefer notes,

> The holiness of the people is also envisioned, binding the health of the group to laws and to its members' imitation of the Lord (Lev 19:9–18). Although the people's holiness is not prominently observed in Proverbs, this concept perforates the book's moral fabric with references to the Lord as 'the Holy one' (Prov 9:10; 30:3) and becomes a possible aim in view of efforts to align wisdom with *imitatio Dei*.[18]

The phrase "knowledge of the Holy" appears to refer to Yhwh through the logical coordination of the phrases in these verses. In addition, the parallel within Prov 2:5 and 9:10 indicates it is referring to Yhwh (דַעַת אֱלֹהִים / דַעַת קְדֹשִׁים).[19] However, the use of קְדֹשִׁים is uncommon, only occurring twice outside of Proverbs with God as the referent (Josh 24:19; Hos 12:1). As observed, Hosea 12:1 and Josh 24:19 parallel "God" with the plural term קְדֹשִׁים.[20]

---

[17] For further analysis of the imitative foundations for this phrase, see Excursus: Leviticus and the Holiness of God. Cf. Waltke, *Proverbs (1–15)*, 441.

[18] Arthur J. Keefer, *The Book of Proverbs and Virtue Ethics: Integrating the Biblical and Philosophical Traditions* (Cambridge: Cambridge University Press, 2021), 157.

[19] Waltke, *Proverbs*, 428.

[20] Some scholars, such as Dearman, Andersen, Freedman, and Nogalski, believe Hos 12:1 means "holy ones" with God as the faithful one. However, it seems quite logical to see this very tight syntactical unit with a single subject, Judah. While Judah is soon after given a warning, the *niphal* of the verb "faithful" often means "made firm" or "established" which would be semantically antithetical to the previous verb in this verse (BDB). Yet, this would create an even closer syntactical connection between the lines. He walks with God and is established with the Holy One. So, although Hos 11:9 uses the sg. in parallel with God, it seems this instance too should be paralleled with God. See J. Andrew Dearman, *The Book of Hosea*, NICOT (Grand Rapids: Eerdmans, 2010), 295; Francis I. Andersen and David Noel Freedman, eds., *Hosea: A New Translation with Introduction and Commentary*, AB 24 (Garden City: Doubleday, 1980), 603; James Nogalski, *The Book of the Twelve: Hosea--Jonah*, SHBC 18a (Macon, GA: Smyth & Helwys, 2011), 166.

Hos 12:1	וִיהוּדָה עֹד רָד עִם־אֵל וְעִם־קְדוֹשִׁים נֶאֱמָן	And Judah walks with God and he is faithful with *the Holy One*
Josh 24:19	לֹא תוּכְלוּ לַעֲבֹד אֶת־יְהוָה כִּי־אֱלֹהִים קְדֹשִׁים הוּא אֵל־ קַנּוֹא הוּא	You are not able to serve Yhwh for he is *a holy God*, he is a jealous God

As these examples illuminate, it is likely that the plural form *qedoshim* (קְדֹשִׁים) mimics the plural form for "God" (אֱלֹהִים), a form common throughout the HB.[21] This implies that the substantival use of the adjective is an important though surprisingly uncommon title for God.[22]

The phrase in Prov 9:10 is a verbless clause that not only parallels wisdom and insight,[23] a common overlap in Proverbs, but also uses a similar concept from Prov 1:7, "The fear of Yhwh is the beginning of knowledge" (יִרְאַת יְהוָה רֵאשִׁית דָּעַת). Although the words used for "beginning" in these two verses are different, there is a semantic overlap in meaning throughout the HB.[24] Putting these verses together helps to build a conceptual picture of what this knowledge might mean. Since Prov 1–9 is a distinct corpus,[25] Prov 1:7 and 9:10 likely serve as an inclusio to this section. These chapters set forth the building blocks of wisdom, which are not merely practical and anthropocentric but religious and theocentric.[26] At first glance, it may seem that Proverbs equivocates on the word "knowledge," which occurs thirteen times in the first

---

[21] Schmitt argues that the idea of an abstracted title "holy one" was not present until the Second Temple Period. Prior, Yhwh's holy character was always used as a "concrete modifier." If this were correct, it would simply mean that "holy" (קְדֹשִׁים) was shorthand for "holy God" (אֱלֹהִים קְדֹשִׁים) as seen in Josh 24:19. See John J. Schmitt, "The God of Israel and the Holy One," *HS* 24 (1983): 27–31.

[22] The phrase more commonly found in the HB uses the sg. "holy one of Israel" (קְדוֹשׁ יִשְׂרָאֵל), primarily found throughout Isaiah. Oswalt notes the phrase parallels a number of other phrases and characteristics of God. In his evaluation, Oswalt seems to touch on the imitative reflection of Yhwh as a fatherly teacher, commenting, "If one wishes to turn aside into crookedness, corruption and evil, it involves no less than a conscious rejection of God's teaching (Isa 5:24; 30:12; 48:17), and a rejection of God himself and his character (Isa 1:4). ... God intends to share his holy character with his followers. This means that we humans can be faithful as he is." Similarly, he says, "God's holiness is displayed in the righteousness of his children's lives. ... Isaiah mocks the whole idea of a holiness which does not bear the mark of God's character."

Goldingay makes many similar connections in Isaiah, "The powerful are the people who should have been exercising authority in the right way, exercising *mišpāṭ* and *ṣĕdāqâ* (cf. Isa 56:1). ...Yahweh has 'made himself holy' or manifested holiness (*qādaš* niphal). Holiness manifests itself in *mišpāṭ* and *ṣĕdāqâ*. There is thus a positive aspect to this manifestation of holiness; it means taking action on behalf of people who are abused." By this, it seems he makes a clear imitative connection between the active holiness, justice, and righteousness of God and the people, parallel with the instruction from the proverbial father.

See John N. Oswalt, *The Holy One of Israel: Studies in the Book of Isaiah* (Cambridge: James Clarke & Co., 2014), 41–58; John Goldingay, *The Theology of the Book of Isaiah* (Downers Grove: IVP, 2014), 101–5.

[23] For more discussion on 9:10, see Lesson 15.

[24] S. Rattray and J. Milgrom, "רֵאשִׁית," *TDOT* 13:269.

[25] Alastair Hunter, *Wisdom Literature* (SCM, 2006), 18.

[26] Longman, *Proverbs*, 100.

nine chapters.[27] In many places, "knowledge" appears to mean information, which if used wisely will produce good. However, it is likely since both wisdom and knowledge are equated with the "fear of Yhwh" that both terms are actually meant to be taken primarily as religious or theocentric concepts and only secondarily as practical or anthropocentric (cf. Exod 36:1–2).[28] This seems to be the case in Prov 30:3.[29] As discussed in Lesson 1, hating knowledge is parallel to rejecting the "fear of Yhwh" (Prov 1:29). Therefore, it is understood that the "fear of Yhwh" begins the journey of wisdom which simultaneously begins the process of knowing God, who is the telos of the wisdom pathway. Thus, as one grows in "fear of Yhwh" one also grows in wisdom and begins to know God, all of which are further developed along a relational and reflective pathway.

As the only other occurrences, Hos 4:1 and 6:6 use the phrase "knowledge of God" in similar contexts and for similar purposes as Prov 2:5.[30] For Hosea, the phrase is paralleled with "steadfast love" (חסד) twice and "faithfulness" (אמת) once.[31] Although Hosea does not parallel the phrase with "fear of Yhwh," the prophet does parallel the idea with common religious terms that typically imply a covenantal relationship with Yhwh. Furthermore, the phrase is given as an idiomatic phrase similar to "fear of Yhwh,"[32] which implies more than the mere words that comprise the phrase. Such an

---

[27] Prov 1:4, 7, 22, 29, 2:5, 6, 10, 3:20, 5:2, 8:9, 10, 12, 9:10.

[28] Gemser explains Zimmerli's anthropocentric view of wisdom literature and the thread of scholarship that followed. Yet, he does not follow Zimmerli's but Von Rad's religious view. Zimmerli was the dominant view until Von Rad's minor corrective which allowed Prov 1–9 to be considered theological. However, Von Rad believed theological wisdom to be rather late. Jenks provides a substantive argument that the theological aspect was not late but original. See Berend Gemser, "The Spiritual Structure of Biblical Aphoristic Wisdom: A Review of Recent Standpoints and Theories," in *Studies in Ancient Israelite Wisdom*, ed. James L. Crenshaw, The Library of Biblical Studies (New York: Ktav, 1976), 208–19; Gerhard von Rad, *Wisdom in Israel* (Nashville: Abingdon, 1972), 55; Alan W. Jenks, "Theological Presuppositions of Israel's Wisdom Literature," *HBT* 7.1 (1985): 43–75.

[29] Proverbs 30:3 is particularly challenging to translate since several options are viable. The LXX translates Prov 30:2–3, "I am more void of understanding than all men, and understanding of men is not in me; God has not taught me wisdom, and I have not known knowledge of the holy [one/ones/things]." The MT of Prov 30:3 could be read in a variety of ways, though: "I have not learned wisdom nor know knowledge of the Holy one;" "… nor know knowledge of holy things;" "Have I not learned wisdom that I shall know the Holy one?;" "I have not learned wisdom that I may truly know the Holy one;" "Oh that I had learned wisdom that I might know the Holy one;" or "I have not learned wisdom yet I shall know the Holy one." Whybray believes Agur is falsely confessing his ignorance of God, who he should know as the creator and covenant God of Israel. Longman follows Prov 30:1–3 in the MT and proposes that Agur's self-effacing statements are a sign of humility and his wisdom, or a sign of one on the proper path. Plöger follows Prov 30:4 of the MT that Agur is simply pointing to the inaccessibility of God. McKane follows the LXX and affirms the theocentric source of proper wisdom rather than wisdom taught by men. See Longman, *Proverbs*, 520–21; McKane, *Proverbs*, 643–47; Plöger, *Spruche Salomos (Proverbia)*, 358–59; Whybray, *Proverbs (1972)*, 407–9.

[30] Treier also points out that Prov 2 is replete with covenantal language, including commandments, righteousness, and loving-kindness, though several more words could be added. See Childs, *Isaiah: A Commentary*, 104; Daniel J. Treier, *Proverbs & Ecclesiastes*, Brazos Theological Commentary on the Bible (Grand Rapids: Brazos, 2011), 24.

[31] For further analysis of Hosea, see Excursus: Hosea and the Knowledge of God.

[32] Michael V. Fox, "The Pedagogy of Proverbs 2," *JBL* 113.2 (1994): 238.

implication gives more credence to interpreting "knowledge of God" as a functional unit, with significant connotations.[33] Within the context of Hosea, there is a strong emphasis on the relationality of knowing Yhwh rather than mere moralism. At the heart of Hosea's prophetic word, the marital metaphor emphasizes that the goal of the "betrothal" – in "righteousness," "justice," loving-kindness," and "faithfulness" – is that Israel "will know Yhwh" (Hos 2:19–20 [21–22]). This image not only illuminates the intended connection between faithfulness/loving-kindness and the "knowledge of God," but it further elicits the personal connotation underlying the phrase.[34] Since the knowledge of God is relational in Hosea, it is likely that Prov 2:5 also intends the son to know God, the telos of the wise path. As it will be further discussed for the good path section, the result of knowing God in Prov 2:5 is that the son will "understand righteousness and justice" (2:9), an illuminating parallel with Hosea.

The syntactical relationship within the phrase "knowledge of God" (דעת אלהים) is another important aspect. The LXX, Syr., and Vulg. read it as a construct (genitive). The strongest indicator of the relationship between "knowledge" and "God" is the parallelism with "fear of Yhwh" (Prov 2:5). In this latter phrase, the construct implies an objective genitive sense, "one who fears Yhwh."[35] If this is carried over to the next line, the objective genitive for the phrase *da'at elohim* (דעת אלהים) would imply "one who knows God."[36] Such a parallel would make the most sense, despite the Targum's altered reading. In Prov 2:5b, the Tg. translates, "And you will find knowledge *from before* God" (וידיעתא מן קדם אלהא תשכח). This reading initially seems quite odd; and, it certainly seems to imply a particular sense of the phrase. However, upon further investigation, the use of "before" (קדם) or "from before" (מן קדם) preceding "God" (אלהא) or "Yhwh" (ווי) is actually rather common in the Targumim. Though the translation practice covers many stock phrases, quite often it is the way "word of Yhwh" (דְּבַר־יְהוָה) is communicated, especially in the prophets (e.g., Hos 1:1). Such an addition to the Hebrew text has warranted some scholars to attribute this to the Tg. writers' interest in removing anthropomorphic language from God.[37] In an article addressing the use of קדם in the Targumim, Klein argues that this is actually not the case. He instead believes it is simply a stock way of communicating deference before a higher-ranking individual.[38] This phrase, though often used with respect to Yhwh, is

---

[33] Zoltán S Schwáb, "The Value of a Curious Translation: Revisiting Proverbs 2:5," *JBL* 133.4 (2014): 744.

[34] Dearman, *Book of Hosea*, 126–30, 196–97.

[35] Ronald J. Williams and John C. Beckman, *Williams' Hebrew Syntax*, 3rd ed. (Toronto: University of Toronto Press, 2007), 13.

[36] See Schwáb, "The Value of a Curious Translation," 744.

[37] Alexander Sperber, ed., *The Bible in Aramaic: based on old manuscripts and printed texts*, 3rd ed. (Leiden; Boston: Brill, 2013), 37; T. Walker, "Targum," in *A Dictionary of the Bible*, ed. James Hastings et al., vol. 4 (New York: Scribner's; T&T Clack, 1911); M. L. Klein, "The Preposition קדם ('before') a Pseudo-Anti-Anthropomorphism in the Targums," *JTS* 30.2 (1979): 503.

[38] Cathcart, McNamara, and Maher discuss this preposition and its use in light of Klein's article. They agree with the deferential use of קדם but also believe it is used in anti-

also used when referring to human kings (e.g., Gen 14:4, 27:29, 43:15; Dan 2:24–25, 3:13, 4:3, 5, 5:13, 15, 23, 6:19). In many cases, it is used with respect to serving idols, crying out to someone, or meaning a causal relationship between two events (Gen 7:7; Exod 9:11, 10:5; Num 11:1, 12, 18).

Hosea provides a helpful comparison with Prov 2:5a regarding this phrase. For Hos 10:3, the MT reads "we will not fear Yhwh" (לֹא יָרֵאנוּ אֶת־יְהֹוָה) while the TgJ reads "we do not fear *from before* Yhwh" (לָא דְחֵילְנָא מִן קֳדָם יוי). It appears then that the phrase can be used to indicate a direct object. In Prov 2:5a, the MT has "you will understand the fear of Yhwh" (תָּבִין יִרְאַת יְהֹוָה) and the TgProv has "you will understand the fear of *God*" (תתביין דחלתא דאלהא). So, in the case of Prov 2:5, the first line of the TgProv maintains the noun construct phrase from the MT and does not convert it into a verbal phrase nor does it implant the preposition מִן קדם. Yet, the second line alters the noun construct phrase into a clause with the preposition. In Hos 4:1, the MT has "and there is no knowledge of God in the land" (וְאֵין־דַּעַת אֱלֹהִים בָּאָרֶץ) while the TgJ reads "there are none *who walk in the fear of Yhwh* in the land" (וְלֵית דִמהַלְכִין בְּדַחלְתָא דיוי בְּארעָא). This particular change seems to indicate that the TgJ translators may have had some issue with the phrase "knowledge of God," such that they saw it necessary to change the phrase to "those walking in the fear of Yhwh." The idea of knowing God in the Hosea TgJ is not only changed in Hos 4:1 but altered in every other case in which it occurs (2:22, 4:1, 5:4, 6:3, 6, 8:2, 13:5). This suggests that there is a conceptual and possible theological issue going on with this phrase. While the TgProv did not take issue with the "fear of Yhwh," despite changing it to "God" in Prov 2:5, it appears the translator did take issue when it came to the "knowledge of God." This tendency may inform the curious use of מִן קדם in Prov 2:5. The distinction suggests that the TgProv and TgJ translators believed there was an interpretive distinction between fearing Yhwh and knowing him, despite Klein's attempt to say otherwise.[39] This would suggest that the translators of TgProv fully understood the direct relational implications of the phrase in the MT, which likely triggered their desire for a more deferential or transcendent view of God here.

Furthermore, Prov 2:5 is a chiastic parallel. The verse is set up as a grammatical inversion with V-O-O-V.[40] Both verbs are the same grammatically and are connected to construct noun phrases with proper names. The parallelism is synonymous with the verbs as the grammatical inclusio. There is likely a grammatical parallel between the construct noun phrases as well, both with objective genitive relationships. However, while the grammatical and syntactical relationships are the same between the lines, it must be considered if this is true for the semantic qualities as well. In lines

---

anthropomorphic ways as well, especially when the glory of God or seeing him or some tangible terminology is used. See Kevin J. Cathcart and R. P. Gordon, eds., *The Targum of the Minor Prophets*, ArBib 14 (Wilmington: M. Glazier, 1989), 5.

[39] The *Aramaic Bible* notes, "'Knowledge of God' is avoided" which "implies a theological revision." See John F. Healey, "The Targum of Proverbs," in *The Aramaic Bible*, ed. Kevin J. Cathcart, Michael Maher, and Martin McNamara (Collegeville, MN: Liturgical, 1991), 15; Klein, "The Preposition קדם ('before') a Pseudo-Anti-Anthropomorphism in the Targums," 504.

[40] I.e., verb – object – object – verb.

Prov 2:5a and 5b, the verbs are quite different in their meaning and type. The verb "to understand" is typically used in an internal, noetic sense and the other "to find" expresses an external sense. Yet, this antithetical parallel relationship is perhaps part of the poetic and conceptual lesson, implying that the first phrase is personal and internal to the son while the latter is external or extra-personal. Likewise, the nouns of Prov 2:5a and 5b are quite different. There does not seem to be much semantic relationship between fear and knowledge, except that they are likely complementary. Fear can cause a person to seek knowledge and knowledge can assist in properly assessing fear. Finally, the only clear semantic parallel in the verse is the relationship of the proper nouns, Yhwh and God. These are meant to be synonymous, though not without their connotative implications as well.[41]

While this web of parallelism is intricate, it seems the intent for the phrases "fear of Yhwh" and "knowledge of God" is to be understood as grammatically parallel but semantically unique.[42] Both phrases serve as centralizing principles for the wise path. The first is inward while the latter is outward.[43] Estes comments on the verse, saying,

> Knowledge of God, then, is not divorced from everyday life, as though belonging to a sacred sphere separate from the secular life. Instead, the knowledge of God is the pre-eminent goal that is the integration point for all of life. ... The ultimate goal for education in Proverbs 1–9 is the knowledge of God. Just as the fear of Yahweh is the beginning of wisdom (9:10), so it is the end of wisdom as well (2:5). The knowledge of God is the supreme goal that draws all of education and life together into an integrated whole.[44]

As it is in Hosea, knowing God is akin to a marital relationship or perhaps a friendship (e.g., Exod 33:11; Isa 41:8).[45] This type of knowledge is not a matter

---

[41] See, for example, R. K. Harrison, *Introduction to the Old Testament* (196; repr., Peabody, MA: Hendrickson, 2016), 580–82; Martin Rose, "Names of God in the OT," in *AYBD* (New York: Doubleday, 1992), 4:1001–11.

[42] Schipper holds that the parallelism between the lines and scholarship by Kratz on Hosea indicates the phrase "special knowledge that is bestowed upon the scribal sage ... insights about God" (Schipper, *Proverbs 1–15*, 109). While some knowledge about God is certainly necessary, the marital and sexual metaphors used in both Hosea and Proverbs lean toward a more personal sense.

[43] Fox notes the internal or cognitive orientation of Prov 2:5a, "This 'understanding' consists in a mature insight into what it means to fear God. At a certain level of development, one can understand (and not just feel) the fear of God, for it has cognitive content or subject matter. ... When the object of *hebin* is a mental state (such as fear of God) or a cognitive faculty, the verb means to acquire the designated object in an insightful, cognitive way. ... The verb *hebin*, like English 'understand,' always denotes an apprehension (or teaching) of meanings, causes, workings, or implications, and not only a knowledge of facts" (Fox, *Proverbs 1–9*, 110–11).

[44] Daniel J. Estes, *Hear, My Son: Teaching and Learning in Proverbs 1–9*, NSBT 4 (Grand Rapids: Eerdmans, 1997), 85–86.

[45] Frame notes that "Knowing a person involves knowing facts about him ... but most often it means being involved with him either as a friend or as an enemy. ... When scripture speaks of God 'knowing' men, generally the reference is not to factual knowledge at all ... In such

of fact but a matter of interpersonal process.[46] Knowing God, however, also necessitates adherence to his ways, "To know what God does means to do it."[47] Together, then, Prov 2:5a and 5b form a comprehensive anthropology and theology – man's relation to God, himself, and the covenant community.

The Source of Wisdom (2:6–8)

The proverbial teacher provides the son with both the initial path, characterized by listening and seeking (Prov 2:1–4), and the goal of that path, God (2:5). For Prov 2:5, the resultative "then" (אָז) indicates that listening or seeking wisdom is not an end in itself. Rather, the telos is to understand proper covenantal relationship with Yhwh (יִרְאַת יְהוָה) and to know him personally (דַּעַת אֱלֹהִים). In other words, the teacher provides a framework for "the pattern or shape of a way of life lived in the presence of God," i.e., one that reflects his ways.[48] Following this high point, the teacher goes on to provide the son with the underlying logic. The reason one will find or know God by listening to *torah* and seeking wisdom is that Yhwh is the source (Prov 2:6). In a reminiscent contemplation, Job laments that man does not know wisdom or its source (Job 28:12, 20). Yet, as Job says, "God understands its path and he himself knows its place" (Job 28:23).[49] The teacher of Proverbs implies that God knows wisdom and its path because he is in fact its source and giver (Prov 2:6; cf. Sir 1:1).[50]

The teacher expounds upon Prov 2:5 with the "for" (כִּי) clause in 2:6. He states, "For Yhwh will give wisdom, from his mouth knowledge and

---

contexts, knowing generally means 'loving' or 'befriending'. ... Man's knowledge of God, then, is very similar to God's knowledge of man" (John M. Frame, *The Doctrine of the Knowledge of God* (Phillipsburg, NJ: P&R, 1987), 46–47).

[46] Terrien remarks on the knowledge of God, saying, "It designates the involvement of man's total personality in the presence of Yahweh" (Samuel L. Terrien, *The Elusive Presence: Toward a New Biblical Theology*, RP 26 (San Francisco: Harper & Row, 1978), 40).

[47] Fox, *Proverbs 1–9*, 112.

[48] Remarking on OT ethics, Barton goes on to say, "Ethics is not so much a system of obligations as a way of communion with God" (John Barton, "Approaches to Ethics in the Old Testament," in *Beginning Old Testament Study*, ed. John Rogerson (Philadelphia: Westminster, 1982), 128, 130).

[49] Turner observes that God both "establishes" and "seeks" wisdom, which seems contradictory (Job 28:27). In light of Proverbs, however, the idea of God seeking wisdom may connect with the son's searching for wisdom as an imitative act after God. The lexemes are different, though; Prov 2:4 uses "seek" (בקש) and "search" (חפש) and while Job 28:27 uses "search" (חקר). If the connection is present, then the collection of lexemes would simply mean to pursue, perhaps in the sense of examine. See Marie Turner, "Wisdom as Encounter with God," *LTJ* 50.2 (2016): 138–39.

[50] As the curious chapter concludes, "He said to the man, 'Behold, the fear of the Yhwh is wisdom and to turn from evil is insight'" (Job 28:28)." The terminology of this verse finds a number of parallels in Prov 1–9. Cf. Kenneth T. Aitken, *Proverbs* (Philadelphia: Westminster, 1986), 29.

understanding."[51] A reasonable and probable allusion is Solomon's gift from Yhwh, "God gave to Solomon wisdom and understanding" (1 Kgs 4:29 [5:9]). In a minor variant, the LXX of Prov 2:6 uses the phrase "from his presence [face]" (ἀπὸ προσώπου αὐτοῦ) rather than the MT's "from his mouth" (מִפִּיו). Although "presence" fits and could be the result of losing the *nun* (מפניו), the use of "mouth" is fairly common throughout the HB and Proverbs. Following the LXX, the phrase would imply that these gifts are derived from being in the presence of God. Alternatively, the phrase "mouth of Yhwh" occurs often in the Torah for God's direct instruction and in the prophets for his utterances.[52] For example:

Num 9:23	According to *the mouth of Yhwh* they camped and according to *the mouth of Yhwh* they set out. They kept the service of Yhwh according to *the mouth of Yhwh* by the hand of Moses.
Deut 1:26	You did not go up but you rebelled *the mouth of Yhwh.*
Deut 8:3b	Man does not live by bread alone but man lives by everything *the mouth of Yhwh* brings forth.
Isa 40:5	The glory of Yhwh will be revealed and all flesh together will see for *the mouth of Yhwh* has spoken.
Mic 4:4b	None shall be afraid for *the mouth of Yhwh* of armies has spoken.
Jer 9:11a	Who is the man who is wise and understands this? And who has *the mouth of Yhwh* spoken to?

As these examples elsewhere in the MT illuminate, there is an inherent sense of God's "presence" associated with the phrase "mouth of Yhwh." Therefore, in accordance with the Torah and prophetic tradition, Proverbs implies that wisdom, knowledge, and understanding are not only taught by Yhwh, but they are inextricably dependent on his presence. This presence implies proper relation with him, which necessitates obedience and listening.[53] Due to its broad use, the phrase in Prov 2:6 likely alludes to covenant-faithful prophets, such as Moses, Isaiah, Micah, and Jeremiah, who served as the "mouth of

---

[51] Moss notes the implication that Yhwh is himself a wisdom teacher (Moss, "Wisdom as Parental Teaching in Proverbs 1–9," 430).

[52] Keefer remarks on Proverbs' intertextual relationships, "The links of Proverbs 1–9 with law and Deuteronomy may attest not to its introductory function but to its aim of integrating Proverbs with other portions of the OT. The Deuteronomic ties occur in Proverbs 1–9 and 10–31 and in both are largely assumed conceptions, appearing like icebergs, protruding at particular places and harbouring much more underneath. I have called such formations 'assumptions' whereby a little shows atop the text's surface and implies information or a framework that might draw out latent insights. The Deuteronomic allusions often appear in a similar way – as assumptions" (Keefer, *Proverbs 1–9 as an Introduction to the Book of Proverbs*, 36). With "assumptions," this may be broader and more of a shared, theological coherence than a direct reliance.

[53] Schipper, *Proverbs 1–15*, 110.

Yhwh" for the people.[54] The teacher, then, is pointing the proverbial son to God for the path and telos of wisdom but also God's prophetic mouth-pieces, who were reliable intermediate sources and noble examples to follow.[55] In other words, against all mundane empirical epistemological theories, the teacher believes that true wisdom is characterized by seeking, finding, and receiving from the covenant God, Yhwh.[56]

Although the initial gifts from seeking and finding God are internal – wisdom, knowledge, and understanding – the teacher then turns to external or practical aspects. Of particular importance, here, is the poetic interplay between God and the one receiving his blessings (Prov 2:7–8).

2:7	יִצְפֹּן לַיְשָׁרִים תּוּשִׁיָּה מָגֵן לְהֹלְכֵי תֹם:	And he will store up success for the upright, a shield for those walking blameless,
2:8	לִנְצֹר אָרְחוֹת מִשְׁפָּט וְדֶרֶךְ חֲסִידָו יִשְׁמֹר:	protecting paths of justice; and he will guard the way of his faithful.

In this dense poetic unit, God promises to "store up" (צפן) and to "guard" (שמר), the first and last words of Prov 2:7–8. The term "store up" is used in 2:1b. There, the son is to "store up" (צפן) the father's "commandments" (מצוה). It is not an accident then that God promises to "store up" blessings if the son will "store up" his instructions. Although this imitative parallel is reversed in a sense, the poetic logic implies personal interchange and covenant relationship rather than rote mimicry. The teacher goes on to identify three recipients of God's blessings. These all begin with a ל – the upright (לַיְשָׁרִים), those walking blamelessly (לְהֹלְכֵי תֹם), and the one protecting paths of justice (לִנְצֹר אָרְחוֹת מִשְׁפָּט).[57] All of these, as opposed to Prov 2:6, are external, social, civil, covenantal actions. Unfortunately, the LXX and Syr. flatten these lines into simply God

---

[54] See William McKane, *Prophets and Wise Men*, SBT 44 (SCM, 1965), 65–78.

[55] For differing nuances on divine inspiration here, see Loader, *Proverbs 1–9*, 117–18; Waltke, *Proverbs (1–15)*, 223–24; Meinhold, *Die Sprüche*, 65.

[56] Longman rightly notes, "According to Proverbs, observation and experience, tradition, and learning from one's mistakes—all are important sources of human wisdom. However, at the heart of wisdom is God himself. Apart from God there is no true insight into the world. God is the only source of true wisdom. Even the ability to observe and experience comes from the Lord. ... If wisdom depends on understanding the world correctly, how can that be achieved if one does not acknowledge that God is the center of the cosmos? Everything must be understood in relationship to Yahweh himself" (Longman, *Proverbs*, 78–79).

[57] The phrase "to guard" (לִנְצֹר) could be pointed as a participle with "one guarding" (לְנֹצֵר). Alternatively, the MT infinitive pointing could function as a complement to the preceding participle "those walking" (לְהֹלְכֵי). Loader understands the term "shield" to be in apposition to "success" (תּוּשִׁיָּה) the subject for "those walking" and "guarding." In this way, Yhwh does not "himself do the shielding" nor involve "himself in the daily quarrels and conflicts" (Loader, *Proverbs 1–9*, 119). This view does not rightly do justice to the conceptual interplay between God and man. Rather, it renders God in a deistic fashion, merely providing insight but not involvement. Likewise, the analogy of "shielding" is directly applied to Yhwh later in Prov 30:5, thus undermining Loader's premise in 2:7.

acting.[58] The MT, however, maintains the poetic and conceptual interplay from the teacher by couching the actions of the recipients within the inclusio of Yhwh's actions (cf. Lesson 4). Furthermore, just as God will "store up" if the son will, so also in Prov 2:8 God will "guard" (שמר) if the son will "guard" (נצר). Again, the reflective or imitative relational interplay shows the mutuality between God and the one who seeks him and receives his wisdom.[59] In reality, though, these identified recipients of blessing are embodiments of the characteristics of God's own ways and in accordance with his expectations – being upright, blameless, and just (cf. Prov 2:21).[60] So, in a reciprocal sense, God imitates those who imitate him. By walking in the ways of Yhwh, the son will both know God and subsequently receive his blessings. By knowing Yhwh, the son will walk in his ways and find wisdom, knowledge, and understanding.[61] The wise path, then, is not linear but more like a spiral process, since it is an interpersonal pursuit.[62]

It is important to consider what may be intended by the sense of source here, as it pertains to Yhwh. Three possibilities are considered here. Yhwh as the source of wisdom, knowledge, and understanding could mean that he creates and manifests such things, then gives them out. The son would receive and use them as one might a farm tool. This sense would be a transfer of informational or noetic tools. Another sense could be that God is the source of these in that he defines the parameters for what constitutes wisdom, knowledge, and understanding. In other words, this would be a special revelation view, due to the son's hampered epistemological capacity to define these qualities on his own. Finally, Yhwh as the source could imply that God is himself the embodiment and exemplar of these qualities.[63] In this view, one would receive the divine qualities as far as they know and reflect God in their character, desires, and actions.[64] Although an amount of special revelation is

---

[58] I.e., "guarding" (ﻧﻄﺮ) or "storing" (θησαυρίζω), "shielding" (ὑπερασπίζω), and "guarding" (φυλάσσω).

[59] Estes, *Hear, My Son*, 68.

[60] Wright says, "Justice was the social foundation of Israel not only because the initiative of God's redeeming power was an act of righteousness, but also because it called forth a response of imitative righteousness and justice among the Israelites themselves. Having been put 'right,' so to speak, the Israelites were to maintain righteousness. Having experienced justice, they were to 'do justice'" (Wright, *Old Testament Ethics for the People of God*, 261).

[61] As Birch understands, "The knowledge of God is prior to and encompasses the knowledge of God's will." Likewise, "Moral norms arise out of knowing God. 'I will take you as my people, and I will be your God. You shall know that I am Yahweh.'" See Bruce C. Birch, "Moral Agency, Community, and the Character of God in the Hebrew Bible," *Semeia* 66 (1994): 29; Bruce C. Birch, "Divine Character and the Formation of Moral Community in the Book of Exodus," 구약논단 *(Old Testament Discussion)* 8 (2000): 299.

[62] See Fox, *Proverbs 1–9*, 111; Longman, *Proverbs*, 120; Stuart Weeks, *An Introduction to the Study of Wisdom Literature* (London: T&T Clark, 2010), 120–21. In contrast, Weeks proposes a linear process from wisdom to the fear of Yhwh.

[63] See Richard W. Medina, "Life and Death Viewed as Physical and Lived Spaces: Some Preliminary Thoughts from Proverbs," *ZAW* 122 (2012): 205.

[64] Birch rightly observes, "The Hebrew Bible understands that Israel finds its focus as moral community in relation to its God. ... Ethics in the Hebrew Bible are theocentric. ... The wisdom tradition with its emphasis on human capacity to seek wisdom and learn from

necessary to rightly know God and adhere to his ways, there is a sense in this chapter through the spiraling path to Yhwh that the good path is not mere blind obedience by fiat. Rather, it is akin to walking behind and with someone on a road or perhaps watching and participating in the farming techniques of one's father.

The Two Paths (2:9–22)

In Prov 2:9, the third main structural movement begins with the second use of the term "then" (אָז). This term is followed by a "for" (כִּי) clause in Prov 2:10, which mirrors the structure of 2:5–6. Furthermore, the structure of this section (Prov 2:9–22) proceeds in four parts. First, there are three verses (Prov 2:9–11) that give a positive view of the practical blessings in seeking and knowing God. The second and third parts are each four verses long (Prov 2:12–15, 16–19) and both begin with "to deliver you" (לְהַצִּילְךָ). These two parts are blessings in the sense of protection from the wayward path and those who walk on it. Finally, Prov 2:20 begins with "in order that" (לְמַעַן), which creates a minor, conclusive section (2:20–22). These final verses provide both a positive promise of blessing and a negative promise of protection. With 2:5–8 included, there are nine positive verses for blessing (2:5–11, 20–21) and nine negative verses for warning (2:12–19, 22), creating thematic balance for the apodoses of this lesson.

Walking on the Good Path (2:9–11, 20–21)

Although Prov 2:5 initiates the path of blessing, the good path continues structurally with 2:9. In addition to "then" (אָז), this section starts with "you will understand" (תָּבִין) just as Prov 2:5 began. In other words, the teacher poetically affirms that if the son will listen to instruction, he will "understand the fear of Yhwh" and he will "understand righteousness, justice, uprightness – every good path" (Prov 2:5, 9). The parallel between these verses helps to illuminate the implication of Prov 2:5 and the conditioned promise of 2:1–2. Likewise, the parallel illuminates a similar set of phrases found in Prov 1:3 and 7, "to receive wise *musar*, righteousness, justice, and uprightness … the fear of Yhwh is the beginning of knowledge, the fool despises wisdom and *musar*." Although the introductory verses do not make a clear connection between these elements, Prov 2:5 and 9 build a bridge. By putting these together, the case for "knowledge" in Prov 1:7 as an elided form of "knowledge

---

experience understands the source of wisdom and the order of all things to be in God" (Birch, "Divine Character," 281).

of God" from 2:5 is strengthened. The phrase in Prov 1:7, then, could be understood as "the fear of Yhwh is the beginning of the knowledge [of God]."

The path of blessing, as proffered in Prov 2:9, is not an abstract set of rules. Rather, the path is central to and based on the way of Yhwh himself. In the Psalms, "righteousness" and "justice" are inextricably related to Yhwh, calling them "the foundation of your throne" (Ps 89:14, 97:2). It is also said that Yhwh "loves righteousness and justice" (Ps 33:5) and that Yhwh "establishes uprightness and does justice and righteousness" (Ps 99:4; cf. 103:6). In a prophetic declaration, Zephaniah says, "Yhwh is righteous within [Jerusalem]. He does not make perversity. Every morning he gives his justice" (Zeph 3:5). In Isaiah, the prophet says that Yhwh is "a God of justice" and will "fill Zion with justice and righteousness" (Isa 30:18, 33:5). The picture within the HB is that God is not only the commander of these ways but expects them of his people since they are based on his own character and behavior. In fact, the ancient Song of Moses (Deut 32:4) identifies these characteristics with Yhwh, likely a root for the other uses in the HB.[65]

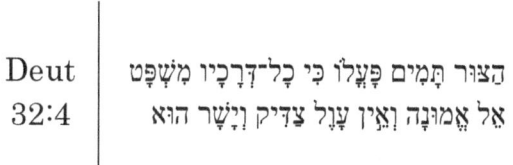

| Deut 32:4 | הַצּוּר תָּמִים פָּעֳלוֹ כִּי כָל־דְּרָכָיו מִשְׁפָּט אֵל אֱמוּנָה וְאֵין עָוֶל צַדִּיק וְיָשָׁר הוּא | The Rock, his deeds are blameless, for all his ways are just; a God of faithfulness without perversity. He is righteous and upright. |

In this way, then, the son is promised to grow in the likeness of Yhwh as he listens, seeks, and walks in the ways of Yhwh. Wright proposes an insightful reflection on this point, "If the motto of Proverbs is 'The fear of [Yhwh] is the beginning ... of wisdom,' it would be appropriate to add that 'the imitation of [Yhwh] is the application of wisdom.' This emerges in the way that so many of the little details of behaviour commended in the book do indeed reflect the character of God himself."[66]

To further understand the poetic logic of this lesson, it is important to see that Prov 2:10 connects with the relational aspect of 2:5b, similar to 2:9 with 2:5a. The teacher states in Prov 2:10, "Wisdom will enter your heart and knowledge will please your soul." According to Estes, this means, "[Wisdom]

---

[65] For discussions on its origins and influences, see Craigie, *The Book of Deuteronomy*, 373–80; Patrick W. Skehan, "Structure of the Song of Moses in Deuteronomy (Deut 32:1–43)," *CBQ* 13.2 (1951): 153–63; William F. Albright, "Some Remarks on the Song of Moses in Deuteronomy 32," *VT* 9.4 (1959): 339–46; William L. Moran, "Some Remarks on the Song of Moses," *Bib* 43.3 (1962): 317–27; James R. Boston, "Wisdom Influence upon the Song of Moses," *JBL* 87.2 (1968): 198–202; Matthew Thiessen, "The Form and Function of the Song of Moses (Deuteronomy 32:1–43)," *JBL* 123.3 (2004): 401–24; Mark Leuchter, "Why Is the Song of Moses in the Book of Deuteronomy?," *VT* 57.3 (2007): 295–317.

[66] Specifically on Proverbs, Wright notes that the righteousness of Yhwh is a central component to the teacher's subtle instruction to imitate God, particularly as a king and judge. As he goes on to say, "Political and judicial justice matter as much to the sage as to the law-giver and prophet. Here is an area where the social and moral health of the wider community depends very much on the integrity and commitment of individuals and the decisions they make" (Wright, *Old Testament Ethics for the People of God*, 41, 370).

can function as the dominant factor controlling the person's thoughts, emotions, and decisions."[67] Similarly, Ross says, "When a person assimilates wisdom, doing right becomes attractive and delightful; for he sees the advantage of it."[68] Likewise, Waltke comments, "Though presented in two stanzas, the religious and ethical benefits are inseparable. A personal relationship with [Yhwh] (Prov 2:5–8) entails an intuitive understanding of what is right in human relationships (2:9–11)."[69] Continuing the metaphor in Prov 2:11, the teacher overlays the actions of God and the son. Two terms used previously, "guard" (שׁמר) and "protect" (נצר), appear here, as well. In Prov 2:8, the terms indicate the reciprocal interplay between God and the son. Here, the metaphor extends the guardianship of God to "Wisdom," partially anthropomorphizing her. Elsewhere in Prov 1–9, the son is commended to "guard" or "protect" the instruction (Prov 4:4, 21, 5:2, 7:1, 2, 8:32; 2:8, 11, 3:1, 21, 4:13, 23, 5:2, 6:20). In Prov 4:6, the teacher echoes 2:11 by saying that "Wisdom" will "guard" him. Similarly, in 3:26, the teacher echoes Prov 2:8 saying that "[Yhwh] will guard your foot from being caught." So, in this network of passages, the reciprocal and imitative relationship between the parties is displayed for the son's proper consideration. On one hand, it likely connotes that the path of wisdom, or the way of Yhwh, is not an individualistic one but necessarily communal. It is also likely that the metaphorical use of "wisdom" here – alongside "knowledge," "understanding," and "discretion" – is simply a poetic way of saying that God will be the guide, protector, and blessing for the son in his journey.[70] This perspective is especially poignant since the teacher has already established that Yhwh is the source and goal of wisdom, knowledge, and understanding.

As the blessed path section continues, it skips Prov 2:12–19 and concludes in 2:20–21. As a summarizing and logically informed plea, Lesson 2 overtly commends ideal examples, those individuals worthy of imitating.[71] In Prov 2:20, the father says that the son ought to "walk in the way of the good [ones] and keep the paths of the righteous [ones]." Bland gives an insightful perspective.

> The internal character of the upright governs their life (cf. Prov 6:20–23). Character is viewed not as a single act, but as a way of life. The following proverb indicates how integrity is cultivated: 'The righteous walk in integrity — happy are the children who follow them!' (20:7) Parents who walk in integrity will pass on that lifestyle to their

---

[67] Estes, *Hear, My Son*, 75.

[68] Allen P. Ross, "Proverbs," in *The Expositor's Bible Commentary: Proverbs – Isaiah*, rev. ed. (Grand Rapids: Zondervan, 2008), 59.

[69] Waltke, *Proverbs (1–15)*, 217.

[70] Schipper, *Proverbs 1–15*, 113.

[71] Keefer argues that these conclusive verses "draw attention not to behaviours as such but to the ethical evaluation of behaviours and their association with character types" (Keefer, *Proverbs 1–9 as an Introduction to the Book of Proverbs*, 58). The focus of his study elicits this evaluation, which seeks to understand character types in Prov 10–22. In this way, whether the "righteous" or "good" are real or ideal they serve as models for the son to emulate and follow after as they walk in the way of Yhwh.

children, who in turn will be blessed by such an example. Children imitate parents. [72]

The first two types of exemplar individuals are the "good" (טובים) and the "righteous" (צדיקים). [73] The grammar of these words within their phrases requires that they are nouns or substantive adjectives, referring to persons or groups. [74] These terms also parallel the "upright" (ישרים) and "blameless" (תמימים) in Prov 2:21, which are pluralized categories of exemplar persons. The particular form for "righteous" here is always used to mean "righteous people." Alternatively, the term "good ones" is a plural adjective that can occur with an adjectival function, [75] an abstract plural function, [76] or a substantival function for persons.[77] Proverbs 14:19 uses the plural to imply persons by contrasting the term with "the wicked" and "the evil." It states, "The evil [ones] bow before the good [ones] and the wicked [ones] at the righteous gates" (שַׁחוּ רָעִים לִפְנֵי טוֹבִים וּרְשָׁעִים עַל־שַׁעֲרֵי צַדִּיק). So, in Prov 2:20, the teacher directly instructs the son to do as the "good" and "righteous" do.[78] They are on the right path that leads to the knowledge of God and, in turn, will result in his protective, relational presence. It is not sufficient for the son to merely hear. He must engage in imitative patterning, which he learns from following those on the same righteous path.[79]

Immediately after commending imitation, the teacher informs the son that "the upright (וִישָׁרִים) will dwell in the land and the blameless (תְּמִים) will remain in it" (Prov 2:21).[80] Although Prov 2:20–21 does not explicitly state the

---

[72] Whether or not the "righteous" were thought to be parents or just persons acting in appropriate ways, their point lends toward the fundamental role of family and community in character formation. See Bland, *Proverbs and the Formation of Character*, 57.

[73] Loader refers to these types as a "class of people" contrasted with the wicked class of people (Loader, *Proverbs 1–9*, 134). While it may imply different types of classes, the proper image is two paths or those on two distinct paths. The righteous and good types of persons are on the path of wisdom, walking in the way of Yhwh. Those who do wicked things are those walking on the evil way which will lead to death.

[74] The LXX seems to misunderstand the HB and translates the plurals in Prov 2:20 as adjectives modifying "path" (τρίβος) rather than as human categories for ideal models.

[75] E.g., Deut 8:12; 2 Sam 15:3; 1 Kgs 12:7; Ezek 20:25, 36:31; Zech 1:13, 8:19; Song 1:3; Eccl 4:9, 7:10; Lam 4:9; Neh 9:13; 2 Chron 10:7, 12:12, 19:3.

[76] E.g., Jer 44:17; Song 1:2; Eccl 11:6.

[77] E.g., Prov 2:20, 14:19.

[78] Birch claims, "Character formation requires emulation as a necessary part of its dynamic. ... In moral development this process might focus on parents, friends, leaders, communities, or even the mediated example of persons in novels or biographies" (Birch, "Moral Agency," 32). In Prov 1–9, the teacher utilizes both positive and negative models to guide the son.

[79] Lyu says, "Proverbs' character of the righteous is to be studied, mimicked, and internalized in the pupil's life. Proverbs 1–9 gives a structured 'theory of learning' and guiding principles for using the raw material in the rest of the book.... The binary anthropology of Proverbs, coupled with its ardent emphasis on wisdom, is the crystallization of Israelite wisdom that enables moral imagination to bloom into moral character" (Sun Myung Lyu, *Righteousness in the Book of Proverbs*, FAT 55 (Tübingen: Mohr Siebeck, 2012), 74–75).

[80] Keefer differs with Schipper on the centralization of Prov 2:21. Structurally, Prov 2:20 provides the result but 2:21 the benefit in a "for" (כִּי) clause. Persistence in the land is merely a benefit for walking in the right way, the more important point. See Schipper, *Proverbs 1–15*,

source of security, it is implicitly the direct result of covenantal and relational protection from God. Earlier, the father says in Prov 2:7–8 that Yhwh blesses and protects "the upright" (יְשָׁרִים) and those "walking blamelessly" (הֹלְכֵי תֹם). So, if the son is to dwell in the land, or securely (בֶּטַח) in Prov 1:33, he must be like them. By emulating these models, he will listen to the teacher's instruction, seek wisdom, understand the fear of Yhwh, know God, and walk in their ways of righteousness, justice, and uprightness (Prov 2:9). In these verses, then, the son is both explicitly and implicitly instructed to be like these four types of ideal persons.[81] These groups collectively represent the ways of Yhwh by which the son will choose life (cf. Deut 30:19–20).[82]

A word can be said here in Prov 2:21 about the imagery of dwelling in the land (יִשְׁכְּנוּ־אָרֶץ). The Torah repeatedly promised entry and security in the land if Israel would walk in the way of Yhwh and reject the ways of the nations (e.g., Deut 4:1–2, 25–31, 5:31–33, 9:4–6, 11:8–9, 30:16, 20).[83] A key implication for security in the land was the presence of God there. In fact, many of the Torah commands for covenant fidelity emphasized an environment for God to dwell with them (e.g., Deut 6:15, 7:21, 23:14–16, 32:51). For properly informed and aligned ancient Israelites, there was no security apart from the presence of God, which was foundationally centered in the land of Israel (cf. Ruth 1:1–5). This reality was relevant for the proverbial father and his instruction, as well. In the latter portion of Proverbs, the importance of security in the land is also stated in Prov 10:30, "The righteous [one] will not be moved forever, and the wicked will not inhabit the land" (צַדִּיק לְעוֹלָם בַּל־יִמּוֹט וּרְשָׁעִים לֹא יִשְׁכְּנוּ־אָרֶץ). Furthermore, the metaphorical images in Prov 2 for 'walking' and 'seeking' imply conclusive ends. That is, seeking leads to finding and walking leads to a destination. As analogies, the two metaphors overlap in the sense that walking in the way of Yhwh is akin to seeking wisdom, both of which conclude with finding God in the land – the implicit end of both pursuits. As it will be seen in the negative path, dwelling in the land and finding God are actually a matter of life and death,[84] not simply prosperity or intellectualism.

104–6, 120; Bernd U. Schipper, *Hermeneutik der Tora: Studien zur Traditionsgeschichte von Prov 2 und zur Komposition von Prov 1–9*, ZAW 432 (Berlin: De Gruyter, 2012), 75; Keefer, *Proverbs 1–9 as an Introduction to the Book of Proverbs*, 108–9.

[81] Waltke, *Proverbs (1–15)*, 234.

[82] Wright correctly understands, "[Israel was] to be a people who would imitate the character of [Yhwh] himself ('the way of [Yhwh]') by their commitment to 'righteousness and justice.' ... That sphere, as all spheres of their corporate life, was to be governed by justice, because that is precisely God's own way" (Wright, *Old Testament Ethics for the People of God*, 221).

[83] Aitken, *Proverbs*, 33.

[84] Waltke makes the case, "Life in this book mostly refers to the abundant everlasting life that outlasts clinical death, which is only a shadow along the path of life." This is particularly important in contrast to other national religions and their gods, e.g., Egypt. Thus, the path of life in Proverbs, as elsewhere in the HB, is according to its relation to the God of life (cf. Gen 2:7; Eccl 12:7). In contrast, Fox and Medina do not find reason to see immortality in Proverbs. Medina proposes that Proverbs teaches "transgenerational longevity," or a sense of perpetuity through progeny. However, his primary view is the immediate benefits of life, or fullness of life. Though Fox and Medina's views are understandable, Waltke's view provides broader explanatory power

Deliverance from the Bad Path (2:12–19, 22)

While the positive vision for the path of blessing is the intent of the teacher's instruction, it is pedagogically and theologically necessary to inform the son of the alternative path. As previously discussed, the two-path motif originating in Gen 2 served as both an opportunity and a warning. In Prov 2, the dual path is contrasted explicitly, receiving equal treatment. The warning against the bad path is two-fold. This path is treacherous along the way and its end is death. If the son becomes like those on this deadly path, he is guaranteed to share their fate. The way and fate of this evil path is, instead, meant to propel the son toward the good path, one characterized by the righteous and Yhwh.

The two primary warning stanzas (Prov 2:12–15, 16–19) address those on the bad path and the "foreign woman," both of which appear elsewhere in Prov 1–9. In Prov 2:12–15, the teacher creates a strong picture similar to that in Lesson 1 regarding the way of sinners (1:10–19).[85] Lesson 1 explicitly calls the son to "not walk in the way with them" (Prov 1:15). Lesson 2 does not give an explicit command. Rather, the whole lesson is couched in conditional and resultative language. This rhetorical device shifts the tone from a 'call to obedience' to an 'appeal for sensible logic.' Here, in Prov 2:12–15, the teacher lists seven types of persons walking on the "bad path" (דֶּרֶךְ רָע). The seven overlapping categories are: "men of perverse speech," "those abandoning the upright path," "those who walk in paths of darkness," "those rejoicing to do evil," "they revel in evil perversities," "those whose ways are crooked," and "those whose ways are devious." Although the son is certainly not to engage in these wicked practices, the teacher's negative exemplars, just as in Lesson 1, serve as models. He must not imitate or become like them in action or desire. These seven types embody the numeric symbol of perfection for wicked fools (cf. Prov 6:16–19). They and their ways will not result in wisdom, let alone knowing God. In fact, the teacher says that the relational knowledge of God and the internalization of his ways will "deliver" (נצל) the son from both the destructive consequences of those along the bad path and from the deleterious end in becoming like them.

The teacher also invokes the metaphorical "foreign woman" (אִשָּׁה זָרָה, נָכְרִיָּה).[86] According to scholars, this figure may represent an adulterous or

---

for the complex use of life and justice, particularly in light of other HB passages and ANE concepts. See Waltke, *Proverbs (1–15)*, 104–7, 233; Medina, "Life and Death Viewed as Physical and Lived Spaces: Some Preliminary Thoughts from Proverbs," 207–9; Fox, *Proverbs 1–9*, 143.

[85] Cf. Loader, *Proverbs 1–9*, 123.

[86] The LXX for Prov 2:16 is quite different than the MT or any other text tradition, apparently extending the previous stanza (2:12–15). The verse reads, "To make you far from the straight path and a stranger of righteous purpose." As Cook contends, the LXX is not avoiding sexuality, which appears later. Rather, the translator is avoiding confusion with the metaphor "in order to make a theological point, it is not the sexual that leads astray, but bad counsel, not things external but what lies within." See Johann Cook, "אִשָּׁה זָרָה (Proverbs 1–9 Septuagint): A Metaphor for Foreign Wisdom?" *ZAW* 106 (1994): 463–64; Johann Cook, "A Theology of the Greek Version of Proverbs," *HvTSt* 71.1 (2015): 6.

interracial affair (e.g., Exod 34:16; Deut 5:18, 7:3; Josh 23:12–13), a foreign goddess and paganism, or generically seductive paths in opposition to Yhwh.[87] Although a reasonable case can be made for each option, the third is a more broadly applicable and generally encompassing view, which subsumes the others.[88] In fact, going after foreign gods and unsanctioned sexual affairs were both in opposition to Yhwh and his way, both of which were aberrations to his covenant and punishable by death in the Torah (e.g., Deut 13:5–11, 22:22). If there is to be any sensible correlation between Prov 2:12–15 and 16–19, however, then the metaphor of this "foreign woman" and her ways must also complement those figures on the "bad path" (2:12). Both Prov 2:12 and 16 begin with the phrase "to deliver you" (לְהַצִּילְךָ). The structural overlay here reflects in a sense the parallel structure of Prov 2:5–6 and 2:9–10 (כִּי ... אָז תָּבִין). The result of listening and seeking is two-fold, not to be seen as mutually exclusive. The two sections were mutually dependent or logically related. In a similar way, the "bad path" and the "foreign woman" should be seen as overlapping or interrelated realities.[89] The overlap between the two negative results is especially clear from Prov 2:22. The concluding verse of the lesson combines the two stanzas by mentioning the wicked and the mortal danger, the latter only explicitly mentioned in the "foreign woman" stanza (Prov 2:18–19).

With this in mind, it is important to see how the "foreign woman" stanza (Prov 2:16–19) expands upon a few key concepts. First of all, deliverance from her is a blessing for those who listen, seek, and walk in the way of God. In Lesson 1, the father warns the son of the enticement of sinners and their bad path: he must not let them "persuade" him and he must not "walk in the way with them" (Prov 1:10, 15). The father in Lesson 2, however,

---

[87] Fox identifies six possibilities in his view: 1) foreign prostitute, 2) cult prostitute, 3) foreign goddess, 4) foreigner, 5) Hebrew prostitute, or 6) an adulterous wife. Following Whybray, he believes the adulterous wife is the only convincing option. Schipper appeals to parallels in ANE wisdom which warn of a love for foreign women as well. He also points out the emphasis on adultery and interracial marriage in the HB. Longman, along with Estes, connects the strange woman to Woman Folly, a contrast to Woman Wisdom who represents Yhwh himself. As a contrast, Folly and the strange woman function as a "metaphor for all the false gods and goddesses." Hengel proposes this "foreign woman" is symbolically representing "foreign wisdom." See Fox, *Proverbs 1–9*, 134–41; Longman, *Proverbs*, 58–61, 123–25; Schipper, *Proverbs 1–15*, 115–18; Whybray, *Composition of the Book of Proverbs*, 16–17; Martin Hengel, *Judentum und Hellenismus*, 2nd ed. (Tübingen: Mohr, 1973), 281; Estes, *Hear, My Son*, 54–55.

[88] Weeks rightly understands the intentional ambiguity of this "foreign" woman rather than as an explicit category. He says, "It seems likely that the author is using the 'foreignness' of the woman primarily in a poetic way, exploiting the connotations of the term, not setting out an exclusivist agenda." Likewise, he adds, "The broader message is that learning and internalizing the Law enables one to recognize and resist attempts to lure one aside from the way of life approved by God." Seemingly against his view in Prov 2:16–17, Whybray does note the contrasting seductions presented to the son throughout Prov 1–9, "The young man is warned against the fatal attraction of a whole range of women; and as counter-attractions he is presented with the persuasiveness of the father's teaching and of Wisdom." See Weeks, *Instruction and Imagery in Proverbs 1–9*, 141, 143; Whybray, *Composition of the Book of Proverbs*, 57–58.

[89] Murphy makes a case that the "foreign woman" is meant to contrast Woman Wisdom, as seen elsewhere in Prov 1–9 (Roland E. Murphy, "Wisdom and Eros in Proverbs 1–9," *CBQ* 50.4 (1988): 603).

breaks that composite warning into its two metaphorical, rhetorical aspects. Here in Lesson 2, the warning for the imitative path of sinners appears in Prov 2:12–15 while the enticement aspect is addressed in 2:16–19. The foreign woman characterizes one who is deceptive with words, seeking to persuade the naïve to commit unfaithful acts. She is said to "abandon the companion of her youth and forgets the covenant of her God" (Prov 2:17; cf. Deut 4:23). The parallel lines in this verse seem to be synonymous, invoking a double entendre.[90] Adultery is the abandonment of one's spouse and it breaks a marital covenant.[91] Metaphorically speaking, breaking the covenant of God is akin to adultery and, therefore, abandonment of God.[92] Elsewhere in the HB, Israel is referred to as a young bride of Yhwh, especially from the Sinai epoch, where she broke her covenant through idolatrous and unjust practices (cf. Hos 2:13–20; Isa 54:4–7; Jer 2:2–3, 3:1–5; Ezek 16:22–26, 59–63). The Torah explicitly warned Israel not to become like the nations of the land nor to make illegitimate covenants with them, which is akin to adultery and prostitution (e.g., Exod 34:12–16; Deut 31:16). Just as the son is to be wary of the sinners' persuasion, then, he is to be on guard against the seduction of the "foreigner," who will seek to lead him away from Yhwh and his ways.[93]

In this "foreign woman" stanza, she also perpetuates the bad path motif, one that leads to "death" and the "Rephaim" (Prov 2:18; cf. 9:18).[94] The finality of this path is expressed in the phrase, "The one entering her will not return and they will not reach the paths of life" (Prov 2:19; cf. 7:27). In contrast, these negative metaphors are ultimately meant to provoke the son to walk in the good path. This implies that the way of Yhwh or the teacher's instruction is the opposite, a path characterized by life and covenant faithfulness. So, the son is warned that joining in the path of the "foreign woman," or imitating her ways, will end in death. Furthermore, the phrase "enter her" (בָּאֶיהָ) is likely a double entendre for both unfaithful sexual behavior and for death, which is the inescapable conclusion of the bad path. In Lesson 1, the father also warns the son not to "enter" (תבא), referring to the persuasion of the sinners (Prov 1:10). Here in Lesson 2, the term is poetically associated with sexuality. Both uses are associated with persuasion and indicative of the bad path, which results in death (Prov 1:18–19, 2:18–19, 22). As it is with the sinners and the seven types of wicked people on the bad path, the son must not unite himself to this metaphorical adulterer so that he may avoid becoming like her. If he does, however, his actions will lead to reflecting her reality, one who "abandons the companion of her youth and forgets the covenant of her God" (Prov 2:17). By imitating her in these aberrations, he

---

[90] Cf. Schäfer, *Die Poesie der Weisen*, 61; Schipper, *Proverbs 1–15*, 116.

[91] Waltke, *Proverbs (1–15)*, 231.

[92] Whybray, *Proverbs (1972)*, 23.

[93] The theme of the *zarah* and her seductive ways is a central focus in Lessons 9, 10, 12, and 13.

[94] These references may be poetic allusions to Canaanite mythology (Waltke, *Proverbs (1–15)*, 232–33). While one may infer a positive correlation to such practices, the opposite is just as possible. The teacher may have implied that following in the evil way was related to following in the ways of the nations. For further discussion on the "Rephaim," see Lesson 15.

will follow in her deadly fate (Prov 2:18–19). The heart of the father's instruction, then, is for the son to walk on the good path, reflecting the righteous and wise on it (Prov 2:20–21). These good examples are those who know Yhwh and follow in his ways instead.

Conclusion

In Lesson 2, the father provides vitally important guidance in several ways. He shows the son that the path of wisdom ultimately concludes in God (Prov 2:5). This is because he is its source, the embodiment of divine wisdom and its preeminent teacher (Prov 2:6). So, for the son to grow in wisdom, he must grow in the knowledge and likeness of God (Prov 2:5–8). This wisdom spiral is further complemented by Yhwh's reciprocal giving and protection, or his presence on the wise path, as the son properly responds and pursues (Prov 2:7–11). The father also encourages the son by highlighting the types of people who have gone before and walked in the wisdom and knowledge of God (Prov 2:20–21). These righteous and upright people ought to be emulated, those who are antithetical to the evil way and the fools on it (Prov 2:12–19, 22). Therefore, if the son desires blessing and life, he must seek to be like God and those on the wise path. In failing to do so, he will share the fate of those destined for the grave. While this second lesson focuses on finding the God of the good path, the third lesson encourages the son to express this newly found knowledge of God through the way he lives.

EXCURSUS

Hosea and the Knowledge of God

Hosea's prophetic account is a deeply profound exposé on the relational reality of Israel and Yhwh. Through a network of metaphors and theological imagery, the prophet communicates Yhwh's disdain for his covenant people and their aberrant ways. They have abandoned him and his ways for other lovers and bore "strange" (זר) children. Although their rebellion will result in *musar*, he assures them that he will still be true to his promises and would eventually restore the people – though mixed with others – to be a holy and obedient people. In the meantime, they must see the gravity of their situation, with all its graphic deviations.

As it pertains to our study here, the unique phrase "knowledge of God" only occurs in Hosea (4:1, 6:6) and Proverbs (2:5). While the two accounts provide unique contexts, they both intuitively connect "knowing God" to "walking in his ways." The Book of Hosea is an excellent study of the interplay between a gracious God and a foolish people. Just as an unfaithful spouse stumbles in delusion and selfish proclivities, so Israel misunderstood the essence of God's ways, presuming they could exchange relationship and divine imitation with empty and perfunctory practices. Yet, as the prophet clarifies, the "ways of Yhwh are upright" and so the wise are characterized by walking in these same upright ways (Hos 14:9; cf. Prov 2:7, 21, 3:6, 32, 4:11).

Metaphors

In this 8th c. prophetic work,[1] the author focuses on several issues for the people, the most relevant phrases being "knowledge of God" (דעת אלהים) and

---

[1] See J. Andrew Dearman, *The Book of Hosea*, NICOT (Grand Rapids: Eerdmans, 2010), 3–5; Francis I. Andersen and David Noel Freedman, eds., *Hosea: A New Translation with Introduction and Commentary*, AB 24 (Garden City: Doubleday, 1980), 31–39, 317; Hans Walter Wolff, *Hosea: A Commentary on the Book of the Prophet Hosea*, Hermeneia (Philadelphia: Fortress, 1974), xxi–xxiii.

"know Yhwh" (ידע את־יהוה).[2] The grammar of the latter implies a direct object relationship, implying personal knowledge of Yhwh rather than mere "knowledge" about or perhaps from. [3] It is likely that the phrases are equivalent in their sense, though perhaps highlighting nuanced aspects of such knowledge.[4] As will be explored, the general concept is that of a complex web, one integrating relational, ethical, and covenantal aspects. Perhaps the most striking dissonance, though, is Israel's claim to know God, presuming their religious practices alone were equated with the knowledge of God (Hos 8:1–14). Yet, the whole of Hosea serves as an indictment against such a claim. They were the adulterous wife analogous to Hosea's own personal situation, having broken their covenant and pursued illicit ways antithetical to the *torah* way of Yhwh.

Although metaphors are not always explicit or given explanations in the HB, Hosea's prophecy provides the reader with both a coterie of images and what they analogize.[5] First, it is explicit that Yhwh is presented as a husband and Israel as his wife (Hos 2:2).[6] She is envisioned more personally as a mother of the collective people. This naturally implies that Yhwh is their father (e.g., Hos 1:10, 11:1), though tenuous in their legitimacy (1:2). Likewise, literal adultery and prostitution, embodied by Hosea's wife, are meant to metaphorically represent Israel's disregard for Yhwh's covenant and even idolatrous, pagan practices (e.g., Hos 1:2–3, 2:5, 16, 3:1).[7] The latter half of this prophecy is built on the imagery of Hosea's children and their mixed heritage (Hos 1:10–11, 2:4–5, 5:7). Despite the desecration of Israel and the impending *musar* (Hos 5:2, 10:10), they will be redeemed and once again know only Yhwh (Hos 13:4) and do so according to his *torah* way (Hos 2:19–20).

Knowing God

As mentioned, the language of knowing God is a complex metaphor in Hosea. The terms "to know" (ידע) and "knowledge" (דעת) appear collectively twenty

---

[2] Stuart says that knowledge of God is critical to Hosea and "represents the essence of the covenant relationship" (Douglas K. Stuart, *Hosea-Jonah*, WBC 31 (Waco: Word Books, 1987), 75).

[3] Andersen and Freedman, *Hosea*, 319.

[4] John L. McKenzie, "Knowledge of God in Hosea," *JBL* 74.1 (1955): 23.

[5] For discussions of the complex literary and metaphorical aspects in Hosea, see Allan Rosengren, "Knowledge of God According to Hosea the Ripper: The Interlacing of Theology and Social Ideology in Hosea 2," *SJOT* 23.1 (2009): 122–23; Ehud Ben Zvi, "Reading Hosea and Imagining YHWH," *HBT* 30.1 (2008): 43–57; Yvonne Sherwood, *The Prostitute and the Prophet: Hosea's Marriage in Literary-Theoretical Perspective*, JSOTSup 212 (Sheffield: Sheffield Academic, 1996), 134, 307.

[6] Ben Zvi, "Reading Hosea and Imagining YHWH," 47–48; Dearman, *Book of Hosea*, 56.

[7] For a discussion on the use of "know" (ידע) or in treaty language in the ANE and biblical literature, see Herbert B. Huffmon, "The Treaty Background of Hebrew Yāda'," *BASOR* 181 (1966): 31–37.

times in the book.[8] The range of connotations includes sexual, informational, relational, personal, and covenantal.[9] It is difficult to fully parse the overlap between the uses in Hosea's account, which is perhaps an intentional rhetorical function for the reader. To better understand the implications and interpretation of the idea, several key passages will be examined (Hos 2:19–20, 4:1–6, 5:4–6, 6:3–6, 8:1–2, 13:4–5, 14:9). Each passage interweaves the central idea of knowing God with what that entails. In other words, if one does indeed know God that person will reflect him and his ways.

Hosea 2:19–20 [21–22]

"I will betroth you to myself forever. I will betroth you to myself in righteousness and justice and in steadfast love and mercy. I will betroth you to myself in faithfulness. You will know Yhwh."

While the first occurrence of "know" in Hosea (2:8 [10]) refers to Israel's ignorance of Yhwh's goodness, the second likely serves as the centralizing use for the book broadly (Hos 2:20 [22]). This use is found in a distinct five-verse unit (Hos 2:16–20 [18–22]), indicated by the phrase "and it will be in that day" (2:16 [18]; cf. 21 [23]).[10] Following a long diatribe describing the foolishness and wickedness of Israel, against all reasonability, the Lord declares that a day is coming when he will restore her to be his wife once again (Hos 2:16 [18]).[11] In fact, he promises that this second or renewed marriage will be forever (Hos 2:19 [21]). Several important elements are apparent. First, he will remove other gods from their midst (Hos 2:17 [19]). Second, he will establish a covenant of protection and "safety" (בטח) (Hos 2:18 [20]).[12] Third, this new marriage will be characterized by righteousness, justice, steadfast love, mercy, and faithfulness (Hos 2:19–20 [21–22]).[13] Fourth, he clarifies that

---

[8] (ידע) Hos 2:10, 22, 5:3, 4, 9, 6:3, 7:9, 8:2, 4, 9:7, 11:3, 13:4, 5, 14:10; (דעת) Hos 4:1, 6, 6:6.

[9] M. Douglas Carew, "To Know and Not to Know: Hosea's Know/Ledge in Discourse Perspective" (Trinity International University, PhD diss., 2000), iv.

[10] Wolff, *Hosea*, 46–47.

[11] Drawing on Exod 33:12–14, Crotty posits that the divine initiative is central to both the initial covenant and this latter version (Robert B. Crotty, "Hosea and the Knowledge of God," *ABR* 19 (1971): 10–11).

[12] While seemingly innocuous, Wolff rightly identifies the covenantal insinuations for this promise. Likewise, the assurance of "safety" (בטח) is an important promise from Wisdom in Prov 1:33, as well, central to the son's relationship with her and his presence in the Land. See Wolff, *Hosea*, 51.

[13] Dearman, following Wolff, sees this list as a type of bride-price, a *beth pretii* rather than a *beth essentiae*. While perhaps an analogous image, it does not fit the situation here. Israel broke covenant, meaning they abandoned God's ways. So, he will renew the covenant and ensure the second instance will not falter from the original qualities which are necessary. The qualities and character of God are central and necessary for participants in this covenant. It is possible, though, that the bride-price analogy simply signifies Yhwh will supply his own qualities to his "wife" in order to maintain the covenant. Stuart slightly amends the implications based on the preposition ב to infer that Yhwh as both husband and father of Israel makes the marital

all of this will result in Israel's knowledge of Yhwh, saying, "You will know Yhwh" (וְיָדַעַתְּ אֶת־יְהוָה) (Hos 2:20 [22]).[14] The final statement encapsulates the complex nature of "know" in Hosea. Here, elements of marital intimacy, personal and relational knowledge, and even ethical or covenantal aspects are intertwined.[15]

For the purposes of this study, it is most noteworthy to identify the interrelated nature of knowing Yhwh with his character qualities.[16] The Torah established that the character and even nature of Yhwh is to be merciful (רחם), just (משפט), faithful (אמונה), righteous (צדק), and full of steadfast love (חסד), beginning in Exod 33:12–34:9 and subsequently found throughout the rest of the HB.[17] Up to this point in Hosea, idolatry or pagan worship were the only issues raised. Israel was certainly adulterous in her affection for other gods. However, the ethical qualities in Hos 2:19–20 are not an arbitrary insertion. As it will be discussed later in Hosea, the paganism of Israel was intimately entangled with and perhaps causally related to her abandonment of Yhwh's *torah* ways.[18] One of the great concerns of the Torah was that upon entering the land the people would become just like the nations they were to remove (e.g., Exod 23:24; Lev 18:24–30, 20:22–26; Deut 18:9). This was not only for explicitly cultic practices but also in their conduct and character. For the people to exist in covenantal relationship with Yhwh, envisioned as marriage in Hosea, it was necessary for them to walk in his ways as well. As indicated in Hosea, one could not simply claim to know him apart from imitating and reflecting his inherent character qualities, particularly those explicitly identified in the Torah and here in Hosea.

---

agreement with himself. In his view, the implication of the preposition is "accompaniment" and "response." However, the "ongoing marriage relationship" favors the response aspect and perpetual embodiment of such covenantal qualities. Carew's view is preferable, which sees the list as qualities which will "characterize the new relationship." See Dearman, *Book of Hosea*, 127; Wolff, *Hosea*, 52–53; Stuart, *Hosea-Jonah*, 59–60; M. Douglas Carew, "To Know or Not to Know: Hosea's Use of Yd‘/D‘t," in *The Old Testament in the Life of God's People* (Winona Lake: Eisenbrauns, 2009), 77.

[14] Macintosh makes an interesting note that Israel will know "Yhwh" rather than saying "me." On one hand, this may allude to the covenantal character of God rather than personal knowledge. On the other, it could be a mere literary and covenantal concession to engender identity and clarity, along with the literary motif later in the prophecy. Either is amenable. See A. A. MacIntosh, *A Critical and Exegetical Commentary on Hosea*, ICC (Edinburgh: T&T Clark, 1997), 85.

[15] Dearman, following the majority view, sees the phrase in its personal and intimate implications. Contra the majority view, Kelle prefers the translation "acknowledge Yhwh," insinuating Israel's proper view of Yhwh as opposed to other gods. Certainly, properly knowing God, according to the majority view, would lead to Kelle's idea. However, this is only a secondary result of the more central, majority view for this phrase. See Dearman, *Book of Hosea*, 128; Brad E. Kelle, *Hosea 2: Metaphor and Rhetoric in Historical Perspective*, AcBib 20 (Atlanta: SBL, 2005), 279.

[16] Cf. MacIntosh, *Hosea*, 83–85.

[17] Dearman rightly understands Hosea to be deeply influenced by and related to the self-revelation of Yhwh. This is expressed in both his amicable qualities and his justice. As discussed in Exod 33, the nature of God is intimately related to knowing him and requires imitation of him. See Dearman, *Book of Hosea*, 128, 380.

[18] MacIntosh, *Hosea*, 84.

Hosea's prophecy to Israel of a future reality recapitulates the essence of God's desire and expectations from his Torah (Deut 5:29–33, 30:1–4, 19–20; cf. Isa 11; Ps 46:10–11).[19] Prior to the official Sinai covenant, Abraham was chosen and explicitly charged to maintain the Lord's way, "I have known (ידע) him in order that he might command his sons and house after him that they shall guard *the way of Yhwh*, doing righteousness and justice" (Gen 18:19; cf. Hos 12:6). From the time of Abraham to Moses to Hosea, the central motif was that those in covenant with Yhwh were to walk in his way by explicitly embodying or imitating his character, which at the most basic level was expressed in righteousness and justice. Yet, according to Hosea, knowing Yhwh was a complex reality. On one hand, the actual marriage practices within Israel's cultural situation had significant civil and social implications.[20] On the other, this was not a typical human marriage but one steeped with ethical and theological implications.[21] Thus, to know Yhwh included both social and civil parameters alongside ethical and theological fidelity.

Hosea 4:1b, 2, 6

"There is no faithfulness and no steadfast love and no <u>knowledge of God</u> in the land. Swearing, deception, murder, thievery, and adultery spread out. Blood flows on blood. ... My people are destroyed from lack of the knowledge. Because you rejected the knowledge, I will reject you from being a priest to me. You forgot the torah of your God; I too will forget your sons."

The examination of Hosea is especially appropriate in light of its overlap with Prov 2:5.[22] Thus, understanding the phrase "knowledge of God" in the prophet's usage will better coordinate its potential meaning or conceptual range for Proverbs. As already observed, the notion of knowing Yhwh in Hosea is a complex reality. For the prophet, the first three chapters present a poignant metaphor and prophecy of Israel's relationship with Yhwh, embodied

---

[19] Ehud Ben Zvi, *Hosea*, FOTL 21A/1 (Grand Rapids: Eerdmans, 2005), 65, 73–74.

[20] For further explanation of covenant and marriage formulas in the ANE and Israel, see Dearman, Dearman, *Book of Hosea*, 56–59.

[21] Kelle has proposed, against the majority view, that Hosea 2 is largely if not primarily pertaining to the socio-political situation of 8th c. Israel. While certainly appropriate as the historical background, the covenantal relation between Yhwh and Israel is more properly understood in the majority view (Kelle, *Hosea 2*, 19–20).

[22] McKenzie discusses the essence of the phrase and its variations. Drawing from Eichrodt, he says, "[It] is not the reflective consideration and theoretical knowledge of the divine will, but an acceptance of the revealed divine essence and will in its proper spiritual being which is seen as penetrated and determined by the divine reality." In context of his historical evaluation, he intends to differentiate biblical knowledge of God from mere philosophy, implying a covenantal and spiritual aspect. In other words, it is not simply cognitive information. See McKenzie, "Knowledge of God in Hosea," 22–23, 27; Walther Eichrodt, *Theologie des Alten Testaments* (Berlin: Evangelische Verlagsanstalt, 1948), 178.

in Hosea's own marital strife. Beginning in chapter four, however, the book takes a turn.[23] It is no longer a mere martial analogy but utilizes a more typical prophetic tone and structure, found in many other places (e.g., 2 Kgs 7:1; Isa 1:10; Jer 2:4; Ezek 13:2; Am 3:1; 2 Chron 18:18).[24]

Although Hos 1–3 was primarily concerned with the imagery of fornication as pagan worship, Hos 4 picks up on the essence of Hos 2:19–20. The prophet claims, "There is no knowledge of God in the land" (Hos 4:1).[25] The immediate and necessary question is what does this mean or imply? In context, the phrase is placed in parallel or sequence with several character qualities and ethical practices. A lack of "knowledge of God" (דַּעַת אֱלֹהִים) is paralleled directly with a lack of "faithfulness" (אמת) and "steadfast love" (חסד) (cf. Ps 25:10).[26] Furthermore, the phrase is equated in the following verse with cursing (אלה), deception (כחש), murder (רצח), theft (גנב), adultery (נאף), and bloodshed (דמים). While the first two are against Yhwh's personal character, the secondary group is explicitly in violation of the Torah and God's covenantal expectations.[27]

In interpreting the meaning, one option is to see the phrase "knowledge of God" as merely one of the aberrations, though distinct and isolated from the others mentioned. In this view, it is not possible to explicate any particular meaning from the phrase. However, as seen in Hos 2:20, knowing Yhwh was already set in parallel with two of God's character qualities, "steadfast love" and "faithfulness."[28] While the occurrence of "know" in Hos 2:20 was in the verbal form, the nominal form in 4:1 likely implies an objective genitive relationship for the Hebrew construct phrase, paralleling the direct object relationship from earlier.[29] In other words, the "knowledge of

---

[23] Dearman, *Book of Hosea*, 145.

[24] John Goldingay, "Hosea 4 and 11, and the Structure of Hosea," *TynBul* 71.2 (2020): 184–85; MacIntosh, *Hosea*, 128.

[25] Freedman and Andersen view this passage against the eschatological, parallel antithesis in Isa 11:9, "The earth will be filled with the knowledge of Yhwh" (Andersen and Freedman, *Hosea*, 334).

[26] Dearman comments on this passage saying, "The charge is that among the people of God there is no conduct or character in accord with God's revealed will and consistent with his character. Loving-kindness and faithfulness are a recognized word pair in ancient Israel. The word pair typically describes attributes of YHWH" (Dearman, *Book of Hosea*, 147).

[27] Dearman, *Book of Hosea*, 150–51; MacIntosh, *Hosea*, 130; Stuart, *Hosea-Jonah*, 75; Andersen and Freedman, *Hosea*, 337; Carew, "To Know or Not to Know," 80.

[28] Here, Macintosh rightly sees the connection between these passages, acknowledging the moral and covenantal implications (MacIntosh, *Hosea*, 128; Wolff, *Hosea*, 67).

[29] Carew uses "subjective" to mean personal but also for subjective genitive with Yhwh as the giver of knowledge. Likewise, he uses "objective" to mean an external or concrete thing, implying mere cognitive information. The use of "objective" in this study intends the grammatical function similar to those phrases which utilize the *et* (את) as a direct object marker. Carew does not accept the objective genitive category for the phrase, though it seems he means in the sense of content rather than syntactical grammar. The verbal phrases in Hos 2:20 and 6:3 place Yhwh in the objective position utilizing the et (את), which Carew and most others see as related to Hos 4:1 and 6:6. For a discussion on the debates regarding this grammatical feature, see Carew, "To Know or Not to Know," 73–74, 79, 83–84.

God" implies "one who knows God," God being the implicit direct object.[30] Such a view would be against a mere informational or source view for the function of this construct.[31] As Freedman and Andersen rightly commented,

> Knowledge [of God] means understanding of his ways as revealed in the covenant ... These qualities are expressed in personal relationships. In Yahweh's covenant, they are shown by loving obedience to his ways; but his 'ways' are his own treatment of his creatures – he is good to them. ... When the three covenant virtues fail, the crimes listed in v. 2 follow.[32]

Thus, knowledge of God is not simply information about or from God. Rather, it implies a complex reality intertwined with relational, ethical, and covenantal knowledge,[33] where God is the object of knowledge. Likewise, it implies Israel must conduct itself in the way God does. This imitative correspondence is at the heart of what Hosea and Proverbs see as knowing God.

Hosea's prophecy goes on to supply a judgment (Hos 4:6) based on the reality of Israel's condition (4:1–2). In Hos 4:6, the prophet states, "My people are destroyed from lack of the knowledge (knowing). Because you rejected the knowledge (knowing), so I will reject you from my priesthood. Since you forgot the *torah* of your God, I myself will also forget your sons." In this passage, the term "knowledge" is associated negatively with forgetting God and his *torah*, or his *torah* way as described in Hos 4:1–2.[34] The article is likely an anaphoric connection to the full phrase "knowledge of God," which is presumably definite.[35] In a similar situation, Wisdom claims in Lesson 1 that because

---

[30] Bruce K. Waltke and M. O'Connor, *An Introduction to Biblical Hebrew Syntax* (Winona Lake: Eisenbrauns, 1990), 146–47.

[31] Wolff rightly suggests a web of connections between this use of "knowledge" with the other significant occurrences, e.g., Hos 2:20, 6:6. However, he makes a confused statement regarding the phrase and this verse, "'Knowledge of God' is not a second, different kind of 'religious' sphere in addition to the 'ethical' ... the phrase means knowledge of his teachings as the source of a harmonious community life within Israel. ... דעת אלהים signifies the intimate knowledge of the revealed law of God." On one hand, he is correct to see the connection between the phrase and God's *torah*. Yet, he incorrectly divorces *torah* from God. By doing so, he renders the entire marital analogy of Hos 1–3 meaningless. God's ways are reflected in his *torah* and his people are expected to reflect his ways by maintaining his *torah*. As will be seen throughout the rest of Hosea, the motif is central to Hosea's prophecy. Wickedness and immorality are the other side of the coin for lack of knowing God. See Wolff, *Hosea*, 67.

[32] Andersen and Freedman, *Hosea*, 336.

[33] Dearman, *Book of Hosea*, 147.

[34] MacIntosh, *Hosea*, 139; Dearman, *Book of Hosea*, 158. Dearman suggests that "the instruction of your God is interchangeable with knowledge/knowledge of God." This suggestion is due to the parallel structure and converse significance in the Torah between forgetting and remembering.

[35] The use of *hada'at* (הַדַּעַת) is unusual. It only occurs a handful of times (Gen 2:9, 17; 1 Kgs 7:14; Jer 22:16; Dan 12:4). Used twice here in Hos 4:6, it does not indicate the subject of the verb as it does in Dan 12:4. In Gen 2:9, it specifies the definite construct phrase "the tree of knowledge of good and evil." In 1 Kgs 7:14, it is preceded by a direct object marker in sequence with several other attributes of a craftsman. The only other similar use is from Jer 22:16, which

"fools hate knowledge" and reject her calls and counsel she will reject their calls (Prov 1:22–29). To further clarify his meaning of "knowledge" or "knowledge of God," Hosea indicts Israel on both ethical and cultic grounds, "They sinned against me … I will visit on account of [the people's] ways and deeds … They prostituted apart from their God. On the tops of their hills, they sacrificed … Ephraim is joined with idols" (Hos 4:7, 9, 12, 13, 17).[36] Thus, they had become thoroughly wicked and did not know Yhwh.[37] Because of this, Israel would be punished for both its pagan worship and its moral, relational abandonment of God and his way of life.[38] By imitating the aberrant practices of the nations, they had rejected Yhwh and his character.

Hosea 5:3, 4, 6

"Surely, I know Ephraim and Israel is not hidden from me. For, now, you have fornicated, O Ephraim; Israel is defiled. Their deeds do not allow to return to their God. For a spirit of fornication is within them and they do not know Yhwh. … With their sheep and cattle, they go to seek Yhwh but they will not find. He withdrew from them."

Continuing the indictment from the previous chapter,[39] Hosea reiterates the problem in Israel as both pagan practices and unethical behavior. In a unique occurrence, Hosea says that Yhwh "knows" Ephraim. While on the surface this may seem like a relational use, the parallel line indicates that "Israel is not hidden" (Hos 5:3). So, the parallel line clarifies that Yhwh knows the sin and deviations of Ephraim and Israel. Thus, he declares that "they do not know

---

is an interesting and important phrase for this study, "He judged the judgment of the humble and poor, then it was well. Is this not the knowledge of (to know) me?" The phrase in Hos 4 could also be a noun (or substantive infinitive) with an article or an unusual case of a definite infinitive construct. The typical infinitive form, found nearby in Jer 24:7, is "to know me" (לָדַעַת אֹתִי), which is also very similar to the message and intent of Hosea. Either way, the phrase is taken grammatically in Jer 22, it seems to imply knowing God in a direct object sense. This use accords well with Hos 2:20 and 4:6, as well. See Waltke and O'Connor, *Biblical Hebrew Syntax*, 600–603; McKenzie, "Knowledge of God in Hosea," 26.

[36] Andersen and Freedman, *Hosea*, 323.

[37] Wolff mistakes the import of this verse because of his myopic view of "knowledge" in Hosea. He rejects Weiser's "subjective" view of the phrase which would imply "attitudes of 'heartfelt devotion' and of an 'inward relationship to God.'" His basis for the rejection is the term "reject" (מאס), which he believes always has a "concrete object." For him, this would necessitate "knowledge" to be of God's legal commands. Similar to the mistake in Hos 4:1, divorcing *torah* from Yhwh is exactly the opposite of the point of Hosea. To reject *torah* is to reject the ways of God. To reject the ways of God is to reject God. See Wolff, *Hosea*, 78–79; A. Weiser, *Das Buch der zwölf kleinen Propheten*, ATD 24 (Göttingen: Vandenhoeck & Ruprecht, 1949), 41–45; Georg Fohrer, "Umkehr und Erlösung beim Propheten Hosea," *TZ* 11.3 (1955): 169; Eberhard Baumann, "'Wissen um Gott' bei Hosea als Urform von Theologie?" *EvT* 15.8–9 (1955): 426–31.

[38] Ben Zvi, *Hosea*, 95.

[39] Stuart, *Hosea-Jonah*, 90.

Yhwh" because "the spirit of prostitution is within them" (Hos 5:4; cf. 4:12).[40] It is important to note the literary semantic play by Hosea and God in these few verses. God knows them, though only in the sense of information regarding their sin rather than in the sense of covenantal relationship as seen elsewhere in Hosea. Conversely, Israel and Ephraim do not know Yhwh, likely in the relational and covenantal sense.[41] It would seem their own lack of knowledge led them to project ignorance on God, as though he did not see the truth of their lives.[42] This deluded projection is similar to the charge found in Ps 94:7, "They slay the widow and sojourner and they murder the fatherless. But they say, 'Yah does not see and the God of Jacob does not understand.'" To this foolish notion, Hosea clarifies that although they have separated themselves from God's covenant, they cannot escape his justice.

Several verses later, Hosea indicts his audience for their unethical, anti-*torah* practices such as moving a boundary marker (Hos 5:10), again an injustice in direct violation of Torah (Deut 19:14; cf. 27:17; Job 24:2; Prov 22:28). In fact, their lack of knowledge will not only result in *musar* (Hos 5:2; cf. Prov 3:11–12) but will prevent them from returning to or finding Yhwh (cf. Isa 59:2).[43] The prophet states, "They will go to seek Yhwh and they will not find. He has withdrawn from them" (Hos 5:6; cf. 7:10).[44] Not only does this statement parallel Wisdom in Prov 1:28 but it highlights the deeply relational and covenantal aspect of knowing God. In other words, their profligate ways caused a separation between them and Yhwh.[45] Going after other gods and abandoning the *torah* way will result in, or is perhaps evidence of, their lack of knowledge.

Hosea parallels the inability of Israel to return to God with their wicked deeds. As a result, they do not and cannot know Yhwh. Thus, their lack of knowing God is directly related to his ways.[46] In other words, abrogation of the covenant through a corrupt will and way caused a real, relational divide. From the Torah, however, God desired Israel to seek him, even after they had strayed (Deut 4:29; cf. Prov 1:28, 8:35; Jer 29:13–14). Seeking him was a fundamental aspect of relational fidelity. Much like the promises in Deuteronomy, Hosea provides a hopeful future for the rebellious nation, "I will return to my place when they atone for guilt and seek my face"

---

[40] Freedman and Andersen suggest that "spirit of prostitution" is an explicit reference to rival gods, which necessarily creates ignorance of the Lord (Andersen and Freedman, *Hosea*, 391).

[41] Dearman, *Book of Hosea*, 174.

[42] Cf. Isa 29:15; Ezek 8:12, 9:9; Ps 10:11, 59:7; 64:5, 73:11, 94:7; Job 22:13.

[43] Regarding the idea of seeking God, Dearman suggests that it indicates the failed attempt to receive blessings. God has "withdrawn from them" (Hos 5:6). Because of this, they do not have access to his blessings. While this certainly could be an aspect or even the motive underlying Ephraim/Israel, Hos 5:3–4 intimate the disparity of covenantal relationship. The inability to find God is akin to relational separation and thus to him treating Israel like any other nation. See Dearman, *Book of Hosea*, 176.

[44] As MacIntosh notes, "To seek (the face of) God … i.e., a personal communion with him" (MacIntosh, *Hosea*, 186).

[45] Dearman, *Book of Hosea*, 173.

[46] Macintosh builds a conceptual and instructive motif between Hos 5:4 and 2:20, indicating the covenantal and relational ramifications (MacIntosh, *Hosea*, 184).

(Hos 5:15). As the prophet makes clear, the Lord's desire and plan is for restoration and knowledge, unlike the bleak fate of the wicked fools in Prov 1–9.

Hosea 6:3a, 6

"'May we know, may we pursue <u>to know Yhwh</u>' ... I desire steadfast love and not sacrifice and <u>knowledge of God</u> more than burnt offerings."

As described in Hos 2, Israel was characterized as fickle in her affections and pursuits.[47] She was with the Lord but then chased after other lovers (Hos 2:5 [7]). After her tryst, though, she naively declared, "I will return to my first husband for it is better for me than now" (Hos 2:7 [9]).[48] This unstable characteristic arises again in Hos 6. The prophet dramatizes a hypothetical statement from Israel. In this rhetorical declaration, Israel says, "Let us return to Yhwh ... Let us know, let us pursue to know Yhwh" (Hos 6:1, 3). While this sounds quite noble *prima facie*, it is clear that the intent is the same as it was in Hos 2, "Your steadfast love (חסד) is like a morning cloud and dew which goes early" (Hos 6:4; cf. 7:11–16, 13:3). Ironically, inconsistency and being fickle is exactly the opposite of חסד, which implies loyalty and commitment. Israel's fickle desire for blessings without relational fidelity is also apparent, "He will come to us as the rain; he will bring forth on the land as spring showers" (Hos 6:3). On one hand, the Lord did promise to restore Israel after their *musar*, if they would seek him. However, the prophet clarifies their vacuous desire to "know Yhwh" in the rest of this chapter.

Several verses later, Hosea put forth a powerful statement from Yhwh, "I delight in steadfast love (חסד) and not sacrifice, and knowledge of God (דַּעַת אֱלֹהִים) more than burnt offerings" (Hos 6:6). As previously mentioned, the phrase "knowledge of God" is unique. In its occurrence in Hos 4, the phrase parallels both ethical and behavioral aspects of God and his way.[49] Similarly, here, the phrase is placed alongside a covenantal character quality of God.[50] The parallel structure of the verse implies that the head verb "I delight" applies also to the second line. Likewise, the term "steadfast love" is paralleled with "knowledge of God." Finally, the contrasted element is synonymously paralleled between "sacrifice" and "burnt offerings." Although parallelism is often difficult to identify, the prophet provides a fairly clear example of incomplete synonymous parallelism. The comparison of "steadfast love" and "knowledge of God" is of particular importance since the same two terms

---

[47] Carew, "To Know or Not to Know," 82.

[48] MacIntosh, *Hosea*, 226.

[49] Andersen and Freedman, *Hosea*, 430.

[50] MacIntosh equates the phrase with "Yahweh's ethical nature" along with "moral integrity" and "decency" (MacIntosh, *Hosea*, 234–35).

appear together in Hos 4:1,[51] along with a similar phrase in 2:19. Understanding the network of phrases together, it becomes apparent that to "know God" it is not only necessary to abandon other gods but also to live in the way of God and to imitate his character.[52] Mere cultic obedience is not sufficient,[53] as it was expressed to Saul three centuries prior (1 Sam 15:22).[54] Knowing God is a complex reality that necessitates personal, ethical, covenantal, and theological aspects.

Immediately after condemning Israel's sacrifice – namely sacrifice void of knowledge – he compares their treachery to Adam's breaking of the covenant (Hos 6:7).[55] Although the text does not provide much explanation for mentioning Adam, it perhaps points to a few critical underlying ideas. First, sacrifice did not exist before Adam and Eve rebelled and were cursed. Second, Adam and Eve existed in perfect relational harmony with God, implying that they knew God. Third, prior to their fall, they properly imitated God and embodied his characteristics as co-regents, enacting God's dominion on the earth. Fourth, the sin they committed was both disobedience to God's *torah* and a desire for improper imitation. Finally, their seemingly small sin cascaded into a world filled with rebellion, sin, murder, etc.

Hosea adds to the indictment against Israel by identifying some specific atrocities. Their priests were wicked like thieves and murderers waiting to ambush the innocent (Hos 6:9; cf. Prov 1:11).[56] Not only is this a direct violation of the Torah (e.g., Exod 20:13, 15), it results in or is evidence of a lack of knowledge of God. Certainly, robbing and killing do not cohere with God's quality of steadfast love or mercy. Because of their fickle return and rejection of God's *torah* way, the prophet promises that judgment for the people is fixed (Hos 6:11). It was not acceptable for them to engage in cultic practices found in the Torah while simultaneously rejecting the *torah* way.[57] As Hos 6:6 makes it clear, the cultic practices were never the goal or an end in themselves. Following in the way of Yhwh was always the objective, just as it was with Adam in the Garden.

---

[51] Stuart, *Hosea-Jonah*, 110.

[52] Against previous statements, Wolff comments, "The concept of חסד indicates how completely the right covenant relationship with God forms the basis of the Old Testament ethos (cf. v 4 and 4:1f). The parallel concept דעת אלהים shows that this relationship to God – indeed, this communion ... is the foundation of everything. ... To know him is to experience him and to live in communion with him in trust and obedience. For the Hebrew thought, these existential components are inseparably bound to the cognitive functions" (Wolff, *Hosea*, 120).

[53] MacIntosh, *Hosea*, 188.

[54] Andersen and Freedman, *Hosea*, 431.

[55] Stuart, *Hosea-Jonah*, 111.

[56] Stuart suggests a few metaphorical alternatives such as "murder of orthodoxy" or priestly strife between rival groups. Though plausible, a straightforward reading is not problematic and captures sentiments elsewhere in Hosea (Stuart, *Hosea-Jonah*, 111).

[57] Carew, "To Know or Not to Know," 83.

Hosea 8:1b-2

"They transgressed my covenant and against my torah *they rebelled. To me they cry out, 'My God, <u>we Israel know you.</u>'"*

Hosea's indictment of Israel continues through Hos 7 and 8. In language similar to earlier passages, he condemns their capricious ways and desires (Hos 7:11–14).[58] Chapter 8 then heightens the self-deception that was taking place in Israel. In their blinding wickedness, they cry out, "My God, we know you, Israel" (Hos 8:2). At this point in the prophecy, the claim is patently absurd. From the beginning of the book to now, they have been nothing but adulterous and wicked, rejecting both God and his ways. Even here in this passage, the prophet points out that they have idols and in Samaria an official golden calf (Hos 8:4, 5; cf. 11:2, 13:1–2). Altogether, these aberrations confirm what Yhwh says, "They have transgressed my covenant and against my *torah* they have rebelled" (Hos 8:1).[59] The Lord makes it clear that they do not know him, regardless of what they may think or claim. Perhaps most important for the reader, this clarification is closely connected with God's covenant and *torah*. In other words, one cannot know or claim to know God apart from walking in his *torah* way. The knowledge of God is inextricably tied to imitating and obeying him.

Hosea 13:4–5

"I am Yhwh, your God from the land of Egypt. <u>You shall only know me.</u> There is no one who saves apart from me. It was I who knew you in the wilderness, in the land of drought."

Established at the outset of Hosea's prophecy, the central theme of the whole book was fidelity to Yhwh, the covenant God of Israel. It is appropriate that near the end he reiterates and emphasizes the exclusivity of God. Hosea utilizes a subtle framing for a covenant formula from the Torah (Hos 13:4–5; e.g., Exod 20:2; Lev 26:13; Deut 5:6; cf. 1 Sam 2:2; Isa 45:5, 21).[60] Up until Hos

---

[58] Dearman, *Book of Hosea*, 219.

[59] Wolf states, "[*torah*] denotes the entire disclosure of Yahweh's will, already fixed in writing ... It describes that attitude and conduct appropriate to the covenant ... the Torah can also mediate the entire 'knowledge of God'" (Hos 4:6) (Wolff, *Hosea*, 138).

[60] As Craigie illuminates, "[The Decalog] was the legal aspect of the covenant relationship in a sense similar to the role a legal wedding contract plays in a marriage. ... It was representative of God's love for men and it called in turn for a response of love (6:4–5). The Decalog was representative of God's love in that its injunctions, both negative and positive, led not to restriction of life, but to fullness of life. It demanded a response of love, not because obedience would somehow accumulate credit in the sight of God, but because the grace of God, experienced already in the liberation from Egypt and in the divine initiative in the covenant

13:5, the emphasis had been on the people knowing God. Here, the focus turns to God's knowledge of the people.[61] Thus, the marital metaphor as a covenant from Hos 1–3 returns to the Lord's appeal to Israel.[62] From a theological perspective, if God is omniscient then his knowledge of Israel cannot simply mean information here (cf. Jer 23:24). Rather, in the vein of marriage, Yhwh's knowledge of Israel is covenantal and personal. For genuine knowledge of this kind, however, they needed to be like God in order to have "a God so near" (Deut 4:7). Apart from the *torah* way, it was not only that Israel did not know God but that God could not know them. Relational knowledge is inherently bidirectional. One cannot say they have relational knowledge of a tree or rock, due to a lack of relational capacity. Similarly, Israel had abdicated their relational capacity to know God, and conversely for God to know them, by seeking other gods and by refusing to walk in the way of Yhwh. His desire for them to reflect his ways was inherent to his desire for them to know him and vice versa.

Hosea 14:9 [10]

"Who is wise, he will understand these things, discerning, he will know them: upright are the ways of Yhwh, the righteous will walk in them but rebels will stumble in them."

Just as the Torah had predicted (e.g., Deut 8:12–14, 32:15), once Israel entered the land, they no longer felt a need for God. They clearly abandoned him and his covenant way (Hos 13:6). In spite of this rebellion, the prophet concludes on a high note with a future restoration. There is a promise for restoration, security, and blessing (Hos 14:3–7). This blessing, though, is part and parcel of God's restored presence and relation with Israel (Hos 14:5, 7, 8). As Wolff notes, "Yahweh himself is the gift of salvation to his people."[63] In his kindness and grace, he promises to heal and love them (Hos 14:2, 4).

To conclude the whole prophetic book, this curious epilogue appears as the final verse.[64] Regardless of the verse's authorship,[65] its message highlights a central though subtle theme. As the verse says, "The ways of Yhwh are upright, the righteous will walk in them but rebels will stumble in

---

promise, elicited such a response from man in gratitude" (Peter C. Craigie, *The Book of Deuteronomy*, NICOT (Eerdmans, 1976), 149–50; Dearman, *Book of Hosea*, 380).

[61] Dearman rejects the textual emendation from the LXX and Syr. which replace "know" with "shepherd" on the grounds that *yada'* (ידע) is an important motif in Hosea. This would also be strengthened by the parallel passages. See Dearman, *Book of Hosea*, 321–22.

[62] Dearman, *Book of Hosea*, 321.

[63] Wolff, *Hosea*, 236.

[64] Ben Zvi sees this epilogue as the "interpretive key" for the rest of the prophetic book (Ben Zvi, *Hosea*, 315).

[65] Opinions differ widely on a specific date; however, most permit that it is possible the passage is original to Hosea and the 8th c. For some discussion of the issue, see Wolff, *Hosea*, 239; Dearman, *Book of Hosea*, 16–21; MacIntosh, *Hosea*, 582–83; Stuart, *Hosea-Jonah*, 219.

them" (Hos 14:9). The way of Yhwh and stumbling are found at important places previously. The term "stumble" (כשל) occurs at Hos 4:5 and 5:5 (cf. Prov 4:12, 16, 19). In Hos 4:5, as discussed earlier, the context is the natural result of not knowing God or lacking knowledge. Likewise, this lack was akin to *torah* violation and their lack of God's characteristics. Similarly, as discussed in Hos 5:5, the stumbling of Israel is because they do not know Yhwh. Their ignorance is due to cultic fornication and violation of the Torah. As a result, Yhwh withdrew and rejected them. The entire import of Hosea's message is for the reader to walk in the ways of Yhwh, the *torah* way. In doing so, Israel will exist in a proper covenant relationship with Yhwh, allowing for the knowledge of God. Hosea 14:9, then, is a summation and recapitulation of 2:19–20. One particular difficulty regarding the ways of Yhwh is that even perfunctory or partial obedience is not sufficient. Rather, walking in the ways of Yhwh and knowing him is a complex reality that necessitates the totality of a person, their will, and their ways.[66] As Dearman notes, "There is a sense in which YHWH is his ways."[67] Thus, the author's point is that to reject his ways is to reject him.[68] So, if the reader accepts and walks in the ways of Yhwh by imitating him, he is in essence accepting Yhwh himself.

Conclusion

In this highly charged message, the prophet Hosea provides Israel with a dense call for both warning and hope. On one hand, they had abandoned Yhwh and his ways while simultaneously claiming to know him. As Hosea sharply clarifies, their actions proved otherwise, which necessitated his *musar*. Yet, despite their profligate ways, God's good nature promised them a future hope, a time when the people would be characterized by God's characteristics through their relational knowledge. In this future, they would not revel in injustice and idolatry but would join in the way of the righteous (cf. Prov 2:20–21). As seen in Prov 1–9, this way of the righteous necessarily reflects Yhwh and Wisdom in their own walking on this path (e.g., Prov 8:20). Likewise, the proverbial father exerts a great deal of focus on the problematic issue of infidelity (Lessons 1–2, 9–13), particularly as it relates to the wisdom program and figured in the contrast between Widom and the *zarah* (זרה). In a variety of ways, Hosea's condemnations of Israel parallel the warnings for the proverbial son, which exhort him not to walk in such foolish ways. Rather, as a wise and upright son, he is to follow in the *torah* way in order that he might truly know God.

---

[66] Ben Zvi suggests that the whole of Hosea was a picture of a wise God teaching his children. In return, the audience of Hosea's prophecy were to reflect and imitate God in his divine ways (Ben Zvi, "Reading Hosea and Imagining YHWH," 55).

[67] Dearman, *Book of Hosea*, 346.

[68] Wolff divorces *torah* from God, suggesting "ways of Yhwh" only implies obedience to commands (Wolff, *Hosea*, 240). While part of the equation, mere obedience fails to capture the metaphor of marriage and the personal nature of covenantal fidelity.

LESSON 3

Analysis of Proverbs 3:1–10
"Keeping commandments is life"

As the wisdom student is learning adherence to instruction and rules, the proverbial father focuses on the inherent relational aspect in this early stage of the wisdom program, similar to Lesson 2. In Lesson 3, the father appeals to the well-worn Torah path, which implicitly espouses the long tradition of transgenerational instruction and imitation (Prov 3:1–4), a key point also promoted in Lessons 6, 12, and 13. At the heart of the lesson, though, the son is primarily expected to express and grow in his knowledge of God by walking in the divine path (Prov 3:5–7). Of course, this path is both internal and external. Just as God operates internally and externally, so the son is to reflect his ways. This expression of divine knowledge is drawn from Prov 2:5 and Hosea,[1] teaching a relational reality that necessitates a divine way of life – including character, desires, and behaviors (Prov 3:6). Furthermore, this lesson teaches that the relational connection expressed in this instruction is bidirectional and even reciprocal (Prov 3:9–10). In a curious way, God imitates man as he imitates God. Thus, the son's educational process is further expanded along the imitative, wisdom trajectory from the proverbial father toward the divine Father, preeminently figured as such in Lesson 4.

Structure of Lesson 3

Unlike Lesson 2, the third lesson is less formally structured.[2] However, it is often noted by scholars that there is a symmetry of couplets that form its poetic structure. While Lesson 2 was an extended conditional, these couplets are driven by imperatives and jussives, comprised of two verses each where

---

[1] For more discussion, see Excursus: Hosea and the Knowledge of God.

[2] Nel makes an unnecessarily bold claim, "[Prov 3:1–12] reveals a highly poetic structure. This poem is deliberately structured and without the recognition of this structure any attempted interpretation is in jeopardy" (Philip Johannes Nel, *The Structure and Ethos of the Wisdom Admonitions in Proverbs*, BZAW 158 (New York: De Gruyter, 1982), 59).

the first is a command or teaching followed by a benefit or result from adhering to the command.[3] Most commentators divide this lesson at 3:12, creating a twelve-verse unit to start Prov 3. However, as discussed in the "Structure of Proverbs 1–9," this study divides the section at 3:10.[4] For most, the lesson is comprised of six couplets (Prov 3:1–12). However, five couplets are formed by dividing at 3:10.[5] While six may seem symmetrically appealing prima facie, the five-couplet structure illuminates two thematic units: 3:1–4 serve as "the blessing of *torah*" and 3:5–10 serve as "the blessing of Yhwh."

I. The Blessing of *torah* (3:1–4)
II. The Blessing of Yhwh (3:5–10)
    a.   Trust & Know Yhwh (5a)
    b.   Fear Yhwh (7b)
    c.   Honor Yhwh (9a)

Although Yhwh is central in Prov 3:11–12, this couplet fits better as an inclusio with the divine couplet in 3:19–20, surrounding the wisdom poem of 3:13–18. In fact, if the schema for command-blessing in each couplet were correct, Prov 3:11–12 would break from the pattern with a command-explanation instead. Likewise, the initial command of 3:11 is more similar to 3:1 in form than 3:2–10, implying it is a new unit.[6] As mentioned in the "Structure," it is possible that Prov 3:11–12 serves as a soft break or transition between lessons, passing elements from one lesson to the next (cf. Prov 7:24–

---

[3] Strangely, Fox states that "there are no true *miṣwot* ('precepts,' 'commands') in this lecture." By this, it seems he means legal, civil, and social prescriptive behaviors. Of course, the commands to trust, know, fear, turn, and honor are divinely oriented and pietistic but commands nonetheless. Such pietistic "commands" are not foreign to Torah either (e.g., Deut 6:5). See Fox, *Proverbs 1–9*, 143.

[4] Kidner similarly divides his third broad section of Prov 1–9, titled "The wholehearted disciple," into three sections: 3:1–10, 11–20, 21–35. Unfortunately, he does not provide discussion on the logic or purpose of these units. Weeks divides the section as Kidner, appealing to the "my son" division and the MT's section mark. See Derek Kidner, *Proverbs: An Introduction and Commentary*, TOTC (IVP, 1964), 60–62; Weeks, *Instruction and Imagery in Proverbs 1–9*, 50–51.

[5] Although Whybray includes Prov 3:11–12 as a division in his structure, he equivocates on the relationship between 3:1–10 and 11–12. Because of the distinction of content, he says, "Only vv. 11–12, which constitute a fourth admonition, appear to be a later addition to this instruction: these verses are concerned not with duties towards God but with the pupil's proper reaction to God's actions towards him. Without them the instruction comprises [five] couplets." Fox also includes Prov 3:11–12 with 3:1–10 but notes his uncertainty, "The MT marks a new section (pisqaʾ) here, beginning the verse on a new line. In terms of content, there is undoubtedly a certain shift in topic, but unless we take vv. 11–12 as a stray epigram or a later addition, it must be joined to Lecture III." See Whybray, *Composition of the Book of Proverbs*, 19; Fox, *Proverbs 1–9*, 152.

[6] In Prov 3:7, the verse uses the second masculine singular imperfect (*yiqtol*) "you must not be" (אַל־תְּהִי). This hortatory, jussive form matches with Prov 3:1 (אַל־תִּשְׁכָּח) and 3:11 (אַל־תִּמְאָס). However, Prov 3:1 and 11 both include "my son" (בְּנִי). Thus, Prov 3:7 is likely connecting the commands of 3:1 with 3:7, rather than indicating that 3:11–12 are a part of 3:1–10.

27, 8:32–36).[7] The second section of Lesson 3 can also be broken down into three central teachings.[8] These are indicated by imperatives with Yhwh functioning as the coordinating refrain.

Furthermore, the three teachings include additional imperatives that emphasize the essence of the lesson. In Prov 3:5–6, there are two imperatives: "trust Yhwh" (בְּטַח אֶל־יְהוָה) and "know him" (דָעֵהוּ). In 3:7, the second line has two imperatives: "fear Yhwh" (יְרָא אֶת־יְהוָה) and "turn from evil" (וְסוּר מֵרָע). Finally, Prov 3:9 has one imperative but it is implied or elided from 3:10, "honor Yhwh" (כַּבֵּד אֶת־יְהוָה).

The Blessing of *torah* (3:1–4)

In Waltke's view, the structure and theme of this lesson illuminate a covenantal duality between the two involved, illuminating responsibilities for both the human and divine partners.[9] The lesson begins with a montage of Torah language.[10] In particular, the teacher implores the son in Prov 3:1 to

---

[7] Pemberton argues that Prov 3:11–12 must be part of 3:1–10, due to thematic and lexical connections. However, even in his schema, Prov 3:3–10 are distinct from 3:11–12, which he refers to as the "Epilogue." Likewise, despite some valid points, his argument overlooks the verses' value for the next section, 3:13–20. Thus, it is likely Prov 3:11–12 were intended and structured as a bridge between Lessons 3 and 4, both of which emphasize the importance of Yhwh and overlay the proverbial father with the Fatherhood of God. See Glenn D. Pemberton, "The Rhetoric of the Father: A Rhetorical Analysis of the Father/Son Lectures in Proverbs 1–9" (University of Denver; Colorado Seminary, PhD diss., 1999), 160–71.

[8] See Waltke, *Proverbs (1–15)*, 240.

[9] Waltke states, "In theological terms, the admonitions in the odd verses of Prov 3:1–12 present the obligations of the son, the human covenant partner; the argumentation in the even verses shows the obligations of the Lord, the divine covenant partner. The human partner has the responsibility to keep ethics and piety, and the divine partner the obligation to bless his worshiper with peace, prosperity, and longevity" (Bruce K. Waltke, "Does Proverbs Promise Too Much?" *AUSS* 34.2 (1996): 321).

[10] Scholars such as G. E. Wright, struggled to connect biblical wisdom to their OT theology schemas. As Wright said, "In any attempt to outline a discussion of Biblical faith it is the wisdom literature which offers the chief difficulty because it does not fit into the type of faith exhibited in the historical and prophetic literatures. In it there is no explicit reference to or development of the doctrine of history, election, or covenant."

Toombs contended instead, "The Law, then, takes its religious significance, not from its content, but from its context; from the fact that it originated in, and was itself an integral part of the act of God by which he worked a deliverance for his people. ... Wisdom, like the Law, was hypostatized and regarded as the preexistent instrument of God in the creation of the world. In estimating the theological significance of the Law, it has been found necessary to look beyond both the specific commandments which make up the legal codes and the metaphysical glorification of the place of Torah in God's universal plan, and to focus attention on the context in which the Law was given. It is thus *a priori* probable that the theological meaning of wisdom will be found in the process by which wisdom comes to men." See G. E. Wright, *God Who Acts: Biblical Theology as Recital*, SBT 8 (London: SCM, 1952), 103; Lawrence E. Toombs, "O.T. Theology and the Wisdom Literature," *JBR* 23.3 (1955): 193–96; Graeme Goldsworthy, "Wisdom and Its Literature in Biblical-Theological Context," *SBJT* 15.3 (2011): 42–55.

not "forget" (שכח) his *torah* or "commands" (מצות).[11] Together, the lexemes find a strong basis in Deuteronomy.[12] This coordination is especially important for Lesson 3 because it establishes the conceptual framework for the teacher's intent. Whybray states, "The contents of this teaching are however wholly concerned with the pupil's relationship with Yahweh."[13] In Deuteronomy, Yhwh is the teacher of Israel (cf. Ps 25:4–5, 86:11, 119:66).[14] Moses was the intermediary merely delivering God's teaching.[15] Likewise, it has been observed that "forgetting" is not a passive or accidental event, which is contrasted with "protect" (נצר).[16] Rather, it is a conscious abandonment of God's ways, figured as a wayward path. The blessing itself is Deuteronomic as well. In Prov 3:2, the son is provided with the hopeful or ideal results of following the *torah* way. By walking in the ways of God, the son will experience "length of days," "years of life," and *shalom*. Although such terms were likely colloquial blessing statements,[17] Deut 30:20 places life in direct connection with a relationship with Yhwh, "He is your life and length of days." Regarding life with Yhwh, Waltke notes, "In biblical theology 'full' life is essentially a relationship with God. According to Gen 2:17 disruption of the proper relationship with the One who is the source of life means death. Wisdom is concerned with this proper relationship and so with this kind of life."[18] Interestingly, in Prov 1–9, Wisdom and the teacher's *torah* are given as the sources of life and length of days (Prov 3:16, 18, 22, 4:10, 13, 22, 6:23, 8:35, 9:11). Rather than driving a wedge between Yhwh, Wisdom, and the teacher's *torah*, it is more cohesive to see an intentional and necessary overlap between them.[19] If "path" is the proper metaphor, then the son is called to walk this righteous and divine path, equivalent to seeking God (cf. Ps 119:1–2). In so doing, he will find God and the source of wisdom and life (cf. 2:5–6).

---

[11] Fox claims, "*Torah* in Proverbs does not refer to law or legally enforceable ordinances." In contrast, Loader rightly rejects Fox's implications, "... that does not deny the religious impact of its use." Whether or not "proverbs" or "instructions" were enforceable is unknown, though improbable. Yet, if the teacher's reference point for his *torah* was the Torah, then they could in a sense be obligatory according to Fox's notion. The proverbial *torah* is presented as fatherly instruction rather than judicial absolutes, which Walton and Walton claim is true of the Torah as well. See Fox, *Proverbs 1–9*, 142; Loader, *Proverbs 1–9*, 146–47; Walton and Walton, *Lost World of the Torah*, 5–6, 37–45.

[12] See Overland, "Did the Sage Draw from the Shema?"; McKane, *Proverbs*, 291; Schipper, *Proverbs 1–15*, 125–26.

[13] Whybray, *Composition of the Book of Proverbs*, 18; J. H. Potgieter, "The (Poetic) Rhetoric of Wisdom in Proverbs 3:1–12," *HvTSt* 58.4 (2002): 1367.

[14] J. W. McKay, "Man's Love for God in Deuteronomy and The Father/Teacher – Son/Pupil Relationship," *VT* 22.4 (1972): 435.

[15] Potgieter, similar to Whybray, remarks, "The content of the exhortation [3:1–4] is to follow in the footsteps of the wise father, to enter into a specific mode of existence, a way of life that has been proven to provide success and prosperity. The father is portrayed as a Moses-like figure giving teaching and commands." See Potgieter, "The (Poetic) Rhetoric of Wisdom in Proverbs 3:1–12," 1368; R. N. Whybray, *Proverbs: Based on the Revised Standard Version*, NCBC (Grand Rapids: Eerdmans, 1994), 59.

[16] Fox, *Proverbs 1–9*, 142.

[17] Schipper, *Proverbs 1–15*, 127–28.

[18] Waltke, "Does Proverbs Promise Too Much?" 328.

[19] See Whybray, *Composition of the Book of Proverbs*, 59.

The teacher then adds an unclear statement to his initial command. Verse 3 uses a third plural rather than the second singular as in Prov 3:1. The plural seems to reference "steadfast love" (חסד) and "faithfulness" (אמת). Likewise, the verb "abandon" (עזב) is in the active rather than passive voice. The second line uses two imperatives, "bind them" (קָשְׁרֵם) and "write them" (כָּתְבֵם). The plural "them" in the second line could reference either "steadfast love" (חסד) and "faithfulness" (אמת) or *torah* (תורה) and "commands" (מצוה). The poetic structure may imply a conditional "if" between 3a and 3b. By reading "them" as anaphoric for *torah* and "commands," the terms "steadfast love" and "faithfulness" become the conditioned blessings.[20] In other words, Prov 3:3 would read, "Steadfast love and faithfulness will not abandon (עזב) you [if] you bind [*torah* and *mitsvah*] ... and write [*torah* and *mitsvah*]." The import for "steadfast love" and "faithfulness" likely goes beyond mere humanistic pleasantries, as well.[21] The terms are categorically related to Yhwh and his divine ways.[22] Thus, if the son abandons God's ways, this will result in the loss of his presence and relational benefits, i.e., his "steadfast love" and "faithfulness."[23] As discussed elsewhere, these terms are intrinsic to God's nature and the way he conducts his affairs.[24] In fact, Abraham's servant in Gen 24:27 used the same language to say, "Blessed be Yhwh ... who did not abandon (עזב) his steadfast love (חסד) and his faithfulness (אמת) from my lord." With similar syntax, the teacher encourages the son to be like Abraham, who enjoyed Yhwh's "steadfast love" and "faithfulness," serving as an exemplar for walking in the ways of God (e.g., Gen 17:1; cf. Gen 5:22, 6:9; Mic 6:8; Mal 2:6).

To further emphasize the son's adoption of the teacher's *torah*, he is instructed to internalize the commands (Prov 3:3b; cf. Jer 31:33). Much can be said about the theological and prophetic nature of this principle. However, in

---

[20] Loader and Waltke espouse the view that *hesed* (חסד) and *emet* (אמת) are the antecedents of "them." Yet, if considered logically, this is quite unlikely. From Deuteronomy, the people were to bind the "commands" to their hands and foreheads (Deut 6:8, 11:18). It is questionable what it would even mean to bind "steadfast love" or "faithfulness" around the neck (or fingers). Instead, *hesed* (חסד) and *emet* (אמת) are relational benefits or blessings rather than precepts, as are *torah* and "commands." Likewise, the parallel phrases in Prov 6:21 and 7:3 explicitly refer to the "commands" (מִצְוֹת), rendering Waltke and Loader's view untenable. See Fox, *Proverbs 1–9*, 144–45; Whybray, *Proverbs (1972)*, 61; Plöger, *Spruche Salomos (Proverbia)*, 33; Waltke, *Proverbs (1–15)*, 241; Loader, *Proverbs 1–9*, 149; Whybray, *Proverbs (1994)*, 61.

[21] Whybray, *Composition of the Book of Proverbs*, 18.

[22] Schipper notes there is a strong correlation not only to the pair in relation to Yhwh's nature but his care for his anointed (Schipper, *Proverbs 1–15*, 129; McKane, *Proverbs*, 291).

[23] Fox holds a peculiar view of *hesed* (חסד). He states, "*Hesed* is always conferred by a superior upon an inferior. ... This understanding of *hesed* runs counter to the widely accepted theory of N. Glueck (1927), who defined *hesed* as covenantal loyalty. In my view, *hesed* has no covenantal reference, nor is it essentially loyalty. ... *Hesed* within a covenantal relationship is a benefit not mandated by the terms of the covenant." While חסד may extend beyond formal covenants (e.g., Judg 8:35), it does seem to operate as an expected interpersonal component of relationship, whether formal or informal (e.g., 2 Sam 7:15, 9:7). Prinsloo provides a broader and more preferable definition, "[חסד] refers to solidarity between two parties, whether it is in the sphere of family life, between friends, in marriage or in the relationship with Yahweh." See Fox, *Proverbs 1–9*, 144; G. T. M. Prinsloo, "Reading Proverbs 3:1–12 in Its Social and Ideological Context," *HvTSt* 58.4 (2002): 1392.

[24] See Excursus: Exodus and God's Leading in His Way. Cf. Perdue, *Proverbs*, 101.

the current discussion, the point is to again lead the son away from hypocritical, merely external religiosity and sapiential-ism (cf. Prov 2:3–4; Deut 10:16, 30:6; Isa 29:13). In the framework of Deuteronomy, binding and writing the instructions is akin to training in the Torah, or the ways of Yhwh (cf. Deut 6:6–9, 11:18–21).[25] In an elemental sense, the training framework is a process between a father and son or in Proverbs perhaps a teacher and student. Primarily, though, these paradigm relationships point to Yhwh's role as father and teacher (cf. Prov 3:11–12).[26] The implication of Prov 3:1–2, then, is that if the son will follow and internalize God's ways, he will walk in perpetuity with God. His blessings are a complex matrix, inextricably rooted in Yhwh, but most simply described as "favor in the eyes of God and man" (Prov 3:4).[27]

The Blessing of Yhwh (3:5–10)

After subtly promoting God's way in Prov 3:1–4, the teacher more explicitly turns theological and personal.[28] As mentioned, the three couplets of this section center on Yhwh and expand upon what was previously offered. In Prov 3:5–10, there is a logical and theological progression from greater to lesser, though intended as interconnected extensions. Together, the teacher explains to the son that remembering *torah* is akin to trusting, knowing, fearing, and honoring Yhwh.

The first couplet in this section gives a dual, parallel command (Prov 3:5–6; cf. Ps 37:3–6). The son is to "trust Yhwh" (בְּטַח אֶל־יְהוָה) and to "know him" (דָעֵהוּ).[29] The corresponding parallel lines are "with all your heart" (בְּכָל־לִבֶּךָ)[30] and "with all your ways" (בְּכָל־דְּרָכֶיךָ). Of course, the phrase "with all your heart" is a favorite expression for covenantal relationship and faithfulness in Deuteronomy (4:29, 6:5, 10:12, 11:13:13:3, 26:16, 30:2, 6, 10; cf. Josh 22:5; 1

---

[25] Schipper, *Proverbs 1–15*, 128; Weeks, *Instruction and Imagery in Proverbs 1–9*, 155.

[26] Schipper, *Proverbs 1–15*, 126; McKay, "Man's Love for God in Deuteronomy and The Father/Teacher – Son/Pupil Relationship," 432; Weeks, *Instruction and Imagery in Proverbs 1–9*, 153.

[27] The phrase "in the eyes of God and man" was likely a stock idiom in the ANE, appropriated by the teacher to inculcate the Yahwistic root of both wisdom and favor, particularly as universal rather than local or ethnic. See Schipper, *Proverbs 1–15*, 130; Fox, *Proverbs 1–9*, 147–48; Meinhold, *Die Sprüche*, 75.

[28] Newsom, "Woman and the Discourse of Patriarchal Wisdom: A Study of Proverbs 1–9," 149–51; Waltke, "Does Proverbs Promise Too Much?" 320–21.

[29] The expression *da'ehu* (דָעֵהוּ) in the MT is often translated as if it were causative (*hiphil*) "acknowledge him" rather than as "know him," which is the ground form (*qal*) given in the text. The LXX does use the more impersonal "know" (γνωρίζω) rather than "know" (γινώσκω), though. The TgProv and Syr. use ground form (*qal*) equivalents of "know" (ידע). In the shadow of Prov 2:5, it seems the teacher is further connecting the principles of knowing God, fearing him, and walking in his ways. See Waltke, *Proverbs (1–15)*, 244–45; Perdue, *Proverbs*, 98–100.

[30] Psalm 119:1–2 parallels "those walking in the *torah* of Yhwh" with "they seek him with all the heart" (בְּכָל־לֵב יִדְרְשׁוּהוּ).

Sam 7:3, 12:20, 24; Jer 29:13; Joel 2:12).[31] While the prepositional phrases likely imply a synonymous meaning, the command to "trust" and "know" are complementary more than synonymous. Trusting with the heart, the son will internalize the *torah* and commands of God. In doing so, he will commit himself to the path of God, which consequentially includes knowing God.[32] This sense is further ensconced by declaring that the benefit of trusting and knowing is an "upright" or "straight" (ישׁר) path. The double entendre implies that the path is not crooked or misleading nor is it evil or wicked.[33] The way of Yhwh is upright and straight (cf. Deut 32:4). Where does this path lead? It leads to life (Prov 3:2), favor (3:4), healing (3:8), and blessings (3:10).[34] The ultimate end of these though is their source. As they flow from God, so they lead to him. Lesson 2 explicitly connects "fear of Yhwh" and "knowledge of God." Here in Lesson 3, the ideas are more obliquely related in Prov 3:6–7 but nevertheless continue the teacher's intent.[35] The two are inextricably related, both leading to one another.[36] Knowing God through one's path bridges the potential disconnect between right-actions and right-relationship.[37]

Thus, trusting Yhwh, knowing him, and the straight path are mutually dependent. In fact, the preposition (בְּ) found in the Heb. phrase בְּכָל־דְּרָכֶיךָ (Prov 3:6a) is likely being used as a *beth instrumenti*, parallel to the phrase in 3:5a.[38] The first command is relatively straight forward, "Trust Yhwh *with* all your heart." The *lev* (לֵב) is the center and conduit for the son's trust. However, the sense is more difficult in Prov 3:6a because the logic is less apparent, "Know him (*in / with / through*) all of your ways."[39] The difficulty

---

[31] Schipper, *Proverbs 1–15*, 130.

[32] Toombs commenting on Prov 2:5, though relevant for 3:6–7, makes the observation, "The search for wisdom, demanding as it is, does not lead directly to wisdom, but to God. It brings, not a sense of *achievement*, but of *reverence* ... The end of the quest is also that intimate personal fellowship with the Eternal which is 'the knowledge of God'" (Toombs, "O.T. Theology and the Wisdom Literature," 194).

[33] Loader, Waltke, and Fox take the *piel* of ישׁר to mean "make smooth" in the sense of an easy, trouble-free life. However, Schipper rightly connects this to Hos 14:10 which commends the straight-way of Yhwh and those who walk it. The way of Yhwh is not easy but free from evil. Waltke does go on to add, "However, to know [Yhwh] one must abstain from evil for there is no evil in him, that relationship also makes one walk 'straight.'" In this sense, the teacher is not commending ease as much as upright character and behavior. Walking with God in his ways, namely trusting and knowing him, will necessarily produce the same results that God experiences in his own ways. See Loader, *Proverbs 1–9*, 154; Fox, *Proverbs 1–9*, 150; Waltke, *Proverbs (1–15)*, 245; Schipper, *Proverbs 1–15*, 131.

[34] Nel says of this path, "[Yhwh] himself is the one who guides life to its fulfillment" (Nel, *The Structure and Ethos of the Wisdom Admonitions in Proverbs*, 47).

[35] Waltke, *Proverbs (1–15)*, 238; Loader, *Proverbs 1–9*, 142.

[36] Estes, *Hear, My Son*, 84–85.

[37] Loader, *Proverbs 1–9*, 154.

[38] See Williams and Beckman, *Williams' Hebrew Syntax*, 97–98; Bruce K. Waltke and M. O'Connor, *An Introduction to Biblical Hebrew Syntax* (Winona Lake: Eisenbrauns, 1990), 196–97.

[39] The phrase "in all his ways" is commonly coupled with "walk" in Deuteronomy and Joshua regarding Yhwh's commands (Deut 5:33, 10:12, 11:22; Josh 2:22, 22:5; cf. 1 Kgs 8:58; Jer 7:23; Ps 145:17). Weeks expounds on the Deuteronomic imagery of a path in Proverbs, saying, "['Way'] is also used by most biblical writers to refer to human behaviour, either in terms of actions, or more commonly, in terms of a general pattern of behaviour. ... It is possible to 'walk

is, what does it mean to know God 'with' your ways? While the phrase is often simplified by translating "know" as "acknowledge" or through the *beth locale* sense "in,"[40] these adjustments obfuscate the teacher's import. The point is that the son will "know" God by walking in his ways with him. Again, the operative metaphor is walking on a path. Reversing the sense helps to illuminate the point, "You do not know God if you do not walk in his ways." In other words, the son must "trust" God internally with his heart and he must "know" God through his behaviors, decisions, desires, and ultimately his commitment to walking the "straight" path. In this sense, then, knowledge is embodied action rather than abstracted intellectualism.[41] Thus, by refusing to do as the teacher instructs, the fool not only forfeits the path of God but the God on that path. Thus, the son's behavior serves as a conduit and center for his knowledge, in this case a relational knowledge with God.[42]

In Prov 3:7–8, the father turns to "fear Yhwh." Here, the son learns that he cannot be the source of wisdom, "Be not wise in your own eyes, fear Yhwh."[43] The lesson parallels Isaiah's warning, "Woe to those wise in their own eyes" (Isa 5:21). Isaiah's prophetic condemnation focuses on the wickedness and injustice of Israel and Judah (Isa 5:7–24). In fact, Isaiah gives the root of these aberrant ways, "They have rejected the *torah* of Yhwh" (Isa 5:24). Similarly, the teacher in Prov 3 expands on the solution or root cause by commanding the son to "fear Yhwh" and "turn from evil" (cf. Job 1:1, 28:28). Implicitly, the *torah* way necessitates fear of Yhwh, which implies covenantal relationship. Likewise, Prov 3:7 connects these commands with the broader straight-way metaphor. Not only does Prov 3:6 commend the straight path, but later in 4:27 (Lesson 8) the teacher creates a bridge between "do not turn right or left" and "turn your foot from evil" (הָסֵר רַגְלְךָ מֵרָע). The motif of turning left or right was central to covenantal faithfulness, particularly for leaders who were to be a model for the people by walking in the ways of Yhwh.[44] Perhaps one of the most important aspects of Prov 3:7a is the external orientation. If the son is not the source of wisdom, he must look or seek it elsewhere. In doing so, the son will necessarily listen to the teacher's *torah*,

---

in the way' of others by imitating what they do." He goes on to say that there was a common association between "the divine way and the Law" (Weeks, *Instruction and Imagery in Proverbs 1–9*, 150, 151–52).

[40] See Williams and Beckman, *Williams' Hebrew Syntax*, 97–98; Waltke and O'Connor, *Biblical Hebrew Syntax*, 196–97.

[41] See O'Dowd, *The Wisdom of Torah*, 3, 48.

[42] Waltke rightly notes, "'To know' in this book means personal knowledge, intimate experience with a person's reality. ... The noted connections between the spiritual consequences in Lecture 2 and the spiritual admonitions in ch. 3 infer that 'know' in 3:6a has the same sense as in 2:5b" (Waltke, *Proverbs (1–15)*, 244–45).

[43] McKane impugns "old wisdom" as "intellectual self-determination." This view leads him to see Prov 3:7 as an attack on such wisdom, deriving from the prophetic tradition. However, Fox, along with Whybray, argues that McKane's view is misguided, on account of both ANE material and proverbs from "early collections." As mentioned elsewhere, the prophets and sages both condemned illegitimate prophecy and wisdom, characterized by their disconnect from Yhwh and his way. See McKane, *Proverbs*, 292; Loader, *Proverbs 1–9*, 154–55; Fox, *Proverbs 1–9*, 150–51; Whybray, *Proverbs (1994)*, 62.

[44] See Lesson 8 for further analysis.

embodying the training process. The son will then imitate the teacher, as sons do their fathers, ultimately seeking to be wise as God is. Following in the external path of wisdom, the son will have "healing" and "rejuvenation" (Prov 3:8). This blessing may be a reference to mere physical well-being. However, both terms imply restoration. Thus, the proverb could imply physical healing and well-being (cf. Gen 20:17; Deut 28:27; 2 Kgs 20:5; Ps 103:3)[45] or God's restoration after judgment (cf. Deut 32:39; Isa 30:26).[46] In most instances, there is a relational and spiritual aspect of this term (cf. Isa 53:5; Jer 3:22; Hos 14:5; Ps 103:3).[47] The son's expectation, then, is a path marked by repentance and restoration (cf. Isa 6:10, 57:18; Ps 23:3; 2 Chron 7:14).

Finally, the lesson ends with a couplet extolling the benefits of honoring Yhwh. This honor is not abstract but practically expressed. The teacher utilizes a familiar idea that only occurs as a command in the Torah as part of the Decalogue, "Honor your father and mother" (Exod 20:12; Deut 5:16). This foundational command is associated with "lengthened days" (יַאֲרִיכֻן יָמֶיךָ), similar to the notion presented at the beginning of Lesson 3 (Prov 3:2). Despite common indirect use in the prophets and psalms, the command to honor Yhwh in this couplet is the only explicit occurrence in the HB. One close implicit use appears in Ps 22:23, "Those who fear Yhwh, praise Yhwh. All the offspring of Jacob, honor him" (cf. Isa 24:15). A telling post-exilic statement draws a connection between Yhwh and the command to honor one's parents, "A son honors a father and a slave his lord. But if I am a father, where is my honor and if I am the great lord where is my fear?" (Mal 1:6). Although the fatherhood of God will be discussed more in Lesson 4, the connection even here

---

[45] Most understand this verse in a purely physical sense, including Waltke. He does, however, emphasize the totality of well-being, including spiritual and psychological which is "toward eternal life." See Loader, *Proverbs 1–9*, 157–58; Waltke, *Proverbs (1–15)*, 246–47; Fox, *Proverbs 1–9*, 151; Schipper, *Proverbs 1–15*, 132–33; Murphy, *Proverbs*, 21.

[46] See M. L. Brown, "רָפָא," *TDOT* 13:598; Mason Lancaster, "Wounds and Healing, Dew and Lions: Hosea's Development of Divine Metaphors," *CBQ* 83.3 (2021): 407–24; D. F. O'Kennedy, "The Metaphor of Yahweh as Healer in the Prophetic Books of the Old Testament," *IDS* 41.3 (2007): 443–55.

[47] There is a strong correspondence between elements of Pss 103 and 104 with Proverbs. The psalmist commends himself not to "forget," which is connected later with "guarding [Yhwh's] covenant and remembering to do [Yhwh's] statutes" (Ps 103:17–18; cf. Prov 2:17, 20, 3:1). Also, he mentions healing in relation to not forgetting, forgiveness, redemption, and God's character – "steadfast love and mercy ... gracious, slow to anger" (Ps 103:2–5, 8; cf. Prov 3:3, 8). Likewise, Yhwh is declared as one who "does righteousness" (Ps 103:6; cf. Prov 2:9). There is, also, a direct allusion to Exod 33:13, when he "made known his ways to Moses," as discussed in Excursus: Exodus and God's Leading in His Way (Ps 103:7). Then in Ps 103:13, Yhwh is compared with a compassionate father (cf. Prov 3:11–12). The blessings mentioned are for "those fearing him" and guarding his ways (Ps 103:17–18). Psalm 104 goes on to extol Yhwh as the great creator who made all things "by wisdom," seemingly summarized in Prov 3:19–20.

Dating for Pss 103–104 is unclear. However, Ross mentions a few reasons some see it as earlier rather than later, particularly pre-exilic. Kidner believes the prophets Isaiah and Jeremiah draw echoes from them. Longman, with Ross and Kidner, note that Ps 104 may draw from an early Egyptian Hymn to Aten (ca. 1379–1352 BCE). However, if there is a connection to the Egyptian hymn, the psalmist only loosely borrows in order to extol Yhwh, the God of Israel. See Allen P. Ross, *A Commentary on the Psalms*, Kregel Exegetical Library (Grand Rapids: Kregel Academic, 2011), III: 228–40; Tremper Longman III, *Psalms*, TOTC (Nottingham: IVP, 2014), II: 358–59; Derek Kidner, *Psalms*, TOTC (Leicester: IVP, 1975), II: 397–406.

is important for understanding the teacher's use of "honor." Furthermore, in one oblique reference to honoring Yhwh, God prophesies of Eli's fallen house, saying, "Those honoring me, I will honor; and those despising me will be cursed" (1 Sam 2:30). The divine reciprocal relationship is reminiscent of Lesson 2 in Proverbs.

The term used for "storehouse" (אָסָם) in Prov 3:10 is uncommon, only occurring elsewhere in Deut 28:8, "Yhwh will command the blessing for you, in your storehouse and in all that your hand goes out to do. And he will bless you in the land which Yhwh your God is giving you." Moses outlines the various blessings in this pericope that will result if "You will guard the commands (מצוה) of Yhwh your God and walk in his ways" (Deut 28:9).[48] This blessing passage concludes with the motif explicitly given in Lesson 8, "You shall not turn from all these words which I am commanding you today, right or left, to walk after other gods to serve them" (Deut 28:14). In the Torah, giving one's "firstfruits" (רֵאשִׁית) or the primacy of their "produce" (תְּבוּאָה) is necessary for proper alignment with the covenant (Exod 23:19, 34:26; Lev 23:10; Deut 14:22, 28, 26:2, 10, 12).[49] Thus, it was equivalent to following the instructions or walking in the ways of Yhwh, which included offering one's firstfruits to God. Though only implicit, Proverbs aligns walking in Yhwh's ways with honoring him.[50] The covenantal relationship here is again reversed in relational reciprocity.[51] God will do as the people do, or in Proverbs as the son does. If the son will honor God, he will be honored by God.[52] Conceptually, though, the people including the son are only able to give back to Yhwh what he provided to them in the first place.[53] In this way, man's imitation of God results in God's reciprocal imitation of man, in this case for blessing.

---

[48] See Weeks, *Instruction and Imagery in Proverbs 1–9*, 150–55.

[49] The LXX says "from the fruit of your righteousness" (ἀπὸ σῶν καρπῶν δικαιοσύνης) rather than simply "from your produce." To this, Lang notes that the MT does not drive a wedge between cult, wisdom, and ethics. Yet, the LXX perhaps attempts to minimize the cultic insinuations with pure ethics. Aitken also notes the importance of this "formal act of worship" as a reminder of the connection between the land, God's provision, and covenant faithfulness (Bernhard Lang, *Die weisheitliche Lehrrede: eine Untersuchung von Sprüche 1–7*, SBS 54 (Stuttgart: KBW-Verlag, 1972), 84–85; Aitken, *Proverbs*, 42–43).

[50] Although Whybray notes the cultic aspect of Prov 3:9–10, he draws an unnecessarily hard line against the motivation for honoring Yhwh. Here, he states, "This is the most blatant expression in the OT of the principle of *do ut des* – the offering of gifts to God solely in order to elicit material rewards from him. ... The motive for the admonition to acknowledge Yahweh and submit to his demands was to obtain success and happiness in life rather than a pious desire to serve him" (Whybray, *Proverbs (1994)*, 63). Knowledge of God and blessings need not be mutually excluded motivations. The essence of covenantal fidelity was to maintain God's presence, implying access to both him and his favor.

[51] Arndt Meinhold, "Gott und Mensch in Proverbien 3," *VT* 37.4 (1987): 474, 476–77.

[52] Prinsloo argues that divine reciprocity in this passage implies the broader ancient idea of patronage, particularly in light of honor/shame social norms (Prinsloo, "Reading Proverbs 3:1–12 in Its Social and Ideological Context," 1392; J. J. Pilch and B. M. Malina, eds., *Handbook of Biblical Social Values*, updated. (Peabody: Hendrickson, 1998), 106–15, 151–55).

[53] Perdue, *Proverbs*, 99; Nel, *The Structure and Ethos of the Wisdom Admonitions in Proverbs*, 47.

Conclusion

As Lesson 3 teaches, the proverbial father does not want the son to misunderstand the knowledge and ways of God. Rather, he proffers a God who is intimately involved with his people and known by his ways. While the divine path is challenging, it is not hidden. The Lord had given to Moses his *torah* and commands, those faithfully passed from generation to generation (Prov 3:1–4). Similarly, the father extends the blessings of the Torah to the blessings inherent to life in the path with Yhwh. Thus, if the son internalizes these divine instructions through his character and externalizes them through his actions, he will be wise and walk in the way of God with him. To this end, the son is instructed to trust, know, fear, and honor Yhwh. In particular, the path metaphor becomes a figurative way for the son to express the divine qualities through all of his ways, or the totality of his life (Prov 3:6). By living the ideal characteristics, he would also continue to grow in and express his knowledge of God (Prov 2:5, 3:5–7). As the father desired, the son must understand that to know God is to do as he does and to do as God does is to know him. Prior to analyzing Lesson 4, we will look at a similar view taught by Jeremiah, which provides a few complementary ideas about knowing God through expressing his ways. Finally, in an interesting aspect of Lesson 3, the father reflects on the reciprocity of God, implying that he himself reflects the ways of those who honor him. This reciprocal relationality, introduced in Lesson 2, is central to the son's understanding of the wise path (Prov 3:9–10; cf. 2:7–11). Despite a strong emphasis on Yhwh in Lessons 2–3, Lesson 4 draws the son to an even higher point in his divine attention. In his next lesson, a central and underlying principle for the wisdom program is presented. God is the ultimate father and teacher, one who masterfully utilizes the exalted Wisdom in his own ways.

EXCURSUS

Jeremiah and Knowing the Ways of Yhwh

T he exilic prophet Jeremiah provides his readers with a trove of memorable and stark statements, many of which are quite comfortable with the message of 8th c. prophets and the Deuteronomic tradition. He focuses on the dual sin of Israel, namely improper cultic and social behavior. For these aberrations, they will be disciplined (e.g., Jer 30:11, 46:28). Yet there would be hope for a future restoration (e.g., Jer 32:37–41). Just as Hosea taught, these sins revolved around covenantal and relational rebellion.[1] Despite a claim to innocence (e.g., Jer 2:35), the prophet makes it clear they were not. The people had gone after other gods and abandoned the ways of Yhwh. Because of this dual sin, Jeremiah declared, in the spirit of Hosea, that they do not know the God of Israel, a topic central to his broader prophetic message.[2] Fidelity to this God is not merely in rote cultic practice or by including Yhwh among their gods but in knowing and reflecting the only God of Israel and the characteristics of his divine nature. In other words, according to Jeremiah, likeness-to-Yhwh was central to a proper knowledge and relationship with him.

Although the full prophetic book holds a great deal of important and relevant passages, for the sake of focus this brief analysis will primarily

---

[1] Thompson notes, "Both Hosea and Jeremiah believed strongly that true religion consists in a personal and existential knowledge of God, and in commitment to those qualities displayed by Yahweh himself – unfailing loyalty, justice, and right dealing" (J. A. Thompson, *The Book of Jeremiah*, NICOT (Grand Rapids: Eerdmans, 1980), 318).

[2] Wolff, Huffmon, and Brueggemann prefer the covenantal perspective of "know" seeing Yhwh primarily as suzerain. Carroll sees the term as "confessional" in the sense of "acknowledging Yahweh." Thompson prefers the personal, intimate, and theological view. Holladay holds to a moderated view as "both intimacy and a covenantal bond." All acknowledge the importance and centrality of the topic to Jeremiah. See William L. Holladay, *Jeremiah 1: A Commentary on the Book of the Prophet Jeremiah, Chapters 1–25*, Hermeneia (Philadelphia: Fortress, 1986), 33, 89, 163, 317–18; Walter Brueggemann, "The Epistemological Crisis of Israel's Two Histories (Jer 9:22–23)," in *Israelite Wisdom: Theological and Literary Essays in Honor of Samuel Terrien* (Missoula: Scholars, 1978), 95; Hans Walter Wolff, "'Wissen um Gott' bei Hosea als Urform von Theologie," *EvT* 12.12 (1953): 533–54; Herbert B. Huffmon, "The Treaty Background of Hebrew Yāda'," *BASOR* 181 (1966): 31–37; Thompson, *Book of Jeremiah*, 145, 229, 318–19, 479; Robert P. Carroll, *Jeremiah: A Commentary*, OTL (Philadelphia: Westminster, 1986), 248–49.

highlight Jer 9 and 22. These passages are particularly poignant for the broader study of wisdom, knowledge, and imitation. They also provide a window into Jeremiah's prophetic theology regarding *torah* and proper relationship with Yhwh.[3] Thus, just as Yhwh was characterized as righteous, just, and deeply concerned for the proper treatment of the vulnerable, so those who know him must likewise be and do, as they reflect his wise and divine ways. The prophetic sentiments of Jeremiah closely align and reflect several of the proverbial father's instructions and desires for the son. Primarily, as Lesson 3 highlighted, the son was to "know [Yhwh] with all his ways" (Prov 3:6). To an extent, Jeremiah's desire for Judah and his rebukes for their failures paint him as a public instantiation of the proverbial teacher.

Jeremiah 9:23–24 [22–23]

"Thus says Yhwh, 'The wise shall not boast in his wisdom and the mighty shall not boast in his strength. The rich shall not boast in his riches. Rather in this, the one who boasts will boast in understanding and knowing me. For I am Yhwh, one who does steadfast love, justice, and righteousness in the land. For in these things, I delight,' declares Yhwh."

Despite its complex literary structure and compositional history, Jeremiah's prophetic message is consistent.[4] The central issue is the violation of God's covenant and subsequently his plan to remedy this problem. In Jer 11:2–5, the prophet proclaims the word of Yhwh to the current generation but is rooted in the ancient covenant made with the Exodus generation.[5] While much of the first half of the book declares the myriad ways they had violated this relationship, the prophet also communicates God's future plan to make a "new covenant," which will be better than the one made with the Exodus generation (Jer 31:31–34; cf. Deut 30:5–6).[6] This new covenant will be characterized by an internalized obedience to *torah* (cf. Prov 2:10, 3:3, 7:3) and a personal, ubiquitous knowledge of God (cf. Prov 2:5, 3:6). Although the first covenant was intended to bring about obedience and knowledge of God, this prophecy implies that it failed in doing so, as Jeremiah and the prophets clearly intimate.

Within Jeremiah's broad warning, the prophet provides an important glimpse into the underpinnings of their failure. Chapter 9 falls within one of

---

[3] See Thompson, *Book of Jeremiah*, 107–13.

[4] Holladay notes that the sapiential nature of Jeremiah's prophecies often led earlier commentators to reject its authenticity. However, this sentiment has shifted, Holladay and Brueggemann claiming the exact opposite. Thompson acknowledges that the passage seems to be an editorial insertion. In his view, though, this was likely done by Jeremiah (Holladay, *Jeremiah 1*, 317; Brueggemann, "The Epistemological Crisis of Israel's Two Histories," 85, 89–90; Thompson, *Book of Jeremiah*, 318).

[5] Thompson, *Book of Jeremiah*, 344.

[6] Thompson, *Book of Jeremiah*, 580–81.

these prophetic warnings (Jer 7–10). The broader warning begins by giving a call to repentance rooted in the Torah, "If you indeed make your ways and deeds good, if you indeed make justice between a man and his neighbor, you do not oppress the sojourner, fatherless, and widow, and you do not shed innocent blood in this place, and do not go after other gods to your harm, behold I will make you dwell in this place" (Jer 7:5–7; cf. Exod 22:21–22; Deut 10:18, 16:11–14, 24:19–21).[7] However, such hope for repentance was not realized, "'They are all adulterers, a treacherous assembly. They shoot their tongue as a bow, lies and not truth grow strong in the land; for they go from evil to evil but they do not know me,' declares Yhwh. ... 'Your seat is in the midst of fraud; in fraud they refuse to know me,' declares Yhwh" (Jer 9:3[2], 6[5]).[8] Jeremiah then clarifies that their wickedness was indeed a generational, imitative rejection of Yhwh, "They have abandoned my *torah* which I gave to them but they did not listen to my voice and did not walk in it, but they walked after their stubborn hearts and after Baals, which their fathers taught them" (Jer 9:13–14[12–13]). The people were wicked and did not know God because they had followed their wicked fathers in their rejection of Yhwh and his *torah* way.[9] As Yhwh says in Jer 7:28, reminiscent of Wisdom's call and the fool's rejection, "They did not listen to the voice of Yhwh their God nor did they receive (לקח) *musar*" (cf. Prov 1:3, 5:12–13, 8:10). Important to note here, Jeremiah understood that their failure was in part due to generational imitation, which should have been in proper relationship and obedience to God (cf. Deut 6:4–7; Prov 4:1–4). In the next chapter, he adds, "You shall not learn the way of the nations ... for the statutes of the peoples are vanity" (Jer 10:2). In other words, the ways of their fathers were akin to the ways of the nations, which were in opposition to the way of Yhwh.

The people were not only deluded in their presumed innocence, they were also deluded in their wisdom, might, and wealth (Jer 9:23[22]; cf. 8:8–9).[10] As Proverbs makes clear, wisdom is only wisdom and even possible as far as it is properly and covenantally related to Yhwh (cf. Prov 1:7, 2:5–6, 9:9–

---

[7] See Holladay, *Jeremiah 1*, 243.

[8] Thompson comments on the idea of knowing God here, "The verb ידע 'know' denotes much more than intellectual knowledge but rather that deep intimate knowledge that follows on the personal commitment of one life to another" (Thompson, *Book of Jeremiah*, 310).

[9] Thompson notes, "Yahweh looked for a similar quality in his people. A particular way of life was right and fitting for them. The norm was not merely social custom, but rather the character and will of the God of the covenant. Nothing less than the 'righteousness of Yahweh' would suffice. Yahweh's ultimate purpose was that his 'righteousness' should prevail over the whole earth" (Thompson, *Book of Jeremiah*, 321).

[10] Brueggemann, with McKane and later Longman, rightly notes that Jeremiah does not reject wisdom or the sapiential tradition but rather the false sages who operated from "epistemological consensus" to achieve "assured results." While this assessment seems correct, Brueggemann defines wisdom as "the deposit of the best observations coming from a long history of reflection on experience." In his view, the prophets sought to provide new "epistemological questions which may have been screened out" by this conservative approach. Such a view seems to overly dichotomize the wisdom and prophetic traditions. See Brueggemann, "The Epistemological Crisis of Israel's Two Histories," 85; Tremper Longman III, *The Fear of the Lord Is Wisdom: A Theological Introduction to Wisdom in Israel* (Grand Rapids: Baker Academic, 2017), 70–73; William McKane, *Prophets and Wise Men*, SBT 44 (London: SCM, 1965), 65–91.

10).[11] As Longman states, "True wisdom comes from centering one's thinking not in oneself, but in God."[12] Yet, the wise had become fools due to their secular view of success and wisdom along with their dissociation from walking in the *torah* way of Yhwh.[13] Earlier in Jer 4:22, he states, "My people are foolish for they do not know me. They are sons of stupidity and have no understanding. They are wise for evil and do not know good." Holladay captures the underlying truth from Jeremiah, "To know Yahweh is to know how to do good: ethical decisions flow from the knowledge of Yahweh. It is a nice anticipation of Augustine's maxim, 'Dilige, et quod vis fac' ['Love (God), and do what you like]."[14] But, Judah did not know God and their ways were proof. So, in response, Jeremiah goes on to declare, "Cursed is the man whose trust is in humanity ... Blessed is the man who trusts (בטח) in Yhwh and his security (מבטח) is Yhwh" (Jer 17:5, 7). Jeremiah's rebuke was a wise word reflecting the proverbial command, "Trust (בטח) in Yhwh with all your heart ... Know him with all your ways ... Do not be wise in your own eyes" (Prov 3:5, 6, 7).

In order to correct their blind and misguided foolishness, Jeremiah provides "a succinct summary of the religion of Israel at its highest."[15] Clarifying God's primary desire, he says, "The one who boasts shall boast in understanding and knowing me. For I am Yhwh, one who does (עשה) steadfast love, justice, and righteousness in the land. For in these things, I delight" (Jer 9:24[23]; cf. Mic 7:18).[16] The prophet brings together an important insight in this verse. God himself does the qualities associated with his personal nature (e.g., Exod 34:6–7) and he desires for his covenant people to do likewise.[17] The two cannot be separated. As Huey rightly observes, "[This is] the very heart of Hebrew religion. They are not only the attributes of God; he delights in those who manifest these same qualities."[18] Separating the covenant way or one's actions from the nature and ways of God, according to Jeremiah, is in

---

[11] Longman remarks on the nature of wisdom, "Wisdom is not simply a matter of learning certain principles of life and applying them mechanistically. Wisdom begins with a relationship with God. ... Based on 1:7, they still would not judge pagan wisdom teachers as truly and authentically wise, because they lack fear of Yahweh. The bottom line is that there is no wisdom apart from a relationship with Yahweh. The very concept of wisdom is a theological concept, and it runs throughout the book" (Tremper Longman III, *Proverbs*, BCOTWP (Grand Rapids: Baker Academic, 2006), 57–58).

[12] Longman, *The Fear of the Lord Is Wisdom*, 72.

[13] Longman, *The Fear of the Lord Is Wisdom*, 73.

[14] Holladay, *Jeremiah 1*, 163.

[15] Thompson, *Book of Jeremiah*, 321.

[16] This triad is found together in some variation only a few times (Ps 33:5, 89:14; Isa 16:5; Jer 9:24; Hos 2:19). However, Holladay notes that the three appear quite often in paired combinations. In his view, the verb "make" (עשה) actually implies Yhwh "creates" these qualities in the earth which he himself does, indicating his universal authority and goodness. Brueggemann believes Jeremiah is dependent on Hosea or at least his prophetic tradition, calling them "prophets most deeply sensitive to the pathos of God" and the only two who "dare to entertain the alternative 'knowing Yahweh,' with will bring new life" (Holladay, *Jeremiah 1*, 317, 318; Brueggemann, "The Epistemological Crisis of Israel's Two Histories," 96).

[17] Cf. William McKane, *A Critical and Exegetical Commentary on Jeremiah*, ICC (T&T Clark, 1986), 212–13.

[18] F. B. Huey Jr., *Jeremiah, Lamentations*, NAC (Nashville: Broadman, 1993), 122.

fact at the heart of foolishness. One cannot claim wisdom or knowledge of God apart from walking in his ways. Yhwh himself was the exemplar of proper character and behavior, which Israel had utterly failed to reflect.

Jeremiah 22:3, 16

"Thus says Yhwh, 'Do justice and righteousness. Deliver the robbed from the hand of the oppressor. You shall not oppress the sojourner, fatherless, or widow. You shall not be violent and you shall not spill innocent blood in this place. ... He judged the afflicted and poor then it was well. Is this not to know me,' declares Yhwh."

Although a unique prophecy is captured in Jer 21–23, its message resonates with those prior. This particular vision declares the impending doom for Jerusalem, especially for the leaders or shepherds of the people. Besides Josiah, the kings and noble class of Judah were largely unfaithful to God and wicked against the people of Judah. Yet, there was hope for a future, though, after their impending discipline. After this discipline, God would raise up a "righteous branch" from the line of David who would rule in the ways of Yhwh, through wisdom, justice, and righteousness (Jer 23:5[4]).[19]

This prophetic word from Yhwh echoes an earlier message as well, "I will give you shepherds after my heart (כְּלִבִּי) and they will shepherd you with knowledge and understanding" (Jer 3:15). As Thompson understands, these two verses (Jer 3:15, 23:4) should be seen as complementary.[20] In only a few occurrences of "after my heart" (כלבי), David is described as one whose heart was after or according to Yhwh (1 Sam 13:14).[21] Conversely, it was said of Solomon, "His heart was not fully with Yhwh his God, *according to the heart* (כִּלְבַב) of David his father" (1 Kgs 11:4). Also, of Abijam, it was said, "He walked in all the sins of his father which he did before him and his heart was not fully with Yhwh his God, *according to the heart* (כִּלְבַב) of David his father" (1 Kgs 15:3). Together, it appears the Davidic pattern or expectation for kings was covenant fidelity, which necessarily included walking in the ways of Yhwh himself – wisdom, knowledge, justice, and righteousness – as Jeremiah further illuminates. Implied within this network of passages, there is also the subtle insinuation of reflecting one's father, David and those like him were sons to Yhwh (cf. 2 Sam 7:14; Ps 2:7, 89:26; Prov 3:11–12).[22] Jeremiah uses this fatherly metaphor for God (Jer 3:19; cf. Isa 63:16) but as a condemnation against Judah. The prophet states from Yhwh, "I said you shall call me 'my father' and shall not turn from after me. ... [but] they have corrupted their

---

[19] Longman, *The Fear of the Lord Is Wisdom*, 74.

[20] Thompson, *Book of Jeremiah*, 202.

[21] Timothy S. Laniak, *Shepherds after My Own Heart: Pastoral Traditions and Leadership in the Bible*, NSBT 20 (Downers Grove: IVP, 2006), 22–23, 132–33.

[22] See the discussion in Lesson 8. Cf. Laniak, *Shepherds after My Own Heart*, 108–9.

way; they have forgotten Yhwh their God. Return, O rebellious sons" (Jer 3:19b, 21b, 22a). So, in God's promise to provide shepherds "according to my heart" (Jer 3:15), the prophet implies they will be those who reflect Yhwh as proper and faithful sons. This message is the essence of the proverbial program.

But what was the cause for Judah's impending discipline? The prophet inveighs against their dual sin, "They abandoned the covenant of Yhwh their God and they worshiped and served other gods" (Jer 22:9; cf. Deut 29:25–26).[23] Reiterating his message from earlier, Jeremiah gives another conditional call for repentance, again rooted in the Torah, "Do justice and righteousness, deliver the robbed from the hand of the oppressor; you must not oppress the sojourner, fatherless, or widow. You must not do violence or shed innocent blood in this place" (Jer 22:3–4; cf. Deut 10:17–19).[24] The people, though especially the leaders, had forsaken God's covenant ways.[25] They were not reflecting his character and nature but were in direct defiance to him and his *torah*.

Because of this disobedience, Jeremiah gives a prophetic warning against Shallum (Jehoahaz; cf. 1 Chr 3:15) and Jehoiakim, who had not walked in the way of their father Josiah (2 Kgs 23:32, 37). Both kings and sons of Josiah are indicted for their departure from Josiah and ultimately the way of Yhwh.

> 'Woe to the one who builds his house without righteousness and his upper rooms without justice. He works with his neighbor freely and he does not give him his wage (cf. Prov 3:27–29). ... Are you a king because you compete in cedar? Did not your father eat and drink and

---

[23] Strangely, most scholars myopically focus on the idolatrous aspect of Jeremiah's indictment. While idolatry is certainly an aspect, the covenantal component is much more comprehensive. Although Jeremiah seems to echo Deut 29:25–26, the more common refrain is found in Deut 28:9 and 14, part of the blessing pronouncement, which states, "Yhwh will establish you for himself, a holy people, as was sworn to you, if you will keep the commands of Yhwh your God and walk in his ways. ... and if you do not turn from all the words which I commanded you today, right or left, to go after other gods to serve them." This passage is reflected elsewhere as well (e.g., 11:28). Israel was not only to avoid idolatry but to walk in all the ways of Yhwh. For a myopic treatment of Jer 22:9, see Carroll, *Jeremiah*, 421; Walter Brueggemann, *To Pluck up, to Tear down: A Commentary on the Book of Jeremiah 1–25*, ITC (Grand Rapids: Eerdmans, 1988), 190; Holladay, *Jeremiah 1*, 586; Thompson, *Book of Jeremiah*, 475.

[24] Thompson, *Book of Jeremiah*, 473–74.

[25] Brueggemann uses Mendenhall's "two histories" paradigm to understand the approach of Jeremiah. Regarding the prophet's approach, he states, "It is history with a covenant-making God that is the only history. Every other history is an illusion and a deception." This assertion is based on Mendenhall's dichotomy between the "Mosaic-covenantal" view of history versus the "Davidic-royal" view of history among Judahites in Jeremiah's time. The royal view according to Mendenhall was a self-interested, "paganization of Israel" due to its accommodation to the royal practices and intentions of the surrounding ANE nations. In Brueggemann's view, this false view of the Davidic throne was largely propagated by the self-interested nobility class consisting of sages, prophets, priests, etc. See Brueggemann, "The Epistemological Crisis of Israel's Two Histories," 86–87, 91; George E. Mendenhall, "The Monarchy," *Int* 29.2 (1975): 160.

make justice and righteousness then it was well for him? He judged the case of the afflicted and poor then it was well. Is this not to know me?' declares Yhwh. 'Yet, your eyes and heart are only for profit and shedding innocent blood and oppression and crushing' (Jer 22:13–17; cf. Prov 1:11, 19, 6:17).

As seen in this passage, the prophet contends against their self-interested desires.[26] Primarily, these wicked kings had failed to possess the desires of God and to properly express his ways. Yhwh was the righteous king (e.g., Jer 23:6) who at the behest of Israel had relinquished to Saul and the line of David his direct rule.[27] Yet, it was always the case that they were to rule not as kings but as a "prince" (1 Sam 9:16, 10:1, 13:14; cf. Judg 8:23) under the great king, Yhwh (cf. 1 Sam 8:7). As brothers among the people (Deut 17:20), they were to be exemplars of the *torah* way of Yhwh (Jer 33:15–22; cf. Isa 11:2–5; Prov 16:1–15).[28] Regarding the proper Davidic paradigm, Laniak rightly notes, "A good shepherd is one who sees what the Owner sees and does what the Owner does. He is a follower before he is a leader. He is a leader because he is a follower. The shepherds whom God judges in the Bible are those who forget that the people in their care are not their own."[29] Jeremiah lamented that the leaders of his day had failed, sharply contrasting them with God's own love and care for the vulnerable (Deut 10:17–19).[30] In their failure to uphold the Torah, they not only broke covenant but as a result did not know God. A core message from Jeremiah, then, is that knowledge of Yhwh is not feasible apart from reflecting his ways.[31]

Conclusion

The message of Jeremiah is in close continuity with both the proper prophetic and sapiential traditions yet is diametrically opposed to false versions of both. Those wicked and foolish leaders had sought profit and security apart from God, his ways, and the knowledge of God, consequently receiving neither. Ironically, if they had instead sought God and his way, he promised to provide them with blessing and security, available only to those who would reflect him and obey his *torah* (e.g., Deut 5:28–33, 30:15–20; cf. Prov 1:33, 2:20–22, 3:13–18, 33, 4:26–27, 8:32–36). As Jeremiah and Yhwh express to Shallum, the explicit definition for "knowing me [Yhwh]" (הַדַּעַת אֹתִי נְאֻם־יְהוָה) is to do righteously, justly, and to judge fairly, especially for the vulnerable (Jer

---

[26] Brueggemann, *To Pluck up, to Tear Down*, 193.

[27] Holladay, *Jeremiah 1*, 615.

[28] Dali Luo, "Proverbs 16:1–15: An Invitation to Adopt the Royal Way of Life" (Trinity International University, PhD diss., 2010); Thompson, *Book of Jeremiah*, 473–74.

[29] Laniak, *Shepherds after My Own Heart*, 22.

[30] Cf. Thompson, *Book of Jeremiah*, 278.

[31] Brueggemann, *To Pluck up, to Tear Down*, 193.

22:15–16). This is because such instruction was reflective of Yhwh's own desire and ways (e.g., Deut 10:17–19). It is not surprising, then, that Jeremiah's rebukes accord well with the proverbial father's instruction. The son was to listen and to receive *musar* in the proper way of God, that "in all of his ways, he will know Yhwh" (Prov 3:6). Just as Jeremiah understood, the proverbial father taught the son that true wisdom and knowledge of God must primarily accord with the heart and way of God.

LESSON 4

Analysis of Proverbs 3:11–20
"Wisdom is a tree of life"

I n continuation of prior lessons, the proverbial father centers the son's
vision on a critical aspect of Yhwh. While the proverbial father is the
student's first point of reference for studying and growing in wisdom, it
is ultimately the divine Father who embodies the primary role of teacher and
father (Prov 3:11–12). Even the preeminent Wisdom is subsumed within the
power and will of Yhwh in this lesson, both literarily and theologically (Prov
3:19–20). So, both in his greatness as the creator and his nearness as a father,
Yhwh models the proper use of wisdom in his creativity, dominion, and
instruction. In a way, even the proverbial father is seen as a student before
God here. Likewise, through the path of emulating God's use of Wisdom, the
son can restore the proper Edenic relationship lost in the Garden (Prov 3:13–
18). This relationship and the wise path were lost due to the first couple's
improper imitation of God. If the son will reflect God as the divine Father,
then he will find the life and blessing inherent to the divine path. Thus, this
lesson serves the wisdom program by proffering Yhwh as the central figure
and exemplar for Prov 1–9, partially revealed already in Lessons 2 and 3.

Structure of Lesson 4

The structure of Lesson 4 is discussed in more detail in the "Structure of Prov
1–9" section. In a condensed form, the lesson begins with Yhwh as a father
(Prov 3:11–12) and concludes with Yhwh as the creator (Prov 3:19–20). Within
the midst of these couplets, a highly structured poem extols the supremacy
and blessedness of wisdom (Prov 3:13–18). The sense of the poem is an
encomium for the value of wisdom, which Yhwh himself knows and uses (Prov
3:19).

I. Yhwh as Father (3:11–12)
II. Supremacy of Wisdom (3:13–18)
III. Yhwh as Creator (3:19–20)

As it will be observed, the lesson overlays the role and significance of the father, Wisdom, and Yhwh. However, Yhwh is explicitly central in this lesson, serving implicitly as the ultimate exemplar for the son.

Yhwh as Father (3:11–12)

The fourth lesson lays the foundation for a key conceptual and metaphorical image that serves all of Prov 1–9. Here, the process of the son's formation is moved beyond the proverbial father and Wisdom to directly involve Yhwh. The Lord is not simply to be feared, trusted, honored, and known by the son. He himself walks with the son as a father, *the* Father. His fatherly care will oversee the son's well-being and growth, as one steeped in biblical, divine wisdom. Here, the son is given the most explicit connection between his three teachers. Lesson 4 signals the literary and metaphorical convergence of the three primary sources of instruction for the wisdom program.[1] While this is important, the author of Proverbs is clear to maintain some necessary distinctions in the metaphor. In other words, the teacher does not want to conflate or collapse the three figures. To avoid this confusion, the comparative (כְּ) is utilized to avoid implying direct fatherhood. This could have blurred the lines of essence and role, particularly problematic in its ANE context.[2]

Although Marmorstein pointed to Prov 10:1 as an indicator of Yhwh's role as the father in Proverbs, in actuality, 3:11–20 better serves this purpose.[3] What was only speculative up to this point becomes more explicit. In fact, the entire program began with the words, "My son, listen to your father's *musar* (שְׁמַע בְּנִי מוּסַר אָבִיךָ)" (Prov 1:8a; cf. 6:23). The disconnected grammar of "your father" with "my son" comes into focus in 3:11. Here, the teacher makes a connection through parallel, "My son, do not reject the *musar* of Yhwh and do not despise his rebukes (תּוֹכַחְתּ). For those he rebukes Yhwh loves and as a father he delights in the son." Although the son should listen to his father or teacher, the parallel clarifies that the wisdom program instruction is

---

[1] See Weeks, *Instruction and Imagery in Proverbs 1–9*, 44.

[2] See John N. Oswalt, "Theology of the Pentateuch," in *DOTPe* (Downers Grove: IVP, 2003), 854; David R. Tasker, *Ancient near Eastern Literature and the Hebrew Scriptures about the Fatherhood of God*, StBibLit 69 (New York: Peter Lang, 2004), 86.

[3] See Arthur Marmorstein, *The Doctrine of Merits in Old Rabbinical Literature; and The Old Rabbinic Doctrine of God: I. The Names and Attributes of God and II. Essays in Anthropomorphism* (1920; repr., New York: Ktav, 1968), 202.

ultimately rooted and modeled in Yhwh. The primary proverbial figure for fatherhood is in fact Yhwh himself, the "ultimate teacher of wisdom."[4] As Tasker comments, "The fatherhood of God" served as a "model for human fatherhood."[5] Just as the proverbial father is connected to Yhwh, Wisdom is also subsumed. As discussed in Lesson 1, she declared, "Turn to my rebukes (תּוֹכַחַת)" (Prov 1:23 // 3:11). Later in Lesson 14, she says, "Receive my *musar*" (Prov 8:10 // 3:11). Thus, in light of these parallels, it is evident that Lesson 4 serves as a metaphorical key to draw the two central figures of instruction under Yhwh, the ideal father and model of wisdom.

To begin unpacking this significant biblical anthropomorphism,[6] the fatherhood of God or the gods was a well-attested concept throughout the ANE.[7] Often the title was ascribed to a high-god in authority within a pantheon or as the progenitor of other gods and men.[8] In an intriguing imitative example in the ANE, the people ascribed their sleep at night as parallel to their god's slumber, literally the sun setting for night.[9] The concept of "father" was also typically associated with kingship, the king being understood as a son of the gods.[10] This relationship constituted the basis of authority and the responsibility to rule properly. It was also common for "father" to be applied to those in the role of counselor, sage, expert, or patron, both in the human and divine realms.[11] While the fatherhood of various gods

---

[4] McKay, "Man's Love for God in Deuteronomy and The Father/Teacher – Son/Pupil Relationship," 432; Schipper, *Proverbs 1–15*, 126; Meinhold, *Die Sprüche*, 77. Meinhold says this fatherly image of God is unique. Yet, the HB, particularly in the psalter, is replete with language referring to Yhwh as father and teacher (e.g., Ps 25:4–5, 27:11, 34:11, 51:6, 86:11, 119:1–176).

[5] Tasker, *Fatherhood of God*, 5.

[6] Clines argues for the value of anthropomorphic language, "Anthropomorphic language is not some element in the Biblical texts for which excuses have to be made, or a network of metaphors that must be reduced to plain language, but part of the Biblical apprehension of God. It is to be evaluated, not negatively as accommodation to human language or divine condescension to human understanding, but positively, as a vital element of our knowledge of God" (David J. A. Clines, "Yahweh and the God of Christian Theology," *Theology* 83.695 (1980): 326, 330).

[7] Philip J. Nel, "The Concept of 'Father' in the Wisdom Literature of the Ancient Near East," *JNSL* 5 (1977): 62. For more discussion and examples, see Chapter Two: Historical Survey of *Imitatio Dei*.

[8] As Oswalt notes, Israel understood the fatherhood of Yhwh differently than the broader ANE may have thought, "It was not uncommon for the high god, such as Anu among the Sumerians or El among the Canaanites, to be referred to as the father of the gods. But here the emphasis is upon the engendering function of the father. This god sexually engendered all the others through Ki or Asherah, his wife" (John N. Oswalt, "God," in *DOTPr* (Downers Grove: IVP, 2012), 291).

[9] Samuel Noah Kramer, *Sumerian Mythology: A Study of Spiritual and Literary Achievement in the Third Millennium B.C.* (Philadelphia: University of Philadelphia Press, 1972), 42; Tasker, *The Fatherhood of God*, 26. The Sumerian line reads, "O Utu, shepherd of the land, father of the black-headed people, when thou liest down, the people, too, lie down." Of course, the HB distinguishes Yhwh in this regard as one who does not sleep or slumber (Ps 121:3–4; cf. 1 Kgs 18:27).

[10] Tasker, *Fatherhood of God*, 40, 59.

[11] Tasker observes that "the Sumerians initially saw the fatherhood of their gods procreatively and secondarily as the source of wisdom," a rather common motif in the ANE. See Nel, "Concept of 'Father,'" 64–65; Tasker, *Fatherhood of God*, 17–18, 29, 33, 39–40.

had parallels with the biblical concept of Yhwh, there was less intimacy between the gods and the people than the HB describes of Yhwh.[12] The biblical picture elicits a more compassionate perspective,[13] like a human father who loves rather than one who merely generates.

This biblical picture of divine fatherhood has at times been demurred in the OT as trivial or problematic.[14] Yet, the passages that it appears within seem to presume the notion as common knowledge rather than as a surprising addition. While there are a number of passages that mention or allude to the fatherhood of Yhwh,[15] several are of particular significance due to their lexical and thematic relation to Prov 3:11–12.

Prov 3:11–12	מוּסַר יְהוָה בְּנִי אַל־תִּמְאָס וְאַל־תָּקֹץ בְּתוֹכַחְתּוֹ: כִּי אֶת אֲשֶׁר יֶאֱהַב יְהוָה יוֹכִיחַ וּכְאָב אֶת־בֵּן יִרְצֶה:	My son, do not reject [מאס] the *musar* of Yhwh and do not despise his rebukes [יכח]. For those he rebukes [יכח] Yhwh loves [אהב] and as a father he delights in the son.
Prov 13:24	חוֹשֵׂךְ שִׁבְטוֹ שׂוֹנֵא בְנוֹ וְאֹהֲבוֹ שִׁחֲרוֹ מוּסָר:	The one who withholds his rod, hates his son; and the one who loves [אהב] him, seeks for him *musar*.
Deut 8:5–6	וְיָדַעְתָּ עִם־לְבָבֶךָ כִּי כַּאֲשֶׁר יְיַסֵּר אִישׁ אֶת־בְּנוֹ יְהוָה אֱלֹהֶיךָ מְיַסְּרֶךָּ: וְשָׁמַרְתָּ אֶת־מִצְוֹת יְהוָה אֱלֹהֶיךָ לָלֶכֶת בִּדְרָכָיו וּלְיִרְאָה אֹתוֹ:	And you will know with your heart that just as a man disciplines [יסר] his son, Yhwh your God disciplines [יסר] you. And you will guard the commands of Yhwh your God, walking in his ways and fearing him.

---

[12] The idea of divine fatherhood in the ANE was often associated with law and order, as well as origins. Furthermore, Tasker notes among the Sumerians, "Their relationship with the father-gods was not a personally satisfying one, but a relationship considered necessary to ensure abundant harvests, fertile herds, and social harmony. ... The personal gods in turn expected honor and obedience" (Tasker, *The Fatherhood of God*, 23–25).

[13] While this is generally true for the ANE, there was perhaps an element of compassion and mercy ascribed to El in Canaan. Tasker quotes from an unpublished thesis by Henri A. Drouault, "El is the good and kind god; he is the god of mercy. This is an unusual quality among the ancient gods of the Near East, a sort of foreign element. In fact, if it were not for El, the words 'kindness, compassion, and mercy,' would have been practically left out of the language of the pantheon" (Tasker, *The Fatherhood of God*, 64).

[14] For some negative views on the fatherhood of God or its dismissal in the OT, see Wilhelm Bousset, *Jesu Predigt in ihrem Gegensatz zum Judentum: ein religiongeschichtlicher Vergleich* (Göttingen: Vandenhoeck & Ruprecht, 1892); Sigmund Freud, *Moses and Monotheism*, trans. Katherine Jones (London: Hogarth, 1951); Rudolf Bultmann, *Primitive Christianity in Its Contemporary Setting*, trans. R. H. Fuller (New York: Meridian, 1956); Joachim Jeremias, *The Prayers of Jesus* (Naperville: Allenson, 1967); Mary Daly, *Beyond God the Father: Toward a Philosophy of Women's Liberation* (Boston: Beacon, 1973); Robert Hamerton-Kelly, *God the Father: Theology and Patriarchy in the Teachings of Jesus* (Philadelphia: Fortress, 1979); Johann Baptist Metz, Edward Schillebeeckx, and Marcus Lefébure, eds., *God as Father?*, Concilium 143 (New York: Seabury, 1981); Thomas McGovern, "John Paul II on the Millennium and God as Father," *Homiletic and Pastoral Review* 99.7 (1999): 8–17.

[15] E.g., Exod 4:22; Deut 8:5, 32:6; 2 Sam 7:14; Isa 63:16, 64:8; Jer 3:4, 19, 31:9; Hos 11:1; Mal 1:6, 2:10; Ps 2:7, 68:5, 89:26, 103:13; Prov 3:12; 1 Chr 17:13, 22:10, 28:6, 29:10.

2 Sam 7:14	אֲנִי אֶהְיֶה־לּוֹ לְאָב וְהוּא יִהְיֶה־לִּי לְבֵן אֲשֶׁר בְּהַעֲוֺתוֹ וְהֹכַחְתִּיו בְּשֵׁבֶט אֲנָשִׁים וּבְנִגְעֵי בְּנֵי אָדָם:	I will be for him a father and he will be for me a son. When he sins, I will rebuke [יכח] him with the rod of men and with marks of the sons of man.
Ps 103:13	כְּרַחֵם אָב עַל־בָּנִים רִחַם יְהֹוָה עַל־יְרֵאָיו:	As a father is compassionate [רחם] over sons, Yhwh is compassionate [רחם] over those who fear him.
Job 5:17–18	הִנֵּה אַשְׁרֵי אֱנוֹשׁ יוֹכִחֶנּוּ אֱלוֹהַּ וּמוּסַר שַׁדַּי אַל־תִּמְאָס:	Behold, blessed is the man God rebukes [יכח] and he does not reject [מאס] the *musar* of Shaddai.
Ps 94:12	אַשְׁרֵי הַגֶּבֶר אֲשֶׁר־תְּיַסְּרֶנּוּ יָּהּ וּמִתּוֹרָתְךָ תְלַמְּדֶנּוּ:	Blessed is the man whom Yah disciplines [יסר] and you teach [למד] him from your *torah*.

These passages exemplify either literary borrowing or shared cultural concepts and language for the fatherhood of God. Proverbs 13:24 indicates that "love" through *musar* is a typical function between a human father and son, making the metaphor for Yhwh very personal and real. In Moses' instruction regarding God's covenant, Yhwh's discipline is connected with his functional fatherhood and with walking in his ways. As an early passage from the Torah, Deut 8 may serve as the catalyst for the biblical motif broadly (cf. Deut 4:36, 11:2), particularly in Prov 3.[16] However, the motif does appear first more subtly in Gen 1–3[17] and Exod 4:22,[18] serving to anchor the metaphor fundamentally in the Israelite mind. In fact, the parallel between these passages proves difficult to discern directionality, perhaps indicating the shared religious and cultural concepts and language more so than direct literary borrowing.[19] The historical account of David's covenant, perhaps

---

[16] Schipper and Brown, among others, remove the historical weight and prevalence of the motif by placing Deut 8 in "late-Deuteronom(ist)ic thought." Alternatively, Weeks says, "When it evokes the Deuteronomic idea of God as instructor, it is hard to believe that the writer would not expect his Jewish readership to see in this a reference to the Torah." Despite this view, he cautions against Delitzsch who he believes creates too strong of an intertextual dependence on Deuteronomy. See Schipper, *Proverbs 1–15*, 125; William P. Brown, "The Law and the Sages: A Reexamination of Tôrâ in Proverbs," in *Constituting the Community: Studies on the Polity of Ancient Israel in Honor of S. Dean McBride Jr.*, ed. John T. Strong and Steven S. Tuell (Winona Lake: Eisenbrauns, 2005), 266; Weeks, *Instruction and Imagery in Proverbs 1–9*, 104).

[17] Oswalt, "Theology of the Pentateuch," 854.

[18] "And you will say to Pharaoh, 'Thus says Yhwh, 'My son, my firstborn is Israel'" (Exod 4:22).

[19] Regarding inter-biblical allusions, Schaefer states, "Allusions are limited to a word, a brief phrase, or an image that constitutes an indirect reference but can sometimes be traced to a source. Allusive reference may be intentional, or it may be an echo. The essence of the conscious allusion is the author's intention to recall previous oracles with their context; once the reader recognizes the references, the horizons for comprehension are expanded." For this network of passages, it is perhaps more appropriate to understand their correspondence according to the categories of a common use motif or metaphor, though direct allusion is possible. For a lively and complex debate over the validity and terminology of intertextuality, see Konrad R. Schaefer, "Zechariah 14: A Study in Allusion," *CBQ* 57.1 (1995): 68–69; Michael Fishbane,

unsurprisingly, includes the metaphor of Yhwh as a father, especially as one who rebukes like a teacher. In this passage, the formative purpose for the discipline is indicated by the conjunctive clause, "And my steadfast love (חסד) will not turn from you as I turned from Saul" (2 Sam 7:15). The Lord dealt with Saul through judgment but would deal with David's offspring through discipline as a son, illuminating an important biblical distinction. Similarly, Ps 103 intuitively understands and communicates the biblical principle of God's mercy/compassion (רחם) in his fatherhood, likely bringing together various instances of this motif from Exodus (cf. 33:13, 19, 34:6–7).[20] Together, the passages paint a clear picture of Yhwh's role and function as a father, which included all covenant-faithful Israelites, Davidic kings, the proverbial son, and those whom "Yhwh loves." Surprisingly, the teacher does not indicate what qualifies as one whom the Lord loves. Implicitly, it seems most appropriate for it to be those who are his children. In light of this network of passages and Prov 1–9, it would seem the children of God are those in covenant with him, expressed by wisely walking with him in his ways.

Throughout the Hebrew scriptures, a myriad of titles, names, and ascriptions are attached to Yhwh, all expressed in an active and relational sense.[21] However, there are three that carry particular, overarching, and relational weight throughout. Although he was the creating, saving God of Israel, he is known most eminently through the metaphors king, husband, and father.[22] Each of these metaphors has overlapping qualities but also implies unique aspects of his role. The concept of divine kingship, also known in the ANE, carried the sense of law and order, or justice and righteousness, often in the affiliated metaphor of a shepherd.[23] Likewise, the divine husband, also known in the ANE, carried the sense of covenant faithfulness, protection, and

---

Biblical Interpretation in Ancient Israel (New York: Oxford University Press, 1985); Richard B. Hays, *Echoes of Scripture in the Letters of Paul* (New Haven: Yale University Press, 1989); Lyle Eslinger, "Inner-Biblical Exegesis and Inner-Biblical Allusion: The Question of Category," *VT* 42.1 (1992): 47–58; Paul R. Noble, "Esau, Tamar, and Joseph: Criteria for Identifying Inner-Biblical Allusions," *VT* 52.2 (2002): 219–52; Jeffery M. Leonard, "Identifying Inner-Biblical Allusions: Psalm 78 as a Test Case," *JBL* 127.2 (2008): 241–65; Geoffrey D. Miller, "Intertextuality in Old Testament Research," *CurBR* 9.3 (2011): 283–309; Russell Meek, "Intertextuality, Inner-Biblical Exegesis, and Inner-Biblical Allusion: The Ethics of a Methodology," *Bib* 95.2 (2014): 280–91; Lesley DiFransico, "Identifying Inner-Biblical Allusion through Metaphor: Washing Away Sin in Psalm 51," *VT* 65.4 (2015): 542–57.

[20] Fox makes an unnecessarily strong statement regarding God's mercy, "God's forgiveness and mercy (raḥǎmim, as distinct from his kindness, ḥesed), which are central to personal piety, have no role in Prov 1–9 and are scarcely mentioned elsewhere in Proverbs." He unfortunately approaches the passage myopically and in light of Egyptian piety, thus missing the broad network of other biblical passages that indicate the fatherhood of God motif actually carries with it the inherent sense of compassion/mercy (Fox, *Proverbs 1–9*, 155).

[21] Oswalt, "Theology of the Pentateuch," 852.

[22] Weinfeld discussed these metaphorical images through the paradigmatic language "master-vassal," "husband-wife," and "father-son." However, regarding the "master-vassal" motif, he based it on the idea of Yhwh as "sovereign God-King." Also, these categories in his view were closely related to the expression of covenant relationship. See Moshe Weinfeld, "Ancient Near Eastern Patterns in Prophetic Literature," *VT* 27.2 (1977): 188.

[23] Oswalt, "God," 291–92.

providence.[24] The fatherhood of God, however, carried elements of the other two metaphors but seems to highlight his role as creator and teacher, one who is compassionate and patient as with a son. The fatherhood image also carries the possibility of passing on one's traits or trade to a son, as was often the case. Genesis 1 and 5 seem to indicate that a son's reflection of his father's image is not so much tied to his appearance as to his character and conduct.[25] The picture in Genesis indicates the universality of God's fatherly relation to all humans. However, he is most intimately related to those who properly imitate him by walking in his ways.[26]

The divine fatherhood motif is picked up and amplified later by the early biblical interpreters in the NT.[27] Of course, the NT views Jesus as the preeminent son of the Father, who obeys, imitates, and knows his father (e.g., John 5:18–20, 8:55). While much could be said of this salient parallel, several passages in the NT directly connect the fatherhood of God with imitation and walking in his ways.[28]

Eph 4:32–5:1	γίνεσθε [δὲ] εἰς ἀλλήλους χρηστοί, εὔσπλαγχνοι, χαριζόμενοι ἑαυτοῖς, καθὼς καὶ ὁ θεὸς ἐν Χριστῷ ἐχαρίσατο ὑμῖν. γίνεσθε οὖν μιμηταὶ τοῦ θεοῦ ὡς τέκνα ἀγαπητὰ καὶ περιπατεῖτε ἐν ἀγάπῃ, καθὼς καὶ ὁ Χριστὸς ἠγάπησεν ἡμᾶς	Be kind to one another, compassionate, gracious to each other just as God in Christ was gracious to you. Therefore, be imitators of God as beloved children and walk in love just as Christ also loved you.

[24] Oswalt notes the unique qualities of Yhwh's covenantal relation with Israel, "This nuptial understanding of the covenant, especially as expressed in Ezekiel and Hosea, underlines that the basis of the covenant between Yahweh and Israel is radically different from that of the Hittite suzerainty treaties upon which the Sinai covenant is formally modeled. ... If this marriage metaphor shows that grace is understood by the prophets to be both the basis and the modus operandi of the covenant, it also underlines a point that Deuteronomy makes very clear: the motivation for keeping the terms of the covenant is love, not coercion. If the imagery of sovereign and servant provides one apt metaphor for the relation between God and humans, it is by no means the only metaphor, and perhaps not always the best one" (Oswalt, "God," 290).

[25] Beale, *We Become What We Worship*, 130.

[26] For rabbinic teachings on the relationship between God's fatherhood and his imitation, see Israel Abrahams, *Studies in Pharisaism and the Gospels* (1917; repr., New York: Ktav, 1967), 169.

[27] Thompson makes the case for continuity in the NT from the OT for this foundational metaphor. See Marianne M. Thompson, *The Promise of the Father: Jesus and God in the New Testament* (Louisville: Westminster John Knox, 2000).

[28] Holmes builds on the patristic theologians to say, "Christian faith does not simply benefit from talk about imitation of God; the pursuit of God, and of saying things that are true of God, assumes imitation." Similarly, Gregory of Nyssa observes, "It is necessary for anyone desiring to be closely united with another to take on the ways of that person through imitation." See Christopher R. J. Holmes, *A Theology of the Christian Life: Imitating and Participating in God* (Grand Rapids: Baker Academic, 2021), 47, 50, 54; Gregory of Nyssa, *On the Christian Mode of Life*, trans. Virginia Woods Callahan (Washington, DC: Catholic University of America Press, 1967), 133.

1 Pet 1:14–17	ὡς τέκνα ὑπακοῆς μὴ συσχηματιζόμενοι ταῖς πρότερον ἐν τῇ ἀγνοίᾳ ὑμῶν ἐπιθυμίαις, ἀλλὰ κατὰ τὸν καλέσαντα ὑμᾶς ἅγιον καὶ αὐτοὶ ἅγιοι ἐν πάσῃ ἀναστροφῇ γενήθητε, διότι γέγραπται, Ἅγιοι ἔσεσθε, ὅτι ἐγὼ ἅγιος. Καὶ εἰ πατέρα ἐπικαλεῖσθε τὸν ἀπροσωπολήμπτως κρίνοντα κατὰ τὸ ἑκάστου ἔργον, ἐν φόβῳ τὸν τῆς παροικίας ὑμῶν χρόνον ἀναστράφητε	As obedient children, do not be conformed to the passions of your former ignorance, but according to the Holy One calling you, you also ought to be those who are holy in all conduct, for it was written, 'You shall be holy for I am holy.' And if you call him father, who judges impartially according to one's work, in fear conduct yourselves in the time of your sojourning.
Matt 5:48	Ἔσεσθε οὖν ὑμεῖς τέλειοι ὡς ὁ πατὴρ ὑμῶν ὁ οὐράνιος τέλειός ἐστιν.	Therefore, you shall be perfect as your heavenly father is perfect.
Luke 6:35–36	πλὴν ἀγαπᾶτε τοὺς ἐχθροὺς ὑμῶν καὶ ἀγαθοποιεῖτε καὶ δανίζετε μηδὲν ἀπελπίζοντες· καὶ ἔσται ὁ μισθὸς ὑμῶν πολύς, καὶ ἔσεσθε υἱοὶ ὑψίστου, ὅτι αὐτὸς χρηστός ἐστιν ἐπὶ τοὺς ἀχαρίστους καὶ πονηρούς. Γίνεσθε οἰκτίρμονες καθὼς [καὶ] ὁ πατὴρ ὑμῶν οἰκτίρμων ἐστίν.	But, love your enemies and do good and lend without expecting return and your reward will be great and you will be sons of the Most High, for he is kind to the ungracious and evil. Be compassionate just as your father is compassionate.

Similar to the HB, there is a presumption of the fatherhood of God in the NT.[29] It is not surprising that several of the occurrences of the motif in the NT also uncritically parallel this notion with imitation of or likeness with God. This implies that the concept was endemic and readily understood without further explanation or argumentation. The passage in Eph 4:32–5:1 fits within a broader pericope eliciting the two-path metaphor as well. Here, the two paths are defined negatively with ignorance and various immoralities – "You must no longer walk just as the gentiles also walk ... those being darkened in understanding, those estranged from the life of God" (Eph 4:17, 18) – and positively with a new life or self which is "created in accordance with God" and expressed by walking in his character and behaviors (Eph 4:24, 5:1). Similarly, Peter appeals to the fatherhood of God as an obvious basis for ordering one's conduct. His reference to Leviticus, which does not mention the fatherhood of

---

[29] Buber states, "We need only transfer ourselves by intermediary links. We from mediacy to immediacy, from the imitation of Jesus to his imitation of our Father, and we are standing on Jewish soil ... The imitation, not of a mediator in human form but of God himself—this is the central paradox of Judaism" (Martin Buber, *Israel and the World: Essays in a Time of Crisis* (New York: Schocken Books, 1948), 71).

God, indicates that the concept of God's ways and his exemplar status as Father were stock concepts (Lev 11:44–45, 19:2). Finally, in Matt 5 and Luke 6, Jesus alludes to the same conceptual tradition from the HB. Likeness to God was mediated primarily to his people through the metaphor of Fatherhood.[30] This connection is, of course, central in the transgenerational education commanded in the Torah (e.g., Deut 6:7, 11:19). Yet, it is clearly rooted in the ideal expression of fatherhood, Yhwh being a father with *musar* and "love."

It is important at this point to elucidate the fatherhood metaphor in Prov 3:11–12 more directly. While many of the passages referenced thus far may appear tangential, the concept of *musar* here must be considered in order to rightly understand why the teacher inserted Yhwh as the Father. Of particular importance is the question, what is the goal of *musar*? On a basic, simplistic level, *musar* is related to obedience and *torah*. Yet, it is important to understand that *musar* is not an end but a means to an end. As taught throughout the HB, *musar* is more akin to guidance and leading on a path than a mere event or quality. Indeed, *musar* is at the heart of formation or walking the straight path. The ideal, of course, is to be or become like the one guiding and instructing. One of the major complaints from the prophets was the blindness, foolishness, and wickedness of the supposed sages and leaders. They were not exemplars in the least. Rather, the proverbial son is to pattern his character and conduct according to his father who is preeminently derived from and concluded in God, the supreme Father.[31] As Bland notes, "The truly wise ones humbly submit themselves to God. ... They see life as a journey in which God's discipline molds them into his image."[32] Similarly, through parallel, the son is to be like the father as all of Israel is to be like the divine-Father.[33] Thus, in this introductory verses of Lesson 4, a great deal is communicated through the seemingly simple fatherhood metaphor.[34]

---

[30] Feldmeier says, "The evangelist has positioned exactly in the center of Jesus's discourse the double characterization of God by means of kindness and mercy that the followers of Jesus are to reflect in their own conduct. In this way, they will enter into a father-child relationship, and thereby into the closest conceivable fellowship with God." Likewise, Carroll comments, "This way of life, though subversive and countercultural, mirrors God's own character and commitments and is therefore the mode of living adopted by those who are truly God's children." See Reinhard Feldmeier, "'As Your Heavenly Father Is Perfect': The God of the Bible and Commandments in the Gospel," *Int* 70.4 (2016): 439; John T. Carroll, *Luke: A Commentary*, NTL (Louisville: Westminster John Knox, 2012), 153.

[31] Bland confirms this imitative trajectory, "Parents follow God's example by observing how God disciplines." In this sense, it is not only the son who is being formed in Prov 1–9 through an imitative schema but also parents – or any other parental, teaching figure. See Bland, *Proverbs and the Formation of Character*, 25–26.

[32] Bland, *Proverbs and the Formation of Character*, 6.

[33] McKay, "Man's Love for God in Deuteronomy and The Father/Teacher – Son/Pupil Relationship," 432.

[34] Derousseaux calls it the "pedagogy of the divine father." Keefer adds to this the emphasis on divine imminence rather than transcendence at this point, "the affective, familial care of a father to a son." See Louis Derousseaux, *La crainte de Dieu dans l'Ancien Testament: royauté, alliance, sagesse dans les royaumes d'Israël et de Juda* (Paris: Éditions du Cerf, 1970), 328; Keefer, *Proverbs 1–9 as an Introduction to the Book of Proverbs*, 150.

Supremacy of Wisdom (3:13–18)

The second occurrence of Wisdom, metaphorically imaged as a person, occurs here in Lesson 4 (cf. Prov 1:20–33, 4:6–9, 13, 8:1–9:12). Much of the language and imagery in this six-verse poem occurs elsewhere in Prov 1–9.[35] There is an emphasis on seeking and finding (Prov 3:13; cf. 2:4–5, 3:13, 4:22, 7:15, 8:9, 17, 35–36),[36] holding on to her (3:18; cf. 4:13), her incomparable value (Prov 3:14–15; cf. 2:4, 8:10–11, 18–19), the gift of life (Prov 3:16, 18; cf. 3:2, 4:10, 13, 22, 6:23, 8:35, 9:11),[37] and the blessing of following her ways (Prov 3:17; cf. 1:15–16, 2:20, 4:11, 8:20, 32, 9:6; Isa 59:7–8). The only particularly unique idea used here is the metaphor "She is a tree of life" (Prov 3:18a).[38] Duvall and Hays comment,

> The mention of the 'tree of life' seems to be a clear reference back to the tree of life in Genesis 2–3. Ironically, while it was the unauthorized and disobedient desire for knowledge that resulted in the banishment of Adam and Eve from the garden, the tree of life, and the presence of God in Genesis 2–3, in Proverbs God offers a way back to the garden, to his presence, and to the tree of life, through Woman Wisdom.[39]

---

[35] Whybray, *Composition of the Book of Proverbs*, 37.

[36] In Prov 3:13, interestingly, the word for "obtain" (פוק) in all of its other uses in Proverbs (8:35; 12:2; 18:22) occurs in the phrase "obtains favor from Yhwh" (רָצוֹן מֵיְהוָה יָפִיק). This perhaps implies a conceptual framework for the sense of "receive" as a gift or reward. A similar or parallel phrase is in 8:32–35, which likely indicates Wisdom is the speaker there, "Blessed are those guarding my ways ... the one finding me finds life and he will receive (פוק) favor from Yhwh." Although Wisdom does not speak or address the son in 3:13–18, the content and message are almost identical.

[37] An important parallel occurs in Prov 24:13–14, "My son, eat honey for it is good and honey sweet to the mouth. Thus, know wisdom is for your soul if you find it. There is an end, but your hope will not be cut off" (cf. Prov 23:18). Here, there is an association between finding wisdom and immortality, similarly described.

[38] Marcus early on, followed by Fox and others, dismissed the metaphor as dead and disconnected from Gen 2–3, only referring to the "medicinal" aspect in late Jewish idiom, partly dependent on ANE equivalents. Osborne, however, corrects the over dependence on ANE equivalents and the deadness of the metaphor. He notes that the reference likely does point back to Gen 2–3, indicating both general wellness and immortality. Likewise, he notes that the apparent parallels to ANE wisdom is due to shared cultural imagery rather than appropriation, "If we join the notion of cognitive environment with the metaphor theory of cognitive linguistics, the result is that both Egypt and Israel employed a similar conceptual metaphor." See Ralph Marcus, "The Tree of Life in Proverbs," *JBL* 62.2 (1943): 117–20; Fox, *Proverbs 1–9*, 159; William R. Osborne, "The Tree of Life in Ancient Egypt and the Book of Proverbs," *JANER* 14.1 (2014): 114–39.

[39] J. Scott Duvall and J. Daniel Hays, *God's Relational Presence: The Cohesive Center of Biblical Theology.* (Grand Rapids: Baker Academic, 2019), 106; Richard S. Hess, *Israelite Religions: An Archaeological and Biblical Survey* (Downers Grove: IVP, 2007), 76; Meinhold, *Die Sprüche*, 80–81. Alternatively, Hess draws a somewhat similar yet contradicting picture of Wisdom stating, "The female characteristics of Yahweh and some background to the personification of Wisdom (e.g., Prov. 3) owe their origins to Asherah." Meinhold proposes that with Prov 3:16, the symbolism reflects *Ma'at* in Egyptian circles.

The first couple sought to be like God in an unauthorized manner (Gen 3:5).[40] Likeness to God was not the problem in Gen 3, though, clearly indicated by Gen 1:26–27.[41] Rather, it is the aberrant pathway, symbolized with a tree, which seeks the benefits of divinity apart from God and his ways. Thus, the path in Proverbs sets out to restore humanity to a proper imitative or reflective relationship with God, which was lost in Genesis.[42] The son is encouraged and persuaded in Proverbs to walk in the ways of Wisdom, equivalent to the ways of Yhwh guided by his *musar*. In doing so, he will have access to the "tree of life," symbolizing the proper path of likeness.[43] On this path, the son will seek to imitate God as a son rather than as a usurper.[44]

The metaphorical connection between the father, Wisdom, and Yhwh is important both in their distinctions and similarities. Unfortunately, misunderstanding the role of Wisdom often leads to confusion. Brown makes this mistake in an article discussing several wisdom psalms, "Torah is nowhere given personified status in the Psalter. The metaphorical richness that vivifies wisdom in Proverbs is lacking in psalmic treatments of Torah. ... [T]he psalmists placed great value on God's unmediated agency in teaching. ... [A] personification of Torah comparable to that of wisdom would have compromised such singular theocentric focus."[45] Brown's comparison is problematic, in part due to the difference between Torah and Wisdom. Wisdom is not simply a personification of an abstract concept but is related to Yhwh more as an anthropomorphism. Thus, *torah* is different, not to be confused with God. *Torah* cannot logically be an anthropomorphism since it is simply instruction that comes from and through Wisdom/Yhwh. The metaphorical nature of Wisdom, though, allows for her to provide much that is typically associated with God, as discussed in Lesson 1. Weeks more closely approaches the metaphor, "In chapter 3, the father and personified Wisdom are now linked more poetically to YHWH ... Wisdom herself is identified as an

---

[40] Day argues their desire was to be like "gods" in the generic plural rather than like God. This view is certainly part of the problem but does not negate their unholy desire to usurp the creator rather than reflect him. See Beale, *We Become What We Worship*, 21, 41, 44, 46, 129–34; John Day, "Wisdom and the Garden of Eden," in *Perspectives on Israelite Wisdom: Proceedings of the Oxford Old Testament Seminar*, ed. John Jarick, LHBOTS 618 (London: T&T Clark, 2016), 337.

[41] Najman, "Imitatio Dei," 313.

[42] See Waltke, *Proverbs (1–15)*, 259–60.

[43] The phrases between Gen 3:24 and Prov 3:18 are slightly different. The Genesis account says the cherubim guarded "the way of the tree of life" (אֶת־דֶּרֶךְ עֵץ הַחַיִּים). The phrase in Gen 3 is a definite construct, which could indicate the "way," the "tree," or both. The phrase in Prov 3:18 is a nominal sentence, however, which says, "She is a tree of life" (עֵץ־חַיִּים הִיא). The predicate phrase is indefinite, possibly implying multiple "trees." It would seem through the intertextual play that the proverbial poem envisions Wisdom as "the way" (דֶּרֶךְ) from Gen 3. The trees may be the same or different but it is Wisdom that is in focus, here. She is the restorer of humanity to a proper relationship with the divine.

[44] As Najman notes, "The human must exercise dominion over other creatures but must not misunderstand this dominion as absolute. To be created in the image of God is to be called to imitate God, but not to be God. Both the blood prohibitions are meant to signify the limitations placed on the image of God" (Najman, "Imitatio Dei," 316).

[45] Brown, "Come, O Children," 100–101.

attribute of YHWH. ... wisdom and instruction are attributes of YHWH."[46] While Weeks more appropriately understands Wisdom, he unnecessarily identifies "instruction" as an attribute as well. Again, the proverbial father is careful to distinguish wisdom and instruction. Wisdom is an anthropomorphic attribute or representation of Yhwh while *torah* is simply guidance and tools for properly walking in his ways.

Yhwh as Creator (3:19–20)

Despite the anthropomorphic use of Wisdom in Prov 1–9, the father's description of her in 3:19–20 enters the liminal space between anthropomorphism and personification. Wisdom is in focus and exalted in 3:13–18. Then, the uniqueness and ultimacy of Yhwh are clarified, given immediately after the incredible Wisdom poem. The proximity of these verses is not accidental but intentional. Wisdom is used metaphorically for God's own wise and instructive ways. There is an aspect of instrumentality inherent to wisdom, available to all who properly seek.[47] In this sense, Wisdom must be differentiated from Yhwh since he actually utilizes wisdom, a pervasive idea associated preeminently in his creative works (cf. Prov 8:22–23; Ps 104:24).[48] Thus, Wisdom is understood as a "faculty or skill" of God more so than as an abstract idea.[49] Likewise, as Schipper notes, Wisdom clearly is not to be viewed as an "independent agent" or a divine being.[50] This distinction is important regarding this lesson. The son is expected throughout the fifteen lessons to find and utilize wisdom. Although he would not be expected to create his own world, there is a rhetorical force behind the connection. In other words, the son is to attain and utilize wisdom just as God does, learning and

---

[46] Weeks, *Instruction and Imagery in Proverbs 1–9*, 101; Schipper, *Proverbs 1–15*, 139–40. Despite identifying Wisdom as an attribute, shortly after, Weeks also refers to Wisdom as simply something created (107). Schipper identifies "insight" and "knowledge" along with "wisdom" as attributes of Yhwh. However, though a number of words are associated and paralleled with wisdom in Proverbs, only wisdom is given an explicit anthropomorphic qualification, one closely identified with Yhwh himself. While this may be incidental or arbitrary, it may have been a careful nuance in the conceptual framework for the proverbial teacher.

[47] Weeks comments regarding the dual use of Wisdom as a tool and person, "Wisdom itself remains a concept that transcends the individual: when the divine attribute of wisdom comes into being, so, simultaneously, does the whole concept of wisdom, the general arising from the first instance of the particular" (Weeks, *Instruction and Imagery in Proverbs 1–9*, 123). While he attempts to construct a bridge, it may go further than a mere metaphor of a divine attribute can be understood. If indeed a divine attribute, it would follow that wisdom did not have a "first instance," except in the sense of its relation to the created world diachronically speaking. As discussed here, the metaphor may simply be used to express a divine attribute available to all who imitate and walk in the father's ways.

[48] Fox, *Proverbs 1–9*, 161; Schipper, *Proverbs 1–15*, 147–48; Whybray, *Composition of the Book of Proverbs*, 37.

[49] Meinhold, *Die Sprüche*, 81; Weeks, *Instruction and Imagery in Proverbs 1–9*, 101.

[50] Schipper, *Proverbs 1–15*, 147.

participating in his faculties and skills.[51] Thus, the comparative imitation is not in the results but rather in the means. God is a wise father whose ways are characterized by Wisdom. Thus, the son should also be wise and walk in his ways. This metaphor is intimated through the relational, anthropomorphism of Wisdom, a faculty and way inextricably related to Yhwh. The divine and fatherly inclusio for Lesson 4 draws these elements tightly around the centrality of Yhwh for the entirety of the pedagogical enterprise. The inclusio is similar in this sense to how Prov 1–9 begins and ends the whole program with the fear and knowledge of Yhwh (Prov 1:7, 2:5, 9:10).

Conclusion

In this lesson, the proverbial father steps aside and points to God as the ultimate figure and source of Wisdom and instruction (Prov 3:11–12). While the father provides necessary teaching, he does so only as one who transmits what was taught to him. This chain of instruction is primarily sourced in Yhwh. Even the great Wisdom is presented in this lesson as a mere tool of God in his creative and kingly ways (Prov 3:19–20). Thus, the son is to reflect his heavenly Father in the proper use of Wisdom, a core aspect of the father-son metaphor. In doing so, the son will find the tree of life, returning humanity to its Edenic roots (Prov 3:13–18). Elements of this lesson, particularly the fatherhood of God, serve the rest of the wisdom program by elevating the basis of the son's instruction. Although mundane instruction and blessings are a benefit, they are only indirect benefits of walking in familial connection with Yhwh, the primary concern of the proverbial father throughout the wisdom program. After this extended look at the knowledge and closeness of Yhwh in Lessons 2–4, Lesson 5 moves the focus to a more mixed teaching on Yhwh. Following a number of admonitions, the son is warned not to become an abomination to God by emulating the ways of sinners.

---

[51] Meinhold, *Die Sprüche*, 79.

LESSON 5

Analysis of 3:21–35
"Yhwh is with the upright"

After several lessons highlighting the knowledge of and filial closeness to Yhwh, the proverbial father issues a somber warning for the son in Lesson 5. While blessing and relationship are inherent for the one following in the ways of Yhwh, those who deviate from the wise way will become an abomination to him (Prov 3:32–35). In brief, the son must avoid walking in the way of sinners or desiring to be like the man of violence (Prov 3:27–31). Instead, he must reflect the character and behaviors of the wise, particularly rooted in the nature and ways of God. In fact, the father says that God will be with the son in his way and protect him if he will be one of the "upright" and properly guard his fatherly instruction (Prov 3:23, 26). Thus, this fifth lesson continues the emphasis on Yhwh from Lessons 2–4 but revisits the concerns and warnings of Lesson 1 regarding the ways of sinners. As the son progresses in his training, this lesson is vital for putting into perspective the physical and relational consequences of his choices, whether for good or bad. If he emulates sinners, he will suffer. If he emulates Yhwh and the upright, he will be blessed.

Structure of Lesson 5

While Lesson 3 focuses on positive commands for the son, Lesson 5 provides seven admonitions, along with eight blessings and four curses.[1] The structure of this lesson is clear but not quite as symmetrical as Lesson 4.[2] In Prov 3:21,

---

[1] Weeks sees Prov 3:1–10 and 21–35 as complementary sections, the first focusing on the son's orientation toward Yhwh and the second with his orientation toward humanity (cf. 3:4). While the sections may indeed be complementary, it is also true that Lesson 5 orients the son toward Yhwh and his ways, in contrast with wicked ways. See Weeks, *Instruction and Imagery in Proverbs 1–9*, 99.

[2] Schipper, *Proverbs 1–15*, 151; Achim Müller, *Proverbien 1–9: der Weisheit neue Kleider*, BZAW 291 (Berlin: De Gruyter, 2000), 169.

the lesson begins with the typical literary marker "my son" with a third masculine plural negated imperfect (*yiqtol*) "may they not deviate," serving as a familiar opening introduction and directive.[3] Following, Prov 3:22–24 appear to be blessings that will accompany the son through proper adherence to instruction. For Prov 3:25–31, the teacher provides the seven admonitions in a seven-verse unit.[4] However, the last two admonitions occur in Prov 3:31, which perhaps influences the insertion of 3:26, bringing the total verse count to seven. Likely an intentional insertion, Prov 3:26 provides a relational encouragement to the son by commending the presence of Yhwh with him along the proper path.[5] Finally, the lesson ends with four verses in couplet lines contrasting those whom the Lord is with and those he is against. Structurally, then, the lesson places the seven-verse admonition unit between two four-verse units which open and close the lesson.

---

21 Intro & Command
  22 Blessing 1
  23 Blessing 2
  24 Blessing 3
25 Admonition 1
  26 Blessing 4
27 Admonition 2
28 Admonition 3
29 Admonition 4
30 Admonition 5
31 Admonitions 6 & 7
  32 Curse 1 & Blessing 5
  33 Curse 2 & Blessing 6
  34 Curse 3 & Blessing 7
  35 Blessing 8 & Curse 4

Despite thoughtful attention to structure, a grammatical difficulty occurs with the opening of the lesson. Though the teacher uses the typical "my son," he once again utilizes the third masculine plural, similar to 3:3. However, in Prov 3:3, the reference was fronted with "steadfast love and faithfulness." Here, the referent is less apparent. Several reasonable options are possible: 1. "wisdom"

---

[3] Although Whybray notes this as the introduction, he extends it to include 3:21–24 (Whybray, *Composition of the Book of Proverbs*, 19–20).

[4] Whybray separates out 3:25–26 from 27–31, claiming the body of the lesson consists of only five admonitions (Whybray, *Composition of the Book of Proverbs*, 20).

[5] Overland argues that Prov 3:13–26 should be considered a unit, rather than dividing at 3:21. His reasoning is thematic, picking up on the generally positive quality of these verses. He titles this unit "The Value of Wisdom." As discussed in the structural analyses, the break at Prov 3:21 is preferable for multiple reasons. Overland's attention to the blessings ending with Prov 3:26 is misguided since the blessings serve as an inclusio to Lesson 5 including 3:32–35. See Overland, "Literary Structure in Proverbs 1–9," 285–90.

(Prov 3:13–20);[6] 2. "steadfast love and faithfulness" (3:3); 3. the father's commands and *torah* (3:1);[7] 4. "words" and "sayings" (4:20–21);[8] 5. the admonitions (3:25–31);[9] or 6. "sound wisdom and discretion" (3:21b).[10] Following Prov 3:21, the verb of 3:22 is also in the third masculine plural, though with the *weqatal* form. This initial blessing seems to coordinate with the other nine blessings as related results of the opening line. For the first option, several scholars prefer the referent to be "wisdom," which is drawn from Prov 3:13–20.[11] While possible, it is not clear why the plural is used then, which could imply wisdom and understanding or knowledge, though quite distant (Prov 3:13).[12] Murphy also attempts to appeal to the gift of "life" appearing in 3:2, 16, and 18, along with similar imagery in 1:9, "a grace for your head … a necklace for your neck," to coordinate the referents. For Prov 1:9 and 3:2, the referent is actually *torah* and "commands," not "wisdom." This would be a confused and conflated reference, not fitting well in 3:21 or Lesson 5 broadly. Wisdom and the father's instruction are identified as givers of life, which serve as a coordinating theme overall. In Lesson 5, though, their prominence is subdued. For the second option, if the referent were from 3:3, the line would also have to be read as, "My son, steadfast love and faithfulness will not deviate from your eyes if you protect sound wisdom and discretion" (Prov 3:21). While similar in form, the great distance and different sense from 3:3 implies the similarity is probably not intended for its parallel content but for poetic cohesion. Similarly, for the third option, the father's *torah* and "commands" are certainly central to the whole program and implicitly present but are quite distant from this point.

For the fourth option, Fox appeals to the identical phrase in 4:21a as the key to 3:21. In Prov 4:20–22, there are several similarities as in 3:21–22, "My son, ponder my words; turn your ear to my sayings. *May they not deviate from your eyes;* guard (שׁמר) them within your heart. For they are life to those finding them." Fox proposes that 3:21 originally included 4:20, which would allow "words" and "sayings" to be the natural referent in 3:21. Likewise, Prov 3:22 does mention "life" as a result of adherence as it does in 4:22. Despite this possible emendation by Fox, there is no textual history available for support and it contains several divergences between the passages despite the parallel phrase. Thus, it would only be conjecture and not relevant to the passage as it has been received. For the fifth option, the admonitions could be understood

---

[6] Fox notes this was an option proposed by a few medieval rabbis but believes it would not fit with the sense of Prov 3:21. See David A. Hubbard, *Mastering the Old Testament: Proverbs* (Waco: Word Books, 1989), 76; Meinhold, *Die Sprüche*, 84; Murphy, *Proverbs*, 23; Waltke, *Proverbs (1–15)*, 263; Loader, *Proverbs 1–9*, 177; Fox, *Proverbs 1–9*, 163.

[7] See Plöger, *Spruche Salomos (Proverbia)*, 39.

[8] See Fox, *Proverbs 1–9*, 163.

[9] See Schipper, *Proverbs 1–15*, 151.

[10] See McKane, *Proverbs*, 298; Meinhold, *Die Sprüche*, 84; Whybray, *Composition of the Book of Proverbs*, 19–20; Whybray, *Proverbs (1994)*, 70; Perdue, *Proverbs*, 105, 110; Longman, *Proverbs*, 140–41.

[11] Murphy, *Proverbs*, 23; Waltke, *Proverbs (1–15)*, 263; Overland, "Literary Structure in Proverbs 1–9," 285–90. Waltke bases his structure on the work by Overland.

[12] Whybray, *Proverbs (1994)*, 70.

collectively as the referent in 3:21, though only implicitly. However, most of the blessings and curses are not clearly related to the admonitions, individually or collectively. Thus, the admonitions more likely serve as practical examples of the opening charge in 3:21.

For the final option, the terms "sound wisdom and discretion" seem to best coordinate as referents to the third masculine plural opening line, though the grammar is difficult in all the options.[13] First, the phrase "protect sound wisdom and discretion" occurs in close proximity and intent, located in the second line of 3:21.[14] Poetically, the terms are likely elided but implied in the first half.[15] This would necessitate a conditional promise, perhaps rearranged to say, "Sound wisdom and discretion shall not deviate from your eyes if you protect them."[16] Second, and perhaps more interesting thematically, the terms "sound wisdom" (תּוּשִׁיָּה) and "discretion" (מְזִמָּה) only occur a few times in Prov 1–9.[17] Their other occurrences point to the relational connection with Yhwh and Wisdom along with divine reciprocity inherent in the proper path.[18] The term for "sound wisdom" occurs three times: "[he] stores up sound wisdom for the upright" (Prov 2:7); "guard sound wisdom and discretion" (Prov 3:21); and "counsel and sound wisdom are mine; I have insight and strength" (Prov 8:14). The first use describes a blessing from Yhwh for those who seek, find, and know him. The third use comes from Wisdom as a first-person rhetorical ploy to encourage the son to seek and find her. Here in Lesson 5, the term is used in a command to the son. In the broader context, "sound wisdom" is understood as a relational gift or result from walking in the way of Yhwh and Wisdom. This is perhaps why the teacher carefully says to "protect" (נצר), assuming it has already been received through finding and knowing God (Prov 2:5, 3:6). The term for "discretion" occurs five times: "to give prudence to the naïve, to the youth knowledge and discretion" (Prov 1:4); "discretion will guard over you, understanding will protect you" (2:11); "protect sound wisdom and discretion" (3:21); "to guard discretion and your lips will protect knowledge" (5:2); and "I, Wisdom, dwell with prudence; I find knowledge and discretion"

---

[13] Whybray says, "The reference is clearly to the nouns mentioned in the second line which originally came first, namely 'sound wisdom' (tūšiyyâ) and 'prudence' (mezimmâ). Secondly, in MT this introduction differs from that of the other instructions in that the father in his address to his son does not state that it is his own teaching to which he is referring (contrast, e.g., 'my words,' 'my commandments,' 2:1 and parallels). This may, of course, be implied; but it is interesting that LXX has 'my counsel and understanding' here" (Whybray, *Composition of the Book of Proverbs*, 19–20).

[14] Loader contends against this view claiming that Hebrew never utilizes a cataphoric referent. He bases this on Toy's brief statement, "against Heb. usage," but is certainly not true generally. Cataphora is an established feature, according to Waltke/O'Connor, which is perhaps even more likely in poetic, structurally complex literature. Interestingly, Toy's comments actually reject Loader's overall view as impossible since "wisdom, understanding, and knowledge are attributes of God." See Loader, *Proverbs 1–9*, 165–66; Waltke and O'Connor, *Biblical Hebrew Syntax*, 690; Toy, *Proverbs*, 73–74.

[15] Whybray, *Proverbs (1994)*, 70.

[16] McKane prefers to reverse the order of lines in 3:21, though he maintains the jussive rather than an implied conditional (McKane, *Proverbs*, 298).

[17] (תּוּשִׁיָּה) – Prov 2:7, 3:21, 8:14; (מְזִמָּה) – Prov 1:4, 2:11, 3:21, 5:2, 8:12.

[18] See Kidner, *Proverbs*, 63.

(8:12). [19] As discussed in Lesson 2, there is a parallel and reciprocal relationship between "discretion" guarding the son and the son guarding "discretion." Although not as explicitly associated with Yhwh or Wisdom, the context of Prov 2:11 is Yhwh's blessing and 8:12 is part of Wisdom's rhetorical charge to seek and find her, as well. Thus, the term does carry with it a similar sense of the divine path.

The Admonitions

As most agree, the admonitions form the baseline of this unit. They point the son to important behaviors and attitudes incumbent on the one walking in the ways of the Lord. Interestingly, though, Yhwh is not directly named in the admonition verses. Rather, his name is invoked within the blessings and curses at the beginning and end (Prov 3:26, 32, 33).[20] While subtle, the lesson does in fact intertwine the entirety of the lesson with the son's adherence to the ways of God. As Kidner remarks, "Wisdom means walking with God."[21] In Prov 3:21 and 32, the term "deviate" (לוז) is used, both in the introduction (3:21) and in the conclusive blessings and curses section (3:32–35). For the introductory use, the rare term connotes the loss of "sound wisdom" (תּוּשִׁיָּה) and "discretion" (מְזִמָּה) if the son does not actively protect them. In this use, the term does not directly imply the son's waywardness. However, in the latter use, "deviate" appears in the passive (*niphal*) participle in parallel with "abomination of Yhwh." The term in this use is also negatively paralleled with the "upright" (יְשָׁרִים), confirming the "deviation" or "crooked" sense of the term (cf. Prov 2:15).[22] It is important to understand that in this latter use, the *niphal* participle implies one who did not follow the instruction or warning of 3:21. In this way, the entirety of Lesson 5 revolves around an instruction to the son on how *not* to become an abomination. Thus, the admonitions along with the blessings and curses are proposed as encouragements and warnings for properly adhering to 3:21.

Although each of the admonitions is important to the path, several are particularly relevant to this study. The second admonition, or first according to some, commends the son to be both just and good. The verse commands the son, "Do not withhold good from the one it is due when it is in the power of

---

[19] Interestingly, the term in its nominal form only occurs 19x in the HB. Almost all occurrences are negative in the sense of schemes and plotting evil. The only positive uses are in Jer 11:15 and 23:20 regarding the Lord's plans. Though, these plans are for the discipline of his people.

[20] Schipper rightly believes the blessing/cursing theme of this lesson is an intentional allusion to the Deuteronomic theme, particularly in parallel to Deut 6 and 27–28. However, Longman does caution against an over-emphasis on the connection or reliance, preferring a more subtle and implicit allusion. See Schipper, *Proverbs 1–15*, 153; Longman, *Proverbs*, 144.

[21] Kidner, *Proverbs*, 62–63.

[22] Schipper, *Proverbs 1–15*, 162.

your hand to do" (Prov 3:27).[23] The verse has several components with parallels elsewhere in the HB. First, the phrase "power of your hand" is a rare idiom that seems to connote the sense of "ability" (Gen 31:29; Deut 28:32; Mic 2:1; Prov 3:27; Neh 5:5). Second, and more interesting, the idea of "withholding good" appears in Ps 84:11–12 [12–13], "Yhwh God is a sun and shield; Yhwh gives favor and honor. *He will not withhold good to those walking in purity.* Yhwh of hosts, Blessed (אַשְׁרֵי) is the man who trusts in you" (cf. Prov 20:7). It is clear in this psalm, which uses the same phrase, that Yhwh is commended and praised for this behavior or character trait.[24] In a similar promise, Ps 34:9–10 [10–12] says, "Fear Yhwh, O his saints, for *there is no lack for those fearing him.* Young lions crave and hunger; but *those seeking Yhwh will not lack any good.* Come, O sons, listen to me; I will teach you the fear of Yhwh." In other words, Yhwh providentially gives good to those walking in his ways, namely his sons.[25] The context of Ps 34 is certainly wisdom-oriented and elicits many parallel ideas.[26] However, Ps 84 also utilizes several terms or ideas found in Prov 1–9.[27] The idea of God as a "shield" (מָגֵן) occurs in both (Ps 84:10, 12; Prov 2:7, 30:5). The theme of the "blessed man" characterizes both contexts (Ps 84:5, 6, 13; Prov 3:13, 8:34, 20:7, 28:14). Likewise, Ps 84:5 [6] uses an uncommon term "highway" (מְסִלָּה) which likely occurs in Prov 3:26, as will be discussed in the blessings. In the Psalm passage, the phrase connotes an important parallel for understanding the type of person who is "blessed." The psalmist in Ps 84:5 [6] says, "Blessed (אַשְׁרֵי) is the man whose strength is in you; in their heart are the paths (מְסִלּוֹת)." The "paths" here likely imply either Zion's or God's, either of which connotes a similar sense (cf. Ps 84:7 [8]).[28] They are those who seek the Lord and walk in his ways.[29] Although the psalmist

---

[23] Schipper notes that "good" could mean a material item or just "good" in a more generic sense. He rightly leans toward the generic sense as it relates to a divine blessing. This sense, perhaps as a double entendre, would then preempt the following admonitions. Loader likewise associates the phrase with the term "to do" which he finds broad evidence in the HB for syntagmatic relation with words like justice and righteousness. See Schipper, *Proverbs 1–15*, 158; Loader, *Proverbs 1–9*, 186–87.

[24] DeClaissé-Walford, Jacobson, and Tanner, *Book of Psalms*, 653.

[25] Allen notes that "good" is initially mentioned as an attribute of God to be experienced (Ps 34:8 [9]). However, goodness of God as an attribute is known or demonstrated by his good provisions. Thus, good character is not abstract but enacted or embodied. See Ross, *Commentary on the Psalms*, 752–53.

[26] Jacobson et al. locate the place and purpose of the psalm around a cultic worship experience. The occasion would include overlapping physical and religious or spiritual aspects. Likewise, there would be instruction in the Torah alongside divine presence (DeClaissé-Walford, Jacobson, and Tanner, *Book of Psalms*, 326–27).

[27] Hossfeld and Zenger note the "wisdom perspective" of the psalm, particularly at this point. The imagery implies a cultic orientation on the one hand; yet, it defies being "restricted to the cult, but rather projects a comprehensive spirituality of daily life" (Hossfeld and Zenger, *Psalms 2*, 356).

[28] Tate mentions the double entendre of the walking metaphor used here, "Those who walk in pilgrimage and those who 'walk' with obedience and faith in the way of Yahweh" (Tate, *Psalms 51–100*, 360–61).

[29] Hossfeld and Zenger comment on the path of the blessed saying that "their whole life is a 'pilgrim path' to the living God," implying that God is the goal (Hossfeld and Zenger, *Psalms 2*, 355).

does not command the audience to "not withhold good" as the proverbial father does, the psalmist does provide another characteristic of Yhwh that ought to serve as a model for those seeking to be like him. At its core, the implication is that Yhwh justly gives to men as is right and what they deserve. This principle is a common theme throughout the HB (e.g., Prov 24:12; Ps 62:13; Job 31:16, 34:11; Jer 17:10; Ezek 33:20). Thus, the proverbial teacher points the son to a wise behavior or character trait that he ought to emulate, ultimately rooted in the Lord.[30] As Yhwh properly adjudicates and does not withhold justice, so the son ought to as well. In doing so, he will walk in God's ways, protecting "sound wisdom and discretion."

The teacher concludes his admonitions with a command similar to Lesson 1.[31] In Prov 3:31, the teacher says, "Do not envy a man of violence and do not choose (בחר) any of his ways."[32] The Vulg. actually translates the verse, "Do not emulate (aemulor) an unjust man; do not imitate (imitor) his ways."[33] In 1:15, the father similarly warned the son, "My son, do not walk in the way with [sinners]; withhold (מנע) your foot from their paths." Likewise, Wisdom warned, "They hated knowledge and did not choose (בחר) the fear of Yhwh." As discussed earlier, Lesson 1 emphasized the danger of imitating the wicked, metaphorically conveyed through the imagery of joining their path.[34] Loader astutely explains the admonition in Prov 3 against "jealousy to emulate those who live by the principle of antisocial violence. ... The violent man has success. That is where the temptation to imitate him comes from."[35] Of course, the intent of the admonition is to point the son toward the proper path, to choose the knowledge and fear of Yhwh instead. In both lessons, the path of the wicked is characterized by violence, particularly against the "innocent" (נָקִי) in 1:11.[36] This violence is unjust, indicated by the term "without reason" (חִנָּם) found in both lessons (Prov 1:11, 3:30). In Lesson 1, the proper path is associated with the proverbial father and Wisdom.[37] In Lesson 5, the proper

---

[30] Regarding the Lord's just and compassionate ways, Perdue says, "The wisdom tradition never teaches the renunciation of possessions in order to pursue a life of poverty, but it does stress the importance of supporting those in need. In so doing, sages were *emulating* the compassion and charity of Yahweh" (Perdue, *Proverbs*, 108. Italics added).

[31] Perdue, *Proverbs*, 107; McKane, *Proverbs*, 300.

[32] The BHS and BHQ propose reading the term "angered" (חרה) instead of "choose" (בחר). The basis for this is due to a similar phrase in Prov 24:19 and Ps 37:1: "Do not be angered (חרה) by the evil, do not be jealous (קנא) of the wicked" and "Do not be angered (חרה) by the evil, do not be jealous (קנא) of the deeds of the perverse." The BHQ states that the LXX translator influenced a later copyist by supplying "jealous" (ζηλόω). While those phrases are similar, the term קנא occurs in both parallel lines. However, Prov 3:31 seems to positively parallel both lines in this verse, "jealous // choosing" and "man of violence // his ways." Thus, the sense of choosing is more appropriate to this context.

[33] Toy says that the Vulg. interpretation "represents the Hebrew" in its intended sense (Toy, *Proverbs*, 80).

[34] Hubbard and Waltke both use the term "emulate" to describe the admonition against the wicked in this verse. Schipper refers to them negatively as "models." See Hubbard, *Proverbs*, 69; Schipper, *Proverbs 1–15*, 152; Waltke, *Proverbs (1–15)*, 269.

[35] Loader, *Proverbs 1–9*, 192–93.

[36] Meinhold takes the "violent man" as a general or collective term for the way of the wicked in Prov 1–9 (Meinhold, *Die Sprüche*, 87).

[37] Schäfer, *Die Poesie der Weisen*, 103.

path is associated with Yhwh (Prov 3:26, 32–34).[38] Although the son initially encountered this instruction according to the father (Prov 1:8–19), he then encountered it according to Wisdom (Prov 1:20–33). Following Lesson 2, the son encounters Yhwh (Prov 2:5–6) and begins to grow in his knowledge and likeness of him, particularly as his father (Prov 3:6, 11–12). In the process of his development, he is now reintroduced to a similar lesson encountered earlier but with an advanced perspective. One who is characterized by unjust violence not only deviates from the proper path and endangers his life but is an abomination to Yhwh and his ways. Yhwh is always righteous and just, treating men according to their ways. Thus, the son is to avoid imitating the ways of sinners and instead must imitate the ways of God, also embodied by the father and Wisdom.[39] The implicit intention for the lesson is that the son would not only avoid the ways of the violent man but would instead choose the ways of Yhwh.[40]

The Blessings and Curses

As mentioned, the blessings and curses of Lesson 5 are tangential to the admonitions. Only one of the blessings is clearly related to an admonition (Prov 3:25–26). The first four blessings and the final set of both blessings and curses appear to be a result of the introductory instruction from the teacher. The point of this separation is likely to avoid placing direct connections between admonitions and specific blessings or curses. Rather, the whole

---

[38] Murphy and Habel also observe this movement from father, to Wisdom, to Yhwh. Murphy says of this unit and Prov 3:31, "YHWH takes over the role of wisdom, preserving the youth on the way." Habel similarly comments, "Yahweh is the actual guardian of the way walking at the disciple's side, keeping his feet free from entanglements. ... He assumes the function previously served by the wisdom teacher, authentic teaching, or wisdom itself. ... Thus, Yahweh becomes the source of true instruction, a higher teacher than the wisdom teacher. The way of wisdom becomes the religious way of Yahweh. He is the companion and guardian who blesses the traveler through life." See Norman C. Habel, "Symbolism of Wisdom in Proverbs 1–9," *Int* 26.2 (1972): 144–45; Murphy, *Proverbs*, 24.

[39] Although Schipper does not make the implicit connection with God, he does rightly note, "[The wicked person] cannot serve as a model for the wisdom student. ... v. 31 [has] a summarizing character [of vv. 27–30], explicitly emphasizing that one should not look to such a person as a role model." Similarly, Aitken notes, "His temptation is to envy such men; worse still, to imitate them. That is what the sage now warns against in verses 31–35, developing it along much the same lines as 2:20–22. Psalm 37 deals with the same theme." See Schipper, *Proverbs 1–15*, 160–61; Aitken, *Proverbs*, 51.

[40] The Heb. phrase "any of his ways" (בְּכָל־דְּרָכָיו) is unique in form and occurrence (3:31; cf. Deut 10:12, 11:22; Josh 22:5; 1 Kgs 8:58; Ps 145:17). Schipper says the phrase implies "following the way of the divine law." Although he says Ps 145:17 is an exception, it is rather more likely an insightful divine grounding for the divine law, "Yhwh is righteous in all his ways, and kind in all his deeds" (Ps 145:17). In other words, Yhwh himself is the exemplar for the wise way, which includes his *torah*. This phrase appears with the way of the kings, as well. See the discussion in Lesson 8 for more on this point. Cf. Schipper, *Proverbs 1–15*, 161.

instructional program or two-path metaphor is in view.[41] The first two blessings mentioned are already familiar to the father's instruction and found elsewhere in Prov 1–9. The theme of life is positively associated with the father's teachings (Prov 3:2, 4:10, 22, 6:23) and with Wisdom (3:16, 18, 4:13, 8:35, 9:11). Negatively, life is lost by walking in the way of sinners and pursuing the foreign woman (Prov 1:19, 2:19, 5:6, 11, 7:23). However, in Prov 3:22, the theme of life is a result of protecting "sound wisdom and discretion." Elsewhere in the HB, "sound wisdom" (תּוּשִׁיָּה) is uncommon but typically associated with God. In Isa 28:29, the prophet says, "[Yhwh] is wonderful in counsel, great in sound wisdom." Then in Job, the term is paralleled with other attributes of God several times, including wisdom, understanding, and counsel (Job 11:6, 12:16, 26:3). As the second blessing, in Prov 3:23, the idea of walking or dwelling "securely" (בֶּטַח) occurs as a blessing both here and in Lesson 1, which was a gift from Wisdom (Prov 1:33). However, "security" in the HB is quite often a direct blessing of Yhwh for those walking in his ways (e.g., Lev 25:18–19, 26:5; Deut 33:12; Jer 23:6, 32:37; Ezek 28:26, 34:25). The second and third blessing have a close parallel in Ps 4:9, "I will lie down in peace and sleep, for you alone O Yhwh cause me to dwell securely."[42] Lesson 5 separates sleep and security into sequential verses. While it is not necessary to demonstrate direct borrowing, the shared concept is that Yhwh provides security and peace to those who trust in him and walk in his ways. The higher implication for all three of these blessings, however, is the association with God, who does not die, is always secure, and is perpetually at peace. The idea of sweet sleep for the son need not imply divine sleep (cf. Ps 121:3–4), as it did for the Ugaritic gods, but simply the lack of anxiety and a sense of security (e.g., Prov 6:4, 10; Ps 127:2).[43] The sense of peace for "sleep" is contrasted with the term "fear" (פחד) in 3:24.[44] Likewise, Wisdom's blessing of security in 1:33 is also contrasted with the term "fear" (פחד), central to walking in her ways. Thus, these blessings point to the son's affiliation with God in his path, which the fourth blessing intimates more clearly.

The oddly placed fourth blessing is both pivotal and plagued by a textual quandary (3:26). It begins with a "for" (כִּי), likely indicating a

---

[41] Müller, *Proverbien 1–9*, 173; Plöger, *Spruche Salomos (Proverbia)*, 40; Raymond C. Van Leeuwen, "Liminality and Worldview in Proverbs 1–9," *Semeia* 50 (1990): 113, 116; Habel, "Symbolism of Wisdom in Proverbs 1–9," 144–45. Van Leeuwen contends against the "nuclear symbol" of Prov 1–9 as two-paths, previously argued by Habel. Instead, he proposes that Prov 1–9 is "primarily concerned to inculcate a particular Yahwistic worldview." By this, it seems he has in mind a created world with built-in limitations and a "bi-polar human *eros* for the beauty of wisdom." He roots this theory largely in ANE concepts of order. While he is perhaps right to highlight the orderliness inherent to the book, as this study demonstrates, the path metaphor is indeed central, drawing its roots from beyond Proverbs itself. However, the path metaphor does communicate limitations. The path metaphor is not simply about motion or direction but association in nature, character, and behavior, reflecting Yhwh who exemplifies and maintains this path. Since Yhwh is orderly and the imagery of a path necessarily includes the inherent boundaries which define it, Van Leeuwen is not incorrect, only misguided in emphasis.

[42] Schipper notes the high occurrence of allusions and parallel language between this lesson and the psalter (Schipper, *Proverbs 1–15*, 153).

[43] See the discussion on 3:11–12 in Lesson 4.

[44] Loader, *Proverbs 1–9*, 179.

relationship with the previous verse. Verse 25 starts the admonitions unit with a charge, "do not fear sudden trouble (פחד)," which seemingly draws from Prov 3:23 before that, "you will not tremble (פחד)." In Prov 3:25, the initial line is paralleled with an instructive second line, "when the ruin of the wicked comes." This first admonition is self-oriented rather than others-oriented as are the following six admonitions. Though, of course, all the admonitions are inextricably tied together under the introductory instruction. So, the causal clause of 3:25 provides the reason the son ought not to be fearful of ruin or calamity. It is only the wicked or those in the way with sinners who will experience such an end. Instead, the teacher promises that "Yhwh will be with your *way* and guard your foot from being captured." The term "way" has at least four options from the textual traditions. First, the MT seemingly uses the rare term "confidence" (כֶּסֶל). This word has an alternative meaning as "loin" or "side," which the Vulg. apparently follows in its translation. The more common form of this lexeme is "fool" (כְּסִיל), especially popular in Proverbs and Ecclesiastes.[45] Perhaps attempting to avoid the textual uncertainty, the Syr. omits the term and simply states, "Yhwh will be with you." The LXX instead uses the term "path" (ὁδός). While seemingly quite different, as the BHS indicates, the term could have been an orthographic mistake of letters, the alternative forms being "with your foolishness/confidence" (בְכִסְלְךָ) or "in your path" (בִמְסִלָּתֶךָ).[46] The mistake between the "m" (𐤌) and "k" (𐤊) is quite possible due to their similarity in the paleo-Hebrew script. Though the term "path" (מְסִלָּה) is uncommon, it does occur later in Prov 16:17, "The path (מְסִלַּה) of the upright turns from evil, one guarding his soul, who protects (נצר) his way (דרך)." This verse echoes a number of phrases and ideas central to the lessons of Prov 1–9, particularly the "path" metaphor and "guarding." In either reading of Prov 3:26, the emphasis is on the presence and providence of Yhwh with the son. The strong path theme in Prov 1–9, the LXX textual tradition, and the correspondence with 16:17 may incline the reading here toward "path." In this view, Yhwh will not just be a hope for the son but he will be *with* the son in his way.[47] As Lesson 3 instructed, the son is to "know Yhwh in all of his ways." Thus, the mirrored connection implies that Yhwh will be with him in his ways as the son walks in the Lord's ways, presumably with him. This promise of nearness and relation serves as the fourth blessing, which will "guard" the son's foot from capture. As discussed in Lesson 2, the notion of "guarding" (שמר) or "protecting" (נצר) occurs often in Prov 1–9 both as a charge to the son and as a promise from Yhwh or Wisdom.[48] In both Lessons 2 and 5, the uncommon term "discretion" (מְזִמָּה) is used in reversed perspective. Here, in

---

[45] Out of the term's 28 occurrences, 22 are in Proverbs.

[46] If the term "confidence" is original, the preposition would be a *beth essentiae* (Schipper, *Proverbs 1–15*, 157). If it is "path," then the preposition is accompaniment.

[47] Longman follows the "confidence" reading but rightly comments on the implications for divine presence, "Confidence that follows from a life of wisdom: the presence of Yahweh in one's life. God himself will guarantee one's protection. The presence of Yahweh is likely to be connected to the teaching explicit elsewhere in Proverbs that those who are wise are in relationship with Yahweh (Prov 1:7)" (Longman, *Proverbs*, 142).

[48] Schipper, *Proverbs 1–15*, 151.

Prov 3:21, the term serves as one of the overarching qualities the son is to "protect" (נצר). However, in Prov 2:11, it says, "Discretion (מְזִמָּה) will guard (שמר) over you; understanding will protect (נצר) you." Now that the son has been protected by discretion, he must also protect discretion. As this lesson clarifies, discretion is a quality of God and is available for those walking in his ways.

The lesson concludes with four curses and blessings (Prov 3:32–35).[49] Although this section begins with a "for" (כִּי), it does not seem to uniquely appeal to the content of 3:31 except as its final line summates the whole intent of Lesson 5.[50] In Prov 3:31, the last two admonitions charge the son not to "envy the violent man" nor to "choose any of his ways." The blessings and curses that follow seem to build on the parallel term "deviate" (לוז) from 3:21, which implicitly draws on the path metaphor and the ways of the wicked.

The emphasis of the lesson is on the danger of deviation which would turn the son into an "abomination of Yhwh."[51] "Abomination" (תּוֹעֵבָה) in the HB is a difficult term to define.[52] The term occurs 21x in Proverbs always with an ethical perspective,[53] indicative of the wicked and their ways.[54] In fact, the term appears again in Lesson 11 (Prov 6:16) preceding a list of seven ethical violations that "Yhwh hates," implying the path of the wicked is not just socially problematic but inextricably against God and his ways.[55] Near the end of Proverbs, a verse in 29:27 highlights the two paths as equally detestable to the other, "A man of perversity is an abomination to the righteous but the upright way is an abomination to the wicked" (cf. Prov 13:19). Outside Proverbs, the terms for "abomination" and "abhor," which occur 117x as a noun and twenty-two times as a verb, apply to a wide variety of situations perhaps best understood as "detestable," "violation," or "incompatible."[56]

---

[49] Loader divides the unit to be Prov 3:27–35 rather than 3:21–35 but he does acknowledge the general sapiential language in the final section (Loader, *Proverbs 1–9*, 184).

[50] Plöger, *Spruche Salomos (Proverbia)*, 42.

[51] The phrase in this form only occurs in Deuteronomy and Proverbs, 8x and 12x respectively. While this points to the likelihood of source, McKane prefers to point to the Egyptian equivalent instead. This is due to his view that the phrase applies to the cultic in Deuteronomy and moral in Proverbs. In this, he assents with Weinfeld that if dependence is present, it is Deuteronomy that adapts the Proverbial use and "pressed it into the service of a new cause ... the exclusiveness of the cult of Yahweh." See McKane, *Proverbs*, 301; Weinfeld, *Deuteronomy and the Deuteronomic School*, 266–69.

[52] The term, even in its divine formula, was not unique to Israel but found in various sister cultures including those of Egypt and Ugarit. See H. Dietrich Preuss, "תּוֹעֵבָה," *TDOT* 15:591–604; Waltke, *Proverbs (1–15)*, 271; Meinhold, *Die Sprüche*, 87.

[53] R. E. Clements, "The Concept of Abomination in the Book of Proverbs," in *Texts, Temples, and Traditions: A Tribute to Menahem Haran*, ed. Michael V. Fox et al. (Winona Lake: Eisenbrauns, 1996), 212.

[54] Here is a summarized list of various abominations and parallels in the Book of Proverbs: one who deviates from instruction, scorners, arrogance, lying, a false witness, sowing discord, a false balance, injustice, wickedness, scheming evil, thoughts of the wicked, a crooked heart, a sacrifice by the wicked, the wicked path, shedding innocent blood.

[55] As Toy notes, the term typically connotes something "incompatible with the nature of Yahweh" (Toy, *Proverbs*, 80–81).

[56] As it is found in Proverbs, Schipper uses the phrase "unacceptable to God" (Schipper, *Proverbs 1–15*, 161).

In its initial biblical occurrences, the term is applied to the Israelites in contrast to the social and religious customs of the Egyptians (Gen 43:32, 46:34; Exod 8:22). It is also used as an explanation for a wide spectrum of Torah violations. The spectrum included cultic, religious, social, civil, ethical, sexual, and dietary instructions. While the spectrum of what constituted an abomination was expansive, the result of and purpose for avoiding such abominations were the social and relational ramifications. In many of the uses, the inherent idea, whether explicit or implicit, was the "separative" quality.[57] In Deut 23:8, Moses commands Israel, "Do not abhor an Edomite, for he is your brother; do not abhor an Egyptian, for you were a sojourner in his land." The implication is clearly one of social ostracization. In fact, the first occurrences mentioned previously are in the context of social ostracization between Egyptians and Israelites due to differing customs.[58] In many of the cases, the abomination is due to intermixing with the nations and their practices. In other words, the Israelites' lack of social and religious distinction from the nations conversely led to their relational ostracization from God, their covenant Lord.

One particularly interesting reference seems to illuminate this social aspect, "All my close companions (סוֹד) abhor (תעב) me; and the one I love has turned against me" (Job 19:19). Here, it is clear the sense is social and relational separation, as Job describes his status as a social pariah. Though not explicit, the narrative implies that Job's friends and family believe he is guilty of an abomination and is receiving an appropriate curse. Thus, they are separating themselves from him and his disgrace. In Prov 3:32, the teacher ties these ideas to the way of the wicked. First, the teacher inversely parallels "the one who deviates" (נָלוֹז) with "the upright" (יְשָׁרִים) and "abomination of Yhwh" with "his intimate companion" (סוֹדוֹ). It is important to note that the text does not say that the deviant has "done" an abomination but "is" an abomination. This characterization is then inversely paralleled with a close, relational term. The term "companion" (סוֹד) is also difficult to define with certainty but does allude to a common sentiment. Typically, the word implies a council, company, or friendship. In a discerning example, the psalmist declares, "Who is the man who fears Yhwh? He will instruct (ירה) him in the way he should choose (בחר). ... Companionship (סוֹד) with Yhwh is for those who fear him and to those he makes known his covenant" (Ps 25:12, 14).[59] Perhaps not surprisingly, the context of this verse is Ps 25:8–9, "Good and upright (ישׁר) is Yhwh; therefore, he will instruct (ירה) sinners in his way. He leads the humble (עָנָו) in justice and he teaches (למד) the humble (עָנָו) his way. All the

---

[57] Preuss, "Tôʿēḇâ," 602–3.

[58] Pinker attempts to determine the precise cause of the Egyptians view toward the Hebrews. However, he is only able to provide a number of tentative possibilities which boil down to cultural differences that "led to some distancing between the Hebrews and Egyptians" (Aron Pinker, "'Abomination to Egyptians' in Genesis 43:32, 46:34, and Exodus 8:22," *OTE* 22.1 (2009): 172).

[59] Commenting on Prov 3:32, Fox rightly notes, "A sense of what disgusts God is essential to the fear of God" (Fox, *Proverbs 1–9*, 167). Put in a different way, those who fear God emulate him as they abhor what God abhors.

paths of Yhwh are steadfast love and mercy, for those protecting (נצר) his covenant and testimonies." [60] In this psalm, there is an inextricable relationship between Yhwh, his ways, and his companions. The psalmist clarifies that the "companion" of Yhwh is one who knows and walks in his ways, with God as his teacher leading the way.[61] In other words, as God and his ways are good, upright, just, merciful, and faithful, so is the one in a covenant relationship with him.[62] However, as the proverbial teacher clarifies, violation of God's attributes and behaviors, or his way, is to abhor him and become relationally separate.[63] While subtle, the point is quite profound in the educational development of the son. The immediate context of becoming an abomination to Yhwh in Prov 3:32 is the warning not to imitate or desire the way of the wicked in 3:31. This juxtaposition is not incidental but instructive. As Waltke says, "The one who mimics *any of his ways* (see Prov 1:15) is his comrade and as such is under the LORD's curse (3:32–35)."[64] Conversely, then, anyone who mimics the ways of Yhwh is his comrade and will receive the blessings inherent to walking the wise path with him. Thus, the father teaches that friendship with the wicked is to be an enemy of God but the upright friend of God is opposed to the wicked way. God himself is said to espouse this orientation in the concluding verses. He blesses the righteous but curses the wicked (Prov 3:33). He favors the humble (עָנָו) but scoffs at the scoffer (Prov 3:34).

Conclusion

In Lesson 4, the father provides a dynamic and poetic instruction focused on the greatness of Wisdom and Yhwh. While more subdued in presentation, Lesson 5 espouses several teachings of equal weight. Here, the father focuses on contrasting examples, couched in the language of admonitions, curses, and blessings. Primarily, the son is to embody the ways of Yhwh, doing good and giving justice (Prov 3:27–29). In deviating from this path, though, he will emulate the violent man and those under the curse of God (Prov 3:31–35). As a wise son, he must not become an abomination to the "upright" and Yhwh (Prov 3:32). If he does follow in the ways of sinners, he will be relationally ostracized from the covenant community. To avoid this dreadful fate, he is to reflect the divine qualities inherent to the wise path. As a guide and reward,

---

[60] As Allen comments, "If God is good and upright, then the way that he teaches sinners to follow will be the same" (Ross, *Commentary on the Psalms*, 601).

[61] Müller, *Proverbien 1–9*, 190; Peter C. Craigie, *Psalms 1–50*, 2nd ed., WBC (Grand Rapids: Zondervan, 2004), 220. Craigie says, "The way of wisdom … is the way of covenant … the more profound blessing was to be found in the 'friendship' of God (v. 14), for the covenant was not merely a conditional contract, offering rewards in return for obedience; more than that, it was a privileged and intimate relationship, offered by God to his covenant people."

[62] Ross, *Commentary on the Psalms*, 601.

[63] Meinhold, *Die Sprüche*, 87.

[64] Waltke, *Proverbs (1–15)*, 270.

the Lord will walk with him in his path, providing protection and relationship (Prov 3:23, 26, 32). Thus, the son will render himself one of the righteous who dwells securely as a close companion with God. In Lessons 2–5, the proverbial father desires that the son feel the full weight and centrality of Yhwh in this wise path. For Lessons 6–8, however, the father once again focuses on the role of a human father and the historical sequence of godly and wise models who have passed along the divine way to him.

LESSON 6

Analysis of 4:1–9
"The wise embrace Wisdom"

After several lessons with Yhwh at the center, Lesson 6 makes an abrupt shift by not directly naming him. In fact, his name does not reappear until Lesson 10 (Prov 5:21). This suppression, however, does not mean that he is unrelated or irrelevant to the teacher's content.[1] Rather, in the educational process, the son has already been thoroughly catechized on the centrality of Yhwh and his ways (Lesson 2–5). Now, the father seeks to personalize the path and persuade the son to follow him. Lesson 6 illuminates two primary threads, one earthly and one divine. First, the father commends the transgenerational nature of this wisdom instruction that he received from his father and presumably those before him (Prov 4:3–4). Second, he promotes the necessity of imitating God's own proximity to Wisdom (Prov 4:5–7). Thus, both the grandfather and all preceding wise figures serve as models for the son in learning to pass on the wisdom tradition. Likewise, God serves as a model of one who knows and possesses Wisdom, despite not being named. By following these instructions, the son will be one who reflects his father, grandfather, and ultimately the divine Father.

Structure of Lesson 6

In the sixth lesson, the teacher provides several positive and negative commands. The first occurs as the typical, opening call (Prov 4:1–2). While many aspects of these verses are typical, the opening call addresses "sons" in the plural rather than the singular as used thus far. Following the opening

---

[1] McKane unduly drives a wedge between the instruction derived from generational transmission versus Yhwh (William McKane, *Proverbs: A New Approach*, OTL (London: SCM, 1970), 303). As demonstrated up to this point already, the source of wisdom has been clearly delineated and necessarily rooted in Yhwh and his ways.

call, the father goes on to provide several vital commands, which he himself learned from his father (Prov 4:3–9).[2]

I.   The Father's Instruction (4:1–2)
II. The Grandfather's Instruction (4:3–9)
   a. Possess Wisdom (3–5)
   b. Wisdom's Protection (6–7)
   c. Wisdom's Honor (8–9)

The commands of this lesson center around the son(s) obtaining or possessing Wisdom. While this divine figure is not explicitly anthropomorphized, the grandfather does wrap her in marital imagery, perhaps as a rhetorical device.[3] Echoing language from other lessons, Wisdom will honor and bless the son if he will be faithful to her. This reciprocal relationship was previously observed with Yhwh and Wisdom. The overlay between the father's and the grandfather's instruction likewise implies that the transgenerational instruction found in this wisdom program is likely drawn from the Torah, ultimately sourced in Yhwh himself.[4]

The Father's Instruction (4:1–2)

While much of the language in the opening instruction is typical, found throughout the fifteen lessons, there is an oddity present in all textual traditions. The teacher provides an appeal to "sons" (בָּנִים) in the plural rather than the singular. Although the final "m" (ם) could be explained by an orthographic mistake due to the following word "discipline" (מוּסָר) beginning with a "m" (מ), no text tradition supplies the more expected singular form of "son" nor the singular verb form for "listen."[5] The implication is that the lesson is not simply for the proverbial son in Prov 1–9.[6] So, two primary options are

---

[2] Michael V. Fox, *Proverbs 1–9: A New Translation with Introduction and Commentary*, AYBC 18A (New York: Doubleday, 2000), 171.

[3] Roland E. Murphy, *Proverbs*, WBC 22 (Dallas: Thomas Nelson, 1998), 26.

[4] Cf. Bernd U. Schipper, *Proverbs 1–15: A Commentary on the Book of Proverbs 1:1–15:33*, Hermeneia (Minneapolis: Fortress, 2019), 166.

[5] The BHS proposes reading with the singular. While the plural is abrupt, it is not without parallel in Prov 1–9 (5:7, 7:24, 8:32). Furthermore, the plural pronominal suffix (לָכֶם) is used anaphorically for "sons" in 3:2, along with the second masculine plural verb form. According to the structure proposed in this study, all four of these plural occurrences of "sons" represent the start of new lessons. So, it is preferable to maintain the MT's reading here.

[6] A parallel seems to occur between Lesson 6 and 10, highlighting similar phrases and grammatical shifts. In Lesson 6, the "sons" are addressed in Prov 4:1 with the singular father implied in 4:2, "my *torah*." Then in Prov 4:5b, the teaching from the grandfather says, "Do not turn (נטה) from the words (אמר) of my mouth." In Lesson 10, the "sons" are again addressed in Prov 5:7 with a parallel phrase from the father this time, "Now, O sons, listen to me and do not

likely.[7] The "sons" in view could be contemporaneous with the son and teacher, implying a school setting or a generic audience.[8] Alternatively, as Waltke argues, the plural for "sons" may intend the generational succession of this lesson, or diachronic rather than synchronic.[9] While Prov 4:1–2 begins in the plural, 4:4–9 uses the singular for the audience, portrayed as the father with his father. The oscillation between audiences perhaps parallels and signals a pattern in the Torah, especially since the term is expressly used here (ירה / תורה).[10] In this case, it is possible the teacher took his queues from the Torah, "This is the command, statutes, and judgments, which Yhwh your (pl.) God commanded to teach you (pl.) ... So that, you (sg.) may fear Yhwh your (sg.) God, guarding all his statutes and commands which I am commanding you, you and your sons and your sons' sons ... You (sg.) shall repeat them to your sons and you shall speak of them in your sitting, in your house, in your walking in the way, and in your lying and your rising" (Deut 6:1, 2, 7).[11] In this appeal from Moses, the transgenerational command is both collective and singular, intended both for fathers-to-sons and sons-to-their sons for each

turn (סור) from the words (אמר) of my mouth." In both, there is a shift to the plural "sons" with a parallel command. Although Lesson 6 focuses on obtaining Wisdom, Lesson 10 focuses on staying away from the strange woman. While Lesson 6 commends the faithful transmission of the teaching of the father and grandfather, Lesson 10 notes the danger of departing from the instruction of teachers (5:13).

[7] Murphy proposes a few options, without landing on any definitively: "variation of the customary address," the universality of the instruction, or the plurality of mother and father in the instruction and transmission process. McKane, who favors the familial setting for Proverbs, notes the tension between 4:1 and 3 creates, since "sons" is mentioned in the context of father and mother. While the plural according to him implies a school setting, the parental reference pushes back against this theory, confounding any strict view. See Murphy, *Proverbs*, 27; McKane, *Proverbs*, 303.

[8] Fox prefers the generic audience view, stating, "The author seems indifferent to the grammatical number of his addresses to the audience. This is undeniable in Prov 9:4–5, where Lady Folly speaks in the plural to a simpleton. Such fluctuations show that the father-son address in Proverbs is a generic convention. A father is ostensibly speaking to his son but through him the author is actually addressing all boys" (Fox, *Proverbs 1–9*, 172; James Alfred Loader, *Proverbs 1–9*, HCOT (Leuven: Peeters, 2014), 201–2). While the generic audience is perhaps the underlying view, especially in the later uses, the context of Prov 4:1 is a generational transmission of instruction. Thus, it may serve dual purposes.

[9] Bruce K. Waltke, *The Book of Proverbs: Chapters 1–15*, NICOT (Grand Rapids: Eerdmans, 2004), 276.

[10] Scholars in the 19th c. used the oscillation between sg. and pl., referred to as Numeruswechsel, to define overlapping textual histories. However, later scholarship rejected this notion. As Weinfeld notes, "The change may simply be a didactic device to impress on the individual or collective listener, or it may reflect the urge for literary variation." For discussion on the topic, see Moshe Weinfeld, "Deuteronomy, Book Of," in *AYBD* (New York: Doubleday, 1992), 168–83; Christopher T. Begg, "The Significance of the Numeruswechsel in Deuteronomy the 'pre-History' of the Question," *ETL* 55.1 (1979): 116–24; Hans Ausloos, "The Risks of Rash Textual Criticism Illustrated on the Basis of the Numeruswechsel in Exod 23,20–33," *BN* 96 (1999): 5–11.

[11] Tasker and McCarthy make the case that the father-son relationship, expressed between Yhwh and Israel in Deuteronomy, was not ancillary or contradictory to the covenant but quite central, particularly in respect to fatherly instruction. See D. J. McCarthy, "Notes on the Love of God in Deuteronomy and the Father-Son Relationship between Yahweh and Israel," *CBQ* 27.2 (1965): 144–47; David R. Tasker, *Ancient near Eastern Literature and the Hebrew Scriptures about the Fatherhood of God*, StBibLit 69 (New York: Peter Lang, 2004), 176–77.

family and for the whole of Israel. The appeal not only grounds the authority of the proverbial instruction in Yhwh,[12] but it also promotes the means of its reception, a cascade of imitative succession.[13]

Related to this notion, a second curious feature of Prov 4:1 is the Heb. phrase *musar av* (מוּסַר אָב). Although nearly identical to Prov 1:8, the phrase in Lesson 1 was specifically, "My son, listen to your father's *musar.*" Whereas, here in 4:1, it is, "My sons, listen to fatherly *musar.*" The important difference was the identification of the father by the pronoun "your" in Lesson 1. It is likely that the phrase of Prov 4:1, in contextual relation to "sons," is a descriptive use of the construct, implying "fatherly *musar.*" The import could signify the authoritative essence of the instruction or perhaps signal its relational source and imitative implications.[14] Newsom rightly notes,

> There is always a measure of identification between father and son, so that a son understands and thinks 'when I grow up, that's what I will be.' … Chapter 4 speaks of the transformation of the sons into the fathers in the chain of tradition. The male subject is to a certain degree apportioned between father and son.[15]

While an exclusive view of either a generic school setting or family is not necessary,[16] the overarching point embedded within this lesson is the expectation of sons to both imbibe and transmit the image of their fathers. In this sense, the teacher of this lesson seeks to relate the succession of wisdom

---

[12] Stuart Weeks, *Instruction and Imagery in Proverbs 1–9* (New York: Oxford University Press, 2007), 123; Loader, *Proverbs 1–9*, 208; David A. Hubbard, *Mastering the Old Testament: Proverbs* (Waco: Word Books, 1989), 82.

[13] Educationists and psychologists have noted three modes of learning: "imitative learning," "instructive learning," and "collaborative learning." Although these categories are often assigned to age ranges, they seem to observe fundamental roots to the educational process, common throughout humanity. For further discussion, see Jeroen Dekker, "Cultural Transmission and Inter-Generational Interaction," *International Review of Education* 47.1/2 (2001): 82; Michael Tomasello, Ann C. Kruger, and Hilary H. Ratner, "Cultural Learning," *Behavioral & Brain Sciences* 16.3 (1993): 495–511; Gergely Csibra and György Gergely, "Sylvia's Recipe: The Role of Imitation and Pedagogy in the Transmission of Cultural Knowledge," in *Roots of Human Sociality: Culture, Cognition, and Human Interaction* (Oxford: Berg, 2006), 229–55; Michael Tomasello, "Emulation Learning and Cultural Learning," *Behavioral & Brain Sciences* 21 (2002): 703–4.

[14] The authority imbued within this lesson is signaled as well by the final phrase of Prov 4:5, which has parallels in Moses (Deut 32:1) and Wisdom (Prov 8:8) (Schipper, *Proverbs 1–15*, 171).

[15] Carol A. Newsom, "Woman and the Discourse of Patriarchal Wisdom: A Study of Proverbs 1–9," in *Gender and Difference in Ancient Israel,* ed. Peggy L. Day (Minneapolis: Fortress, 1989), 151.

[16] Stepping into the long debate over the social setting of Israelite education, Vayntrub declares, "There exists no available data on the social or educational function of the biblical book of Proverbs." By this, she intends external corresponding evidence which might definitively place early Israelite education and the book of Proverbs. Instead, until further developments occur, the question remains ambiguous and speculative. See Jacqueline E. Vayntrub, "The Book of Proverbs and the Idea of Ancient Israelite Education," *ZAW* 128.1 (2016): 98.

to those walking in the righteous way. Though not explicit, it is implicit that Yhwh is the origin of both the way and the instruction.

The Grandfather's Instruction (4:3–9)

Distinct from other lessons in Prov 1–9, the teacher builds on the idea of transgenerational transmission. [17] In Prov 4:3–4, the teacher explicitly mentions the intermediate source of his instruction. He states, "When I was a son with my father, tender and alone before my mother, he taught (ירה) me and said, 'May your heart hold fast to my words; guard my commands and live.'" The grandfather's lesson presumably begins in Prov 4:4b and continues through 4:9. Perhaps surprisingly, the common term for "word" (דבר) only occurs four times in Prov 1–9.[18] First, it appears as "words of the wise" in the opening introduction (Prov 1:6) and then from Wisdom as a promised gift to those who listen to her (1:23). The other two are in chapter 4 as the instruction from the grandfather (Prov 4:5) and then as the opening call for Lesson 8 from the teacher to the son (4:20). This last use actually combines the terms used by the grandfather in Lesson 6 and the opening instruction for Lesson 7 (Prov 4:10). Lesson 7 says to "receive my words (אמר)" and Lesson 8 says to "consider my words (דבר), turn your ear to my words (אמר)." Together, the inference is that his lessons are derived from his father, likely derived from his father. In other words, he has been faithful to do as his father did. Thus, the son ought to follow him by faithfully obeying and transmitting this generational instruction, as well.[19]

In Lesson 6, the prime directive of the father's instruction from the grandfather is that the son would obtain wisdom. This teaching cascades in four movements. First, the lesson highlights the typical charge to guard the instruction, which is essential to life (Prov 4:1–2). Then, the lesson compels the son to get wisdom, also necessary for life (4:3–5). The result will be Wisdom's protection (4:6–7). Finally, the grandfather provides an inherent additional blessing associated with embracing Wisdom – she will exalt and honor the one who does so (Prov 4:8–9). The language of this instruction is found throughout the fifteen lessons from the three teachers (including the grandfather now), connoting the unity of message and source.

In a unique expression, the grandfather charges his son (and indirectly the proverbial son) to "obtain/possess" (קנה) wisdom and insight (4:5, 7). The term qanah (קנה) occurs six times in Prov 1–9, four of which are in this lesson,

---

[17] Pemberton notes the uniqueness of the explicit mention of a grandfather in the didactic process (Glenn D. Pemberton, "The Rhetoric of the Father: A Rhetorical Analysis of the Father/Son Lectures in Proverbs 1–9" (University of Denver; Colorado Seminary, PhD diss., 1999), 136).

[18] There are also two occurrences of the vb. form (Prov 2:12, 8:6).

[19] Cf. Catherine Petrany, "Fathers, Mothers, Sons, and Silence: Rhetorical Reconfiguration in Proverbs," *BTB* 50.3 (2020): 157.

highlighting its centrality. In the opening prologue, the framework of the book utilized the term in 1:5, "May the wise listen and increase instruction (לֶקַח) and may the understanding obtain/possess (קנה) guidance." It is interesting to note that the term "instruction" (לֶקַח) occurs in both 1:5 and 4:2, as well (cf. Prov 1:5, 4:2, 7:21, 9:9). So, the first use orients the student towards the wisdom program generally. The final use of the term *qanah* (קנה) occurs in Prov 8:22 and seems to highlight an important parallel between the son and Yhwh in Lesson 6. This final use in Prov 8, though, is more contested due to its association between Wisdom and Yhwh.[20] Earlier in this study, it was proposed that Wisdom is likely meant as an anthropomorphic attribute of God.[21] At the least, Wisdom is seen in very close association with God,[22] often behaving and speaking as God.[23] So, in Lesson 14, after a long rhetorical

---

[20] A long, complex historical discussion has developed over the millennia in hopes of identifying and defining Wisdom in Prov 8:22–31. Typically, the debate has revolved around whether she was created, a separate divine entity, a divine wife, Christ pre-figured, a divine attribute, or a poetic personification of the abstract concept of wisdom. Unfortunately, the debate will not be conclusively solved here. For extensive theories, histories, and alternative views, see R. B. Y. Scott, "Wisdom in Creation: The 'Amôn of Proverbs 8:30," *VT* 10.2 (1960): 213–23; Jean de Savinac, "La Sagesse en Proverbes 8:22–31," *VT* 12.2 (1962): 211–15; R. N. Whybray, "Proverbs 8:22–31 and Its Supposed Prototypes," *VT* 15.4 (1965): 504–14; Mitchell Dahood, "Proverbs 8:22–31: Translation and Commentary," *CBQ* 30.4 (1968): 512–21; McKane, *Proverbs*, 351–58; Gerhard von Rad, *Wisdom in Israel* (Nashville: Abingdon, 1972), 146–76; Bruce Vawter, "Prov 8:22: Wisdom and Creation," *JBL* 99.2 (1980): 205–16; Bernhard Lang, *Wisdom and the Book of Proverbs: A Hebrew Goddess Redefined* (New York: Pilgrim, 1986), 113–56; Daniel H. Williams, "Proverbs 8:22–31," *Int* 48.3 (1994): 275–79; R. N. Whybray, *The Composition of the Book of Proverbs*, JSOT 168 (Sheffield: JSOT, 1994), 41–42; Fox, *Proverbs 1–9*, 279–81; Waltke, *Proverbs (1–15)*, 406–23; Alan C. Lenzi, "Proverbs 8:22–31: Three Perspectives on Its Composition," *JBL* 125.4 (2006): 687–714; Loader, *Proverbs 1–9*, 344–51; Michael P. Barrett, "Wisdom: Person or Personification? Thoughts on Proverbs 8," *Puritan Reformed Journal* 8.1 (2016): 5–12; Tremper Longman III, *Proverbs*, BCOTWP (Grand Rapids: Baker Academic, 2006), 203–7; Gerlinde Baumann and Christl M. Maier, "Personified Wisdom: Contexts, Meanings, Theology," in *The Writings and Later Wisdom Books*, ed. Nuria Calduch-Benages and Christl M. Maier (Atlanta: Society of Biblical Literature, 2014), 57–76; Schipper, *Proverbs 1–15*, 286–94, 308–15; Christine Roy Yoder, "Personified Wisdom and Feminist Theologies," in *The Oxford Handbook of Wisdom and the Bible* (New York: Oxford University Press, 2021), 273–85; Susannah Ticciati, "Wisdom in Patristic Interpretation: Scriptural and Cosmic Unity in Athanasius's Exegesis of Proverbs," in *The Oxford Handbook of Wisdom and the Bible* (New York: Oxford University Press, 2021), 187–203.

[21] Lang notes this view but prefers a more poetic or mythological perspective in Proverbs, rejecting Larcher's statement regarding the Wisdom of Solomon, "Wisdom is a part of the *ego* of the divine personality and reflects several aspects of the richness in God. ... Her actions are none other than God's himself. The author, therefore, ascribes the very same activities to God and to his Wisdom." See Lang, *Wisdom and the Book of Proverbs*, 114, 138, 140; Chrysostome Larcher, *Études sur le Livre de la Sagesse*, Études bibliques (Paris: Gabalda, 1969), 409.

[22] Longman discusses Wisdom and Yhwh, referring to her closeness as a synecdoche, "Thus, at a minimum, Woman Wisdom personifies YHWH's wisdom. Therefore, in ch. 9, to choose to dine with Woman Wisdom is to choose to learn from YHWH himself. But perhaps we can go even further and say that Woman Wisdom represents YHWH himself by means of synecdoche" (Tremper Longman III, "Theology of Wisdom," in *The Oxford Handbook of Wisdom and the Bible*, ed. Will Kynes (Oxford: Oxford University Press, 2021), 396).

[23] R. N. Whybray, *Proverbs: Based on the Revised Standard Version*, NCBC (Grand Rapids: Eerdmans, 1994), 17.

monologue by Wisdom (Prov 8:4–21) intending to persuade the son to seek and find her, Wisdom describes her supremacy and association with the Lord.[24] She says in Prov 8:22,

MT	יְהוָה קָנָנִי רֵאשִׁית דַּרְכּוֹ קֶדֶם מִפְעָלָיו מֵאָז	Yhwh possessed me, the beginning of his way; before his deeds, since then.[25]
LXX	κύριος ἔκτισέν με ἀρχὴν ὁδῶν αὐτοῦ εἰς ἔργα αὐτοῦ	The Lord created me, the beginning of his way for his deeds.

Although the LXX clearly understood the initial phrase to mean "create" (κτίζω),[26] several meanings for *qanah* (קנה) are possible: "buy,"[27] "possess,"[28] or "create."[29] The final use is more contested and limited but may find a parallel in Ug., which implies the sense of "bring forth." The first use is a typical function of the term in the sense of "acquire" while the second implies the

[24] Waltke makes an interesting structural observation in 8:22–31, noting the bookends of "Yhwh" and "sons of men" for this section. The poetic implication is the mediating and shared function of Wisdom between both Yhwh and humans. See Waltke, *Proverbs (1–15)*, 406; Arthur J. Keefer, *Proverbs 1–9 as an Introduction to the Book of Proverbs* (London: T&T Clark, 2020), 158.

[25] The interpretive sense of the verse has several options. The phrase "beginning of his way" could be appositional to "me" implying Wisdom was the beginning of Yhwh's way. Or, it could be in an adverbial sense, though the preposition is missing, that God possessed Wisdom "at" the beginning, taking a temporal sense. The LXX seems to read it as appositional. Also, the last word (מֵאָז) in poetic relation to the second line of 8:22 likely implies "and ever since," which may imply a contrast between past direction and future direction. So, together the first and second lines could be read, "Yhwh has possessed me [head of his way] from before his deeds and ever since." This added second line places the proximity of Wisdom to Yhwh in an eternal or non-temporally bounded relationship. Yhwh has always had Wisdom, which served as the foundation for the wise path and his means for creatively ordering the world. While distinct in some sense, Yhwh and Wisdom are co-eternal, one a divine being and the other a divine quality.

[26] Cook notes, "[T]he Hebrew text, at least as far as the translator was concerned, leaves the impression that wisdom actually has a more independent function in the creation process – a notion that was unacceptable to the Greek translator ... the Hebrew probably intended to state that wisdom had a secondary and even inactive role in respect of the creation ... it is evident that [the translator] actually tried to play down the role wisdom was seen to have in the creation process" (Johann Cook, *The Septuagint of Proverbs: Jewish and/or Hellenistic Proverbs?* VTSup 69 (New York: Brill, 1997), 222).

[27] Although the term normally carries the sense of "buy" in the OT, it appears in eleven verses in Proverbs with a more poetic, connotative sense. While a monetary sense of "buy" is likely present in a few (Prov 16:16, 17:16, 23:23), most occurrences imply the sense of "acquire/possess" instead (1:5, 4:5, 7, 8:22, 15:32, 18:15, 19:8, 20:14). In Ruth 4:5, the term connotatively applies to both "buy" and "acquire" regarding the land and Ruth, the kinsman redeemer possessing Ruth through the land purchase from Naomi.

[28] The Vulg. translates with the sense of "possess" (*possideo*). Similarly, Aquila, Symmachus, and Theodotian translate with the sense of "acquire" (κτάομαι).

[29] McKane and Waltke amend this use to "procreate" (McKane, *Proverbs*, 352; Waltke, *Proverbs (1–15)*, 418). Only 6 uses of the term are typically associated with the sense of "create" (Gen 4:1, 14:19, 22; Deut 32:6; Ps 78:54, 139:13; Prov 8:22). In several, though, the sense of "possess/acquire" is perhaps preferable.

sense of "ownership." If wisdom is an anthropomorphic attribute of God (cf. Prov 3:19),[30] then the first would probably not make sense here since it is not something that can be bought.[31] The latter two options are equally plausible, though. Shortly after Prov 8:22, Wisdom goes on to further describe her supremacy using perhaps a parallel term "I was brought forth" (חוֹלָלְתִּי) twice in 8:24–25, though often used to mean "give birth" or "to writhe."[32] The term *hil* (חיל), appearing in the passive intensive (*polal*) here, only occurs one other place in Proverbs, "A northern wind brings forth (תְּחוֹלֵל) rain and a secretive tongue [brings forth] an indignant face" (Prov 25:23).[33] In this example, the term cannot mean to create, give birth, or to writhe. Rather, there is an associative presence implied. It could mean causation but does not require such a strict connotation. In a reverse parallel, the associative quality of *hil* (חיל) would imply that Wisdom was with Yhwh in his bringing about his creative acts, even as an active force in the process. In fact, Prov 8:27a and 30a seem to make this associative connection, "When he established the heavens, I was there (בַּהֲכִינוֹ שָׁמַיִם שָׁם אָנִי) ... I was beside him, a craftsman (וָאֶהְיֶה אֶצְלוֹ אָמוֹן)" (cf. Wis 7:22, 8:6).[34] The overarching sense of Wisdom's self-

---

[30] Cf. Loader, *Proverbs 1–9*, 349; Weeks, *Instruction and Imagery in Proverbs 1–9*, 101, 123; Schipper, *Proverbs 1–15*.

[31] Alternatively, in reference to Prov 4:5, Loader proposes the term can be used in the sense of gaining a wife (cf. Ruth 4:8, 10) (Loader, *Proverbs 1–9*, 204). Such a sense seems implied in Prov 4:5–9 yet is theologically suspect in 8:22, which suggests another option may be preferable.

[32] Job is ridiculed for his supposed arrogance in 15:7. Eliphaz says to him, "Are you the first man born and were you brought forth (חוֹלָלְתָּ) before the hills?" The language parallels that of Prov 8 and Ps 90, insinuating that only Wisdom/God is supreme in knowledge/wisdom. Cf. Murphy, *Proverbs*, 51–52.

[33] The MT points Prov 25:23 with the active intensive (*polel*) but 8:24–25 with the passive intensive (*polal*). It is possible the pointing for Prov 8:24–25 was mistaken and should represent the *polel*. There is no textual evidence for this alternative. However, the slight emendation would imply that Wisdom was an active co-creator rather than implying she was created. In Prov 8:30, Wisdom is subtly implied as a fellow creator with Yhwh. This change to the active would likely also apply to the *niphal* נִסַּכְתִּי (either *niphal* or *piel* in form), "I anointed/established ... I brought forth" (Prov 8:23–24). A similar phrase is used in Ps 90:2, which says, "Before the mountains were born and you brought forth (תְּחוֹלֵל) earth and world, you are God from everlasting." The *polel* is used but could be read as a *polal* implying the earth was passively brought forth as the LXX tradition follows. Although either would make sense here, certainty is difficult to establish for the form in any of the uses. Thus, it is plausible to say in Prov 8 either that Wisdom was brought forth by God or that Wisdom brought forth with God. Interestingly, later in this psalm ascribed to Moses though reminiscent of Ecclesiastes, the poet requests, "Make us know to rightly count our days and wisdom will enter the heart" (Ps 90:12). This last phrase is very close to Prov 2:10, "Wisdom will enter your heart." Though directionality is difficult to assess, there appears to be shared language and ideas, which are personified in Prov 1–9.

[34] The first phrase of 8:30 is notoriously difficult and debated. Several options exist for the phrase and term *amon* (אמן). First, "I was a craftsman at his side." Second, "I was beside him, the craftsman [Yhwh]." Third, "I was nursed at his side." Fourth, "I was beside him continually/faithfully." Each reading is plausible and is represented in various textual traditions and commentaries. Thus, Rendsburg argues all three are in view as a "brilliant display of polysemy." Regardless of the view taken, the text emphasizes the closeness of Wisdom to Yhwh and her primacy over creation and humanity. See Scott, "Wisdom in Creation"; Dahood, "Proverbs 8," 519; Michael V. Fox, "Amon Again," *JBL* 115.4 (1996): 699–702; Waltke, *Proverbs*

description in Prov 8:22–31 is her intimate association with Yhwh, both in temporal primacy and supremacy (cf. Prov 3:19).[35] Thus, the term *qanah* (קנה) in Prov 8:22, whether "brought forth" or "possessed" in meaning, likely intends her associative presence with Yhwh. On one hand, Yhwh possessed Wisdom as an eternal attribute, in the sense of essence.[36] On the other, he brought her forth as a means for crafting and guiding the world, in the sense of function. Related to the functional sense, Prov 8:23 goes on to describe Wisdom with unique imagery and language, "From before the ages, I was anointed/poured out (נסך); from the start, from before the earth" (cf. Sir 1:9).[37] The LXX uses the term "establish" (θεμελιόω), perhaps paralleling the sense of "create" (κτίζω) in the previous verse. However, the term in Heb. does not attest to this sense. An intriguing, connotative use of this term is found in Ps 2:6, "I myself have poured out (נסך) my king, over Zion, my holy mountain."[38] In both Ps 2 and Prov 8, the sense could imply "anoint," insinuating the associative connection between the king/Wisdom and Yhwh. Common imagery in the ANE, a king was divinely anointed for the purpose of identification, authority, and commission.[39]

The importance of this discussion, regarding the peculiar contents of Lesson 14 at this point, is the parallel created with Lesson 6. In Lesson 14, it declares, "Yhwh possessed (קנה) me, the beginning (רֵאשִׁית) of his way" (Prov 8:22).[40] Although the verse does not directly name who or what was possessed,

---

(1–15), 417–21; Schipper, *Proverbs 1–15*, 312–13; Gary A. Rendsburg, "Literary and Linguistic Matters in the Book of Proverbs," in *Perspectives on Israelite Wisdom: Proceedings of the Oxford Old Testament Seminar*, ed. John Jarick, LHBOTS 618 (London: T&T Clark, 2016), 117–18).

[35] Waltke, *Proverbs (1–15)*, 417.

[36] Fox emphasizes the created quality of Wisdom, going so far as to say, "Prior to creation God did not have wisdom ... Wisdom is therefore an accidental attribute of godhead, not an essential or inherent one." This view goes beyond the biblical text and is likely an anachronistic compartmentalization of God. Rather, the purpose of this passage is not to create a taxonomy of the essential versus accidental attributes of God but to highlight the primacy of Wisdom, which God himself uses and bestows on those who walk in his ways. See Fox, *Proverbs 1–9*, 279; Loader, *Proverbs 1–9*, 347–48.

[37] Fox lists four views for the term: "anointed," "made princess," "appointed," and "formed." Following his view for Prov 8:22, he prefers "formed." Schipper argues for the alternative root *sakak* (סכך) meaning "woven, formed" as well (Fox, *Proverbs 1–9*, 281; Schipper, *Proverbs 1–15*, 309). In Sir 1:9, the author clearly follows the creative sense and imagery for pouring wisdom out, "The Lord himself created her and saw and counted her and poured her over all his works" (κύριος αὐτὸς ἔκτισεν αὐτὴν καὶ εἶδεν καὶ ἐξηρίθμησεν αὐτὴν καὶ ἐξέχεεν αὐτὴν ἐπὶ πάντα τὰ ἔργα αὐτοῦ).

[38] See Otto Plöger, *Spruche Salomos (Proverbia)*, BKAT 17 (Neukirchen-Vluyn: Neukirchener Verlag, 1984), 86.

[39] Waltke points out the reflective correspondence between God's rule, Wisdom's, and those who listen to her, quoting from Eliade, "The house ... is the universe that man constructs for himself by imitating the paradigmatic creation of the gods, the cosmogony" (Waltke, *Proverbs (1–15)*, 407–8; Mircea Eliade, *The Sacred and the Profane: The Nature of Religion*, trans. Willard R. Trask (New York: Harper & Brothers, 1961), 56–57, 172–79).

[40] It is quite possible the use of *qanah* (קנה) in Lesson 6 influenced the word choice in Lesson 14. The author could have chosen a different term to specifically mean Wisdom was "created" (ברא) or "birthed" (ילד) or something else but instead used one that is less definitive with great semantic range. Thus, the author may have intentionally built a conceptual and imitative bridge between Yhwh and the son here.

the use of a first-person pronoun links back to Prov 8:12, which clarifies, "I, Wisdom" (cf. 8:13–20). In fact, the first-person pronoun is used in every verse from Prov 8:12–36 except in four. It is important to identify that Yhwh "possessed" (קנה) "Wisdom" because this idea is uniquely paralleled in Prov 4:5 and 7.[41] Lesson 6 appears to recount the instruction of the grandfather to the father who is now passing it on to the son. Here, the highly emphasized command is to "obtain/possess" (קנה) Wisdom (Prov 4:5). The lesson again reiterates this in Prov 4:7, "The beginning (רֵאשִׁית) of wisdom, obtain/possess (קנה) wisdom." Although these verses also include the phrase "obtain/possess" (קנה) for "insight" in addition to "wisdom," Wisdom is ostensibly the primary focus. In Prov 4:6 and 8–9, the third feminine pronoun is used. While this could apply to either feminine word, "wisdom" (חָכְמָה) or "insight" (בִּינָה), only Wisdom is given an anthropomorphized (or personified) sense elsewhere in Prov 1–9.[42] This suggests Wisdom is primarily in view. It is equally salient that Lesson 14 also focuses on an anthropomorphized Wisdom who is possessed by Yhwh. Likewise, Wisdom is identified as the "beginning of his way" (Prov 8:22).[43] Thus, together, the broader context of Lesson 6 encourages the son to follow in the way of his father who is following in the way of his father who are all ultimately following in the way of Yhwh, the preeminent possessor of Wisdom.[44]

After the command to possess Wisdom, Lesson 6 goes on to envision her as both a guardian and a wife. Of course, these metaphors on a mundane level are meant to persuade the son to seek, possess, and use wisdom. However, the language implies a divinely mediated relationship. The son is called to "love" (אהב) and "embrace" (חבק) Wisdom (Prov 4:6, 8).[45] This relational portion of the lesson connects to Lesson 2 and the bookends of Prov

---

[41] The LXX for these verses differs greatly from the MT. In Prov 4:5, the grandfather says "guard the command" (LXX) in place of "obtain wisdom, obtain insight" (MT). For Prov 4:7, the entirety of the verse is missing in the LXX. However, the Vulg. and Syr. both follow the MT. It is unclear why the LXX does not include these phrases. The BHQ suggests it is theologically motivated as implied in similar variances in Prov 16:16 and 23:23.

[42] Lang discusses types of personification in the ANE, which he often brought to life abstract ideas which he calls "realm-as-personality" (Lang, *Wisdom and the Book of Proverbs*, 132–36).

[43] Fox discusses a variety of alternative meanings for *derek* (דרך) but prefers the more generic, metaphorical sense. Similarly, Loader comments, "דרך is a well-established metaphor for human conduct or behaviour and lifestyle ... God can also have a 'way'" (cf. Job 40:19) (Loader, *Proverbs 1–9*, 350; Fox, *Proverbs 1–9*, 280).

[44] Speaking on the relationship between wisdom, covenant, Yhwh, and humanity, Van Leeuwen remarks, "Humans create micro-cosmic kingdoms, cities, houses, and persons ... This human *imitatio Dei* presupposes that creation is in some sense revelatory, that it speaks with the voice of divine, cosmic wisdom ... and that creatures themselves speak wisdom, rightness, and praise ... Human wisdom echoes the divine wisdom" (Raymond C. Van Leeuwen, "Theology: Creation, Wisdom, and Covenant," in *The Oxford Handbook of Wisdom and the Bible* (New York: Oxford University Press, 2021), 66).

[45] Regarding the bridal imagery, McKane prefers to see instead an "influential patron by her protégé" who opens the "pathway to advancement" (McKane, *Proverbs*, 306). Certainly, the metaphor is not to be taken overly literally or strictly for bridal love. Yet, the parallel with Lesson 10 does at least lend toward the lover imagery while also incorporating atypical elements such as guarding and exalting.

1–9, indicating its broader vision. As discussed in previous lessons, there is a reciprocal relationship between those who guard Wisdom and her guarding of them (Prov 4:6 // 2:7–8, 11). In particular, the overlap between Wisdom and Yhwh signifies the son's relational and covenantal inclusion within their ways and care.[46] Likewise, the unique primacy phrase for the "beginning," with both *reshit* (רֵאשִׁית) and *tehilah* (תְּחִלָּה), connects the grandfather's instruction to the whole of the program (Prov 4:7 // 1:7, 8:22, 9:10).[47] Similarly, the uncommon term "embrace" (חבק) only occurs elsewhere in Proverbs with the foreign woman of Lesson 10 (Prov 5:20).[48] As mentioned, though sexual immorality is certainly foolish and against *torah*, the wily and seductive metaphor seems to imply also the ways and gods of those foreign peoples. Thus, the son is positively persuaded to "embrace" (חבק) the way of Wisdom and Yhwh in Lesson 6 but negatively persuaded not to "embrace" (חבק) the way of the nations and Folly in Lesson 10 (Prov 5:20, 23). As discussed in the "Structure of Prov 1–9," these lessons are paralleled in the chiastic schema of Prov 1–9, further emphasizing and illustrating this point.

Wisdom is also described as giving honor to those who love and embrace her at the end of this lesson.[49] Similar phrasing is used in Lesson 1 (Prov 1:9), likely connecting this lesson with the whole, both in its generational transmission and Wisdom's mediatorial role.[50] Interestingly, in 1 Sam 2:30, Yhwh speaks to Eli, "I will honor those honoring me and curse those despising me." The pronouncement comes through a "man of God" as a rebuke to Eli because of his sons who "did not know Yhwh" (לֹא יָדְעוּ אֶת־יְהוָה) (1 Sam 2:12, 27). While honoring is not a uniquely divine action, it is a behavior that Yhwh bestows on those who properly walk in his ways and know him.[51]

---

[46] Van Leeuwen notes, "Love of Wisdom was tantamount to the love of God, for though cosmic Wisdom had a certain independence from YHWH, she was not separable from God" (Van Leeuwen, "Theology: Creation, Wisdom, and Covenant," 72).

[47] Pemberton identifies several possible renditions: 1) "Wisdom comes first; therefore, get wisdom;" 2) "The beginning of wisdom is this: Get Wisdom;" 3) "The beginning of wisdom? The acquisition of wisdom?" 4) "At the first of your wealth acquire wisdom" (Pemberton, "The Rhetoric of the Father," 132–33). While these options are debatable, the implicit connection with "beginning" elsewhere, especially in the pinnacle Wisdom poem, suggests the thematic and theological intent is supreme. In fact, the son is to "possess/obtain" wisdom at the "beginning" of his ways just as God did (Prov 4:7 // 8:22).

[48] Dorsey also notices this parallel. However, his schema for Prov 1–9 is different, paralleling all of Prov 4:1–27 with 5:1–23 (David A. Dorsey, *The Literary Structure of the Old Testament: A Commentary on Genesis–Malachi* (Grand Rapids: Baker Academic, 2004), 191).

[49] While "love" can have a romantic use, it is also central to the covenant and Torah. The double entendre mingles the imagery of both as a rhetorical device (e.g., Deut 4:37, 5:10, 6:5). See William L. Moran, "Ancient Near Eastern Background of the Love of God in Deuteronomy," *CBQ* 25.1 (1963): 77–87; Waltke, *Proverbs (1–15)*, 280.

[50] Keefer argues for the mediatorial function of Wisdom. Commenting on Prov 3:19–26 and 8:22–31, he says, "I argue that wisdom functions as a mediator between God and humans, 'bridging the gap' so to speak between the Lord's prudent governance and human planning, to render them complementary so long as humans heed wisdom" (Keefer, *Proverbs 1–9 as an Introduction to the Book of Proverbs*, 44, 157).

[51] Cf. Schipper, *Proverbs 1–15*, 173. Schipper also includes the connection with Ps 37:34, which uses similar language as Prov 4:8, indicating Yhwh is the one who "exalts" (רום) "the one guarding his way."

Similarly, Deuteronomy uses the ideas of loving and guarding several times in regard to Yhwh's way and covenant with the people, which was mutual or bidirectional (Deut 4:37, 5:10, 6:5, 7:8–9, 10:12, 15, 11:1, 22, 19:9, 23:6, 30:16, 20).[52] Near the end of Deuteronomy, Moses seeks to persuade the people to keep the Lord's ways, saying, "Love Yhwh your God and guard his word and cling (דבק) to him for he is your life and length of days" (30:20).[53] The term for "cling" (דבק) is slightly different from the term "embrace" (חבק) in Prov 4:7. However, the two have much overlap semantically and phonologically, perhaps regarded as poetic synonyms in Lesson 6. The parallel with Lesson 10 possibly influenced Prov 4:7 to use the more mundane, romantic lexeme in order to evoke a more explicit marital image while echoing the Deuteronomic covenantal paradigm. This connection could assist in explaining the oddly juxtaposed metaphor for both guardian and wife ascribed to Wisdom (Prov 4:6), which would actually suggest divine covenantal relationship and care. The connection to Yhwh here may be further strengthened through the parallel actions of both Yhwh and Wisdom in honoring the son (Prov 3:9–10, 4:8–9). In other words, if the son will honor Yhwh in Lesson 3, he will be honored by Wisdom in Lesson 6.

Conclusion

The focus of Lesson 6 is two-fold. The son is to love and guard Wisdom, metaphorically implying a faithful and persistent relationship with Yhwh, who in reciprocal reflection loves, guards, and blesses the son (Prov 4:5–9). The wise path, however, is not an austere accumulation of data or neutral, mundane forms of success. Rather, the process and pathway of the wise are inherently relational and transgenerational (Prov 4:1–4). For the son to properly adhere to the transgenerational instruction of his grandfather, he will need to cling to and possess Wisdom (Prov 4:5, 7). By following this path, he will reflect his ancestors and Wisdom's ultimate divine possessor. This sixth lesson is a vital transition for the son's wisdom development, further highlighting the human models he must imitate, though still maintaining the underlying divine thread. As the instruction moves into Lesson 7, the father focuses further on his personal role in "leading" the son along this wise path. Although he highlights the distinctiveness of these two paths in prior lessons, the father emphasizes a few critical metaphors to further clarify this point.

---

[52] Mutual, covenantal "love" was central to marriage imagery, including Israel with God. Schipper rightly notes this relationship implied in Prov 4, "Yhwh's love for Israel corresponds to the people's love for Yhwh. Thus, in Prov 4:1–9, Wisdom claims for herself an authority that is otherwise ascribed only to Yhwh and Yhwh's revealed word" (Schipper, *Proverbs 1–15*, 172).

[53] Schipper argues for a strong connection between Prov 1–9 and Deuteronomy, especially Deut 30 (Schipper, *Proverbs 1–15*, 290).

LESSON 7

Analysis of 4:10–19
"The way of wisdom is life"

As the wisdom program nears its fulcrum (Lesson 8), the son is increasingly made aware in Lesson 7 of the choice he has before him. He will either walk on the path of the wicked, marked by darkness and ignorance (Prov 4:14–17, 19), or he will walk on the path of the righteous, marked by light and wisdom (Prov 4:10–13, 18). Of course, the proverbial father desires that he will follow his own "leading" and experience, presumably as one of the righteous (Prov 4:11). By doing so, the son will also walk with Yhwh, rather than stumble over him (Prov 4:12, 16, 19). Just as Yhwh is righteous, the "way of Wisdom" is characterized by righteousness. Conversely, the son must not imitate the "way of the evil" (Prov 4:14). As a student of wisdom, the son must seek to emulate his father and the righteous models before him (Prov 4:11, 18). Their path is the way of life (Prov 4:10, 13). All who take a different path will stumble and end in darkness (Prov 4:19).

Structure of Lesson 7

As in Lesson 6, the name of Yhwh does not appear in Lesson 7. Similarly, this lack does not imply that the Lord is not in view or relevant.[1] Rather, the lesson serves as a personal instruction from a father to a son, commending his own engagement and experience along the wise and righteous path.[2] In fact, the central theme of the lesson is the dueling pathways,[3] utilizing two contrasting metaphors: wicked/righteous and darkness/light. Though Wisdom was a

---

[1] McKane, *Proverbs*, 309–10.

[2] Waltke notes the similar intimacy of this lesson with Lesson 6 (Prov 4:3), "encouraging the son to identify with his father" (Waltke, *Proverbs (1–15)*, 287).

[3] See McKane, *Proverbs*, 306–7; Loader, *Proverbs 1–9*, 209–10, 212; Kenneth T. Aitken, *Proverbs* (Philadelphia: Westminster, 1986), 59. Aitken notes the corresponding two-paths imagery directly related to life or death in Deut 30:15–20.

divine figure to be loved and embraced in Lesson 6, here wisdom is only referred to as a "path" (דרך) (Prov 4:11; cf. 3:18–19). This path, of course, is one traveled by the wise and ultimately reflective of God and his ways (cf. Prov 8:22).

Although the structure of Lesson 6 was less formalized, the structure here is more easily observed.[4] The opening charge is typical, calling on "my son" in the first singular (Prov 4:10). However, it is coupled with a personal word from the father figure also in the first singular "I," much like in Prov 4:2–3, which perhaps indicates an overlap between lessons. Following the opening lines, the father provides four grammatically linked verses (Prov 4:12–15). In these verses, the driving feature is the second masculine singular "you" and "your." The lesson then transitions into four verses utilizing the third masculine plural "they" (Prov 4:16–19). The last four-verse section is further divided into two parts, the ways of the wicked (Prov 4:16–17) and the contrast between the righteous/wicked (4:18–19).[5] These divisions create a poetic symmetry of ten verses, reminiscent of previous structures (cf. Prov 3:11–20).

---

    a. First Person:
                10 Intro – "Hear my son … accept my words"
                11 Intro – "I taught … I led"

    b. Second Person:
                12 – "you will not stumble"
                13 – "you shall not let go"
                14 – "you shall not enter … you shall not walk"
                15 – "you shall not pass"

    c. Third Person:
                16 – "[the wicked] cannot sleep"
                17 – "[the wicked] eat … and drink"

                18 – "the path of the righteous is like light"
                19 – "the path of the wicked is like darkness"

---

[4] Loader makes a few similar observations on structure but misses the grammatical pattern. This results in an improperly arranged schema. Toy comes close perhaps incidentally by simply dividing the ten verses into five bicola. Historically, commentators have sought to rearrange the verses and identify added or interpolated verses within this lesson to fit their sensibilities. However, all attempts are unnecessary and do damage to the poetic, thematic logic. See Loader, *Proverbs 1–9*, 210–11; C. H. Toy, *A Critical and Exegetical Commentary on the Book of Proverbs*, ICC (New York: C. Scribner's Sons, 1899), 91; Whybray, *Composition of the Book of Proverbs*, 22.

[5] Whybray refers to the last two as the conclusion (Whybray, *Composition of the Book of Proverbs*, 21).

The structure naturally lends towards a poetic progression from "I" to "you" to "they." This poetic sense of progression is perhaps intentionally affiliated with the metaphor of Prov 3:18, which pictures the wise rising as the sun.[6]

The use of כשל

The curious use of "stumble" (כשל) is an important thematic feature in this lesson, which occurs several times (Prov 4:12, 16, 19).[7] Perhaps surprisingly, the term only appears in Proverbs here and twice much later in 24:26–27, "For seven times the righteous falls and rises but the wicked stumble (כשל) in evil. When your enemy falls, do not rejoice; and when he stumbles (כשל), may your heart not rejoice." Several reminiscent and important thematic parallels occur between the disparate sections of Proverbs.[8] These latter verses fall within a section using the charge "my son" (Prov 24:13, 21; cf. 23:15–28). There is also a focus on the contrast between the wicked and the righteous (Prov 24:15, 16, 19, 20). Additionally, this is one of the few places "fear Yhwh" (יְרָא־אֶת־יְהוָה) occurs (Prov 24:21; cf. 3:7). As in Lesson 7, there is a promise that wisdom will bring perpetuity of life (Prov 24:14; cf. 4:10).[9] In the latter use of "stumble," the proverbial teacher only links the term to the "wicked" and "enemy" (Prov 24:16–17). In Lesson 7, it is used in three ways: as the fate of the wicked, as the intentions of the wicked for others, and as incompatible with the way of the wise, upright, and righteous. The actions of the wicked in 4:16, who seek to cause stumbling, are a direct violation of Torah in Lev 19:14.[10] Their

---

[6] Brown notes, "For the righteous and the wise, the pathway connotes formation of character, 'shining brighter and brighter.' As for the wicked, their way is one stumble after another in the dark." Fox similarly says, "This dynamism suggests the education and moral growth of a youngster." See William P. Brown, "Virtue and Its Limits in the Wisdom Corpus: Character Formation, Disruption, and Transformation," in *The Oxford Handbook of Wisdom and the Bible*, ed. Will Kynes (Oxford: Oxford University Press, 2021), 50, 54; Fox, *Proverbs 1–9*, 182.

[7] Harding discusses the wordplay in Q from the HB between "stumble" (כשל) and "successful" (שכל). While his focus is on Daniel's use, this thematic contrast is likely present in Proverbs as well. The wise, righteous, faithful son will be "successful" or "insightful" (שכל) while the fool will "stumble" (כשל). Goldberg notes that the sense of "successful" (שכל) is that "wise behavior means conforming one's life to the character of God," which is precisely the opposite of the fool and those who stumble. See James E. Harding, "The Wordplay Between the Roots כשל and שכל in the Literature of the Yahad," *RevQ* 19.1 (1999): 69–82; Louis Goldberg, "שכל," in *TWOT* (Chicago: Moody, 1999), 877.

[8] There is also a unique term used for "honey" (נפת) both in 24:13 and 5:3, which is the chiastic parallel of Lesson 7.

[9] There is actually a very similar phrase found between Prov 2:10 and 24:14: "Wisdom will come into your heart and knowledge will be pleasant to your soul" and "Know wisdom is [sweet] to your soul; if you find, then there is a future and your hope will not be cut off."

[10] As Lev 19:14 says, "You shall not curse the deaf nor place before the blind a stumbling block; for you shall fear your God. I am Yhwh." Levine comments here that the seemingly trivial law actually embodied "a general norm of behavior" that Israel was not to prey on others' weaknesses, whether physically or cognitively. While those who were caused to stumble by the wicked cannot hear or see (understand) the violation, "God sees and hears on their behalf and will punish their tormentors" (Baruch A. Levine, *Leviticus: The Traditional Hebrew Text with*

intentions and deeds, even passion, are not only socially problematic but ultimately a violation against God and his *torah*. The verse in Lev 19 concludes the verse with the theological and relational reason they must not cause others to stumble, "You shall fear your God, I am Yhwh" (Lev 19:14).

In an interesting prophetic reversal, Isaiah warns that Israel as a people will "stumble" (כשל) on a rock of "stumbling" (מִכְשׁוֹל), which is actually the Lord himself (Isa 8:14–15).[11] Leading up to this pronouncement, Isaiah mentions Yhwh's rebuke not "to walk in the way of this people" (Isa 8:11). The implication is that Isaiah is to walk in the way of Yhwh, trusting in him. Because Israel rejects Yhwh, they subsequently reject his "teaching" (תּוֹרָה), "testimony" (תְּעוּדָה), and "word" (דָּבָר), which would result in "darkness" (אֲפֵלָה) and loss of "dawn" (שָׁחַר) (Isa 8:20, 22). In Prov 4:19, the "way of the wicked" is directly compared with "darkness" (אֲפֵלָה) while in Isa 8:22 those who curse God will be thrust into the "darkness" (אֲפֵלָה).[12] As it pertains to Lesson 7, the unique concept of "stumble" is used outside of Proverbs with a spiritual connotation, inversely related to walking in the way of Yhwh. Thus, Prov 4:10–19 without mentioning the name of the Lord cleverly intertwines him with the lesson.

Following the Father

At this point in the pedagogical program, the son has been introduced to a number of important principles and figures. The son learned about the centrality of Yhwh in his walk and ways.[13] In this path, he is to follow figures such as Wisdom, the righteous and upright, the grandfather, and even Yhwh. The son has learned many teachings but in Prov 4:11 the father mentions, "I instructed (ירה) you in the way of Wisdom; I led (דָּרַךְ) you in the paths of uprightness."[14] Of particular importance is the statement that the father not

---

the *New JPS Translation*, The JPS Torah Commentary (Philadelphia: Jewish Publication Society, 1989), 128).

[11] The NT picks up on this metaphor, developing it into what is known as "stone Christology." Though God was normally thought of as a rock of refuge, in this Isaianic prophecy he instead becomes a source of stumbling for those who refuse his word or instruction (cf. Isa 28:16; Ps 118:22; Matt 21:42–44; Mark 12:10; Luke 20:17–18; Acts 4:11; Rom 9:32–33; 1 Pet 2:6–8). See Dietrich-Alex Koch, "The Quotations of Isaiah 8,14 and 28,16 in Romans 9,33 and 1 Peter 2,6.8 as Test-Case for Old Testament Quotations in the New Testament," *ZNW* 101.2 (2010): 223–40; Frank Thielman, "Paul's View of Israel's Misstep in Rom 9.32–3: Its Origin and Meaning," *NTS* 64.3 (2018): 362–77; Abba Hillel Silver, *A History of Messianic Speculation in Israel: From the First through the Seventeenth Centuries* (Boston: Beacon, 1959), 3–13.

[12] Charles L. Feinberg, "אפל," in *TWOT* (Chicago: Moody, 1999), 64–65. Feinberg notes that the term typically "symbolizes moral failure and its punishment" and "apostasy from God."

[13] Weeks, *Instruction and Imagery in Proverbs 1–9*, 153.

[14] Fox argues for the "emphatically moralistic" implications of this verse against McKane, noting, "Yošer is never used of actual physical straightness, but only of moral rectitude" (Fox, *Proverbs 1–9*, 179; McKane, *Proverbs*, 307–8).

only "instructed" but he himself "led" the son (cf. Prov 6:22).[15] In other words, he not only verbalized the way but exemplified it – not merely a "do as I say" but a "do as I do."[16] While subtle, the statement indicates that the instruction is not simply abstract information.[17] Rather, it is a developmental process that necessitates both verbal and exemplary instruction. The Deuteronomic instruction from Moses was given for the generational transmission of the Lord's ways (Deut 4:9–10). However, it was clearly expected for them, including their children, "to do" (לעשות) all that was in the covenant, particularly in the land promised to their forefathers (Deut 4:13–14). In fact, Moses recounts in the Sinai event, "Yhwh said to me, 'Gather the people to me that I may cause them to hear my words that they may learn to fear me all their days ... and may teach their sons'" (Deut 4:10). The fathers were to teach the words of God both verbally and physically in their own obedience and imitation of Gods ways. In Proverbs, the father reminds the son that he himself has done just that. He has led the son in the ways of his teaching, both verbally and personally.[18] The term used here is somewhat unusual, however. While the verb *darak* (דָּרַךְ) is fairly common, it only occurs once in Proverbs and is rarely used in the sense of "lead" elsewhere (Isa 11:15, 42:16, 48:17; Ps 25: 5, 9, 119:35). Typically, the word simply means to "walk," "tread," or idiomatically to "pull a bow." Interestingly, the uses of *darak* (דָּרַךְ) with the sense of "lead" have Yhwh as the subject. One, in particular, is similar to Prov 4:11, "Thus says Yhwh your redeemer, the Holy One of Israel, 'I am Yhwh your God who teaches (למד) you to profit, who leads (דרך) you in the way you shall walk'" (Isa 48:17).[19] Similar language is also used in Ps 25:5 and 9, "Lead

---

[15] Although Lesson 7 uses the term *darak* (דרך) for "lead" (Prov 4:11), Lesson 12 uses the term *nachah* (נחה) for "lead" (Prov 6:22). In this earlier lesson, it is the father who leads the son. In Lesson 12, it is Wisdom who leads the son, perhaps signaling the progression from father/mother to Wisdom/Yhwh as the primary instructor/example in the son's development (cf. Lessons 14 and 15). For further discussion on the topic of leading, see Lesson 12 and Excursus: Exodus and God's Leading in His Way

[16] In Prov 23:26, a similar imitative statement is made, "My son, give me your heart and may your eyes delight in my ways." The son is to watch and learn from the proverbial father and teacher.

[17] Estes states, "The goal of the wise teacher is to guide the learner to live within Yahweh's world. The focus is upon the development of the inner person, not just upon compliance with a pattern of external actions. The teacher endeavours to bring the learner to personal maturity" (Daniel J. Estes, *Hear, My Son: Teaching and Learning in Proverbs 1–9*, NSBT 4 (Grand Rapids: Eerdmans, 1997), 131).

[18] Estes observes, "The ultimate goal, however, is that the learner will develop independent competence in living responsibly in Yahweh's world. The teacher's progression from expert authority to facilitator parallels the intellectual and moral development of the learner" (Estes, *Hear, My Son*, 133). While Estes' point appears on track, it may be nuanced a bit. Rather than independence, the son is taught perpetual dependence on Yhwh and his ways. Likewise, he is not simply to live in Yhwh's world but with Yhwh as his likeness in his world.

[19] Oswalt expands on the teaching and leading metaphor for Yhwh, "Character is what his behavior teaches. He is characteristically a teacher and a guide. ... he has shown himself to the human race in order to show us what we were made for and how we can return to that goal. ... God's leading of his people in their wanderings became an apt metaphor for his ultimate purpose of leading us to himself and our own true selves" (John N. Oswalt, *The Book of Isaiah*, NICOT (Grand Rapids: Eerdmans, 1986), 281).

(דרך) me in your truth and teach (למד) me, for you are the God of my salvation … He leads (דרך) the humble in justice and teaches (למד) the humble his way." As observed, there is a fundamental correspondence between teaching and the metaphor of leading on a path. Although the causative (*hiphil*) of *darak* (דֶּרֶךְ) could merely represent a causative effect, parallels elsewhere with the more explicit term *nachah* (נחה) point to the likelihood of a metaphorical correspondence (e.g., Isa 57:18, 58:2–11; Ps 5:9, 23:3, 27:11, 73:24, 139:24, 143:10).[20] Thus, the proverbial father is personally guiding the son in the way (Prov 4:11) just as his father did for him (4:3–4) and ultimately as God does for all his people, like sons (3:11–12).[21]

Although Lesson 6 referred to Wisdom anthropomorphically, Lesson 7 does not exalt her as such. Rather, wisdom is a path, paralleled with the "way of uprightness" and the "path of the righteous" (Prov 4:11, 18). In 4:13, however, the father makes a similar remark of *musar* as was said of Wisdom, "Hold onto *musar*, do not abandon (רפה); protect (נצר) it (her) for it (she) is your life." In 4:6, the grandfather says, "Do not abandon (עזב) her and she will guard (שמר) you; love her and she will protect (נצר) you." The Heb. grammar, of course, uses the feminine pronoun in Prov 4:13 but contextually does not seem to imply a similar metaphor for *musar* as for Wisdom.[22] Yet, what is important is the definitive statement regarding *musar*. In Lesson 4, the *musar* of the father and Proverbs was ultimately linked to Yhwh, the preeminent Father. However, only one other place in the HB makes such a definitive statement regarding life, "He is your life," referring to Yhwh (Deut 30:20).[23] So, while the father's words will add "years of life" (Prov 4:10), the *musar* he is passing on is of mortal significance.[24] By implication, *musar* is not only practically efficient but is relationally necessary for walking in the way of Yhwh.[25]

---

[20] See Lesson 12 and Excursus: Exodus and God's Leading in His Way.

[21] Cf. McKane, *Proverbs*, 307–8.

[22] Fox claims that the personified feminine pronoun for Wisdom is extended to include *musar*, "In these cases, *musar* is equivalent to wisdom, and the feminine gender of *ḥokmah* is maintained in speaking about *musar*, though that word is formally masculine" (Fox, *Proverbs 1–9*, 180; Schipper, *Proverbs 1–15*, 180).

[23] Schipper, *Proverbs 1–15*, 177, 180.

[24] Waltke believes the metaphor implies more than mere mortality, "The road metaphor does not depict life from the cradle to the grave, but the road to eternal life versus the road to eternal death" (Waltke, *Proverbs (1–15)*, 289).

[25] Waltke observed, "The house of the wicked is annihilated because it is built on the flimsy foundation of human epistemology, the relative truth accessible to human sight. Only the omniscient, omnipotent God knows the true road that leads to life, reality as it actually is. Truth is beyond the reach of finite humanity; the Lord himself must reveal the right way through his inspired sage, and the disciple must accept that revelation by faith" (Waltke, *Proverbs (1–15)*, 592).

Following the Righteous

Lesson 7 draws on patterns and metaphors from earlier lessons in order to create a continuity of message. In particular, the proverbial father points back to the beginning of Lesson 1 and the end of Lesson 2. After providing a promise and command derived from following in his way, he launches into a negative admonition for the son to abstain from following in aberrant ways. The teacher warned the son, "Do not enter (אֵל־תָּבֹא) with sinners ... do not walk (הלך) in the way (דרך) with them" (Prov 1:10, 15). Now, he similarly rebukes, "Do not enter (אֵל־תָּבֹא) in the path (אֹרַח) of the wicked and do not walk (אשר) in the way (דרך) of the evil" (Prov 4:14).[26] For both, the plural terms רְשָׁעִים and רָעִים are grammatically substantive adjectives, functioning as construct absolutes for "path" and "way." The grammar requires that it is not abstractly "evil" or "wicked" paths but the ways of evil and wicked people. This idea finds a correlation in Prov 22:24–25, including an imitative expansion, "Do not befriend a man of anger and do not enter (לֹא תָבוֹא) with a man of wrath lest you shall learn (אלף) his ways (אֹרְחֹתָיו) and a snare capture your soul." In this proverb, it was understood that association leads to imitation. Thus, Lesson 7 implies that the father was as much concerned with the son's imitation of wicked people as with the abstract path and its consequences.[27] In other words, the son was to be led by the father, implicitly in the path of wisdom, rather than to be led by wicked examples whose ways are aberrant.[28] Just as there was an emphasis in Lesson 1 on not becoming like sinners in their ways, so Lesson 7 re-emphasizes the principle.[29]

The focus on exemplar individuals as models both for the right way or the wrong way is seen later in this lesson, as well. The final two verses (Prov 4:18, 19) use similar language to contrast types of people more so than the paths they tread. In Prov 4:18, it says that "the path of the righteous (צַדִּיקִים) is like light." Similarly, in Prov 4:19, it says that "the way of the wicked (רְשָׁעִים) is like darkness."[30] Much like Prov 4:14, these plurals are necessarily substantive adjectives due to the grammar of the construct phrases. As in Prov 4:14, the last two refocus the son's attention not merely on the results or the path, per se, but on those influencing him, whether for good or evil. The son is to follow those on the wise path by imitating the righteous, who progressively

---

[26] The lexeme used here *ashar* (אשר) normally carries the sense of "blessed" in the form *ashre* (אַשְׁרֵי), but only in a few rare occasions appears to mean "guide," "lead," or "walk." These rare uses only appear in Isa (1:17, 3:12, 9:15) and Prov (4:14, 9:6, 23:19). Since the term is used elsewhere in the wisdom literature with the sense of "blessed" in Prov (3:13, 8:34, 20:7, 28:14), it perhaps serves as a double entendre, implying that the son ought not to seek blessedness through walking in the way of evil.

[27] Cf. Keefer, *Proverbs 1–9 as an Introduction to the Book of Proverbs*, 79–80.

[28] Cf. Fox, *Proverbs 1–9*, 180.

[29] Murphy, *Proverbs*, 27.

[30] Perdue notes the association of darkness and this particular term (אֲפֵלָה) with judgment and even the Day of Yhwh (Leo G. Perdue, *Proverbs*, IBC (Louisville: John Knox, 2000), 116). This perhaps implies more than just a lack of success but their positional relationship against Yhwh outside the covenant.

grow in light,[31] an idiom for knowledge and wisdom. As Lyu comments, "One gets closer to being righteous by doing what is righteous."[32] In other words, the righteous are both defined and shaped by the fruit of their desire and deeds. Conversely, the wicked person is trapped in darkness, an idiom for lack of knowledge and wisdom.[33] This type of person is characterized and shaped by the fruit of their deeds, as Fromm says, "The longer we continue to make the wrong decisions, the more our heart hardens ... and eventually freedom is lost."[34]

The lesson is buttoned up with the final word "stumble" (כשל), meant to contrast the way and instruction of the father. The wicked "stumble" because their sight, or understanding, is hindered and darkened, the blind leading the blind (Isa 56:10; Mal 2:8; cf. Matt 15:14; Luke 6:39).[35] In fact, Jesus later utilized a similar proverbial metaphor,[36] adding a poignant lesson worth noting, "A disciple is not above the teacher; but when fully trained up he shall be like his teacher" (Luke 6:40). As a teacher himself, Jesus understood the imitative trajectory of a disciple, culminating in one's reflection of their teacher.[37] A blind teacher creates blind disciples. Conversely, a teacher of light creates disciples of light. In Lesson 7, the father is the one who possesses light and wisdom. If the son will follow the father, he will walk the smooth path, ultimately rooted in following the ways of Yhwh who is the author of light (e.g., Gen 1:3; Isa 2:5, 45:7; Ps 27:1, 37:6, 43:3, 56:14, 119:105).[38] In Isaiah, a few helpful parallels surface as well. The Lord says in

---

[31] Keefer observes in Prov 1–9, "The reader is encouraged to practice and emulate the ideal person, and as a result, to become one. For those who set their course to follow the journey, the righteous person provides a paradigm of life." Similarly, Lyu mentions, "The character of the righteous person is the sages' chosen exemplar of the ethical and pious life, and as such he serves as a paradigm of life to emulate." See Keefer, *Proverbs 1–9 as an Introduction to the Book of Proverbs*, 63; Sun Myung Lyu, *Righteousness in the Book of Proverbs*, FAT 55 (Tübingen: Mohr Siebeck, 2012), 62.

[32] Lyu, *Righteousness*, 74.

[33] Schipper proposes that the metaphor of light and dark "symbolize the realm of the dead, where light is a symbol for life." While death and life are certainly in view, the metaphor here uses the progression of dawn against those in darkness without knowledge to emphasize the cognitive, moral, and spiritual growth of the son rather than life directly. However, metaphorically speaking, life and wisdom are inextricably connected, as the beginning of this lesson presumes (4:10). See Plöger, *Spruche Salomos (Proverbia)*, 48; Fox, *Proverbs 1–9*, 183; Schipper, *Proverbs 1–15*, 182.

[34] Erich Fromm, *The Heart of Man: Its Genius for Good and Evil* (New York: Harper & Row, 1964), 135–36.

[35] Cf. Schipper, *Proverbs 1–15*, 177. Schipper emphasizes the strong metaphorical connections between Prov 4:18–19 and Isa 56–66, also highlighting its presence in the Qumran scrolls.

[36] Marshall and Green note the common proverbial usage of the blind leading the blind in antiquity, perhaps rooted in the biblical tradition. See I. Howard Marshall, *The Gospel of Luke: A Commentary on the Greek Text*, NIGTC (Exeter: Paternoster, 1978), 268–70; Joel B. Green, *The Gospel of Luke*, NICNT (Grand Rapids: Eerdmans, 1997), 277–78.

[37] As Bock rightly understands, "[Jesus] is warning us to watch which teacher we follow. If we follow someone who takes in no light, we will stumble. So, we are to consider carefully who our teacher is" (Darrell L. Bock, *Luke*, IVP New Testament Commentary (Downers Grove: IVP, 1994), 127).

[38] Cf. Waltke, *Proverbs (1–15)*, 292.

Isa 42:16, "I will cause the blind to walk in the way they do not know; in paths they do not know I will lead (דרך) them. I will make the darkness before them into light and their crookedness into straightness."[39] Likewise, in several places, God promised that the nation of Israel would one day become the source of light to the nations, passing on to them the ways of Yhwh, much like the father is doing for the son here (e.g., Isa 2:2–4, 42:6, 49:6, 51:4).[40] Thus, the proverbial father of Lesson 7 invokes the light metaphor in order to highlight the distinction between the exemplars for the two paths, which lay before the son. He must choose who will train him and who he will emulate.

Conclusion

Lesson 7 makes it plain that the path of life is one fraught with challenges, temptations, and obstacles, an unfortunate reality for all of humanity. To effectively navigate these challenges, the son learns that he must have clear vision. As this lesson suggests, the way of the righteous is full of light while the path of the wicked is saturated by darkness (Prov 4:18–19). So, the son must take care to walk in the righteous way so that he may navigate the myriad of hidden snares (Prov 4:14–17, 19). Yet, he is not alone in this journey. The father has "led" him thus far, and the son will continue to be led by Wisdom and Yhwh as he develops (Prov 4:10–13; cf. 6:22). Likewise, there are many wise and righteous examples who have gone before and are on the wise path with him (Prov 4:11, 18). Thus, he must actively refuse the way of the wicked and hold closely to the instruction of the father (Prov 4:10, 14). This personal instruction is able to make him wise unto life, walking securely on the path of the righteous. After presenting Yhwh, Wisdom, himself, the grandfather, and the righteous as those on the wise path, the father then takes the son a step further in Lesson 8 at the center of his program. In this next lesson, the son is not only explicitly encouraged to consider his path carefully but is also implicitly encouraged to observe the straight-way of Moses, Joshua, and David, among other historical figures he should carefully consider.

---

[39] Leading up to this statement, the Lord also promised of his coming servant, "I appoint you to be a covenant people, to be a light of nations, to open the eyes of the blind, to release the prisoner from prison, those sitting in darkness from bondage" (Isa 42:6b-7). The Lord and his servant are paralleled as bringers of light for those in darkness.

[40] Oswalt notes the irony of Isaiah's prophecy that it is the blind who will be "bearers of light for the nations" once God reveals to them his salvation through the servant (Oswalt, *The Book of Isaiah*, 126–27).

LESSON 8

Analysis of 4:20–27
"Walk the straight path"

At the heart of Prov 1–9, the father further hones in on the path metaphor in Lesson 8, a central thread throughout the wisdom program. Instead of elaborating on the dangers or aberrations of foolish ways, however, the father instructs the son to carefully consider his way and to evaluate it against the righteous models who have come before him (Prov 4:26–27). On one hand, the path metaphor points to a person's myriad desires and characteristics as they progress through life (Prov 4:23). Yet, as the father poetically instructs, it is also an embodied reality, a physical expression of mental concepts (Prov 4:21, 24–27). So, the son is to direct and guard himself properly in order to maintain his advancement along the wisdom trajectory. In doing so, he will imitate patriarchal figures such as David who had reflected Yhwh (Prov 4:27; cf. 5:21; 1 Sam 13:14). Thus, this central lesson, though seemingly modest in its instruction, serves as a spindle for the other lessons, weaving them around the father's imitative intent. Of course, at the heart of the straight-way is Yhwh, though unnamed, who both exemplifies the ideal characteristics and establishes the way of those who walk in them.

Structure of Lesson 8

The eighth lesson is both typical and unique from the other lessons of Prov 1–9. In the initial fatherly calls, Lessons 8 and 9 (Prov 4:20, 5:1) begin with nearly identical language. The only variation is the replacement of "words" and "sayings" with "wisdom" and "understanding." These differences are likely meant to signal continuity and expansion between the lessons and their authority rather than in distinction.[1] In other words, the father's teaching is wisdom and wisdom is the father's teaching. While a potentially bold claim, as seen elsewhere, there is an intentional overlap between the teaching of the father and Wisdom, ultimately sourced in Yhwh.[2]

4:20	בְּנִי לִדְבָרַי הַקְשִׁיבָה לַאֲמָרַי הַט־אָזְנֶךָ	My son, consider my *words*; turn your ear to my *sayings*.
5:1	בְּנִי לְחָכְמָתִי הַקְשִׁיבָה לִתְבוּנָתִי הַט־אָזְנֶךָ	My son, consider my *wisdom*; turn your ear to my *understanding*.

Despite bearing many similarities with other lessons in the highly structured program, there is not an easily observable schema to this lesson.[3] Rather, there are a number of features that serve to highlight it from among the other lessons and implant it in the son's heart. To begin, this eighth lesson is the only one with eight verses. Likewise, it contains eight grammatical imperatives, which create a sense of flow and structure, though not mechanically or perfectly symmetrical. [4] From the lexical and thematic perspective, the lesson is saturated with bodily language, used metaphorically. [5] More densely than elsewhere, the teacher layers bodily terms, several of which are used multiple times: ear (אֹזֶן), eyes (עַיִן), eyelids (עַפְעַפִּים), mouth (פֶּה), lips (שְׂפָתַיִם), heart (לֵבָב), flesh (בָּשָׂר), feet (רֶגֶל), and life (חַיִּים).[6]

---

[1] Fox, however, sees this as the universalizing of the source of his wisdom (Fox, *Proverbs 1–9*, 190).

[2] Although Yhwh is not mentioned in this section, Murphy rightly notes, "There is no question but that the figure of God/the Lord lurks behind these chapters." Longman similarly says, "It does not mention God explicitly but ... the father's path is the one that is associated with God." See Murphy, *Proverbs*, 29; Longman, *Proverbs*, 155.

[3] Scholars almost unanimously identify Prov 4:20–27 as a distinct unit but have floundered in identifying a satisfying structural pattern. Although Schipper initially proposed a two-fold structure, he quickly then questioned its validity. Schäfer divided it into four-verse halves, the first titled "receptive" and the other "active." However, it is not clear whether these categories actually align with the bodily terms proposed. See Loader, *Proverbs 1–9*, 223; Schipper, *Proverbs 1–15*, 185; Rolf Schäfer, *Die Poesie der Weisen: Dichotomie als Grundstruktur der Lehr und Weisheitsgedichte in Proverbien 1–9*, WMANT 77 (Neukirchen-Vluyn: Neukirchener Verlag, 1999), 120–21.

[4] Nel proposes a multi-layered structure that centers on Prov 4:23, an admonition to guard the heart (Philip Johannes Nel, *The Structure and Ethos of the Wisdom Admonitions in Proverbs*, BZAW 158 (New York: De Gruyter, 1982), 61). However, while the heart is certainly important, his case is thin and does not warrant such a strong stance. Several thematic elements work together to weave the author's purpose, primarily interested in the son's way.

[5] Fox refers to the metaphorical use of body imagery as the "student's moral self-image" used to "encourage the youth's incorporation of a certain self-image, an inner carriage, a sense of being straightforward" (Fox, *Proverbs 1–9*, 188).

[6] While all the body parts complement the poetic instruction, the "heart" may serve as the most important part. Waltke says it is the "director of the rest of the body." Fox appeals to the broader ANE use of the heart as the seat of one's thoughts and personhood. This use lends to the importance of "consideration" in this lesson. Toy viewed it as a synecdoche to represent the "self" or the person holistically. Despite the heart's importance, it is all the metaphorical

Yet, all of these terms primarily serve as metaphors, alluding to ideas such as understanding, obedience, wisdom, will, choice, and conduct.[7] This emphasis on bodily metaphors at the center of the chiasm seems to signal the overall metaphorical sense of the whole program, utilizing concrete and personally relatable terms to insinuate important poetic truths. Whybray notes a similar density of these bodily terms in Ps 115:5–6.[8] Though he rightfully says the psalm has a different purpose than Prov 4:20–27, the passages are ostensibly related in their underlying imitative concept. As an invective against idolatry, the psalmist writes, "They have a mouth but do not speak. They have eyes but do not see. They have ears but do not hear. They have a nose but do not smell. They have hands but do not feel. They have feet but do not walk and their throat makes no utterance. Those making them become like them, all who trust in them" (Ps 115:5–8; cf. 135:15–18). The passage illuminates the imitative relationship between idolaters and their idols.[9] On a literal and physical level, idols are inert. So, their makers and worshippers end up reflecting their inertness, understood through their moral and religious ways. This reversal condemns the aberrant path as one that places the idolater beneath the animal, equivalent to the fool or wicked on the wisdom hierarchy. Thus, the fool may be tempted to follow the teachings of the father for merely bodily gains – physical, earthly, selfish – but the true path requires the reader to understand the teacher's deeper intentions (cf. Matt 11:15). It seems then that at the heart of the proverbial program, there is an underlying reversal of the lifeless way of the idolater, which is supplanted by the way of the living God. In all of his ways, the wise will reflect the active embodiment of life, one that cannot be counterfeited.

These formative implications are further amplified by the thematic emphasis on the dual concepts of turning and consideration. Lesson 5 similarly utilized the term "deviate" (לוז), found twice here as well (Prov 4:21, 24). Additionally, the two synonymous terms for "turn" – natah (נטה) and sur (סור) – serve as a backbone and as an inclusio to the lesson (4:20, 24, 27).[10] Like the body metaphors, this lesson is densely littered with directional language. Also, several overlapping terms are used to encourage the son to consider (קשב), look (נבט), watch (פלס), and guard (נצר) the father's teaching in order to avoid deviating from the Torah way, or God's ways.[11] In fact, with a

---

body parts together that serve the teacher's poetic point. See Schipper, *Proverbs 1–15*, 185; Loader, *Proverbs 1–9*, 222–23; Fox, *Proverbs 1–9*, 186; Waltke, *Proverbs (1–15)*, 295; Toy, *Proverbs*, 98.

[7] Perdue proposes that the use of a full coterie of bodily terms insinuates the way of wisdom and life is holistic, "Through the course of study one's entire being, including especially one's character, is formed and transformed" (Perdue, *Proverbs*, 118; Whybray, *Composition of the Book of Proverbs*, 34).

[8] Whybray, *Proverbs (1994)*, 81.

[9] Cf. Allen P. Ross, *A Commentary on the Psalms*, Kregel Exegetical Library (Grand Rapids: Kregel Academic, 2011), 769.

[10] Cf. Waltke, *Proverbs (1–15)*, 294; Schäfer, *Die Poesie der Weisen*, 125.

[11] As Hinkle rightly observes, "The Pentateuch is used as a means of equating the instructions of the father figure with those of Yahweh. It serves as a reminder of the instructions the readers have learned from instructions derived from Yahweh" (Adrian E. Hinkle,

hint of irony perhaps, the father uses the connotative stock phrase "turn your ear" (Prov 4:20) as a protective measure against turning from the straight path (4:26–27).[12] Together, these various poetic, thematic, and lexical features form a highly focused lesson, instructing the son to follow in his father's ways.

Consider the Path

As a wise teacher, the father understands that the straight path is neither easy nor automatic.[13] In fact, there are many distractions and influences that may lead the son astray if he is not careful. To this point, the father crafts an important message to the son, "May your eyes look forward and your eyelids be straight in front of you. Consider the path of your feet and all your ways will be established" (Prov 4:25–26). While seemingly innocuous and simple, the message connects with several elements elsewhere, which serve to illuminate its implications. First, the son is to keep his eyes "forward" or "to the front" (לְנֹכַח). The term is typically used to imply "in front of" or "opposite," a close synonym of the final term of the verse *neged* (נגד) (Prov 4:25). The connection later in Prov 5:21 helps illuminate the importance here, using the uncommon term *nokach* (נֹכַח) again but for the "eyes of Yhwh."[14] The second half of 5:21 is similar to 4:26, implying the two are intentionally parallel. In Prov 4:25, the instruction is for the son to keep his eyes to the front while 5:21 says that "all the ways of a man are in front of (נֹכַח) the eyes of Yhwh." The context of this statement is complex. On one hand, the implication seems to be a warning that nothing is hidden from the Lord, speaking of the danger in embracing the foreign woman. Yet, the broader context of the lesson is that the son(s) would listen to his teachers (Prov 5:13) and not hate *musar* (5:23). With this contextual view, Prov 5:21 takes on a more fatherly and protective tone.[15] In other words, Yhwh's eyes are watching over the son's path. More to

---

Pedagogical Theory of Wisdom Literature: An Application of Educational Theory to Biblical Texts (Eugene: Wipf & Stock, 2017), 96).

[12] In a very similar passage, the psalmist of Ps 119 includes an ironic use of both terms to imply the same sense found in Prov 4:20 and 27, "I do not turn (סור) from your judgments, for you teach me. ... I turn (נטה) my heart to do your statutes until the everlasting end" (Ps 119:102, 112). While this may imply one intentionally borrowing from the other, it at least confirms a poetic synonymous usage.

[13] Fox emphasizes the two-path metaphor which summarizes the many individual ways of behavior that align with either the path of life or the path of death. Weeks contends, however, that there is only one path, which is characterized by wisdom and righteousness. Everything else is simply a deviation from that path. From the diversity of "path" imagery used in Prov 1–9, it would seem both have grounds for their views. It is likely that in a real sense, the path of death is not really a path as much as missing *the path*. However, the idea of paths is often used more generically for human behaviors, character, and desires which do constitute alternative directions or paths. See Weeks, *Instruction and Imagery in Proverbs 1–9*, 75–76; Fox, *Proverbs 1–9*, 129–31.

[14] Schipper, *Proverbs 1–15*, 214; Achim Müller, *Proverbien 1–9: der Weisheit neue Kleider*, BZAW 291 (Berlin: De Gruyter, 2000), 76–78.

[15] Schipper, *Proverbs 1–15*, 214.

the point, just as the Lord's eyes are "forward," fixed on the son, in imitative reflection the son's eyes ought to be "forward," fixed on Yhwh and his ways. If the son rejects Yhwh and his father's teaching, then the eyes of Yhwh will be on him in the negative sense for judgment. But if the son follows in the straight-way, then the eyes of the Lord are for corrective guidance and protection as a father.

The dueling function of the Lord's eyes is further highlighted by Prov 4:26. While Prov 4:25 was interested in the straightness of the path, 4:26 uses the uncommon term *pales* (פלס) in close relation to *magal* (מעגל) to instruct the son's careful consideration of his path.[16] The father says, "Consider (פלס) the path (מעגל) of your feet." The term *pales* (פלס) only occurs three times in Proverbs (4:26, 5:6, 5:21) and three other times elsewhere in the HB (Isa 26:7; Ps 58:3, 78:50). The root sense seems to be related to the nominal idea of a "balance" or "scale" (פלס), which only occurs twice (Isa 40:12; Prov 16:11).[17] In this way, the son is to weigh out or carefully examine the various aspects of his ways to see if they align with the straight-way. Isaiah spoke a similar phrase in a prophetic song for Judah, "The way of the righteous is straight; You consider (פלס) the path (מעגל) of the righteous" (Isa 26:7). For Isaiah, the righteous are those who are faithful to God (26:2; cf. Prov 3:3, 8:7), seek him (26:9; cf. Prov 1:28, 8:17), and trust in Yhwh (26:3–4; cf. Prov 3:5).[18] The use of *pales* (פלס) in Isa 26:7 is similar to Prov 5:21b, "and [Yhwh] considers (פלס) all his ways (מעגל)," speaking of the "ways of a man" from the first half. While Prov 5:21 seems to carry a dual sense of both warning and fatherly comfort, the Isaianic passage only implies the Lord's consideration in a positive and affirmative sense for the faithful. Much like the reciprocal connection for Prov 5:21a, this second half also implies that the son is to imitate Yhwh in his careful considerations. Implicit here is that Yhwh is a wise teacher who carefully considers his own way and is able to guide and assist the student by carefully considering his way, as well. The positive correlation with Yhwh is further highlighted by the negative instance of the word pair found in 5:6, "The path of life she does not consider (פלס); she does not know her paths (מעגל) are unstable."[19] This use describes the way of the strange woman. Of course, it is exactly opposite to the father's instruction for the son.[20] The father says to "consider the path of your feet" (Prov 4:26) and that his instruction is "life

---

[16] Cf. Fox, *Proverbs 1–9*, 187. Fox initially argues for the verse to mean "make level" but quickly acknowledges it likely carries the sense of "weigh" or "consider."

[17] The term *pales* (פלס) is found with an Akk. root (palāsu) in the sense of "to see, look" (HALOT). This may suggest that the idea of "weigh" or "scale" was a secondary, connotative, idiomatic, or derivative inference from the sense of "carefully look, examine," though others have proposed the Akk. sense of "bore through." Cf. McKane, *Proverbs*, 311; Whybray, *Proverbs (1994)*, 83; Loader, *Proverbs 1–9*, 229.

[18] Oswalt notes the reflective quality of those God saves, "God will certainly not act on behalf of the unrighteous, but those who have a passion for the same character as God's (righteousness and faithfulness, cf. 11:5) may depend upon him in patient hope" (John N. Oswalt, "God's Determination to Redeem His People (Isaiah 9:1–7, 11:1–11, 26:1–9, 35:1–10)," *RevExp* 88.2 (1991): 161).

[19] Cf. Schipper, *Proverbs 1–15*, 214.

[20] Cf. Weeks, *Instruction and Imagery in Proverbs 1–9*, 208.

to those finding" (4:22). So, the coordination of these three verses places into juxtaposition the two paths. One path is characterized by a foolish, haphazard strange woman. The other is characterized by the instruction of the father and Yhwh, who embody and teach the "path of life." In fact, the father promises the son that "all your ways will be established (כון)" if he will consider his path. The proverbial father leaves the question of who or how the son's ways will be established. Yet, the ambiguity leans toward the Lord being the one responsible, particularly for his covenant people.[21] This sense is strengthened by the popular aphorism later in Prov 16:9, "A man's heart plans his way, but Yhwh establishes (כון) his step."[22] So, the son and the surety of his way are ultimately dependent on Yhwh. In order to find this surety, he must keep his eyes to the front and carefully consider his path, just as the Lord does. In doing so, he will imitate the father and Yhwh rather than the strange woman.

Walking the Straight Path

As clarified in this lesson, it is necessary for the son to carefully consider the straight path, which ultimately leads to life (Prov 4:22). Yet, it is not clearly identified what the straight path is or what it entails. Presumably, all fifteen lessons centered around Lesson 8 are for the purpose of guiding the son and illuminating this path. However, Lesson 8 surprisingly does not provide many specifics, other than mentioning "a crooked mouth" and "devious lips" (Prov 4:24). As mentioned in the structure and themes of this lesson, there is a strong emphasis on the straight-way, though. This thread crescendos in the final verse, "Do not turn right or left; turn your feet from evil" (4:27). The phrase directs the son to a deeply important theme elsewhere in the HB.[23] Beginning in Deut 5, a motif that is centered on the faithfulness of Israel and the leader of Israel utilizes the admonition not to turn "right or left."[24] The parallel of this passage with Deut 5:32–33 and its various features was

---

[21] The LXX adds to the end of this lesson, following 4:27. It seems the translator sought to clarify the involvement of Yhwh in this process by adding, "And he will make straight your paths and he will lead your way in peace" (Prov 4:27β, LXX). While the verses are likely an addition, lacking in the MT and Syr., the final verse does capture elements related to the proverbial program for the son to be led by God in his ways. Lang argues that despite the LXX attempt to clarify the passage, this should not imply that the idea of Yhwh's involvement was a later gloss. Rather, Yhwh was central even in the original. See Bernhard Lang, *Die weisheitliche Lehrrede: eine Untersuchung von Sprüche 1–7*, SBS 54 (Stuttgart: KBW-Verlag, 1972), 79–80.

[22] Similarly, Moses rebuked a disobedient Israel, saying, "They are a crooked and twisted generation. Shall this foolish and unwise nation repay Yhwh? Is he not your father, he who obtained (קנה) you, made you, and established (כון) you?" (Deut 32:5–6).

[23] Cf. Schipper, *Proverbs 1–15*, 191; Waltke, *Proverbs (1–15)*, 301.

[24] Cf. A. Robert, "Les Attaches Littéraires Bibliques de Prov. I-IX," *RB* 43.1 (1934): 61–62; Whybray, *Proverbs (1994)*, 83; McKane, *Proverbs*, 311. Without much reasoning except that it is common shared language, Whybray and McKane disagree with Robert that the passage has any relation to Deuteronomy.

discussed in the "Structure of Prov 1–9" section. To avoid redundancy, many of these salient aspects will not be restated.

In Moses' exhortation, he commands the people of God to "walk in the whole way" which Yhwh commanded them (Deut 5:33). This passage concludes the re-giving of the Ten Commandments in preparation for the people to enter the land with their God, focusing on the covenantal imperative.[25] A similar preparatory statement resurfaces in Deut 17:20 with the well-known kingly regulations.[26] Once the covenant people are given peace in the land, the Lord will choose a king to rule not as a typical ANE monarch but as one among brothers (Deut 17:15, 20). The key marker of such a reign is to be the straightness of his path, to not "turn (סור) from the commandment, right or left" (Deut 17:20). Similarly, at the conclusion of the Mosaic speeches, the covenantal feature known as the blessing and cursing, typical in the ANE,[27] once again reemphasizes this admonition, including its correlation with worshiping other gods (Deut 28:14). Perhaps unsurprisingly, the phrase occurs twice in Joshua at the beginning and end in order to remind the people of its importance. As Joshua assumes leadership over Israel, the Lord both comforts and exhorts him. Although seemingly innocuous within a well-loved passage, he is told to uphold and do *torah*, paralleled with the idea of not turning from it "right or left" (Josh 1:7). Then at the end, he gives his final plea to the people to do as he did by keeping the *torah* of Moses, again paralleled with not turning "right or left" (Josh 23:6).[28] After Joshua, though, the theme becomes less common. The paucity is perhaps representative of the chaotic and unrestrained behavior of Israel during the Judges period and even the monarchy.[29] Interestingly, Isaiah makes one oblique use of the phrase. In Isa 30:21–22, the prophet presents a teacher, presumably God or his servant, who warns the people of the allure of false paths, "'This is the way, walk in it,' when you go right or left."[30] These other paths to the "right or left" are characterized by idols and representative of moral and religious apostasy.

---

[25] Peter C. Craigie, *The Book of Deuteronomy*, NICOT (Eerdmans, 1976), 149–50.

[26] In a nearby verse, a similar phrase is used to warn the people from rebelling against the verdicts of priests and judges, presumably as mediators of God's instruction, "You shall not turn (סור) from the word which they declare to you, right or left" (Deut 17:11).

[27] E.g., Kenneth A. Kitchen and Paul J. N. Lawrence, *Treaty, Law and Covenant in the Ancient Near East* (Wiesbaden: Harrassowitz Verlag, 2012), 244, 253–54; Christopher B. Hays, *Hidden Riches: A Sourcebook for the Comparative Study of the Hebrew Bible and Ancient Near East* (Louisville: Westminster John Knox, 2014), 179–80.

[28] In Ps 119:51, the psalmist utilizes similar language without mentioning left or right, "I did not turn (נטה) from your *torah*."

[29] One adjacent use of the phrase does occur in 1 Sam 6:12. This use describes the straight travel of cattle carrying the ark of the covenant. Implicitly, "they did not turn right nor left" because they were instinctively led by God their master, unlike the rebellious Israelites. Much like Isaiah's prophecy against Judah (Isa 1:2–3), these ignorant animals were more wise than humans, a strong condemnation against the people. Cf. Christopher R. J. Holmes, *A Theology of the Christian Life: Imitating and Participating in God* (Grand Rapids: Baker Academic, 2021), 54–55.

[30] The term for "teacher" (מוֹרֶיךָ) may be understood in the sg. or pl. (cf. LXX, Syr., Q). Motyer (cf. Oswalt, Childs) argues that "teacher" should be a sg. for God due to the sg. verbs. This is referring to the personal care of Yhwh, "the divine law/instruction-giver" (cf. Isa 2:3,

The last clear use of this motif appears in the introduction for Josiah, who interestingly became king at eight years old (2 Kgs 22:1). The author describes his reign and life by three descriptors, "He did what was right (הַיָּשָׁר) in the eyes of Yhwh, he walked in the whole way of David his father, and he did not turn (סור) right or left" (2 Kgs 22:2). The three-fold parallel helps illuminate the overlap between them, particularly as they arise elsewhere in the HB. The Deut 5 passage mentions the people were to obey the command of Yhwh.[31] Underlying the whole arc and metaphor of walking in the way is the notion of imitation, particularly as people follow their leader or as a son reflects his father. This idea becomes linked with Josiah in 2 Kgs 22. Walking in the straight path – not turning right or left – implied walking in the way of David his father, or acting as David did.[32] Likewise, walking in the way of his father necessarily implied doing right in the eyes of Yhwh.[33] Of course, David is promised that his son will be like God's son (2 Sam 7:14). Even David himself is curiously said to have a heart like God (כִּלְבָבוֹ), implying a certain type of relation and reflection (1 Sam 13:14).[34] The phrase "walked in the way of his father" is not only used of Josiah, however. A number of kings are

28:26). In this way, it would be an elative or plural of majesty. Blenkinsopp, however, preferred the view that "teacher" was "an expression of divine favour in the form of the teaching, guidance, and example of a prophetic figure, a leader." Beuken, after noting the varied views in rabbinic literature, proposed the two uses of "your teacher" (מוֹרֶיךָ) in Isa 30:20 as different referents, one being human prophets and the other God. In either case, Blenkinsopp's notion that the teacher(s) serves as a guiding example is helpful for its relation to the broader motif of turning "right or left." See J. A. Motyer, *The Prophecy of Isaiah: An Introduction & Commentary* (Downers Grove: IVP, 1993), 250; Oswalt, *The Book of Isaiah*, 560; Joseph Blenkinsopp, *Essays on the Book of Isaiah*, FAT 128 (Tubingen: Mohr Siebeck, 2019), 153; Willem A. M. Beuken, "What Does the Vision Hold: Teachers or One Teacher? Punning Repetition in Isaiah 30:20," *HeyJ* 36.4 (1995): 457–63; Brevard S. Childs, *Isaiah: A Commentary*, OTL (Louisville: Westminster John Knox, 2001), 227.

[31] Commenting on 1 Sam 6:12, Klein observes that the phrase is "used in Deuteronomistic literature to express total obedience (Deut 5:32, 17:11, Josh 1:7)" (Ralph W. Klein, *1 Samuel*, WBC 10 (Waco: Word Books, 1983), 58–59).

[32] Paul House, *1, 2 Kings*, NAC (Nashville: B&H, 1995), 381.

[33] The end of Josiah's story further clarifies the language and relation of the Deuteronomic connection, "And there was not a king before him like him who turned (שׁוּב) to Yhwh with his whole heart and with his whole soul and with all his might according to the *torah* of Moses and after him none arose like him" (2 Kgs 23:25; cf. Deut 6:5). Cf. Mordechai Cogan and Hayim Tadmor, *II Kings: A New Translation*, AB 11 (Garden City: Doubleday, 1988), 281; Iain W. Provan, *1 and 2 Kings* (Grand Rapids: Baker Books, 2012), 270.

[34] There has been some debate as to the meaning of the phrase "according to his heart" (כִּלְבָבוֹ). Johnson and Athas have argued that it refers only to God's election, not David's relation or reflection of Yhwh and his ways. However, DeRouchie and Long propose a middle-way or both-and approach. The selection of God for covenant and service necessarily implies conformity and reflection. Furthermore, it is not enough to say this phrase only means God chose David because God also chose Saul. Yet, he was not referred to in this way. Likewise, as seen in the motif throughout Kings, David is a patriarch and an exemplar for those who walk in God's ways. See Jason S. DeRouchie, "The Heart of YHWH and His Chosen One in 1 Samuel 13:14," *BBR* 24.4 (2014): 467–89; George Athas, "'A Man after God's Own Heart': David and the Rhetoric of Election to Kingship," *JESOT* 2.2 (2013): 191–97; Benjamin J. M. Johnson, "The Heart of YHWH's Chosen One in 1 Samuel," *JBL* 131.3 (2012): 455–66; V. Philips Long, *The Reign and Rejection of King Saul: A Case for Literary and Theological Coherence*, SBLDS 118 (Atlanta: Scholars, 1989), 92.

described with this phrase, both positively and negatively. Amon is said to have "walked in the whole way which his father walked," speaking of Manasseh's idolatry (2 Kgs 21:21). Prior to this, Jehoram is said to have "walked in the way of Israel's kings, just as the house of Ahab," doing what was "evil in the eyes of Yhwh" (2 Kgs 8:18). In a positive example, Jehoshaphat is said to have "walked in the whole way of Asa his father. He did not turn (סור) from it, doing right (הַיָּשָׁר) in the eyes of Yhwh" (1 Kgs 22:43). In fact, it says that he was "buried with his fathers in the city of David, his father" (1 Kgs 22:51). Almost immediately after, Ahaziah is said to have done what was evil in the eyes of Yhwh, summarized as, "He walked in the way of his father and in the way of his mother and in the way of Jeroboam" (1 Kgs 22:52). As the preeminent negative example, Jeroboam is named as the patriarch of four other aberrant kings of Israel, in the early stages of separation, who walked in his evil ways – Nabab, Baasha, Zimri, and Omri (1 Kgs 15:26, 34, 16:19, 26). Although only Nadab is his actual son, the rest are treated as though they were sons due to their reflection of his ways. The entirety of the motif perpetuates the notion that individuals are associated with others through an imitative relationship characterized by a father-to-son relation. [35] The metaphorical idiom would not have had any value if it were not a readily understood idea, without the need for explanation. Though Josiah and Jehoshaphat were not direct sons, they are figured as such due to their reflection of David's ways.

Near the end of Solomon's demise, the Lord mingles the actions of Solomon and the people, saying, "Behold, I am tearing the kingdom from the hand of Solomon ... because they have abandoned me and worshiped Ashtoreth ... they did not walk in my ways doing right (הַיָּשָׁר) in my eyes, my statutes and judgments, as David his father" (1 Kgs 11:31, 33). Both Solomon and the people were guilty of not being proper reflections of their father, that is David and Yhwh. [36] Despite the prominence and dire consequences of Solomon's aberrant path, this negative example actually began with Samuel's unrighteous sons, who brought about Israel's desire for a human monarch. Though Samuel was a righteous prophet and judge, "His sons did not walk in his way but they turned (נטה) after profit and took bribes and twisted (נטה) justice" (1 Sam 8:3). The implication is that Samuel did not pervert justice or take bribes but walked faithfully in the way of Yhwh. Thus, from Samuel to

---

[35] The example of Zimri highlights the generic use of the statement to imply that imitation was not thought of in exact or mechanical ways. Rather, as House notes, "This comment reflects Zimri's overall life and activity, not just his brief reign" (House, *1, 2 Kings*, 201). Similarly, the concept for walking in the ways of David, or of Yhwh, did not mean to do everything he did but the overall trajectory of his ways, likely focused on character and adherence to God's ways.

[36] As Provan notes with respect to the intermingling of Solomon and the people, "Kings are characteristically models for and representative of the behavior of their subjects." Cogan unnecessarily takes an undefended stance that the plural is a mistake, "The original text was no doubt read with verbs in the singular." But Provan more appropriately understands the intentional, subtle implications in this text. Cf. Provan, *1 and 2 Kings*, 95; Mordechai Cogan, *1 Kings: A New Translation with Introduction and Commentary*, AB 10 (New York: Doubleday, 2000), 340.

Josiah, a long list of positive and negative examples is present. Without stating it definitively as imitation, these individuals are identified as sons of their fathers by their behavior and character. It would seem then that the metaphor operates as an idiom for the idea of imitation, or fatherly reflection.

As the metaphor relates to Proverbs, Josiah's description highlights three key, overlapping ideas. Although the phrase "turn right or left" is not accompanied directly by the phrases "walk in the whole way of his father" or "did right in the eyes of Yhwh," both ideas are central to the educational program of Prov 1–9 and do appear in various forms elsewhere in this section. Furthermore, as it was elucidated earlier, the proverbial son is expected to follow in the way of his father, which ultimately implies the way of Yhwh. Here in Lesson 8, at the center of the wisdom program, the son is given a highly instructive metaphor that only the wise and considerate son would understand. By evaluating his path, he must compare it with the path of those who came before to determine if he is indeed walking in the way of Yhwh and doing right in his eyes, as a wise son.

Conclusion

In Lesson 8, the son is instructed to reflect the active embodiment of the wise who pattern their lives on the ways of God, utilizing the dual metaphors of path and body. In all of his ways, the son is to adhere to and closely consider his persistence on the straight way, one that cannot be counterfeited (Prov 4:26–27). In doing so, he will become like God, one whose eyes are forward and who considers his way (cf. Prov 5:21). He will be a true son of his father and of David, along with all the wise and righteous examples who walk this path. He will become one after God's own heart, a heart that reflects the divine Father (cf. 1 Sam 13:14). As a benefit to this path, the son will find and be characterized by life (Prov 4:22), unlike the lifeless fate of foolish idolaters and their idols (cf. Ps 115:5–8). This central lesson, then, contributes to the deepening of the path metaphor in Prov 1–9 and its reflection of key concepts from elsewhere in the HB. While the straight-way metaphor has immediate value in this lesson, it primarily serves the whole wisdom program by subtly pointing the wisdom student to the path's underlying ancestral and divine source as well as its mortal significance. While the father's message is a positive encouragement in Lesson 8, he takes on a more negative tone in Lessons 9–13. This is primarily in order to make the son aware of the seductive dangers that will seek to lead him astray from the wise path.

LESSON 9

Analysis of 5:1–6
"The way of folly is death"

N ow that the son has received a substantial amount of positive instruction, the father moves the son through the darker side of the wisdom pedagogy in Lessons 9–13. Similar to the message of Lesson 5, the father teaches in Lesson 9 that aberrant ways are not only deleterious but are in opposition to Yhwh and life. Perhaps the greatest danger of this foolish path, however, is the deception and ignorance that characterize those who walk on it (Prov 5:3–4, 6). In order for the son to continue on the path of the wise, he will need to sharpen his wit and actively pursue the "path of life" (Prov 5:6). In Lesson 9, the father utilizes a primary foil initially introduced in Lesson 2 (Prov 5:3; cf. 2:16). This *zarah* serves as one of the father's key metaphorical threads throughout the wisdom program, one who seeks to lead the son away from the straight path of Lesson 8. Just as Wisdom assumes many rhetorical roles, the *zarah* embodies a variety of figures and ways that contrast with the divine path, collectively embodied by Woman Folly (Prov 5:5–6; cf. 7:25–27, 9:13–18). The father in Lesson 9 provides the son with an inverse or indirect instruction. He must consider the way of Yhwh and those who follow in his ways, unlike the *zarah* (Prov 5:5–6). While the positive examples seen up to this point are essential, the father understands the reality of deceptive influences that may entice the son to abandon the way of the righteous, leading him on the deadly path of fools. As a vital remedy, the son must instead listen to and emulate the father and Wisdom (Prov 5:1–2).

Structure of Lesson 9

As the shortest lesson, often enveloped into the next by scholars,[1] Lesson 9 has a fairly simple structure. In Prov 5:1–2, the father gives his familiar

---

[1] E.g., Whybray, Meinhold, Fox, Waltke, Loader, and Schipper. Delitzsch broke the sections into Prov 4:1–5:6 and 5:7–23. See "Structure of Prov 1–9" for further discussion.

introductory call (cf. 4:20). Then, Prov 5:3–6 provide a stark, though ambiguous, warning of the *zarah* (זָרָה) and her ways.[2] Ultimately, there is a contrast here between following the father's teaching and following the foreign woman.[3] Following the *zarah* will ultimately lead to death while, implicitly, following the father will lead to life.

In the ninth lesson, the tone of the pedagogical program takes a more negative turn. While negative warnings were also featured in the teaching of the first eight lessons (Lessons 1, 2, 5, 7), the second half of the program (Lessons 9, 10, 12, 13, 15) focuses largely on the destructive ways of the foreign, strange, adulteress woman, who is contrasted against Wisdom.[4] Thus, while much of the imitative imagery is positive in the first half, the second half is understandably contrasted in this respect. Despite this shift, a unifying continuity is found through the opening instructions given from the father to the son(s), found at the outset of all fifteen lessons. As mentioned in Lesson 8, this lesson begins with an identical call, only substituting "words" and "sayings" with "wisdom" and "understanding."[5] The father is directing and guiding the son to grow and develop into a wise man by focusing on the potential dangers along the righteous, wise path. Deviation from this proper path, as emphasized in the previous lesson, is tantamount to rebellion against Yhwh and his ways, a sure road to destruction.

---

[2] Despite the various views, Tan captures the overarching sense of this proverbial figure, "She is a representation of the way of 'foreignness' and apostasy; those who choose her ways therefore abandon the covenant of Yahweh." Similarly, she says that Prov 5 is "not about admonitions of fidelity to one's spouse as much as it is about fidelity to the 'true' Jewish community and Yahweh ... [foreign women] corrupt Israel and cause them to leave the ways of Yahweh." Regarding the variety of related terms for this figure, Schipper mentions, "The female figure ultimately symbolizes the deceptive potential of the wrong path ... contrasted in 5:18 with 'the wife of one's youth,' who represents the 'path of wisdom' and a proper relationship to God." See Nancy Nam Hoon Tan, *The "Foreignness" of the Foreign Woman in Proverbs 1–9: A Study of the Origin and Development of a Biblical Motif*, BZAW 381 (New York: De Gruyter, 2008), 87, 104–5; Schipper, *Proverbs 1–15*, 199.

[3] The contrastive parallel to Wisdom accumulates a number of related designations, metaphorically describing her with overlapping and familiar language: "foreign woman" (אִשָּׁה זָרָה), "stranger" (נָכְרִיָּה), "woman of evil" (אֵשֶׁת רָע), "woman of a neighbor" (אֵשֶׁת רֵעַ), "prostitution woman" (אִשָּׁה זוֹנָה), and "woman of folly" (אֵשֶׁת כְּסִילוּת) (Prov 2:16, 5:3, 6:24, 26, 29, 7:5, 9:13).

[4] The contrast with Wisdom also implies by extension the teacher and Yhwh. Estes provides a lengthy discussion of the possibilities for what *zarah* (זרה) may mean according to a number of scholars, often taken in a literal/historical sense. Fox is one who argues she is merely an adulteress type of person. However, Estes amply refutes this unnecessarily narrow view and describes the literary parallel she has with Wisdom, indicating the contrasting personification of Folly. As Perdue observes, she represents "a prostitute, a fertility priestess, an adulteress, a worshiper of a fertility goddess, and folly" and only "obedience to the wisdom of the teacher may preserve ... from the entrapment of this personification of folly, pagan religion and culture, and sexual misconduct." Murphy and Longman confirm this literary interplay between Wisdom and Folly as well. Additionally, Tan rightly identifies Wisdom as "symbolic of the way of Torah and piety leading to Yahweh." See Daniel J. Estes, "What Makes the Strange Woman of Proverbs 1–9 Strange?: Ethical and Unethical in the Old Testament: God and Humans in Dialogue," in *Ethical and Unethical in the Old Testament: God and Humans in Dialogue* (New York: T&T Clark, 2010), 151–69; Fox, *Proverbs 1–9*, 252–63; Roland E. Murphy, "Wisdom and Eros in Proverbs 1–9," *CBQ* 50.4 (1988): 603; Tan, *"Foreignness" of the Foreign Woman in Proverbs 1–9*, 104; Longman, *Proverbs*, 159.

[5] Cf. Müller, *Proverbien 1–9*, 86–87.

Imitation of Wisdom

By this point in the pedagogical program, the son understands he is to listen to the father by following in his wise ways. As it has been demonstrated elsewhere, there is often an overlay between the proverbial father with both Wisdom and Yhwh, often blurring the lines.[6] In the opening of Lesson 9, the son receives a familiar call to "consider" (קשׁב) and even "turn" (נטה) to his father's instruction (cf. Prov 4:20). However, while the resultative clause "to guard" seems innocuous (Prov 5:2), it in fact ties into a broader motif in Prov 1–9. First, throughout these chapters, there is a reciprocal relationship between the son and Wisdom. If he will seek and guard her, he will find and be guarded by her. This relationship was especially prominent in Lesson 2, which also implied an underlying relation with Yhwh. It is not until Prov 8:12, though, that 5:2 comes into imitative focus.[7] Here, Wisdom declares that she finds "knowledge and discretion" (וְדַעַת מְזִמּוֹת).[8] While *da'at* (דַעַת) is relatively common, the term for "discretion" (מְזִמָּה) is not. The terms together interestingly occur three times in Prov 1–9 (1:4, 5:2, 8:12). The first is in the prologue for the pedagogical program. The last is Wisdom's declaration of her own ways. Then, there is this middle occurrence at the shift in the program toward focusing on the *zarah*. It is instructive for the son to understand the contrast the father seeks to instill in him. Unlike the foreign woman, Wisdom is known by her honorable speech (Prov 8:6, 7, 8, 9, 13).[9] Thus, the son is to not only listen to her instruction, much like the father's, but he ought to follow her in her ways, becoming like her or even one with her. Discussing Wisdom's self-description, Perdue says, "Since Woman Wisdom herself walks in the paths of 'righteousness' and 'justice,' the rewards of material gifts are offered to the sages who seek to emulate her behavior and to follow her instruction" (cf. Prov 8:6–9, 20).[10] Thus, in parallel, the son must not only find "knowledge and discretion" as Wisdom has done but he must guard them too (Prov 5:2). In doing so, he will then be guarded by Wisdom (and discretion) from the "way of evil," "perverse speech," and the deadly path of the *zarah* (cf. Prov 2:10–13).

---

[6] According to Waltke, the father's identification of the teaching as "my wisdom ... understanding" is unique and reminiscent of Prov 2:6 from Yhwh. This implies literary and conceptual overlap between the two figures. Similarly, Longman says, "[The father's wisdom] is not to be differentiated from divine wisdom ... he is a conduit of divine wisdom to the son." However, Loader and Fox believe the unique phrasing merely implies the universality of the instruction. See Waltke, *Proverbs (1–15)*, 306–7; Longman, *Proverbs*, 158–59; Loader, *Proverbs 1–9*, 234; Fox, *Proverbs 1–9*, 190.

[7] Cf. Schipper, *Proverbs 1–15*, 200.

[8] In Prov 5:2, the terms are in a slightly different syntactical relation (מְזִמּוֹת וְדַעַת).

[9] On Wisdom's teaching here, Whybray rightly observes, "[These terms are] frequently used in the Old Testament of God and of those who conform their conduct to his standards" (Whybray, *Proverbs (1994)*, 123).

[10] Perdue, *Proverbs*, 142.

Following the Foreigner

After proposing the proper way, the teacher then launches into the bulk of the lesson, a very metaphorical and poetic warning. It seems the purpose is to highlight whom the son ought not to follow. The imagery utilizes a stark, affective contrast between sweet and bitter. This contrast on one hand parallels Lesson 7 in its light versus dark dichotomy.[11] However, in Prov 5:3–6, there is a twist. Unlike the light, the sweetness proposed here is in fact bitterness, despite its appearance. To accentuate the subtle deception, the teacher utilizes the literary pairing of "foreign" (זרה) and "smooth" (חלק), found in two other places as well (Prov 2:16, 7:5). The passage in Lesson 2 uses similar language and imagery to paint a parallel picture.[12] If the son will seek and find the ways of Wisdom and Yhwh, he will be delivered from the foreign woman (זרה) and her smooth (חלק) words (Prov 2:16). Likewise, it mentions that the *zarah* is marked by her rejection of God's covenant and will ultimately result in her descent to "death" (מָוֶת) far from the "paths of life" (אָרְחוֹת חַיִּים), which is indicative of God's ways (Prov 2:17–19).[13] Lesson 9, likewise, warns of the *zarah* and her descent to "death" (מָוֶת) and her failure to walk the "path of life" (אֹרַח חַיִּים), demonstrating the deception of her "smooth" speech (Prov 5:5–6). In Lesson 2, the warning was coupled with a positive inversion. There, the son was instructed not only to avoid the *zarah* and her ways but positively to walk in and "guard" the "paths" (אָרְחוֹת) of the "righteous" and the "good" (Prov 2:20). In other words, the son is to imitate the ways of those following the straight path and not those who are evil.[14] Similarly in Lesson 9, though without a positive alternative, the emphasis is essentially the same. He must not follow in the ways of the *zarah*, namely imitating her foolish and deceptive ways. In doing so, he will end up sharing the same reward with her. Fox rightly notes of the one following this woman, "Her twisted desire is an expression of her depravity. The death-loving wicked man has similar perverted values."[15] By this, Fox implies an imitative or reflective relationship between the wicked woman and those who follow her. Though less directly connected, this picture also mirrors the imitative implications of Lesson 1 and the sinners' demise (Prov 1:10–19).[16]

Embedded within this *zarah* warning, the teacher alludes to the deceptive nature of her words. The term "honey" (נֹפֶת) is relatively rare (Prov 5:3, 24:13, 27:7; Ps 19:11; Song 4:11). For the use in Prov 24:13, the context includes one of the few "my son" statements outside Prov 1–9. It also uses the term "honey" to describe the effects of "wisdom" on the son. More than that, by savoring wisdom as honey, the son will find life in perpetuity (Prov 24:14).

---

[11] Plöger not only sees the relation between metaphors but the entanglement between the ways of the wicked and the *zarah*. See Plöger, *Spruche Salomos (Proverbia)*, 54–55.

[12] Plöger, *Spruche Salomos (Proverbia)*, 54–55.

[13] Tan, *"Foreignness" of the Foreign Woman in Proverbs 1–9*, 87.

[14] Lyu, *Righteousness*, 74–75; Bruce C. Birch, "Moral Agency, Community, and the Character of God in the Hebrew Bible," *Semeia* 66 (1994): 32.

[15] Fox, *Proverbs 1–9*, 193.

[16] Cf. Tan, *"Foreignness" of the Foreign Woman in Proverbs 1–9*, 85–86.

Such imagery is essentially the inverse of the *zarah* in Lesson 9. Also, the term appears in a nearly identical phrase in Song 4:11, "Your lips drip honey, my bride" (נֹפֶת תִּטֹּפְנָה שִׂפְתוֹתַיִךְ כַּלָּה). In Lesson 9 (Prov 5:3), the phrase says, "For the lips of the foreign woman drip honey" (כִּי נֹפֶת תִּטֹּפְנָה שִׂפְתֵי זָרָה). Depending on the dating of these passages, it is possible that one drew language from the other.[17] Regardless, the imagery certainly overlaps between the two romantic situations, though one is understood positively and the other as deceptive. Finally, there is an interesting connection between Lesson 9 and Ps 19:11. The psalm is a well-known creation and wisdom poem. On one hand, it exalts God as the universal creator who imbued his creation with "knowledge," which continually proclaims his glory (Ps 19:1–3). It is important to note that the psalm explicitly states the metaphorical sense of nature's "speech" as "without words" yet it gives its voice nonetheless.[18] The second part of the psalm then expounds on the personal and covenantal side of God through the name Yhwh.[19] He is not only known in part by creation but relationally known through his *torah*, his instructive ways.[20] In this praise, the psalmist extols the value of God's ways in making one wise.[21] As part of this commendation, the psalmist uses the term "honey" (נֹפֶת) as a comparative descriptor for the *torah* of Yhwh.[22] In fact, the comparative language of "better than" in Ps 19 is found in a combination of imagery from Prov 3:13–18, 5:3, 8:10–11, and 8:19. Other than 5:3, the proverbial uses are comparative descriptors for Wisdom.

---

[17] For discussions on the connections between Prov 1–9 and Song of Songs, see Annette Schellenberg, "'May Her Breasts Satisfy You at All Times' (Prov 5:19): On the Erotic Passages in Proverbs and Sirach and the Question of How They Relate to the Song of Songs," *VT* 68.2 (2018): 259–63; Schipper, *Proverbs 1–15*, 196–97.

[18] The explicit use of "speech" and "words" in the metaphorical sense indicates that the terms in Prov 1–9 need not be taken in an overly literalistic way. The "words" and "speech" of the proverbial father and Wisdom need not be confined to a particular, proscribed curriculum but likely imply a more generic instructive purpose. Likewise, the "words" and "speech" of the *zarah* need not only be understood as actual seductive words from a prostitute or adulteress. Rather, the terms can be more poetically understood, whether explicit or implicit, pointing to the ways of the *zarah* or Folly.

[19] Benjamin D. Sommer, "Nature, Revelation, and Grace in Psalm 19: Towards a Theological Reading of Scripture," *HTR* 108.3 (2015): 390–91, 396–97.

[20] The term *torah* likely has a few connotations. In Ps 19, Sommer believes it "refers both to behavioral *torah* (it means 'law') and to that *torah* that embodies wisdom (it also means 'teaching'). And this *torah* is first of all a matter of covenant, a meaning that fits both the legal and pedagogical senses of the term" (Sommer, "Nature, Revelation, and Grace in Psalm 19," 380).

[21] Sommer makes an interesting distinction regarding the central issue being addressed in Ps 19. While pagan, polytheism was patently wrong, there was also the subtle sin of worshiping and praying to "the right God the wrong way." As he says in another way, "It is not apostasy but monotheism gone awry." This point seems instructive for Prov 1–9 as well. While there is certainly a clearly wrong way (apostasy), there is also a way that may seem right but is indeed just as wrong. See Sommer, "Nature, Revelation, and Grace in Psalm 19," 387–88.

[22] Sommer focuses on the sun imagery in Ps 19 as indicative of the pagan worship in non-Israelite religions. Yet, he notes with Mark Smith that this is likely not a polemic against polytheism or a rejection of Yhwh. Rather, there were Israelites that were worshiping the sun as Yhwh, a subtle aberration rather than a direct affront. See Sommer, "Nature, Revelation, and Grace in Psalm 19," 382–86; Mark S. Smith, "'Seeing God' in the Psalms: The Background to the Beatific Vision in the Hebrew Bible," *CBQ* 50.2 (1988): 171–83.

So, Prov 5:3 stands out in its negative connotation. Rather than describing the value of Wisdom (or *torah*), it serves to indicate that the ways of *zarah* are actually counterfeit. This distinction is important to notice. It is not merely that the ways of *zarah* are unfavorable but that they are an affront to the ways of Wisdom and even Yhwh.[23] Thus, the son is to be wise and able to discern not only the patently false and wicked way but also the "way that seems right to a man but her end is the paths of death (דַּרְכֵי־מָ֫וֶת)" (Prov 14:12, 16:25).[24]

The lesson concludes with an important imitative instruction in the last verse. Here, the father enlightens the son that despite the seemingly smooth ways of the *zarah*, she is ignorant and does not understand the folly of her path.[25] In Lesson 8, attention was given to the term "consider" (פלס). The word is paralleled with the son and Yhwh. The son was instructed to "consider" the path he is on, as does Yhwh (Prov 4:26, 5:21). However, the foil to this motif occurs with the *zarah* who does not.[26] In fact, she not only does not consider her path but she is marked by a general lack of knowledge. Grammatically, Prov 5:6b implies she does not know that her paths are aberrant. However, poetically, it is possible the father intentionally begins the verse with "paths of life" and ends with "she does not know" in order to imply that she does not know the paths of life.[27] Thus, she lacks both information and the desire to correct her ways. A similar attack occurs at the end of Prov 1–9 against Woman Folly, "She does not know what" (Prov 9:13).[28] This ignorance is likewise indicative of the one who follows her, "He does not know" (Prov 9:18). Of course, by Lesson 9 in the pedagogical program, the son is already well aware of the importance of knowledge and knowing, particularly as it pertains to following proper teachers. While wisdom is indeed central, knowledge is typically associated with divinity.[29] Thus, the way of ignorance

---

[23] As Tan argues, adultery and involvement with "foreign" women were not only against Torah (e.g., Exod 20:14, 34:15–16; Lev 18:20; Deut 5:18, 7:3–4, 22:22) but was understood as indicative of apostasy, particularly in the Torah and Deuteronomic literature (Tan, *"Foreignness" of the Foreign Woman in Proverbs 1–9*, 81–82, 87, 90, 95, 99, 103–5).

[24] The phrase meaning "her end" (וְאַחֲרִיתָהּ) is the same in Prov 5:4, 14:12, and 16:25 as well.

[25] The Heb. grammar for both תְּפַלֵּס and תֵדָע in Prov 5:6 could be either second masculine singular or third feminine singular. Thus, the verse could be a warning to the son or a description of the *zarah*. Considering its proximity and conclusive function along with similar language used elsewhere, it is preferable to understand this verse in relation to the *zarah* and her ways. Likewise, the use of פלס here gives a negative parallel contrasting the positive uses in Prov 4:26 and 5:21. For more on the view that is a warning for the son, see Whybray, *Proverbs (1994)*, 86; Murphy, *Proverbs*, 30; Tan, *"Foreignness" of the Foreign Woman in Proverbs 1–9*, 89–90; Loader, *Proverbs 1–9*, 237–38.

[26] Fox identifies the term "lest" (פֶּן) as a "negative optative." This sense retains the *zarah* as the subject but implies that she desires not to consider the "paths of life" (5:6). See Fox, *Proverbs 1–9*, 193.

[27] Fox identifies that some rabbinic interpretations (e.g., Tur-Sinai) have followed this view, though he believes the phrase "her ways wander" is the appropriate object due to proximity (Fox, *Proverbs 1–9*, 192–93).

[28] Cf. Arndt Meinhold, *Die Sprüche*, ZBK (Zürich: Theologischer Verlag, 1991), 102.

[29] "Knowledge" alongside wisdom serves as one of the close associates with divinity. "Fear of Yhwh is the beginning of *knowledge*" (Prov 1:7a). "For they hated *knowledge* and did not choose the fear of Yhwh" (Prov 1:29). "Then you will understand the fear of Yhwh and find

is necessarily in opposition to the way of God. As Lesson 7 conveyed through the metaphor of darkness, "The way of the wicked is like darkness; they do not know on what they stumble" (Prov 4:19).[30] The father, however, desires for the son to "guard knowledge" (Prov 5:2),[31] not merely for its pragmatic purpose but as a relational indicator. For the son to know and be full of knowledge implies proper alignment between himself, his father, Wisdom, God, and his ways.

Conclusion

After an attentive focus on the straight-way in Lesson 8, the son receives a short but intense lesson on a real and dangerous alternative path. While not new to the son, the father highlights the deceptive, even seductive, quality of this aberrant way (Prov 5:3–4). It is a path marked by counterfeit illusions and ignorance as well as a disregard for life and wise consideration (Prov 5:5–6). Tragically, the end of this godless path is death and Sheol. Yet, if the son will reflect the ways of the father, Wisdom, and Yhwh, he will instead be marked by knowledge and walk the "path of life," both of which are central to the divine path (Prov 5:6). At the start of the second half of the wisdom program, this little lesson packs a mighty punch by contrasting these two ways before the son. He can either emulate the *zarah* and her foolish ways or he can emulate Wisdom and her wise ways (Prov 5:2, 5–6). Choosing and maintaining the straight-way, however, will not be easy or automatic. He must continually adhere to the father's instruction (Prov 5:1–2) and consider his character, desires, and behavior in order to determine if he is indeed reflecting his father, Wisdom, and Yhwh. In continuity with this thread, Lesson 10 further emphasizes the destructive and unwise ways of the *zarah*. She represents the path of those who reject the father's *musar*, an instruction that ultimately comes from the divine Father and teacher.

---

the *knowledge* of God for Yhwh gives wisdom, from his mouth knowledge and understanding" (Prov 2:5). "In all your ways, *know* him and he will make your paths straight" (Prov 3:6). "The fear of Yhwh is the beginning of wisdom and *knowledge* of the Holy One is insight" (Prov 9:10).

[30] Cf. Fox, *Proverbs 1–9*, 194.

[31] A similar phrase occurs in Mal 2:7–8, "For the lips of the priest shall guard knowledge and they shall seek *torah* from his mouth for he is the messenger of Yhwh of hosts. But you have turned (סור) from the way, you have caused many to stumble in the *torah*, you have spoiled the Levite covenant." Although likely much later in dating, the prophet uses language very similar to Prov 1–9, particularly in relating the ideas *torah*, knowledge, the way, and turning. In fact, this rebuke immediately follows a commendation for Levi, presumably the tribe by his name, which says, "True *torah* was in his mouth and perversity was not found in his lips. In peace and uprightness, he walked with me and he turned many from guilt" (Mal 2:6). Here, it is explicit that there is a necessary correlation between following *torah* and walking with God in his ways. Interestingly, the emphasis on perverse speech in Malachi is likewise central in Prov 1–9, including Lesson 9. Also, Levi was commended for acting as a proper teacher for Israel, guiding her in the proper way.

LESSON 10

Analysis of 5:7–23
"The fool embraces disaster"

A fter reintroducing the highly negative *zarah* figure in Lesson 9 (Prov 5:3, 20; cf. 2:16), a thread that drives Lessons 9–13, the father provides a more balanced instruction for the son(s). Central to the wisdom program, the father encourages the son here in Lesson 10 to receive *musar* with joy and to maintain fidelity to the wise path (Prov 5:12, 23), just as he is to be faithful to a beloved spouse. As seen previously (Lessons 1, 4, 6), *musar* is a key thread that serves the son's growth along the wisdom trajectory. The wise path is not only beneficial, keeping the son from harm (Prov 5:9–11, 14, 22–23), but is indicative of those who know Yhwh and his way (Prov 5:12–13, 21). This form of fidelity will help him grow in the deeper more abstract ways of Wisdom and Yhwh, as well. On the other hand, the son is exhorted to flee from Folly, instead loving and embracing Wisdom (Prov 5:8, 19–23). In this pursuit, he will reflect not only his father and wise teachers but also Yhwh himself, the preeminent teacher and husband.

Structure of Lesson 10

The tenth lesson provides an illuminating extension of Lesson 9. In the father's desire to persuade the son(s) to follow his teachers, he divides the lesson into four structurally defined sections. It begins with the introduction and call (Prov 5:7). Then, an imperative starts the second unit with negative, hypothetical results (Prov 5:8–14). The third section uses a second imperative to give a positive charge (Prov 5:15–20). Finally, the lesson concludes with a summarizing warning marked with the causal "for" (כִּי) (5:21–23).

Furthermore, just as in Lesson 6, the first verse is set in the plural, while the rest of the lesson uses the singular.[1]

I.	Introduction & Call (5:7)
II.	Negative Imperative (5:8–14)
III.	Positive Imperative (5:15–20)
IV.	Warning (5:21–23)

The unit break at Prov 5:7 is not typically observed by scholars formally but does provide a useful opportunity for the author to poetically and thematically allude to several elements outside of Lesson 10. On one hand, the lesson continues thematically with the *zarah* warning, which extends through Lesson 13.[2] There is, however, a minor ambiguity at the beginning of Lesson 10 referencing "her" (Prov 5:8) without clearly providing who the father has in mind. The "stranger" (זָרָה) and "foreigner" (נׇכְרִיָּה) are not explicitly mentioned until nearly the end (Prov 5:20).[3] So, the pronoun at the start likely serves as both an anaphoric and cataphoric reference, thematically linking the two lessons.[4] However, despite this thematic link, there are elements that create important connections elsewhere, as well. In particular, as mentioned previously, Lesson 10 (Prov 5:7–23) is chiastically paired with Lesson 6 (4:1–9). Interestingly, the two lessons begin with unique and similar calls from the father: "Now, O sons, listen to me (וְעַתָּה בָנִים שִׁמְעוּ־לִי)" (Prov 5:7a) and "Listen, O sons, to fatherly *musar* (שִׁמְעוּ בָנִים מוּסַר אָב)" (Prov 4:1). Both reference the plural "sons" (בָּנִים) with a call to "listen" (שִׁמְעוּ). Similarly, the second introductory statement provides another close parallel, "Do not turn from the words of my mouth (וְאַל־תָּסוּרוּ מֵאִמְרֵי־פִי)" (Prov 5:7b). The grandfather also states in Lesson 6,

---

[1] The plural בָּנִים occurs four times in Prov 1–9 (4:1, 5:7, 7:24, 8:32). The LXX and Vulg. remove the plurals, likely for harmonization. The term אַל־תָּסוּרוּ in the second line of Prov 5:7 only occurs in one other curious passage, "Samuel said to the people, 'Do not fear; you have surely done all this evil. But you must not turn (אַל־תָּסוּרוּ) from after Yhwh and you must serve Yhwh with all your heart. You shall not turn (לֹא תָּסוּרוּ) after empty things which will not profit and will not deliver for they are empty'" (1 Sam 12:20–21). In this farewell address, Samuel seemingly alludes to the call from both Moses and Joshua regarding the straight-way motif with only slightly different language (Deut 5:32, 17:20, 28:14; Josh 1:7, 23:6). If the proverbial father indeed has the farewell of Samuel in mind, the initial call of this lesson would take on a far more substantive and authoritative tone. It would also directly connect the lesson with the broader straight-way motif from Lesson 8 and the kings of Israel. Cf. Schipper, *Proverbs 1–15*, 195.

[2] Cf. Longman, *Proverbs*, 157–58.

[3] Interestingly, the roots of these terms appear in the masculine form near the beginning of the lesson in Prov 5:10, "strangers" (זָרִים) and "foreigner" (נָכְרִי). The father's use here is perhaps indicative of his broader intent for the terms with metaphorical, literary implications.

[4] Schipper and Plöger argue for a thematic coherence for the whole of Prov 5. While certainly true, they along with most other scholars miss the subtle shifts and implications for Lesson 10's distinctiveness. See Schipper, *Proverbs 1–15*, 196; Plöger, *Spruche Salomos (Proverbia)*, 54.

"Do not turn from the words of my mouth (וְאַל־תֵּט מֵאִמְרֵי־פִי)" (Prov 4:5).[5] Thus, Lesson 10 begins with a composite call from both the father and grandfather of Lesson 6. In light of several important thematic parallels, the two lessons seem to contain not only unique terms and phrases but serve to further interpret each other. In order to ultimately propel the son towards Wisdom and the way of Yhwh, he utilizes the dangerous *zarah* theme from Lesson 9 to contrast the requisite fidelity theme of Lesson 6.[6] By refusing to listen to and imitate his positive exemplars (Prov 5:13), the son will lose his well-being and even his life (4:4, 5:23).

The Way of *Musar*

Just as Lesson 6 sets the tone with a call to listen to "fatherly *musar*," Lesson 10 likewise wraps the teaching around *musar*. Throughout Prov 1–9, the idea of *musar* is always positive and is identified as either "your father's" or "Yhwh's" (Prov 1:8, 3:11). Here, though, the term is used in a negative setting. As mentioned in the previous lesson, the second half of the pedagogical program tends to be more negative in its orientation, particularly with parallels from the first half. The father and grandfather had defined faithfulness to *musar* as faithfulness to Wisdom, who was pictured as a guardian wife (Prov 4:1, 5–9). Yet, at this point in the program, the lesson ends with an ominous statement, "He will die without *musar*" (Prov 5:23). The "he" here is likely referencing the "wicked" person of Prov 5:22. While this does not seem to directly implicate the son, the father does give a hypothetical warning if the son were to follow in the way of the *zarah*, "Then you will say, 'O how I hated *musar*'" (Prov 5:12).[7] In other words, the way of *zarah* is antithetical to *musar* and thus antithetical to life.[8] As described in Lesson 4,

---

[5] The nuanced interplay of the two terms for "turn" may additionally link this lesson with Lesson 8 and the interchange of these terms in the straight-way motif. Cf. Schipper, *Proverbs 1–15*, 204.

[6] Meinhold observes the parallel language between Lessons 6 and 10, which he likewise sees as a signal of the author's intent – a contrast between the way of Wisdom and the way of the *zarah* (Meinhold, *Die Sprüche*, 105).

[7] The father uses "lest" twice (Prov 5:9, 10) to set the hypothetical situation, serving as the potential result of not adhering to the stern command of 5:8. In Prov 5:15, a second imperative is used to mark the second half of the lesson.

[8] Waltke argues, "Will die (yāmût) refers to eternal death in opposition to the eternal life of the righteous, not merely to either a premature death (see v. 11) or clinical death. ... The immoral are robbed of life, which is rooted in the true love and loyalty found in God and his people both now and forevermore." As Holmes deftly remarks, "We ought not to yearn for what will one day pass away. Accordingly, our intellects must be trained to see temporal goods as signifying eternal goods. If we are to see rightly, we must progress morally, seeing all that is good in a temporal sense—for example, friendship—as pointing to and sharing in the absolute good. 'Moral progress' involves re-formed desire, the longing for gifts that are truly important." In this, he envisions God as the prime exemplar and goal. Thus, the fragmented and incomplete version of life experienced now is merely a foyer to the eternal progress of the wise and righteous in imitating God. See Waltke, *Proverbs (1–15)*, 324; Holmes, *Theology of the Christian Life*, 92.

the *musar* of Prov 1–9 is ultimately from Yhwh, as a father to his son (Prov 3:11–12). This means to hate *musar* is to hate Yhwh and his way. In similar language, Wisdom had said of fools that "they hate knowledge and do not choose the fear of Yhwh" (Prov 1:29). As an introduction to the program, knowledge and *musar* are overlayed with the centralizing statement, "The fear of Yhwh is the beginning of knowledge, fools despise wisdom and *musar*" (Prov 1:7).[9] Thus, the father teaches that the son must not follow in the way of the *zarah* because it is antithetical to the way of Yhwh – knowledge, wisdom, and *musar*.

Furthermore, the focus on *musar* is emphasized in the immediate verse (Prov 5:13). The father continues the hypothetical path of one who follows the *zarah* and rejects *musar*. Such a person would not only lament having rejected *musar* but also having disobeyed (לֹא־שָׁמַעְתִּי) and turned (נטה) from the teaching of his "instructors" (מוֹרַי) and "teachers" (מְלַמְּדָי). These two terms for "teacher" are rare in the HB, only occurring in six verses: (מְלַמְּדַי) Ps 119:99, Prov 5:3; (תַּלְמִיד) 1 Chron 25:8; (וּמוֹרֶךָ) Isa 30:20, Hab 2:18, Job 36:22, and Prov 5:3. Two of these are of particular relevance. Elihu says, "Behold, God is highly exalted in his power. Who is a teacher like him?" (Job 36:22). While "God" is not used in Prov 5, the author of Job clearly understood God to be the perfect and preeminent "teacher," whom all human teachers merely imitate to a lesser degree.[10] Second, the psalmist praises the *torah* of Yhwh in Ps 119:97–104. The core intent of the passage is to show the superiority of God's *torah* to all other instruction, including from his human teachers (Ps 119:99). Yet, the passage does not demean the role of a teacher. God himself is described several verses later as the psalmist's ultimate teacher (Ps 119:102).[11] Interestingly, the psalmist declares at the end of the unit (Ps 119:104) that he hates every false path (שָׂנֵאתִי כָּל־אֹרַח שָׁקֶר). This hate is of course the exact opposite of the one described in Prov 5:12–13, who hated *musar* (or knowledge in 1:29). Following the straight-way motif, the psalmist also mentions, "I did not turn (סור) from your judgments" (Ps 119:102). The "turn" metaphor plays a central role in identifying righteous or wicked leaders throughout Kings and serves to identify those who are wise or foolish in Proverbs. In Lesson 10, these "teachers" are not clearly identified but from the rest of Prov 1–9 would at least include the father, grandfather, Wisdom, and Yhwh.[12] If the diachronic perspective for the plural "sons" is in view (Prov

---

[9] Loader, *Proverbs 1–9*, 249.

[10] Cf. Schipper, *Proverbs 1–15*, 208.

[11] While Yhwh is not clearly referred to as a "teacher" in Lesson 10, the father subtly alludes to his guiding role. As discussed in Lessons 8 and 9, the language of considering (פלס) one's ways is linked to the son, the *zarah*, and Yhwh (Prov 4:26, 5:6, 21). The son is instructed to "consider" his path. The *zarah* does not "consider" her path. But Yhwh does "consider," likely in an instructor-type capacity for both the son and mankind generally.

[12] The LXX changes these terms to singular. While the father is one of his teachers, he is not the only one. Schipper, however, takes the terms in an overly scholastic sense, perhaps due to his late dating of the material. Rather than specific terminology for a "type of professional group," the terms imply the multiplicity of legitimate instructors along the son's path, which may have included formal teachers as well. Fox and Waltke rightly view the terms as generic for any instructive figure, whether formally or informally. Meinhold takes a neutral stance. Cf.

5:7),[13] this would also imply the fatherly lineage of all those who have followed in the ways of Yhwh throughout the generations.

In the second major section of the lesson (Prov 5:15–20), the father focuses on positively encouraging fidelity rather than merely avoiding the unchaste ways of the *zarah* (5:8, 20). To do this, he envelops his instruction with the language of intimacy and marriage. The metaphor seems to propel a triple entendre (or three referential implications).[14] These referents are fidelity to a spouse, Wisdom, and Yhwh (or his *torah*).[15] On a very basic, mundane level, the son is to observe *torah* regulations for fidelity to a spouse.[16] Yet, the passage does not merely instruct the son to obey but to "rejoice in the wife of his youth" (Prov 5:18). The relationship is to be one of passion and pursuit rather than drudgery and restriction. It is perhaps no surprise, then, that language from Song of Songs finds several parallels here.[17] The proverbial father begins with an ambiguous discussion about water (Prov 5:15–18), which may imply sexual connotations.[18] However, the father seamlessly moves into clearly intimate imagery of a sensual, marital relationship (Prov 5:18–20).[19] While the term "spring" (מַעְיָן) in Prov 5:16 often carries the literal sense, Song of Songs utilizes it with a relational and perhaps sexual connotation (Song 4:12). Also, much like the use of "breast" (שַׁד) in Song 4:5, the proverbial father uses an uncommon term for "breast" (דַּד) to heighten the sensual desire of the son (Prov 5:19). As Schellenberg argues, eroticism need not be intellectualized or spiritualized away since it is not inherently negative but a positive desire in the proper framework of fidelity.[20] Thus, the father's base level instruction is for the son to learn and practice fidelity with his wife, a failure lamented in the prophets as well (e.g., Mal 2:14). If the son

Fox, *Proverbs 1–9*, 198; Schipper, *Proverbs 1–15*, 208; Waltke, *Proverbs (1–15)*, 315; Toy, *Proverbs*, 110; Meinhold, *Die Sprüche*, 104.

[13] See Lesson 6 for further discussion. Waltke argues for the diachronic transmission but Loader is skeptical, preferring the general or universal intent (Waltke, *Proverbs (1–15)*, 276, 311; Loader, *Proverbs 1–9*, 238–39).

[14] Schipper notes the tri-level intent of the passage as well. Also, Steen provides an interesting discussion on polyvalent metaphors and reader comprehension. See Gerard Steen, "How to Do Things with Metaphor in Literature," *RBPH* 68.3 (1990): 658–71; Schipper, *Proverbs 1–15*, 213–14.

[15] Schipper refers to these three levels as the "erotic/sexual level," "sapiential knowledge," and the "religious dimension" (Schipper, *Proverbs 1–15*, 215–16).

[16] See the discussion in Lesson 9.

[17] On this point, Schellenberg remarks, "The thesis that these connections are all coincidental is no longer convincing." For a discussion and resources on the numerous connections between Song of Songs and Proverbs, see Schellenberg, "'May Her Breasts Satisfy You at All Times' (Prov 5)," 259–60.

[18] Fox, *Proverbs 1–9*, 199–201; Paul A. Kruger, "Promiscuity or Marriage Fidelity: A Note on Prov 5:15–18," *JNSL* 13 (1987): 61–68; Waltke, *Proverbs (1–15)*, 319.

[19] For a study on water imagery and its gendered place throughout ancient iconography, see Carole R. Fontaine, "Visual Metaphors and Proverbs 5:15–20: Some Archaeological Reflections on Gendered Iconography," in *Seeking Out the Wisdom of the Ancients: Essays Offered to Honor Michael V. Fox on the Occasion of His Sixty-Fifth Birthday*, ed. Ronald L. Troxel, Kelvin G. Friebel, and Dennis R. Magary (Winona Lake: Eisenbrauns, 2005), 185–202.

[20] Schellenberg, "'May Her Breasts Satisfy You at All Times' (Prov 5)," 257.

could not manage this basic form of covenantal faithfulness, he could not possibly uphold the more ethereal and religious forms.[21]

In a subtle but clever sapiential way, the father alludes to the second layer of his lesson, fidelity to Wisdom.[22] As discussed in Lesson 6, the paired lesson persuades the son to pursue Wisdom as one would a wife, even to obtain her just as Yhwh had.[23] Lesson 10 in Prov 5:19–20 makes this connection through the uncommon term "embrace" (חבק).[24] While Lesson 6 used this term in the positive for Wisdom, Lesson 10 turns it negative as an absurd hypothetical. Rather than be "inebriated" (שׁגה) by the *zarah* and "embrace" her, he ought to be "inebriated" by his wife.[25] Likewise, in similar language, he is to be satisfied by his wife's love just as he is called to love Wisdom (Prov 4:6, 5:19). Of course, Wisdom herself later explicitly states, "The one who loves me, I will love ... there is an inheritance for the one loving me" (Prov 8:17, 21). However, this marital imagery for the sake of fidelity not only extended to Wisdom as a wife but ultimately in fidelity to Yhwh's covenant way.[26] In Lesson 14, the author describes Wisdom as Yhwh's "delight" (שַׁעֲשֻׁעִים) and helper (Prov 8:30).[27] While not explicitly marital (cf. Gen 2:18), in light of Lessons 6 and 10, it is suggestive of Yhwh's relation with Wisdom,[28] meant as a metaphorical example for the son to follow. Furthermore, as Schipper mentions, "In light of the Deuteronom(ist)ic tradition and the marriage metaphor in the book of Hosea, the statements in Prov 5:18–19 could be interpreted as alluding to one's relationship to God."[29] To arrive at this view, he rightly sees the intentional parallel or contrast between the *zarah* and the

---

[21] Murphy states regarding the dual intent of the lesson, "Fascination with the 'stranger' destroys a double love: the love for one's wife, and also for Wisdom" (Murphy, *Proverbs*, 33; Fox, *Proverbs 1–9*, 205).

[22] As Murphy remarks, "If the youth is guided by wisdom, he will catch those characteristics and refuse to be caught himself." Though he does not explicitly refer to the imitative reflection of Wisdom, his teacher, the notion of guidance and catching onto characteristics embodied within Wisdom certainly leads to this conclusion. See Murphy, *Proverbs*, 34; Schipper, *Proverbs 1–15*, 210; Schäfer, *Die Poesie der Weisen*, 147.

[23] See the discussion in Lesson 6. Also, Murphy, *Proverbs*, 279.

[24] It is only used twice in Proverbs (4:8, 5:20).

[25] Zalcman argues that there was an intentional poetic play on two very similar roots, used in Prov 5:19 and 20. The term שׁגה almost always has a negative use, such as "stagger," "stray," or "inebriated." However, the nearly identical lexeme שׂגה is used positively for "grow" or "increase." Thus, the son ought to "increase" in his love for the wife (5:19) and not be "inebriated" by the *zarah* (5:20). The argument is quite plausible, though the poetic play could apply from either root. See Lawrence Zalcman, "Prov 5,19c," *ZAW* 115.3 (2003): 433–34.

[26] McKane demurs the final verses (Prov 5:21–23) as ad hoc and a late edition for a Yahwistic re-interpretation of an otherwise mundane, untheological lesson on sexuality. However, there is no clear evidence that the various parts existed separately or that Yahwism is somehow incompatible with the multifaceted metaphor being used throughout by a masterful, ancient literati. Longman rightly argues here for Yahwistic continuity throughout Prov 1–9. See McKane, *Proverbs*, 312–13; Longman, *Proverbs*, 164–65.

[27] It is perhaps not surprising this rare term for "delight" is mostly found in Ps 119: "your *torah* is my delight" (119:77); "If your *torah* was not my delight then I would perish in humility" (119:92); "your *mitsvot* are my delight" (119:143); and "I desire your salvation, O Yhwh; your *torah* is my delight" (119:174).

[28] Cf. Fontaine, "Visual Metaphors and Proverbs 5:15–20," 187.

[29] Schipper, *Proverbs 1–15*, 197.

"wife of your youth (נְעוּרִים)" in Lesson 10 with the *zarah* who "abandons the companion of her youth (נְעוּרִים) and forgets the covenant of her God" in Lesson 2 (Prov 2:16–17).[30] This connection implies that the *zarah* stands for foolish infidelity generically and is contrasted with the fidelity of the wise. In a hopeful prophecy for Zion, Isa 62:4–5 utilizes this fundamental, marital metaphor for God's relation to Israel, "You shall be called 'my delight is in her' and your land will be married, for Yhwh delights in you … as a bridegroom rejoices over a bride, your God will rejoice over you." As Isaiah declared, God is the preeminent example of a faithful husband who pursues and delights in his covenantal wife.[31] The son, therefore, is to admire and follow in his ways, both in the literal and figurative sense.

At this point, it should be emphasized that the literal level of the marital imagery in Prov 5 need not be perceived as mutually exclusive to the metaphorical reference to Wisdom or Yhwh.[32] The prophet Hosea presumably had a real wife who was caught up in promiscuity and prostitution (Hos 1:2–3, 3:1–3). Yet, it is the literal nature of the image that provides gravity for the metaphorical significance of Israel's infidelity to Yhwh. Thus, the father sought to infuse the importance of fidelity with real, understandable language for a young man. This form of fidelity is a visible and tangible signal to those more difficult, internal forms along the straight way. In this vein, Lesson 1 implies that the father and mother are together, serving as an exemplary image of faithfulness as well (Prov 1:8; cf. 4:3, 6:20, 10:1). In other words, they did not abandon the spouse of their youth nor the covenant of their God. Rather, they upheld and walked in *torah* and *musar*, as those of whom they were children by character and deed.[33] As core to the way of Yhwh, the son is to imitate his parents (and grandparents) in his marital fidelity, his love and affection for Wisdom, and by following the ways and *musar* of Yhwh.[34]

The Way of Folly

Although the illusory seduction by the *zarah* seems prominent in this lesson, it is not the focus.[35] The allusion to infidelity merely serves as a contrast or

---

[30] These connections may also help coordinate the unusual terms in the proverbial context – "assembly" (קָהָל) and "congregation" (עֵדָה) – indicating fidelity or infidelity for both a civil and religious setting. See Schipper, *Proverbs 1–15*, 115–18, 197–99; Whybray, *Proverbs (1994)*, 92.

[31] Cf. Longman, *Proverbs*, 164.

[32] Cf. Fox, *Proverbs 1–9*, 204.

[33] See Lesson 8 for more discussion on the straight-way motif and identification with historical figures based on one's reflection of their character, behaviors, and desires.

[34] As Schipper mentions, "The relationship to God is expressed through the image of marriage. Thus, 5:18 deals not only with the contrast between the 'strange woman' and one's own wife but also—on a deeper theological level—with the question of the correct relationship to God" (Schipper, *Proverbs 1–15*, 212).

[35] Schipper observes too that the focus is not on sexual immorality but as he states a "lack of sapiential competence" (Schipper, *Proverbs 1–15*, 215).

foil to the father's lesson on fidelity. However, similar to Lesson 9, the *zarah* way is painted in frightful and undesirable language. The son must not only pursue the way of Wisdom and Yhwh but must actively avoid turning onto destructive paths.[36] As with the literal level of marital delight, there is also the literal level of infidelity, discussed more in Lessons 12 and 13. The father's warning that the son will only receive loss, pain, and bitterness through infidelity is a real possibility. Yet, the warning in this lesson ought not to be left on the mundane level alone. As bookends to the lesson, the father mentions two phrases that indicate Folly is at the heart of this *zarah* way.[37] The first is with the inaugural imperative, "Stay far from her way and do not draw near to the door of her house (אֶל־פֶּתַח בֵּיתָהּ)" (Prov 5:8). In the last section of Lesson 15, the father warns that "Woman Folly (אֵשֶׁת כְּסִילוּת) ... sits at the door of her house (לְפֶתַח בֵּיתָהּ)" (Prov 9:13–14).[38] The cataphoric reference illuminates the heart of the *zarah* path here. She not only stands for adulterous behavior and infidelity but for the way of Folly broadly, the counter to following Wisdom.[39] In light of this, the loss, pain, and bitterness envisioned are not only the result of infidelity but of foolishness generally. The term for Woman Folly (כְּסִילוּת) is only found in Lesson 15 in the HB (Prov 9:13). However, its root "fool" (כְּסִיל) occurs numerous times, though almost exclusively in Proverbs and Qoheleth. In Lesson 1, Wisdom identified "fools" as those who "love simplicity," "delight in scoffing," and "hate knowledge" (Prov 1:22). Similarly, she says, "The turning of the naïve will kill them and the security of fools will destroy them" (Prov 1:32). The language of turning to her way and house is also seen at the start of Lesson 14 (Prov 7:24–27) and the end of Lesson 15 (9:13–18). Lesson 14, as will be discussed later, transitions from the seductress woman's warnings to the delightful Woman Wisdom. The father warns that the son must not "turn to her ways" because "her house is the ways of Sheol" (Prov 7:25, 27). Similarly, Woman Folly calls for the naïve or those walking on the "straight (upright) path" to "turn here," referring to the door of her house. Yet, her house is in reality the gate or path to the "valleys of Sheol" (Prov 9:14, 15, 16, 18). As mentioned, this language and imagery parallels the *zarah* in Prov 2:16–19 as well. So, the father of Lesson 10 masterfully ties the mundane to the sagacious without relegating one or the other. Instead, the son is instructed negatively not to follow after those who are on the way of Folly. Imitating them will only lead to his death and destruction, which is in opposition to Yhwh and Wisdom.

To conclude the lesson, the father alludes to this broader motif of the "fool" by condemning one who lacks *musar*, "He is inebriated (שׁגה) by his great

---

[36] Cf. Schipper, *Proverbs 1–15*, 206.

[37] Schipper notes the generic and multifaceted implication of the *zarah* stating, "The female figure ultimately symbolizes the deceptive potential of the wrong path" (Schipper, *Proverbs 1–15*, 199).

[38] Perdue notes that these references may allude to a prostitute/adulterer's house, a pagan temple, or the "metaphorical world of folly and wickedness, where death dwells." In reality, they may implicate all three, as noted elsewhere. See Perdue, *Proverbs*, 120–21.

[39] Longman, *Proverbs*, 163. The imagery of Prov 5 is primarily sexual in nature while the imagery in Prov 9 is likely cultic, though they overlap in language and intent.

foolishness" (Prov 5:23).[40] The term "foolishness" (אִוֶּלֶת) differs from "fool" (כְּסִיל) or "Folly" (כְּסִילוּת) used elsewhere and actually only appears here in Prov 1–9.[41] However, the term is directly paralleled with "fool" later in Prov 13:16, "The prudent act in knowledge but a fool (כְּסִיל) displays his foolishness (אִוֶּלֶת)." The use in Prov 5 is then a subtle signal to the broader motif. The final term "stagger" (שׁגה) was used positively for delight in one's wife and negatively for embracing the *zarah*. So, not only is infidelity the way of Folly, but the son also learns that rejection of *musar* is as well. The connection with following in the way of the *zarah* (implicitly Folly) is further highlighted by the father's use of the term "held fast" (תמך). The term appears in Prov 5:22 and 5:5. In 5:5, it is said that the steps of the *zarah* "held fast" (תמך) to Sheol. Similarly, the "wicked" is said to "be held fast" (תמך) by his sin (Prov 5:22). Thus, the father explicitly links the way of the *zarah* with the way of the wicked. While there is perhaps a sense of characterization associated, the heart of the path metaphor implies that the son ought not follow or imitate the wicked in the *zarah* way. In doing so, he would in essence be rejecting fidelity and the *musar* of the father, Wisdom, and Yhwh.

Conclusion

The primary desire within Prov 1–9 is, of course, to promote growth in wisdom. However, one of the primary tools and terms used to bring the son into alignment with Wisdom is *musar*. While it is mentioned in previous lessons (Prov 1:8, 3:11, 4:1), the vital importance of *musar* is highlighted as a necessary prophylactic against the deceptive and deadly ways of the *zarah* in Lesson 10 (Prov 5:8–13, 20, 22–23). Instead of embracing the *zarah*, the son is to joyously embrace his spouse and the father's *musar*. Likewise, the *musar* mentioned in this lesson is not merely from the father but from all those faithful teachers who have either directly or indirectly provided guidance for the son in the way of fidelity (Prov 5:12–13). According to this instruction, the wisdom student must walk in faithfulness to his spouse, emulating God's own faithfulness to his bride Israel (Prov 5:15–19). Yet, at a deeper level, he is encouraged to flee from Folly and instead pursue Wisdom (Prov 5:8, 19–20, 23; cf. 4:6–8). By walking on this path of fidelity, the son will not only reflect his wise teachers but Yhwh himself, the ultimate example of a husband and teacher. After this explicit lesson on fidelity, the father moves the son to observe a more subtle example in Lesson 11. In a modest thematic break from the *zarah* theme, the son is taught that the wicked man who does not embrace Wisdom and the father's *musar* is on a relational descent away from Yhwh into abject ostracization.

---

[40] The term for "inebriated" or "stray" (שׁגה) only occurs in this lesson for Prov 1–9 (5:19, 20, 23).

[41] Goldberg notes the synonymous use and overlap of these terms, though the term אִוֶּלֶת tends to have a moral quality to the foolishness rather than a merely intellectual or neutral one (Louis Goldberg, "אִוֶּלֶת," in *TWOT* (Chicago: Moody, 1999), 20).

LESSON 11

Analysis of 6:1–19
"Yhwh is against the wicked"

After focusing on the necessity of fidelity and *musar* in Lesson 10, the father paints a jarring picture for the son using a stark compilation of images in Lesson 11. Although foolishness is problematic and does not yield the fruit that it purports (Prov 6:9–15), there is yet a greater danger in that foolish path. Just as the righteous walk in the way of and emulate Yhwh, the foolish and wicked are in opposition to Yhwh (Prov 6:16). Thus, they are outside of his covenantal and relational protection, receiving the end they have earned. As a countermeasure, the father gives the son lowly yet instructive examples to follow, which indirectly point him to greater examples (Prov 6:5, 6). By following concrete, even simplistic figures such as ants and gazelle, the son will learn not only how to avoid numerous disasters and snares along the foolish path but he will also begin to reflect Yhwh and will persist in proper relation to him. The wise path, then, is an upward trajectory toward Yhwh, while the foolish path is a descent toward becoming one of the wicked and abominable that God hates (Prov 6:12, 16). In Lesson 10 relational fidelity was explicit, but here in Lesson 11, it is more implicit, though still fundamental.

Structure of Lesson 11

Couched between four lessons focused on *zarah* warnings, Lesson 11 may seem like a disjointed break. This lesson does not discuss or warn of the *zarah* and her deathly ways as do Lessons 9, 10, 12, and 13.[1] Furthermore, the lesson seems to be a hodgepodge of randomly placed wisdom sayings, akin to Prov

---

[1] For clarification, Lesson 12 does not mention the *zarah* but does discuss the theme, instead using the terms "evil woman" (אֵשֶׁת רָע) and "stranger" (נָכְרִיָּה). The latter term is of course paralleled with the *zarah* elsewhere (Prov 2:16, 5:20). Lesson 11 is distinct from those surrounding it in its glaring absence of any allusion to sexuality.

10–31.[2] In fact, the peculiarity of this unit has been so perplexing for scholars that Murphy declared, "There is no connection among them," implying the sections within Lesson 11 are merely late, haphazard insertions.[3] At this point in the program, however, the careful placement and consideration of all prior and following lessons lead to the opposite conclusion. What may seem an aberration to cursory observation instead promotes continuation and connection, even beyond the lesson itself.[4] First, it is important to note that this lesson parallels Lesson 5, as discussed previously. On this level alone, there are several components of this lesson that parallel the prior lesson. Second, though there is not a *zarah* (זרה) warning, the lesson begins (Prov 6:1) with a conditional clause based on a parallel between "neighbor" (רֵעַ) and "stranger" (זָר). Though subtle, this opening provides continuity with the surrounding lessons yet with distinction. The masculine form of "stranger" only occurs elsewhere in Prov 1–9 in Lesson 10 where it is used for the potential recipients of the fool's household.[5] Likewise, the term "neighbor" is only found in Lessons 5, 11, and 12. The use in Lesson 12 (Prov 6:29), though, is an off comment for the fool who commits adultery with his neighbor's wife. Thus, the opening of Lesson 11 provides both an important lexical bridge and thematic break between units.[6]

Despite this bridge, there is a change in literary cohesion. Until this point, the only lessons with a clearly segmented structure are Lesson 1 (Prov 1:8–19, 20–33) and Lesson 4 (3:11–12, 13–17, 18–19). Yet in both, the thematic continuity is still reasonably clear. Here, though, Lesson 11 divides into four distinct thematic units. While continuity is still present, it is less apparent.

---

[2] C. F. Keil and Franz Delitzsch, *Commentary on the Old Testament*, rev. ed. (repr., Peabody: Hendrickson, 1996), 6:97; Stuart Weeks, *Instruction and Imagery in Proverbs 1–9* (New York: Oxford University Press, 2007), 224–25.

[3] Fox wrongly calls it a "miscellany with little direct bearing on the lectures." See Roland E. (Roland Edmund) Murphy, *Wisdom Literature: Ruth, Esther, Job, Proverbs, Ecclesiastes, Canticles* (Eerdmans, 1981), 59; R. N. Whybray, *The Composition of the Book of Proverbs*, JSOT 168 (Sheffield: JSOT, 1994), 48–49; Michael V. Fox, "Ideas of Wisdom in Proverbs 1–9," *JBL* 116.4 (1997): 616.

[4] Harris refers to the literary patterning contained as "mimetic representation." He draws from Sternberg who saw a need for different modes of information, ordering, and expression to be represented through different mediums or modes giving different effects. As he says, "The ordering imposed on the unordered is a representational ('mimetic') junction where art, world, and language meet ... Action and description are not so much discrete segments as functions of discourse – representational ('mimetic') functions that relate to complementary aspects of the world" (72–73). With this, Harris uses Sternberg's observations to coordinate the disjunctive sections of Prov 6:1–19 as an intentional whole. See Scott L. Harris, *Proverbs 1–9: A Study of Inner-Biblical Interpretation*, SBLDS 150 (Atlanta: Scholars, 1996), 126–34; Meir Sternberg, "Ordering the Unordered: Time, Space, and Descriptive Coherence," *Yale French Studies*.61 (1981): 60–88.

[5] Arndt Meinhold, *Die Sprüche*, ZBK (Zürich: Theologischer Verlag, 1991), 108.

[6] The break may orient the son's understanding of the *zarah* warnings or avoid overemphasis of the sexuality metaphor. Cf. James Alfred Loader, *Proverbs 1–9*, HCOT (Leuven: Peeters, 2014), 251.

Each unit of this lesson is marked by the coordinating subject of its content: "my son" (Prov 6:1, 3), "sluggard" (6:6, 9), "worthless man" (6:12), and "abomination" (6:16). The first two sections are linked with the idea of "sleep" (שֵׁנָה) as well as a lesser-to-greater metaphor using animals (Prov 6:4–5, 6–10).[7] The second and third units are linked with an undesirable result "coming" (בוא) as the result of foolish ways (Prov 6:11, 15). The third and fourth units are linked by a number of body imagery terms and the same unique phrase "one who sows discord" (Prov 6:14, 19).[8] Furthermore, in the literary flow, there is a relational movement from near to far,[9] serving as a poetic device to illuminate the descent of the foolish way into abject opposition to Yhwh. The initial address is "my son," which is stated twice.[10] This doubled address to "my son" (Prov 6:1, 3) only occurs elsewhere in Lesson 1 (1:8, 10, 15) and Lesson 10 (5:7, 20). It implies knowledge, concern, care, and personal interest, perhaps even hope for a return to the wise path. The second figure addressed is the "sluggard," which is specific – second masculine singular with a doubled address, as well (Prov 6:6, 9) – but not as personal. Here, there is concern and perhaps hope for such a person, but it is not as intimate as the first filial call. The third section merely references the ways of a "worthless man" in a third-person description, coming across as very generic and impersonal. Finally, the fourth section is completely disconnected, serving as a general declarative statement of actions and individuals with no relation to the father or Yhwh. This hopeless and conclusive fate of the wicked parallels the end of several earlier lessons (Prov 2:22, 4:19, 5:6, 22–23).[11]

---

[7] Though necessarily distinct, the metaphorical concept is a literary device perhaps akin to the later interpretive and philosophical tools *qal wahomer*, *a minori ad maiorem*, and *a fortiori*. See Richard N. Longenecker, *Biblical Exegesis in the Apostolic Period*, 2nd ed. (Grand Rapids: Eerdmans, 1999), 52; Michael V. Fox, *Proverbs 1–9: A New Translation with Introduction and Commentary*, AYBC 18A (New York: Doubleday, 2000), 216.

[8] Shipper notes the unity between these units, citing Delitzsch's three-unit schema. See Bernd U. Schipper, *Proverbs 1–15: A Commentary on the Book of Proverbs 1:1–15:33*, Hermeneia (Minneapolis: Fortress, 2019), 218; Keil and Delitzsch, *Commentary on the Old Testament*, 6:97; Bruce K. Waltke, *The Book of Proverbs: Chapters 1–15*, NICOT (Grand Rapids: Eerdmans, 2004), 341.

[9] Cf. Otto Plöger, *Spruche Salomos (Proverbia)*, BKAT 17 (Neukirchen-Vluyn: Neukirchener Verlag, 1984), 65–66; Meinhold, *Die Sprüche*, 108; Whybray, *Composition of the Book of Proverbs*, 51. These scholars note the progressive movement in seriousness but do not mention the relational distancing.

[10] Loader and Meinhold note the double address to both "my son" and the "sluggard" (Prov 6:1, 3, 6, 9). This connection further draws the units together, perhaps illuminating the cause of the duplicate "my son." See Loader, *Proverbs 1–9*, 251; Meinhold, *Die Sprüche*, 108–9, 113–14.

[11] Cf. Waltke, *Proverbs (1–15)*, 329; Meinhold, *Die Sprüche*, 108.

Through the literary flow, there is a palpable and intuitive sensation of growing danger, climaxing in the utter "hate" (שׂנא) of Yhwh,[12] which may itself be a play on the term "sleep" (שׁנה) signaling cohesion across the lesson. Of course, the term for "hate" occurs a few times in Prov 1–9 from fools (Prov 1:22, 29, 5:12, 8:36, 9:8) or from Yhwh and Wisdom (6:16, 8:13). It is intriguing that what one hates defines, or perhaps manifests, which path they are on.[13] In parallel language, Wisdom states, "The fear of Yhwh is hatred of evil. I hate pride, arrogance, an evil way, and a mouth of perversity" (Prov 8:13). Much of this language is used to describe the ways of a "worthless man" or the abominations that Yhwh hates here in Lesson 11. This connection further amplifies the intimate overlay between Yhwh and Wisdom, on one hand, and the utter separation for those who do not follow in their ways. As Wisdom poetically defines, "All who hate me have loved death" (Prov 8:36). In the proverbial program, hating wisdom is to hate her ways and to hate her ways is to hate Yhwh and his ways. The father of course desires for his son to be wise, that is, to walk in the way of Yhwh, Wisdom, and himself. Thus, in a clever and subtle way, the author weaves together a deep and profound lesson for the son, both in its complex literary connections and its weighty theological implications.

Hope for the Son and a Sluggard

While much could be said of this lesson, several elements are of particular interest to this study. To begin, the proverbial father wants the son to be wise, that is, able to avoid the many traps and aberrations along the way. The danger in the first section is not only of giving a pledge (Prov 6:1; cf. 11:15, 17:18, 20:16, 22:26, 27:13) but also the frivolity of one's word and oath, "If you are caught in the words of your mouth" (6:2).[14] The final two sections (Prov 6:12–19) emphasize God's disdain for false or deceptive words as well. In the Torah, though, the topic of proper oath-making and keeping is an important social feature (e.g., Lev 27, Num 6, 30, Deut 23). Although it is permitted, the examples of Joshua (Josh 9:14–16), Jephthah (Judg 11:29–31, 35), and Saul (1 Sam 14:24–30), among others, warn against vows, particularly for rash

---

[12] In Mal 1:2–3, Yhwh is said to "hate" Esau but "love" Jacob. The terms seem to imply relationship rather than emotion or hostility. Jacob was chosen as the conduit of God's covenant. Esau was not. Later the NT's reflection on this narrative implies it was due to Esau promising his birthright in a rash, unwise agreement. In the words of Lesson 11, he was caught in the words of his mouth, an early negative exemplar of rash deals. The proverbial son was not to emulate Esau and his ways.

[13] As Harris mentions, "The character of the 'man' is manifested by their speech or actions" (Harris, *Proverbs 1–9*, 119).

[14] Numbers 30:2 states, "If a man vows a vow to Yhwh or swears an oath, to a binding vow, according to his soul he shall not defile his word; according to all that has proceeded from his mouth he shall do" (cf. 30:3–15). Schipper notes that the term "snare" (יקשׁ) was used connotatively in reference to idolatry in Deut 7:25, which uses the term "abomination" (תוֹעֵבַת) immediately after. Likewise, it is perhaps important that two of the three places "snare" is used with "captured" (לכד) are in Isa 8:15 and 28:13 (Schipper, *Proverbs 1–15*, 222).

ones.[15] The inherent danger is that the finite knowledge and power of a human could not provide any true guarantee of outcome. [16] Only God had the knowledge and power to perfectly make and keep an oath (e.g., Num 23:19). Likewise, pledges have a history of limits and danger, particularly in Genesis (cf. Exod 22:25–27; Deut 24:10–13). Judah gives a "pledge" to Tamar after using her as a prostitute (Gen 38:17–20). Also, during the Joseph episode in Egypt, Judah once again vows himself as a "pledge" to return with Benjamin (Gen 43:8–9, 44:30–34). Of course, in both instances, he is caught by his pledge and words.[17] Despite being the patriarch of the Davidic monarchy, Judah serves as a glaring negative exemplar in this regard. In an indirect way, then, the son is instructed not to imitate Judah, Joshua, Jephthah, or Saul by making vows or pledges. This characteristic is associated with a foolish and dangerous path, as attested by biblical history.

To further highlight the incredulity of this dangerous endeavor, the father once again turns to a lesser-to-greater metaphor. The first instance of this appears in Lesson 1 (Prov 1:17–18). There, wicked men who seek to ambush and spill innocent blood are analogously shown to be more foolish than birds. In a similar metaphor, the proverbial father in Lesson 11 uses two animals in precarious situations that are able to evade the schemes of hunters.[18] In Prov 6:5, the son is commanded to "be delivered," paralleled with the same term (הִנָּצֵל) in the initial coordinating command of 6:3 (cf. 2:12, 16).[19] Thus, the animal metaphor is intended to expand on his primary warning. What is most important, however, is the literary function of the metaphor. As

---

[15] Cf. David A. Hubbard, *Mastering the Old Testament: Proverbs* (Waco: Word Books, 1989), 97–98.

[16] Fox, like others, takes this in a somewhat simplistic manner, focusing on the relationship around the "surety" or pledge. While pledges and loans could be seen as handing power over to another, in the context of this unit there is more concern over the son getting trapped in any deal or vow more generally. The animal metaphor does not imply a particular view of pledges but the evasive abilities of the gazelle and bird to elude traps. Whether in word or pledge, the son ought to avoid binding deals which as a finite being he cannot guarantee. See Fox, *Proverbs 1–9*, 213–16.

[17] Harris makes a lengthy case for the inner-biblical allusion from this passage to the Joseph narrative in Genesis. While the allusion is difficult to determine with certainty, he is not alone in his view. Several writers from the rabbinic period made similar connections (*Gen. Rab.*, XCIII:1; LXXXIV:18; *Yal. Sh. Misle Shlomo*, 6:1–5). For further discussion, see Harris, *Proverbs 1–9*, 111–57.

[18] As Day notes, the use of animal proverbs in proximity to the numerical proverb is similar to portions of *Ahiqar* (70–100). The dating of this ANE wisdom may indicate its familiarity with Proverbs or the universality of these forms. See John Day, "Foreign Semitic Influence on the Wisdom of Israel and Its Appropriation in the Book of Proverbs," in *Wisdom in Ancient Israel: Essays in Honour of J. A. Emerton*, ed. Robert P. Gordon, H. G. M. Williamson, and John Day (New York: Cambridge University Press, 1995), 64–65; James H. Charlesworth, *The Old Testament Pseudepigrapha and the New Testament* (New Haven: Yale University Press, 1985), 2:498–99; Schipper, *Proverbs 1–15*, 220.

[19] Although Schipper says this verse does not deal with a "higher form of sapiential knowledge," it is perhaps the exact opposite in light of the intra-textual connection with Lesson 2. The fact that "deliver" (נצל) only occurs in both of these lessons points the son toward the ultimate source of deliverance, Yhwh and his instruction. Lesson 2 implied preemptive deliverance while Lesson 11 hypothesizes about post-error deliverance. See Schipper, *Proverbs 1–15*, 223.

discussed in Lesson 1, this type of metaphor appeals to the son's most basic and concrete level of comprehension. Furthermore, it relies on a fundamental, though implicit, wisdom hierarchy view of the world from highest to lowest: Yhwh/Wisdom, the father/wise, creatures, and then fools.[20] In this way, the son is not only to look to the lesser as an object lesson but also ultimately to seek the greater. In other words, the novitiate may not be able to understand the ways and deep things of God, but he should at least be able to observe the simple ways of creatures. However, if he is not able to understand even these simple things or refuses to consider them, he will inevitably go the way of the fool. As the metaphor would imply, a fool is more foolish than a gazelle or bird who are able to avoid hunters.[21] While the gazelle and bird are not necessarily the intent of the lesson, they do serve as a mediating example. The son ought to be like or imitate the gazelle and bird who are wily and hard to capture.[22] Of course, the ultimate goal is for the son to be so wise that he is never snared. In the finite human state, it is most wise to simply avoid pledges and vows, since it is only God in his perfection who can guarantee his word (cf. Matt 5:33–37). As the psalmist declared, "Your word is established in the heavens forever, O Yhwh" (Ps 119:89). In context, the psalmist states that his salvation from those who seek to ambush him rests in his knowledge of God and trust in his word (Ps 119:94–95). The lesson here in Prov 6 is that the son will be less like Judah, Jephthah, and Saul and more like the father and Yhwh.

With rhetorical intentionality, this type of metaphor is used again in the following verse (Prov 6:6). Here, the proverbial father states, "Go to the ant, O sluggard, see her ways and become wise" (cf. Prov 30:24–28). [23] Although the previous metaphor used the comparative preposition "as" (כְּ) to relate the animals to the son, the father explicitly directs the sluggard in this example to observe and do.[24] Without an exact Heb. equivalent for "imitate," this is about as close as one could get.[25] As Whybray rightly observes, the creatures are a "model to be imitated."[26] The father perceptively understood what pedagogical scholars have stumbled upon over the last eighty years.[27]

---

[20] Waltke notes, "The sluggard is useless ... who stands far below the animal, which does not need a reproach." As Waltke alludes, the sluggard places himself beneath animals in the wisdom hierarchy by acting unwise. See Waltke, *Proverbs (1–15)*, 336.

[21] Hubbard, *Proverbs*, 98.

[22] Cf. Waltke, *Proverbs (1–15)*, 335. Though difficult to capture, these animals could be outsmarted of course.

[23] The term for "ant" (נְמָלָה) only occurs in Prov 6:6 and 30:25. Daube makes an interesting though loose case that the two passages allude to the "pre-monarchic period" and to "Saul and David." See D. Daube, "A Quartet of Beasties in the Book of Proverbs," *JTS* 36.2 (1985): 386.

[24] As Harris observes, "The sluggard who fails to model himself upon the industrious ant will meet poverty." Fox calls the ant a "paragon of enterprise." Schipper calls the ant a "role model." See Harris, *Proverbs 1–9*, 121; Fox, *Proverbs 1–9*, 216; Schipper, *Proverbs 1–15*, 219.

[25] Forti notes, the sluggard was to observe, internalize, and imitate. Loader similarly states that "humans [are to] imitate ants." See Tova Forti, *Animal Imagery in the Book of Proverbs*, VTSup 118 (Leiden: Brill, 2008), 12, 103–4; Loader, *Proverbs 1–9*, 263).

[26] Whybray, *Composition of the Book of Proverbs*, 50.

[27] Adrian E. Hinkle, *Pedagogical Theory of Wisdom Literature: An Application of Educational Theory to Biblical Texts* (Eugene: Wipf & Stock, 2017), 11.

Three crucial steps underlie the basis of human learning: observe, remember, and imitate.[28] However, the father obviously does not want the son to merely imitate ants.[29] Rather, it is intended as a lesser-to-greater metaphor that would point the son toward both the underlying principle and those human examples who demonstrate their wisdom through their hard work and preparation.[30] Of course, it is also understood that Yhwh is not a sluggard. In fact, he does not sleep or slumber at all (Ps 121:3–4). As 1 Kgs 18:27 intimates, Elijah mocked the prophets of Ba'al on the possibility that their god(s) was sleeping and needed to be awakened (1 Kgs 18:27). The implication is that Yhwh God is not like their god(s) but is always eternally and eminently aware. In this regard, he is the polar opposite of the sluggard who is characterized and captured by sleep. Thus, the son is to reflect Yhwh to the degree it is proper for a finite human to do. In doing so, he would be industrious and not lazy, qualities of the wise and Yhwh.

Regarding the principle of hard work and preparation, the Joseph story arises with some parallels.[31] The term for "ruler" (מֹשֵׁל) is used of him, both as a boy and as the governor of Egypt (Gen 37:8, 45:8, 26).[32] Likewise, his wisdom was renowned (אֵין־נָבוֹן וְחָכָם כָּמוֹךָ), particularly due to his adherence

---

[28] Hinkle notes three steps derived from educational scholarship, "Because observation is the first critical step in social cognitive learning, the ability of the learner to notice the modeled behavior is a crucial component of the process. Furthermore, the degree to which the learner focuses his or her attention contributes to the propensity to commit the action to memory. The second stage in learning through modeled behavior is memory retention. Once a learner notices a behavior, it must be committed to memory for it to be later imitated. Biehler and Snowman suggest the memory may solely include the behavior itself or may encompass the behavior as well as its rationale. Third, the modeled behavior must be reproduced or imitated. Finally, the behavior must be reinforced. As previously stated, this reinforcement may take place directly (affecting the learner himself) or vicariously (affecting someone else with a similar behavior). Both direct and vicarious reinforcement produce similar affects for memory retention and determining whether the behavior is repeated based on the negative or positive reinforcement" (Hinkle, *Pedagogical Theory of Wisdom Literature*, 27).

[29] Forti observes, the purpose is to teach "diligence in pursuit of an ordered and upright life" (Forti, *Animal Imagery in the Book of Proverbs*, 103).

[30] Regarding the ant lesson, Schipper states that "simply observing nature allows one to achieve the same goal [as] educative wisdom." While natural revelation has its role, that is not the rhetorical function of these types of metaphors or this passage. Instead, they are intended to be a rebuke, as Hubbard rightly understood. In other words, if even an ant has some wisdom, how much more should a human, let alone someone supposedly walking on the path of Yhwh. It must be remembered that these metaphors occur as a result of unwise behavior not as the first lesson in their studies. Forti finds that Menachem Meiri understood the rebuke aspect of this proverb as well. See Schipper, *Proverbs 1–15*, 225; Forti, *Animal Imagery in the Book of Proverbs*, 104; Hubbard, *Proverbs*, 99.

[31] Loader and von Rad enumerate many parallels between the Joseph narrative and Proverbs. However, Loader is skeptical of its value specifically in this passage, by virtue of dilution. He prefers to see the Joseph narrative as influenced by Proverbs or its "sapiential mentality" instead. However, it seems unnecessary to create an absolute intertextual dependence here rather than, as he coins, a certain "sapiential mentality" and perhaps "pedagogical mentality" that is sourced and predicated on the historical Joseph narrative of which Judah was part as well. See Loader, *Proverbs 1–9*, 254–55; Gerhard Von Rad, "Josephsgeschichte und ältere Chokma," in *Congress Volume: Copenhagen 1953*, vol. I of *VTSup* (Copenhagen: Brill, 1953), 120–27.

[32] Daube, "A Quartet of Beasties in the Book of Proverbs," 381–82.

to God's word and purity of ways (Gen 41:39). Because of this, he was like the ant who prepared ahead of time for famine and provided security for the masses during the time of scarcity (Gen 41:1–57). Whether or not the proverbial author intended an allusion to the Joseph story, this patriarch certainly would have served as a positive exemplar in Israelite history. He was not rash but humbly and wisely followed in the ways of Yhwh. Joseph, and others like him, would have been the greater example for the son ultimately to imitate, to which the ant served only as a metaphorical signal.

Furthermore, in this ant-metaphor, it is important to consider the father's additional line, "Which do not have a chief (קָצִין) or officer (שֹׁטֵר) or ruler (מֹשֵׁל)" (Prov 6:7; cf. Hab 1:14).[33] The force of the lesser-to-greater metaphor here is the fact that these tiny, non-human creatures are able to do all that they do with such wisdom yet are not forced or commanded to do so.[34] In a similar lesser-to-greater metaphor, Isaiah begins his prophetic book by indicting Judah as less obedient or more foolish than an "ox" and a "donkey," who know and presumably obey their master (Isa 1:3).[35] So, on the wisdom hierarchy, these livestock are above Judah. Then, in a proverbial type call, Isaiah goes on to say, "Hear the word of Yhwh, O chiefs (קָצִין) of Sodom, give ear to the *torah* of our God, O people of Gomorrah" (Isa 1:10).[36] Following this, he explains as the mouthpiece of Yhwh that the people's cultic practices are a wasteful burden because he ultimately desires proper justice. He lists several of their offenses, similar to those found in Prov 6:12–19, alongside his desire for positive traits that are also expected from the proverbial father throughout Prov 1–9 (Isa 1:10–31). While unforced adherence to the ways of Yhwh is the desire, Ezekiel prophesies that this would only happen when Yhwh will one day remove the people's hearts of stone and place his Spirit within them (Ezek 11:19–20, 36:25–32; cf. Deut 30:6; Jer 31:33). After this, they would loathe their prior "abominations" and instinctively walk in his ways, much like the ants and all creation do (Ezek 36:27, 31; e.g., Ps 19:2; Job 38–41). For the proverbial father, the commands of the Torah are only helpful markers along the way of Yhwh, which involve the whole person, including their will. As the ant is willfully wise and industrious so the son ought to be.[37] Furthermore,

---

[33] Healey notes that the term for "chief" (קָצִין) may have originally been "harvest" (קָצִיר). In his view, this would harmonize the later teaching from Jesus regarding the birds who do not harvest yet are preserved (Matt 6:26). While this view may fit in the LXX, as even he notes, it would not fit the context of Prov 6 in the MT. Rather, the two passages are using a lesser-to-greater metaphor in very different ways. As Jones rightly observes, they are "quite antithetical" though likely echoed on purpose. In Jesus's teaching, there is no sense of imitation. But, in Prov 6, the son or sluggard is specifically intended to imitate the animals. See John F. Healey, "Models of Behavior: Matt 6:26 (//Luke 12:24) and Prov 6:6–8," *JBL* 108.3 (1989): 2; John N. Jones, "'Think of the Lilies' and Prov 6:6–11," *HTR* 88.1 (1995): 175–77.

[34] As Waltke notes, "The ant possesses a God-given wisdom to work." It may also be appropriate to say an instinctively God-*reflective* wisdom and work ethic. See Waltke, *Proverbs (1–15)*, 337.

[35] As Fox notes, this connection was observed by 13th c. rabbinic scholar Menachem Meiri as well (Fox, *Proverbs 1–9*, 216).

[36] Cf. Waltke, *Proverbs (1–15)*, 337.

[37] As Fox rightly observes regarding desire or will, "Wisdom has an attitudinal or emotional as well as an intellectual component. That is why the son is urged not only to learn

just as Yhwh operates without compulsion, so the wise son is to do likewise. In doing so, he will more properly reflect the character, desires, and behaviors of his father along with all the sages who had come before him.

A Hopeless Man of Abomination

Although the first two sections (Prov 6:1–5, 6–11) are relatively hopeful in their orientation, the last two are quite negative (6:12–15, 16–19). Despite warnings against pledges and being a sluggard, the father uses the lesser-to-greater metaphor to provide simple yet positive examples to follow. For these latter examples, they serve only for negative contrast. According to the hierarchy, fools and the wicked are at the bottom, even beneath creatures. Thus, to an extent, the description of a "worthless man" also serves as a lesser-to-greater metaphor to highlight the worst place to be. Likewise, his impersonal description works as a foil to point the son toward those who are noble and worthy to emulate.[38] More than that, he serves as the metaphorical embodiment of all that Yhwh hates (cf. Ps 11:5).[39]

In a subtle but clever way, the father weaves together the seemingly distinct units for the "worthless man" and the "abominations." In both sections, the term "devise" (חֹרֵשׁ) appears (Prov 6:14, 18), only occurring elsewhere in Prov 1–9 in Lesson 5 (3:29). As mentioned, the unique phrase "one who sows discord" (מְשַׁלֵּחַ מְדָנִים) appears in these two sections and only once elsewhere in the HB (Prov 6:14, 19, 16:28). The term "wicked" (אָוֶן) only occurs in these two sections in Prov 1–9 (6:12, 18). Furthermore, both sections use similar imagery and language: a crooked mouth, a lying tongue, a heart that devises evil, deceptive or proud eyes, feet bent toward evil, and hands or fingers used for deception and death (cf. Prov 1:11, 16; Isa 59:7).[40]

---

wisdom but to love and desire it (4:6–8). Wisdom is a configuration of soul; it is moral character. And fostering moral character, it is no overstatement to say, it is at all times the greatest goal of education. It is also the greatest challenge, for moral character comes down to desiring the right things, and how can we teach desire? The author of the lectures tries to do so, in part, by delivering his thoughts through an affective rhetorical persona, that of the father" (Fox, "Ideas of Wisdom in Proverbs 1–9," 620). Of course, the teacher's persuasive use of affective rhetorical persona extends beyond the father figure, including the animal kingdom in this passage.

[38] Meinhold calls this character "a paragon of evil" (der Ausbund von schlechtigkeit), implying the character's use as a negative role model (Meinhold, *Die Sprüche*, 108).

[39] Cf. Schipper, *Proverbs 1–15*, 233; Meinhold, *Die Sprüche*, 108–9.

[40] Cf. Plöger, *Spruche Salomos (Proverbia)*, 65; Loader, *Proverbs 1–9*, 270; Leo G. Perdue, *Proverbs*, IBC (Louisville: John Knox, 2000), 126.

	Worthless Man	Abominations	
6:12	a crooked (עִקֵּשׁ) mouth	a lying tongue	6:17
		a false witness	6:19
		who breathes out lies	
6:13	winks his eyes	proud eyes	6:17
6:13	signals his feet	feet hurry to evil	6:18
6:13	teaches with his fingers	hands shed blood	6:17
6:14	a perverse heart that devises evil	a heart that devises wicked plans	6:18
6:14	one who sows discord	one who sows discord	6:19

Clearly, the father intends to give the son a sharp example of one he must not become nor emulate. McKane calls him a "model of malevolence." [41] By imitating a "worthless" or "wicked" man, he would likewise become an abomination.[42] As discussed in Lesson 5, this was ultimately understood as social and relational ostracization from Yhwh.[43] The term for "worthless" (בְּלִיַּעַל) is found a number of times throughout the HB. However, in the story of Eli, his sons are described as "sons of worthlessness" (בְּנֵי בְלִיַּעַל), which is immediately connected to the statement, "They did not know Yhwh" (1 Sam 2:12). By calling them "sons of," the author implies that they are characterized by their foolish and wicked ways rather than implicating Eli their father to be evil.[44] In fact, by giving this separation of paternal relation, it implies that they did not reflect or imitate the ways of their biological father but instead emulated those who practice wickedness (e.g., Deut 13:14, 15:9; Judg 19:22, 20:13). This pattern parallels those in 1–2 Kings who reflect good or bad kings, as discussed in Lesson 8. Likewise, to know Yhwh is to walk in his ways. So, they demonstrate their lack of knowledge and affiliation by walking in evil and reflecting their true, wicked fathers.

In a contrasting example, a Davidic psalm that mixes the words of the psalmist and Yhwh has similar language to Lesson 11, exemplifying a positive alternative. In Ps 101, the psalmist says that he considers and walks in the

---

[41] William McKane, *Proverbs: A New Approach*, OTL (London: SCM, 1970), 325.

[42] The numerical proverb type (e.g., "six ... seven") is only attested a couple of times in the HB (e.g., Prov 30; Amos 1–2; Hos 6:2). While there are no examples in Egyptian wisdom, Day notes the occurrence in Ugaritic and West Semitic wisdom (cf. KTU 1.4.III.17–21; *Ahiqar* 92–93). See Day, "Foreign Semitic Influence on the Wisdom of Israel and Its Appropriation in the Book of Proverbs," 64; Nicolas Wyatt, *Religious Texts from Ugarit*, BibSem 53 (London: Sheffield Academic, 2003).

[43] Meinhold notes there is a sense of "incompatibility" (unvereinbar) with him. Similarly, Whybray says, "It destroys the possibility of a positive relationship with Yahweh." See Meinhold, *Die Sprüche*, 115; R. N. Whybray, *Proverbs: Based on the Revised Standard Version*, NCBC (Grand Rapids: Eerdmans, 1994), 100.

[44] Martens refers to this use as "people or items belonging in a category or group" (E. A. Martens, "בֵּן," in *TWOT* (Chicago: Moody, 1999), 114). Also, although Eli is not directly indicted for evil ways as his sons are, he does receive rebuke and judgment for improperly teaching and leading his sons in the way of Yhwh (1 Sam 2:29, 3:14).

pure (תמים) way and that he turns (סור) from a crooked (עקש) heart (Ps 101:2, 4).[45] Also, he says that he hates (שׂנא) evil deeds and will not set his eyes on a "worthless" (בְּלִיַּעַל) thing (Ps 101:3).[46] Finally, as a summary he says that he will not know evil (Ps 101:4). The second half of the psalm could be from the perspective of Yhwh or the psalmist, who reiterates disdain for those who lie, deceive, and are proud (Ps 101:5–8; cf. Prov 6:12–19). This psalm engenders the type of person whom the father in Prov 6:1–19 would have lauded as a proper example to follow. Similarly, the psalms attributed to David in 2 Sam 22–23 capture much of the proverbial father's sentiment as well, "I kept the ways of Yhwh ... I did not turn (סור) from his statutes. ... with the crooked (עקש) you are harsh ... God is pure (תמים) in his way" (2 Sam 22:22, 23, 27, 31; cf. Prov 2:21).[47] Near the end of these psalms, he adds, "The worthless (בְּלִיַּעַל) are cast away like thorns" (2 Sam 23:6). In light of these psalms, there is a sense that the son ought to reject the path of the "worthless" man in order to walk in the "pure" way of Yhwh. By doing so, he would walk the righteous path as a son of his father and David instead. As motivation, the end of these paths is completely opposite. In Prov 6:15, the "worthless" man will find disaster suddenly (cf. 3:25). Yet, David proclaims that "God made an everlasting covenant" with him which was "guarded" (2 Sam 23:5). Thus, the foolish way is marked by suddenness, insecurity, and disaster due to separation from God.[48] Yet, the way of the wise is marked by eternity, security, and relationship with God. In the latter part of Proverbs, a cluster of verses seem to reiterate this, "The path of life is upward for the prudent, to turn (סור) from Sheol downward. Yhwh tears down the house of the proud ... evil plans are an abomination of Yhwh" (Prov 15:24–26).[49] Opposite to the

---

[45] Longman notes the proverbial parallels in this psalm (Tremper Longman III, *Psalms: An Introduction and Commentary*, TOTC (Nottingham: IVP, 2014), 350).

[46] Cf. Waltke, *Proverbs (1–15)*, 342.

[47] Longman and Youngblood note the connections between 2 Sam and Ps 101 (Longman, *Psalm*, 351–52; Ronald F. Youngblood, "1, 2 Samuel," in *The Expositor's Bible Commentary: 1 Samuel–2 Kings*, ed. Tremper Longman III and David E. Garland, Rev. ed. (Grand Rapids: Zondervan, 2009), 581).

[48] In Prov 6:11 (6:10–11 // 24:33–34), the final phrase of this verse has eluded translators due to its odd usage. The phrase "your lack (will come) like a man of shield" (וּמַחְסֹרְךָ כְּאִישׁ מָגֵן). As Fox notes, there has been uncertainty with the term "shield" seemingly parallel to "your poverty will go/come as a wanderer" (6:11a). He argues that it should be read from the Ug. root meaning "to beg," or here a "beggar man." Loader instead says that it "can only mean an armed man," emphasizing the speed and indefensibility of the sluggard's fate. While Fox's view is uncertain, the lexeme in Heb. was certainly a common term for "shield," also serving as a common metaphor for Yhwh (e.g., Prov 2:7, 30:5; cf. Gen 15:1; Deut 33:29; Ps 33:20, 59:12, 84:10, 115:9–11, 119:114, 144:2). The Davidic psalm in 2 Sam 22:3, 31, and 36 calls God a "shield" as well (מָגֵן הוּא לְכֹל הַחֹסִים בּוֹ), almost identical to Prov 30:5. Perhaps in a play on words and/or usage (Prov 2:7 // 6:11), the proverbial father alludes to the insecurity of the sluggard in contrast to Yhwh's security. The implication, of course, would be that God is a מָגֵן in the positive, protective sense but the sluggard is a מָגֵן in the negative, beggar sense. See Fox, *Proverbs 1–9*, 217–18; McKane, *Proverbs*, 324; Loader, *Proverbs 1–9*, 265.

[49] Waltke discusses the "path of life" of this passage and its implications, "The rewards of righteousness from present joy to everlasting life in relationship with the LORD. The path (see 1:15, 19) of life refers to the state or condition that affects everlasting fellowship with the living God. Leads [lit. "is"] upward as an antithesis to downward in connection with the grave

progression of this lesson, the proverbial father desires for the son to instead ascend the trajectory of wise exemplars even to Yhwh himself, who is the source of life and its path (cf. Ps 16:10–11).

Conclusion

Through several lesser-to-greater metaphors, the father instructs the son in Lesson 11 to be like the wise. By following the wise, he will avoid not only the disasters of folly but the many harmful snares along that foolish path. Positively, the son is to learn from the wise behaviors of even simple creatures, such as ants and gazelles (Prov 6:5, 6). Negatively, he must not imitate the ways of the "sluggard" or the "worthless man," who is an abomination to Yhwh (Prov 6:6, 9, 12, 16). While relational infidelity is the explicit focus of Lesson 10, this lesson espouses the same sentiment against infidelity to Yhwh. This form of infidelity, though, is presented through negative association with the "worthless man." Therefore, just as the son is instructed to pursue fidelity by following his teachers in Lesson 10, couched in the image of marriage, he is instructed in Lesson 11 to pursue fidelity by imitating wise examples, ultimately manifesting God's own ways. Although the dangers of foolishness are presented as internal and personal snares here in Lesson 11, the deceptive and seductive ways of the *zarah* are again highlighted in Lessons 12 and 13.

---

implies eternal life above and beyond the grave." In contrast, "The plans of an evil person (see 1:16) are an abomination to the LORD (see 3:32). Repulsed by them, the LORD withdraws his beneficent presence, abandoning the wicked to a certain and eternal death (cf. 1:20–33; 6:16–19; cf. Ps. 1:6)" (Waltke, *Proverbs (1–15)*, 634–37).

LESSON 12

Analysis of 6:20–35
"Torah is the path of life"

A fter an important thematic hiatus with Lesson 11, the father returns to the theme of relational and sexual fidelity.[1] Lesson 12 saturates the son's imagination with relatable metaphors and imagery. Yet, just as in Lessons 9 and 10, the father ultimately intends Wisdom and Yhwh to be the underlying focus of his training (Prov 6:20–23, 34–35). The strange woman, also called an "evil woman" here, is merely a foil to the instruction (Prov 6:24). Just as Yhwh is the leader and teacher of Israel, Wisdom too guides and instructs the son (Prov 6:22). Similarly, though, just as the son's ancestors were prone to apostasy by imitating the nations, the father knows that the proverbial son is also in danger of leaving the "path of life" (Prov 6:23). To counter this aberration, Lesson 12 connects the path of life to the *torah* and "commands" of the father, which contrast the ways of the "foreign" and "evil" woman (Prov 6:24–33).

Structure of Lesson 12

The goal of Lesson 12 seems to be tri-level, as it was in Lesson 10. Certainly, the son is not to be physically and socially unfaithful or adulterous, which would be against the Torah and end in real trouble (Prov 6:29, 32–35; cf. Exod 20:14; Lev 20:10; Deut 5:18, 22:22, 24).[2] Instead, the son is expected to be

---

[1] Cf. Roland E. Murphy, "Wisdom and Eros in Proverbs 1–9," *CBQ* 50.4 (1988): 603; Roland E. Murphy, *The Tree of Life: An Exploration of Biblical Wisdom Literature*, 2nd ed. (Grand Rapids: Eerdmans, 1996), 17–18.

[2] The exact phrase from Prov 6:29, "neighbor's wife" (אֵשֶׁת רֵעֵהוּ), appears nine times in the HB (Lev 20:10; Deut 22:24; Jer 5:8; Ezek 18:6, 11, 15, 22:11, 33:26; Prov 6:29), all of which refer to violations of the Torah way. It is also important to note that at the end of the list of unlawful behaviors of Lev 20 it states, "You shall not walk in the customs of the nations I am casting out" (Lev 20:23). The verse implies the imitative path Israel must not walk, which is central to the proverbial pedagogy and intent as well. Cf. Meinhold, *Die Sprüche*, 117.

faithful to Wisdom and the wise path, which finds its end in Yhwh and his "way of life" (Prov 6:23; cf. 2:19, 5:6, 10:17, 15:24).[3] To get the son to see this instruction, the father creates a three-part lesson.[4] The first portion is a positive command, intended to highlight the role and value of *torah* and *mitsvah* (Prov 6:20–24). Then, the father gives a negative command, which is meant to parallel the first (Prov 6:25–31). Finally, as a general statement, the father gives a wise, prophetic, and Torah-adherent expectation concerning the adulterous way (Prov 6:32–35).

    I.   Positive Command: follow *torah* and *mitsvah* (6:20–21)
        a. Result – Reason – Purpose (6:22–24)
   II.   Negative Command: resist the evil woman and stranger (6:25)
        a. Reason – Analogy (6:26–31)
  III.   Declarative Statement: adultery is foolish and dangerous (6:32)
        a. Result – Reason (6:33–35)

The lesson's theme and interpretation are signaled by a key structural feature. Functioning as an inclusio for the first section,[5] the father parallels *torah* and *mitsvah* with "evil woman" and "stranger" (Prov 6:20, 24).[6] By giving the parallels in this way, he provides the antithetical poles of his instruction. If the son guards *torah,* he will be guarded against the "stranger" and instead find life. But if he chooses the "stranger," he will be destroyed (Prov 6:20–25, 32). The son can only choose one path. As the father intends, the son ought to walk in the way of *torah*, that is, the "way of life" and Yhwh.[7]

---

[3] Perhaps surprisingly, the exact phrase used "way of life" (דֶּרֶךְ חַיִּים) only occurs here in the HB. Its close equivalent (אֹרַח חַיִּים) is used elsewhere in Proverbs and the HB (e.g., Prov 2:19, 5:6, 10:17, 12:28, 15:24). The closest match is in Gen 3:24 with the phrase "to guard the *way* of the tree of *life*" (לִשְׁמֹר אֶת־דֶּרֶךְ עֵץ הַחַיִּים). With such a paucity of use, the reference may signal the reader to consider Gen 3 and the prime negative example of divine imitation.

[4] Whybray deconstructs the section into a variety of disparate added verses. However, most argue for a cohesive tripart structure. Despite this, most divide the sections slightly differently than presented here. See Whybray, *Composition of the Book of Proverbs*, 25; Loader, *Proverbs 1–9*, 273–74; Waltke, *Proverbs (1–15)*, 350; Plöger, *Spruche Salomos (Proverbia)*, 68.

[5] Cf. Schipper, *Proverbs 1–15*, 236.

[6] There is considerable debate over the proper reading of "evil woman" (אֵשֶׁת רָע) in Prov 6:24. Two primary alternatives have been argued. The LXX reads it re-vocalized as "neighbor's wife" (אֵשֶׁת רֵעַ) or "married woman" (γυναικὸς ὑπάνδρου) and the BHS proposes "strange woman" (אִשָּׁה זָרָה). The term נָכְרִיָּה at the end of Prov 6:24 is intentionally coupled with the lexeme "smooth" (חלק) which is coupled in a similar phrase in 2:16 that parallels אִשָּׁה זָרָה. Since the phrase in question is paralleled with "stranger" (נָכְרִיָּה) in Prov 6:24, it is likely meant as a clever literary bridge between the common "strange woman" motif throughout Prov 1–9 and the adulterous or prostitute neighbor-wife imagery later in the lesson (Prov 6:26, 29, 32). For more detailed debates, see Fox, *Proverbs 1–9*, 230; McKane, *Proverbs*, 328–29; G. Boström, *Proverbiastudien*, Lunds Universitets Årsskrift N.f., Avd. 1, Bd. 30, Nr. 3 (Lund: C.W.K. Gleerup, 1935), 144–46; Schipper, *Proverbs 1–15*, 236, 241–42; Loader, *Proverbs 1–9*, 277–79.

[7] Schipper rightly notes the dichotomous paths in this section. The "evil woman" is indicative of "the path of destruction" and a "transgression of God's commandment." The goal is to provide a "torah-oriented concept of wisdom" (Schipper, *Proverbs 1–15*, 236).

Deuteronomic Allusions

Lesson 12 uses a few key terms and phrases. The most notable and unique appears in Prov 6:21, "Bind them on your heart always; tie them around your neck." The phrase is quite similar to the one in Prov 3:3 and 7:3 (Lessons 3 // 13). As mentioned previously, the phrase from these verses harkens back to Deut 6:5–8 (cf. Deut 11:18–22).[8] In Deut 6, Moses says, "May these words which I am commanding you today be on your heart ... You shall bind them as a sign on your hand" (6:6, 8). Though there are minor differences, the terminology is strikingly similar. Furthermore, Moses commands the parents to "teach" Yhwh's instruction to their children, as he says, "When you dwell in your house, when you walk on the way, when you lie down, and when you rise" (Deut 6:7). In Deut 11:22, Moses adds to this parallel statement, "You shall guard this whole *mitsvah* ... loving Yhwh your God, walking in all his ways and clinging (דבק) to him." With slightly different terms and perspectives, the proverbial father tells the son that *torah* and *mitsvah* "will lead you when you walk, guard over you when you lie down, and speak to you when you arise" (Prov 6:22). Again, the clever literary interlacing of Deut 6 with Prov 6 is hard to miss.[9] With the Deuteronomic allusion, the father highlights the underlying role of the generational transmission of the instruction that he is providing. Perhaps as a synecdoche, *torah* and *mitsvah* point the son to those who give the instruction, both in their word and deed. In other words, he is teaching his son just as he was taught, stretching all the way back to Moses on the plains of Moab. This faithful sequence itself is worthy of following and imitating, Moses being the exemplary teacher of Israel. It is notable that the lesson begins with the composite or parallel use of *torah* and *mitsvah,* likely a hendiadys here.[10] The use of these terms together outside of Proverbs is always in reference to Yhwh or the teaching from Moses. The first use is actually prior to Moses, however, when God reaffirmed the Abrahamic covenant with Isaac (Gen 26:5). The use in Genesis indicates that the terms

---

[8] Murphy refers to this allusion as a "deliberate recall" and Weeks says it is "surely a deliberate reminiscence." Fox withholds a strong stance on source, saying, "Whether [from] a shared wisdom tradition or to the influence of one text on the other is a moot point. ... Prov 6:20–22 formulates a commonplace of education." See Roland E. Murphy, *Proverbs*, WBC 22 (Dallas: Thomas Nelson, 1998), 38–39; Weeks, *Instruction and Imagery in Proverbs 1–9*, 143; Fox, *Proverbs 1–9*, 230; McKane, *Proverbs*, 326–27.

[9] Regarding the allusion, Murphy states, "The parental teaching is presented in the same light as the fundamental Yahwistic document of Deuteronomy. The passage 'actualizes' the traditional law ... it attempts formation of moral character." This actualization is not abstract but the well-worn pedagogy of imitation and reflection of one's parents and teachers. See Murphy, *Proverbs*, 40.

[10] Fox notes that the two terms are used interchangeably for both father and mother (e.g., Prov 1:8, 3:1, 4:2, 7:2, 31:1), indicating there is not a specific connection for either term with a particular parent or person. Schipper also proposes that they may be "synonymous" in this verse. According to Cook, the LXX translator viewed the terms for the dangerous woman (Prov 6:24) as a metaphorical hendiadys rather than distinct persons. See Fox, *Proverbs 1–9*, 228; Schipper, *Proverbs 1–15*, 239, 240; Johann Cook, *The Septuagint of Proverbs: Jewish and/or Hellenistic Proverbs?* VTSup 69 (New York: Brill, 1997), 184–86.

together do not merely refer to the mosaic law but more generally to instruction from Yhwh. So, the four occurrences in Prov 1–9 likely imply the same divine instructional intent as everywhere else (Prov 3:1, 6:20, 6:23, 7:2). With this in mind, it is important that the proverbial father words his initial call as, "My son, guard the *mitsvah* of your father and do not forsake the *torah* of your mother" (Prov 6:20). The use of "father" and "mother" are likely a hendiadys as well, functioning as a composite allusion to the son's faithful instructors, which include his parents (cf. Prov 1:8).[11] It is also probable that the father and mother are meant to parallel Yhwh and Wisdom.[12] If the allusion to Wisdom is underlying this lesson, it would add another referent to her metaphorical use in Prov 1–9, functioning as a mother, a Moses-like teacher, a faithful wife, the proper path, and as an anthropomorphism of Yhwh.

Allusions to Yhwh

An important example of sexual immorality and idolatry appears in Num 25.[13] For the wandering Israelites, Shittim resulted in a great testing and purge. As the narrative recounts, "The people began to prostitute (זנה) with the daughters of Moab [cf. Prov 6:26]. And they called for the people to sacrifice to their gods ... and the anger of Yhwh burned against Israel" (Num 25:1–3). In response, Yhwh authorized the killing of all those who had participated. After Phineas and Moses addressed the aberration, Yhwh commends Phineas, saying, "[He] has turned my wrath (חמה) from over the sons of Israel, in his jealousy (קנא) he was jealous (קנא) in their midst, so I did not extinguish the sons of Israel in my jealousy (קנא)" (Num 25:11). This tragic account is mentioned by Moses in his Deuteronomic preparation for Israel's entrance into the land. The passage is well known for intertwining *torah* with proverbial language in a few respects.[14] First, Moses recounts the episode with its purpose in Deut 4, "Yhwh your God destroyed from among you all who followed after (הָלַךְ אַחֲרֵי) Ba'al of Peor. But you who clung (דבק) to Yhwh your God are alive today. See, I have taught (למד) you the statutes and judgments ... Keep them and do them for it is your wisdom (חָכְמָה) and insight (בִּינָה) to the

---

[11] Cf. Perdue, *Proverbs*, 128–29.

[12] Cf. Meinhold, *Die Sprüche*, 117; Nancy Nam Hoon Tan, *The "Foreignness" of the Foreign Woman in Proverbs 1–9: A Study of the Origin and Development of a Biblical Motif*, BZAW 381 (New York: De Gruyter, 2008), 95.

[13] The Num 25 story serves as a primary instantiation of the Israel-as-adulterous-wife motif. As Fishbane comments, "The motif of a faithless Israel who whores after false gods, and confuses Ba'al with YHWH, is retrojected in the period of the desert wanderings—where it assumes a paradigmatic form" (Michael A. Fishbane, "Accusations of Adultery: A Study of Law and Scribal Practice in Numbers 5:11–31," *HUCA* 45 (1974): 40).

[14] Fishbane concludes a long discussion on the legal aspects and motif of adultery in the Torah with a reflection on Proverbs, "The reflex of the law of adultery in Prov 6:20–23 ... an inner-biblical midrash on the Decalogue ... a general warning against adultery—or, more specifically, in the light of the seduction of false wisdom" (Fishbane, "Accusations of Adultery," 44).

people" (Deut 4:3–6).[15] The illuminating passage is bookended by the terms *mitsvah* and *torah*, which are representative of all the related terms used for God's instructions (Deut 4:2, 8). In fact, Moses specifically uses the singular term *torah* collectively in Deut 4:8, "Like this whole *torah* which I place before you today" (כָּל הַתּוֹרָה הַזֹּאת אֲשֶׁר אָנֹכִי נֹתֵן לִפְנֵיכֶם הַיּוֹם). Lesson 12 seems to use the terms in a similar way (Prov 6:20, 23), possibly invoking the Deuteronomic sense.[16] This formative passage serves to bring together the correlational connections between adultery, idolatry, apostasy, *torah*, and wisdom.[17] Thus, Prov 6, Num 25, and Deut 4 all emphasize the deadliness of adulterous and idolatrous folly tantamount to rejecting Yhwh's *torah*.

Furthermore, in Deut 4, Moses uses the phrase "walked after" to summarize the actions of the rebellious and unfaithful Israelites.[18] What did he mean by "walk after," though? The Israelites at Shittim seem to have engaged in both sexual immorality and idolatrous practices. These practices were at the behest of the local people.[19] They not only invited Israel to watch but included them and taught them their ways (cf. Exod 34:11–16).[20] In contrast, Moses wanted to "teach" them the righteous way, namely the instructions and ways of Yhwh. By learning his ways, they would be wise and live, or walk in the "way of life" as Proverbs puts it (Prov 6:23). In fact, those who lived from the Num 25 story were those who "clung" to Yhwh (Deut 4:4), a term often affiliated with a marital and relational covenant, as previously discussed (Prov 4:8, 5:20; cf. Gen 2:24; Deut 30:20). In contrast, 1 Kgs 11 says later that Solomon "clung" to the gods of his wives because of love (11:2). In

---

[15] Krüger regards this passage as the "transformation of [law] into a sapiential teaching of life" (Thomas Krüger, "Law and Wisdom According to Deut 4:5–8," in *Wisdom and Torah: The Reception of "Torah" in the Wisdom Literature of the Second Temple Period*, ed. Bernd U. Schipper and D. Andrew Teeter, JSJSup 163 (Leiden: Brill, 2013), 43).

[16] Murphy says of the Deuteronomy allusion in Prov 6 that "sapiential and 'Yahwistic' teaching do not differ ... the teaching of the parents are ... analogous to the commands of Moses" (Murphy, *Proverbs*, 39).

[17] Moses weaves multiple streams together in this passage. Much like Deut 6 and 11, he says they must pass on and teach the *torah* to their subsequent generations (Deut 4:9–10). However, surrounding the praise of Torah (Deut 4:5–8), he reminds Israel of their prior apostasy and the perennial temptation to do likewise.

[18] Tigay connects this passage (Deut 4:2) to a similar warning against apostasy in Deut 12:29–13:18, which he observes warns "not to imitate pagan practices" or the idolatrous ways of the nations (cf. Deut 12:30). It is important to note the direct parallel between following "after" other gods with the imitative language of "How do these nations serve their gods that I may also do likewise?" (Deut 13:30). This implication seems to hold throughout the various instances where "following after" is used in the HB. See Jeffrey H. Tigay, *Deuteronomy: The Traditional Hebrew Text with the New JPS Translation*, The JPS Torah Commentary (Philadelphia: Jewish Publication Society, 1996), 44.

[19] Cole rightly notes the progression from physical fornication to spiritual apostasy, which may have included cult prostitution (R. Dennis Cole, *Numbers*, NAC (Nashville: B&H, 2000), 435). The same warning is likely envisioned by the proverbial teacher, as well.

[20] In this passage, Moses renews the covenant with Israel after their idolatrous apostasy, which invoked the second use of God's moniker "jealous" (קַנָּא) regarding their polytheism or poly-latry (Exod 20:5, 34:14). The passage warns of their intermarrying with non-Israelites who "prostitute after their gods and cause your sons to prostitute after their gods" (Exod 34:16). Again, the sense is that they would teach the Israelite sons to do as they do or imitate their foreign ways in apostasy to Yhwh and his covenant.

doing so, he "walked after (הלך אחרי) Ashtoreth," and other gods, rather than "fully after (אחרי) Yhwh as David his father" (11:5).[21] While the term דבק does not appear in Lesson 12, the sentiment certainly does, both in the positive and negative (Prov 6:20–24).[22] The proverbial son is tempted to follow in aberrant ways by desiring the "evil woman" and being captured by her, a form of apostasy and folly (Prov 6:25).[23] In the passage from Num 25, it is important to see that their adulterous behavior provoked Yhwh to "anger" (חמה) and "jealousy" (קנא) (25:11).[24] Although the term for "jealousy" does not appear with Solomon, the term is used of Judah and Rehoboam who caused Yhwh to be "jealous" (קנא) due to following Solomon in his aberrant worship and various "abominations of the nations" (1 Kgs 14:22–24). Interestingly, the terms for "anger" and "jealousy" appear in Prov 6:34 for the offended man, which parallel Num 25. While the use here seems to imply the mundane level for the husband of an adulterous woman,[25] it must not be removed from the context of the "evil woman" and broader "stranger" motif that is found throughout Prov 1–9 (2:16, 5:3, 20, 7:5; cf. Exod 34:13–16; Num 5:14–30; Deut 7:2–5).[26] The proverbial teaching weaves together the practical and the theological. Committing adultery and sexual violations are unwise both in their affront to the Torah and in their inevitable natural destructive results. However, the proverbial picture utilizes specific terminology in order to evoke the ancient picture of Israel's aberration against the Lord. The perennial draw of the Israelites away from the way of *torah* to the ways of the nations was a real threat.[27] Thus, the son is to be wary not to imitate his aberrant ancestors as they imitated the ways of the Moabites. In doing so, he would provoke the

---

[21] Interestingly, Solomon seems to serve as both a positive and negative exemplar for wisdom. The wisdom student will determine by his choices which version of Solomon he will imitate and follow. Cf. Tan, *"Foreignness" of the Foreign Woman in Proverbs 1–9*, 103–4.

[22] Lesson 4 instead uses the more proverbial term "grasp" (תמך) while Lesson 6 uses "embrace" (חבק) to indicate a similar sentiment (Prov 3:18, 4:8; cf. Prov 4:4, 5:5, 5:20, 5:22; Song 2:6, 8:3).

[23] The following verse (Prov 6:26) mentions the cost of prostitution as a "loaf of bread" and that a "married woman hunts for life." Similar language is used in Ezek 13:17–23 regarding women who use magic and divination. If the terms carried this imagery generally, it would further condemn and identify the ways of the "evil woman" with the pagan practices of the nations. See Fox, *Proverbs 1–9*, 232.

[24] These terms appear together only a few times, always in reference to Yhwh except once (Num 25:11; Ezek 5:13, 16:38, 42, 23:25, 36:6; Zech 8:2; Prov 6:34, 27:4).

[25] Tan rightly notes the "association of apostasy with adultery" in the first half of the lesson but then goes on to incorrectly say that the "foreign woman" motif has no use or association in the latter half of the lesson, which deals only with adultery. See Tan, *"Foreignness" of the Foreign Woman in Proverbs 1–9*, 95.

[26] Weeks rightly notes, "What the woman seems to represent, after all, does not involve her having a fixed or specific marital status, merely the capacity to corrupt and ruin. ... Adultery, after all, is the classic biblical figure for apostasy" (Weeks, *Instruction and Imagery in Proverbs 1–9*, 142–43).

[27] Reflecting on the various depictions of "foreign women" in the HB, Tan observes that they are primarily seen as "bad because they corrupt Israel and cause them to leave the ways of Yahweh" (Tan, *"Foreignness" of the Foreign Woman in Proverbs 1–9*, 104–5). This fact is further established by the intentional inclusion of "foreign women" such as Ruth in a positive light. The foreignness motif was primarily a literary and theological indicator of religious corruption rather than a mere sexual or social aberration.

jealousy and anger of Yhwh, a dire position in which to put oneself. In fact, as the proverbial father notes in Lesson 12 (Prov 6:34), the one caught in an illicit affair will experience the divine attribute of "vengeance" (נקם). Yhwh says in a notorious statement, related to pagan practices, "Vengeance (נקם) is mine" (Deut 32:35, 37–39; cf. Isa 59:18). Similarly, Ps 94:1 calls Yhwh a "God of vengeance" (אֵל־נְקָמוֹת) in the context of being a righteous judge.[28] Even more interestingly, the term appears in Prov 6:34 as the phrase "a day of vengeance" (בְּיוֹם נָקָם).[29] This phrase is used several times in Isaiah for God's future judgment and restoration (Isa 34:8, 61:2, 63:4). So, in an unexpected reversal, it is the offended husband, or jealous man, who acts in imitative reflection of Yhwh by upholding *torah*, both in "jealousy" and "vengeance" here.[30] Similarly, Prov 6:34 says that the offended man will not "lift his face" (לֹא־יִשָּׂא פָנִי) or accept any "bribe" (שֹׁחַד), a key image from the Torah also derived from Yhwh's character (Deut 10:17; cf. Exod 23:8; Deut 16:19; Josh 24:19).[31] Thus, the wayward adulterers, who remain in the anonymous and generic third-person, serve as an abject contrast to the Torah way and the character of God.[32]

---

[28] Set within a prominent set of divine kingship psalms, the psalmist praises God's "vengeance" as a form of justice against the wicked and their deeds. Interestingly, the psalmist uses proverbial language as well, such as, "Blessed is the man whom you discipline, O Yah, and you teach him from your *torah*" (94:12). While the term "vengeance" carries a negative sentiment for many in the modern era, Peels notes that it was neutral in its origin, even positive in its divine or judicial use. See H. G. L. Peels, "נקם," in *NIDOTTE*, ed. Willem VanGemeren (Grand Rapids: Zondervan, 1997), 154; H. G. L. Peels, "Passion or Justice? The Interpretation of Beyôm Nāqām in Proverbs vi 34," *VT* 44.2 (1994): 270–74.

[29] Peels rightly argues that the phrase was not unrestrained, personal revenge but the proper maintenance of legal justice (Peels, "Passion or Justice?" 270–74).

[30] Durant provides a substantive discussion of the term "vengeance" from Ps 94. As a manifestation of justice and righteousness, she proposes the divine attribute should ideally be imitated. Just as God vindicates the offended by judging the wicked, so the reader is to reflect his desire for justice. Although, later in the NT, Paul cautioned against imitating this attribute in light of the example given by Jesus (Rom 12:19; cf. Heb 10:30). Paul does not explicitly delineate his reasoning but shortly after (Rom 13:4) uses the same lexical root "vengeance" (ἔκδικος; cf. ἐκδίκησις) for the role of a human governor acting as a "servant of God," who rewards the good and punishes the evil. The governor, then, imitates the divine attribute in his appointment by God to serve justice (Rom 13:1–2). See Karen Elizabeth Durant, "Imitation of God as a Principle for Ethics Today: A Study of Selected Psalms" (University of Birmingham (UK), PhD diss, 2010), 188–204.

[31] The divine quality of impartiality is established in Deut 10:17 with the declaration, "Yhwh your God, he is God of gods and Lord of lords, the great and mighty God, and one feared, who will not lift his face (לֹא־יִשָּׂא פָנִים) and will not take a bribe (שחד)." The parallel language between Deut 10:17 and Prov 6:34 is quite striking. The phrase "he will not lift" also appears in the final warning passage from Joshua, which refers to Yhwh as a "jealous God" (אֵל־קַנּוֹא), carrying on the tradition of Moses as a faithful student. Joshua's plea to Israel was in the context of a warning against idolatry (Josh 24:14–18). He specifically says, "If you abandon Yhwh and serve strange (נכר) gods" (Josh 24:20). As mentioned previously, the lexeme for "strange" parallels the one used for the "strange woman" (נָכְרִיָּה) of Prov 6:24, further highlighting the implicit connection.

[32] Despite this general address, Waltke notes the return to the second person in the final phrase, serving as a literary inclusio for the lesson (Prov 6:35) (Waltke, *Proverbs (1–15)*, 350).

Allusions to Wisdom

The parallel between Lessons 4 and 12 illuminates a few intriguing points regarding Yhwh and Wisdom as well. In Lesson 4, the teacher elevates Wisdom in a great encomium. The poem speaks of her incomparable value and that her path is one of life (Prov 3:14–18). Likewise, she possesses and gives both riches and honor to those who find and hold onto her (Prov 3:16, 18). In Lesson 12, Wisdom is not mentioned. Yet, her inverse is described as the "evil woman" and "stranger" (Prov 6:24).[33] She is as cheap and common as a "loaf of bread" (Prov 6:26).[34] The one who pursues her will get dishonor, harm, and destruction (Prov 6:32–35).[35] Her way is adulterous and will not be set free (Prov 6:29, 32–35). This is antithetical to the "blessed" way of Wisdom (Prov 3:13, 18).[36] In fact, the initial call of the father in Lesson 12 sounds quite similar to ideas given to the son regarding Wisdom. Although the lesson calls the son to "bind them" to his heart (Prov 6:21), mentioning *mitsvah* and *torah* (6:20), it curiously goes on to state, "She will lead you in your walking, guard you in your lying, and talk to you in your waking" (Prov 6:22).[37] The third feminine singular is an unusual usage since there is no clear grammatical referent.[38] Some have understood the singular to be a poetic collective for both *torah* and *mitsvah*.[39] While this is perhaps partly the answer, Wisdom is the expected referent for the third feminine singular from elsewhere.[40] The anthropomorphic figure of Wisdom is often given personal qualities that are not attributed to *torah* or *mitsvah*.[41] Here, this unnamed feminine figure is

---

[33] Despite a lexical departure from the MT, the LXX translator was perhaps intentionally building a more cohesive and progressive case against the different versions of the dangerous woman in Prov 1–9. As Cook comments, "They are all in some way or another connected to foreign wisdom. In the chapter under discussion the dangerous 'married' woman is one with a foreign tongue" (6:24). See Cook, *The Septuagint of Proverbs*, 468.

[34] As Murphy notes, the direct comparison in Prov 6:20–35 is the positive results of choosing fidelity versus the negative for infidelity. Regarding the debate over the intent of a "loaf of bread," Schipper makes a reasoned argument for transaction from Job 2:4 which uses the preposition בעד twice in this manner. This implies the "loaf of bread" was likely a payment rather than a euphemism for poverty. See Murphy, *Proverbs*, 39; Schipper, *Proverbs 1–15*, 243.

[35] Schipper says of this negative figure in the lesson, "She represents one of the main dangers that the wisdom student faces—human desire, which leads people to sell their soul and robs them of their humanity" (Schipper, *Proverbs 1–15*, 251).

[36] The father cleverly uses the motif of "find" (מצא) here to contrast the call to "find" Wisdom or Yhwh elsewhere (Prov 1:28, 2:5, 3:13, 8:17, 35).

[37] Schipper notes the holistic framing of this verse, which in his view could only properly refer to Yhwh (Bernd U. Schipper, "When Wisdom is not Enough! The Discourse on Wisdom and Torah and the Composition of the Book of Proverbs," in *Wisdom and Torah: The Reception of "Torah" in the Wisdom Literature of the Second Temple Period*, ed. Bernd U. Schipper and D. Andrew Teeter, JSJSup 163 (Leiden: Brill, 2013), 62).

[38] In the Talmud, *b. Sota 21A* refers to this as the Torah, which is a companion even into the eschatological age. See Jacob Neusner, *The Babylonian Talmud: A Translation and Commentary*. (Peabody: Hendrickson, 2011), 11:102.

[39] Plöger, *Spruche Salomos (Proverbia)*, 69.

[40] Fox, *Proverbs 1–9*, 229; C. H. Toy, *A Critical and Exegetical Commentary on the Book of Proverbs*, ICC (New York: C. Scribner's Sons, 1899), 133; Waltke, *Proverbs (1–15)*, 351–52.

[41] See discussion on Prov 3:19.

put within the Deuteronomic reference, functioning in the role of a parent.[42] However, the passage goes beyond Deut 6 to say, "she will lead (נחה) you" (Prov 6:22). Perhaps surprisingly, the term "lead" only appears once in Deuteronomy, "Yhwh alone leads (נחה) you, there is no strange (נֵכָר) god with him" (Deut 32:12). The passage speaks of God's faithfulness to Israel despite their foolishness and unfaithfulness to him. The term for a "strange" god is a lexical parallel with the feminine form "strange woman" (נָכְרִיָּה) of Prov 6:24. Furthermore, while the term נחה is not used much in Deuteronomy, the idea appears several times regarding Yhwh's rescue of Israel out of Egypt (Exod 13:17, 21, 15:13, 32:34, 33:14; cf. Ps 77:21).[43] The Lord's leading (נחה) appears again with numerous examples in the psalter, for example, "Lead (נחה) me in the everlasting way" (Ps 139:24).[44] Thus, the unique interweaving of the transgenerational pedagogy of Deut 6 with imagery often associated with Yhwh implies the proverbial father's practical and theological intent. As an anthropomorphism of Yhwh, Wisdom will lead the son like a parent, or even as Moses, in the wise and faithful way.[45]

Just as sons and kings are to follow in the ways of their forefathers (Lesson 8), so the proverbial son is to follow in the way of Wisdom and Yhwh. This point becomes particularly poignant through the parallel between Prov 3:11–12 and 6:23. Lesson 4 speaks of Yhwh as a father who rebukes (תּוֹכַחַת) a son out of his love (Prov 3:11). The son, however, must not reject Yhwh's *musar* (cf. Deut 11:2).[46] In Lesson 12, the father says that "rebukes (תּוֹכַחַת) of *musar*" are the "way of life" (Prov 6:23). The terms appear together in Prov 1–9 one other time for the hypothetical fool of Lesson 10 who hates both "rebukes" and *musar* (Prov 5:12). So, the proverbial father points the son to the source of this *torah* and *mitsvah* that he is commending.[47] It is not a man-made path but the path of the preeminent Father, Yhwh. As Schipper argues, "*Torah* can be defined as the path of wisdom."[48] Thus, if the son chooses the "evil woman," he is rejecting Yhwh and his ways.[49] Such a way is foolish and unbecoming for the son of a wise and righteous teacher. Finally, in Ps 43:3, the psalmist uses similar language as Prov 6:22–23, "Send your light and truth. They will lead (נחה) me. They will bring me to your holy mountain and your sanctuary." The lesson in Prov 6 says, "She will lead (נחה) you in your walking ... for *mitsvah*

---

[42] Meinhold, *Die Sprüche*, 117.

[43] For a detailed discussion of the term *nachah* (נחה) and the passage's relevance from Exodus, see Excursus: Exodus and God's Leading in His Way.

[44] See Ps 5:9, 23:3, 27:11, 31:4, 43:3, 61:3, 67:5, 73:24, 77:21, 78:14, 53, 72, 107:30, 139:10, 143:10. Schipper notes that the term typically "reflects the metaphor of a shepherd ... to emphasize God's guidance" (Schipper, *Proverbs 1–15*, 240).

[45] Cf. Waltke, *Proverbs (1–15)*, 352.

[46] Cf. Schipper, *Proverbs 1–15*, 241.

[47] McKane argues in light of the Ps 119:105 connection, "your word is a lamp ... light," that *torah* and *mitsvah* are meant to be "equated with the word of Yahweh," paralleled with the father's initial call in 6:20 (McKane, *Proverbs*, 327–28).

[48] Schipper, *Proverbs 1–15*, 251.

[49] Schipper argues that the whole passage "has to do with the 'wrong way'" which the teacher highlights "through the example of the adulterous woman" (Schipper, *Proverbs 1–15*, 238). While adultery is certainly troublesome, the underlying aberration from moral and covenantal fidelity is an even greater threat to the son.

is a lamp and *torah* a light and a path of life are the rebukes of *musar*" (Prov 6:22–23). Both passages use the moral traits of God as a synecdoche. It is ultimately God who leads his followers in his way as they imitate and reflect his traits.[50]

Conclusion

Lesson 12 signals an underlying Deuteronomic pedagogy by starting with a reference to the parental unit and some notable language from the Torah (Prov 6:20; cf. Deut 6:5–8). Building on this allusion, the father goes on to use imagery that exposes parallel examples of apostasy and idolatry, a perennial problem for Israel found in the narratives of the Torah (Prov 6:24–33). Even at the beginning of their covenantal relationship with Yhwh, Israel was prone to abandon him and his ways (e.g., Exod 32; Num 25). The seductive ways of the nations, which included both sexual and religious elements, often persuaded the people of God to imitate their foreign and illicit ways. The proverbial father, however, directs the son in this lesson to consider a negative model as well as the positive Deuteronomic instructions that can prevent him from falling prey to the smooth words that lead to destruction (Prov 6:24). As a wise son, he is to follow Wisdom's leading (Prov 6:22; cf. Exod 33:14) and reflect God's disdain for unfaithfulness (6:34–35). In fact, the son is to adhere closely to the father's instruction and not even flirt with the aberrant ways of the "evil woman" (Prov 6:25–29). Her way will surely end in harm and disgrace, along with all those who follow in her ways (Prov 6:32–33). Yet, if the son will properly hold to the *torah* and *mitsvah* of his father (Prov 6:20), he will find life and walk in the way of Wisdom and Yhwh (6:22–23). At this point in the wisdom program, the son is quite familiar with the aberrant ways of the *zarah*, or "stranger." Yet, in Lesson 13, the proverbial father further expands on the instruction of Lesson 12 and the dangers of this false, even counterfeit, path that opposes Wisdom and Yhwh.

---

[50] In later Egyptian wisdom, Weeks notes the use of "way" for "a personal way that is the way of the god ... which the individual may be guided by the god." Despite this, most uses of "way" or "way of life" in Egypt and Mesopotamia were quite different in their meaning or purpose. Rather, Weeks rightly observes, the proverbial metaphor should be seen in light of other biblical texts. As he states, "A single way, or pattern of behaviour, can be said to characterize whole groups, and it is possible to 'walk in the way' of others by imitating what they do." See Weeks, *Instruction and Imagery in Proverbs 1–9*, 148–51; Didier Devauchelle, "Le Chemin de Vie Dans l'Égypte Ancienne," in *Sagesses de l'Orient Ancien et Chrétien: La Voie de Vie et La Conduite Spirituelle Chez Les Peuples et Dans Les Littératures de l'Orient Chrétien; Conférences IROC 1991–1992*, ed. Rene Lebrun, Sciences Théologiques & Religieuses 2 (Paris: Beauchesne, 1993), 111.

EXCURSUS

Exodus and God's Leading in His Way

T he story of God's miraculous and gracious salvation from Egypt was unique in history (Exod 34:10; Deut 4:32–35). Yet, the idolatrous practices Israel engaged in were anything but unique. The people turned to the idolatry of the nations almost immediately after being liberated, an event nearly as stunning as God's mighty deeds. After Moses ascended Mt. Sinai to receive the stipulations of their newly confirmed covenant with Yhwh, Exod 32 informs the reader that Aaron, at the behest of the Israelite people, crafted a golden calf (32:1). Although the abomination warranted the people's annihilation (Exod 32:10), Moses interceded and God provided a moderated punishment for their wickedness (Exod 32:11–14, 27, 35). Yet, beyond the death and plague that ensued, Moses became concerned that Yhwh would no longer be with them on their journey, as the Lord declared, "I will not go up in your midst, for you are a stiff neck people, lest I consume you in the way" (Exod 33:3).

Within this formative event for Israel, a curious dialogue transpires between Moses and Yhwh. The content of this dialogue, though, was anything but direct. While many interpretations are possible, God's eventual theophanic revelation of his character seems to capture the essence of the narrative's purpose, which became a prominent motif throughout the rest of the HB (Exod 34:5–7). At the heart of this fulcrum point for Israel, Moses cried out to Yhwh, "Make known to me your way and I shall know you" (Exod 33:13; cf. Prov 2:5, 3:6). The following analysis will highlight the revelation of God's way as a means for following, reflecting, and knowing him. Just as Yhwh "led" (נחה) Moses and Israel in his way (Exod 33:14), the figure Wisdom in Proverbs is said to "lead" (נחה) the willing and adherent in her ways (Prov 6:22).

The God Who Leads

After God dismissed Israel (Exod 32:33–33:6), the text provides a historical, explanatory insertion (Exod 33:7–11). The insertion provides the setting for the dialogue that is taking place between Moses and Yhwh.[1] Perhaps, the most interesting aspect of this insertion is the statement, "Yhwh spoke to Moses face-to-face just as a man speaks to his friend" (Exod 33:11). The point of the comment is that Moses had a familiar and regular relationship with Yhwh at the Tent of Meeting. His dialogue at this crucial juncture was not unique in its occurrence but in its content and the weight of its potential consequence for Israel.

As the narrator intended to convey, Moses' concern was not his own well-being but the persistence of Israel as a people, particularly as Yhwh's people (Exod 34:9).[2] So, Moses responds to God's dismissal by questioning his command to "bring up this people" (Exod 32:34, 33:1, 12). The question in Exod 33:12, however, seems to disregard the details of Yhwh's command in 33:1. A few options are possible for what Moses meant by his question. It may have been a mere literary incongruence,[3] a question regarding the identity of the "messenger,"[4] a question of whom Moses was called to lead, or perhaps Moses' subtle rejection of Yhwh's removal of his presence. While each has its merit, the overall context seems to focus on the presence (פני) of Yhwh with the people,[5] seen in Moses' response, "If *your presence* does not go, do not bring *us* up from here" (Exod 33:16). The Lord told Moses twice that his "Angel will go before you" (Exod 32:34, 33:2). Yet, Moses' petition in Exod 33:12 seems to ignore this, "Consider, you say to me, 'bring up this people,' but you have not made known to me who you will send with me" (33:12). He uses the term "you will send" (שלח), implying Yhwh is sending but not going. Thus, it appears Moses is either saying, "Who is going if you've rejected Israel" or "Who from among Israel, if not all of Israel." Although the text does not resolve the tension explicitly, Moses does mention "the people" or "us" several times (Exod 33:13, 15, 16, 34:9).[6] The force of his appeal insists that God not only refrains from destroying Israel or revoking the promised land (Exod 33:1–2) but to be

---

[1] Cf. Cornelis Houtman, *Exodus*, trans. Sierd Woudstra, HCOT (Leuven: Peeters, 2000), 686.

[2] Terence E. Fretheim, *Exodus*, IBC (Louisville: John Knox, 1991), 298.

[3] For theories on the text's compositional history, see Houtman, *Exodus*, 683, 686.

[4] Duane A. Garrett, *A Commentary on Exodus*, Kregel Exegetical Library (Grand Rapids: Kregel Academic, 2014), 647.

[5] Propp highlights and discusses the "face" or "presence" theme in this passage, "Face is inherently ambiguous. Sometimes a part stands for the whole, so that 'face' = 'self,' and sometimes a part is just a part. In my understanding, the Face is not Yahweh's full essence. It is so to speak, an archangel, i.e., a messenger fully empowered to represent God on earth. Depending on the context, it can be regarded as equivalent or non-equivalent to Yahweh, just as, among idolaters, an idol both is and is not the god. ... Yahweh's Face is a hypostasis, i.e., a part of the divine being that stands for the whole. ... If a face is a visible symbol, a pictogram so to speak, a name is an audible symbol. God is not the sound 'Yah-weh,' but these symbols, or the four letters Y-H-W-H, in some contexts represent his presence. ... We are led to equate the divine back with Yahweh's anonymous Messenger (promised in 23:20, 23, 32:34, 33:2), his Glory (33:18), and his Name (34:5–6). (Significantly, while in cognate literatures 'Baal's Face' or 'Baal's Name' can be a goddess, the Torah does not acknowledge female hypostases. These will return in Lady Wisdom (Prov 8:22–31). And gain popularity in later Judaism, e.g., the Shekinah." See William H. C. Propp, ed., *Exodus 19–40: A New Translation with Introduction and Commentary*, AB 2A (New York: Doubleday, 2006), 604, 619–20.

[6] Propp, *Exodus 19–40*, 611.

personally involved and present with them. The disparity of the relationship is highlighted in Yhwh's deferral to Moses, "*you* and the people *you* brought up from the land of Egypt" (Exod 33:1; cf. 32:7). Following the theophany (Exod 34:10), Yhwh agreed to make a covenant "before *your* people" (נֶגֶד כָּל־עַמְּךָ), referring to Moses. In the chapters leading up to Exod 32, the narrator clearly identifies it was Yhwh who brought them up out of Egypt (Exod 12:51, 16:6, 32, 20:2, 29:46). Likewise, Israel is repeatedly called "my people" by Yhwh (e.g., Exod 6:7). So, the reversal of this motif and God's placement of responsibility for the people on Moses cleverly establishes the Lord's utter disdain for Israel. In fact, the transfer of Israel to Moses appears to be an echo of the terms used by the people and Aaron earlier, "Moses, the man who brought us up from the land of Egypt ... these are your gods, O Israel, who brought you up from the land of Egypt" (Exod 32:1, 4). In an attempt to dissuade God's rejection of Israel, Moses then utilized his own favor and relationship with Yhwh, "You said, 'I know you by name and you have found favor in my eyes'" (Exod 33:12; cf. Gen 6:8; Prov 8:35).[7] He desired that God would provide this same blessing to the rest of Israel, in particular, his presence, guidance, and protection.

Within this dialogue exchange, Moses makes a series of requests, one which is particularly intriguing in Exod 33:13. This first request is enigmatic and does not receive an appropriate response from Yhwh in Exod 33:14. The second request (Exod 33:15–16) is an extension of the first (33:13), which results in Yhwh's second response. He affirms in the second response that he will do as Moses has requested. Here, an inclusio is utilized for the brief dialogue and conclusion, used six times in Exod 33:12–17 and 34:9, [8] "[I or you] found favor in [your or my] eyes" (Exod 33:12, 13, 16, 17, 34:9).[9] Moses' third request, then, appears to parallel and further clarify the first request, "[Moses] said, 'please show (ראה) me your glory (כבד)'" (Exod 33:18). The third response from Yhwh is more appropriate to the request. Here, the Lord says, "I will pass all my goodness before you and proclaim the name of Yhwh before you and be gracious to whom I will be gracious and be merciful to whom I will be merciful" (Exod 33:19). The latter portion of the response signals the dialogue's purpose, further expressed in the theophany of Exod 34:5–6, "Yhwh descended in a cloud and stood with him there and proclaimed the name of Yhwh. And Yhwh passed before him and Yhwh proclaimed, 'Yhwh, God, merciful and gracious, slow to anger and full of steadfast love.'" As scholars have noted, the phrase in Exod 33:19 reflects the divine name formulation in 3:14.[10] The name formulation implies Yhwh's divine freedom and aseity.

---

[7] Fretheim discusses the uniqueness of Moses and Noah as the only two said to have "favor in the eyes of Yhwh." He goes on to coordinate the implications of Noah's narrative with Moses, commenting, "God's actions toward Israel are not unique: this is the way of God with the world" (Fretheim, *Exodus*, 304).

[8] Propp believes the chiasm centers on and emphasizes the term "face." For discussion on the literary complexity and potential chiastic structure of 33:12–17, see Nahum M. Waldman, "God's Ways: A Comparative Note," *JQR* 70.2 (1979): 67–68; Propp, *Exodus 19–40*, 605.

[9] Fretheim, *Exodus*, 298.

[10] Fretheim, *Exodus*, 305–6.

Neither Egypt nor Israel could contain him or attempt to manipulate his behavior prior to the exodus. Likewise, neither Israel nor Moses could contain or manipulate him regarding the fate of Israel after they broke his covenant.[11] Furthermore, Stuart discusses the significance of the appositional placement of the name with these attributes, "A general principle is stated rather than merely a personal word to Moses. God's 'mercy' and 'compassion' were granted to all his covenant people (Deut 13:17; cf. Jas 5:11) and should in turn characterize the behavior of all his covenant people (e.g., Zech 7:9), but they are not automatically available to all other people unless they join in covenant with God."[12] In other words, the people were expected to reflect the behavior, character, and desires of their covenant God.

The Lord's first response to Moses, however, has created confusion for most scholars. By establishing the proper text, here, the intentional tension and deflection within the dialogue are more clearly understood.

Exod 33:14 MT	וַיֹּאמַר	and he said,
	פָּנַי יֵלֵכוּ	'My presence will go
	וַהֲנִחֹתִי לָךְ	and I will *lead* you.'
Exod 33:14 LXX	καὶ λέγει Αὐτὸς προπορεύσομαί σου καὶ καταπαύσω σε	and he said, 'I myself will go before you and I will give you rest.'

For Exod 33:14, most translators follow the LXX (Tg. Onq., Syr.), reading with the MT's vocalization וַהֲנִחֹתִי from the root "to rest" (נוח) rather from "to lead" (נחה).[13] The MT's version is certainly attested by the pointing and the various text traditions.[14] Yet, the absence of a *yod* in the middle or at the end of the term allows for either root to be read, which of course was originally without vowel pointing (cf. MT, SP). The difficulty is that for either root there is a defective spelling in this occurrence. The *hiphil* first singular would either need to be וַהֲנִיחֹתִי from נוח or וְהִנְחֵיתִי from נחה.[15] Earlier in Genesis, an interesting parallel is found for the נחה root, "Blessed be Yhwh, God of my lord Abraham, who did not abandon his steadfast love and faithfulness with my lord. Yhwh

---

[11] Nahum M. Sarna, *Exodus*, JPS (Philadelphia: JPS, 1991), 214.

[12] Douglas K. Stuart, *Exodus*, NAC (Nashville: B&H, 2006), 708.

[13] Though largely dismissed by modern scholarship, Ehrlich argued for the lexeme *nachah* (נחה) (Arnold B. Ehrlich, *Randglossen zur Hebräischen Bibel: textkritisches, sprachliches und sachliches* (Leipzig: J.C. Hinrichs, 1908), 405).

[14] The phrase and verse are not extant in the Q mss. Childs rejects the proposition by Ehrlich due to the lack of textual witness support (Brevard S. Childs, *Exodus: A Commentary*, OTL (Philadelphia: Westminster, 1974), 584).

[15] These are the hypothetical forms if morphologically and grammatically correct. The lexeme נחה occurs 40x in the HB. Of the forty, only three (7.5%) appear with the י at the end (Exod 15:13 [נָחִיתָ], Ps 77:21 [נָחִיתָ], Neh 9:12 [הִנְחִיתָם]). Alternatively, the lexeme נוח occurs 141x in the HB and 33x in the Torah. Of the thirty-three in the Torah, nineteen (58%) appear with the י or ו in the middle (Gen 42:33; Exod 16:23, 24, 34, 17:11, 23:12, 32:10; Lev 7:15, 16:23, 24:12; Num 11:25, 15:34, 19:9, 32:15; Deut 3:20, 5:14, 12:10, 25:19, 26:4). Likewise, in the Prophets and Writings, the י or ו are in the middle 43 of the 72 occurrences (60%) and 22 of the 33 occurrences (67%), respectively.

led me in the way [בַּדֶּרֶךְ נָחַנִי], to the house of my lord's brother. ... he led me in the true way [הִנְחַנִי בְּדֶרֶךְ אֱמֶת]" (Gen 24:27, 48). Here, the *qal* and *hiphil* forms of *nachah* (נחה) occur with a suffixed ending yet without the *yod* (י) in the third radical position. Not only do the textual forms parallel Exod 33:14 but the coordination between God's character and his leading are clear as well. In close proximity, Exod 32:10 does utilize the *yod* for the root *nu'ach* (נוח), "Now, let me rest [הַנִּיחָה] since my anger burns against them and will consume them and I will make you a great nation." Although either root would not violate the logic of Exod 33:14, the conceptual relationship between the verbs "lead" and "walk" is more appropriate, [16] a pairing that occurs in a number of key places (e.g., Exod 13:21, 32:34; Prov 6:22; Neh 9:12, 19). [17] Likewise, the promise to give "rest" (נוח) does not seem to fit in Exod 33:14 and has no clear referent or purpose in the broader context. [18] The only use of "rest" in Exodus (or Genesis) is with the Decalogue's prescription for Sabbath (Exod 20:11, 23:12). While the root *nu'ach* (נוח) is not found in the sense of "give rest/peace" elsewhere in Exodus, it does occur in Deuteronomic texts (Deut 3:20, 5:14, 12:10, 25:19; cf. Josh 1:13, 15, 21:44, 22:4, 23:1; 2 Sam 7:1, 11; 1 Kgs 5:18). [19] Additionally, if the use of נוח is original, it would be the only place "rest" was promised in the singular "to you" (לְךָ). [20] But if the phrase was originally "I will lead you," then the singular would fit the context, of course, implying God's agreement to lead Moses.

To further understand Yhwh's first response to Moses, the context provides a clarifying parallel. God's affirmation of his presence and guidance in Exod 33:14 mirrors his own command to Moses in 32:34.

וְעַתָּה לֵךְ נְחֵה אֶת־הָעָם אֶל אֲשֶׁר־דִּבַּרְתִּי לָךְ הִנֵּה מַלְאָכִי יֵלֵךְ לְפָנֶיךָ	And now, **Go, lead** the people of which I spoke to you; behold, my messenger **will go** before you.

---

[16] For a similar discussion, see John S. Kselman, "A Note on W'nhhw in Isa 57:18," *CBQ* 43.4 (1981): 539–42. Kselman appears to find positive interpretive correspondence between Exod 33:14 and Isa 57:18. Although he acknowledges the broad acceptance of "rest" in Exod 33, he prefers the conceptual connection between "go" (הלך) and "lead" (נחה).

[17] Propp notes the possibility of נחה and the potential connection with 13:21 but does not pursue the option or provide any reasoning (Propp, *Exodus 19–40*, 604).

[18] Of the thirty-three occurrences of נוח in the Torah, the lexeme occurs 25x in Gen–Num. However, it is only used in the sense of 'rest/peace' twice, both of which are for the 'Sabbath' command (Exod 20:11, 23:12). The lexeme occurs 7x in Deut, four of them used in the sense of 'rest/peace,' in particular 'rest from enemies.' The Deuteronomic idea is then echoed often throughout the prophets and writings. Irwin similarly agrees that "peace" does not fit the context. See William H. Irwin, "The Course of the Dialogue between Moses and Yhwh in Exodus 33:12–17," *CBQ* 59.4 (1997): 631.

[19] Propp presumes the meaning "rest" which he takes to mean "I will appease you." He bases this largely on the usage in "Deuteronomi(ist)ic literature" (Propp, *Exodus 19–40*, 604).

[20] Alternatively, Fretheim, among others, has understood this to mean that God's presence will leave but he will still give "rest" to Moses (Fretheim, *Exodus*, 297).

In other words, Yhwh declares in Exod 33:14 to Moses that he will do for Moses what he commanded Moses to do for Israel in 32:34. Furthermore, this command and promise from God parallels an earlier description of his own presence and guidance out of Egypt, as seen in Exod 13:21.

וַיהוָה הֹלֵךְ לִפְנֵיהֶם יוֹמָם בְּעַמּוּד עָנָן לַנְחֹתָם הַדֶּרֶךְ	And **Yhwh went** before them daily by a pillar of cloud **to lead them in the way**

Reading Exod 33:14 with the sense of "lead" complements the context and overall theme of the passage and Exodus in general. Yhwh himself leads and instructs his people. Yet, he utilized the mediator Moses and the somewhat mysterious "angel" (מַלְאָךְ). While the ideal was for all Israel to directly interact with, follow, and know Yhwh, their disobedience and fear necessitated mediatorial intervention (cf. Exod 20:18–21). For Moses, the Lord's relationship and guidance would persist regardless of the people's rebellion or obedience (Exod 32:10). Thus, just as he was to be God for Pharaoh (Exod 4:16, 7:1), Moses was now to be God for Israel. In parallel, God instructs Moses to do as he did, leading and teaching the people. Despite Moses' concern, Yhwh did agree to continue to lead him in order that Moses might do so for the people going forward. Thus, Exod 33:14 is more logically coherent with "lead" than "rest." So, the prevalence of textual witnesses for the root נוח "to rest" is likely due to a late, anachronistic reading of Exod 33:14, influenced by the common Deuteronomic motif found later. In Exodus, though, Yhwh was envisioned as the preeminent leader of Israel, though mediated through Moses and his "angel."

The Way and Knowledge of God in Exodus 33:13

Now that the text and context have been established, the curious request of Moses in Exod 33:13 must be addressed. Moses asked to know the Lord's "way." The logical result according to his request is that he would "know" the Lord. However, two questions are in order. What is meant by "way" and what does it mean to "know" Yhwh?[21] Propp provides four options for the meaning of "way:" 1) request for guidance to the land through the desert; 2) knowledge of Yhwh's own travel plans; 3) instruction in Yhwh's expectations for the people; or 4) revelation of Yhwh's own personal character and behavior, including his "judicial principles."[22] While each of these options is possible,

---

[21] As Garrett alludes, it may be that Moses simply wants to know Yhwh's plans for Israel, "This is not a request for an advanced class in theological doctrine; it is simply that Moses is bewildered at how things are turning out." In a similar vein, Durham focuses on the theme of Yhwh's presence. See Garrett, *A Commentary on Exodus*, 647–48; John I. Durham, *Exodus*, WBC (Waco: Word Books, 1987), 647.

[22] Propp, *Exodus 19–40*, 603.

Sarna pulls on the proper thread here, reflecting Propp's third and fourth options, "Moses here asks to comprehend God's essential personality, the attributes that guide His actions."[23] As Sarna rightly observes, as well, Ps 25 and 103 provide commentary on this passage, collapsing the whole dialogue between Moses and Yhwh from Exod 33:13 and 34:6.

Exod 33:13 MT	וְעַתָּה אִם־נָא מָצָאתִי חֵן בְּעֵינֶיךָ הוֹדִעֵנִי נָא אֶת־דְּרָכֶךָ וְאֵדָעֲךָ לְמַעַן אֶמְצָא־חֵן בְּעֵינֶיךָ	And now, if I have found favor in your eyes, *make known to me your way*[24] *and I will know you*,[25] in order that I will find favor in your eyes
Exod 33:13 LXX	εἰ οὖν εὕρηκα χάριν ἐναντίον σου, ἐμφάνισόν μοι σεαυτόν, γνωστῶς ἴδω σε, ὅπως ἂν ὦ εὑρηκὼς χάριν ἐναντίον σου	Therefore, if I have found favor before you, *reveal yourself to me, I shall clearly*[26] *know you*, that I have found favor in your eyes
Ps 25:4–5, 8–10 MT	דְּרָכֶיךָ יְהוָה הוֹדִיעֵנִי אֹרְחוֹתֶיךָ לַמְּדֵנִי: הַדְרִיכֵנִי בַאֲמִתֶּךָ וְלַמְּדֵנִי כִּי־אַתָּה אֱלֹהֵי יִשְׁעִי אוֹתְךָ קִוִּיתִי כָּל־הַיּוֹם: טוֹב־וְיָשָׁר יְהוָה עַל־כֵּן יוֹרֶה חַטָּאִים בַּדָּרֶךְ: יַדְרֵךְ עֲנָוִים בַּמִּשְׁפָּט וִילַמֵּד עֲנָוִים דַּרְכּוֹ: כָּל־אָרְחוֹת יְהוָה חֶסֶד וֶאֱמֶת לְנֹצְרֵי בְרִיתוֹ וְעֵדֹתָיו:	4 *Make known to me your ways*, O Yhwh. 5 *Cause me to walk in your truth* and teach me; for you are the God of my salvation. I wait for you all day. ... 8 Good and upright is Yhwh. Therefore, instruct sinners in your way. 9 Cause the guilty to walk in justice. And teach the guilty his way. 10 *All the paths of Yhwh are steadfast love and faithful*, to those guarding his covenant and testimonies.
Ps 103:6–8 MT	עֹשֵׂה צְדָקוֹת יְהוָה וּמִשְׁפָּטִים לְכָל־עֲשׁוּקִים: יוֹדִיעַ דְּרָכָיו לְמֹשֶׁה	6 One who works righteousness, O Yhwh, and justice for all the oppressed; 7 *One who made known his ways to Moses*,[27] to the sons of

---

[23] Sarna, *Exodus*, 213.

[24] The SP and Tg. Neof. use the plural of the noun "ways." The Tg. Onq. creates the phrase "your good way," perhaps to parallel 33:19.

[25] The Tg. Onq. creates the phrase "and I will know your mercy" (ואידע רחמך). The Tg. Neof. makes the phrase "and I will fear from before you" (ואדחל מן קדמיך).

[26] Term "clearly" (γνωστῶς) only occurs here and Prov 27:23 in the LXX. In Prov, the Greek term seems to be an attempt to translate the emphatic use of a tautological infinitive, a common Hebrew grammatical idiom, "You shall surely know" (יָדֹעַ תֵּדַע).

[27] Propp prefers the plural reading for Exod 33:13 precisely because of Ps 103:7 (Propp, *Exodus 19–40*, 588). While an important parallel, there are other places that change the term "way" to "ways" such as 2 Kgs 22:2 and 2 Chron 34:2, "[Josiah] walked in the whole way (בְּכָל־דֶּרֶךְ) of David his father" // "[Josiah] walked in all the ways (בְּדַרְכֵי) of David his father."

לִבְנֵי יִשְׂרָאֵל עֲלִילוֹתָיו׃	Israel his deeds; 8 ***Merciful and***
רַחוּם וְחַנּוּן יְהוָה	***gracious***, O Yhwh, ***slow to anger and***
אֶרֶךְ אַפַּיִם וְרַב־חָסֶד	***full of steadfast love***.

As an early interpreter of the Exodus dialogue, the psalmist saw that the "way" of Yhwh was his personal character and behavior, manifested to Moses at his request.[28] He also understood that Yhwh was like a father to Israel (cf. Ps 103:13),[29] who teaches, guides, and disciplines, desiring his people to walk in accordance with his own way (cf. Deut 8:5–6; Prov 3:11–12). Up to this point, Moses had conversed with Yhwh. He had seen God's mighty deeds to deliver Israel out of Egypt and to provide in numerous miraculous ways. It appears, however, Moses was not sure what Yhwh was actually like. In other words, were the commands and behaviors arbitrary or inherent to his own way? Would he indeed mercilessly wipe out the people? In Exod 33:19, Yhwh informs Moses of his nature by declaring that he shows "mercy" (רחם) and "grace" (חנן) to whomever he wills. Surprisingly, this is the first revelatory use of these terms explicitly ascribed to Yhwh's action or character in the Torah. The only earlier occurrences are merely indirect blessings between people (Gen 33:5, 11, 42:21, 43:14, 29).[30] As Yhwh explained to Moses prior, he had been known as powerful in past times, the *El-Shaddai* (e.g., Exod 6:3), but was progressively revealing his nature, particularly in his covenant relationship with Israel.[31]

To better understand Moses' request in context, it is important to note that it is progressively linked in Exod 33:13 and 18. He says to Yhwh, "Make known (ידע) to me your way (דרך) and I will know (ידע) you ... Show (ראה) me your glory (כבד)." The Lord responds to the first with, "My presence will go and I will lead you" (Exod 33:14). This strange response to Moses' request seems to be at best a partial answer or perhaps a deflection to Moses' concern

---

[28] The psalmist in Ps 139:23–24 (cf. 5:9, 23:3, 27:11, 31:4, 73:24, 77:21, 78:14, 143:10) appears to pick up on this theme, as well, popular in Psalms, "Search me, O God, and know my heart; examine me and know my thoughts. See if there is a grievous way in me and lead me [וּנְחֵנִי] in the everlasting way." Here, the options are the "grievous" or "toilsome" way versus the "everlasting" way. While little is said of this divine way, the psalmist does contrast it with "the wicked," "men of blood," "evil intent," "those who use the Lord's name in vain," "those who hate Yhwh," and "those who rise against [Yhwh]," all of which are reflected in some capacity within the proverbial wisdom program.

[29] Relevant to the study of Lesson 4 in Proverbs, Ps 103:13 goes on to state, "As a father is merciful to sons, Yhwh is merciful to those fearing him." In other words, those who fear Yhwh are equivalent to or figuratively treated as God's sons, central to the motif for the son to emulate God as a teacher and father.

[30] The nominal form *chen* (חֵן) occurs almost exclusively in the idiomatic stock phrase "favor in the eyes of" several times in the Torah, both for people and God (Gen 6:8, 18:3, 19:19, 30:27, 32:6, 33:8, 10, 15, 34:11, 39:4, 21, 47:29, 50:4; Exod 3:21, 11:3, 12:36, 33:12, 13, 16, 17, 34:9; Num 11:11, 15, 32:5; Deut 24:1). While the idea of "favor" from God was presumed, Moses was not sure if this was indeed true of his nature or ways.

[31] On this point, Propp discusses that the term "way" may have derived from Ugaritic implying God's "power," equivalent to כח (Deut 4:37). Although this connotation may subtly underlie the ambiguous request, Yhwh's own response provides the narrator's intent for the reader. See Propp, *Exodus 19–40*, 603.

regarding God's earlier command.[32] However, Exod 33:18 seems to imply Moses was not fully satisfied with the answer he received in 33:14, likely signaling he had more in mind with the first request. So, Moses rephrases the request (Exod 33:18). To this, Yhwh gives a more complete and appropriate answer to satisfy Moses. The dialogue then transitions into the famous historical narrative describing the "name" theophany episode (Exod 33:19–34:7; cf. Num 14:18; Deut 5:9–10; Jer 39:11; 32:18–19, 46:28, 49:12; Joel 2:13; Jon 4:2; Mic 7:18–20; Nah 1:2; Ps 86:15, 103:8, 17, 145:8; Lam 3:32; Dan 9:4; Neh 9:17).[33] In this episode, the Lord both declares and reveals his character, a proper and perhaps preferable substitute for his "presence" (פָּנַי). Thus, Yhwh's character – the essence of his "way" (דרך) – is what Moses could expect from him. As Hamilton comments, "Everything the Lord says autobiographically is something that God is or does for the benefit of others."[34] Although "way" is often used literally for a road or journey in Exodus, the metaphorical usage for God's covenant stipulations occurs only twice before Moses' request. In Exod 18:20, Yhwh tells Moses, "You will warn them of the statutes and instructions (תורה) and shall make known (ידע) to them the way (דרך) they shall walk and the deed that they shall do." The only other time the metaphor is used prior to 33:13 is in Yhwh's rebuke of Israel for their idolatry, "They turned (סור) quickly from the way (דרך) which I commanded them; they made for themselves a molten calf and they worshiped it and sacrificed to it and they said, 'These are your gods, O Israel'" (Exod 32:8; cf. 23:32).

In context, Moses' first request to know the "way" of Yhwh must be understood against the revelation of God's nature in the following verses.[35] Likewise, Moses' purpose for including the phrase "I will know (ידע) you" is significant. As mentioned previously, the narrator interrupts the dialogue with a comment that Moses and Yhwh already had a friendly relationship, which was unique to Moses – "Yhwh spoke to Moses face-to-face" and "a prophet has not yet arisen in Israel like Moses whom Yhwh knew (ידע) face-to-face" (Exod 33:11; Deut 34:10). The primary theme for most contexts in Exodus containing the term "know" (ידע) are informational in nature, though, particularly that Egypt or Israel would know "that I am Yhwh" (כי אני יהוה). As a form of revelation, it is stated in Exod 6:3, "By my name, I did not make

---

[32] Irwin proposes that the strange mismatched requests and responses are a literary technique he calls "delayed response." In his view, the "two currents discernable" are an "ironic playfulness" (Irwin, "The Course of the Dialogue between Moses and Yhwh in Exodus 33:12–17," 633).

[33] Propp discusses several possibilities for the "name" theophany presented here. Against some speculation throughout rabbinic tradition regarding the number of divine attributes, he warns, "I do not believe that we are meant to count anything here" (Propp, *Exodus 19–40*, 610).

[34] Victor P. Hamilton, *Exodus: An Exegetical Commentary* (Grand Rapids: Baker Academic, 2011), 576.

[35] Waldman discusses a number of potential meanings for God's "way." He says it could refer to God's involvement in battle (Deut 33:2; Judg 5:4–5; Hab 3:6; Ps 68:25). Alternatively, based on an Akk. cognate, he proposes it could mean "customary ways, their basic character." Within the broader Mesopotamian and ANE religious tradition, he notes the idea could connote the means by which a human can please the gods, particularly related to shrines. Waldman seems to prefer the last option for Exod 33:13. See Waldman, "God's Ways," 69–70.

myself known." Regarding his covenant stipulations, Yhwh commands Israel, "You shall not oppress a sojourner; you yourself know (ידע) the life of sojourning, for you were sojourners in the land of Egypt" (Exod 23:9). The use of "know" in this example seems to imply a personal, experiential type of knowledge, one which ought to translate into a behavioral reality. The only other significant type of knowledge expressed in Exodus is when both Moses and Yhwh say that Moses is known "by name" (בְּשֵׁם). This phrase is unique, only occurring here with the term "know" (Exod 33:12, 17). In almost all other occurrences in the HB, the phrase uses the idea "call upon" or "speak," even in this passage later (Exod 33:19, 34:5). So, in essence, Moses says of Yhwh, 'You know *me* by name. You have *told* me your name, but I do not know *you* in your fullness of person and character.'

So, although the Lord's responses to Moses' requests – to know his way and glory (Exod 33:13, 18)[36] – may seem strange, in actuality they complete the underlying framework for Moses' requests. To satisfy him, Yhwh informs Moses that he has not and cannot experience his full "presence."[37] God's fullness is too much for a mere human to bear.[38] What Moses can endure is a glimpse or perceptible version.[39] This glimpse centered on "the name Yhwh" (בְּשֵׁם יְהוָה). Yet, inherent to his name is his "way" and "glory," most eminently captured in the statement, "A God of mercy and grace, slow to anger and full of covenant faithfulness and truth, guarding covenant faithfulness for thousands, forgiving iniquity and trespass and sin but he will not set free the guilty, visiting iniquity of fathers on children and children's children, on the third and fourth" (Exod 34:6–7).[40] The Lord's partial revelation to Moses satisfied his desire to know Yhwh and his way, which immediately propels Moses to again implore him to make Israel his "inheritance" (Exod 34:9).

So, to summarize, Yhwh and Moses exchanged several requests and responses. Yhwh's first response seems to be a deflection and a mundane concession. However, Moses goes on to clarify his desire and interest. At first, he clarifies his concern for the people, which God affirms. Then, he clarifies that the heart of his request was to understand and know Yhwh himself

---

[36] Propp discusses the meaning of "glory" used here. While it may simply connote "self," he prefers the sense of "theophany." Additionally, he notes the potential logical connection between this covenantal validation scene in Exodus and Gen 15:8, "by what shall I know" (Propp, *Exodus 19–40*, 606).

[37] Regarding the apparent contradiction in Moses' request to "know" or "see" God, Hamilton notes, "There must have been two mutually exclusive traditions in Israel that were never brought together: God cannot be seen. God can be seen. The other answer is to suggest that 'saw' or 'saw face to face,' like 'seek[ing] God's face,' is the Bible's way of affirming the possibility and reality of an encounter or a relationship with God that is akin to a relationship between lovers." See Fretheim, *Exodus*, 299; Hamilton, *Exodus: An Exegetical Commentary*, 570.

[38] Irwin perceptively notes that Moses omits the danger of God's presence in his appeals until he himself has experienced the theophany in Exod 34:9 (Irwin, "The Course of the Dialogue between Moses and Yhwh in Exodus 33:12–17," 634).

[39] Hamilton, *Exodus: An Exegetical Commentary*, 569–70.

[40] Waldman refers to Maimonides in his understanding of the divine attributes, those that "man must know and imitate." For a discussion on the meaning of "way" in rabbinic tradition, see Waldman, "God's Ways," 67.

better. While Moses may have meant God's "presence," the Lord fulfills his desire by manifesting his nature through his name and characteristics. Although a complicated narrative, the progression of the dialogue builds from pedestrian concerns to a theophany that impacted the rest of biblical history – the nature of Yhwh revealed.

Conclusion

The coordination of the way, character, likeness, and knowledge of God in this passage is a significant contribution to the study of these topics in the HB, particularly as it impacted the proverbial wisdom program. These aspects of God are independent in their own respect but are at the same time interrelated. Yhwh commands his way, which must be kept. Yet, this way is intimately intertwined with his nature.[41] Together, knowing the way of Yhwh and walking in it is to know him, a form of embodied knowledge (cf. Prov 3:6).[42] The relational aspect inherent to the way of Yhwh is highlighted in this passage as well. Those who walk in the way will likewise gain personal and experiential knowledge of Yhwh himself, particularly as they walk with him in his way and emulate his character. However, if they walk contrary to his way, they will forfeit a personal and experiential knowledge of God, as Israel found out through their stumbling in the wilderness.

---

[41] Stuart, *Exodus*, 705–6.

[42] See Ryan O'Dowd, *The Wisdom of Torah: Epistemology in Deuteronomy and the Wisdom Literature*, FRLANT 225 (Göttingen: Vandenhoeck & Ruprecht, 2009), 15, 24.

LESSON 13

Analysis of 7:1–23
"Keeping commandments is life"

Much like Lessons 9, 10, and 12, the father focuses on the metaphor of seduction and adultery in Lesson 13. Through an extended third- and first-person illustration on the ways of the *zarah*, it becomes clear that she is not a passive deviation but an active threat to the son (Prov 7:12–20). The father understands the importance of *torah* and *mitzvah* to properly form awareness, character, and commitment to the way of Yhwh and Wisdom (Prov 7:1–3). Without these, the son will likely fall prey to her seduction. This is in part because she stands as a rival or counterfeit to Wisdom. To avoid such a blunder, the father once again utilizes a lesser-to-greater metaphor in order to persuade the son to imitate the wise and prudent (Prov 7:22–23). This metaphor also emphasizes that the father's instruction is not a trivial warning but one of mortal consequence. As a bridge between thematic sections, Lesson 13 highlights both the *zarah* and Wisdom, the contentious embodiments of the two paths before the son (Prov 7:4–5). Depending on which he chooses, he will align himself to one type of ancestor, either to those who followed after the way of the nations or to those who followed closely in the way of Yhwh.

Structure of Lesson 13

In his address regarding the seductive dangers that await the son, the father uses a three-part structure.[1] First, as is typical, the father exhorts the son to guard *torah* and *mitzvah* (Prov 7:1–3; cf. 3:1, 6:20, 23). Then, with a creative

---

[1] Most use a three-part division but incorrectly ascribe the sections as Prov 7:1–5, 6–23, 24–27. Loader provides a six-strophe structure: Prov 7:1–5, 6–9, 10–13, 14–20, 21–23, 24–27. However, as discussed in the "Structure of Prov 1–9," Prov 7:24–27 serves as a literary and thematic bridge between Lessons 13 and 14. See Schipper, *Proverbs 1–15*, 254; Plöger, *Spruche Salomos (Proverbia)*, 75; Fox, *Proverbs 1–9*, 237–38; Waltke, *Proverbs (1–15)*, 367; Loader, *Proverbs 1–9*, 292.

and detailed diatribe, the father warns the son of the *zarah* and her powerfully seductive and aggressive ways, the direct rival of Wisdom (Prov 7:4–21). Finally, the father provides a conclusive string of metaphors to illustrate the fate of those who succumb to the persuasion of the *zarah* rather than his instruction (Prov 7:22–23).

I. The Exhortation: guard *torah* and *mitzvah* (7:1–3)
II. The Warning: Wisdom's seductive rival (7:4–21)
III. The Naïve's Fate: following the *zarah* to peril (7:22–23)

For "The Warning," there are four sub-sections, as well (Prov 7:4–5, 6–13, 14–19, 21). The first part gives an admonition for the son to identify with Wisdom and not the *zarah*. The second part is the father's first-person observation of the naïve who foolishly fall into her traps.[2] By implication, the son ought to follow in his father's ways by also observing the folly of the naïve and learning from their blunders rather than foolishly following them.[3] The third part is a first-person view from the perspective of the *zarah*, who aggressively pursues and persuades the naïve. The fourth part is a conclusive return to the father's observation. The concluding "Naïve's Fate" is really an extension of the father's observation. However, it takes a literary turn to metaphor rather than as part of his observation per se. It is also important to note that while the imagery of the lesson uses sexual seduction, the father incisively includes the term "teaching" (לֶקַח) in reference to the *zarah* in order to signal that the lesson is not merely about sexual misconduct (cf. Prov 1:5, 4:2, 9:9).[4] Rather, the

---

[2] The LXX and Syr. both read this section with the woman as the subject, looking out of the window. However, the change in perspective to the father's personal observation would seem a more difficult reading to explain from a text-critical perspective. Regardless, there is not a significant difference in interpretation if it were originally feminine. Forti and Talshir argue that despite the LXX shift in gender here, the translator does not intend to change the message or imagery of the lesson. Building on the LXX, though, McKane notes that some have taken the feminine reading to signal the Astarte or Aphrodite cult. They primarily get this from the LXX term παρακυπτουσα, assuming a late date for both the LXX and MT. McKane seems to prefer the feminine reading but with Wisdom as an Israelite queen, a poetic play on the Astarte or Jezebel motif. Both of these theories seem unnecessary. While the mention of vows may be an indication that she is a cult prostitute, as it is widely argued, it does not necessitate the feminine reading in 7:6. See Tova Forti and Zipora Talshir, "Proverbs 7 in MT and LXX: Form and Content," *Text* 22.1 (2005): 129–67; McKane, *Proverbs*, 335–36; Karel Van Der Toorn, "Female Prostitution in Payment of Vows in Ancient Israel," *JBL* 108.2 (1989): 193–205; Boström, *Proverbiastudien*, 103–34; Waltke, *Proverbs (1–15)*, 377; Leo G. Perdue, *Wisdom and Cult: A Critical Analysis of the Views of Cult in the Wisdom Literatures of Israel and the Ancient Near East*, SBLDS 30 (Missoula: Society of Biblical Literature, 1977), 150.

[3] Brown and Bland note the importance of "human experience as a means of incarnating moral character" in the pedagogy of Proverbs (Dave L. Bland, *Proverbs and the Formation of Character* (Eugene: Cascade Books, 2015), 66).

[4] Cf. Fox, *Proverbs 1–9*, 248–49. Fox refers to the *zarah*'s speech as the "Strange Woman's doctrine, the negative counterpart to wisdom's teaching."

zarah and her aberrant ways embody the false and foolish teachings that might lure the son away from walking in the way of the wise.[5]

Parallels with Lesson 3 (7:1–3)

As mentioned previously, Lesson 13 (Prov 7:1–23) parallels Lesson 3 (3:1–10) in the chiastic schema of Prov 1–9. Both lessons implore the son to guard *torah* and *mitsvah* (Prov 3:1, 7:2). While not exclusive to the lessons, their combination is an indication of the linkage (cf. Prov 6:20, 23). Furthermore, the two lessons use a unique phrase "write them on the tablets of your heart" as part of the introductory call from the father (Prov 3:3, 7:3; cf. Deut 6:6–9, 11:18–21).[6] As described in Lesson 3, the implications of these elements signal the reader to the Torah and Yhwh's instruction.[7] In other words, the teaching from the father is not arbitrary but rooted in a long imitative tradition of the wise, leading back to its founder, God and his ways. This parallel then takes the son a step further in his evaluation of the seductive ways of the *zarah*. Lesson 3 is a positive, persuasive case for following, trusting, knowing, and honoring Yhwh. It is open and unhidden in its way, even condemning apparent wisdom which deviates from true wisdom (Prov 3:7). This path is accompanied by wellness and blessings. Yet, Lesson 13 describes a way that is laced with aggressive persuasion and meets in dark hidden corners.[8] It purports purity but only in a false and heartless manner (Prov 7:14). While the one who follows the Lord is blessed, the fate of the naïve who follows the aberrant way is ignorance and death.[9] So, this introductory exhortation from the father serves as a framing device for the lesson to be understood in light of the proper way from Lesson 3. Again, what is generally positive in the first half of Prov 1–9 is often revisited or re-illumined with a negative view in the latter half. In terms of progress, this lesson presumes the son's eventual

---

[5] Fox notes that many medieval rabbinical sources (Maimonides, Malbim, Sa'adia) viewed this *zarah* and her ways as emblematic of worldly, lustful desires or even philosophies that may capture a person rather than a literal warning against adultery or prostitution. He also provides a lengthy discussion on the variety of interpretations for the "strange woman." See Fox, *Proverbs 1–9*, 241, 252–62; Scott C. Jones, "Wisdom's Pedagogy: A Comparison of Proverbs VII and 4Q184," *VT* 53.1 (2003): 68; Plöger, *Spruche Salomos (Proverbia)*, 75–76; Daniel J. Estes, *Hear, My Son: Teaching and Learning in Proverbs 1–9*, NSBT 4 (Grand Rapids: Eerdmans, 1997), 117–18.

[6] Cf. Schipper, *Proverbs 1–15*, 255.

[7] Cf. Murphy, *Proverbs*, 42; Johnny E. Miles, *Wise King - Royal Fool: Semiotics, Satire and Proverbs 1–9* (New York: T&T Clark, 2004), 54.

[8] As Perdue notes, "It is her language more than her actions or appearances that has the power to entrap and destroy" (Perdue, *Proverbs*, 134).

[9] Cf. Richard J. Clifford, *The Wisdom Literature*, Interpreting Biblical Texts (Nashville: Abingdon, 1998), 56.

engagement with aggressive forms of temptation, seducing him to leave the wise path of his father and Yhwh.[10]

Wisdom's Rival (7:4–21)

At the heart of this lesson, the warning against the *zarah* resurfaces with a final crescendo. However, what is interesting in this presentation is her explicit contrast with Wisdom.[11] While subtly present in previous lessons, the father commands the son, "Say to Wisdom, 'You are my sister'" (Prov 7:4).[12] The very next verse intimates that the reason for this is to "guard" the son from the *zarah* and her parallel the "stranger" (נָכְרִיָּה). In the initial exhortation, the father calls on the son to "guard" (שׁמר) his *torah* and *mitsvah* (Prov 7:1–2), subtly overlaying himself and his instruction with Wisdom and Yhwh.[13] Thus, the son's confession of Wisdom in Prov 7:4 would serve as a means to fulfill or actualize the father's command in 7:1–2. The explicit personification of Wisdom here likely serves as a bridge or preview to the following two lessons,[14] which provide the most extensive anthropomorphic descriptions of Wisdom and her counterpart, Folly.[15] However, the father's use of "sister" regarding Wisdom seems a bit incongruous on the surface with the more consistent marital imagery used elsewhere (e.g., Prov 4:4–9).[16] This sentiment is found within the poetic lines of the Song of Songs, as well (Prov

---

[10] Jones argues that the equivalent Qumran lesson in 4Q184 differs in the area of nuance and competence. While the proverbial father intends for the son to progress in his discernment as part of his growth in wisdom, the Qumran teachers sought to avoid ambiguity or "indeterminacy in pedagogical method." See Jones, "Wisdom's Pedagogy," 75–80.

[11] For detailed comparison and contrast, see Gale A. Yee, "'I Have Perfumed My Bed with Myrrh': The Foreign Woman ('iššâ Zārâ) in Proverbs 1–9," *JSOT* 13.43 (1989): 53–68; J. N. Aletti, "Seduction et Parole En Proverbes I-IX," *VT* 27.2 (1977): 129–44; Jones, "Wisdom's Pedagogy."

[12] The command from the father is an offensive or preemptive action meant to contrast the aggressive ways of the *zarah*, in order to fight passivity and naivety (Miles, *Wise King - Royal Fool: Semiotics, Satire and Proverbs 1–9*, 74). This proactive action is meant to parallel the proactive action of the *zarah*. Similarly, Lessons 1 and 15 both note that it is really Wisdom that initiates or embodies the proactive action by calling out to the naïve (Prov 1:20–21, 9:1–4).

[13] Cf. Tremper Longman III, *Proverbs*, BCOTWP (Grand Rapids: Baker Academic, 2006), 186; Schipper, *Proverbs 1–15*, 255.

[14] Cf. Whybray, *Composition of the Book of Proverbs*, 27. Whybray notes a pattern where the lesson content is followed by "poems which are concerned with both personified Wisdom and with Yahweh," implying the intentional placement of Lesson 13 before 14.

[15] Murphy observes similar traits between the seductress of Lesson 13 with Folly in Lesson 15. He also notes that this woman is "beside" (אצל) every corner (Prov 7:12) while Wisdom is "beside" Yhwh (8:30). This subtly implies the proper path the son ought to emulate. See Murphy, *Proverbs*, 43.

[16] McKane, Waltke, and Longman argue the term is actually meant to imply "wife" or "bride" from Song of Songs and ANE love poetry. This would certainly align with the Wisdom as wife imagery, particularly as a deterrent to prostitution. However, Song of Songs explicitly pairs the term with "bride" while in Prov 7 the parallel line uses "kin" (מדע). This difference implies familial rather than marital imagery is intended here as opposed to Song of Songs. See McKane, *Proverbs*, 334; Waltke, *Proverbs (1–15)*, 369–70; Longman, *Proverbs*, 187.

4:9–5:2).[17] As noted previously, though, the metaphorical uses of Wisdom are actually quite wide, including a wife, a mother, a teacher, a prophet, and an aspect or embodiment of Yhwh.[18] So, rather than implicate incestuous behavior (e.g., Lev 18:9–11; Deut 27:22; cf. 2 Sam 13:1–32),[19] the term is better understood as an endearing nod to the familial and friendly relation. This close relationship, even cohabitation, between the son and Wisdom is paralleled with the term "kin" (מֹדָע).[20] Further, it is likely that the use of "sister" and "kin" is meant to explicitly contrast the status of the *zarah* and "stranger" of the next verse (Prov 7:5). In other words, Wisdom is from within the Torah-adherent tradition and covenantal community, like kin, while the alternative ways of the *zarah* are foreign and inherently outside the father's instruction, or the way of Yhwh.[21]

To further implicate the foreign temptress and her seductive, aberrant ways, the father uses language from elsewhere in Prov 1–9. The description of the *zarah* and "stranger" uses the unique phrase "smooth words" (אֲמָרֶיהָ הֶחֱלִיקָה) which appears in parallel with Prov 2:16 (7:5; cf. 6:24).[22] The father goes on to connect one's interest and acceptance of her ways with the image of turning to "her house" (בֵּיתָהּ). This phrase appears several times primarily of the *zarah* (Prov 2:18, 5:8, 7:8, 7:27) but also of Folly (9:14) and even with Wisdom (9:1). As the metaphorical imagery typically implies, there is an association between entering "her house" and a descent into Sheol or "death" (Prov 2:18, 7:27, 9:14). So, the father uses this imagery to imply that entering into or "walking the path of her house" (דְּרָךְ בֵּיתָהּ יִצְעָד), that is the *zarah,* is a sure way to achieve calamity and even death. In fact, the final verse of Prov 1–9 concludes the whole program with this point. The father warns that the naïve who turn to Folly (or the *zarah*) are indeed following after the naïve who have gone before and now reside in Sheol (Prov 9:18).[23] Thus if the son gives

---

[17] Fox, Schipper, and Jones note a number of other allusions as well. See Fox, *Proverbs 1–9*, 240; Schipper, *Proverbs 1–15*, 256; Jones, "Wisdom's Pedagogy," 70–71.

[18] Cf. Fox, "Ideas of Wisdom in Proverbs 1–9," 625; Fox, *Proverbs 1–9*, 341. Fox generally argues for a multi-faceted view of the metaphorical source of Wisdom's imagery, finding elements of trace aspects from the variety of potential sources. However, he arrives at this by ascribing disunity to the text.

[19] In Ugaritic lore, Anat was both the sister and consort of Baal. So, it is less probable that the proverbial father would imply through ambiguity not only a violation to Torah but also an aberrant aspect of Canaanite mythology. See CTA 10:2:10–3:21; Wyatt, *Religious Texts from Ugarit*, 156–59.

[20] The familial language for Wisdom may be an intentional contrast from the highly seductive and erotic language for the *zarah*. Here, the brotherly affection and care for Wisdom as a sister demurs the animalistic lust and violence of those who follow the *zarah*. Cf. Schipper, *Proverbs 1–15*, 262; Loader, *Proverbs 1–9*, 297–98.

[21] Cf. Longman, *Proverbs*, 187; Estes, *Hear, My Son*, 57; Raymond C. Van Leeuwen, "Liminality and Worldview in Proverbs 1–9," *Semeia* 50 (1990): 116; Perdue, *Proverbs*, 133. As Estes says regarding the implicit ways of the *zarah*, "They clearly portray the foolishness of living outside the limits of Yahweh's order."

[22] Cf. Knut Martin Heim, *Poetic Imagination in Proverbs: Variant Repetitions and the Nature of Poetry*, BBRSup 4 (Eisenbrauns, 2013), 94–104.

[23] Estes astutely remarks, "Folly, then, is not regarded in Proverbs as intellectual deficiency, but inability or unwillingness to conform to Yahweh's order" (Estes, *Hear, My Son*,

into the *zarah*, he is, in essence, imitating the naïve fools who have already fallen prey to her aberrant though tempting ways.

Furthermore, as mentioned, the ways of the *zarah* are not passive. This foreign woman and her ways are proactive and even aggressive. It says that she "looks," "seeks," "grasps," and "finds" the naïve (Prov 7:6, 13, 15).[24] All of these traits, however, are indicative of Wisdom and those with her on the proper path (Prov 1:28, 2:5, 3:13, 18, 4:13, 8:9, 12, 17, 35). So, the father informs the son that his temptation to stray will in some sense mirror or reflect his own pursuit for Wisdom, though in an inverse or counterfeit manner. Likewise, the aggressiveness of the *zarah* is further highlighted by the phrase, "She lies in ambush at every corner" (Prov 7:12). The term for "lie in ambush" (ארב) was used in Lesson 1 for the initial foil to the father's way.[25] The way of "sinners" used this term as part of their ploy to the son (Prov 1:10; cf. Mic 7:2–3).[26] Although the group of miscreants was going to ambush the innocent, the tables have now been turned on the son. He is the target of ambush but from the seductive *zarah*.[27] Though the attack by the *zarah* may appear less caustic than the miscreants of Lesson 1, their end is all the same (Prov 1:19, 7:23). In fact, Lesson 1 even describes that the ambush of these sinners was, in reality, a trap set for themselves (Prov 1:18). In a similar way, the father uses an animal metaphor to imply the same thing in Lesson 13 (Prov 7:22–23). Just as the son was commanded there, "Do not walk in the way with them" (Prov 1:15), he is now warned not to follow after or imitate the ways of the *zarah*, or those who do. Following in their ways means sharing in their fate.

Finally, it is clear enough that the father's purpose in this portion of Lesson 13 is primarily to persuade the son to turn away from the *zarah* as she aggressively seeks to "turn" (נטה) him to her way (Prov 7:21; cf. 2:2, 4:5, 20, 27, 5:1, 13).[28] He understands that following and seeking after her will only result in trouble. In fact, the father describes the approach of the *zarah* with the term "persuade" (נדח). The term is used elsewhere in the HB, perhaps not surprisingly, in relation to idolatry and apostasy (Prov 7:21; cf. Deut 4:19, 13:14, 30:17; 2 Chron 21:11). While not exclusively used for idolatry, the term's use with the naïve and his union with the *zarah* does seem equivalent to or indicative of those passages with idolatry and religious apostasy. The most

---

44). In other words, the foolish path which leads to death is marked by an unwillingness to imitate and reflect the ways of Wisdom and Yhwh.

24 Cf. Fox, *Proverbs 1–9*, 247; Schipper, *Proverbs 1–15*, 264.

25 Cf. Richard J. Clifford, *Proverbs: A Commentary*, OTL (Louisville: Westminster John Knox, 1999), 83.

26 Cf. Schipper, *Proverbs 1–15*, 267, 270.

27 Clifford proposes that the naïve fool who follows her will actually be her sacrifice for the vow she will fulfill. This view does make sense of the ox led to slaughter and other imagery he points out but requires a future tense reading of the Piel perfect as "I will fulfill my vows" (שִׁלַּמְתִּי), initially proposed by Boström. Scholarship has been divided on the validity of this reading. See Clifford, *Proverbs*, 88; Schipper, *Proverbs 1–15*, 268–70.

28 Cf. Toy, *Proverbs*, 155–56; Waltke, *Proverbs (1–15)*, 367. Toy draws a parallel between this passage and both 1 Kgs 11:2 and Deut 13:5 with the terms for "turn" (נטה) and "persuade" (נדח), respectively.

appropriate of these is the extended command from Deut 13:1–18 regarding the fate of those who "persuade" fellow Israelites, even kin, to go after other gods.[29] Moses notes that these apostates, who teach others to do the same, actually serve as a tool in order to test the people's "love" (אהב) for Yhwh (Deut 13:3; cf. Prov 3:12, 8:17, 21). Moses commands that they must instead "walk after Yhwh" (Deut 13:4). Lesson 13 poetically recasts this grave danger and command from the Torah in the form of a seductress, who would lead the son to turn and go astray, both into apostasy and death.[30]

The Fate of the Naïve (7:22–23)

To conclude the final lesson on the *zarah*,[31] the father once again uses a string of lesser-to-greater metaphors. Much like before, the metaphors include a deer and a bird (Prov 7:23; cf. 1:17, 6:5). This time, however, he also includes an ox (Prov 7:22; cf. Isa 1:3).[32] Unlike the ant metaphor (Prov 6:6–8), these animals are utilized for their foolish or naïve entrapment (cf. Jer 19:11).[33] Likewise, the fate of each is their demise. The ox is perhaps the most pitiful example, which starts the list here. In this case, the ox is much larger and certainly able to overpower the one leading them. Yet, it willingly follows its leader right into death.[34] The purpose and value of this type of metaphor is to give an easily observable and relatable analogy for his lesson. To do this, the metaphor utilizes the wisdom hierarchy which views animals below the wise but above the fool. In other words, fools are worse or lower than animals. The point is not to exhort the son to be like the animals but to see them as a demeaning example which he must strive to be wiser than. In this case, his animalistic

---

[29] Cf. Toy, *Proverbs*, 155–56; Schipper, *Proverbs 1–15*, 274. As Schipper rightly notes, "The woman stands not only for adultery or seduction, but for the 'other teaching.' This, in turn, represents a path."

[30] In light of the strong Deuteronomic language of Prov 7:1–3, it is reasonable to conclude the father had the Torah in view while developing this lesson. Murphy agrees that the passage "actualizes the traditional law." But he myopically views it only in the literal sense of adultery and sexual immorality. Murphy, *Proverbs*, 45; Perdue, *Proverbs*, 133.

[31] Fox, *Proverbs 1–9*, 239.

[32] As mentioned, Isaiah also utilizes this lesser-to-greater metaphor using an ox and donkey to shame Judah into being wiser. "An ox knows its owner and a donkey his master's pen. Israel does not know; my people do not understand" (Isa 1:3).

[33] Jeremiah uses a similar image to prophetically and poetically describe the conspiracy against him, though he was innocent and perhaps naïve as a youth. Thus, the image of the naïve is not inherently one of wickedness but of one who must seek to subvert the wiles of the wicked and their ways through divine wisdom. "And Yhwh made known to me and I knew; then he made me see their deeds. And I was like a friendly ([אַלּוּף] unsuspecting/naïve) lamb led to slaughter. And I did not know that they devised schemes against me" (Jer 19:18–19).

[34] In Prov 7:22, the MT uses the term "suddenly" (פִּתְאֹם), perhaps echoing the sudden disaster from 3:25 and 6:15. However, the LXX uses the term "naïve, tricked" (κεπφόω), instead reading the Heb. term "naïve, simple" (פְּתִי) found in Prov 7:7 as פְּתָאִים (cf. 1:4, 8:5, 9:6). The Syr. seems to avoid the issue by translating, "And he goes and he is caught." The context would make more sense of the LXX reading in that the ox "naively" follows the *zarah* rather than "suddenly." Prior to the development of the *nikkud*, both consonantal forms would be interchangeable and easily explainable.

desires must be assuaged in order to avoid following in the animals' unfortunate though naïve fate.

In this passage, the animals embody the path of the naïve or blind, which unknowingly but willingly walk right into their own destruction. The son ought not to be so foolish but as a wise student, he must avoid the tempting yet destructive path of the *zarah*. Similar to Lesson 9 (Prov 5:6) and Lesson 15 (9:13; cf. 9:18), the way of the *zarah* is marked by ignorance (7:23; cf. 4:19). This quality directly contrasts the way of the wise which is conversely marked by knowledge and knowing (e.g., Prov 1:2, 7, 2:5, 3:6, 8:12, 9:10). So, the father desires the son to be prudent, expressing wisdom and knowledge by walking in the way of Wisdom and Yhwh.[35] These figures, along with the father, are the greater examples to which the lesser animal metaphors are intended to point the son. If he imitates the wise and their way, then he too will find life.

Conclusion

Lesson 13 concludes the *zarah* lessons. Here, the father once again references Wisdom explicitly, which serves as a bridge to the last two lessons. While Wisdom is seen in a variety of roles elsewhere, she is figured in Lesson 13 as beloved kin (Prov 7:4). In this metaphor, she is the faithful and familial inverse of the foreign *zarah*, who is the embodiment of infidelity and folly (Prov 7:10, 19). Furthermore, the father describes the *zarah* as aggressive in her attempts to persuade the son to follow in her ways (Prov 7:13, 21). If he is not careful, the son will become like, or even worse than, animals who are willingly led to their death (Prov 7:22–23). Instead, he must guard the father's *torah*, which has been passed down through the generations, in order to protect his life (Prov 7:1–3). By walking in this way, he will stay on the straight path, reflecting the ways of Wisdom and Yhwh. As a thematic bridge, the opening of Lesson 14 provides an additional harrowing end for those who follow the *zarah* in Lessons 9–13. Yet, this negative opening is an intentional contrast with the exalted and righteous path of Wisdom, which will lead the son to be like Wisdom and Yhwh (Prov 7:4, 8:1).

---

[35] Estes comments on the totality of the student's imitative trajectory – knowledge, action, desire, "The learner must not only know what wisdom teaches and do what wisdom commands, but he must also love what wisdom values so that his life is shaped in accordance with Yahweh's desires" (Estes, *Hear, My Son*, 67). In his statement, it appears Estes espouses an imitative or reflective relationship between the son and Wisdom or Yhwh.

LESSON 14

Analysis of 7:24–8:31
"Seek wisdom as Yhwh"

Following an extended and colorful exposé of the *zarah* in Lessons 9–13, the father launches into an extended and colorful encomium of Wisdom in Lesson 14. While Wisdom is now the explicit focus of the father's attention, it is really her divine qualities and proximity that he is most interested in promoting. On the one hand, if the son follows in the way of Wisdom, he will avoid harm and Sheol (Prov 7:24–27). Similarly, if he walks in the way of righteousness, as Wisdom does (Prov 8:20), he will restore the original intent of *adam* (אָדָם). As the first humans were to do, he will serve as a prince with God, properly utilizing Wisdom and reflecting his righteous rule (Prov 8:14–18, 30). Yet, as described in previous lessons, the path of Wisdom is fraught with distractions and temptations (Prov 8:10–11). As an underlying poetic image, then, the father draws the student's heart away from the depths of Sheol up to the heights of heaven in order that he might reflect, know, and rule with Yhwh as a beloved son.

Structure of Lesson 14

The focus of the father in Lesson 14 is to provide a positive and exalted example for the son to emulate. Although Wisdom has been promulgated in prior lessons (e.g., Prov 3:13–18), here the father collates all her marvelous qualities, behaviors, desires, and most importantly her relationship with Yhwh, all of which the son should aspire to embody. This goal unfolds through the lesson with four movements.[1] The first section (Prov 7:24–27) is a typical opening call from the father which serves as a thematic bridge both from the *zarah* to Wisdom and as a contrast to the fourth section. The second section (Prov 8:1–11) is a first-person call from Wisdom framed as the father's *musar*

---

[1] For a survey of various attempts to structure Prov 8, see Loader, *Proverbs 1–9*, 319–21.

(8:1–3, 10–11).[2] Then, Wisdom once again gives a first-person pronouncement through a persuasive description of her way and value (Prov 8:12–21). Finally, the father concludes the lesson with an enigmatic first-person account from Wisdom describing not only her preeminence but primarily her proximity to Yhwh (Prov 8:22–31).[3]

   I. The Ways of Sheol (7:24–27)
  II. The Call of Wisdom (8:1–11)
 III. The Way of Wisdom (8:12–21)
 IV. Wisdom with Yhwh (8:22–31)

As mentioned previously, most scholars understandably place Prov 7:24–27 as the conclusion of 7:1–23 and in contrast from 8:1–31.[4] While this placement rightly ascribes the third feminine singular "she, her" (Prov 7:25–27) to the *zarah* of Lesson 13 rather than to Wisdom of Lesson 14, it does not rightly take into consideration the fatherly call of 7:24.[5] This call matches or echoes three others (Prov 4:1, 5:7, 8:33).[6] So, rather than merely dismiss the break, it is better to seek understanding. Why does Prov 7:24 seem to be an insertion into an otherwise logical conclusion of the *zarah* warning? First, Lesson 13, which primarily describes the ways of the *zarah*, begins with a command for the son to call Wisdom his sister (Prov 7:4). With literary and thematic inverted balance, the father begins Lesson 14 which primarily describes the ways of Wisdom with a warning against the *zarah*. Second, an emphasis on the way or path language used elsewhere is contrasted within Lesson 14 (Prov 8:2, 13, 20, 22).[7] Third, Lesson 14 is a progression from the depths of Sheol to presumably the heights of heaven. The lesson begins by describing the deathly descent into Sheol for those who turn to or follow after the *zarah* and her ways

---

[2] The framing by the father is often missed, forcing scholars to misread Prov 8:10–11 as part of Wisdom's call. However, these two verses place "wisdom" in the third person saying that "wisdom is better than ..." and "they do not compare with her." Instead, this framing is likely meant to parallel Prov 1:8 and 4:1, "fatherly *musar*." Also, Lessons 1 and 15 use similar fatherly framing for the Wisdom speeches, as discussed in the next lesson. Against Fox's persuasion, the phrase "my *musar*" should not be seen as a mistake, despite other text traditions. Instead, the fatherly framing of Wisdom's speeches allows them to be understood primarily as the *musar* of the proverbial father, insinuating the intentional overlap between the two wise figures. See Fox, *Proverbs 1–9*, 270–71; Toy, *Proverbs*, 163–64.

[3] Cf. Fox, "Ideas of Wisdom in Proverbs 1–9," 630.

[4] E.g., Fox, *Proverbs 1–9*, 265. Most also include Prov 8:32–36 with 8:1–31 as the conclusion of the same unit. However, the opener in Prov 8:32 indicates the beginning of a new lesson, serving as a bridge into Lesson 15 just as 7:24 does for Lesson 14.

[5] The plural "sons" in the MT (Prov 5:7, 7:24, 8:32) is made into the singular "son" in the LXX and Vulg., presumably seeking harmonization with the other introductory calls from the father.

[6] For more discussion on these similar openings, see the "Structure of Prov 1–9" along with Lessons 6, 10, and 15. Schipper notes the close parallel between 5:7–8 and 7:24–25 but concludes the latter only marks a new subsection. See Schipper, *Proverbs 1–15*, 277; Meinhold, *Die Sprüche*, 131.

[7] Cf. Clifford, *Proverbs*, 94.

(Prov 7:27). The father then provides a call, an alternative path, for the son to observe (Prov 8:1–11). Then, Wisdom gives an exalted description of her way and what it means to follow after her (Prov 8:12–21). Finally, Wisdom describes her closeness or proximity to Yhwh, the ultimate goal and source of wisdom and righteousness.[8] Thus, the opening call from the father in Prov 7:24–27 creates a poetic, though subtle, narrative for one walking along the wise and righteous path, embodying the ways of the father, Wisdom, and Yhwh. The opening, then, provides a stark negative contrast against the rather positive picture painted throughout the rest of the lesson.

The Ways of Sheol (7:24–27)

This opening section (Prov 7:24–27) not only complements the purposes of the lesson as it unfolds but contains several instructive warnings of its own. None of the language and imagery is particularly new here but is reused from prior lessons. A student at this point in their progression who does not "listen" or "consider" the father's instruction will unfortunately "turn" (שׂטה) from the proper path.[9] Such a turn would be a clear repudiation of the father and Wisdom.[10] Interestingly, the father describes (Prov 7:25) the aberration with the plural "ways" (דְּרָכֶיהָ) and "paths" (נְתִיבוֹתֶיהָ).[11] This grammar is further evidence that this unit is intentionally separated from Lesson 13, which describes the *zarah* with a singular "way" (דֶּרֶךְ בֵּיתָהּ). Lesson 14 begins with a more generalizing form of the *zarah* and her ways, likely bridging or foreshadowing the instruction for the naïve and Folly later (Prov 9:6, 13–18).[12] The analogy in Lesson 13, with an aggressive adulterous or prostitute woman, primarily served as a literary device that is now being broadened to include the myriad of false ways which contrast the "way of righteousness" (אֹרַח־צְדָקָה) associated with Wisdom (8:20).[13] Again, this negative example is included not merely to condemn the *zarah* or even Folly, per se, but to persuade the son not to "follow after" or "whore after" these abominable and destructive ways (cf.,

---

[8] Cf. Waltke, *Proverbs (1–15)*, 411, 412, 417.

[9] This term appears in Prov 4:15 of Lesson 7 also and likely alludes to the centralizing principle discussed in Lesson 8 with the terms נטה and סור. The aberration of turning in Prov 1–9 typically implies leaving the straight-way which has been walked by the wise patriarchs who faithfully followed after Yhwh.

[10] Schipper examines a number of parallels between Prov 8, Ps 19, and Ps 119. In the psalter, the role of wisdom is understood through the frame of *torah*. The implication may be that repudiation of the father and wisdom equates to disobedience to Torah. See Schipper, *Proverbs 1–15*, 290–91.

[11] Cf. Schipper, *Proverbs 1–15*, 277.

[12] Cf. Murphy, *Proverbs*, 44; Schipper, *Proverbs 1–15*, 277.

[13] Estes discusses that the qualities espoused by Wisdom in her speeches are intrinsic to the way of Yhwh as well. Thus, the student must conform to righteousness because Yhwh is righteous, displayed through his speech and actions. The path-metaphor of course engenders the "way of life, conduct" of a person, including Yhwh (8:22). See Estes, *Hear, My Son*, 50–52; Loader, *Proverbs 1–9*, 342.

Exod 34:15–16; Deut 31:16; Judg 2:17; 1 Chron 5:25). If one follows after the *zarah* or foolish and disobedient choices, their certain end is death and Sheol. So, the son ought not to follow her but rather Wisdom in the way of righteousness. As Perdue rightly observes, "Since Woman Wisdom herself walks in the paths of 'righteousness' and 'justice,' the rewards of material gifts are offered to the sages who seek to emulate her behavior and to follow her instruction."[14]

The fools of Prov 7:26 serve to further generalize the ways of the *zarah* through a lesser-to-greater metaphor. These fools are a negative imitative example that the son should carefully observe,[15] those at the bottom of the wisdom hierarchy. The naïve that have followed in the ways of the *zarah* previously have now become "fallen carcasses" and have been slain (Prov 7:26). Though subtle, the intent is for the son to not only look to these negative examples but to do the opposite, similar to the animal metaphors of Lesson 13. If he desires to not be like them in their post-death captivity, then he must not emulate them in their pre-death ways. Imitating them in their aberrant ways, much like the sinners of Lesson 1, will lead him to follow in their inevitable descent as well. Fear of this catastrophe is the intent of the father. He desires the son to be wise and ascend to the heights of Wisdom and Yhwh instead. However, such a progression is not possible if the son turns off the path of his instruction onto the myriad of tempting, deceitful paths that lead to death.

The Call of Wisdom (8:1–11)

As the father transitions to Wisdom, he utilizes a similar formula found in Lesson 1 where he provides a first-person call from Wisdom framed by himself (Prov 1:20–21, 8:1–3, 10–11; cf. 9:1–3, 13–15, 18).[16] While the opening lesson was a negative ploy, the father now gives a positive image for the son to observe. Much like his own calls to the son, Wisdom gives her plea for the son or the naïve to learn and hear from her (Prov 8:4–5). What was primarily found in the mouth of the father is now found in the speech of Wisdom.[17] This conflation serves to establish Wisdom as a symbolic embodiment of the ideal characteristics of the wise,[18] namely of the father and Yhwh. The son's

---

[14] See Perdue, *Proverbs*, 143; Schipper, *Proverbs 1–15*, 307.

[15] Cf. Longman, *Proverbs*, 191.

[16] Schipper notes that the place of Wisdom at the "heights" is also true of God elsewhere in the HB (cf. Isa 33:5, 16, 57:15, 58:4; Mic 6:6; Ps 7:8). See Schipper, *Proverbs 1–15*, 295.

[17] As discussed previously, Wisdom and the father often overlap in their instruction. Cf. Fox, "Ideas of Wisdom in Proverbs 1–9," 630; Schipper, *Proverbs 1–15*, 298.

[18] Fox makes the case that the various places of declaration from Wisdom should not be taken as a single event or specific place but a general or typical occurrence. In his view, he believes this also conveys the accessibility of Wisdom, true of "God's commandments in Deut 30:11–14," as well. See Fox, *Proverbs 1–9*, 266–67.

mundane exemplar is the father, but the father desires the son to progress on the upward trajectory toward God as the ultimate example of Wisdom.[19]

In this portion of the lesson, the primary focus is on proper speech. A dominant characteristic of the wise is the speech they utter, which is an indicator of the path that they walk. Wisdom embodies purity of speech that rises to a divine level.[20] She states that "all the words of my mouth are righteous" (Prov 8:8).[21] In biblical understanding, such a claim is only true of God.[22] David, while complaining of the ubiquity of deceit, said, "The words of Yhwh are pure words, refined silver" (Ps 11:2, 7).[23] Similarly, Wisdom states that "wickedness is an abomination of my lips" (Prov 8:7). This language reflects the disdain of Yhwh in Lesson 11 (Prov 6:16–19; cf. 3:32). So, the father boldly proffers Wisdom as a divine figure (cf. Deut 32:4–5).[24] Yet, she is not merely to be admired. She is to be followed and imitated, as Longman rightly observes, "The wise person emulates Woman Wisdom in [their speech]."[25] Just as she embodies pure speech,[26] the son is to aspire to this wise objective. In doing so, he will live out the *musar* of his father and the characteristics of Yhwh.

At the beginning of her speech (Prov 8:5), Wisdom calls for the naïve to understand "prudence" (עָרְמָה). At the end of her call to the son, Wisdom mentions that her speech will only be useful or understandable to those who "find knowledge" (Prov 8:9). As discussed previously, knowledge and knowing are qualities often ascribed to the wise. So, in the next section (Prov 8:12), Wisdom opens her second speech to the son with the phrases, "I dwell with

---

[19] Fox notes that "the teacher is wise, but wisdom itself transcends any human wisdom." This implies that there is an upward movement inherent in the wisdom program. See Fox, "Ideas of Wisdom in Proverbs 1–9," 633.

[20] Cf. Whybray, *Proverbs (1994)*, 123.

[21] The father strings together a number of parallel terms to describe the purity of Wisdom's speech (Prov 8:6–9): "upright" (מֵישָׁרִים), "truth" (אֱמֶת), "righteous" (צֶדֶק), "straight" (נְכֹחַ), "abomination of my lips is wickedness," and "there is no twisting and crookedness in them."

[22] In Ps 33:4–6, the psalmist describes the purity and power of Yhwh's word, "For the word of Yhwh is upright and all his work is true. One who loves righteousness and justice, the steadfast love of Yhwh fills the earth. By the word of Yhwh, the heavens were made; and by the breath of his mouth all their hosts."

[23] The relatively uncommon phrase "children of man" (בְּנֵי אָדָם) appears in both passages, possibly indicating an intentional correspondence (Ps 11:2, 9 // Prov 8:4, 31). Cf. Deut 32:8; 2 Sam 7:14; Jer 32:19; Ezek 31:14; Joel 1:12; Prov 15:11; Dan 10:16; and 11x in Psalms. Schipper holds that the phrase expressed "humanity as a whole," particularly in parallel with "men" (אִישִׁים). See Schipper, *Proverbs 1–15*, 297.

[24] Schipper observes the divine quality of the speech attributed to Wisdom. Also, Meinhold and Fox note the parallel between "I am Wisdom" (אֲנִי־חָכְמָה) and "I am Yhwh" (אֲנִי יְהוָה) common in the divine self–revelatory moniker (8:12; e.g., Gen 15:7; Exod 6:2; Lev 11:44; Deut 5:6). Perdue holds that the imagery of Prov 8:1–21 intentionally implies that "Wisdom, not simply the monarchy or the temple, serves as the link between heaven and earth." See Meinhold, *Die Sprüche*, 139–40; Fox, *Proverbs 1–9*, 271; Schipper, *Proverbs 1–15*, 299; Perdue, *Proverbs*, 140–41; Loader, *Proverbs 1–9*, 329–30.

[25] Longman, *Proverbs*, 200.

[26] Regarding Wisdom's "murmuring" or "meditating" (הגה) on "truth," Schipper notes the relation with Ps 1:2, noting that Wisdom embodies the "righteous person whose life is guided by God's word" (Schipper, *Proverbs 1–15*, 298). Thus, Wisdom does not merely serve as one who dictates true speech but as one who embodies a truth-speaker, worthy of being emulated.

prudence (עָרְמָה)" and "I find knowledge."[27] While serving as a literary device to bridge the units, this claim also signals the son to look to Wisdom as one who possesses and enacts the qualities she purports.[28] Thus, the son is obliged to emulate her, in his pursuit of both prudence and knowledge. Although these particular qualities are important, it is likely that they serve as functional placeholders for all of Wisdom's qualities. Though she is not a real person, this does not denigrate her value as an intermediate between the fallible "children of man" and the ineffable Yhwh.[29] As an ideal, the son ought to be characterized by truth and act as a truth-teller, reflecting the wise whom he aspires to emulate.

The Way of Wisdom (8:12–21)

The second speech (Prov 8:12–21) by Wisdom is similar to the first (8:4–9) but focuses on her value or "fruit," reflecting much of the divine qualities found previously.[30] However, the second speech adds an interesting layer to the lesson. She propounds four characters that utilize her (Prov 8:15–16). These are "kings" (מְלָכִים), "officials" (רוֹזְנִים), "princes" (שָׂרִים), and "nobles" (נְדִיבִים), provided that they qualify as "those judging righteously" (Prov 8:16; cf. Isa 32:1).[31] In other words, it is obvious that not all prominent figures actually utilize wisdom. But those who do would fall into the category of the wise, in

---

[27] Fox remarks, "Wisdom is describing herself in terms of a wise human being, and an attribute of the wise is that they can gain or 'find' knowledge" (Fox, *Proverbs 1–9*, 272). This correlation naturally implies that Wisdom is an exemplar for the son.

[28] As Longman notes, "[Wisdom] serves as a role model for her followers" (Longman, *Proverbs*, 209).

[29] Fox argues that the Wisdom figure does not represent a singular person or even type but a "complex literary figure" who models a variety of desirable characteristics. Also, Aletti observes that the third speech by Wisdom begins with "Yhwh" (Prov 8:22), ends with "children of man" (8:31), and uses a personal pronoun for Wisdom near the middle (8:27). In his view, this poetic structure implies a spatial or conceptual distinction. Yee further demonstrates Wisdom's unifying role through the literary structure. Both Aletti and Yee argue that there is a "dynamic progression in the hymn whereby Wisdom moves from passivity to presence ... to activity itself." This literary structure seems to illuminate a subtle model for the son or naïve to follow as well, moving along a progressive trajectory of wisdom. See Fox, "Ideas of Wisdom in Proverbs 1–9," 625; Fox, *Proverbs 1–9*, 352–59; Jean-Noël Aletti, "Proverbes 8,22–31. Étude de Structure," *Bib* 57.1 (1976): 28, 34; Gale A. Yee, "An Analysis of Prov 8:22–31 According to Style and Structure," *ZAW* 94.1 (1982): 58–66.

[30] The attributes described of Wisdom in Prov 8:14 are explicitly associated with Yhwh in Job 12:13. This association implies that Wisdom embodies the characteristics of Yhwh and that the son must embody these qualities in order to reflect Wisdom and Yhwh. Cf. Murphy, *Proverbs*, 50–51; Schipper, *Proverbs 1–15*, 303; Waltke, *Proverbs (1–15)*, 402.

[31] The "kings" (מְלָכִים) and "rulers" (רוֹזְנִים) also appear in parallel in Ps 2:2, "The kings of the earth erect themselves and the rulers are unified together against Yhwh and against his anointed" (cf. 2:10–11). These characters are exactly the opposite of the figures imagined in Prov 8:15. In Prov, they are qualified as those who govern with "righteousness" (צֶדֶק), necessarily implying wisdom derived from the "fear of Yhwh." In contrast, Ps 2 rightly associates the messianic figure or king as a companion, even a son of God, implying his proximity and reflection of Yhwh. As in Isa 32:1–8, he is an ideal ruler.

part by virtue of proper judging.[32] On the wisdom hierarchy, these figures would be above the naive but below Wisdom and Yhwh.[33] Still, they represent figures who have embodied wisdom and her qualities.[34] Thus, the son is to desire to imitate them in his own progression toward being one of the wise. Although the son may not have had many (if any) real examples of truly wise rulers, they serve as the pedagogical image to which the son should aspire.

As part of Wisdom's personal, divine-like introduction (Prov 8:12–14), she pronounces her disdain for "pride" and "arrogance." These terms actually precede the verses lauding kings and rulers who govern by her. The implication is that anyone who rules by her must necessarily avoid pride or arrogance, perhaps especially kings (cf. Deut 17:20). [35] Likewise, as Schipper notes, it is said elsewhere in the HB that Yhwh has disdain for pride and arrogance as well (e.g., Isa 2:12; Amos 6:8; Prov 15:25).[36] He even claims this disdain is central to her close connection and association to Yhwh. Those who aspire to be wise and ultimately imitate Yhwh, perhaps especially rulers, must also hate pride and arrogance. Furthermore, it is not coincidental that in Lesson 3 it was stated, "By Wisdom, Yhwh founded the earth; by understanding he founded the heavens" (Prov 3:19). While the earthly kings and rulers were wise to utilize Wisdom, in reality, it is Yhwh who is the primary example of a just ruler who utilizes Wisdom. Thus, the son should look to the human examples but only insofar as they lead to the greater goal of emulating Yhwh as the ultimate wise and just ruler.

A mildly perplexing mixture of language and imagery occurs in Wisdom's speech following her endorsement to emulate the wise rulers. In Prov 8:18–21, perhaps in light of the theme regarding kings and rulers, she mentions that wealth and honor are with her and that she will fill the "treasure houses" of those who "love" her (8:18, 21).[37] Previously, though, the father specifically instructed the son to receive *musar* and knowledge rather than silver or gold (Prov 8:10–11; cf. 3:15).[38] It would seem strange that Wisdom would contradict the father here. Rather, in these verses, she

---

[32] Cf. Fox, *Proverbs 1–9*, 274.

[33] Cf. Schipper, *Proverbs 1–15*, 302–3. Schipper refers to 1 Kgs 3:9, 12 to note the divine role assumed by Wisdom in Prov 8:14–16.

[34] Scholars have illuminated the parallels between Wisdom and the eschatological ruler from Isa 11:2 (Plöger, *Spruche Salomos (Proverbia)*, 89–90; Schipper, *Proverbs 1–15*, 303; Waltke, *Proverbs (1–15)*, 402; Whybray, *Proverbs (1994)*, 125). The similar proverbial language in Isa 11 could imply that the son should emulate the messianic figure envisioned there as a righteous judge, endowed with all the appropriate divine characteristics. Alternatively, both passages may simply highlight the ideal image of a ruler who rightly reflects the superior kingship of Yhwh.

[35] As Longman says, "The wise simply emulate Woman Wisdom" (Longman, *Proverbs*, 202).

[36] See Schipper, *Proverbs 1–15*, 302.

[37] Fox discusses the philosophical and reciprocal relationship between Wisdom and the wise, or "the attraction of like for like." However, he rightly correlates this to the Deuteronomic concept of "reciprocal divine-human love." See Fox, *Proverbs 1–9*, 276.

[38] Schipper is uncertain whether Prov 8:11 should be taken as a summary from the narrator or Wisdom. However, the close parallel with Prov 3:15 would imply it is part of the father's instructional framing. See Schipper, *Proverbs 1–15*, 300.

intermingles within the offer of mundane wealth several important qualities that are better than or are the essence of her way. In Prov 8:18, she ends the verse with "righteousness" as the cap of riches, honor, and wealth. Then, in Prov 8:19, she says that her "fruit" is better than "gold" and "silver," implying their triviality. [39] Following this, she states, "I walk in the way of righteousness, amidst the paths of justice." So, while the fool may hear this speech and immediately focus on the riches aspect, Wisdom makes the pursuit of wealth a subdued if not unrelated objective.[40] Those who love Wisdom will find her and walk in her ways.[41] While treasure has its benefits, it does not compare to fidelity and relation to Wisdom and the wise path. [42] This sentiment seems to reflect the idea of Prov 15:16, "Better is a little with the fear of Yhwh than great treasure and tumult with it." In the vein of a riddle, it seems the use of kings and rulers was a foil to lead a foolish student down the path of false aspiration. The son is not to aspire to these kings' greatness in terms of wealth or honor but in their apprehension of Wisdom and their reflection of God's character.[43] Only the wise who rightly fear Yhwh will see past the glitter of gold to the heart of the father's intention and the true path. As Kidner rightly opines, "You have to be good to be wise ... you have to be *godly* to be wise, and this not because it pays."[44] It would seem by "godly" he means one must be God-like, possessing or reflecting his pure intentions and characteristics, in order to rightly know and utilize the divine quality of Wisdom. In other words, one must imitate God to be wise.

Wisdom with Yhwh (8:22–31)

The last portion of Lesson 14 has endured an array of opinions and speculations, primarily seeking to determine the date and identity of the peculiar figure self-described (Prov 8:22–31).[45] While this is not a superfluous endeavor, it seems in the context that the purpose and primary function of the

---

[39] Loader suggests the imagery of Wisdom's "fruit" implies the Garden of Gen 2–3 (cf. Prov 3:18). Thus, imitating her, imagined as partaking of her fruit, is in a sense a primeval return to the Tree of Life (Loader, *Proverbs 1–9*, 341).

[40] Cf. Waltke, *Proverbs (1–15)*, 399.

[41] Waltke rightly notes that "wisdom herself models the role of a believing seeker after virtue" (Waltke, *Proverbs (1–15)*, 400).

[42] In Isa 33:5–6, the prophet wisely states, "Yhwh is exalted for he dwells in the heights. He fills Zion with justice and righteousness. He will be faithful with you, the wealth of salvation, wisdom, and knowledge. The fear of Yhwh is Zion's treasure."

[43] Fox proposes that Prov 8:20–21 implies that Wisdom achieves wealth through "honorable paths." In his view, this insinuates that the wise are to do likewise in imitation. While it is questionable if Wisdom is being envisioned as accumulating wealth, it is important that Fox intuitively implies an imitative relationship between Wisdom and the wise in this respect. See Fox, *Proverbs 1–9*, 278.

[44] Derek Kidner, *Proverbs: An Introduction and Commentary*, TOTC (IVP, 1964), 30.

[45] See the discussion in Lesson 6. Cf. Bernhard Lang, *Wisdom and the Book of Proverbs: A Hebrew Goddess Redefined* (New York: Pilgrim, 1986), 51–82; Whybray, *Composition of the Book of Proverbs*, 60.

passage is more pressing. The father adds a third speech from Wisdom which does not address the son or the audience at all. Yet, undoubtedly, it is part of the speech that began in Prov 8:4.[46] The speech from Wisdom is broken into three portions united by the inclusio which utilizes the phrase "children of man" (Prov 8:4, 8:31).[47]

The first speech by Wisdom is a direct address to the naïve, framed as *musar* from the father. The second speech by Wisdom is a slightly more distant address, only indirectly referring to those who "love me" and "seek me" (Prov 8:17). The third speech moves the audience even further into an indirect address with the only reference to the audience being the generic "children of man" as the final words.[48] Yet, in a poetic and literary movement, the speeches gravitate or ascend towards Yhwh.[49] There is not a direct appeal to him in the first speech. In the second, there is a reference to "fear of Yhwh," which implicitly indicates kings and rulers govern justly by her in reflection of him. Then, in the third speech, Wisdom describes her delightful companionship with Yhwh in great intimacy.[50] In fact, the austere statement in Prov 3:19, which describes Yhwh's establishment of heaven and earth by Wisdom, comes alive here as a first-person witness account from Wisdom, "When he established the heavens, I was there" (Prov 8:27). Wisdom is no longer envisioned as an inanimate tool but as a sentient observer and divine companion.

So, what is the rhetorical value of this third speech for the father's lesson? It seems the primary function is not merely to exalt Wisdom. This conclusion was reached previously in the series of lessons. Rather, it is to exalt Wisdom's proximity,[51] companionship, and cooperation with Yhwh in his creation.[52] The language in this speech mingles several images such as a

---

[46] Cf. Schipper, *Proverbs 1–15*, 308.

[47] An interesting reference occurs in the Psalter, both in the Yahwistic and Elohistic versions, "Yhwh (God) looks down from heaven on the *children of man* to see if there is one who understands, who seeks God" (Ps 14:2, 53:3).

[48] The phrase "children of man" (בְּנֵי אָדָם) is paralleled with "men" (אִישִׁים) in Prov 8:4. The latter is an uncommon form of Heb. "men" (אֲנָשִׁים) and possibly represents a Phoenician-ism as Fox argues. The value of these uncommon terms is to universalize Wisdom, her role, and her applicability. See Fox, *Proverbs 1–9*, 267–68.

[49] Cf. Whybray, *Composition of the Book of Proverbs*, 128–29.

[50] Lang wrongly understands Wisdom or perhaps over-imagines her ANE reflection. He calls her a "goddess" who engages in a proud example of the common ANE genre "self-praise of a god," present in the HB for Yhwh (e.g., Isa 44:24). However, in this passage, Wisdom does not praise herself at all. She rightfully ascribes creative power and glory to Yhwh. She merely describes her blessed position as a companion with, though subservient to, Yhwh. As an anthropomorphism of Yhwh, however, she has spoken truths representative of Yhwh earlier in the lesson and the program. Yet, she remains a noble example for the son to emulate. Thus, if Wisdom is indeed a polemic against such divine figures as Ishtar or Hathor, she does so in a relegating manner before Yhwh, the true source of power and glory. See Lang, *Wisdom and the Book of Proverbs*, 57–61; Waltke, *Proverbs (1–15)*, 418, n. 136.

[51] Fox describes the status of Wisdom by her "residing in angelic proximity to God." See Fox, "Ideas of Wisdom in Proverbs 1–9," 633; Cleon L. Rogers III, "The Meaning and Significance of the Hebrew Word אמון in Proverbs 8,30," *ZAW* 109.2 (1997): 209.

[52] This emphasis is native to the sagacious rhetoric from Moses, as well, "Surely this great nation is a wise and understanding people. For, which great nation has its god so near to

spouse (Prov 8:22),[53] a daughter (8:24–25, 30),[54] a fellow-craftsman (8:27–30),[55] and a joyful worshipper (8:30–31).[56] While each image carries significant interpretive value, it is really Wisdom's proximity to Yhwh that the father intends for the son to observe and desire at this point. It is perhaps the pedagogical climax in the whole of Prov 1–9.[57] Of course, the son cannot imitate Wisdom temporally by returning to the beginning of creation. However, as a son of Adam, he can return in a sense to the primordial world in which "the man" (הָאָדָם) was tasked with working alongside God, subduing and exercising dominion over creation, which included the Garden (Gen 1:28, 2:15–17).[58] Man was the pinnacle of the creation narrative, receiving God's special endowment, blessing, and likeness. Yet, the original innocence and proximity to Yhwh were lost in Gen 3, due to an improper desire to be like God.[59] In an attempt to achieve counterfeit wisdom, the man lost life, safety, honor, wisdom, and ultimately fellowship with Yhwh. Thus, Wisdom in the third speech of Lesson 14 subtly inspires the son to look beyond mundane riches and honor, which even a fool may desire, to fulfill his quest for true wisdom.[60] As Fox astutely observes, "Divine acquisition of wisdom … is the prototype of human acquisition of wisdom."[61] In other words, the father promotes the imitation of God as the pinnacle of the wisdom trajectory.

Conclusion

In Lesson 14 and elsewhere, the enigmatic figure of Wisdom pushes the boundaries of any strict categorization. While this ambiguity has often led scholars into debate, the proverbial father intentionally chose her as a primary example not only because of her innate imitable characteristics but

---

him as Yhwh our God whenever we call out to him" (Deut 4:6b–7). The inherent benefit of proximity to God comes with wisdom, understanding, and obedience to Yhwh's way.

[53] For a more detailed analysis, see the discussion in Lesson 6.

[54] Cf. Lang, *Wisdom and the Book of Proverbs*, 63–64; Fox, "Ideas of Wisdom in Proverbs 1–9," 624; Miles, *Wise King - Royal Fool: Semiotics, Satire and Proverbs 1–9*, 66.

[55] Cf. Longman, *Proverbs*, 209.

[56] Cf. Waltke, *Proverbs (1–15)*, 407; Meinhold, *Die Sprüche*, 143.

[57] Cf. Loader, *Proverbs 1–9*, 324.

[58] The case has been made that Prov 8:22–31 parallels numerous aspects of Gen 1–2. The observations tend to focus, however, only on the creative aspect and not the human component. If the father had in mind Gen 1–2, particularly after mentioning the kings and rulers who governed righteously, it is likely that he had in mind the first *adam* to serve as a model for the proverbial *adam* (8:31), as well. See Michaela Bauks and Gerlinde Baumann, "Im Anfang war … ?: Gen 1,1ff und Prov 8,22–31 im Vergleich," *BN* 71 (1994): 24–52; Schipper, *Proverbs 1–15*, 288–90.

[59] Hindy Najman, "Imitatio Dei and the Formation of the Subject in Ancient Judaism," *JBL* 140.2 (2021): 316.

[60] Fox mentions, "Because Wisdom herself is wise, she typifies the experience of wise humans (Fox, *Proverbs 1–9*, 289). This notion implies the inherent imitative relationship between Wisdom and the wise.

[61] Fox, *Proverbs 1–9*, 280.

also due to her proximity to Yhwh. To an extent, the son is to reflect and love Wisdom as one would a teacher or parent (Prov 8:4–11, 17). Yet, she also serves as a tool used by noble rulers enacting justice, which includes Yhwh (Prov 8:14–16; cf. 3:19–20). Likewise, in seeking Wisdom, the son is promised to find her (Prov 8:17), if he will walk with her along the path of righteousness (8:20). In his emulation and attainment of Wisdom, he will reflect her relationship with Yhwh, as well, becoming a true knower of God (Prov 8:22–34; cf. 2:5).[62] In this reflection of Wisdom, he will join Yhwh in collaboratively shaping the created order and will emulate wise rulers.[63] He will both rejoice in and be the delight of Yhwh, as a beloved child before a father (cf. Prov 3:11–12).

Thus, this restoration or return to an Edenic reality will bring him, and humanity, into a proper imitative correspondence with God.[64] In essence, the climax of this lesson is the exact inverse of its opening, which describes the descent of fools into Sheol (Prov 7:24–27). Rather, the son must follow Wisdom's ascent, where he will find both Wisdom and God.[65] As the wisdom program concludes in Lesson 15, the father draws from the momentum in Lesson 14. The son will be given his final lesson from the father, showing the sharp contrast between the way of the wise and the way of fools. As one who is soon to be a teacher himself, he must discern whom he will emulate and whom he will lead in the way of Wisdom.

---

[62] As Clifford observes, "The relationship between Wisdom and her disciples on earth … mirrors the relationship between Wisdom and Yahweh in heaven" (Clifford, *Proverbs*, 97; Perdue, *Proverbs*, 146).

[63] Drawing on Keel, Waltke finds correspondence between Yhwh's creative ordering and its implications for human society, "The LORD's fixed created order serves as a model of his fixed moral boundaries for human beings to prevent society from collapsing into anarchy. 'The earthly order [in ancient Egypt] emulates the heavenly, and like the heavenly, it is guaranteed by the deity'" (Waltke, *Proverbs (1–15)*, 415; Othmar Keel, *The Symbolism of the Biblical World: Ancient Near Eastern Iconography and the Book of Psalms* (New York: Seabury, 1978), 96).

[64] Fox proposes that "possess" (קנה) in Prov 8:22 is intentionally used in order to promote this correspondence, which was argued in Lesson 6 (Fox, *Proverbs 1–9*, 280).

[65] Wisdom claims in Prov 8:17 that those who seek her will find her. As Schipper rightly notes, the sentiment is true also of Yhwh as Deut 4:29 makes clear, "When you seek Yhwh your God, you will find him, when you seek him with all your heart and with all your soul." See Schipper, *Proverbs 1–15*, 305; Tremper Longman III, "Theology of Wisdom," in *The Oxford Handbook of Wisdom and the Bible*, ed. Will Kynes (Oxford: Oxford University Press, 2021), 396).

LESSON 15

Analysis of 8:32–9:18
"Seek wisdom, find life"

I n Lesson 14, the father gave the son a profound look at the association Wisdom has with Yhwh.[1] At the end of the wisdom program, however, Lesson 15 again focuses on the contrast between the two competing paths.[2] The son must choose whether to follow in the way of Wisdom and Yhwh, equated with life (Prov 8:35, 9:6, 10–11),[3] or to careen off the well-worn path of the righteous straight into the open arms of Folly, equated with death (Prov 8:36, 18).[4] These paths and figures represent the groups and fates that correspond. Therefore, by emulating the righteous, he will find Wisdom and the "knowledge of the Holy One" (Prov 9:10). Yet, by emulating the foolish, he will reflect the counterfeit state of Folly, embodying ignorance and death (Prov 9:13, 18). The father and Wisdom, of course, desire that the son will walk in the "way of insight" and of Yhwh. In Lesson 15, the emphasis also shifts from the father's primary role for instruction and emulation to Wisdom's primary role as the son's teacher and example (Prov 8:32–34). She not only assumes this role for the son but in turn provides guidance for him to become a teacher as well, one who passes along the *torah* he received (Prov 9:7–9). By following her ways, he will become one of the "blessed," namely, one characterized by the life and favor of Yhwh.

---

[1] Cf. Schipper, *Proverbs 1–15*, 317.

[2] Cf. Whybray, *Composition of the Book of Proverbs*, 44; Murphy, *Proverbs*, 61; Longman, *Proverbs*, 215.

[3] Clifford mentions of Prov 9:10, though referring to the wisdom program more broadly, "[Fear of Yhwh] involves Yahweh, Israel's God, who is the guarantor of the way of wisdom. The verse puts the quest for wisdom in explicitly religious terms" (Clifford, *Proverbs*, 106).

[4] Cf. Schipper, *Proverbs 1–15*, 339.

Structure of Lesson 15

At the conclusion of the wisdom program, the father unravels his final lesson in three parts. First, a typical introductory call is given, though now in the voice of Wisdom (Prov 8:32–36).[5] Second, the father gives a sagacious speech from Wisdom (Prov 9:4–12), framed by his guidance (9:1–3). Finally, a brief, contrasting call from Folly is given (Prov 9:16–17), framed by the father (9:13–15, 18).

I. Wisdom's Call: the son's final teacher (8:32–36)
II. Wisdom's Speech: a call to turn (9:1–3, 4–12)
III. Folly's Speech: a call to turn (9:13–15, 16–17, 18)

The opening call (Prov 8:32–36) is a unique instance in Prov 1–9 where Wisdom assumes the role of the father from previous lessons. Although the speaker is not specifically named, the highly theological language spoken in the first-person is likely drawn from Lesson 14, serving as a bridge between lessons. There, Wisdom says in Prov 8:17 that those who love her and seek for her will find her (cf. 1:28, 3:13). Similarly, the opening call in Prov 8:35–36 says that those who find me find life but those who hate me love death (cf. 1:29). So, as the pedagogy has progressed, it seems the father is relinquishing his role for the son's guidance and growth to Wisdom, the exalted teacher.[6] The father has reached the extent of his human ability to train the son. The son must now turn to Wisdom and Yhwh as his primary example to follow. No longer will the mundane model from his father and mother suffice.[7] Fox rightly mentions that Wisdom is envisioned in Prov 8 as one who has been "raised and trained" by Yhwh and can thus "operate as an autonomous thinker and teacher of wisdom."[8] This procession itself, then, implies a model for the father and son to look to in their pursuit of Yhwh as a teacher, imitating God's relationship with Wisdom in their instruction to others.

---

[5] Most observe the transition to Wisdom as a teacher but typically see this section as the conclusion of Prov 8 rather than the start of a new section, that is Lesson 15. Although Schipper follows most others in his view, he does note that the central themes of Prov 9 are initially raised in these verses. Similarly, Waltke says that Prov 8:34 foreshadows 9:1–6. See McKane, *Proverbs*, 358–59; Fox, *Proverbs 1–9*, 290; Schipper, *Proverbs 1–15*, 316; Waltke, *Proverbs (1–15)*, 423, 425, 429.

[6] Cf. Fox, *Proverbs 1–9*, 340–41; Lang, *Wisdom and the Book of Proverbs*, 56–59.

[7] Miles proposes that "Wisdom and Yahweh … as 'mother' and 'father'" are the "collective merismus of parental instruction" (Miles, *Wise King - Royal Fool: Semiotics, Satire and Proverbs 1–9*, 95). In line with this notion, Wisdom and Yhwh serve as the ultimate model for the father and mother as instructors. Wisdom and Yhwh also receive the son as their student now, his divine instructors figured as parents.

[8] Fox, *Proverbs 1–9*, 293–94.

The structuring of Lesson 15 is similar to Lesson 14. Both begin with the phrase "And now, sons, listen to me" (Prov 7:24, 8:32).[9] A similar bridge-type unit is also present at the beginning of both lessons (Prov 7:24–27, 8:32–36). Likewise, both lessons include a speech from Wisdom framed by the father who provides insightful guidance for its reception (Prov 8:1–3, 4–9, 10–11 // 9:1–3, 4–12). However, Lesson 14 progresses in a positive trajectory from Sheol to the climax of Wisdom's intimate association with Yhwh, the opposite of Sheol (Prov 7:27). Lesson 15, by contrast, begins in the favor of Yhwh but ends in the pits of Sheol, which concludes the whole pedagogical program on a rather negative note (Prov 9:18). This decision to end with Folly may be due to the rather negative start in its chiastic parallel, Lesson 1 (Prov 1:10–19). In a similar way, Lesson 1 begins with a warning about the fatal path, which is followed by Wisdom's speech. Whereas in Lesson 15, Wisdom's speech precedes a warning about the fatal path, creating a chiastic reversal. Although positive motivation is ideal, the father seems prescient enough to understand the enduring value of a warning for guiding the son(s) in the wise way.[10] He

---

[9] Whybray devises a complex reorganization of Prov 8:32–36, based partly on the LXX and previous scholarship. However, Fox rightly refutes his unnecessary speculations. See Whybray, *Composition of the Book of Proverbs*, 42–43; Fox, *Proverbs 1–9*, 289; Toy, *Proverbs*, 179–80.

[10] Lawrence Kohlberg popularized a theory of moral development that proposed a progression along six stages (typically associated with age and maturity), the last being the most desirable: punishment, reward, social approval, social-legal adherence, the well-being of society, and concern for ethics in principle. However, since his first proposals, a number of criticisms have arisen questioning a variety of aspects in this theory. While rejecting any divine quality in moral reasoning, he built a relativistic model that overly separated the various stages into a mutually exclusive continuum. Later scholarship, however, demonstrated a great deal of overlap between the elements of his stages for those at various stages of life, education, age, and cultural background.

Furthermore, this interesting discussion raises the question of the role or absence of the "golden rule" (Matt 7:12) within Proverbs. Does Proverbs subscribe to an individualistic, egoist view of morality? Does the biblical sage teach any concern for justice or righteousness as a universal principle, in awareness and for the sake of others or the broader community? While the explicit words of Lev 19:18 or Luke 6:31–36 are not found, both passages are closely associated with divine imitation: "be holy for I am holy" (Lev 19:2) and "be merciful even as your Father is merciful" (Luke 6:36). However, even in the Luke 6 passage, the context promises a "reward" for those that imitate God, implying that these motivations are not mutually exclusive, as Kohlberg presumed. Further, it is important to recall that the divine qualities which the wise embody – righteousness, justice, uprightness, fairness, wisdom, understanding – are inherently communal and socially oriented (e.g., Deut 10:17–19). Similarly, the Torah seems to teach the interconnectedness of the whole congregation's behavior (e.g., Lev 18:24–30; Deut 6:1–5). Nevertheless, the proverbial father does seem to prioritize the benefits and harms of one's choices for themselves (e.g., Prov 9:12) rather than focusing on their effects on others or as a pure principle (cf. Toy, 195; LXX). This may simply be a feature of the literary function of ancient pedagogy or specifically rhetorical motivation for the naïve, who may not find such principles as Lev 19:18 sufficiently compelling yet.

While a thorough discussion regarding the moral philosophy and psychology of Proverbs is beyond the scope of this study, further discussions and critiques of Kohlberg's theory can be found in the following: Lawrence Kohlberg, "Stage and Sequence: The Cognitive-Developmental Approach to Socialization," in Handbook of Socialization Theory and Research, ed. David A. Goslin (Chicago: Rand McNally, 1969); Lawrence Kohlberg, The Philosophy of Moral Development: Moral Stages and the Idea of Justice (San Francisco: Harper & Row, 1981); Lawrence Kohlberg, The Psychology of Moral Development: The Nature and Validity of Moral

will persist in a perpetual struggle between choosing the path of the righteous and refusing the path of sinners.[11]

The Son's Final Teacher (8:32–36)

To begin the lesson, the father hands off his role to Wisdom as the primary teacher. As mentioned, she gives a call in Lesson 1 (Prov 1:22–33), framed by the father (1:20–21). Throughout the intervening lessons, she is mentioned and lauded regularly, taking on a variety of roles and relationships.[12] Yet, it is not until Lesson 14 that she once again speaks, occurring in a three-part monologue (Prov 8:4–9, 12–19, 20–31), framed by the father (8:1–3). Then, in Lesson 15, she again speaks (Prov 9:4–12), framed by the father (9:1–4). So, the introductory call of Prov 8:32–36 is a unique and illuminating transition for the wisdom program. In the same words formerly given by the father, Wisdom now addresses the son. However, Wisdom as the embodiment of Yhwh expands and exalts the language and gravity of adhering to this instruction.[13]

In the opening verse (Prov 8:32; cf. Ps 1:1), she declares that "the ones guarding my ways" (דְּרָכַי יִשְׁמֹרוּ) are those who are "blessed" (אַשְׁרֵי).[14] Perhaps surprisingly, the term "blessed" is relatively uncommon in the HB. Its primary usage is in the Psalter and Proverbs, only appearing a few times elsewhere. While the word is often translated as "blessed" or "happy," it is likely derived from the verbal root "to advance" (אָשַׁר),[15] which actually occurs later in the lesson for those who reflect the way of Yhwh (Prov 9:6). The nominal derivation seems to connote positive movement and success in its various uses. While one may presume that "blessedness" or success implies wealth (physical prosperity), the term almost always has the context of upright

---

Stages (San Francisco: Harper & Row, 1984); Nicholas Wolterstorff, Educating for Responsible Action (Grand Rapids: Eerdmans, 1980); Donald M. Joy, ed., Moral Development Foundations: Judeo-Christian Alternatives to Piaget/Kohlberg (Nashville: Abingdon, 1983); Paul C. Vitz, "Critiques of Kohlberg's Model of Moral Development: A Summary," Revista Española de Pedagogía 52.197 (1994): 5–35; Richard G. Shepard, "Biblical Progression as Moral Development: The Analogy and Its Implications," JPT 22.3 (1994): 182–86; William C. Spohn, "Conscience and Moral Development," TS 61.1 (2000): 122–38; Stephen K. Moroney, "Higher Stages?: Some Cautions for Christian Integration with Kohlberg's Theory," JPT 34.4 (2006): 361–71; Boris Zizek, Detlef Garz, and Ewa Nowak, eds., Kohlberg Revisited, Moral Development and Citizenship Education 9 (Rotterdam: Sense, 2015); Toy, Proverbs, 195.

[11] As Schipper similarly mentions, "The process of sapiential learning is never finished; rather the wise person must study continually" (Schipper, Proverbs 1–15, 331).

[12] Cf. Fox, Proverbs 1–9, 333–41.

[13] McKane says it slightly different, "Wisdom is a teacher authorized by Yahweh, and to submit to her is to do Yahweh's will" (McKane, Proverbs, 358).

[14] It is perhaps relevant that Wisdom begins this final lesson with an appeal to the "blessed." In Ps 1:1, it begins with the blessed who is also contrasted with the "scoffer" (Prov 9:7–8, 12).

[15] The BDB gives אָשַׁר as the root of אַשְׁרֵי while HALOT creates a separate lexical entry. Although HALOT does not see a relation between the terms, the sense of "stride" or "walk" fits well with the concept that the "blessed" is one who progresses on the wise or divine path.

character and relationship with Yhwh, ironically often in the situation of affliction.[16] Thus, it is fitting that Ps 128:1 would say, "Blessed are all who fear Yhwh, those walking in his ways" (cf. Prov 9:10). Likewise, both Job 5:17 and Ps 94:12 commend the faithful teaching role of Yhwh: "Blessed is the man God rebukes and who does not refuse the *musar* of Shaddai" and "Blessed is the man who you, O Yah, instruct (יסר), and you teach (למד) from your *torah*" (cf. Prov 3:11–12, 8:32–33). Regarding the God-like character aspect, Ps 106:3 says, "Blessed are those guarding justice, the one doing righteousness in all times" (cf. Prov 9:9). Similarly, Ps 119:1–2 commends this sense of the "blessed" on the virtuous path as an orientation for the whole psalm, "Blessed are the blameless of way, those walking in the *torah* of Yhwh. Blessed are those guarding (נצר) his testimonies, those who seek him with their whole heart" (cf. Prov 8:17, 20, 35).[17] So, Wisdom here (Prov 8:32–36) pronounces that those who guard her ways and find her are the "blessed." While being in faithful relation with Yhwh has its salvific benefits (e.g., Deut 33:29; Ps 34:9), the relevant contribution for this lesson is two-fold. The son is not directly called "blessed" but encouraged to be like those who are "blessed." On one hand, the son is to imitate and follow in the ways of those who are "blessed," those who have walked in the *torah* way throughout the generations.[18] They are those who have a particular character and faithful way of life, those walking on the path of the wise (e.g., Prov 2:20–21). On the other hand, the character of the "blessed" is not an end but a reflection of the ultimate source and teacher of the "blessed," Yhwh himself. He is the exemplar of righteousness, justice, and the wise path (cf. Isa 30:18).[19] Thus, the son ought to become like the "blessed" in his ways that he might ultimately reflect Yhwh in proper and intimate relation.

Although Wisdom commends the son to "keep my ways," the phrase is likely drawn from those who reflect the "way of Yhwh" elsewhere. In Gen 18:19, a foundational passage, Yhwh speaks rhetorically or to his angelic entourage concerning Abraham, "I have known him so that he shall command his sons and house after him that they shall guard (שמר) the way of Yhwh (דֶּרֶךְ יְהוָה), doing righteousness and justice." Regarding the whole Torah, John Sailhamer argues, "The purpose of the Pentateuch is ... to be a narrative

---

[16] Hamilton on one hand rightly affirms the term's close association with Yhwh and his character. Yet, he also goes on to wrongly ascribe the sense of "envious desire" to the term, which leads him to wrongly state, "God is not man and therefore there are no grounds for aspiring to his state even in a wishful way" (Victor P. Hamilton, "אָשַׁר," in *TWOT* (Chicago: Moody, 1999), 80–82). If "blessed" is understood generically as success (or proper advancing), though particularly in the area of character and divine peace (cf. Prov 3:17), then Yhwh certainly exists in this state perpetually. Thus, he would serve as the ultimate goal of the "blessed" man who does not deviate from the way of Yhwh.

[17] Cf. Schipper, *Proverbs 1–15*, 315.

[18] Cf. Schipper, *Proverbs 1–15*, 316.

[19] In Isa 28:26 and 29, Motyer makes a connection with Isa 30:18 saying, "He guides him for justice; his God instructs him ... he gives marvelous counsel, makes great wisdom (תּוּשִׁיָּה)" (cf. Prov 2:7). As Motyer notes, God is perfect in his decision making and thus bringing about justice. By implication, God not only makes justice and is the example of a proper judge but he instructs and expects his people to do likewise. See J. A. Motyer, *The Prophecy of Isaiah: An Introduction & Commentary* (Downers Grove: IVP, 1993), 250.

admonition to be like Abraham."[20] If he is at all correct, then, it would be quite reasonable for the father (Wisdom) in Prov 1–9 to point the son (students) to Abraham's example, particularly in his pursuit of Yhwh's way. In a later passage, Yhwh conveys a harsh judgment on Israel, "Because this people transgressed my covenant which I commanded their fathers and they did not listen to my voice, I shall not drive out the nations before them … so that they will be a test against them, if they will guard (שמר) the way of Yhwh (דֶּרֶךְ יְהֹוָה), walking in them just as their fathers guarded (שמר)" (Judg 2:20–22; cf. Jer 5:4–5). As seen in the passages with "blessed," there is a strong correspondence between character and relation with Yhwh, expressed as walking in or guarding his ways. So, what is expressed as the ways of Wisdom in Prov 8:32–36 is really the way of Yhwh.[21] In essence, the son is being called to walk in the manner that Wisdom walks, which is the way of Yhwh.[22] Thus, what was expressed as the instruction of the father is now more explicitly associated with Wisdom. In Prov 8:33, Wisdom commands the son to "hear *musar*," reflecting the father (e.g., 1:8, 4:1) and Yhwh (3:11). So, in her mediation and overlapping expression, Wisdom serves as the son's greater, divine-like instructor, providing the next step in his progression to imitating the ineffable God.[23] In this way, then, the father passes the torch to Wisdom as the son's example and guide through life along the wisdom trajectory.

Wisdom's Speech (9:1–12)

In the father's speech from Wisdom, a final plea is given for the son to walk in the way of the wise. At this point in the program, though, the instruction takes a turn, particularly in Prov 9:7–9. After giving a call to the naïve (Prov 9:4–7), similar to her speech in 8:4–5, she launches into an instruction for instructors.[24] The wisdom student is now progressing to the stage where he

---

[20] John Sailhamer, *The Meaning of the Pentateuch: Revelation, Composition, and Interpretation* (Downers Grove: IVP Academic, 2009), 14.

[21] Cf. Schipper, *Proverbs 1–15*, 316.

[22] It is important that Wisdom commends those who find her as those who are favored by Yhwh. In other words, since God himself is wise, those who reflect Wisdom likewise reflect him. As von Rad said, "It is she who brings order to the whole of life in God's eyes" (Gerhard von Rad, *Wisdom in Israel* (Nashville: Abingdon, 1972), 172).

[23] In Lesson 6, a parallel phrase is given by the father, "My son, hear and receive my words that *years of life may be many for you*" (Prov 4:10). In Lesson 15, Wisdom says, "By me, your days *will be many* and *the years of life* will be increased *for you*" (Prov 9:11). Wisdom picks up the instructive torch from the father, providing a more divine quality to it. The father can only recommend that which leads to life while Wisdom not only recommends the way but actually says she is the way of life, sourced in Yhwh alone. Similarly, Waltke says, "The Owner of Life mediates it to those who seek it through the inspired sage's wisdom." See Schipper, *Proverbs 1–15*, 334; Daniel C. Snell, *Twice-Told Proverbs and the Composition of the Book of Proverbs* (Winona Lake: Eisenbrauns, 1993), 37; Heim, *Poetic Imagination in Proverbs*, 104–9; Waltke, *Proverbs (1–15)*, 425.

[24] Although McKane (and Fox) argues for a complex textual history, proposing it is a late insertion, his conclusion for the final form is that the speech of Wisdom (Prov 9:7–12) primarily serves to "enlarge Wisdom's role as an instructress." Fox (cf. Longman and Estes)

must assume the role of the father or teacher, just as his father and teacher did for him.[25] So, Wisdom provides several points on whom to teach and how to teach them.[26] In a dichotomous manner, there are the scoffers and the wise. The scoffer is characterized by hate and wicked abuse of the teacher (cf. Prov 1:22–25, 5:12–13). The wise, on the contrary, are characterized by their love of the teacher and thus growth in learning. The implication is that the student-turned-teacher must discern whom to train and invest in,[27] a skill implied later in Prov 26:4–5.[28] Interestingly, the language of "love" and "hate" is similarly used for those who seek and find Wisdom (Prov 8:35–36, 9:8). In a sense, the newly minted teacher will be the example or embodiment of Wisdom, as the father has been, for his students until they are able to move beyond him to Wisdom and Yhwh as their example.[29] This model is the perpetual cycle for wisdom training.[30]

In Wisdom's speech, she commends her ways as life-giving or at least life-extending (Prov 9:6, 11).[31] However, there is a parallel that directs the gravity of her ways. In Prov 9:6, she states to the naïve, "Walk in the way of insight (בִּינָה)." This "way" seems to equate to her own ways, characterized here as "insight" (cf. Prov 4:5, 7, 7:4, 8:14). Then, shortly after this she states, "Knowledge of the Holy One is insight (בִּינָה)" (Prov 9:10b; cf. 30:3; Hos 12:1).[32]

---

regarded the verses as "Advice to the Adviser" (Prov 9:7–10) implying instruction for instructors, it would seem. Regarding the textual history, Meinhold and Murphy argue for the verses' continuity and relevance in context. Whybray is doubtful but a bit more ambivalent on their originality or relevance. While it is difficult to know whether any of these verses were original or not, the whole speech becomes more logical and smooth once Wisdom's role and the overarching purpose of Prov 1–9 are understood. See McKane, *Proverbs*, 360; Meinhold, *Die Sprüche*, 150; Whybray, *Composition of the Book of Proverbs*, 44–48; Murphy, *Proverbs*, 61; Fox, *Proverbs 1–9*, 306; Longman, *Proverbs*, 218; Estes, *Hear, My Son*, 74.

[25] Schipper makes an unnecessary and misguided statement about Prov 9:8 that the verse is intended for "those who seek sapiential knowledge but who are not necessarily wisdom teachers." This statement is left unsubstantiated and unnecessarily makes the two mutually exclusive. If the wisdom learning process is never finished, as he says, then why would Wisdom not also instruct teachers, particularly the son at the end of his mundane pedagogical training? See Schipper, *Proverbs 1–15*, 331.

[26] Cf. Hubbard, *Proverbs*, 131–32. Hubbard also notes that one plausible view of Prov 9:7–12 is that Wisdom is speaking and thus teaching the teachers. Regardless, though, the unit appears to be instruction for instructors, whether from Wisdom or the father.

[27] Cf. McKane, *Proverbs*, 368.

[28] This verse says, "Do not answer a fool according to his folly lest you become like him. Answer a fool according to his folly lest he become wise in his eyes" (Prov 26:4–5). Similarly, Schipper argues that Prov 9 serves as the "reading guide for what follows," referring to Prov 10–31. See Schipper, *Proverbs 1–15*, 323.

[29] Fox draws from Khonshotep, a 13th c. BCE Egyptian sage, saying, "To teach is to imitate God and it is godly to listen before answering." The Egyptian text says, "Man resembles the god in this way if he listens to a man's answer." Prior to this, the son of Khonshotep says, "I wish I were like you, as learned as you!" (Fox, *Proverbs 1–9*, 314; Miriam Lichtheim, *Ancient Egyptian Literature: Volume II: The New Kingdom* (Berkeley: University of California Press, 1975), 144, 145). Both Fox and Khonshotep mention the imitative relationship between a teacher and student, who ultimately derive their principles from the divine.

[30] As Clifford mentions, "A sage is always a student, ever eager to learn" (Clifford, *Proverbs*, 106).

[31] Cf. Murphy, *Proverbs*, 60.

[32] Waltke, *Proverbs (1–15)*, 442.

While much could be said about this verse, its connection with 9:6 implies a logical comparison. One who "walks in the way of insight" is one who possesses "knowledge of the Holy One."[33] Waltke mentions of this verse, "Wisdom consists in transcending the fallen human world and participating in the divine, the holy." By saying "participating in the divine," it would seem he implies a coterminous and reflective behavior for those on the wise path, the way of Yhwh. So, these verses help illuminate the relational quality of the wisdom program throughout.[34] Just as Lesson 2 taught that seeking wisdom would result in finding the "knowledge of God" (Prov 2:5), Lesson 15 teaches it is the one who listens to Wisdom that has "insight" and thus "knowledge of the Holy One."[35] In other words, those who walk on the path of the wise do so with and in reflection of Yhwh. As mentioned elsewhere, knowledge is a key characteristic of the wise and those walking in proper relation to Yhwh.[36] This is likely why the father inserts a somewhat arbitrary statement describing Folly, "She does not know anything" (Prov 9:13).[37] Similarly, the fools who follow her into Sheol are described as ignorant, both of the corruption in Folly's ways and of the fate for those who walk in them. In contrast, those who walk

---

[33] The subtle implication, here, is that the student in his pursuit of wisdom and knowledge is to reflect the holiness of the Holy One. The term for "holy" (קְדֹשׁ) surprisingly only occurs three times in Proverbs (9:10, 25:20, 30:3). The foundation for imitating the holy God of Israel, of course, began in Lev 11:44–45 and 19:2. There, the people were expected to be like their covenant partner, "You shall be holy for I am holy, Yhwh your God" (19:2; cf. 11:44–45). See Excursus: Leviticus and the Holiness of God for a more extended discussion.

For scholarly views on the topic, see John H. Walton, *Ancient Near Eastern Thought and the Old Testament: Introducing the Conceptual World of the Hebrew Bible*, 1st ed. (Grand Rapids: Baker Academic, 2006), 110, 311; John H. Walton, *Ancient Near Eastern Thought and the Old Testament: Introducing the Conceptual World of the Hebrew Bible*, 2nd ed. (Grand Rapids: Baker Academic, 2018), 71, 292; John H. Walton and J. Harvey Walton, *The Lost World of the Torah: Law as Covenant and Wisdom in Ancient Context* (Downers Grove: IVP, 2019), 11, 44, 54–55, 203–4, 206; Esias E. Meyer, "When Synchrony Overtakes Diachrony: Perspectives on the Relationship between the Deuteronomic Code and the Holiness Code," *OTE* 30.3 (2017): 754–55, 757; John E. Hartley, *Leviticus*, WBC 4 (Dallas: Word Books, 1992), 309–12; Gordon J. Wenham, "The Gap between Law and Ethics in the Bible," *JJS* 48.1 (1997): 27; Robert R. Wilson, "Approaches to Old Testament Ethics," in *Canon, Theology, and Old Testament Interpretation: Essays in Honor of Brevard S Childs* (Philadelphia, 1988), 67; Esias E. Meyer, "The Dark Side of the Imitatio Dei. Why Imitating the God of the Holiness Code Is Not Always a Good Thing," *OTE* 22.2 (2009): 374; Howard Kreisel, "Imitatio Dei in Maimonides' Guide of the Perplexed," *AJS Review* 19.2 (1994): 206; Eryl W. Davies, "Walking in God's Ways: The Concept of Imitatio Dei in the Old Testament," in *In Search of True Wisdom* (Sheffield: Sheffield Academic, 1999), 101; Samson Raphael Hirsch, *The Pentateuch*, trans. Isaac Levy, 2nd ed. (London: Judaica, 1962), 3:499–500; Baruch A. Levine, *Leviticus: The Traditional Hebrew Text with the New JPS Translation*, The JPS Torah Commentary (Philadelphia: Jewish Publication Society, 1989), 125; Jo Bailey Wells, *God's Holy People: A Theme in Biblical Theology*, JSOTSup 305 (Sheffield: T&T Clark, 2000), 70, 93.

[34] Cf. Schipper, *Proverbs 1–15*, 332.

[35] Cf. McKane, *Proverbs*, 368; Fox, *Proverbs 1–9*, 308.

[36] Whybray, *Composition of the Book of Proverbs*, 44.

[37] Fox argues Folly and Wisdom are inverse reflections of the other, particularly in this regard. However, he does note that the sense of "does not know" could be an idiomatic way of saying "shameless." While plausible, the common motif of "knowledge" for the wise and "no knowledge" for the fool would suggest "shameless" is not the primary sense here in Prov 9 (Fox, *Proverbs 1–9*, 301).

in righteousness will have knowledge, both as a result of walking in the light of truth (Prov 4:18) and in their transforming knowledge of God (2:5, 9:10; cf. Ps 1:6).[38]

Folly's Speech (9:13–18)

To conclude the whole wisdom program, the father ends with a stark warning. The speech from Folly parallels Wisdom (Prov 9:4, 16), using the exact same phrase, "Whoever is naïve, turn here" (מִי־פֶתִי יָסֻר הֵנָּה). Both call the naïve to "turn" to their ways, imaged by their respective houses (Prov 9:1, 14; cf. 14:1, 24:3).[39] The parallel calls, however, imply that the naïve are already on a path but able to turn onto one path or the other (cf. Prov 1:22–23, 8:5).[40] Wisdom calls for them to "abandon their naivety, live, and walk in the way of insight" (Prov 9:6). For Folly, the father says that she calls to those who were "walking on the path, making straight their ways" (Prov 9:15).[41] The contrast implies both figures are seeking to persuade travelers to join them. However, the end of their ways is quite polar. The end of Wisdom's way is life and fellowship with the wise and Yhwh. The end of Folly is Sheol and fellowship with the Rephaim (Prov 9:18; cf. 2:18, 21:16).[42] So, the naïve are presented with not only two paths but two groups.[43] These groups serve as the embodiment of their ways. [44] Likewise, their ways are representative of their prime exemplars, Wisdom or Folly. If the naïve will imitate the wise, they will join them in their joyful fate. Yet, if they choose to imitate the fools, they will join them in the depths and darkness of Sheol.

---

[38] The psalmist says that "Yhwh knows (יוֹדֵעַ) the way of the righteous but the way of the wicked will perish" (Ps 1:6). The MT of Ps 1 vocalizes "know" as a participle. This grammar implies either a present, contemporaneous involvement with the righteous or as a descriptor of Yhwh, one in fellowship with the righteous. Either way, the psalmist clearly contrasts the two ways by their fellowship and knowledge of God versus death, which parallels the picture in Prov 9.

[39] Cf. Murphy, *Proverbs*, 58–59.

[40] Schipper believes this malleable quality, particularly of the naïve, is unique here in Prov 9. Fox, however, proposes that there were three views of "learning capacity" in the ANE pedagogical mind: 1) "some people are closed to learning, and there's no point in trying to teach them"; 2) "learning is always possible, because teaching is the imposition of will on resistant material"; and 3) "learning is often problematic, but it is always in principle possible, given the right approach." See Schipper, *Proverbs 1–15*, 317, 322; Fox, *Proverbs 1–9*, 309.

[41] According to Fox, this phrase is an idiom which "always connotes moral virtue." Similarly, Schipper states that it refers to an "an attitude that includes ethically correct behavior as well as an orientation toward God." See Fox, *Proverbs 1–9*, 302; Schipper, *Proverbs 1–15*, 336.

[42] As Schipper describes, Folly's call refers to a "behavior that intentionally seeks to lead someone astray from the worship of Yhwh" (Schipper, *Proverbs 1–15*, 336).

[43] Cf. Schipper, *Proverbs 1–15*, 330, 336.

[44] In discussing the theology of Prov 9, Longman notes, "To be wise means that one acts like one who is in relationship with Yahweh ... [fools] are acting like worshippers of pagan deities" (Longman, *Proverbs*, 223; Estes, *Hear, My Son*, 47). Implicitly, Longman seems to acknowledge the reflective and imitative qualities of the two groups for those walking in their ways.

What is perhaps most confusing for the naïve, however, is the place of both Wisdom and Folly. In the father's framing for both, he uses the exact same phrase, "the heights of town" (מְרֹמֵי קָרֶת), to describe their position (Prov 9:3, 14).[45] These figures occupy the same space and shout similar pleas to those passing by. Yet, the reality of their position could not be more different. As Lesson 14 beautifully elaborates, Wisdom dwells with Yhwh. So, her position in the heights rightly reflects Yhwh and his position (e.g., Isa 2:11; Ps 113:4–6, 138:6).[46] But, Folly is closely associated with the pits of Sheol and the dead. So, her position at the heights is in fact a counterfeit.[47] She is falsely assuming or imitating the place of Wisdom and Yhwh.[48] In Isa 14, a similar image is propounded about the King of Babylon.[49] Here, the prophet declares, "You said in your heart, 'I shall ascend to heaven, above the stars of God; I will exalt my throne and I will sit on the mountain of assembly … I shall become like the Most High.' Yet, you shall be brought down to Sheol, to the deepest pit" (Isa 14:13–15).[50] The figure is notably wrong in his aspiration to imitate God in an improper or counterfeit way, similar to Adam and Eve (Gen 3).[51] In doing so, he is comparable to Folly. The prophecy also mentions the

---

[45] In Ezek 16, the prophet gives the word of Yhwh in language very similar to Folly here. The context is a rebuke against Jerusalem and Judah who built for themselves high-places in every street corner (Ezek 16:23–52). The rebuke seems to interweave a variety of offenses, couched in the language of adultery and prostitution. While the term "idol" is used (16:36), it also seems their error included a variety of practices abhorrent to Yhwh through their assimilation and imitation of the other nations (Egypt, Philistia, Assyria, and Chaldea). Perhaps most condemning is the pronouncement, "You walked in their ways and you did their abominations; in only a short time, you became more corrupt than them in all their ways" (Ezek 16:47). In following the other nations, Judah became like Folly and her companions.

[46] As Longman rightly observes, "In the ancient Near East, only one house is built on the high place of a city, and that is the temple. It is not a stretch, therefore, to suggest that Wisdom is not only the personification of Yahweh's wisdom but also of Yahweh himself." Motyer commenting on Isa 14:13 notes the implicit contrast between Mt. Zaphon and Mt. Zion. Regarding Prov 9, these two mountains may be figuratively behind the two characters Folly and Wisdom in their respective heights. See Longman, *Proverbs*, 222; Motyer, *Prophecy of Isaiah*, 145.

[47] As Fox (cf. Miles) notes, "Folly mimics Wisdom" (Fox, *Proverbs 1–9*, 302; Miles, *Wise King - Royal Fool: Semiotics, Satire and Proverbs 1–9*, 97). This form of mimicry is a counterfeit and central to the false way. Thus, it is not only those who do blatant foolishness but those who appropriate wisdom's forms for foolish ends that are wicked and in opposition to Yhwh.

[48] Longman also describes the mysterious Folly, "She too represents deity, but in her case she stands for all the pagan gods and goddesses who desire to lure Israel away from the true God" (Longman, *Proverbs*, 222). In this false representation of Yhwh, she stands as a foil to the proper imitation of God.

[49] Cf. Schipper, *Proverbs 1–15*, 338.

[50] As Wegner mentions, "He intends to sit with deities … similar to that of those who attempted to build the tower in Shinar (Gen 11:4)" (Paul D. Wegner, *Isaiah: An Introduction and Commentary*, TOTC (Downers Grove: IVP Academic, 2021), 147–48). Isaiah uses the imagery of a "throne on high" and a "mountain of assembly" (14:13). Isaiah contrasts the king's ambition for the "far region" (יַרְכָה) of Zaphon with his fate in the "far region" (יַרְכָה) of Sheol (14:13, 15). This contrast is similar to that of Prov 9, though the sage uses the term "depths" (עֹמֶק) instead.

[51] As Fox discusses, the banquet image contrasts Wisdom and Folly through the results of their blessing or cursing. This metaphor is used in Prov 3:18 for the "tree of life." Thus, partaking in the way of Wisdom was akin to eating from the tree of life, namely properly walking in the way of Yhwh. Conversely, eating of Folly's fruit was akin to that primordial aberration.

absurdity of seeking to subvert God.[52] As judgment for his arrogance, Isaiah says of the emblematic figure, the king of Babylon, "Sheol below is roused to meet you when you come, the Rephaim are stirred, those leaders of the earth … They shall all answer you and say, 'You have become weak like us, you have been made like us" (Isa 14:9–10; cf. Prov 9:18).[53] The attempt to imitate God in an unholy manner was not new.[54] The King of Babylon was just another fool in a long line of fools. So, in his impetuous pride, he follows his fellow fools both in their life and death.[55] His reflection of their ways necessarily results in his reflection of their fate. This path and fate are similarly expressed in Prov 9. It is telling that both passages use similar terms and imagery.[56] While

---

Oswalt compares Isa 14 to Gen 3, "The forbidden fruit was proffered to Adam and Eve as being able to make them like God." Yet, as he says, "The human problem is that we will not accept God's gifts within the limits imposed by him. We wish to be God." See Fox, *Proverbs 1–9*, 305; John N. Oswalt, *The Book of Isaiah*, NICOT (Grand Rapids: Eerdmans, 1986), 323.

[52] Scurlock provides an interesting ANE comparative analysis for the pagan symbolism being polemically appropriated. She argues that the figure in view is Marduk in his rivalry with Anu, who ironically falls victim to his own trap. If correct in her evaluations, the self-inflicted trap motif would fit well with Prov 1–9 (e.g., 1:18). Also, the pagan divinity could easily be overlaid with Longman's proposal that Folly partly represents the non-Yahwistic deities. See Jo Ann Scurlock, "Assyria and Babylon in the Oracles against the Nations Tradition: The Death of a King (Isa. 14:5–20; Isa. 30:27–33)," *JAOS* 140.2 (2020): 395–413; Longman, *Proverbs*, 222.

[53] Although Holladay argues that the departed are other fallen kings, he proposes the judgement of this King of Babylon is not so much his descent to the grave but his loss of honor and remembrance in their company (Isa 14:19–20). It would seem Holladay unnecessarily separates the two, which both work as elements of the same judgment. Nordheim-Diehl observes the variety of biblical text traditions (MT, LXX, Q, Tg.) and their views of Sheol, arguing for a conceptual development from Sheol being a deity to a place which Yhwh has supremacy over. While interesting, the literary and poetic imagery need not imply an actual deity for the mild personification of Sheol, which is viewed both as a mere place and as personified elsewhere in Isaiah (e.g., 5:14, 28:15, 38:18; cf. 7:11, 14:11, 38:10). In Proverbs, Sheol is used in both a personified sense and as a mere place of the dead, as well (e.g., 1:12, 27:20; cf. 15:11, 24). For Prov 9, Sheol is understood as the opposite place of Wisdom, and implicitly of Yhwh. This dichotomous view is seen in Prov 15:11, "The path of life is upward for the prudent, to turn from Sheol below." For a survey of views and ANE literature on the Rephaim (רְפָאִים), as well as Isa 14, see Philip Johnston, *Shades of Sheol: Death and Afterlife in the Old Testament* (Downers Grove: IVP, 2002), 127–49; William Lee Holladay, "Text, Structure, and Irony in the Poem on the Fall of the Tyrant, Isaiah 14," *CBQ* 61.4 (1999): 641–43; Miriam von Nordheim-Diehl, "Wer herrscht in der Scheol?: eine Untersuchung zu Jes 14,9," *BN* 143 (2009): 81–91.

[54] Oswalt opines that "ultimately the battle is not among various manifestations of deity" but between "Creator and creatures" since "making God in our image is the great folly of humanity" (Oswalt, *The Book of Isaiah*, 320).

[55] As Prinsloo says, "Yahweh is portrayed as *deus victor* … he transforms hubris to humility" (Willem S. Prinsloo, "Isaiah 14:12–15 · Humiliation, Hubris, Humiliation," *ZAW* 93.3 (1981): 438).

[56] Avriel and Amzallag note that the prophecy against the King of Babylon is called a "proverb" (משל) in Isa 14:4 (cf. Motyer, Sawyer, Yee, Mizrahi). The term has a number of potential connotative uses but possibly connects it with wisdom literature (Prov 1:1). This connection could imply that Prov 9 is directly paralleled or perhaps related through conceptual correspondence. Interestingly, building on the work of others, Avriel and Amzallag observe a chiasm for the poem (Isa 14:4–20), which centers on 14:12. O'Connell places its center on 14:12–14. See Mikhal Avriel and Nissim Amzallag, "The Cryptic Meaning of the Isaiah 14 Māšāl," *JBL* 131 (2012): 643–62; Robert H. O'Connell, "Isaiah 14:4b-23: Ironic Reversal through Concentric Structure and Mythic Allusion," *VT* 38.4 (1988): 406–18; Gale A. Yee, "The Anatomy of Biblical Parody: The Dirge Form in 2 Samuel 1 and Isaiah 14," *CBQ* 50.4 (1988): 565–86; Noam Mizrahi, "The Textual

Prov 9 does not limit the identity of the Rephaim to Babylon (Prov 9:18), the implication is that the house of Folly is full of such foolish travelers, who thought themselves more wise than Wisdom and more powerful than Yhwh. The King of Babylon perhaps serves as an exemplar or embodiment of Folly in Isaiah. But, as Wisdom declares, it is "by me that your days will be made many and the years of your life multiplied" (Prov 9:11). If the naïve wish to be like the King of Babylon, they will join him in his fall. But, if the naïve desire to be like Wisdom and Yhwh, properly that is, they will enjoy life and "obtain the favor of Yhwh" (8:35).[57] Though the two paths may appear similar to the naïve, they could not be more different.

Conclusion

In his final lesson, the father gives the final plea. Here, he promotes the way of Wisdom and warns of Folly. Likewise, the son learns that he must be wise for himself in order to be a worthy teacher and example for others (Prov 9:7–12). Just as the father has faithfully transmitted his *torah*, as his father did for him (Prov 4:3–4), the son must also do for the next generation. Furthermore, the father served as the son's teacher throughout the program, but now Wisdom assumes the primary role as the son's exalted teacher along the wisdom trajectory (Prov 8:32–33). If the son continues to follow her, he will walk with the wise in the knowledge of God (Prov 9:6, 10; cf. 2:5). This path is mutually exclusive from the way of Folly (Prov 9:4, 16). Her counterfeit path is ultimately rebellion against God and an attempt to subvert his position. The son, therefore, must properly reflect Yhwh instead by faithfully reflecting Wisdom. As he walks in the way of insight, he will walk in the favor, life, and likeness of Yhwh.

History and Literary Background of Isa 14,4," *ZAW* 125.3 (2013): 433–47; John F. A. Sawyer, *Isaiah* (Philadelphia: Westminster, 1986), 100; Motyer, *The Prophecy of Isaiah*, 142.

[57] As Schipper comments, "Although sapiential education still has its value, it alone cannot lead people to life. For this, Yhwh is necessary." Similarly, Oswalt notes, "Because pride denies God, it must deny us what God has given, ultimately life itself." See Schipper, *Proverbs 1–15*, 340; Oswalt, *The Book of Isaiah*, 324.

EXCURSUS

Leviticus and the Holiness of God

As the conclusion of the proverbial wisdom program, Lesson 15 subtly mentions a unique and profound statement, "The fear of Yhwh is the beginning of Wisdom and knowledge of the Holy One is insight" (Prov 9:10). While the term for "holy" is rare in Proverbs (9:10, 20:25, 30:3), the implication in this use is important. The proverbial father teaches the student a great deal about wisdom and the necessity of seeking wisdom in the proper way. This path, however, is not a secular endeavor of mere will and intellect but a relational journey. It is walking with the righteous sages on the wise path.[1] Yet, this particular wise path is not unmoored but rooted in the very character and ways of Yhwh. Though implicitly understood throughout Proverbs, the wise Yhwh is indeed the holy God of Torah, as well. Thus, it is indirectly expected that the student must properly reflect the holiness of God in order to rightly reflect his wisdom. That is to say, holiness and wisdom are intertwined. In other words, for one to be wise, one must be a righteous person, which means upholding the holy ways of *torah*. For the proverbial father, knowledge of the Holy One is central to the wisdom program, which is primarily achieved by reflecting his ways. Therefore, in walking this wise path, the son will be both wise and holy as Yhwh is.

In this brief analysis, the holiness of God is examined primarily in Leviticus and shown to be a quality expected for those in covenant with Yhwh. Although Walton and Walton reject *imitatio Dei* in their view of biblical morality, analysis of the topic in Leviticus and the Torah paints a different picture. Indeed, the HB presents Yhwh as a divine ruler worthy of imitation and one who expects his people to reflect his ways as part of the enduring covenant. While Israel was a holy people by virtue of their covenant, they were also to both pursue and reflect the holiness of their God.

---

[1] Keefer rightly states, "Proverbial character types ... stand as models intended for interpreters to emulate or disparage" (Arthur J. Keefer, *The Book of Proverbs and Virtue Ethics: Integrating the Biblical and Philosophical Traditions* (Cambridge: Cambridge University Press, 2021), 45).

The Waltons' Proposal

In their volume, *The Lost World of the Torah*, John H. Walton and J. Harvey Walton attempt to recalibrate the field of OT law.[2] In this work, the primary thesis is, "The Torah is similar to ANE legal collections and therefore teaches wisdom not legislation."[3] The authors' approach is primarily the *Sitz im Leben* of biblical law and secondarily its implication.[4] Throughout the propositions of their book, they provide a strong case for the place of wisdom at the helm of what is normally called law, which is supported by scholarship on the topic.[5] This would imply that the law is not statutory legislation in modern legal parlance but guidance for what proper behavior and judgment look like, particularly for kings and rulers. The central concern for them is the limitations of biblical and ANE law. In their estimation, it cannot provide a comprehensive and legally binding order.[6] This is especially troubling for them when biblical law is used prescriptively for modern readers and their societies.

Within their proposed understanding of biblical law, they specifically remove any connection of the law to universal morality.[7] For them, the law was closer to divine command theory, though this theory and its universal, timeless implications are formally dismissed. Divine command theory proposes that laws are legally binding by fiat of divine will without necessarily being derived from divine nature or the transcendence of the law. In other words, they contend that God did not give the laws he gave because they were intrinsically right or because they were based on some eternal moral reality.[8] Furthermore, the basis of the law was unrelated to the character or actions of God. So, in their view of *torah*, they redefine the notion of law to be

---

[2] John H. Walton and J. Harvey Walton, *The Lost World of the Torah: Law as Covenant and Wisdom in Ancient Context* (Downers Grove: IVP, 2019).

[3] Walton and Walton, *Lost World of the Torah*, 37.

[4] Walton and Walton, *Lost World of the Torah*, 37–38. Part of their wisdom approach is to differentiate the actions observed in biblical narratives against the biblical law codes. For them, later biblical narratives lack an appeal to laws or legal statutes from the Torah, which implies a lack of use or role in any legal sense.

[5] Their basic premise is that *torah* means "instruction" rather than "law," which is likely quite right. But it seems they perhaps go too far in distancing Yhwh's nature from his instruction, the ultimate teacher of biblical and proverbial principles. For additional support of ANE and biblical views for legal texts in the wisdom genre, see, Raymond Westbrook, ed., *A History of Ancient Near Eastern Law* (Boston: Brill, 2003), 22–26; Christopher B. Hays, *Hidden Riches: A Sourcebook for the Comparative Study of the Hebrew Bible and Ancient Near East* (Louisville: Westminster John Knox, 2014), 140–44, 185; John Sailhamer, *The Meaning of the Pentateuch: Revelation, Composition, and Interpretation* (Downers Grove: IVP Academic, 2009), 561–62.

[6] Walton and Walton, *Lost World of the Torah*, 37.

[7] Walton and Walton, *Lost World of the Torah*, 206.

[8] As a caveat, they do note the possibility that there are some universals, using the example of stealing. Yet, it is not clear how one would come to know such a universal principle in their theory (Walton and Walton, *Lost World of the Torah*, 206).

contextually and culturally dependent.[9] A wise ruler may look to such a law code for wise guidance but without reference to the God behind it, only its practical relevance in fostering societal order. The wisdom of biblical *torah* provides "insights" for societal order,[10] as it pertains or is relevant to a particular people at a particular time.[11]

Now, in the ANE concept of the gods, the non-Israelite nations may not have based their laws and wise ordinances on the character and ethics of their gods, who were anything but holy and pure.[12] As Walton rightly notes, "The gods are perceived in largely human terms ... like humans, [they] were subject to spite, lust, and rage. Each one of them tried to realize his own aims. ... [They] make mistakes and misjudgments and even commit crimes. They can be surprised."[13] Then, as he goes on to describe, "The operative question in their minds, for instance, is not, 'Is deity just?' but, 'Does the deity administer justice?' It is not important whether the deity is inherently good— is the deity doing good for me and my community."[14] In the prologue of Hammurabi's law code, the text makes it clear that the king was tasked with giving the wise judgments that resulted in a law code, "When the god Marduk commanded me to provide just ways for the people of the land (in order to attain) appropriate behavior, I established truth and justice as the declaration of the land, I enhanced the well-being of the people."[15] So, it seems that the gods vested their legal authority in the king, who gave his own judgments and laws, rather than the gods giving the laws themselves. In this way, the laws could not have reflected their own divine character but only the human king's nature and character. Conversely, in the biblical corpus, it was Yhwh who

---

[9] As Walton and Walton state, "If God did not give rules ... there are no rules to follow. ... Order in society was the goal, and it was achieved through wisdom, which had its foundation in the fear of the Lord" (Walton and Walton, *Lost World of the Torah*, 44). For "fear of Yhwh" as the foundation, it seems they mean the procurement of blessings and avoidance of curses.

[10] Commenting on the Ten Commandments, they say, "The Decalogue, then, like the rest of the Torah, is focused on instructing Israel as to the nature of the societal order that would reflect the reputation God desires for himself" (Walton and Walton, *Lost World of the Torah*, 232).

[11] The metaphorical term used in their book to describe this phenomenon is "cultural river." On one hand, they seem to simply mean a need to understand the differences between the original context and the modern reader's context. On the other, regarding culturally informed morality, they state, "Morality is a function of communities, not individuals. Every community desires order, and morality entails establishing behavior, customs, and traditions as well as social norms and taboos that preserve order. ... Our particular morality is a product of our cognitive environment, just as our particular physical cosmology also is; it represents something we have to work within, not something we have to create." They go on to clarify, "Morality may well comprise some universal absolutes (i.e., do not steal), but it is also defined by norms that are culturally relative." See Walton and Walton, *Lost World of the Torah*, 10–11, 206.

[12] See John H. Walton, *Ancient Near Eastern Thought and the Old Testament: Introducing the Conceptual World of the Hebrew Bible*, 2nd ed. (Grand Rapids: Baker Academic, 2018), 62–63, 64, 66.

[13] Walton, *Ancient Near Eastern Thought (2018)*, 62.

[14] Walton, *Ancient Near Eastern Thought (2018)*, 66.

[15] Martha Tobi Roth and Harry A. Hoffner, *Law Collections from Mesopotamia and Asia Minor*, ed. Piotr Michalowski, 2nd ed., WAW 6 (Atlanta: Scholars, 1997), 80; Hays, *Hidden Riches*, 121–45.

served as the direct king and judge of Israel, providing his own wise statutes and judgments (e.g., Deut 5:4, 22; 1 Sam 8:7). This nuanced literary and theological distinction between the biblical and ANE corpora is important for this discussion.

In Walton and Walton's recalibration of biblical law, they are led to dismiss *imitatio Dei* within the biblical corpus,[16] perhaps due to a conflation of the biblical and ANE contexts.[17] They argue that God's character, desires, and actions are unrelated to his commands or laws.[18] While they do concede some incidental similarity of actions between God and humans in the biblical corpus, the book broadly rejects the notion of divine imitation, especially as it pertains to ethics or morality.[19] In other words, the Israelites, along with the ANE and modern society, do not engage or avoid any behavior because of its purported relation to God. Rather, the principle of societal order is the litmus for guidance in various societies and cultures throughout time. At the heart of their dismissal of *imitatio Dei*, they claim the phrase "Be holy for I am holy" (Lev 19:2) is unrelated to imitating God, functioning only as a statement of status.[20] Holiness for Israel was a state of existence rather than a state to be maintained or pursued, a state unrelated to the ideas of piety and morality. Unfortunately, by removing *imitatio Dei* from their broader theory of law and wisdom, they deconstruct the basis for biblical ethics and morality.[21] Yet, if

---

[16] They define this phrase as a moral system in which "right and wrong are defined ... as doing what God does, or perhaps more accurately doing what God would do in your particular circumstance. The point is for [biblical] readers to manifest the same moral character as God so that they will choose to do the same things that God would choose to do" (Walton and Walton, *Lost World of the Torah*, 203).

[17] As they state, "In the ANE, people did not aspire to imitate the gods" (57). Regarding God's character, they say, "Since God's character is only revealed to us in scattered glimpses ... we cannot know the character of God fully. Given this lack of full disclosure, we are not sufficiently informed to define morality based on our understanding of his character" (211). However, in a somewhat conflicting statement, they do mention, "Because of Yahweh's role as their king, the Israelites ...would have aspired to emulate God's wisdom and justice." Despite this unique allowance, they also question human examples for imitation, "Identifying characters as true moral exemplars becomes much more difficult when we are uncertain whether the behavior is to be emulated" (170). See Walton and Walton, *Lost World of the Torah*, 57–58, 170, 211.

[18] Walton and Walton, *Lost World of the Torah*, 203.

[19] Based on an NT passage (1 Cor 11:1), they note that God's character "may be an important consideration for our conduct" (211). Also, they state, "God's people have been given an identity with God and it is our responsibility to honor God as we reflect him in our lives." By using "reflect," however, they do not appear to mean imitate. Rather, they mean enculturated human behaviors that will affect God's reputation among the people within that particular culture. As they note, "The Torah provides Israel wisdom for establishing order that upholds the reputation of Yahweh. ... This is far different from the idea that it provides principles or rules for morality" (213). This view is quite similar to Lindars' notion of delegation and emissaries. See Walton and Walton, *Lost World of the Torah*, 59–60, 205–6, 211, 213; Barnabas Lindars, "Imitation of God and Imitation of Christ: Duty and Discernment," *Theology* 76.638 (1973): 399.

[20] Walton and Walton, *Lost World of the Torah*, 54.

[21] Regarding divine moral reflection from Lev 19, Walton and Walton say, "[Holiness] is assumed to refer to the moral character of God, which people, through obedience to the law, are supposed to imitate. It would be easy for us, then, to assume that reflecting Yahweh's identity entails cultivating a particular moral character (by means of obeying the law), which

they were to build their view of law and wisdom on the nature of the biblical God, their theory would actually prove far more substantive in both its historical, textual context and its universal, conceptual grounding.

God's Imitative Holiness in Leviticus

Perhaps one of the best-known phrases in Leviticus is from 19:2. Israel was told, "Be (you will be) holy for I am holy, Yhwh your God" (קְדֹשִׁים תִּהְיוּ כִּי קָדוֹשׁ אֲנִי יְהוָה אֱלֹהֵיכֶם). Though traditionally taken in a hortatory or imperative sense,[22] Walton and Walton state, "It is common for people to believe that holiness is something that godly people should aspire to achieve as they attempt to imitate God. ... [But] God declares his people holy by election decree. It is a status that he gives."[23] They argue here on the basis of grammar that it is an indicative not an imperative. Therefore, it must only be taken in the sense of status and not as a command or expectation. However, while the grammar could imply mere status here, in the broader context of Leviticus and the Torah, such a theory falls apart.[24] Rather, the statement is likely meant to be

will thereby reflect Yahweh's moral character. However, this is not what the text is talking about" (Walton and Walton, *Lost World of the Torah*, 57).

[22] See Gordon J. Wenham, "The Gap between Law and Ethics in the Bible," *JJS* 48.1 (1997): 27; Robert R. Wilson, "Approaches to Old Testament Ethics," in *Canon, Theology, and Old Testament Interpretation: Essays in Honor of Brevard S Childs* (Philadelphia, 1988), 67; Esias E. Meyer, "The Dark Side of the Imitatio Dei. Why Imitating the God of the Holiness Code Is Not Always a Good Thing," *OTE* 22.2 (2009): 374; Howard Kreisel, "Imitatio Dei in Maimonides' Guide of the Perplexed," *AJS Review* 19.2 (1994): 206; John G. Gammie, *Holiness in Israel*, OBT (Minneapolis: Fortress, 1989), 34; Eryl W. Davies, "Walking in God's Ways: The Concept of Imitatio Dei in the Old Testament," in *In Search of True Wisdom* (Sheffield: Sheffield Academic, 1999), 101; Samson Raphael Hirsch, *The Pentateuch*, trans. Isaac Levy, 2nd ed. (London: Judaica, 1962), 3:499–500; Baruch A. Levine, *Leviticus: The Traditional Hebrew Text with the New JPS Translation*, The JPS Torah Commentary (Philadelphia: Jewish Publication Society, 1989), 125.

[23] Walton and Walton, *Lost World of the Torah*, 54–55; John H. Walton, *Ancient Near Eastern Thought and the Old Testament: Introducing the Conceptual World of the Hebrew Bible*, 1st ed. (Grand Rapids: Baker Academic, 2006), 110, 311. In his earlier work, he endorsed the notion of imitating God's holiness, though he seems to have evolved on the issue.

[24] A myriad of both *yiqtol* and *we-qatal* verbs are used throughout Leviticus with the prescriptive or proscriptive sense, often interchangeably. This would imply that their theory of "indicative" status rather than a future, expected state and maintenance is not sustainable throughout the book. As a dense example, Lev 21:6–8 gives a variety of proscriptions and prescriptions for priests in order to set them apart, saying, "*They will be* (יִהְיוּ) holy for their God and *they will not profane* (וְלֹא יְחַלְּלוּ) the name of their God for they offer the food of their God with the fire of Yhwh and *they will be* (וְהָיוּ) holy. *They will not marry* (יִקָּחוּ) a prostitute and one defiled ... for he [is] holy (קָדֹשׁ הוּא) to his God. And *you will make him holy* (וְקִדַּשְׁתּוֹ) for he offers the food of your God. *He will be* (יִהְיֶה) holy for you, because I Yhwh am holy (קָדוֹשׁ אֲנִי יְהוָה), who makes you holy (מְקַדִּשְׁכֶם)." In fact, so much effort is made throughout Leviticus to provide the means and process for making and maintaining holiness, both for priests and Israel, that it would be difficult to understand the narrow concept of conferred holy status anywhere outside of Lev 19:2. As in Lev 21, it seems to be both status and state, at the very least. They were to make themselves holy and God would likewise make them holy, or vice versa.

both a status and an expectation, both inextricably connected to a covenant relationship with the holy God. In the statement's local context, it is situated at the start of a secondary or expanded version of the Decalogue from Exod 20, implying their holiness was tied to these principal expectations.[25] It is also intimately related to the name formula (אני יהוה) found in many important locations in Leviticus and the Torah.[26] While the status of "holy" may be conferred, the state of holiness comes with commands and expectations found in the laws, those rooted in the very person and nature of God.[27]

This interesting phrase has a parallel in Lev 11:44–45 and 20:7. In these three verses, the phrase is slightly different, using a *we-qatal* (future/imperfective) verb form, "You (pl.) will be holy for I am holy" (וִהְיִיתֶם קְדֹשִׁים כִּי קָדוֹשׁ אָנִי) (Lev 11:44, 45, 20:7).[28] It is typical for this type of verb construction to have a future sense, to refer to an incomplete action, or to have a hortatory function.[29] As expressed in the phrase, there is an expectation – in the plural – to not only be holy but to actively *be* holy. As a holy people, they were set apart but must also actively make themselves set apart (וְהִתְקַדִּשְׁתֶּם).[30] Furthermore, in both versions of the phrase, a finite verb is connected to a causal, nominal clause ("for I am holy"). God's status, signaled by the divine name formula, stands in a similar syntactical relationship with the commandments, seen many times in Leviticus.[31] If Israel's status alone were intended, a declaration of their holiness would have sufficed. Yet, the inclusion of "for I am holy" necessarily implies correspondence with the preceding prescription. In fact, the *we-qatal* form of "to be" in the second masculine plural (וִהְיִיתֶם) is only found a few times in the Torah (Gen 3:5; Exod 19:5; Lev 11:44–45, 20:7, 26; Num 15:40, 32:22), all of which imply a future

---

[25] Esias E. Meyer, "When Synchrony Overtakes Diachrony: Perspectives on the Relationship between the Deuteronomic Code and the Holiness Code," *OTE* 30.3 (2017): 754–55; John E. Hartley, *Leviticus*, WBC 4 (Dallas: Word Books, 1992), 311; Gordon J. Wenham, *The Book of Leviticus*, NICOT (Eerdmans, 1979), 264.

[26] Hartley, *Leviticus*, 309–12.

[27] Meyer, "When Synchrony Overtakes Diachrony," 757; Jo Bailey Wells, *God's Holy People: A Theme in Biblical Theology*, JSOTSup 305 (Sheffield: T&T Clark, 2000), 93. Meyer notes that in Leviticus there is an impetus toward being holy while Deuteronomy begins with the idea of a "holy nation."

[28] The *we-qatal* can imply the future tense or an imperfect aspect. Waltke and O'Connor note, "Leviticus exhibits a high number [of *we-qatal*] because it contains many prescriptions." They refer to the form's time-oriented use by "waw-relative" and the aspect, logical, or conditional use by "waw-copulative." See Bruce K. Waltke and M. O'Connor, *An Introduction to Biblical Hebrew Syntax* (Winona Lake: Eisenbrauns, 1990), 519–25.

[29] Ronald J. Williams and John C. Beckman, *Williams' Hebrew Syntax*, 3rd ed. (Toronto: University of Toronto Press, 2007), 75–76; B. M. Rocine, *Learning Biblical Hebrew: A New Approach Using Discourse Analysis* (Macon, GA: Smyth & Helwys, 2000), 129–32.

[30] Both Lev 11:44 and 20:7 start with the *hitpael* form in the *we-qatal*, implying Israel was to bring about their holy state that reflected the state of their God, "for I am holy" (כִּי קָדוֹשׁ אָנִי). Interestingly, the follow-up verse after Lev 20:7 says that Israel was to maintain the covenant stipulations but it was Yhwh who makes them holy. "You shall guard my statutes and do them. I am Yhwh, the one who makes you holy" (Le 20:8). The implication is that God's holiness compels Israel to bring themselves into alignment with his ways.

[31] E.g., Lev 19:3, 4, 10, 12, 14, 16, 18, 25, 28, 30, 31, 32, 34, 36, 37.

conditioned event or a process.[32] So, it is unlikely that status alone was in view. Even the very idea of being in the same status as God necessarily evokes reflecting and imaging the nature and character of God, if he is indeed the paragon of holiness.

The idea of Israel reflecting God's holiness is found in a web of related passages. As mentioned, Lev 11:44–45 calls for Israel's holiness due to God's own holiness.[33] The context of these verses is the dietary regulations. Though God's holiness is given as the reason for these regulations here, God clarifies in Lev 20:22–27 that the various regulations are to serve as a division for Israel from the nations.[34] Israel was to be set apart and unique as God himself is.[35] Thus, the dietary restrictions served this purpose, as a practical, cultural instantiation, at least in part.[36] During the Sinai and wilderness period, the clean animals viable to eat were to be consumed in the context of ritual purity at the Tabernacle, a type of sacrificial process.[37] Though God did not literally eat the sacrifices, he did partake in a sense, calling it "a pleasing aroma to Yhwh" (Lev 17:6).[38] Thus, in a symbolic way, Israel was to partake of that

---

[32] Genesis 3:5 is the temptation of Adam and Eve to become like God in a counterfeit way by their own means. Exodus 19:5 and Num 32:22 relate to a conditional covenantal relationship, predicated on obedience. Leviticus 11:44, 45, 20:7, 26, and Num 15:40 all have to do with holiness, directly related to God's commands. The occurrence in Num 15:39–40 is a parallel and illuminating use, "And it will be for you a tassel and you will look at it and you will remember all the commands of Yhwh and you will do them and your heart and your eyes shall not follow after that which you prostitute after. So that you will remember and you will do all my commands and you will be holy to your God." This verse necessitates that the state of holiness is conditioned, dependent, and expected. Additionally, the *yiqtol* second masculine plural form (וִהְיִיֶתֶם) also only occurs a few times in the Torah (Gen 34:15, 44:10; Exod 19:6; Lev 19:2, 26:12). Interestingly, in all these cases it is unclear if status or process is in view. In fact, they may all imply both status and a dynamic state of being.

[33] As Gane states, "The reason for observing the Lord's dietary distinctions is to emulate the Lord's holiness, which is opposed to impurity" (Roy Gane, *Leviticus, Numbers*, NIVAC (Grand Rapids: Zondervan, 2004), 204).

[34] Leviticus 20:26 says, "So, you shall be holy to me for I am holy; I separated you from the nations to be mine" (וִהְיִיֶתֶם לִי קְדֹשִׁים כִּי קָדוֹשׁ אֲנִי יְהוָה וָאַבְדִּל אֶתְכֶם מִן־הָעַמִּים לִהְיוֹת לִי).

[35] Wells, *God's Holy People*, 70.

[36] Scurlock notes that while meat was less common for regular people, it was expected for kings and gods. The gods were typically served twice a day. Although many of the animals offered parallel those in the biblical account, Scurlock mentions a variety of animals and creatures that could be offered to the ANE gods that would have been unclean or an abomination in the biblical sacrificial order. See JoAnn Scurlock, "Animal Sacrifice in Ancient Mesopotamian Religion," in *A History of the Animal World in the Ancient Near East*, ed. Billie Jean Collins, HdO 64 (Leiden: Brill, 2002), 390–403.

[37] In the law code of Exodus and Leviticus, all slaughtered animals were to be killed at the altar with the blood poured out there, indicating a low-level sense of sacrifice (Lev 17:3–7). This regulation for the wilderness generation was later amended in Deut 12:15–16 for practicality in the land. Yet, of the clean, edible livestock, their firstborn were perpetually due to Yhwh, even in the Land (Deut 12:17–18). Levine notes, however, a rabbinic debate regarding this issue, primarily between Rabbis Akiba and Ishmael. The contention is whether Lev 17 intended for all animals slaughtered to be sacrificial or for all sacrifices to be at the central altar. While the interpretation of Lev 17 could go either way, the regulation in Deut 12 seems to provide a change of setting and allowances, implying that all meat consumption during the wilderness period needed to include the Tabernacle. See Levine, *Leviticus*, 113.

[38] The notion that Yhwh eats or has needs like the ANE gods is clearly refuted in Ps 50:12–14, "If I were hungry, I would not tell you because the world and everything in it is mine.

which their God partook.[39] In the Deuteronomic code, a similar explanation for Israel's holiness was provided, "For you are a holy people for Yhwh your God. Yhwh chose you to be a people for his possession from all the peoples who are on the face of the earth" (Deut 14:2; cf. 14:21).[40] While the regulations themselves were not irrelevant, they did serve a specific function and means of expressing Israel's imitation of God's otherness.[41] As he was distinct from creation and the nations' gods, so Israel was to be distinct from the nations and their cultures. Perhaps not surprisingly, the basis of God's command for Israel to be a "holy nation" (גוי קדוש) is found in the preface to the Decalogue (Exod 19:5–6).[42] It is clear that there is an intimate connection between covenant, holiness, separation, and reflection of God's nature.[43] The holiness codes dealt with many issues related to bodily wholeness, purity, and cultic practices.[44] Again, while not arbitrary, they primarily served as signals to God's own holiness and the need for Israel's imitation of that holiness as his special people amidst the ANE peoples, cultures, and religions (e.g., Lev 10:10–11, 15:31, 17:6–9, 21:23; Deut 18:13–14, 23:12–14, 26:18–19).

Another important aspect of Israel's holiness was their observance of the Sabbath.[45] The Torah is very clear that Israel was to set apart the seventh day because God himself did at the conclusion of the creation.[46] The phrasing in Exod 20:11 is reflected from Gen 2:2–3, "God finished on the seventh day his work which he made. And he rested on the seventh day ... And God blessed

---

Do I eat the flesh of bulls or drink the blood of goats? Sacrifice thanksgiving to God and pay your vows to the Most High."

[39] Firmage and Gane mention that the types of animals considered clean overlap with those for sacrifice, stating, "God's holy people emulate his sacrificial diet." See Edwin Firmage, "The Biblical Dietary Laws and the Concept of Holiness," in *Studies in the Pentateuch*, ed. J. A. Emerton (Leiden: Brill, 1990), 177–208; M. Douglas, "The Eucharist: Its Continuity with the Bread Sacrifice of Leviticus," *MT* 15 (1999): 211–12; Gane, *Leviticus, Numbers*, 207.

[40] For reference, כִּי עַם קָדוֹשׁ אַתָּה לַיהוָה אֱלֹהֶיךָ וּבְךָ בָּחַר יְהוָה לִהְיוֹת לוֹ לְעַם סְגֻלָּה מִכֹּל הָעַמִּים אֲשֶׁר עַל־פְּנֵי הָאֲדָמָה

[41] Interestingly, Jesus provided a new key marker to set apart his disciples (Jn 13:35). Likewise, it is probably best to understand God's vision to Peter in light of new demarcations for holiness in the new covenant (Acts 10). God's holiness is not nullified or abrogated in these NT references. Rather, the new covenant is redefining how God's people are set apart and reflect his holiness under the new program (2 Tim 2:14–26).

[42] Exodus 19:5–6 says, "And now, if you will indeed listen to my voice and guard my covenant then *you will be* (וִהְיִיתֶם) for me a possession from all the peoples, for all the earth is mine. And surely *you shall be* (תִּהְיוּ) for me a kingdom of priests and a holy nation." The status of "holy" is a conditioned state or reality according to covenantal adherence.

[43] Levenson notes, "The focus of the Mosaic covenant sealed at Sinai is twofold: history and morality. God there formalizes ... a pact through which Israel might come to reflect back to God some of the grace she has known" (Jon Levenson, *Sinai and Zion: An Entry into the Jewish Bible* (New York: Harper Collins, 1985), 101).

[44] Verne H. Fletcher, "Shape of Old Testament Ethics," *SJT* 24.1 (1971): 65; Hartley, *Leviticus*, 163, 323.

[45] Walton and Walton reject the imitative relationship between God's rest and his prescription for Sabbath, "People are commanded to participate in the rest of God on the Sabbath, not to imitate his rest but in recognition of his work of bringing and maintaining order" (Walton and Walton, *Lost World of the Torah*, 251).

[46] Wells, *God's Holy People*, 61; Wenham, *Story as Torah*, 104; Martens, "How Is the Christian to Construe Old Testament Law?" 205; Levine, *Leviticus*, 256; Gammie, *Holiness in Israel*, 9.

the seventh day and he made it holy for he rested from all his work" (cf. Lev 19:2–3).[47] There is a refrain of maintaining this holy day as a signifier of Israel's imitation of and relationship with the holy God.[48] This marker along with the many instructions of the Torah were to make Israel a holy nation and a kingdom of priests as a reflection of their God.[49]

Furthermore, it is apparent much continuity exists within the Torah regarding God's holiness, Israel's holiness, and the laws that foster the relationship. As Oswalt rightly states regarding the essence of the Torah,

> What emerges when these words are studied is that God is calling his covenant partners to manifest a certain kind of character in all areas of life because that is his holy character. So, the Israelites are expected to honor their parents because their Lord is holy; they are expected to be careful of their neighbor's reputation because their Lord is holy; they are expected to preserve the sanctity of sex in heterosexual marriage because God is holy. In short, having become covenant partners with the holy God, they not only belong exclusively to him but are also expected to live in ways appropriate to his character. The most succinct statement of this point is to be found in Leviticus 22:31–33: "Thus you shall keep my commandments and observe them: I am the Lord. You shall not profane my holy name, that I may be sanctified among the people of Israel: I am the Lord. I sanctify you, I who brought you out of the land of Egypt to be your God: I am the Lord." Thus, the Israelites learned that "holy" describes not merely the essence of deity but also the character of deity. And as there is only one holy being, so there is only one holy character. And although we humans cannot share that essence, we can share that character and indeed are expected to, although it is not as simple as the Israelites first thought it would be. In the process of trying to live out God's holy character, the Hebrews learned a great deal about their own character.[50]

Regarding the relationship of holiness between God and Israel, it is possible the Torah sought to reconceptualization the divine basis of law from that

---

[47] Exodus 20:8, 11 says, "Remember the day of sabbath, for it is holy ... For in six days Yhwh made the heavens and the earth, the sea and all that is in them. And he rested on the seventh day. Therefore, Yhwh blessed the sabbath day and he made it holy." Likewise, in close proximity to the Lev 19:2 statement, it says, "You (pl.) will fear each his mother and his father and you (pl.) will guard my sabbaths. I am Yhwh your God" (19:3).

[48] Exodus 31:13–15 says, "Surely you shall guard my sabbaths for it is a sign between you and me for your generations to know that I am Yhwh *who makes you holy*. And you will guard the sabbath *for it is holy to you* ... the seventh day is a special sabbath, *it is holy to Yhwh*" (cf. Lev 23:3). Deuteronomy 5:12–15, which adds a reason for observing Sabbath, begins with the same phrase, "Guard the day of sabbath, for it is holy, just as Yhwh your God commanded you."

[49] Cf. Dali Luo, "Proverbs 16:1–15: An Invitation to Adopt the Royal Way of Life" (Trinity International University, PhD diss., 2010), 223.

[50] John N. Oswalt, "Theology of the Pentateuch," in *Dictionary of the Old Testament: Pentateuch* (Downers Grove: IVP, 2003), 850.

which was found in the ANE. While many of the laws were parallel in some respects, the God who established this biblical law was not parallel to the gods of the nations. As the divine king, his own nature, character, desires, and actions were to be the foundation of Israel's wise legal guidance and covenant maintenance.[51]

Conclusion

The supremely wise God of *torah* was also supremely holy. As the paragon of kingship and justice, he provided rulings and instructions that were good and wise, not in an arbitrary way but due to his own good, wise nature.[52] While Walton and Walton provide many useful contributions to the study of biblical law and ANE thought, their unnecessary dismissal of *imitatio Dei* seems to be an unfortunate mistake. Although God is not fully imitable, he does expect and provide a path for people to reflect his ways according to their human capacities. So, it is not an absurd expectation for God's people to be holy in a similar way as their God. This relation is understood and communicated in the wisdom program of Prov 1–9, as well. Thus, as Israel is to emulate the holiness of their unique God, the student is to emulate the wisdom of the teacher, who is ultimately reflecting the wisdom of the holy God behind *torah*.

---

[51] Even Walton makes the statement, "Honor Yahweh as the embodiment of Justice." Though he rejects divine imitation, the idea that God is the essence, source, or prime example of justice would suggest that he is a model worthy of emulation (Walton, *Ancient Near Eastern Thought (2018)*, 291).

[52] Cf. Luo, "Proverbs 16:1–15," 36, 44–45, 194, 223.

CONCLUSION

T he aim of this study has been to demonstrate that Prov 1–9 utilizes the formative process of imitation in its pedagogy. This pedagogical endeavor intentionally leads the proverbial student along the wisdom trajectory from mundane human exemplars through the intermediate figure of Wisdom and ultimately to God, referred to as *imitatio Dei*. While God is the ultimate example, the wise teacher understands the developmental process that the son must travel through. Thus, he provides a number of positive and negative figures for the student to observe as he develops in wisdom. Simply put, then, this study analyzes the presence of imitative elements in Prov 1–9 in order to illuminate how those elements ultimately point the wisdom student to know and imitate God.

To establish this underlying and centralizing principle in Prov 1–9, the study began with a historical survey canvassing the context for *imitatio Dei*. Then, the complex and intentional structure of the wisdom program in Prov 1–9 was established. Importantly, a key imitative metaphor was shown at the heart of the father's instruction, the straight-way motif. Following these introductory considerations, the study then undertook a careful reading of the fifteen lessons within Prov 1–9. Particular attention was given to the presence and role of several key threads that serve the imitative pedagogy in this section of Proverbs. These threads include the metaphor of father and teacher, the divine relationship of Wisdom, the pathway imagery, the use of lesser-to-greater metaphorical figures, and the numerous indirect divine attributes that the father desires the son to emulate. Together these threads illuminate the sophisticated literary tapestry of these chapters. Without being unduly overt, the proverbial father seeks to move the son from a place of naivety to a place of wisdom, with the hope that he too will teach others the proper way of God, just as the proverbial father has trained him.

With this brief overview in place, we can highlight a few of the specific results of this study. The historical survey of *imitatio Dei* serves two purposes. Though couched within a trove of positive evaluations, a number of scholars over the past few decades have come out against or at least have critically questioned the validity of man's ability to imitate the divine, especially in any prescriptive manner. Many have questioned how mere creatures could ever hope to know, let alone do, as the infinite creator does in his fullness of character or ways. Furthermore, it is argued that the biblical account purportedly describes many actions, reactions, and commands of God that are either not suitable or dangerous for humans to replicate (e.g., creation, anger, jealousy). For some scholars, the hope and goal for humanity's reflection of God is simply to represent him among fellow humans, not in any imitative sense but simply in an oblique sense as emissaries.

This modern skepticism was, in fact, part of the impetus to explore the topic of *imitatio Dei* and the knowledge of God in this study. Is the concept of *imitatio Dei* anachronistic or foreign to the biblical writers? While some concerns expressed by these scholars are not unfounded, the preponderance of historical evidence demonstrates, at the very least, that humanity has consistently looked to the divine as a type of model. The divine fatherhood is one metaphor, for example, common throughout the traditions. Likewise, in the ANE and Greco-Roman traditions, the gods are often seen conducting themselves in similar ways as humans, particularly within the realm of royal affairs. Although the ANE and Greco-Roman traditions may not have seen their gods as perfect exemplars, they did see them as figures with qualities or relationships that could be emulated. Both the church and rabbinic traditions, however, based their notion of *imitatio Dei* on the nature of God espoused in the OT. For both of these traditions, the scriptures were believed to teach the fatherhood of God, which necessarily suggests the idea of imitation and reflection. The question was typically not whether humanity ought to imitate God but how and what effects that will have on a person and the community. As Proverbs and the broader OT affirm, the biblical God is unique from the non-biblical gods in the consistency and supremacy of his character. He is viewed as the paragon of all ideal human traits such as holiness, righteousness, justice, compassion, truth, and wisdom. This notion has persisted throughout the millennia apart from a few notable scholars. Thus, the historical survey serves this study by demonstrating the ubiquity of both imitation and *imitatio Dei* in the history of religious thought. The wisdom program of Prov 1–9, then, is not novel in its use of this concept but rather in its insightful administration for the pedagogical process of growth in biblical wisdom. In other words, one does not become wise merely by gaining mundane success. Rather, wisdom is measured by one's reflection of and knowledge of God, which are inextricably intertwined.

From the perspective of some scholars, a lack of explicit articulation of the principle of *imitatio Dei* may serve as grounds for dismissal. However, the wisdom program in Prov 1–9 is intentionally subtle. This quality suggests that it is insufficient for a wisdom student merely to have knowledge or information. Such bare data in a fool's hands or mouth is in fact dangerous (Prov 26:4–12). The pedagogical process in Prov 1–9 desires for the son to grow in his ability to discern. At the start of Proverbs, this desire is clearly stated (Prov 1:1–7). It is only the student who possesses a heart with the right starting point and end goal that will rightly understand the subsequent proverbial material (Lessons 1, 2). In fact, the proverbial program is crafted in such a way that those with foolish intent will be exposed. Undoubtedly, there are two explicit paths for the son to consider. These are the path of Wisdom and the path of Folly. With strong warning, the path of Folly is described in its destructive and deadly ways, closely figured with the adulterous and lascivious ways of the *zarah* (Lessons 1, 2, 5, 7, 9–15). To an extent, even the naïve can observe the explicit dangers of this path. Yet, the proverbial program alludes to a second dangerous path. This counterfeit path is conceivably even more dangerous than the explicit path of Folly due to its subtlety and seductiveness. That is to say, it is possible for one to exhibit some of the characteristics found along the path of Wisdom (Prov 14:6) yet done without the proper orientation. This variant form of wisdom is a counterfeit path, no different in its essence or end than the path of Folly. The fear of Yhwh, then, is a key illuminating factor for the true path of Wisdom (Prov 1:7, 2:5, 9:10). In other words, the path of Wisdom is inextricably related to God and to his ways. This truth is why the proverbial father desires the son to be wise in a truly wise way, not merely in regard to human success. The father knows from observing the ways of those truly wise from biblical history that there is a way that seems right to a man but in the end results in destruction (Prov 14:12). At the heart of his wisdom program, the son is to learn how to discern the ways of God and to avoid the myriad traps that lie along his journey. He is to recover the proper way of imitating God, which the first human couple failed by attempting to subvert God's authority through improper imitation (Lesson 4, 14). According to the proverbial father, it is only the wise student who has a heart properly aligned with Yhwh who will rightly reflect his ways without seeking to be like God in counterfeit ways (Lesson 15).

Furthermore, throughout Lessons 1–15, the proverbial father uses a number of metaphors and indirect divine attributions to instill his instruction. These masterfully woven threads lead the discerning son along the divine path. Perhaps the closest example of explicit instruction in *imitatio Dei* is the metaphor of divine fatherhood in Lesson 4, a metaphor used in a similar way by the NT. In Lesson 4, the proverbial father explicitly reveals God as the primary fatherly example. It shows the wise son that God is the ultimate source of fatherly instruction and discipline throughout the wisdom program. The proverbial father intends that the son grow in his own likeness to become a true son according to his ways (cf. Lesson 8). Yet, the wise path is blessed not simply because of potential earthly gain but due to Yhwh's presence and guidance along that path. In other words, the way of the wise is not characterized by life because it holds secret knowledge for success or incantations to shape the world according to one's desires. It is characterized by life because the path is marked by God's instructions and is, in fact, a manifestation of his own ways (Lessons 3, 4, 14, 15). By knowing God in his ways, the son will experience divine protection and presence in the divine path. The fatherly instruction, then, points the son to emulate his wise, heavenly Father by emulating his wise, earthly father.

Similarly, the figure of Wisdom plays a vital and complex role in the pedagogical program. While this figure has elicited a long history of speculation, she cannot be placed into a simple, neat box. This elusive quality allows her to serve several rhetorical purposes. First, at her core, she is a poetic representative of biblical "wisdom" (Lesson 4). All the wise, including

God, properly use her, which implies the son ought to do likewise. Second, she is described as something more than a mere personification of an inanimate or abstract concept. She is at times a quality or representative embodiment of Yhwh himself. Yhwh is both the source and goal of biblical, proverbial wisdom (Lesson 2). When she speaks, often her words and authority are parallel with Yhwh's (Lessons 1, 14, 15). She is, therefore, to be obeyed and emulated because she does as God himself does. Third, she represents all the wise, those who walk in the righteous path. In this use, she is to be emulated as a fellow traveler along the wisdom trajectory (Lessons 1, 4, 12, 14). Along this wisdom trajectory or within the wisdom hierarchy, then, she serves as a bridge between the divine and mundane. The novitiate is not aware of or able to conceive of God and his ways. To address this gap, the father presents himself first, as a human model in contrast to fools (Lesson 1, 3, 6, 7). Wisdom is then given as a second, more exalted model to observe. As the proverbial father intimates, though, her status and value are primarily due to her proximity to and use by God, the paragon of a wise and just king (Lessons 4, 14). Thus, she is presented as a worthy model to emulate in the process of finding and following the divine path.

Of course, the most ubiquitous, explicit, and central metaphor in Prov 1–9 is that of the pathway. The two paths before the son are represented by the enigmatic figures of Wisdom and Folly (Lessons 1, 14, 15). The father is astute enough to understand that the son needs perceptible models on those paths to observe. To this end, there are a number of representative, though generic, figures who serve this pedagogical purpose. On the path with Folly, there are the wicked, unjust, unrighteous, rebellious, ignorant, impetuous, materialistic, arrogant, lying fools (Lessons 1, 2, 5, 7, 9–15). On the path with Wisdom, there are the good, righteous, just, obedient, knowledgeable, considerate, holy, humble, truthful wise persons (Lessons 2, 3, 4, 6, 7, 8, 14, 15). The figures on either path, however, are not meant to be specific persons nor do they express all characteristics equally. Rather, the characteristics of the representative figures are inherent to the paths and to those who walk them (e.g., Prov 2:12–16, 20–22). As ideal models, the father appeals to the positive figures because they embody an ideal characteristic or behavior and therefore reflect the ways of God. In contrast, the proverbial father uses the negative figures as foils and as a warning. To strengthen his case, the proverbial father likely alludes to biblical examples in nearly every lesson, whether positive or negative (e.g., Abraham, Joseph, Judah, Moses, David, and Solomon). The imitative sentiment of this pathway metaphor is nicely captured in a later proverb, "The one who walks with the wise will be wise; but the friend of fools will find trouble" (Prov 13:20). Here, the underlying idea is, of course, that humans are instinctively and irresistibly wired to reflect those around them. As Paul reminds his audience, "Bad company spoils good character" (1 Cor 15:33). Although the son ought to avoid bad companions and examples, the father ultimately desires the son to look back and up – back to the good examples who have come before and up to God who is the ultimate exemplar of wisdom. By choosing appropriate individuals to imitate, the son will be shaped into their ideal likeness becoming increasingly wiser as he emulates and grows in the knowledge of Yhwh (Prov 2:5). This endeavor is the hopeful wisdom trajectory and central objective that the father teaches the son in Prov 1–9.

As an extension of this proverbial hope, this study illuminated the father's use of lesser-to-greater metaphors in order to manifest imitative elements at an elemental level, typically involving creatures and fools (Lessons 1, 11, 13). This type of metaphor highlights qualities even the most naïve can understand and discern. As a powerful rhetorical tool, the father is able to communicate a variety of clever though subtle lessons. The son is to observe the creature primarily in order to look to the greater example or ideal underlying the principle, whether positive or negative. Implicit in such metaphors is the wisdom hierarchy, which views fools at the bottom and God at the top. As Lesson 11 explicitly teaches, these creaturely metaphors display vital qualities, such as being industrious, discerning, and able to avoid snares. The goal for the son, though, is to observe and be like the wise and righteous on the proper upward path, those who embody the ideal underlying qualities (cf. Prov 15:24). This divine path necessarily includes following Wisdom and Yhwh since deviation will result in ostracization (Prov 3:32, 6:16). By looking to the greater and wiser models, the son will embody and emulate their ideal, divine qualities.

At the heart of the wise path is, of course, God himself. As Prov 1–9 teaches, God is both the exemplar of ideal human traits and the ultimate source of instruction in those ways (Lesson 2). The concept of *imitatio Dei* is not as explicit in Proverbs as it becomes later in the NT (e.g., Eph 5:1), along with the church and rabbinic traditions. Nevertheless, the underlying principle is expressed in more indirect and intertextual ways. God is understood as the ultimate source of wisdom, justice, righteousness, and knowledge, a thread that weaves through every lesson. For the son to grow in such qualities, therefore, he must possess and express these divine attributes as they are possessed and expressed by God. It is not sufficient for the son simply to think the right things or merely to do the right things. Such anemic versions of wisdom are not adequately expressive of the complex nature of God and his ways. Rather, the son is to walk in the actions, character, and desires of God in the way that God himself does. This notion is aptly captured by the pathway metaphor, especially with the straight-way motif (Lesson 8). The prevalence, yet subtlety, of divine connections to this wise path encourages the son to grow in discernment and to become truly wise. According to the wisdom program, all good and wise traits are derivative of and reflective of God's own ways, a view more explicitly expressed elsewhere in the HB. To grow in wisdom, then, is to grow in the knowledge of God. To know God is to be wise. These concepts are also central in the Torah, Psalms, and Prophets (see Excurses). The proverbial father is merely crafting them into a more palatable and pedagogical format.

To conclude, then, this study has sought to demonstrate that Prov 1–9, the preeminent biblical wisdom program, is intentionally God-oriented. The fool may enjoy a measure of mundane success but he remains a fool since he neither imitates nor knows God. The wise, by contrast, are those who seek to know God by walking in his ways, that is, by imitating him in his divine character, behavior, and desires. In advocating this perspective, Prov 1–9 resonates with the whole biblical picture. The pedagogical goal of Prov 1–9 is not simply the acquisition of practical knowledge and skill but, rather, an intimate participation in the deeply theological, Torah way of life. In other words, the proverbial son is encouraged to follow along the well-worn path of *imitatio Dei*. According to Proverbs, this is the way of wisdom.

BIBLIOGRAPHY

Abrahams, Israel. *Studies in Pharisaism and the Gospels*. 1917. Repr., New York: Ktav, 1967.

Aitken, Kenneth T. *Proverbs*. Philadelphia: Westminster, 1986.

Albright, William F. "Some Remarks on the Song of Moses in Deuteronomy 32." *VT* 9.4 (1959): 339–46.

Aletti, J. N. "Proverbes 8,22–31: Étude de Structure." *Bib* 57.1 (1976): 25–37.

———. "Seduction et Parole en Proverbes I–IX." *VT* 27.2 (1977): 129–44.

Ambrose of Milan. "Select Works and Letters." In vol. 10 of *The Nicene and Post–Nicene Fathers*, Series 2. Translated by H. de Romestin, E. de Romestin, and H. T. F. Duckworth. New York: Christian Literature Co., 1896.

Andersen, Francis I., and David Noel Freedman, eds. *Hosea: A New Translation with Introduction and Commentary*. AB 24. Garden City: Doubleday, 1980.

Ansberry, Christopher B. "Be Wise, My Son, and Make My Heart Glad: An Exploration of the Courtly Nature of the Book of Proverbs." PhD diss., Wheaton College, 2009.

———. "What Does Jerusalem Have to Do with Athens? The Moral Vision of the Book of Proverbs and Aristotle's Nicomachean Ethics." *HS* 51 (2010): 157–73.

Aquinas, Thomas. *Summa Theologica*. Translated by the Fathers of the English Dominican Province. London: Burns Oates & Washbourne, 1921.

Aristides. "The Apology of Aristides the Philosopher." In vol. 9 of *The Ante–Nicene Fathers*. Translated by D. M. Kay. New York: Christian Literature Co., 1897.

Aristotle. "Poetics." In vol. 23 of *Aristotle in 23 Volumes*. Translated by W. H. Frye. Cambridge: Harvard University Press, 1932.

Athanasius of Alexandria. "Select Works and Letters." In vol. 4 of *The Nicene and Post–Nicene Fathers*, Series 2. Translated by Archibald T. Robertson. New York: Christian Literature Co., 1892.

Athas, George. "'A Man after God's Own Heart': David and the Rhetoric of Election to Kingship." *JESOT* 2.2 (2013): 191–97.

Attridge, Harold W. "Pollution, Sin, Atonement, Salvation." Pages 71–83 in *Ancient Religions*. Edited by Sarah Iles Johnston. Cambridge: Harvard University Press, 2007.

Auerbach, Erich. *Mimesis: The Representation of Reality in Western Literature*. Translated by Willard R. Trask. 50th ed. Princeton: Princeton University Press, 2013.

Augustine of Hippo. "Anti–Pelagian Writings." In vol. 5 of *The Nicene and Post–Nicene Fathers*, Series 1. Translated by Peter Holmes. New York: Christian Literature Co., 1887.

———. "On the Holy Trinity, Doctrinal Treatises, Moral Treatises." In vol. 3 of *The Nicene and Post–Nicene Fathers*, Series 1. Translated by Arthur West Haddan. New York: Christian Literature Co., 1887.

———. "Sermon on the Mount, Harmony of the Gospels, Homilies on the Gospels." In vol. 6 of *The Nicene and Post–Nicene Fathers*, Series 1. Translated by William Findlay and David S. Schaff. New York: Christian Literature Co., 1888.

———. "The City of God and Christian Doctrine." In vol. 2 of *The Nicene and Post–Nicene Fathers*, Series 1. Translated by Marcus Dods. New York: Christian Literature Co., 1887.

———. "The Confessions." In vol. 1 of *The Nicene and Post–Nicene Fathers*, Series 1. Translated by J. G. Pilkington. Buffalo, NY: Christian Literature Co., 1886.

Ausloos, Hans. "The Risks of Rash Textual Criticism Illustrated on the Basis of the Numeruswechsel in Exod 23,20–33." *BN* 96 (1999): 5–11.

Avagianou, Aphrodite A. "*Hieros Gamos* in Ancient Greek Religion: The Human Aspect of a Sacralized Ritual." Pages 145–172 in *Sacred Marriages: The Divine–Human Sexual Metaphor from Sumer to Early Christianity*. Edited by Martti Nissinen and Risto Uro. Winona Lake: Eisenbrauns, 2008.

Avriel, Mikhal, and Nissim Amzallag. "The Cryptic Meaning of the Isaiah 14 Māšāl." *JBL* 131 (2012): 643–62.

Bar-Asher, Shalom. "Anthropomorphism." Pages 51–52 in *The Oxford Dictionary of the Jewish Religion*. Edited by R. J. Zwi Werblowsky and Geoffrey Wigoder. Oxford: Oxford University Press, 1997.

Barrett, Michael P. "Wisdom: Person or Personification? Thoughts on Proverbs 8." *Puritan Reformed Journal* 8.1 (2016): 5–12.

Bartholomew, Craig G., and Michael W. Goheen. *Christian Philosophy: A Systematic and Narrative Introduction*. Grand Rapids: Baker Academic, 2013.

Bartholomew, Craig G., and Ryan O'Dowd. *Old Testament Wisdom Literature: A Theological Introduction*. Downers Grove: IVP Academic, 2011.

Barton, John. "Approaches to Ethics in the Old Testament." Pages 113–130 in *Beginning Old Testament Study*. Edited by John Rogerson. Philadelphia: Westminster, 1982.

———. "Imitation of God in the Old Testament." Pages 35–46 in *The God of Israel*. Edited by R. P. Gordon. Cambridge: Cambridge University Press, 2007.

———. "The Basis of Ethics in the Hebrew Bible." *Semeia* 66 (1994): 11–22.

———. "Understanding Old Testament Ethics." *JSOT* 3.9 (1978): 44–64.

———. *Understanding Old Testament Ethics: Approaches and Explorations*. Louisville: Westminster John Knox, 2003.

Basil of Caesarea. "Letters and Select Works." In vol. 8 of *The Nicene and Post-Nicene Fathers*, Series 2. Translated by Blomfield Jackson. New York: Christian Literature Co., 1895.

Bauks, Michaela, and Gerlinde Baumann. "Im Anfang war ... ?: Gen 1,1ff und Prov 8,22–31 im Vergleich." *BN* 71 (1994): 24–52.

Baumann, Eberhard. "'Wissen um Gott' Bei Hosea als Urform von Theologie?" *EvT* 15.8–9 (1955): 416–25.

Baumann, Gerlinde. *Die Weisheitsgestalt in Proverbien 1–9*. FAT 16. Tübingen: Mohr Siebeck, 1996.

Baumann, Gerlinde, and Christl M. Maier. "Personified Wisdom: Contexts, Meanings, Theology." Pages 57–76 in *The Writings and Later Wisdom Books*. Edited by Nuria Calduch-Benages and Christl M. Maier. Atlanta: Society of Biblical Literature, 2014.

Beale, G. K. *We Become What We Worship: A Biblical Theology of Idolatry*. Downers Grove: IVP Academic, 2008.

Begg, Christopher T. "The Significance of the Numeruswechsel in Deuteronomy the 'pre-History' of the Question." *ETL* 55.1 (1979): 116–24.

Ben Zvi, Ehud. *Hosea*. FOTL 21A. Grand Rapids: Eerdmans, 2005.

———. "Reading Hosea and Imagining YHWH." *HBT* 30.1 (2008): 43–57.

Berlejung, Angelika. "Zeichen der Verbundenheit und Medien der Erinnerung: zur Religionsgeschichte und Theologie von Dtn 6,6–9 und Verwandten Texten." Pages 131–166 in *Ex Oriente Lux: Studien zur Theologie des Alten Testaments*. ABIG 39. Leipzig: Evangelische Verlagsanstalt, 2012.

Best, Ernest. *A Commentary on the First and Second Epistles to the Thessalonians*. BNTC. London: Continuum, 1986.

———. *A Critical and Exegetical Commentary on Ephesians*. ICC 36A. Edinburgh: T&T Clark, 1998.

Beuken, Willem A. M. "What Does the Vision Hold: Teachers or One Teacher? Punning Repetition in Isaiah 30:20." *HeyJ* 36.4 (1995): 451–66.

Birch, Bruce C. "Divine Character and the Formation of Moral Community in the Book of Exodus." 구약논단 (*Old Testament Discussion*) 8 (2000): 281–301.

———. "Moral Agency, Community, and the Character of God in the Hebrew Bible." *Semeia* 66 (1994): 23–41.

Bland, Dave L. *Proverbs and the Formation of Character*. Eugene: Cascade Books, 2015.

Blenkinsopp, Joseph. *Essays on the Book of Isaiah*. FAT 128. Tubingen: Mohr Siebeck, 2019.

Block, Daniel I. *Deuteronomy*. NIVAC. Grand Rapids: Zondervan, 2012.

Bock, Darrell L. *Luke*. IVP New Testament Commentary. Downers Grove: IVP, 1994.

Borchert, Gerald L. *John 1–11*. NAC 25A. Nashville: B&H, 1996.

Boston, James R. "Wisdom Influence upon the Song of Moses." *JBL* 87.2 (1968): 198–202.

Boström, G. *Proverbiastudien*. Lunds Universitets Årsskrift N.f., Avd. 1, Bd. 30, Nr. 3. Lund: C. W. K. Gleerup, 1935.

Bousset, Wilhelm. *Jesu Predigt in Ihrem Gegensatz zum Judentum: ein Religiongeschichtlicher Vergleich*. Göttingen: Vandenhoeck & Ruprecht, 1892.

Bowker, John. "Anthropomorphism." Page 74 in *The Oxford Dictionary of World Religions*. Oxford: Oxford University Press, 1997.

Brisch, Nicole. "The Priestess and the King: The Divine Kingship of Šū-Sîn of Ur." *JAOS* 126.2 (2006): 161–76.

Brown, M. L. "רָפָא." Pages 593–602 in vol. 13 of *TDOT*. Grand Rapids: Eerdmans, 1977.

Brown, William P. "'Come, O Children . . . I Will Teach You the Fear of the Lord' (Psalm 34:12): Comparing Psalms and Proverbs." Pages 85–102 in *Seeking out the Wisdom of the Ancients: Essays Offered to Honor Michael V. Fox on the Occasion of His Sixty–Fifth Birthday*. Winona Lake: Eisenbrauns, 2005.

———. "The Law and the Sages: A Reexamination of Tôrâ in Proverbs." Pages 251–80 in *Constituting the Community: Studies on the Polity of Ancient Israel in Honor of S. Dean McBride Jr.* Edited by John T. Strong and Steven S. Tuell. Winona Lake: Eisenbrauns, 2005.

———. "Virtue and Its Limits in the Wisdom Corpus: Character Formation, Disruption, and Transformation." Pages 45–64 in *The Oxford Handbook of Wisdom and the Bible*. Edited by Will Kynes. Oxford: Oxford University Press, 2021.

———. *Wisdom's Wonder: Character, Creation, and Crisis in the Bible's Wisdom Literature*. Grand Rapids: Eerdmans, 2014.

Brueggemann, Walter. *1 & 2 Kings*. SHBC. Macon: Smyth & Helwys, 2000.

———. "The Epistemological Crisis of Israel's Two Histories (Jer 9:22–23)." Pages 85–105 in *Israelite Wisdom: Theological and Literary Essays in Honor of Samuel Terrien*. Missoula: Scholars, 1978.

———. *To Pluck up, to Tear down: A Commentary on the Book of Jeremiah 1–25*. ITC. Grand Rapids: Eerdmans, 1988.

Buber, Martin. *Israel and the World: Essays in a Time of Crisis*. New York: Schocken, 1948.

———. *Kampf um Israel: Reden und Schriften*. Berlin: Schocken, 1933.

———. "Nachahmung Gottes." *Der Morgen Jahrgang* I.6 (1926): 638–47.

Bultmann, Rudolf. *Primitive Christianity in Its Contemporary Setting*. Translated by R. H. Fuller. New York: Meridian, 1956.

Captain, Philip A. "Effect of Positive Reinforcement on Comprehension, Attitudes, and Rate of Bible Reading in Adolescents." *JPT* 3.1 (1975): 49–55.

Carew, M. Douglas. "To Know and Not to Know: Hosea's Know/Ledge in Discourse Perspective." PhD diss., Trinity International University, 2000.

———. "To Know or Not to Know: Hosea's Use of Yd'/D't." Pages 73–85 in *The Old Testament in the Life of God's People*. Winona Lake: Eisenbrauns, 2009.

Carroll, John T. *Luke: A Commentary*. NTL. Louisville: Westminster John Knox, 2012.

Carroll, Robert P. *Jeremiah: A Commentary*. OTL. Philadelphia: Westminster, 1986.

Carroll R., M. D. "Orphan." Pages 619–21 in *Dictionary of the Old Testament: Pentateuch*. Edited by T. Desmond Alexander and David W. Baker. Downers Grove: IVP, 2003.

Cassian, John. "The Works of John Cassian." In vol. 11 of *The Nicene and Post–Nicene Fathers*, Series 2. Translated by Edgar C. S. Gibson. New York: Christian Literature Co., 1884.

Cathcart, Kevin J., and R. P. Gordon, eds. *The Targum of the Minor Prophets*. The Aramaic Bible 14. Wilmington, DE: M. Glazier, 1989.

Charlesworth, James H. *The Old Testament Pseudepigrapha and the New Testament*. New Haven: Yale University Press, 1985.

Childs, Brevard S. *Exodus: A Commentary*. OTL. Philadelphia: Westminster, 1974.

———. *Isaiah: A Commentary*. OTL. Louisville: Westminster John Knox, 2001.

———. *Old Testament Theology in a Canonical Context*. Philadelphia: Fortress, 1994.

Christensen, Duane L. *Deuteronomy 21:10 – 34:12*. WBC 6B. Nashville: Nelson, 2002.

Chrysostom, John. "Homilies on Galatians, Ephesians, Philippians, Colossians, Thessalonians, Timothy, Titus, and Philemon." In vol. 13 of *The Nicene and Post–Nicene Fathers*, Series 1. Translated by Philip Schaff. New York: Christian Literature Co., 1889.

———. "Homilies on the Gospel of St. John and Epistle to the Hebrews." In vol. 14 of *The Nicene and Post–Nicene Fathers*, Series 1. Translated by G. T. Stupart. New York: Christian Literature Co., 1889.

Clarke, Andrew D. "'Be Imitators of Me': Paul's Model of Leadership." *TB* 49.2 (1998): 329–60.

Clements, R. E. "The Concept of Abomination in the Book of Proverbs." Pages 211–25 in *Texts, Temples, and Traditions: A Tribute to Menahem Haran*. Edited by Michael V. Fox, Victor Hurowitz, Avi Hurvitz, M. L. Klein, Baruch J. Schwartz, and Nili Shupak. Winona Lake: Eisenbrauns, 1996.

Clifford, Richard J. *Proverbs: A Commentary*. OTL. Louisville: Westminster John Knox, 1999.

———. *The Wisdom Literature*. Interpreting Biblical Texts. Nashville: Abingdon, 1998.

Clines, David J. A. "Yahweh and the God of Christian Theology." *Theology* 83.695 (1980): 323–30.

Cogan, Mordechai, and Hayim Tadmor. *I Kings: A New Translation with Introduction and Commentary*. AB 10. New York: Doubleday, 2000.

———. *II Kings: A New Translation*. AB 11. Garden City: Doubleday, 1988.

Cohen, Abraham. *Everyman's Talmud*. 1932. Repr., Hawthorne: BN, 2007.

Cole, R. Dennis. *Numbers*. NAC. Nashville: B&H, 2000.

Cook, Johann. "A Theology of the Greek Version of Proverbs." *HvTSt* 71.1 (2015): 1–11.

———. "אִשָּׁה זָרָה (Proverbs 1–9 Septuagint): A Metaphor for Foreign Wisdom?" *ZAW* 106 (1994): 458–76.

———. *The Septuagint of Proverbs: Jewish and/or Hellenistic Proverbs?* VTSup 69. New York: Brill, 1997.

Couroyer, Bernard. "La Tablette du Coeur." *RB* 90.3 (1983): 416–34.

Cox, Dermot. *Proverbs with an Introduction to Sapiential Books*. OTM 17. Wilmington: Michael Glazier, 1982.

Craigie, Peter C. *Psalms 1–50*. 2nd ed. WBC. Grand Rapids: Zondervan, 2004.

———. *The Book of Deuteronomy*. NICOT. Eerdmans, 1976.

Crenshaw, James L. *Old Testament Wisdom: An Introduction*. Rev. and enl. Louisville: Westminster John Knox, 1998.

Crotty, Robert B. "Hosea and the Knowledge of God." *ABR* 19 (1971): 1–16.

Csibra, Gergely, and György Gergely. "Sylvia's Recipe: The Role of Imitation and Pedagogy in the Transmission of Cultural Knowledge." Pages 229–55 in *Roots of Human Sociality: Culture, Cognition, and Human Interaction*. Oxford: Berg, 2006.

Cupitt, Don. "God and Morality: Duty and Discernment, 6." *Theology* 76.637 (1973): 356–64.

Cyril of Jerusalem. "St. Cyril of Jerusalem, St. Gregory Nazianzen." In vol. 7 of *The Nicene and Post–Nicene Fathers*, Series 2. Translated by R. W. Church and Edwin H. Gifford. New York: Christian Literature Co., 1894.

Dahood, Mitchell. "Proverbs 8:22–31: Translation and Commentary." *CBQ* 30.4 (1968): 512–21.

Daly, Mary. *Beyond God the Father: Toward a Philosophy of Women's Liberation*. Boston: Beacon, 1973.

Daube, D. "A Quartet of Beasties in the Book of Proverbs." *JTS* 36.2 (1985): 380–86.

Davies, Eryl W. "Walking in God's Ways: The Concept of *Imitatio Dei* in the Old Testament." Pages 99–114 in *In Search of True Wisdom*. Sheffield: Sheffield Academic, 1999.

Davis, Carl Judson. *The Name and Way of the Lord: Old Testament Themes, New Testament Christology*. LNTS 129. London: Bloomsbury, 1996.

Davis, Michael. *The Poetry of Philosophy: On Aristotle's Poetics*. South Bend: St. Augustine's, 1999.

Day, John. "Foreign Semitic Influence on the Wisdom of Israel and Its Appropriation in the Book of Proverbs." Pages 55–70 in *Wisdom in Ancient Israel: Essays in Honour of J. A. Emerton*. Edited by Robert P. Gordon, H.

G. M. Williamson, and John Day. New York: Cambridge University Press, 1995.

———. "Wisdom and the Garden of Eden." Pages 336–52 in *Perspectives on Israelite Wisdom: Proceedings of the Oxford Old Testament Seminar*. Edited by John Jarick. LHBOTS 618. London: T&T Clark, 2016.

Dearman, J. Andrew. *The Book of Hosea*. NICOT. Grand Rapids: Eerdmans, 2010.

DeClaissé-Walford, Nancy L., Rolf A. Jacobson, and Beth LaNeel Tanner. *The Book of Psalms*. NICOT. Grand Rapids: Eerdmans, 2014.

Dekker, Jeroen. "Cultural Transmission and Inter-Generational Interaction." *International Review of Education* 47.1/2 (2001): 77–95.

Delitzsch, Franz. *The Book of Proverbs*. Translated by M. G. Easton. Grand Rapids: Eerdmans, 1950.

DeRouchie, Jason S. "The Heart of YHWH and His Chosen One in 1 Samuel 13:14." *BBR* 24.4 (2014): 467–89.

Derousseaux, Louis. *La Crainte de Dieu dans l'Ancien Testament: Royauté, Alliance, Sagesse dans les Royaumes d'Israël et de Juda*. Paris: Éditions du Cerf, 1970.

Devauchelle, Didier. "Le Chemin de Vie dans l'Égypte Ancienne." Pages 91–122 in *Sagesses de l'Orient Ancien et Chrétien: La Voie de Vie et la Conduite Spirituelle Chez les Peuples et dans les Littératures de l'Orient Chrétien; Conférences IROC 1991–1992*. Edited by Rene Lebrun. Sciences Théologiques & Religieuses 2. Paris: Beauchesne, 1993.

Dick, Michael B. *Born in Heaven, Made on Earth: The Making of the Cult Image in the Ancient Near East*. Winona Lake: Eisenbrauns, 1999.

DiFransico, Lesley. "Identifying Inner–Biblical Allusion through Metaphor: Washing Away Sin in Psalm 51." *VT* 65.4 (2015): 542–57.

Dorsey, David A. *The Literary Structure of the Old Testament: A Commentary on Genesis–Malachi*. Grand Rapids: Baker Academic, 2004.

Douglas, M. "The Eucharist: Its Continuity with the Bread Sacrifice of Leviticus." *MT* 15 (1999): 209–24.

Durant, Karen Elizabeth. "Imitation of God as a Principle for Ethics Today: A Study of Selected Psalms." PhD diss., University of Birmingham (UK), 2010.

Durham, John I. *Exodus*. WBC. Waco: Word Books, 1987.

Dürr, Lorenz. *Das Erziehungswesen im Alten Testament und im antiken Orient*. MVAG. Leipzig: J. C. Hinrichs, 1932.

Duvall, J. Scott, and J. Daniel Hays. *God's Relational Presence: The Cohesive Center of Biblical Theology*. Grand Rapids: Baker Academic, 2019.

Ehrlich, Arnold B. *Randglossen zur Hebräischen Bibel: textkritisches, sprachliches und sachliches*. Leipzig: J. C. Hinrichs, 1908.

Eichrodt, Walther. *Theologie des Alten Testaments*. 3 vols. Berlin: Evangelische Verlagsanstalt, 1948.

———. *Theology of the Old Testament*. Translated by J. A. Baker. 2 vols. OTL. Philadelphia: Westminster, 1967.

Eliade, Mircea. *The Sacred and the Profane: The Nature of Religion*. Translated by Willard R. Trask. New York: Harper & Brothers, 1961.

Eslinger, Lyle. "Inner-Biblical Exegesis and Inner-Biblical Allusion: The Question of Category." *VT* 42.1 (1992): 47–58.

Estes, Daniel J. *Hear, My Son: Teaching and Learning in Proverbs 1–9*. NSBT 4. Grand Rapids: Eerdmans, 1997.

———. "What Makes the Strange Woman of Proverbs 1–9 Strange? Ethical and Unethical in the Old Testament: God and Humans in Dialogue." Pages 151–69 in *Ethical and Unethical in the Old Testament: God and Humans in Dialogue*. New York: T&T Clark, 2010.

Evans, C. D., W. W. Hallo, and J. B. White. *Scripture in Context: Essays on the Comparative Method*. Pittsburgh: Pickwick, 1980.

Feinberg, Charles L. "אפל." Pages 64–65 in *TWOT*. Chicago: Moody, 1999.

Feldmeier, Reinhard. "'As Your Heavenly Father Is Perfect': The God of the Bible and Commandments in the Gospel." *Int* 70.4 (2016): 431–44.

Firmage, Edwin. "The Biblical Dietary Laws and the Concept of Holiness." Pages 177–208 in *Studies in the Pentateuch*. Edited by J. A. Emerton. Leiden: Brill, 1990.

Fishbane, Michael A. "Accusations of Adultery: A Study of Law and Scribal Practice in Numbers 5:11–31." *HUCA* 45 (1974): 25–45.

———. *Biblical Interpretation in Ancient Israel*. New York: Oxford University Press, 1985.

Fletcher, Verne H. "Shape of Old Testament Ethics." *SJT* 24.1 (1971): 47–73.

Fohrer, Georg. "Umkehr und Erlösung beim Propheten Hosea." *TZ* 11.3 (1955): 161–85.

Fontaine, Carole R. "Visual Metaphors and Proverbs 5:15–20: Some Archaeological Reflections on Gendered Iconography." Pages 185–202 in *Seeking Out the Wisdom of the Ancients: Essays Offered to Honor Michael V. Fox on the Occasion of His Sixty–Fifth Birthday*. Edited by Ronald L. Troxel, Kelvin G. Friebel, and Dennis R. Magary. Winona Lake: Eisenbrauns, 2005.

Forti, Tova. *Animal Imagery in the Book of Proverbs*. VTSup 118. Leiden: Brill, 2008.

———. "The Polarity of Wisdom and Fear of God in the Eden Narrative and in the Book of Proverbs." *BN* 149 (2011): 45–57.

Forti, Tova, and Zipora Talshir. "Proverbs 7 in MT and LXX: Form and Content." *Text* 22.1 (2005): 129–67.

Fox, Michael V. "Amon Again." *JBL* 115.4 (1996): 699–702.

———. "Ideas of Wisdom in Proverbs 1–9." *JBL* 116.4 (1997): 613–33.

———. *Proverbs 1–9: A New Translation with Introduction and Commentary*. AYBC 18A. New York: Doubleday, 2000.

———. "The Pedagogy of Proverbs 2." *JBL* 113.2 (1994): 233–43.

Frame, John M. *The Doctrine of the Knowledge of God*. Phillipsburg, NJ: P&R, 1987.

France, R. T. *The Gospel of Matthew*. NICNT. Grand Rapids: Eerdmans, 2007.

Frayne, Douglas R. "Notes on the Sacred Marriage Rite." *BO* 42 (1985): 5–22.

Frazer, Sir James George. *The Golden Bough*. London: Macmillan, 1890.

Fretheim, Terence E. *Exodus*. IBC. Louisville: John Knox, 1991.

Freud, Sigmund. *Moses and Monotheism*. Translated by Katherine Jones. London: Hogarth, 1951.

Friberg, Joran. "Numbers and Counting." Pages 1139–1146 in vol. 4 of *AYBD*. Edited by David Noel Freedman. New York: Doubleday, 1992.

Fromm, Erich. *The Heart of Man: Its Genius for Good and Evil*. New York: Harper & Row, 1964.

———. *You Shall Be as Gods: A Radical Interpretation of the Old Testament and Its Tradition*. New York: Holt, Rinehart, and Winston, 1966.

Frydrych, Tomáš. *Living under the Sun: Examination of Proverbs and Qoheleth*. VTSup 90. Boston: Brill, 2002.

Gammie, John G. *Holiness in Israel*. OBT. Minneapolis: Fortress, 1989.

Gane, Roy. *Leviticus, Numbers*. NIVAC. Grand Rapids: Zondervan, 2004.

Garrels, Scott R., ed. *Mimesis and Science: Empirical Research on Imitation and the Mimetic Theory of Culture and Religion*. Studies in Violence, Mimesis, and Culture. East Lansing, MI: Michigan State University Press, 2011.

Garrett, Duane A. *A Commentary on Exodus*. Kregel Exegetical Library. Grand Rapids: Kregel Academic, 2014.

Gebauer, Gunter, and Christoph Wulf. *Mimesis: Culture, Art, Society*. Berkeley: University of California Press, 1995.

Geertz, Clifford. "Religion as a Cultural System." Pages 176–217 in *Anthropological Approaches to the Study of Religion*. Edited by M. Banton. ASA Monographs 3. London: Tavistock, 1966.

Gemser, Berend. "The Spiritual Structure of Biblical Aphoristic Wisdom: A Review of Recent Standpoints and Theories." Pages 208–19 in *Studies in Ancient Israelite Wisdom*. Edited by James L. Crenshaw. The Library of Biblical Studies. New York: Ktav, 1976.

Gericke, Jaco. *The Hebrew Bible and Philosophy of Religion*. SBL 70. Atlanta: SBL, 2012.

Gerstenberger, E. S. *Das dritte Buck Mose: Leviticus*. Gottingen: Vandenhoeck & Ruprecht, 1993.

Gibson, John C. L., and Godfrey Rolles Driver, eds. *Canaanite Myths and Legends*. 2nd ed. New York: T&T Clark, 2004.

Goldberg, Louis. "אֱוִלָת." Page 20 in *TWOT*. Chicago: Moody, 1999.

———. "שׂכל." Page 877 in *TWOT*. Chicago: Moody, 1999.

Goldingay, John. *A Critical and Exegetical Commentary on Isaiah 56–66*. ICC. London: Bloomsbury, T&T Clark, 2014.

———. "Hosea 4 and 11, and the Structure of Hosea." *TynBul* 71.2 (2020): 181–90.

———. *The Theology of the Book of Isaiah*. Downers Grove: IVP, 2014.

Goldsworthy, Graeme. "Wisdom and Its Literature in Biblical–Theological Context." *SBJT* 15.3 (2011): 42–55.

———. *The Goldsworthy Trilogy: Gospel & Kingdom, Wisdom & Revelation*. Milton Keynes: Paternoster, 2013.

Gray, George B. *A Critical and Exegetical Commentary on Numbers.* ICC 4. New York: C. Scribner's Sons, 1903.

Gray, Mark. *Rhetoric and Social Justice in Isaiah.* LHBOTS. New York: T&T Clark, 2006.

Green, Gene L. *The Letters to the Thessalonians.* PNTC. Grand Rapids: Eerdmans, 2002.

Green, Joel B. *The Gospel of Luke.* NICNT. Grand Rapids: Eerdmans, 1997.

Gregory of Nyssa. *On the Christian Mode of Life.* Translated by Virginia Woods Callahan. Washington, DC: Catholic University of America Press, 1967.

Gruber, Mayer I. "Image of God." In vol. 2 of *The Encyclopedia of Judaism.* 2nd ed. Edited by Jacob Neusner, Alan J. Avery-Peck, and William S. Green. Boston: Brill, 2005.

Habel, Norman C. "Symbolism of Wisdom in Proverbs 1–9." *Int* 26.2 (1972): 131–57.

Hallo, William W. "Biblical History in Its Near Eastern Setting: The Contextual Approach." Pages 77–97 in *Israel's Past in Present Research: Essays on Ancient Israelite Historiography.* Edited by V. Philips Long. Sources for Biblical and Theological Study 7. Winona Lake: Eisenbrauns, 1999.

———. "The Birth of Kings." *Love and Death in the Ancient Near East. Essays in Honor of Marvin H. Pope.* Edited by J. H. Marks and R. M. Good. Guilford: Four Quarters, 1987.

Hallo, William W., and K. Lawson Younger. *The Context of Scripture.* New York: Brill, 1997.

Hamerton-Kelly, Robert. *God the Father: Theology and Patriarchy in the Teachings of Jesus.* Philadelphia: Fortress, 1979.

Hamilton, Victor P. *Exodus: An Exegetical Commentary.* Grand Rapids: Baker Academic, 2011.

———. *The Book of Genesis.* NICOT. Grand Rapids: Eerdmans, 1990.

———. "אָשֵׁר." Pages 80–82 in *TWOT.* Chicago: Moody, 1999.

Hammer, Reuven. *Sifre: A Tannaitic Commentary on the Book of Deuteronomy.* Yale Judaica Series 24. New Haven: Yale University Press, 1986.

Hardin, Michael. *Mimetic Theory and Biblical Interpretation: Reclaiming the Good News of the Gospel.* Cascade Companions. Eugene: Wipf & Stock, 2017.

Harding, James E. "The Wordplay Between the Roots כשל and שכל in the Literature of the Yahad." *RevQ* 19.1 (1999): 69–82.

Harris, Scott L. *Proverbs 1–9: A Study of Inner-Biblical Interpretation.* SBLDS 150. Atlanta: Scholars, 1996.

Harrison, R. K. *Introduction to the Old Testament.* 1969. Repr., Peabody, MA: Hendrickson, 2016.

Hartley, John E. *Leviticus.* WBC 4. Dallas: Word Books, 1992.

Hauerwas, Stanley. *The Peaceable Kingdom: A Primer in Christian Ethics.* Notre Dame: University of Notre Dame Press, 1983.

Hays, Christopher B. *Hidden Riches: A Sourcebook for the Comparative Study of the Hebrew Bible and Ancient Near East.* Louisville: Westminster John Knox, 2014.

Hays, Richard B. *Echoes of Scripture in the Letters of Paul*. New Haven: Yale University Press, 1989.

Hazony, Yoram. *The Philosophy of Hebrew Scripture: An Introduction*. New York: Cambridge University Press, 2012.

Healey, John F. "Models of Behavior: Matt 6:26 (//Luke 12:24) and Prov 6:6–8." *JBL* 108.3 (1989): 497–98.

———. "The Targum of Proverbs." In vol. 15 of *The Aramaic Bible*. Edited by Kevin Cathcart, Michael Maher, and Martin McNamara. Collegeville, MN: Liturgical, 1991.

Healy, Mary, and Robin A. Parry, eds. *The Bible and Epistemology: Biblical Soundings on the Knowledge of God*. Milton Keynes: Paternoster, 2007.

Heim, Erin M. *Adoption in Galatians and Romans: Contemporary Metaphor Theories and the Pauline Huiothesia Metaphors*. BIS 153. Leiden: Brill, 2017.

Heim, Knut Martin. *Poetic Imagination in Proverbs: Variant Repetitions and the Nature of Poetry*. BBRSup 4. Eisenbrauns, 2013.

Hengel, Martin. *Judentum und Hellenismus*. 2nd ed. Tübingen: Mohr, 1973.

Hermann, L. S. *Die Sprüche Salomos*. 2nd ed. Munich: Beck, 1899.

Hess, Richard S. *Israelite Religions: An Archaeological and Biblical Survey*. Downers Grove: IVP, 2007.

Hinkle, Adrian E. *Pedagogical Theory of Wisdom Literature: An Application of Educational Theory to Biblical Texts*. Eugene: Wipf & Stock, 2017.

Hirsch, Samson Raphael. *The Pentateuch*. Translated by Isaac Levy. 2nd ed. London: Judaica, 1962.

Holladay, William L. *Jeremiah 1: A Commentary on the Book of the Prophet Jeremiah, Chapters 1–25*. Hermeneia. Philadelphia: Fortress, 1986.

———. "Text, Structure, and Irony in the Poem on the Fall of the Tyrant, Isaiah 14." *CBQ* 61.4 (1999): 633–45.

Holmes, Christopher R. J. *A Theology of the Christian Life: Imitating and Participating in God*. Grand Rapids: Baker Academic, 2021.

Hossfeld, Frank–Lothar, and Erich Zenger. *Psalms 2: A Commentary on Psalms 51–100*. Hermeneia. Minneapolis: Fortress, 2005.

House, Paul. *1, 2 Kings*. NAC. Nashville: B&H, 1995.

Houston, Walter J. "The Character of YHWH and the Ethics of the Old Testament: Is *Imitatio Dei* Appropriate?" *JTS* 58.1 (2007): 1–25.

Houtman, Cornelis. *Exodus*. Translated by Sierd Woudstra. HCOT. Leuven: Peeters, 2000.

Hubbard, David A. *Mastering the Old Testament: Proverbs*. Waco: Word Books, 1989.

Huey, F. B., Jr. Jeremiah, *Lamentations*. NAC. Nashville: Broadman, 1993.

Huffmon, Herbert B. "The Treaty Background of Hebrew Yāda'." *BASOR* 181 (1966): 31–37.

Hunter, Alastair. *Wisdom Literature*. SCM, 2006.

Ibn Ezra, Abraham ben Meïr. *Ibn Ezra's Commentary on the Pentateuch.* Translated by H. Norman Strickman and Arthur M. Silver. New York: Menorah, 1988.

Ignatius of Antioch. "The Apostolic Fathers with Justin Martyr and Irenaeus." In vol. 1 of *The Ante–Nicene Fathers.* Translated by Alexander Roberts and James Donaldson. Buffalo: Christian Literature Co., 1885.

Irwin, William H. "The Course of the Dialogue between Moses and Yhwh in Exodus 33:12–17." *CBQ* 59.4 (1997): 629–36.

James, Elaine T. *An Invitation to Biblical Poetry.* New York: Oxford University Press, 2022.

Jenks, Alan W. "Theological Presuppositions of Israel's Wisdom Literature." *HBT* 7.1 (1985): 43–75.

Jeremias, Joachim. *The Prayers of Jesus.* SBT 2/6. Translated by John Bowden, Christoph Burchard, and John Reumann. Naperville: Allenson, 1967.

Johnson, Aubrey R. *The Vitality of the Individual in the Thought of Ancient Israel.* 2nd ed. Cardiff: University of Wales Press, 1964.

Johnson, Benjamin J. M. "The Heart of YHWH's Chosen One in 1 Samuel." *JBL* 131.3 (2012): 455–66.

Johnson, Dru. *Biblical Philosophy: A Hebraic Approach to the Old and New Testaments.* Cambridge: Cambridge University Press, 2021.

Johnston, Philip. *Shades of Sheol: Death and Afterlife in the Old Testament.* Downers Grove: IVP, 2002.

Johnston, Sarah Iles. *Religions of the Ancient World: A Guide.* Harvard University Press Reference Library. Cambridge: Harvard University Press, 2004.

Jones, John N. "'Think of the Lilies' and Prov 6:6–11." *HTR* 88.1 (1995): 175–77.

Jones, Philip. "Embracing Inana: Legitimation and Mediation in the Ancient Mesopotamian Sacred Marriage Hymn Iddin–Dagan A." *JAOS* 123.2 (2003): 291–302.

Jones, Scott C. "Wisdom's Pedagogy: A Comparison of Proverbs VII and 4Q184." *VT* 53.1 (2003): 65–80.

Josephus, Flavius. *The Works of Josephus: Complete and Unabridged.* Translated by William Whiston. New updated. Peabody: Hendrickson, 1987.

Joy, Donald M., ed. *Moral Development Foundations: Judeo–Christian Alternatives to Piaget/Kohlberg.* Nashville: Abingdon, 1983.

Justin Martyr. "The Apostolic Fathers with Justin Martyr and Irenaeus." In vol. 1 of *The Ante–Nicene Fathers.* Translated by Alexander Roberts and James Donaldson. Buffalo: Christian Literature Co., 1885.

Keefer, Arthur J. *Proverbs 1–9 as an Introduction to the Book of Proverbs.* London: T&T Clark, 2020.

———. *The Book of Proverbs and Virtue Ethics: Integrating the Biblical and Philosophical Traditions.* Cambridge: Cambridge University Press, 2021.

Keel, Othmar. *The Symbolism of the Biblical World: Ancient Near Eastern Iconography and the Book of Psalms.* New York: Seabury, 1978.

Keener, Craig S. *The Gospel of Matthew: A Socio–Rhetorical Commentary.* Grand Rapids: Eerdmans, 2009.

Keil, C. F., and Franz Delitzsch. *Commentary on the Old Testament*. Rev. ed. 1866–91. Repr., Peabody: Hendrickson, 1996.

Kelle, Brad E. *Hosea 2: Metaphor and Rhetoric in Historical Perspective*. AcBib 20. Atlanta: SBL, 2005.

Kellner, Menachem. "Ethics of Judaism." In vol. 1 of *The Encyclopaedia of Judaism*. 2nd ed. Edited by Jacob Neusner, Alan J. Avery–Peck, and William S. Green. Boston: Brill, 2005.

Kidner, Derek. *Proverbs: An Introduction and Commentary*. TOTC. IVP, 1964.

———. *Psalms: A Commentary*. TOTC. Leicester: IVP, 1975.

Kinsley, David R. *The Goddesses' Mirror: Visions of the Divine from East and West*. Albany: State University of New York Press, 1989.

Kitchen, Kenneth A., and Paul J. N. Lawrence. *Treaty, Law, and Covenant in the Ancient Near East*. Wiesbaden: Harrassowitz Verlag, 2012.

Klein, Jacob. "Sacred Marriage." Pages 866–70 in *AYBD*. Vol. 5. Edited by David Noel Freedman. New York: Doubleday, 1992.

Klein, M. L. "The Preposition קדם ('before') a Pseudo–Anti–Anthropomorphism in the Targums." *JTS* 30.2 (1979): 502–7.

Klein, Ralph W. *1 Samuel*. WBC 10. Waco: Word Books, 1983.

Koch, Dietrich–Alex. "The Quotations of Isaiah 8,14 and 28,16 in Romans 9,33 and 1 Peter 2,6.8 as Test–Case for Old Testament Quotations in the New Testament." *ZNW* 101.2 (2010): 223–40.

Kohlberg, Lawrence. "Stage and Sequence: The Cognitive–Developmental Approach to Socialization." In *Handbook of Socialization Theory and Research*. Edited by David A. Goslin. Chicago: Rand McNally, 1969.

———. *The Philosophy of Moral Development: Moral Stages and the Idea of Justice*. San Francisco: Harper & Row, 1981.

———. *The Psychology of Moral Development: The Nature and Validity of Moral Stages*. San Francisco: Harper & Row, 1984.

Koptak, Paul E. "Personification." Pages 516–19 in *Dictionary of the Old Testament: Wisdom, Poetry, & Writings*. Edited by Tremper Longman III and Peter Enns. Downers Grove: IVP Academic, 2008.

———. *Proverbs: From Biblical Text to Contemporary Life*. NIVAC. Grand Rapids: Zondervan, 2003.

Köstenberger, Andreas J., and Richard Duane Patterson. *Invitation to Biblical Interpretation: Exploring the Hermeneutical Triad of History, Literature, and Theology*. 2nd ed. Grand Rapids: Kregel Academic, 2021.

Kövecses, Zoltán. *Metaphor: A Practical Introduction*. 2nd ed. New York: Oxford University Press, 2010.

Kramer, Samuel Noah. *Sumerian Mythology: A Study of Spiritual and Literary Achievement in the Third Millennium B.C.* Philadelphia: University of Philadelphia Press, 1972.

Kraus, F. R. "Das altbabylonische Konigtum." Pages 235–61 in *Le Palaise et la Royaute*. Edited by P. Garelli. Archaeology et Civilisation. Paris: Geuthner, 1974.

Kreisel, Howard. "*Imitatio Dei* in Maimonides' Guide of the Perplexed." *AJSR* 19.2 (1994): 169–211.

Kruger, Paul A. "Promiscuity or Marriage Fidelity: A Note on Prov 5:15–18." *JNSL* 13 (1987): 61–68.

Krüger, Thomas. "Law and Wisdom According to Deut 4:5–8." Pages 35–54 in *Wisdom and Torah: The Reception of "Torah" in the Wisdom Literature of the Second Temple Period.* Edited by Bernd U. Schipper and D. Andrew Teeter. JSJSup 163. Leiden: Brill, 2013.

Kselman, John S. "A Note on W'nḥhw in Isa 57:18." *CBQ* 43.4 (1981): 539–42.

Lakoff, George, and Mark Johnson. *Metaphors We Live By.* Chicago: University of Chicago Press, 1980.

Lancaster, Mason. "Wounds and Healing, Dew and Lions: Hosea's Development of Divine Metaphors." *CBQ* 83.3 (2021): 407–24.

Lang, Bernhard. *Die weisheitliche Lehrrede: eine Untersuchung von Sprüche 1–7.* SBS 54. Stuttgart: KBW–Verlag, 1972.

———. "Schule und Unterricht im alten Israel." Pages 186–201 in *La Sagesse de l'Ancien Testament.* Edited by Maurice Gilbert. 2nd ed. BETL 51. Leuven: Leuven University Press, 1990.

———. *Wisdom and the Book of Proverbs: A Hebrew Goddess Redefined.* New York: Pilgrim, 1986.

Laniak, Timothy S. *Shepherds after My Own Heart: Pastoral Traditions and Leadership in the Bible.* NSBT 20. Downers Grove: IVP, 2006.

Larcher, Chrysostome. *Études sur le Livre de la Sagesse.* Études Bibliques. Paris: Gabalda, 1969.

LeMon, J. M., and B. A. Strawn. "Parallelism." Pages 502–15 in *Dictionary of the Old Testament: Wisdom, Poetry, & Writings.* Edited by Tremper Longman III and Peter Enns. Downers Grove: IVP Academic, 2008.

Lenzi, Alan C. "Proverbs 8:22–31: Three Perspectives on Its Composition." *JBL* 125.4 (2006): 687–714.

Leo the Great. "Leo the Great, Gregory the Great." In vol. 12 of *The Nicene and Post–Nicene Fathers*, Series 2. Translated by Charles Lett Feltoe. New York: Christian Literature Co., 1895.

Leonard, Jeffery M. "Identifying Inner–Biblical Allusions: Psalm 78 as a Test Case." *JBL* 127.2 (2008): 241–65.

Leuchter, Mark. "Why is the Song of Moses in the Book of Deuteronomy?" *VT* 57.3 (2007): 295–317.

Levenson, Jon. *Sinai and Zion: An Entry into the Jewish Bible.* New York: Harper Collins, 1985.

Levine, Baruch A. *Leviticus: The Traditional Hebrew Text with the New JPS Translation.* The JPS Torah Commentary. Philadelphia: Jewish Publication Society, 1989.

Levinson, Bernard M. "The Significance of Chiasm as a Structuring Device in the Hebrew Bible." *WW* 40.3 (2020): 271–80.

Lewis, C. S. *Surprised by Joy: The Shape of My Early Life.* San Francisco: HarperOne, 2017.

Lichtheim, Miriam. *The New Kingdom*. Vol. 2 of *Ancient Egyptian Literature*. Berkeley: University of California Press, 1975.

Lindars, Barnabas. "Imitation of God and Imitation of Christ: Duty and Discernment." *Theology* 76.638 (1973): 394–402.

Lipinski, Edward. "Fertility Cult in Ancient Ugarit." Pages 207–16 in *Archaeology and Fertility Cult in the Ancient Mediterranean: Papers Presented at the First International Conference on Archaeology of the Ancient Mediterranean, the University of Malta, 2–5 September 1985*. Edited by Anthony Bonanno. Amsterdam: Gruner, 1986.

Loader, James Alfred. *Proverbs 1–9*. HCOT. Leuven: Peeters, 2014.

Long, V. Philips. *The Reign and Rejection of King Saul: A Case for Literary and Theological Coherence*. SBLDS 118. Atlanta: Scholars, 1989.

Longenecker, Richard N. *Biblical Exegesis in the Apostolic Period*. 2nd ed. Grand Rapids: Eerdmans, 1999.

Longman III, Tremper. *Proverbs*. BCOTWP. Grand Rapids: Baker Academic, 2006.

———. *Psalms: An Introduction and Commentary*. TOTC. Nottingham: IVP, 2014.

———. *The Fear of the Lord Is Wisdom: A Theological Introduction to Wisdom in Israel*. Grand Rapids: Baker Academic, 2017.

———. "Theology of Wisdom." Pages 389–405 in *The Oxford Handbook of Wisdom and the Bible*. Edited by Will Kynes. Oxford: Oxford University Press, 2021.

López, René. "Identifying the 'angel of the Lord' in the Book of Judges: A Model for Reconsidering the Referent in Other Old Testament Loci." *BBR* 20.1 (2010): 1–18.

Lund, N. W. "The Presence of Chiasmus in the Old Testament." *AJSL* 46.2 (1930): 104–26.

Luo, Dali. "Proverbs 16:1–15: An Invitation to Adopt the Royal Way of Life." PhD diss., Trinity International University, 2010.

Lyu, Sun Myung. *Righteousness in the Book of Proverbs*. FAT 55. Tübingen: Mohr Siebeck, 2012.

MacDonald, Nathan. "Listening to Abraham—Listening to Yhwh: Divine Justice and Mercy in Genesis 18:16–33." *CBQ* 66 (2004): 25–43.

MacIntosh, A. A. *A Critical and Exegetical Commentary on Hosea*. ICC 23. Edinburgh: T&T Clark, 1997.

Maier, John. "Sacred Marriage(s) in Mesopotamian Literature." *Proceedings EGL & MWBS* 24 (2004): 17–34.

Malone, Andrew S. "Distinguishing the Angel of the Lord." *BBR* 21.3 (2011): 297–314.

Marcus, Ralph. "The Tree of Life in Proverbs." *JBL* 62.2 (1943): 117–20.

Marmorstein, Arthur. *Studies in Jewish Theology; the Arthur Marmorstein Memorial Volume*. Edited by J. Rabbinowitz and M. S. Lew. New York: Oxford University Press, 1950.

———. *The Doctrine of Merits in Old Rabbinical Literature; and The Old Rabbinic Doctrine of God: I. The Names and Attributes of God and II. Essays in Anthropomorphism*. 1920. Repr., New York: Ktav, 1968.

Marshall, I. Howard. *The Gospel of Luke: A Commentary on the Greek Text.* NIGTC. Exeter: Paternoster, 1978.

Martens, E. A. "How Is the Christian to Construe Old Testament Law?" *BBR* 12.2 (2002): 199–216.

———. "בֵּן." Pages 114–16 in *TWOT.* Chicago: Moody, 1999.

McCarthy, D. J. "Notes on the Love of God in Deuteronomy and the Father–Son Relationship between Yahweh and Israel." *CBQ* 27.2 (1965): 144–47.

McGovern, Thomas. "John Paul II on the Millennium and God as Father." *Homiletic and Pastoral Review* 99.7 (1999): 8–17.

McKane, William. *A Critical and Exegetical Commentary on Jeremiah.* 2 vol. ICC. Edinburgh: T&T Clark, 1986–1996.

———. *Prophets and Wise Men.* SBT 44. London: SCM, 1965.

———. *Proverbs: A New Approach.* OTL. London: SCM, 1970.

McKay, J. W. "Man's Love for God in Deuteronomy and The Father/Teacher – Son/Pupil Relationship." *VT* 22.4 (1972): 426–35.

McKenzie, John L. "Knowledge of God in Hosea." *JBL* 74.1 (1955): 22–27.

Medina, Richard W. "Life and Death Viewed as Physical and Lived Spaces: Some Preliminary Thoughts from Proverbs." *ZAW* 122 (2012): 199–211.

Meek, Esther L. *Longing to Know.* Grand Rapids: Brazos, 2003.

Meek, Russell. "Intertextuality, Inner–Biblical Exegesis, and Inner–Biblical Allusion: The Ethics of a Methodology." *Bib* 95.2 (2014): 280–91.

Meinhold, Arndt. *Die Sprüche.* ZBK. Zürich: Theologischer Verlag, 1991.

———. "Gott und Mensch in Proverbien 3." *VT* 37.4 (1987): 468–77.

Mendenhall, George E. "The Monarchy." *Int* 29.2 (1975): 155–70.

Metz, Johann Baptist, Edward Schillebeeckx, and Marcus Lefébure, eds. *God as Father?* Concilium 143. New York: Seabury, 1981.

Meyer, Esias E. "The Dark Side of the *Imitatio Dei.* Why Imitating the God of the Holiness Code Is Not Always a Good Thing." *OTE* 22.2 (2009): 373–83.

———. "When Synchrony Overtakes Diachrony: Perspectives on the Relationship between the Deuteronomic Code and the Holiness Code." *OTE* 30.3 (2017): 749–69.

Miles, Johnny E. *Wise King – Royal Fool: Semiotics, Satire and Proverbs 1–9.* New York: T&T Clark, 2004.

Milgrom, Jacob. *Leviticus 23–27: A New Translation with Introduction and Commentary.* AB 3B. New York: Doubleday, 2001.

———. *Numbers.* JPSTC. Philadelphia: JPS, 1990.

Miller, Geoffrey D. "Intertextuality in Old Testament Research." *CurBR* 9.3 (2011): 283–309.

Mills, Mary E. *Images of God in the Old Testament.* Collegeville, MN: Liturgical, 1998.

Miroschedji, Pierre de. "At the Origin of Canaanite Cult and Religion: The Early Bronze Age Fertility Ritual in Palestine." *Eretz–Israel* 7 (2011): 74–103.

Mizrahi, Noam. "The Textual History and Literary Background of Isa 14,4." *ZAW* 125.3 (2013): 433–47.

Moor, Johannes C. de, ed. *An Anthology of Religious Texts from Ugarit*. Vol. 16 of Nisaba. New York: Brill, 1987.

———. *New Year with Canaanites and Israelites*. Kampen: Kok, 1972.

Moran, William L. "Ancient Near Eastern Background of the Love of God in Deuteronomy." *CBQ* 25.1 (1963): 77–87.

———. "Some Remarks on the Song of Moses." *Bib* 43.3 (1962): 317–27.

Moreland, James P. *Philosophical Foundations for a Christian Worldview*. Downers Grove: IVP Academic, 2017.

Moroney, Stephen K. "Higher Stages? Some Cautions for Christian Integration with Kohlberg's Theory." *JPT* 34.4 (2006): 361–71.

Morris, Leon. *The Gospel According to John*. Rev. ed. NICNT. Grand Rapids: Eerdmans, 1995.

———. *The Gospel According to Matthew*. PNTC. Grand Rapids: Eerdmans, 1992.

Moss, Alan. "Wisdom as Parental Teaching in Proverbs 1–9." *HeyJ* 38.4 (1997): 426–39.

Motyer, J. A. *The Prophecy of Isaiah: An Introduction & Commentary*. Downers Grove: IVP, 1993.

Müller, Achim. *Proverbien 1–9: der Weisheit neue Kleider*. BZAW 291. Berlin: De Gruyter, 2000.

Murphy, Roland E. *Proverbs*. WBC 22. Dallas: Thomas Nelson, 1998.

———. *The Tree of Life: An Exploration of Biblical Wisdom Literature*. 2nd ed. Grand Rapids: Eerdmans, 1996.

———. "Wisdom and Eros in Proverbs 1–9." *CBQ* 50.4 (1988): 600–603.

———. *Wisdom Literature: Ruth, Esther, Job, Proverbs, Ecclesiastes, Canticles*. Grand Rapids: Eerdmans, 1981.

Murray, John. *The Problem of God: Yesterday and Today*. New Haven: Yale University Press, 1965.

Najman, Hindy. "*Imitatio Dei* and the Formation of the Subject in Ancient Judaism." *JBL* 140.2 (2021): 309–23.

Nasuti, Peter. "Identity, Identification, and Imitation: The Narrative Hermeneutics of Biblical Law." *Journal of Law and Religion* 4.1 (1986): 9–23.

Nel, Philip J. "The Concept of 'Father' in the Wisdom Literature of the Ancient Near East." *JNSL* 5 (1977): 53–66.

———. *The Structure and Ethos of the Wisdom Admonitions in Proverbs*. BZAW 158. New York: De Gruyter, 1982.

Neusner, Jacob. *The Babylonian Talmud: A Translation and Commentary*. Peabody: Hendrickson, 2011.

Newsom, Carol A. "Woman and the Discourse of Patriarchal Wisdom: A Study of Proverbs 1–9." Pages 142–60 in *Gender and Difference in Ancient Israel*. Edited by Peggy L. Day. Minneapolis: Fortress, 1989.

Niles, Daniel T. *We Know in Part*. Philadelphia: Westminster, 1964.

Noble, Paul R. "Esau, Tamar, and Joseph: Criteria for Identifying Inner–Biblical Allusions." *VT* 52.2 (2002): 219–52.

Nogalski, James. *The Book of the Twelve: Hosea–Jonah*. SHBC 18a. Macon, GA: Smyth & Helwys, 2011.

Noll, Stephen F. "מַלְאָךְ." In *NIDOTTE*. Edited by Willem VanGemeren. Grand Rapids: Zondervan, 1997.

Nordheim–Diehl, Miriam von. "Wer herrscht in der Scheol? eine Untersuchung zu Jes 14,9." *BN* 143 (2009): 81–91.

O'Connell, Robert H. "Isaiah 14:4b–23: Ironic Reversal through Concentric Structure and Mythic Allusion." *VT* 38.4 (1988): 406–18.

O'Dowd, Ryan. "A Chord of Three Strands: Epistemology in Job, Proverbs and Ecclesiastes." Pages 65–87 in *The Bible and Epistemology: Biblical Soundings on the Knowledge of God*. Edited by Mary Healy and Robin A. Parry. Milton Keynes: Paternoster, 2007.

———. "Memory on the Boundary: Epistemology in Deuteronomy." Pages 1–22 in *The Bible and Epistemology: Biblical Sounding on the Knowledge of God*. Edited by Mary Healy and Robin A. Parry. Milton Keynes: Paternoster, 2007.

———. *The Wisdom of Torah: Epistemology in Deuteronomy and the Wisdom Literature*. FRLANT 225. Göttingen: Vandenhoeck & Ruprecht, 2009.

O'Kennedy, D. F. "The Metaphor of Yahweh as Healer in the Prophetic Books of the Old Testament." *IDS* 41.3 (2007): 443–55.

Obermann, Julian. *Ugaritic Mythology: A Study of Its Leading Motifs*. New Haven: Yale University Press, 1948.

Olmo Lete, Gregorio del. *Canaanite Religion: According to the Liturgical Texts of Ugarit*. Winona Lake: Eisenbrauns, 2004.

Olyan, Saul M. "The Biblical Prohibition of the Mourning Rites of Shaving and Laceration: Several Proposals." Pages 181–89 in *A Wise and Discerning Mind: Essays in Honor of Burke O. Long*. Edited by Saul M. Olyan and Robert C. Culley. 2nd ed. Brown Judaic Studies 325. Providence: Brown Judaic Studies, 2020.

Osborne, Grant R. *The Hermeneutical Spiral: A Comprehensive Introduction to Biblical Interpretation*. 2nd ed. Downers Grove: IVP, 2006.

Osborne, William R. "The Tree of Life in Ancient Egypt and the Book of Proverbs." *JANER* 14.1 (2014): 114–39.

Oswalt, John N. "God." Pages 280–93 in *Dictionary of the Old Testament: Prophets*. Edited by Mark J. Boda and J. Gordon McConville. Downers Grove: IVP, 2012.

———. "God's Determination to Redeem His People (Isaiah 9:1–7, 11:1–11, 26:1–9, 35:1–10)." *RevExp* 88.2 (1991): 153–65.

———. *The Book of Isaiah*. NICOT. Grand Rapids: Eerdmans, 1986.

———. *The Holy One of Israel: Studies in the Book of Isaiah*. Cambridge: James Clarke & Co., 2014.

———. "Theology of the Pentateuch." Pages 845–59 in *Dictionary of the Old Testament: Pentateuch*. Edited by T. Desmond Alexander and David W. Baker. Downers Grove: IVP, 2003.

Otto, Eckart. *Theologische Ethik des Alten Testaments*. Theologische Wissenschaft. Stuttgart: W. Kohlhammer, 1994.

Overland, Paul B. "Chiasm." Pages 54–57 in *Dictionary of the Old Testament: Wisdom, Poetry & Writings*. Edited by Tremper Longman III and Peter Enns. Downers Grove: IVP Academic, 2008.

———. "Did the Sage Draw from the Shema? A Study of Proverbs 3:1–12." *CBQ* 62.3 (2000): 424–40.

———. "Literary Structure in Proverbs 1–9." PhD diss., Brandeis University, 1988.

Palaver, Wolfgang. *René Girard's Mimetic Theory*. Studies in Violence, Mimesis, and Culture. East Lansing, MI: Michigan State University Press, 2013.

Peels, H. G. L. "Passion or Justice? The Interpretation of Beyôm Nāqām in Proverbs vi 34." *VT* 44.2 (1994): 270–74.

———. "נקם." Page 154 in *NIDOTTE*. Edited by Willem VanGemeren. Grand Rapids: Zondervan, 1997.

Pemberton, Glenn D. "The Rhetoric of the Father: A Rhetorical Analysis of the Father/Son Lectures in Proverbs 1–9." PhD diss., University of Denver; Colorado Seminary, 1999.

Penchansky, David. *What Rough Beast? Images of God in the Hebrew Bible*. Louisville: John Knox, 1999.

Perdue, Leo G. *Proverbs*. IBC. Louisville: John Knox, 2000.

———. *Wisdom and Cult: A Critical Analysis of the Views of Cult in the Wisdom Literatures of Israel and the Ancient Near East*. SBLDS 30. Missoula: Society of Biblical Literature, 1977.

———. *Wisdom Literature: A Theological History*. Louisville: Westminster John Knox, 2007.

Petrany, Catherine. "Fathers, Mothers, Sons, and Silence: Rhetorical Reconfiguration in Proverbs." *BTB* 50.3 (2020): 154–60.

Philo of Alexandria. *The Works of Philo: Complete and Unabridged*. Translated by Charles Duke Yonge. Peabody: Hendrickson, 1995.

Pilch, J. J., and B. M. Malina, eds. *Handbook of Biblical Social Values*. Updated. Peabody: Hendrickson, 1998.

Pinker, Aron. "'Abomination to Egyptians' in Genesis 43:32, 46:34, and Exodus 8:22." *OTE* 22.1 (2009): 151–74.

Plantinga, Alvin. *Warranted Christian Belief*. New York: Oxford University Press, 2000.

Plato. *Euthyphro; Apology; Crito; Phaedo; Phaedrus*. Translated by Harold North Fowler. 1914. Repr., Cambridge: Harvard University Press, 2005.

Plöger, Otto. *Spruche Salomos (Proverbia)*. BKAT 17. Neukirchen–Vluyn: Neukirchener Verlag, 1984.

Polycarp of Smryna. "The Apostolic Fathers with Justin Martyr and Irenaeus." In vol. 1 of *The Ante–Nicene Fathers*. Translated by Alexander Roberts and James Donaldson. Buffalo: Christian Literature Co., 1885.

Potgieter, J. H. "The (Poetic) Rhetoric of Wisdom in Proverbs 3:1–12." *HvTSt* 58.4 (2002): 1357–74.

Preuss, H. Dietrich. "Tôʿēḇâ." Pages 591–604 in *TDOT*. Grand Rapids: Eerdmans, 2006.

Prinsloo, G. T. M. "Reading Proverbs 3:1–12 in Its Social and Ideological Context." *HvTSt* 58.4 (2002): 1375–1400.

Prinsloo, Willem S. "Isaiah 14:12–15 – Humiliation, Hubris, Humiliation." *ZAW* 93.3 (1981): 432–38.

Pritchard, James B., ed. *The Ancient near Eastern Texts Relating to the Old Testament, with Supplements*. 3rd ed. Princeton: Princeton University Press, 1969.

Propp, William H. C., ed. *Exodus 19–40: A New Translation with Introduction and Commentary*. AB 2A. New York: Doubleday, 2006.

Provan, Iain W. *1 and 2 Kings*. Grand Rapids: Baker Books, 2012.

Pseudo–Clement of Rome. "Fathers of the Third and Fourth Centuries." In vol. 8 of *The Ante–Nicene Fathers*. Translated by B. P. Pratten. Buffalo: Christian Literature Co., 1886.

Rendsburg, Gary A. "Literary and Linguistic Matters in the Book of Proverbs." Pages 111–47 in *Perspectives on Israelite Wisdom: Proceedings of the Oxford Old Testament Seminar*. Edited by John Jarick. LHBOTS 618. London: T&T Clark, 2016.

Rikala, Mia. "Sacred Marriage in the New Kingdom of Ancient Egypt: Circumstantial Evidence for a Ritual Interpretation." Pages 115–44 in *Sacred Marriages: The Divine–Human Sexual Metaphor from Sumer to Early Christianity*. Edited by Martti Nissinen and Risto Uro. Winona Lake: Eisenbrauns, 2008.

Ringgren, Helmer. "יתם." Pages 477–81 in vol. 6 of *TDOT*. Edited by G. Johannes Botterweck, Helmer Ringgren, and Heinz–Josef Fabry. Grand Rapids: Eerdmans, 1974.

Robert, A. "Les Attaches Littéraires Bibliques de Prov. I–IX." *RB* 43.1 (1934): 42–68.

Roberts, Alexander, and James Donaldson, trans. "The Epistle of Mathetes to Diognetus." In vol. 1 of *The Ante–Nicene Fathers*. Buffalo: Christian Literature Co., 1885.

Robertson, O. Palmer. *The Books of Nahum, Habakkuk, and Zephaniah*. NICOT. Grand Rapids: Eerdmans, 1990.

Rocine, B. M. *Learning Biblical Hebrew: A New Approach Using Discourse Analysis*. Macon, GA: Smyth & Helwys, 2000.

Rodd, Cyril S. *Glimpses of a Strange Land: Studies in Old Testament Ethics*. OTS. Edinburgh: T&T Clark, 2001.

———. "Shall Not the Judge of All the Earth Do What Is Right? (Gen 18:25)." *ExpTim* 83.5 (1972): 137–39.

Rogers III, Cleon L. "The Meaning and Significance of the Hebrew Word אמון in Proverbs 8,30." *ZAW* 109.2 (1997): 208–21.

Rose, Martin. "Names of God in the OT." Pages 1001–11 in vol. 4 of *AYBD*. New York: Doubleday, 1992.

Rosengren, Allan. "Knowledge of God According to Hosea the Ripper: The Interlacing of Theology and Social Ideology in Hosea 2." *SJOT* 23.1 (2009): 122–26.

Ross, Allen P. *A Commentary on the Psalms*. 3 vol. Kregel Exegetical Library. Grand Rapids: Kregel Academic, 2011.

———. "Proverbs." Pages 21–251 in *The Expositor's Bible Commentary: Proverbs–Isaiah*. Rev. ed. Grand Rapids: Zondervan, 2008.

Roth, Martha Tobi, and Harry A. Hoffner. *Law Collections from Mesopotamia and Asia Minor*. Edited by Piotr Michalowski. 2nd ed. WAW 6. Atlanta: Scholars, 1997.

Rowley, H. H. *The Unity of the Bible*. Westport, CT: Greenwood, 1978.

Ruark, Joel D. "Toward an Old Testament Theology of Light: From Physical Concept to Metaphysical Analogy." PhD diss., Stellenbosch University, 2019.

Sailhamer, John. *The Meaning of the Pentateuch: Revelation, Composition, and Interpretation*. Downers Grove: IVP Academic, 2009.

Sandoval, Timothy J. "Revisiting the Prologue of Proverbs." *JBL* 126.3 (2007): 455–73.

Sarna, Nahum M. *Exodus*. JPS. Philadelphia: JPS, 1991.

Savinac, Jean de. "La Sagesse en Proverbes 8:22–31." *VT* 12.2 (1962): 211–15.

Sawyer, John F. A. *Isaiah*. Philadelphia: Westminster, 1986.

Schaefer, Konrad R. "Zechariah 14: A Study in Allusion." *CBQ* 57.1 (1995): 66–91.

Schäfer, Rolf. *Die Poesie der Weisen: Dichotomie als Grundstruktur der Lehr und Weisheitsgedichte in Proverbien 1–9*. WMANT 77. Neukirchen–Vluyn: Neukirchener Verlag, 1999.

Schellenberg, Annette. "'May Her Breasts Satisfy You at All Times' (Prov 5:19): On the Erotic Passages in Proverbs and Sirach and the Question of How They Relate to the Song of Songs." *VT* 68.2 (2018): 252–71.

Schipper, Bernd U. *Hermeneutik der Tora: Studien zur Traditionsgeschichte von Prov 2 und zur Komposition von Prov 1–9*. ZAW 432. Berlin: De Gruyter, 2012.

———. *Proverbs 1–15: A Commentary on the Book of Proverbs 1:1–15:33*. Hermeneia. Minneapolis: Fortress, 2019.

———. "'Teach Them Diligently to Your Son!' The Book of Proverbs and Deuteronomy." Pages 21–34 in *Reading Proverbs Intertextually*. Edited by Katharine J. Dell and Will Kynes. London: T&T Clark, 2019.

———. "When Wisdom Is Not Enough! The Discourse on Wisdom and Torah and the Composition of the Book of Proverbs." Pages 55–79 in *Wisdom and Torah: The Reception of "Torah" in the Wisdom Literature of the Second Temple Period*. Edited by Bernd U. Schipper and D. Andrew Teeter. JSJSup 163. Leiden: Brill, 2013.

Schmidt, B. B. *Israel's Beneficent Dead*. Winona Lake: Eisenbrauns, 1996.

Schmitt, John J. "The God of Israel and the Holy One." *HS* 24 (1983): 27–31.

Schockenhoff, Eberhard. "The Theological Virtue of Charity (IIa IIae, Qq. 23–46)." *The Ethics of Aquinas*. Edited by Stephen J. Pope. Washington, DC: Georgetown University Press, 2002.

Schwáb, Zoltán S. "The Value of a Curious Translation: Revisiting Proverbs 2:5." *JBL* 133.4 (2014): 739–49.

———. *Toward an Interpretation of the Book of Proverbs: Selfishness and Secularity Reconsidered*. JTISup 7. Winona Lake: Eisenbrauns, 2013.

Scott, R. B. Y. "Wisdom in Creation: The 'Amôn of Proverbs 8:30." *VT* 10.2 (1960): 213–23.

Scott, William R. *A Simplified Guide to BHS: Critical Apparatus, Masora, Accents, Unusual Letters & Other Markings*. 4th ed. North Richland Hills, TX: Bibal, 2007.

Scurlock, JoAnn. "Animal Sacrifice in Ancient Mesopotamian Religion." Pages 390–403 in *A History of the Animal World in the Ancient Near East*. Edited by Billie Jean Collins. HdO 64. Leiden: Brill, 2002.

———. "Assyria and Babylon in the Oracles against the Nations Tradition: The Death of a King (Isa. 14:5–20; Isa. 30:27–33)." *JAOS* 140.2 (2020): 395–413.

Seitz, Christopher R. *Isaiah 1–39*. Interpretation. Louisville: Presbyterian, 2011.

Shepard, Richard G. "Biblical Progression as Moral Development: The Analogy and Its Implications." *JPT* 22.3 (1994): 182–86.

Sherman, Steven B. *Revitalizing Theological Epistemology: Holistic Evangelical Approaches to the Knowledge of God*. Princeton Theological Monograph Series. Eugene, OR: Pickwick, 2008.

Sherwood, Yvonne. *The Prostitute and the Prophet: Hosea's Marriage in Literary–Theoretical Perspective*. JSOTSup 212. Sheffield: Sheffield Academic, 1996.

Silver, Abba Hillel. *A History of Messianic Speculation in Israel: From the First through the Seventeenth Centuries*. Boston: Beacon, 1959.

Skehan, Patrick W. "Structure of the Song of Moses in Deuteronomy (Deut 32:1–43)." *CBQ* 13.2 (1951): 153–63.

———. *Studies in Israelite Poetry and Wisdom*. CBQMS 1. Washington, DC: Catholic Biblical Association of America, 1971.

Smith, Mark S. "Sacred Marriage in the Ugaritic Texts? The Case of KTU/CAT 1.23." Pages 93–114 in *Sacred Marriages: The Divine–Human Sexual Metaphor from Sumer to Early Christianity*. Edited by Martti Nissinen and Risto Uro. Winona Lake: Eisenbrauns, 2008.

———. "'Seeing God' in the Psalms: The Background to the Beatific Vision in the Hebrew Bible." *CBQ* 50.2 (1988): 171–83.

———. *The Rituals and Myths of the Feast of the Goodly Gods of KTU/CAT 1.23: Royal Constructions of Opposition, Intersection, Integration, and Domination*. Society of Biblical Literature Resources for Biblical Study 51. Atlanta: SBL, 2006.

Schutz, E. "Knowledge, Experience, Ignorance." Pages 390–409 in vol. 2 of *NIDNTTE*. Edited by Colin Brown. Grand Rapids: Zondervan, 1976.

Snell, Daniel C. *Twice–Told Proverbs and the Composition of the Book of Proverbs*. Winona Lake: Eisenbrauns, 1993.

Sommer, Benjamin D. "Nature, Revelation, and Grace in Psalm 19: Towards a Theological Reading of Scripture." *HTR* 108.3 (2015): 376–401.

Sperber, Alexander, ed. *The Bible in Aramaic: based on old manuscripts and printed texts*. 3rd ed. Leiden; Boston: Brill, 2013.

Spohn, William C. "Conscience and Moral Development." *TS* 61.1 (2000): 122–38.

Steen, Gerard. "How to Do Things with Metaphor in Literature." *RBPH* 68.3 (1990): 658–71.

Steinsaltz, Adin Even–Israel. *Sota*. Edited by Tzvi Hersh Weinreb, Shalom Zvi Berger, and Joshua Schreier. Koren Talmud Bavli 20. Jerusalem: Koren, 2012.

Sterling, Gregory E. "*Imitatio Dei* (Eph 5:1–2): The Soteriological Basis for Ethics." Pages 345–60 in *Sōtēria: Salvation in Early Christianity and Antiquity: Festschrift in Honour of Cilliers Breytenbach on the Occasion of His 65th Birthday*. Edited by Cilliers Breytenbach, David S. Du Toit, Christine Gerber, and Christiane Zimmermann. NovTSup 175. Leiden: Brill, 2019.

Stern, David. "*Imitatio Hominis*: Anthropomorphism and the Character(s) of God in Rabbinic Literature." *Proof* 12.2 (1992): 151–74.

Sternberg, Meir. "Ordering the Unordered: Time, Space, and Descriptive Coherence." *Yale French Studies* 61 (1981): 60–88.

Stewart, Anne W. *Poetic Ethics in Proverbs: Wisdom Literature and the Shaping of the Moral Self*. New York: Cambridge University Press, 2016.

Stol, Marten. *Women in the Ancient Near East*. Boston: De Gruyter, 2016.

Stuart, Douglas K. *Exodus*. NAC. Nashville: B&H, 2006.

———. *Hosea–Jonah*. WBC 31. Waco: Word Books, 1987.

Sweeney, Marvin A. *I & II Kings: A Commentary*. OTL. Louisville: Westminster John Knox, 2007.

Sweet, R. F. G. "A New Look at the 'Sacred Marriage' in Ancient Mesopotamia." Pages 85–105 in *Corolla Torontonensis: Studies in Honor of Ronald Morton Smith*. Edited by E. Robbins and S. Sandahl. Toronto: TSAR, 1994.

Tan, Nancy Nam Hoon. *The 'Foreignness' of the Foreign Woman in Proverbs 1–9: A Study of the Origin and Development of a Biblical Motif*. BZAW 381. New York: De Gruyter, 2008.

Tasker, David R. *Ancient Near Eastern Literature and the Hebrew Scriptures about the Fatherhood of God*. StBibLit 69. New York: Peter Lang, 2004.

Tate, Marvin E. *Psalms 51–100*. WBC 20. Waco: Word Books, 2000.

Tenney, Merrill C., and Moisés Silva, eds. *The Zondervan Encyclopedia of the Bible*. Rev. ed. Grand Rapids: Zondervan, 2009.

Terrien, Samuel L. *The Elusive Presence: Toward a New Biblical Theology*. RP 26. San Francisco: Harper & Row, 1978.

Thielman, Frank. "Paul's View of Israel's Misstep in Rom 9.32–3: Its Origin and Meaning." *NTS* 64.3 (2018): 362–77.

Thiessen, Matthew. "The Form and Function of the Song of Moses (Deuteronomy 32:1–43)." *JBL* 123.3 (2004): 401–24.

Thompson, J. A. *The Book of Jeremiah*. NICOT. Grand Rapids: Eerdmans, 1980.

Thompson, Marianne M. *The Promise of the Father: Jesus and God in the New Testament*. Louisville: Westminster John Knox, 2000.

Ticciati, Susannah. "Wisdom in Patristic Interpretation: Scriptural and Cosmic Unity in Athanasius's Exegesis of Proverbs." Pages 187–203 in *The Oxford Handbook of Wisdom and the Bible*. New York: Oxford University Press, 2021.

Tigay, Jeffrey H. *Deuteronomy*. The JPS Torah Commentary. Philadelphia: Jewish Publication Society, 1996.

Tinsley, E. J. *Imitation of God in Christ: An Essay on the Biblical Basis of Christian Spirituality*. Philadelphia: Westminster, 1960.

Tomasello, Michael. "Emulation Learning and Cultural Learning." *Behavioral & Brain Sciences* 21 (2002): 703–4.

Tomasello, Michael, Ann C. Kruger, and Hilary H. Ratner. "Cultural Learning." *Behavioral & Brain Sciences* 16.3 (1993): 495–511.

Toombs, Lawrence E. "O.T. Theology and the Wisdom Literature." *JBR* 23.3 (1955): 193–96.

Toy, C. H. *A Critical and Exegetical Commentary on the Book of Proverbs*. ICC 16. New York: C. Scribner's Sons, 1899.

Treier, Daniel J. *Proverbs & Ecclesiastes*. Brazos Theological Commentary on the Bible. Grand Rapids: Brazos, 2011.

Trible, Phyllis. "Wisdom Builds a Poem: The Architecture of Proverbs 1:20–33." *JBL* 94.4 (1975): 509–18.

Trujillo, J. Ivan. "The Ugaritic Ritual for a Sacrificial Meal Honoring the Good Gods." PhD diss., Johns Hopkins University, 1973.

Turner, Marie. "Wisdom as Encounter with God." *LTJ* 50.2 (2016): 136–45.

Van Der Toorn, Karel. "Female Prostitution in Payment of Vows in Ancient Israel." *JBL* 108.2 (1989): 193–205.

Van Leeuwen, Raymond C. "Liminality and Worldview in Proverbs 1–9." *Semeia* 50 (1990): 111–44.

———. "Theology: Creation, Wisdom, and Covenant." Pages 65–82 in *The Oxford Handbook of Wisdom and the Bible*. New York: Oxford University Press, 2021.

Vawter, Bruce. "Prov 8:22: Wisdom and Creation." *JBL* 99.2 (1980): 205–16.

Vayntrub, Jacqueline E. "The Book of Proverbs and the Idea of Ancient Israelite Education." *ZAW* 128.1 (2016): 96–114.

Vitz, Paul C. "Critiques of Kohlberg's Model of Moral Development: A Summary." *Revista Española de Pedagogía* 52.197 (1994): 5–35.

Von Rad, Gerhard. "Josephsgeschichte und ältere Chokma." Pages 120–27 in *Congress Volume: Copenhagen 1953*. VTSup 1. Copenhagen: Brill, 1953.

———. *Wisdom in Israel*. Nashville: Abingdon, 1972.

Wakeman, Mary K. "Sacred Marriage." *JSOT* 22 (1982): 21–31.

Waldman, Nahum M. "God's Ways: A Comparative Note." *JQR* 70.2 (1979): 67–72.

Walker, C. B. F., and Michael B. Dick. *The Induction of the Cult Image in Ancient Mesopotamia: The Mesopotamian Mīs Pî Ritual*. Vol. 1 of State Archives of

Assyria Literary Texts, 1457–9189. Helsinki: University of Helsinki Press, 2001.

Walker, T. "Targum." Pages 678–83 in in vol. 4 of *A Dictionary of the Bible*. Edited by James Hastings, John A. Selbie, A. B. Davidson, and H. B. Swete. Vol. 4. New York: C. Scribner's Sons, 1911–1912.

Waltke, Bruce K. "Does Proverbs Promise Too Much?" *AUSS* 34.2 (1996): 319–36.

———. "The Book of Proverbs and Ancient Wisdom Literature." *BSac* 136.543 (1979): 221–38.

———. *The Book of Proverbs: Chapters 1–15*. NICOT. Grand Rapids: Eerdmans, 2004.

———. *The Book of Proverbs: Chapters 16–31*. NICOT. Grand Rapids: Eerdmans, 2004.

Waltke, Bruce K., and M. O'Connor. *An Introduction to Biblical Hebrew Syntax*. Winona Lake: Eisenbrauns, 1990.

Walton, John H. *Ancient Near Eastern Thought and the Old Testament: Introducing the Conceptual World of the Hebrew Bible*. 1st ed. Grand Rapids: Baker Academic, 2006.

———. *Ancient Near Eastern Thought and the Old Testament: Introducing the Conceptual World of the Hebrew Bible*. 2nd ed. Grand Rapids: Baker Academic, 2018.

Walton, John H., and J. Harvey Walton. *The Lost World of the Torah: Law as Covenant and Wisdom in Ancient Context*. Downers Grove: IVP, 2019.

Weeks, Stuart. *An Introduction to the Study of Wisdom Literature*. London: T&T Clark, 2010.

———. *Instruction and Imagery in Proverbs 1–9*. New York: Oxford University Press, 2007.

Wegner, Paul D. *Isaiah: An Introduction and Commentary*. TOTC. Downers Grove: IVP Academic, 2021.

Weigel, Gustave, and Arthur G. Madden. *Religion and the Knowledge of God*. Englewood Cliffs, NJ: Prentice–Hall, 1961.

Weinfeld, Moshe. "Ancient Near Eastern Patterns in Prophetic Literature." *VT* 27.2 (1977): 178–95.

———. *Deuteronomy and the Deuteronomic School*. Winona Lake: Eisenbrauns, 1972.

———. "Deuteronomy, Book Of." Pages 168–83 in *AYBD*. New York: Doubleday, 1992.

———. "Feminine Features in the Imagery of God in Israel: The Sacred Marriage and the Sacred Tree." *VT* 46 (1996): 516–29.

Weiser, A. *Das Buch der zwölf kleinen Propheten*. ATD 24. Göttingen: Vandenhoeck & Ruprecht, 1949.

Welch, John W., ed. *Chiasmus in Antiquity: Structures, Analyses, Exegesis*. Hildesheim: Gerstenberg, 1981.

Wells, Jo Bailey. *God's Holy People: A Theme in Biblical Theology*. JSOTSup 305. Sheffield: T&T Clark, 2000.

Wenham, Gordon J. *Story as Torah: Reading Old Testament Narrative Ethically.* Baker Academic, 2004.

———. *The Book of Leviticus.* NICOT. Eerdmans, 1979.

———. "The Gap between Law and Ethics in the Bible." *JJS* 48.1 (1997): 17–29.

Westbrook, Raymond, ed. *A History of Ancient Near Eastern Law.* Boston: Brill, 2003.

White, Stephen L. "Angel of the LORD: Messenger or Euphemism?" *TynBul* 50.2 (1999): 299–305.

Whittaker, J., and Pierre Louis. *Alcinous: Enseignementdes Doctrines de Platon.* Collection des Universités de France. Paris: Belles Lettres, 1990.

Whybray, R. N. "Proverbs 8:22–31 and its Supposed Prototypes." *VT* 15.4 (1965): 504–14.

———. *Proverbs: Based on the Revised Standard Version.* NCBC. Grand Rapids: Eerdmans, 1994.

———. *The Book of Proverbs.* New York: Cambridge University Press, 1972.

———. *The Composition of the Book of Proverbs.* JSOT 168. Sheffield: JSOT, 1994.

———. *The Intellectual Tradition in the Old Testament.* BZAW 135. New York: De Gruyter, 1974.

———. *Wisdom in Proverbs: The Concept of Wisdom in Proverbs 1–9.* Naperville: SCM, 1965.

Wild, Robert A. "'Be Imitators of God': Discipleship in the Letter to the Ephesians." Pages 127–43 in *Discipleship in the New Testament.* Edited by Fernando F. Segovia. Philadelphia: Fortress, 1985.

Williams, Daniel H. "Proverbs 8:22–31." *Int* 48.3 (1994): 275–79.

Williams, Ronald J., and John C. Beckman. *Williams' Hebrew Syntax.* 3rd ed. Toronto: University of Toronto Press, 2007.

Wilson, Gerald H. "'The Words of the Wise': The Intent and Significance of Qoheleth 12:9–14." *JBL* 103 (1984): 175–92.

Wilson, Robert R. "Approaches to Old Testament Ethics." Pages 62–74 in *Canon, Theology, and Old Testament Interpretation: Essays in Honor of Brevard S Childs.* Philadelphia, 1988.

Wolff, Hans Walter. *Hosea: A Commentary on the Book of the Prophet Hosea.* Hermeneia. Philadelphia: Fortress, 1974.

———. "'Wissen um Gott' bei Hosea als Urform von Theologie." *EvT* 12.12 (1953): 533–54.

Wolkstein, Diana, and Samuel Noah Kramer. *Inanna: Queen of Heaven and Earth.* New York: Harper & Row, 1983.

Wolterstorff, Nicholas. *Educating for Responsible Action.* Grand Rapids: Eerdmans, 1980.

Wright, Christopher J. H. *Old Testament Ethics for the People of God.* Downers Grove: IVP, 2004.

Wright, G. E. *God Who Acts: Biblical Theology as Recital.* SBT 8. London: SCM, 1952.

Wyatt, Nicolas. *Religious Texts from Ugarit.* 2nd ed. BibSem 53. London: Sheffield Academic, 2002.

Yee, Gale A. "An Analysis of Prov 8:22–31 According to Style and Structure." *ZAW* 94.1 (1982): 58–66.

———. "'I Have Perfumed My Bed with Myrrh': The Foreign Woman ('iššâ Zārâ) in Proverbs 1–9." *JSOT* 13.43 (1989): 53–68.

———. "The Anatomy of Biblical Parody: The Dirge Form in 2 Samuel 1 and Isaiah 14." *CBQ* 50.4 (1988): 565–86.

Yoder, Christine Roy. "Personified Wisdom and Feminist Theologies." Pages 273–85 in *The Oxford Handbook of Wisdom and the Bible*. New York: Oxford University Press, 2021.

Youngblood, Ronald F. "1, 2 Samuel." *The Expositor's Bible Commentary: 1 Samuel–2 Kings*. Edited by Tremper Longman III and David E. Garland. Rev. ed. Vol. 3. Grand Rapids: Zondervan, 2009.

Zabán, Bálint Károly. *The Pillar Function of the Speeches of Wisdom: Proverbs 1:20–33, 8:1–36 and 9:1–6 in the Structural Framework of Proverbs 1–9*. BZAW 429. Berlin: Walter de Gruyter, 2012.

Zalcman, Lawrence. "Prov 5,19c." *ZAW* 115.3 (2003): 433–34.

Zimmermann, Ruben. *Geschlechtermetaphorik und Gottesverhaltnis: Traditionsgeschichte und Theologie eines Bildfelds im Urchristentum und antiker Umwelt*. WUNT 2. Tubingen: Mohr Siebeck, 2001.

Zizek, Boris, Detlef Garz, and Ewa Nowak, eds. *Kohlberg Revisited*. Moral Development and Citizenship Education 9. Rotterdam: Sense, 2015.

www.ingramcontent.com/pod-product-compliance
Lightning Source LLC
Chambersburg PA
CBHW082139120626
46553CB00010B/2711